Readings in Comparative Politics

Political Challenges
and
Changing Agendas

Mark Kesselman

Columbia University

Joel Krieger

Wellesley College

D0089600

Houghton Mifflin Company   Boston   New York

Publisher: Charles Hartford
Sponsoring Editor: Katherine Meisenheimer
Senior Development Editor: Jeffrey Greene
Editorial Assistant: Kristen Craib
Project Editor: Reba Libby
Editorial Assistant: Deborah Berkman
Senior Art and Design Coordinator: Jill Haber
Executive Marketing Manager: Nicola Poser
Marketing Associate: Kathleen Mellon

Typographical errors in the original published versions of readings have been corrected in the versions excerpted here.

Cover image: digitally created globes, © Image Source Photography/Veer.com

Printed in the U.S.A.

Library of Congress Control Number: 2003110157

ISBN: 0-618-42625-6

123456789-CS-09 08 07 06 05

CONTENTS

PREFACE

What a period to be studying comparative politics! The Chinese proverb that expresses a hope for interesting times has been amply fulfilled in the current period—too much so, some might say. Never more than in this new millennium do students need to step back from the whirl of the daily headlines and nightly news and gain help in separating the wheat from the chaff. But what is wheat? What is chaff? That is, how can we determine which events are of more enduring significance and which will be forgotten by the time this book is published?

Readings in Comparative Politics (RCP) samples some of the most important work in the sub-discipline. Unlike international relations, for example, with its trinity of realism, liberal institutionalism, and constructivism, comparative politics is gloriously—or lamentably (depending on the observer)—catholic, eclectic, and sprawling. In our view, so much the better. We do not aim to provide a coherent picture of a field that we believe reflects the messiness of the political world. Nor do we claim to survey comprehensively the many methodological, theoretical, regional, or political perspectives to be found in comparative politics. We will have succeeded, however, if the rich array of readings in RCP serves to educate, provoke, and invite further study.

RCP provides articles with diverse perspectives on a substantial—but not exhaustive—range of issues within comparative politics. We do not assume that students have extensive background in comparative politics or political science. Nor do we seek to impart professional training. Our aim is to provide students with a wide range of influential, thoughtful, and well-written articles that focus on key issues within comparative politics.

The book opens with an Introduction that describes the scope of the field (but not its methods: RCP focuses on substantive, not methodological, issues). Following the Introduction, we provide three widely cited articles that provide alternative frames for analyzing comparative politics. The next six chapters, comprising the body of RCP, focus on major issues in the field. Each chapter opens with a brief introduction that identifies some important questions. The articles that follow are preceded by an introduction that helps students situate the article and identify its major arguments.

Chapter 2 analyzes states and regimes. We have selected articles that suggest that state formation and survival are political processes—neither inevitable nor benign. The articles in Chapter 3 highlight the fact that economies, whether they are presumably private (capitalist) or not, are governed; that is, political choices and institutions help to constitute and affect economic outcomes. Chapter 4 surveys aspects of democratic development. These articles stress that democracy is contingent, imperfect, and shaped by the context in which it is embedded. Chapter 5 stresses the rich, variable, and constructed nature of political identities. Chapter 6 suggests that institutions are both shaped by political struggle, arenas in which struggles occur, and are influential in shaping political conflicts and outcomes. The book concludes, in Chapter 7, with articles that highlight some current challenges in comparative politics as well as others that invite reflection on how to make better political choices.

RCP is in part an outgrowth of our co-editorship (along with William Joseph) of *Introduction to Comparative Politics* (ICP), an introductory textbook. The four core themes of ICP—a world of states, governing the economy, the democratic challenge, and political identities—have a counterpart in four of the chapters in RCP. Instructors may find it useful to assign RCP in a course in which ICP is the core text. The two books complement each other, in that RCP provides some in-depth and comparative analyses of issues surveyed in more systematic fashion in the country chapters of ICP.

We are grateful for research assistance provided by Kyla Pollack and Sara Fritsch and are once again fortunate to have benefited from the expert assistance of the Houghton Mifflin editorial and production team. Many thanks for the fine help provided by Katherine Meisenheimer, sponsoring editor; Fran Gay and Jeff Greene, senior development editors; Reba Libby, project editor; Deborah Berkman, editorial assistant; Nicola Poser, executive marketing manager; and the following colleagues who provided valuable advice:

Gaspare M. Genna, *University of South Florida*
Hashim Gibrill, *Clark Atlanta University*
Willie Hamilton, *Mount San Jacinto College*
Erik Herron, *University of Kansas*
Matthias Kaelberer, *Iowa State University*
Steven L. Taylor, *Troy University*

Mark Kesselman
Joel Krieger

 Chapter 1

INTRODUCTION

Brave New World

We borrow the title of Aldous Huxley's satirical novel, *Brave New World,* to describe the first decade of the twenty-first century. New it certainly is: No work of science fiction could have predicted some of the watershed political events in world politics as the twentieth century drew to a close and a new century began. Some of the most notable developments contributed to making the world more peaceful, just, and prosperous; for example, the implosion of the Soviet Union, beginning with the fall of the Berlin Wall in 1989, followed by a sharp decline in the Cold War, that is, intense hostility between the Soviet Union (later transformed into Russia) and the United States; widening and deepening of democratic changes in many countries; and technological advances that promote economic growth, health, and well-being. However, these positive changes were often overshadowed by far more disturbing developments: ethnic cleansing, organized rape, and genocide in Rwanda and former Yugoslavia; civil wars; interstate wars; and terrorist attacks inspired by religious, ethnic, economic, and political grievances. Although the twentieth century has been called the most violent in history, the twenty-first century may eventually claim that dubious title. *Readings in Comparative Politics* (RCP) includes a range of articles that aim to make sense of our present turbulent epoch.

In past years, the United States was often a major participant in the world's violent conflicts, but those conflicts were fought on foreign territory. The United States dispatched military forces to other regions of the world and exerted political and economic influence abroad. American soil, however, was a sanctuary protected from foreign incursion. This situation was virtually unique: there were few countries in the world that have not been a site for armed conflict. America's good fortune in this respect ended with a crash, or rather, four crashes, on September 11, 2001. On that day, terrorists hijacked four U.S. airplanes with several hundred civilian passengers aboard. They crashed two planes into the twin towers of the World Trade Center in New York City, causing three thousand deaths and reducing these massive buildings to a mountain of smoking rubble. A third plane crashed into the Pentagon in Washington, D.C. Passengers on the fourth plane thwarted the hijackers' plan to attack the Capitol building or the

White House, and the plane crashed in a Pennsylvania field. In one fateful hour, American politics and culture were changed in fundamental ways for decades to come. In the most diverse spheres, from immigration to security, to criminal justice, to popular culture, Americans live in the shadow of the September 11 attacks. Moreover, repercussions of September 11 ripple throughout the world. One important result was that President George W. Bush ordered attacks on Afghanistan and Iraq, on the grounds that their regimes were linked to terrorism—actions that provoked intense controversy in the United States and abroad.

Although one cannot attach such precise dates to some of the other current transformative developments, they are no less influential: the AIDS pandemic, which has ravaged Africa and other regions, and global warming, which threatens the stability and well-being of the global village in coming decades—to name just two.

The terms "globalization" and "the global era" are frequently applied as general catch phrases to identify the growing depth, extent, and diversity of cross-border connections that are a key feature of the contemporary world. Discussions of globalization often begin with accounts of economic activities, including the reorganization of production and the global redistribution of the workforce (the "global factory") and the increased extent and intensity of international trade, finance, and foreign direct investment. Globalization involves the movement of peoples due to migration, employment, business, and educational opportunities.

The term "globalization" links a highly diverse set of changes. Consider the attacks in the United States on September 11. The hijackers were members of al-Qaida, a thoroughly transnational network with cells in many continents. The hijackers trained and lived in locations thousands of miles apart. They communicated by cell phone and courier, and transferred funds through a sophisticated system linking international banks and traditional moneychangers based in bazaars.

Globalization includes other profound changes that are less visible but equally significant. For example, new applications of information technology (such as the Internet and CNN) blur the traditional distinction between what is around the world and what is around the block, instantly transforming cultures and eroding the boundaries between the local and global. These technologies make instantaneous communication possible. They link producers and contractors, headquarters, branch plants, and suppliers in "real time" anywhere in the world. Employees may be rooted in time and place, but employers can shop for what will bring them the greatest advantages in a global labor market. Employees who have an apparently secure job today may be unemployed tomorrow as employers downsize or move their operations offshore. But job destruction in one region may be offset by job creation elsewhere.

The dilemma that globalization represents can be illustrated by the theme chosen by the American Political Science Association (the official organization of American political scientists) for its 2004 annual meeting: "Global Inequalities." The program for the meeting declared, "While inequalities are hardly new, their relevance has become newly visible as the fading memory of the Cold War is replaced by the omnipresence of various North-South clashes. This invites systematic reflection. The enormous concentration of wealth and power in some parts of the world coexists with the marginalization of other countries and people."

Globalization forges new forms of international governance, from the European Union to the World Trade Organization. And as described above, international terror networks can strike anywhere—from New York to Bali to Madrid. In an attempt to regulate and stabilize the myriad international flows, an alphabet soup of international organizations—NATO, the UN, IMF, WTO, OECD, NAFTA, to name but a few—have been enlisted. Globalization also involves grassroots movements from around the world that challenge the construction of globalization from above. The first such protest occurred when the World Trade Organization sponsored a meeting of government ministers in Seattle in 1999 that was disrupted by thousands of protesters. Ever since, conferences called to develop rules for global commerce and investment have been the site of demonstrations by far-flung coalitions of environmental, labor-based, and community activists.* Thus, to Seattle, one can add the names of cities around the world— Washington, D.C., Prague, Genoa, Miami, and Cancun—where activists have assembled to protest the activity of international financial institutions.

The varied elements of globalization erode the ability of even the strongest countries to control their destinies. No state can fully guarantee economic and psychological security for its citizens. None can preserve pristine national models of economic governance—or distinctly national cultures, values, understandings of the world, or narratives that define a people and forge their unity.

In the brave new world in which we live, countries face a host of challenges simultaneously from above and below. The capacities of states to control domestic outcomes and assert sovereignty are compromised by regional and global technological and market forces, as well as growing security concerns. Countries are assaulted by ethnic, nationalist, and religious challenges that often involve both internal and external components. The challenge of democratic self-government is heightened when many of the decisions that fundamentally affect citizens' lives are made by organizations located far outside a country's borders.

Globalization is like the elephant described differently by every member of a group of blind people. Its extent, meaning, and impact are among the most hotly debated topics in popular discourse and scholarly arenas. One of the most important—and challenging—questions that one can ask about globalization is whether it is a blessing, a curse—or a complex and variable mixture of the two. It may be a blessing, because globalization can be associated with powerful benefits, including cultural richness deriving from exposure to new ideas and artistic expression, a widening of opportunities, and increased well-being from the diffusion of technology and mutual gains from international trade. It may be a curse,

---

* For recent descriptions by sympathetic participant-observers, see John Cavanagh and Jerry Manders, eds., *Alternatives to Economic Globalization: A Better World Is Possible* (San Francisco: Berrett-Koehler, 2004), and Robin Broad, ed., *Global Backlash: Citizen Initiatives for a Just World Economy* (Lanham, MD: Rowman & Littlefield, 2002). For a spirited defense of globalization, see Jagdish Bhagwati, *In Defense of Globalization* (New York: Oxford University Press, 2004).

because globalization has involved immense social dislocations, increased economic and political inequalities, and reduced autonomy for many people throughout the world.

The hard and fast distinction between domestic and international politics has
been blurred by the complex set of cross-border economic, cultural, technological, governance, and security processes, institutions, and relations that constitute the contemporary global order. Because the study of comparative politics
has been profoundly influenced by globalization, and it studies some aspects of
globalization, we have opened this Introduction by highlighting the brave new
world of globalization. But comparative politics is not identical to globalization. It
does not study all aspects of globalization, and it studies some topics not directly
related to globalization. What, then, is comparative politics? What are its scope
and methods? Where does it fit within the broader discipline of political science?
What kinds of issues do specialists in comparative politics address?

What—And How—Comparative Politics Compares*

To compare and contrast is one of the most common human exercises, whether
in the classroom study of literature or politics or animal behavior—or in selecting
dorm rooms or listing your favorite movies. In the observation of politics, the use
of comparisons is very old, dating at least from Aristotle, the ancient Greek
philosopher. Aristotle categorized Athenian city-states in the fifth century B.C. according to their form of political rule: rule by a single individual, rule by a few, or
rule by all citizens. He added a normative dimension (a claim about how societies
should be ruled), by comparing ("contrasting") good and corrupt versions of each
type. The modern study of comparative politics refines and systematizes the age-
old practice of evaluating some feature of X by comparing it to the same feature
of Y in order to learn more about it than isolated study would permit.

The term "comparative politics" refers to a subfield within the academic discipline of political science, as well as to a method or approach to the study of
politics.[†] The subject matter of comparative politics is the domestic politics of
countries or peoples. Within the discipline of political science, comparative
politics is one area of specialization. In addition, most political science (or

---

* Portions of this and other sections of the Introduction are drawn from "Introducing Compara-
tive Politics," chap. 1 in *Introduction to Comparative Politics: Political Challenges and Changing
Agendas,* third ed., edited by Mark Kesselman, Joel Krieger, and William A. Joseph (Boston:
Houghton Mifflin, 2004).

[†] For analyses of the scope and methods of comparative politics, see Philippe Schmitter, "Comparative Politics," in *The Oxford Companion to Politics of the World,* second ed., edited by Joel
Krieger (New York: Oxford University Press, 2001), 160–165; and several essays in *Political Science: The State of the Discipline,* edited by Ira Katznelson and Helen V. Milner (New York: W.W.
Norton & Company, and Washington, D.C., American Political Science Association, 2002).
These essays provide a comprehensive and insightful discussion of the methods of comparative
politics and its evolution, and several elements of the discussion here are drawn from them.

government) departments in U.S. colleges and universities include courses and academic specialists in three other subfields: political theory, international relations, and American politics. Political economy and methodology are also sometimes identified as subfields within political science.

More generally, the subfields of political science usefully highlight important clusters of concerns and encourage specialized study. But one should not regard the subfields as airtight compartments. Nor should the boundaries among subfields be erected into barriers to understanding. For example, because it is widely believed that students living in the United States should study American politics intensively and with special focus, the fields of American and comparative politics often remain separate. The pattern of distinguishing the study of politics at home from politics abroad is also common elsewhere, so students in Canada may be expected to study Canadian politics as a distinct specialty, and Japanese students would likewise be expected to master Japanese politics.

Yet there is no logical reason why study of the United States should not be included within the field of comparative politics—and there is good reason to do so. We therefore include several readings that analyze American politics in RCP. (See readings by Marx, Coates, Katzenstein, Howard, and Putnam.) Indeed, many important studies in comparative politics (and an increasing number of courses) have integrated the study of American politics with the study of politics in other countries. Comparative study can place U.S. politics in a much richer perspective and, at the same time, make it easier to recognize what is distinctive and most interesting about the United States and other countries.

Comparative politics—the study of what occurs within national borders—is typically distinguished from international relations, commonly defined as the study of interactions among states as well as the study of international institutions like the United Nations. Up to a point, this distinction makes sense. In order to study in depth, one must limit the scope of what is studied. But the distinction can also hinder understanding if carried too far. Important issues like immigration, nationalism, economic development, and the conduct and impact of war straddle the fence between comparative politics and international relations. This is especially true in the era of globalization, in which cross-border exchanges are dense and influential. (For examples, see the selections by Tilly, Sassen, Stiglitz, Mansfield and Snyder, and Sanderson.) Indeed, fuller understanding of these concerns can be gained by applying insights and tools from other disciplines, such as sociology, economics, and history.

Yet, however useful broad, interdisciplinary study may be, it requires building upon the contributions developed in more specialized fields. Let us return to the question of how to understand the field of comparative politics.

The comparative approach seeks to identify similarities and differences among countries, as well as political institutions, processes, and policies. As students of comparative politics (we call ourselves comparativists), we believe that we cannot make reliable statements about most political observations by looking at only one case. We often hear statements such as: "The United States has the best health care system in the world." Comparativists immediately wonder what kinds of health care systems exist in other countries, what they cost and how they are financed, who is covered by health insurance, and so on. Besides, what does "best" mean when it comes to health care systems? Is it the one that provides the widest access? The one that is the most technologically advanced? The one that is the most cost-effective? The one that produces the healthiest population? We would not announce the "best movie" or the "best car" without considering other alternatives or deciding what specific factors enter into our judgment. (The selection by Stepan and Skach, comparing the impact of presidential versus parliamentary systems on political stability, provides a fine example of this kind of comparison.)

Theory and Method in Comparative Politics

How do comparativists go about comparing? The comparativist looks at similarities and differences among countries, states, institutions, policies, and conflicts. An important approach within comparative politics tries to develop causal theories—hypotheses that can be expressed formally in a causal mode: "If X happens, then Y will be the result." Such theories include factors (the independent variables, symbolized by X) that are believed to influence some outcome, and the outcome (the dependent variable, symbolized by Y) to be explained. For example, it is commonly argued that if a country's economic pie shrinks, conflict among groups for resources will intensify. This hypothesis suggests what is called an inverse correlation between variables: as X varies in one direction, Y varies in the opposite direction. As the total national economic product (X) decreases, then political and social conflict over economic shares (Y) increases. Even when the explanation does not involve the explicit testing of hypotheses (and often it does not), comparativists try to identify similarities and differences among countries and to identify significant patterns.

Many comparativists do not believe in the possibility of developing causal theories based on general laws that explain specific events (what are called "covering laws"). They argue that this is an impossible project and suggest other ways of understanding politics. Some comparativists suggest that the goal should be to engage in sophisticated statistical analysis to identify patterns or correlations among different elements without claiming causal importance among these correlations. Other comparativists assert that maximum understanding can be gained by developing deductive models to understand how political participants engage in strategic decision-making. Some comparativists seek to identify specific mechanisms that contribute to producing particular outcomes in specific settings. And yet other comparativists claim that the goal of comparative politics should be to interpret the motivations of political actors and the incredible richness and complexity of political activity. Again, this approach rejects the possibility of covering laws to explain political outcomes. The debate among comparativists is wide open. We do not highlight this important methodological debate in RCP, although selections reflect all of the approaches that we have just identified. The major focus of RCP, however, is on substantive problems rather than theoretical or methodological debates.

We do wish to emphasize, however, the limits on just how "scientific" political science—and thus comparative politics—can be. Two important differences exist between the "hard" (or natural) sciences like physics and chemistry and the social sciences. First, social scientists study people who exercise free will. Because people have a margin for free choice, their choices, attitudes, and behavior cannot be fully explained by causal analysis. This does not mean that people choose in an arbitrary fashion. We choose within the context of material constraint, institutional dictates, and cultural prescriptions. Indeed, comparative politics analyzes how these and other factors orient political choices in systematic ways. But there will probably always be a wide gulf between the natural and social sciences because of their different objects of study.

A second difference between the natural and social sciences is that, in the natural sciences, experimental techniques can be applied to isolate the contribution of distinct factors to a particular outcome. It is possible to change the value or magnitude of a factor—for example, the force applied to an object—and measure how the outcome has consequently changed. Like other social scientists, however, political scientists, including comparativists, rarely have the opportunity to apply such experimental techniques.

In the real world of politics, unlike in a laboratory, variables cannot easily be isolated or manipulated. Some political scientists employ techniques that attempt to identify the specific causal weight of a variable in explaining a political outcome. But it is difficult to measure precisely how, for example, a person's ethnicity, gender, or income influences choosing a candidate when casting a ballot. Nor can we ever know for sure what exact mix of factors—conflicts among elites, popular ideological appeals, the weakness of the state, the organizational capacity of rebel leaders, or the discontent of the masses—precipitates a successful revolution.

Despite these difficulties and limitations, the study of comparative politics involves the attempt to strike the right balance in an explanation between the specifics of individual cases and universal patterns. One common goal of comparativists is to develop what is called "middle-level theory." Such a theory explains phenomena found in a limited range of cases, which in comparative politics means a specific set of countries with the same or similar characteristics, political institutions, or processes. If we study only individual countries without any comparative framework, then comparative politics would become merely the study of a series of isolated cases. It would be impossible to recognize what is most significant in the collage of political characteristics that we find in the world's many countries. As a result, the understanding of patterns of similarity and difference among countries would be lost, along with an important tool for evaluating what is and what is not unique about a country's political life.

If we go to the other extreme and try to make universal claims that something is always true in all countries, we would either have to stretch the truth or ignore the interesting differences and patterns of variation. For the political world is incredibly complex, shaped by an extraordinary array of factors and an almost endless interplay of variables. Indeed, after a brief period in the 1950s and 1960s when many comparativists tried—and failed—to develop a grand theory that would apply to all countries, most comparativists have seen the attempt to develop middle-level theory as the most promising.

For example, comparativists have worked hard to analyze the efforts in many countries to replace (or attempt to replace) authoritarian forms of government, such as military dictatorships and one-party states, with more democratic regimes. In studying democratic transitions, comparativists do not treat each national case as unique or try to construct a universal pattern that ignores all differences. Applying middle-level theory, we identify the influence on the new regime's political stability of specific variables such as institutional legacies, political culture, levels of economic development, the nature of the regime before the transition, and the degree of ethnic conflict or homogeneity. Comparativists have been able to identify patterns in the emergence and consolidation of democratic regimes in southern Europe in the 1970s (Greece, Portugal, and Spain) and have compared them to developments in Latin America, Asia, and Africa since the 1980s, and in Eastern and Central Europe since the revolutions of 1989. (But see the selection by Bunce, highlighting the importance of differences among these settings.)

Conclusion

The study of comparative politics has never been more timely, important—or fascinating. The brave new world of the twenty-first century cries out for disciplined analysis. RCP presents a diverse selection of articles and excerpts from books that take a step back from the often bewildering whirl of daily politics to analyze in depth a wide range of issues.

Following this Introduction and three readings that provide overviews of the current shape of world politics, six chapters identify important issues within comparative politics: states and regimes, governing the economy, the challenge of democracy, collective identities, political institutions and policies, and political challenges and changing agendas. For each, we provide an introduction and readings on important issues within the topic. The topics we have identified are key areas within comparative politics, and the readings among the best in the field. However, we do not claim that the organization of RCP represents the only way to organize the material. Moreover, many other excellent articles could be included. We have tried to choose readings that are accessible to students without extensive background in political science, and we include a broad range of current approaches and claims. The analyses range from theoretical explorations of general issues to descriptions of specific events. Some selections reflect a detached perspective; others seek to combine scholarly rigor and political engagement. The diversity of topics, approaches, and positions reflects the current ferment in the field of comparative politics, the complexity of its subject matter, and the fast-changing state of politics in the world.

The turmoil of the brave new world of the twenty-first century suggests the need for humility on the part of students and scholars. As a social scientist has remarked, partly in jest, it is easier to predict the past than the future. Our aim in this Introduction, and throughout RCP, is not to develop a blueprint for predicting (or creating) the future but to provide analyses of important issues within comparative politics. We hope that these readings stimulate you to think more deeply and develop your own position on the many important issues analyzed in *Readings in Comparative Politics.*

1.1

The End of History?

Francis Fukuyama

This influential article was written as the Soviet Union was disintegrating and the cold war ending. Professor Fukuyama ventured a bold prediction: that the end of communism spelled the end of any alternative on the world stage that could compete with the dominant form of political and economic organization championed by the West: democratic capitalism. Critics (including the other selections in Chapter 1) have pointed out that, even in the relatively short time since the end of the cold war, history has changed in extensive and unpredictable fashion, fueled by conflicts over religion, ethnicity, and globalization. Yet Fukuyama did not claim that the future would be conflict-free, only that there would be no broad-based ideological vision comparable to democratic capitalism that could command support throughout the world. Do you think his argument is valid?

I n watching the flow of events over the past decade or so, it is hard to avoid the feeling that something very fundamental has happened in world history. The past year has seen a flood of articles commemorating the end of the Cold War, and the fact that "peace" seems to be breaking out in many regions of the world. Most of these analyses lack any larger conceptual framework for distinguishing between what is essential and what is contingent or accidental in world history, and are predictably superficial. . . .

And yet, all of these people sense dimly that there is some larger process at work, a process that gives coherence and order to the daily headlines. The twentieth century saw the developed world descend into a paroxysm of ideological violence, as liberalism contended first with the remnants of absolutism, then bolshevism and fascism, and finally an updated Marxism that threatened to lead to the ultimate apocalypse of nuclear war. But the century that began full of self-confidence in the ultimate triumph of Western liberal democracy seems at its close to be returning full circle to where it started: not to an "end of ideology" or a convergence between capitalism and socialism, as earlier predicted, but to an unabashed victory of economic and political liberalism.

Francis Fukuyama, "The End of History?" *The National Interest* 16 (Summer 1989), reprinted in Foreign Affairs Agenda, *The New Shape of World Politics: Contending Paradigms in International Relations* (New York: W. W. Norton, 1997): 1–25. Reprinted by permission of the author.

The triumph of the West, of the Western *idea*, is evident first of all in the total exhaustion of viable systematic alternatives to Western liberalism. In the past decade, there have been unmistakable changes in the intellectual climate of the world's two largest communist countries, and the beginnings of significant reform movements in both. But this phenomenon extends beyond high politics and it can be seen also in the ineluctable spread of consumerist Western culture in such diverse contexts as the peasants' markets and color television sets now omnipresent throughout China, the cooperative restaurants and clothing stores opened in the past year in Moscow, the Beethoven piped into Japanese department stores, and the rock music enjoyed alike in Prague, Rangoon, and Tehran.

What we may be witnessing is not just the end of the Cold War, or the passing of a particular period of postwar history, but the end of history as such: that is, the end point of mankind's ideological evolution and the universalization of Western liberal democracy as the final form of human government. This is not to say that there will no longer be events to fill the pages of *Foreign Affairs'* yearly summaries of international relations, for the victory of liberalism has occurred primarily in the realm of ideas or consciousness and is as yet incomplete in the real or material world. But there are powerful reasons for believing that it is the ideal that will govern the material world *in the long run.* . . .

III

Have we in fact reached the end of history? Are there, in other words, any fundamental "contradictions" in human life that cannot be resolved in the context of modern liberalism, that would be resolvable by an alternative political-economic structure? If we accept the idealist premises laid out above, we must seek an answer to this question in the realm of ideology and consciousness. Our task is not to answer exhaustively the challenges to liberalism promoted by every crackpot messiah around the world, but only those that are embodied in important social or political forces and movements, and which are therefore part of world history. For our purposes, it matters very little what strange thoughts occur to people in Albania or Burkina Faso, for we are interested in what one could in some sense call the common ideological heritage of mankind.

In the past century, there have been two major challenges to liberalism, those of fascism and of communism. The former* saw the political weakness,

------

* I am not using the term "fascism" here in its most precise sense, fully aware of the frequent misuse of this term to denounce anyone to the right of the user. "Fascism" here denotes any organized ultra-nationalist movement with universalistic pretensions—not universalistic with regard to its nationalism, of course, since the latter is exclusive by definition, but with regard to the movement's belief in its right to rule other people. Hence Imperial Japan would qualify as fascist while former strongman Stoessner's Paraguay or Pinochet's Chile would not. Obviously fascist ideologies cannot be universalistic in the sense of Marxism or liberalism, but the structure of the doctrine can be transferred from country to country.

materialism, anomie, and lack of community of the West as fundamental contradictions in liberal societies that could only be resolved by a strong state that
forged a new "people" on the basis of national exclusiveness. Fascism was destroyed as a living ideology by World War II. This was a defeat, of course, on a
very material level, but it amounted to a defeat of the idea as well. What destroyed fascism as an idea was not universal moral revulsion against it, since
plenty of people were willing to endorse the idea as long as it seemed the wave
of the future, but its lack of success. After the war, it seemed to most people that
German fascism as well as its other European and Asian variants were bound to
self-destruct. There was no material reason why new fascist movements could
not have sprung up again after the war in other locales, but for the fact that expansionist ultranationalism, with its promise of unending conflict leading to dis-
astrous military defeat, had completely lost its appeal. The ruins of the Reich
chancellory as well as the atomic bombs dropped on Hiroshima and Nagasaki
killed this ideology on the level of consciousness as well as materially, and all of
the proto-fascist movements spawned by the German and Japanese examples
like the Peronist movement in Argentina or Subhas Chandra Bose's Indian
National Army withered after the war.

The ideological challenge mounted by the other great alternative to liberalism, communism, was far more serious. Marx, speaking Hegel's language, asserted that liberal society contained a fundamental contradiction that could not
be resolved within its context, that between capital and labor, and this contradiction has constituted the chief accusation against liberalism ever since. But
surely, the class issue has actually been successfully resolved in the West. As
Kojève (among others) noted, the egalitarianism of modern America represents the essential achievement of the classless society envisioned by Marx. This
is not to say that there are not rich people and poor people in the United States,
or that the gap between them has not grown in recent years. But the root causes
of economic inequality do not have to do with the underlying legal and social
structure of our society, which remains fundamentally egalitarian and moderately redistributionist, so much as with the cultural and social characteristics of
the groups that make it up, which are in turn the historical legacy of premodern
conditions. Thus black poverty in the United States is not the inherent product
of liberalism, but is rather the "legacy of slavery and racism" which persisted long
after the formal abolition of slavery.

As a result of the receding of the class issue, the appeal of communism in the
developed Western world, it is safe to say, is lower today than any time since
the end of the First World War. This can be measured in any number of ways: in the
declining membership and electoral pull of the major European communist
parties, and their overtly revisionist programs; in the corresponding electoral
success of conservative parties from Britain and Germany to the United States
and Japan, which are unabashedly pro-market and antistatist; and in an intellectual climate whose most "advanced" members no longer believe that bourgeois society is something that ultimately needs to be overcome. This is not to

say that the opinions of progressive intellectuals in Western countries are not deeply pathological in any number of ways. But those who believe that the future must inevitably be socialist tend to be very old, or very marginal to the real political discourse of their societies.

One may argue that the socialist alternative was never terribly plausible for the North Atlantic world, and was sustained for the last several decades primarily by its success outside of this region. But it is precisely in the non-European world that one is most struck by the occurrence of major ideological transformations. Surely the most remarkable changes have occurred in Asia. Due to the strength and adaptability of the indigenous cultures there, Asia became a battleground for a variety of imported Western ideologies early in this century. Liberalism in Asia was a very weak reed in the period after World War I; it is easy today to forget how gloomy Asia's political future looked as recently as ten or fifteen years ago. It is easy to forget as well how momentous the outcome of Asian ideological struggles seemed for world political development as a whole.

The first Asian alternative to liberalism to be decisively defeated was the fascist one represented by Imperial Japan. Japanese fascism (like its German version) was defeated by the force of American arms in the Pacific war, and liberal democracy was imposed on Japan by a victorious United States. Western capitalism and political liberalism when transplanted to Japan were adapted and transformed by the Japanese in such a way as to be scarcely recognizable.* Many Americans are now aware that Japanese industrial organization is very different from that prevailing in the United States or Europe, and it is questionable what relationship the factional maneuvering that takes place with the governing Liberal Democratic Party bears to democracy. Nonetheless, the very fact that the essential elements of economic and political liberalism have been so successfully grafted onto uniquely Japanese traditions and institutions guarantees their survival in the long run. More important is the contribution that Japan has made in turn to world history by following in the footsteps of the United States to create a truly universal consumer culture that has become both a symbol and an underpinning of the universal homogenous state. V. S. Naipaul traveling in Khomeini's Iran shortly after the revolution noted the omnipresent signs advertising the products of Sony, Hitachi, and JVC, whose appeal remained virtually irresistible and gave the lie to the regime's pretensions of restoring a state based on the rule of the *Shariah*. Desire for access to the consumer culture, created in large measure by Japan, has played a crucial role in fostering the spread of economic liberalism throughout Asia, and hence in promoting political liberalism as well.

---

* I use the example of Japan with some caution, since Kojève late in his life came to conclude that Japan, with its culture based on purely formal arts, proved that the universal homogenous state was not victorious and that history had perhaps not ended. See the long note at the end of the second edition of *Introduction à la Lecture de Hegel*, 462–3.

The economic success of the other newly industrializing countries (NICs) in Asia following on the example of Japan is by now a familiar story. What is important from a Hegelian standpoint is that political liberalism has been following economic liberalism, more slowly than many had hoped but with seeming inevitability. Here again we see the victory of the idea of the universal homogenous state. South Korea had developed into a modern, urbanized society with an increasingly large and well-educated middle class that could not possibly be isolated from the larger democratic trends around them. Under these circumstances it seemed intolerable to a large part of this population that it should be ruled by an anachronistic military regime while Japan, only a decade or so ahead in economic terms, had parliamentary institutions for over forty years. Even the former socialist regime in Burma, which for so many decades existed in dismal isolation from the larger trends dominating Asia, was buffeted in the past year by pressures to liberalize both its economy and political system. It is said that unhappiness with strongman Ne Win began when a senior Burmese officer went to Singapore for medical treatment and broke down crying when he saw how far socialist Burma had been left behind by its ASEAN neighbors.

But the power of the liberal idea would seem much less impressive if it had not infected the largest and oldest culture in Asia, China. The simple existence of communist China created an alternative pole of ideological attraction, and as such constituted a threat to liberalism. But the past fifteen years have seen an almost total discrediting of Marxism-Leninism as an economic system. Beginning with the famous third plenum of the Tenth Central Committee in 1978, the Chinese Communist party set about decollectivizing agriculture for the 800 million Chinese who still lived in the countryside. The role of the state in agriculture was reduced to that of a tax collector, while production of consumer goods was sharply increased in order to give peasants a taste of the universal homogenous state and thereby an incentive to work. The reform doubled Chinese grain output in only five years, and in the process created for Deng Xiao-ping a solid political base from which he was able to extend the reform to other parts of the economy. Economic statistics do not begin to describe the dynamism, initiative, and openness evident in China since the reform began.

China could not now be described in any way as a liberal democracy. At present, no more than 20 percent of its economy has been marketized, and most importantly it continues to be ruled by a self-appointed Communist party which has given no hint of wanting to devolve power. Deng has made none of Gorbachev's promises regarding democratization of the political system and there is no Chinese equivalent of *glasnost*. The Chinese leadership has in fact been much more circumspect in criticizing Mao and Maoism than Gorbachev with respect to Brezhnev and Stalin, and the regime continues to pay lip service to Marxism-Leninism as its ideological underpinning. But anyone familiar with the outlook and behavior of the new technocratic elite now governing China knows that Marxism and ideological principle have become virtually irrelevant as guides to policy, and that bourgeois consumerism has a real meaning in that country for the first time since the revolution. The various slowdowns in the pace of reform, the campaigns against "spiritual pollution" and crackdowns on political dissent are more properly seen as tactical adjustments made in the process of managing what is an extraordinarily difficult political transition. By ducking the question of political reform while putting the economy on a new footing, Deng has managed to avoid the breakdown of authority that has accompanied Gorbachev's *perestroika*. Yet the pull of the liberal idea continues to be very strong as economic power devolves and the economy becomes more open to the outside world. There are currently over 20,000 Chinese students studying in the U.S. and other Western countries, almost all of them the children of the Chinese elite. It is hard to believe that when they return home to run the country they will be content for China to be the only country in Asia unaffected by the larger democratizing trend. The student demonstrations in Beijing that broke out first in December 1986 and recurred recently on the occasion of Hu Yao-bang's death were only the beginning of what will inevitably be mounting pressure for change in the political system as well.

What is important about China from the standpoint of world history is not the present state of the reform or even its future prospects. The central issue is the fact that the People's Republic of China can no longer act as a beacon for illiberal forces around the world, whether they be guerrillas in some Asian jungle or middle class students in Paris. Maoism, rather than being the pattern for Asia's future, became an anachronism, and it was the mainland Chinese who in fact were decisively influenced by the prosperity and dynamism of their overseas co-ethnics—the ironic ultimate victory of Taiwan. . . .

If we admit for the moment that the fascist and communist challenges to liberalism are dead, are there any other ideological competitors left? Or put another way, are there contradictions in liberal society beyond that of class that are not resolvable? Two possibilities suggest themselves, those of religion and nationalism.

The rise of religious fundamentalism in recent years within the Christian, Jewish, and Muslim traditions has been widely noted. One is inclined to say that the revival of religion in some way attests to a broad unhappiness with the impersonality and spiritual vacuity of liberal consumerist societies. Yet while the emptiness at the core of liberalism is most certainly a defect in the ideology—indeed, a flaw that one does not need the perspective of religion to recognize*— it is not at all clear that it is remediable through politics. Modern liberalism itself was historically a consequence of the weakness of religiously-based societies which, failing to agree on the nature of the good life, could not provide even the minimal preconditions of peace and stability. In the contemporary world only Islam has offered a theocratic state as a political alternative to both liberalism and

---

* I am thinking particularly of Rousseau and the Western philosophical tradition that flows from him that was highly critical of Lockean or Hobbesian liberalism, though one could criticize liberalism from the standpoint of classical political philosophy as well.

communism. But the doctrine has little appeal for non-Muslims, and it is hard to believe that the movement will take on any universal significance. Other less organized religious impulses have been successfully satisfied within the sphere of personal life that is permitted in liberal societies.

The other major "contradiction" potentially unresolvable by liberalism is the one posed by nationalism and other forms of racial and ethnic consciousness. It is certainly true that a very large degree of conflict since the Battle of Jena has had its roots in nationalism. Two cataclysmic world wars in this century have been spawned by the nationalism of the developed world in various guises, and if those passions have been muted to a certain extent in postwar Europe, they are still extremely powerful in the Third World. Nationalism has been a threat to liberalism historically in Germany, and continues to be one in isolated parts of "post-historical" Europe like Northern Ireland.

But it is not clear that nationalism represents an irreconcilable contradiction in the heart of liberalism. In the first place, nationalism is not one single phenomenon but several, ranging from mild cultural nostalgia to the highly organized and elaborately articulated doctrine of National Socialism. Only systematic nationalisms of the latter sort can qualify as a formal ideology on the level of liberalism or communism. The vast majority of the world's nationalist movements do not have a political program beyond the negative desire of independence *from* some other group or people, and do not offer anything like a comprehensive agenda for socio-economic organization. As such, they are compatible with doctrines and ideologies that do offer such agendas. While they may constitute a source of conflict for liberal societies, this conflict does not arise from liberalism itself so much as from the fact that the liberalism in question is incomplete. Certainly a great deal of the world's ethnic and nationalist tension can be explained in terms of peoples who are forced to live in unrepresentative political systems that they have not chosen.

While it is impossible to rule out the sudden appearance of new ideologies or previously unrecognized contradictions in liberal societies, then, the present world seems to confirm that the fundamental principles of socio-political organization have not advanced terribly far since 1806. Many of the wars and revolutions fought since that time have been undertaken in the name of ideologies which claimed to be more advanced than liberalism, but whose pretensions were ultimately unmasked by history. In the meantime, they have helped to spread the universal homogenous state to the point where it could have a significant effect on the overall character of international relations. . . .

V

The passing of Marxism-Leninism first from China and then from the Soviet Union will mean its death as a living ideology of world historical significance. For while there may be some isolated true believers left in places like Managua,

Pyongyang, or Cambridge, Massachusetts, the fact that there is not a single large state in which it is a going concern undermines completely its pretensions to being in the vanguard of human history. And the death of this ideology means the growing "Common Marketization" of international relations, and the diminution of the likelihood of large-scale conflict between states.

This does not by any means imply the end of international conflict *per se*. For the world at that point would be divided between a part that was historical and a part that was post-historical. Conflict between states still in history, and between those states and those at the end of history, would still be possible. There would still be a high and perhaps rising level of ethnic and nationalist violence, since those are impulses incompletely played out, even in parts of the post-historical world. Palestinians and Kurds, Sikhs and Tamils, Irish Catholics and Walloons, Armenians and Azeris, will continue to have their unresolved grievances. This implies that terrorism and wars of national liberation will continue to be an important item on the international agenda. But large-scale conflict must involve large states still caught in the grip of history, and they are what appear to be passing from the scene.

The end of history will be a very sad time. The struggle for recognition, the willingness to risk one's life for a purely abstract goal, the worldwide ideological struggle that called forth daring, courage, imagination, and idealism, will be replaced by economic calculation, the endless solving of technical problems, environmental concerns, and the satisfaction of sophisticated consumer demands. In the post-historical period there will be neither art nor philosophy, just the perpetual caretaking of the museum of human history. I can feel in myself, and see in others around me, a powerful nostalgia for the time when history existed. Such nostalgia, in fact, will continue to fuel competition and conflict even in the post-historical world for some time to come. Even though I recognize its inevitability, I have the most ambivalent feelings for the civilization that has been created in Europe since 1945, with its north Atlantic and Asian offshoots. Perhaps this very prospect of centuries of boredom at the end of history will serve to get history started once again.

1.2

The Clash of Civilizations?

Samuel Huntington

Writing in 1993, Professor Huntington claimed that the world would primarily be divided in the future not by conflicts among states but by conflicts among major religious and ethnic groups. He predicted that the most important cleavage of all would pit "the West versus the rest." This influential article was often cited after the September 11, 2001, attacks on the Pentagon and World Trade Center. Critics, however, have asserted that cultures are not the homogeneous entities implied by "The Clash of Civilizations"; they are complex, internally divided, and changing. Moreover, many scholars argue that states remain central actors in world conflicts. How well does Huntington's thesis withstand these criticisms?

The Next Pattern of Conflict

World politics is entering a new phase, and intellectuals have not hesitated to proliferate visions of what it will be—the end of history, the return of traditional rivalries between nation states, and the decline of the nation state from the conflicting pulls of tribalism and globalism, among others. Each of these visions catches aspects of the emerging reality. Yet they all miss a crucial, indeed a central, aspect of what global politics is likely to be in the coming years.

It is my hypothesis that the fundamental source of conflict in this new world will not be primarily ideological or primarily economic. The great divisions among humankind and the dominating source of conflict will be cultural. Nation states will remain the most powerful actors in world affairs, but the principal conflicts of global politics will occur between nations and groups of different civilizations. The clash of civilizations will dominate global politics. The fault lines between civilizations will be the battle lines of the future.

Conflict between civilizations will be the latest phase in the evolution of conflict in the modern world. For a century and a half after the emergence of the modern international system with the Peace of Westphalia, the conflicts of the Western world were largely among princes—emperors, absolute monarchs

---

and constitutional monarchs attempting to expand their bureaucracies, their armies, their mercantilist economic strength and, most important, the territory they ruled. In the process they created nation states, and beginning with the French Revolution the principal lines of conflict were between nations rather than princes. In 1793, as R. R. Palmer put it, "The wars of kings were over; the wars of peoples had begun." This nineteenth-century pattern lasted until the end of World War 1. Then, as a result of the Russian Revolution and the reaction against it, the conflict of nations yielded to the conflict of ideologies, first among communism, fascism-Nazism and liberal democracy, and then between communism and liberal democracy. During the Cold War, this latter conflict became embodied in the struggle between the two superpowers, neither of which was a nation state in the classical European sense and each of which defined its identity in terms of its ideology. . . .

. . . With the end of the Cold War, international politics . . . becomes the interaction between the West and non-Western civilizations and among non-Western civilizations. In the politics of civilizations, the peoples and governments of non-Western civilizations no longer remain the objects of history as targets of Western colonialism but join the West as movers and shapers of history.

The Nature of Civilizations

During the cold war the world was divided into the First, Second and Third Worlds. Those divisions are no longer relevant. It is far more meaningful now to group countries not in terms of their political or economic systems or in terms of their level of economic development but rather in terms of their culture and civilization.

What do we mean when we talk of a civilization? A civilization is a cultural entity. Villages, regions, ethnic groups, nationalities, religious groups, all have distinct cultures at different levels of cultural heterogeneity. The culture of a village in southern Italy may be different from that of a village in northern Italy, but both will share in a common Italian culture that distinguishes them from German villages. European communities, in turn, will share cultural features that distinguish them from Arab or Chinese communities. Arabs, Chinese and Westerners, however, are not part of any broader cultural entity. They constitute civilizations. A civilization is thus the highest cultural grouping of people and the broadest level of cultural identity people have short of that which distinguishes humans from other species. It is defined both by common objective elements, such as language, history, religion, customs, institutions, and by the subjective self-identification of people. People have levels of identity: a resident of Rome may define himself with varying degrees of intensity as a Roman, an Italian, a Catholic, a Christian, a European, a Westerner. The civilization to which he belongs is the broadest level of identification with which he intensely identifies. People can and do redefine their identities and, as a result, the composition and boundaries of civilizations change.

Civilizations may involve a large number of people, as with China ("a civilization pretending to be a state," as Lucian Pye put it), or a very small number of people, such as the Anglophone Caribbean. A civilization may include several nation states, as is the case with Western, Latin American and Arab civilizations, or only one, as is the case with Japanese civilization. Civilizations obviously blend and overlap, and may include subcivilizations. Western civilization has two major variants, European and North American, and Islam has its Arab, Turkic and Malay subdivisions. Civilizations are nonetheless meaningful entities, and while the lines between them are seldom sharp, they are real. Civilizations are dynamic; they rise and fall; they divide and merge. And, as any student of history knows, civilizations disappear and are buried in the sands of time.

Westerners tend to think of nation states as the principal actors in global affairs. They have been that, however, for only a few centuries. The broader reaches of human history have been the history of civilizations. In *A Study of History*, Arnold Toynbee identified 21 major civilizations; only six of them exist in the contemporary world.

Why Civilizations Will Clash

Civilization identity will be increasingly important in the future, and the world will be shaped in large measure by the interactions among seven or eight major civilizations. These include Western, Confucian, Japanese, Islamic, Hindu, Slavic-Orthodox, Latin American and possibly African civilization. The most important conflicts of the future will occur along the cultural fault lines separating these civilizations from one another.

Why will this be the case?

First, differences among civilizations are not only real; they are basic. Civilizations are differentiated from each other by history, language, culture, tradition and, most important, religion. The people of different civilizations have different views on the relations between God and man, the individual and the group, the citizen and the state, parents and children, husband and wife, as well as differing views of the relative importance of rights and responsibilities, liberty and authority, equality and hierarchy. These differences are the product of centuries. They will not soon disappear. They are far more fundamental than differences among political ideologies and political regimes. Differences do not necessarily mean conflict, and conflict does not necessarily mean violence. Over the centuries, however, differences among civilizations have generated the most prolonged and the most violent conflicts.

Second, the world is becoming a smaller place. The interactions between peoples of different civilizations are increasing; these increasing interactions intensify civilization consciousness and awareness of differences between civilizations and commonalities within civilizations. North African immigration to France generates hostility among Frenchmen and at the same time increased receptivity to immigration by "good" European Catholic Poles. Americans react far more negatively to Japanese investment than to larger investments from Canada and European countries. Similarly, as Donald Horowitz has pointed out, "An Ibo may be . . . an Owerri Ibo or an Onitsha Ibo in what was the Eastern region of Nigeria. In Lagos, he is simply an Ibo. In London, he is a Nigerian. In New York, he is an African." The interactions among peoples of different civilizations enhance the civilization-consciousness of people that, in turn, invigorates differences and animosities stretching or thought to stretch back deep into history.

Third, the processes of economic modernization and social change throughout the world are separating people from longstanding local identities. They also weaken the nation state as a source of identity. In much of the world religion has moved in to fill this gap, often in the form of movements that are labeled "fundamentalist." Such movements are found in Western Christianity, Judaism, Buddhism and Hinduism, as well as in Islam. In most countries and most religions the people active in fundamentalist movements are young, college-educated, middle-class technicians, professionals and business persons. The "unsecularization of the world," George Weigel has remarked, "is one of the dominant social facts of life in the late twentieth century." The revival of religion, "la revanche de Dieu," as Gilles Kepel labeled it, provides a basis for identity and commitment that transcends national boundaries and unites civilizations.

Fourth, the growth of civilization-consciousness is enhanced by the dual role of the West. On the one hand, the West is at a peak of power. At the same time, however, and perhaps as a result, a return to the roots phenomenon is occurring among non-Western civilizations. Increasingly one hears references to trends toward a turning inward and "Asianization" in Japan, the end of the Nehru legacy and the "Hinduization" of India, the failure of Western ideas of socialism and nationalism and hence "re-Islamization" of the Middle East, and now a debate over Westernization versus Russianization in Boris Yeltsin's country. A West at the peak of its power confronts non-Wests that increasingly have the desire, the will and the resources to shape the world in non-Western ways.

In the past, the elites of non-Western societies were usually the people who were most involved with the West, had been educated at Oxford, the Sorbonne or Sandhurst, and had absorbed Western attitudes and values. At the same time, the populace in non-Western countries often remained deeply imbued with the indigenous culture. Now, however, these relationships are being reversed. A de-Westernization and indigenization of elites is occurring in many non-Western countries at the same time that Western, usually American, cultures, styles and habits become more popular among the mass of the people.

Fifth, cultural characteristics and differences are less mutable and hence less easily compromised and resolved than political and economic ones. In the former Soviet Union, communists can become democrats, the rich can become poor and the poor rich, but Russians cannot become Estonians and Azeris cannot become Armenians. In class and ideological conflicts, the key question was "Which side are you on?" and people could and did choose sides and change sides. In conflicts between civilizations, the question is "What are you?" That is a given that cannot be changed. And as we know, from Bosnia to the Caucasus to the Sudan, the wrong answer to that question can mean a bullet in the head. Even more than ethnicity, religion discriminates sharply and exclusively among people. A person can be half-French and half-Arab and simultaneously even a citizen of two countries. It is more difficult to be half-Catholic and half-Muslim.

Finally, economic regionalism is increasing. The proportions of total trade that were intraregional rose between 1980 and 1989 from 51 percent to 59 percent in Europe, 33 percent to 37 percent in East Asia, and 32 percent to 36 percent in North America. The importance of regional economic blocs is likely to continue to increase in the future. On the one hand, successful economic regionalism will reinforce civilization-consciousness. On the other hand, economic regionalism may succeed only when it is rooted in a common civilization. The European Community rests on the shared foundation of European culture and Western Christianity. The success of the North American Free Trade Agreement depends on the convergence now underway of Mexican, Canadian and American cultures. Japan, in contrast, faces difficulties in creating a comparable economic entity in East Asia because Japan is a society and civilization unique to itself. However strong the trade and investment links Japan may develop with other East Asian countries, its cultural differences with those countries inhibit and perhaps preclude its promoting regional economic integration like that in Europe and North America.

Common culture, in contrast, is clearly facilitating the rapid expansion of the economic relations between the People's Republic of China and Hong Kong, Taiwan, Singapore and the overseas Chinese communities in other Asian countries. With the Cold War over, cultural commonalities increasingly overcome ideological differences, and mainland China and Taiwan move closer together. If cultural commonality is a prerequisite for economic integration, the principal East Asian economic bloc of the future is likely to be centered on China. This bloc is, in fact, already coming into existence. . . .

Culture and religion also form the basis of the Economic Cooperation Organization, which brings together ten non-Arab Muslim countries: Iran, Pakistan, Turkey, Azerbaijan, Kazakhstan, Kyrgyzstan, Turkmenistan, Tadjikistan, Uzbekistan and Afghanistan. One impetus to the revival and expansion of this organization, founded originally in the 1960s by Turkey, Pakistan and Iran, is the realization by the leaders of several of these countries that they had no chance of admission to the European Community. Similarly, Caricom, the Central American Common Market and Mercosur rest on common cultural foundations. Efforts to build a broader Caribbean-Central American economic entity bridging the Anglo-Latin divide, however, have to date failed.

As people define their identity in ethnic and religious terms, they are likely to see an "us" versus "them" relation existing between themselves and people of different ethnicity or religion. The end of ideologically defined states in Eastern Europe and the former Soviet Union permits traditional ethnic identities and animosities to come to the fore. Differences in culture and religion create differences over policy issues, ranging from human rights to immigration to trade and commerce to the environment. Geographical propinquity gives rise to conflicting territorial claims from Bosnia to Mindanao. Most important, the efforts of the West to promote its values of democracy and liberalism as universal values, to maintain its military predominance and to advance its economic interests engender countering responses from other civilizations. Decreasingly able to mobilize support and form coalitions on the basis of ideology, governments and groups will increasingly attempt to mobilize support by appealing to common religion and civilization identity.

The clash of civilizations thus occurs at two levels. At the micro-level, adjacent groups along the fault lines between civilizations struggle, often violently, over the control of territory and each other. At the macro-level, states from different civilizations compete for relative military and economic power, struggle over the control of international institutions and third parties, and competitively promote their particular political and religious values.

The Fault Lines Between Civilizations

The fault lines between civilizations are replacing the political and ideological boundaries of the Cold War as the flash points for crisis and bloodshed. The Cold War began when the Iron Curtain divided Europe politically and ideologically. The Cold War ended with the end of the Iron Curtain. As the ideological division of Europe has disappeared, the cultural division of Europe between Western Christianity, on the one hand, and Orthodox Christianity and Islam, on the other, has reemerged. The most significant dividing line in Europe, as William Wallace has suggested, may well be the eastern boundary of Western Christianity in the year 1500. This line runs along what are now the boundaries between Finland and Russia and between the Baltic states and Russia, cuts through Belarus and Ukraine separating the more Catholic western Ukraine from Orthodox eastern Ukraine, swings westward separating Transylvania from the rest of Romania, and then goes through Yugoslavia almost exactly along the line now separating Croatia and Slovenia from the rest of Yugoslavia. In the Balkans this line, of course, coincides with the historic boundary between the Hapsburg and Ottoman empires. The peoples to the north and west of this line are Protestant or Catholic; they shared the common experiences of European history—feudalism, the Renaissance, the Reformation, the Enlightenment, the French Revolution, the Industrial Revolution; they are generally economically better off than the peoples to the east; and they may now look forward to increasing involvement in a common European economy and to the consolidation of democratic political systems. The peoples to the east and south of this line are Orthodox or Muslim; they historically belonged to the Ottoman or Tsarist empires and were only lightly touched by the shaping events in the rest of Europe; they are generally less advanced economically; they seem much less likely to develop stable democratic political systems. The Velvet Curtain of culture has replaced the Iron Curtain of ideology as the most significant dividing line in Europe. As the events in Yugoslavia show, it is not only a line of difference; it is also at times a line of bloody conflict.

Conflict along the fault line between Western and Islamic civilizations has been going on for 1,300 years. After the founding of Islam, the Arab and Moorish surge west and north only ended at Tours in 732. From the eleventh to the thirteenth century the Crusaders attempted with temporary success to bring Christianity and Christian rule to the Holy Land. From the fourteenth to the seventeenth century, the Ottoman Turks reversed the balance, extended their sway over the Middle East and the Balkans, captured Constantinople, and twice laid siege to Vienna. In the nineteenth and early twentieth centuries as Ottoman power declined Britain, France, and Italy established Western control over most of North Africa and the Middle East.

After World War II, the West, in turn, began to retreat; the colonial empires disappeared; first Arab nationalism and then Islamic fundamentalism manifested themselves; the West became heavily dependent on the Persian Gulf countries for its energy; the oil-rich Muslim countries became money-rich and, when they wished to, weapons-rich. Several wars occurred between Arabs and Israel (created by the West). France fought a bloody and ruthless war in Algeria for most of the 1950s; British and French forces invaded Egypt in 1956; American forces went into Lebanon in 1958; subsequently American forces returned to Lebanon, attacked Libya, and engaged in various military encounters with Iran; Arab and Islamic terrorists, supported by at least three Middle Eastern governments, employed the weapon of the weak and bombed Western planes and installations and seized Western hostages. This warfare between Arabs and the West culminated in 1990, when the United States sent a massive army to the Persian Gulf to defend some Arab countries against aggression by another. In its aftermath NATO planning is increasingly directed to potential threats and instability along its "southern tier."

This centuries-old military interaction between the West and Islam is unlikely to decline. It could become more virulent. The Gulf War left some Arabs feeling proud that Saddam Hussein had attacked Israel and stood up to the West. It also left many feeling humiliated and resentful of the West's military presence in the Persian Gulf, the West's overwhelming military dominance, and their apparent inability to shape their own destiny. Many Arab countries, in addition to the oil exporters, are reaching levels of economic and social development where autocratic forms of government become inappropriate and efforts to introduce democracy become stronger. Some openings in Arab political systems have already occurred. The principal beneficiaries of these openings have been Islamist movements. In the Arab world, in short, Western democracy strengthens anti-Western political forces. This may be a passing phenomenon, but it surely complicates relations between Islamic countries and the West.

Those relations are also complicated by demography. The spectacular population growth in Arab countries, particularly in North Africa, has led to increased migration to Western Europe. The movement within Western Europe toward minimizing internal boundaries has sharpened political sensitivities with respect to this development. In Italy, France and Germany, racism is increasingly open, and political reactions and violence against Arab and Turkish migrants have become more intense and more widespread since 1990.

On both sides the interaction between Islam and the West is seen as a clash of civilizations. The West's "next confrontation," observes M. J. Akbar, an Indian Muslim author, "is definitely going to come from the Muslim world. It is in the sweep of the Islamic nations from the Maghreb to Pakistan that the struggle for a new world order will begin." Bernard Lewis comes to a similar conclusion:

> We are facing a mood and a movement far transcending the level of issues and policies and the governments that pursue them. This is no less than a clash of civilizations—the perhaps irrational but surely historic reaction of an ancient rival against our Judeo-Christian heritage, our secular present, and the worldwide expansion of both.*

Historically, the other great antagonistic interaction of Arab Islamic civilization has been with the pagan, animist, and now increasingly Christian black peoples to the south. In the past, this antagonism was epitomized in the image of Arab slave dealers and black slaves. It has been reflected in the ongoing civil war in the Sudan between Arabs and blacks, the fighting in Chad between Libyan-supported insurgents and the government, the tensions between Orthodox Christians and Muslims in the Horn of Africa, and the political conflicts, recurring riots and communal violence between Muslims and Christians in Nigeria. The modernization of Africa and the spread of Christianity are likely to enhance the probability of violence along this fault line. Symptomatic of the intensification of this conflict was the Pope John Paul II's speech in Khartoum in February 1993 attacking the actions of the Sudan's Islamist government against the Christian minority there.

On the northern border of Islam, conflict has increasingly erupted between Orthodox and Muslim peoples, including the carnage of Bosnia and Sarajevo, the simmering violence between Serb and Albanian, the tenuous relations between Bulgarians and their Turkish minority, the violence between Ossetians and Ingush, the unremitting slaughter of each other by Armenians and Azeris, the tense relations between Russians and Muslims in Central Asia, and the deployment of Russian troops to protect Russian interests in the Caucasus and Central Asia. Religion reinforces the revital of ethnic identities and restimulates Russian fears about the security of their southern borders. This concern is well captured by Archie Roosevelt:

> Much of Russian history concerns the struggle between the Slavs and the Turkic peoples on their borders, which dates back to the foundation of the Russian state more than a thousand years ago. In the Slavs' millennium-long confrontation with their

---

* Bernard Lewis, "The Roots of Muslim Rage," *The Atlantic Monthly,* vol. 266, September 1990, p. 60; *Time,* June 15, 1992, pp. 24–28.

> eastern neighbors lies the key to an understanding not only of Russian history, but Russian character. To understand Russian realities today one has to have a concept of the great Turkic ethnic group that has preoccupied Russians through the centuries.*

The conflict of civilizations is deeply rooted elsewhere in Asia. The historic clash between Muslim and Hindu in the subcontinent manifests itself now not only in the rivalry between Pakistan and India but also in intensifying religious strife within India between increasingly militant Hindu groups and India's substantial Muslim minority. The destruction of the Ayodhya mosque in December 1992 brought to the fore the issue of whether India will remain a secular democratic state or become a Hindu one. In East Asia, China has outstanding territorial disputes with most of its neighbors. It has pursued a ruthless policy toward the Buddhist people of Tibet, and it is pursuing an increasingly ruthless policy toward its Turkic-Muslim minority. With the Cold War over, the underlying differences between China and the United States have reasserted themselves in areas such as human rights, trade and weapons proliferation. These differences are unlikely to moderate. A "new cold war," Deng Xaioping reportedly asserted in 1991, is under way between China and America.

The same phrase has been applied to the increasingly difficult relations between Japan and the United States. Here cultural difference exacerbates economic conflict. People on each side allege racism on the other, but at least on the American side the antipathies are not racial but cultural. The basic values, attitudes, behavioral patterns of the two societies could hardly be more different. The economic issues between the United States and Europe are no less serious than those between the United States and Japan, but they do not have the same political salience and emotional intensity because the differences between American culture and European culture are so much less than those between American civilization and Japanese civilization.

The interactions between civilizations vary greatly in the extent to which they are likely to be characterized by violence. Economic competition clearly predominates between the American and European subcivilizations of the West and between both of them and Japan. On the Eurasian continent, however, the proliferation of ethnic conflict, epitomized at the extreme in "ethnic cleansing," has not been totally random. It has been most frequent and most violent between groups belonging to different civilizations. In Eurasia the great historic fault lines between civilizations are once more aflame. This is particularly true along the boundaries of the crescent-shaped Islamic bloc of nations from the bulge of Africa to central Asia. Violence also occurs between Muslims, on the one hand, and Orthodox Serbs in the Balkans, Jews in Israel, Hindus in India, Buddhists in Burma and Catholics in the Philippines. Islam has bloody borders. . . .

---

* Archie Roosevelt, *For Lust of Knowing,* Boston: Little, Brown, 1988, pp 332–333.

The West Versus the Rest

The West is now at an extraordinary peak of power in relation to other civilizations. Its superpower opponent has disappeared from the map. Military conflict among Western states is unthinkable, and Western military power is unrivaled. Apart from Japan, the West faces no economic challenge. It dominates international political and security institutions and with Japan international economic institutions. Global political and security issues are effectively settled by a directorate of the United States, Britain and France, world economic issues by a directorate of the United States, Germany and Japan, all of which maintain extraordinarily close relations with each other to the exclusion of lesser and largely non-Western countries. Decisions made at the U.N. Security Council or in the International Monetary Fund that reflect the interests of the West are presented to the world as reflecting the desires of the world community. The very phrase "the world community" has become the euphemistic collective noun (replacing "the Free World") to give global legitimacy to actions reflecting the interests of the United States and other Western powers.* Through the IMF and other international economic institutions, the West promotes its economic interests and imposes on other nations the economic policies it thinks appropriate. In any poll of non-Western peoples, the IMF undoubtedly would win the support of finance ministers and a few others, but get an overwhelmingly unfavorable rating from just about everyone else, who would agree with Georgy Arbatov's characterization of IMF officials as "neo-Bolsheviks who love expropriating other people's money, imposing undemocratic and alien rules of economic and political conduct and stifling economic freedom."

Western domination of the U.N. Security Council and its decisions, tempered only by occasional abstention by China, produced U.N. legitimation of the West's use of force to drive Iraq out of Kuwait and its elimination of Iraq's sophisticated weapons and capacity to produce such weapons. It also produced the quite unprecedented action by the United States, Britain and France in getting the Security Council to demand that Libya hand over the Pan Am 103 bombing suspects and then to impose sanctions when Libya refused. After defeating the largest Arab army, the West did not hesitate to throw its weight around in the Arab world. The West in effect is using international institutions, military power and economic resources to run the world in ways that will maintain Western predominance, protect Western interests and promote Western political and economic values.

---

* Almost invariably Western leaders claim they are acting on behalf of "the world community." One minor lapse occurred during the run-up to the Gulf War. In an interview on "Good Morning America," Dec. 21, 1990, British Prime Minister John Major referred to the actions "the West" was taking against Saddam Hussein. He quickly corrected himself and subsequently referred to "the world community." He was, however, right when he erred.

That at least is the way in which non-Westerners see the new world, and there is a significant element of truth in their view. Differences in power and struggles for military, economic and institutional power are thus one source of conflict between the West and other civilizations. Differences in culture, that is basic values and beliefs, are a second source of conflict. V. S. Naipaul has argued that Western civilization is the "universal civilization" that "fits all men." At a superficial level much of Western culture has indeed permeated the rest of the world. At a more basic level, however, Western concepts differ fundamentally from those prevalent in other civilizations. Western ideas of individualism, liberalism, constitutionalism, human rights, equality, liberty, the rule of law, democracy, free markets, the separation of church and state, often have little resonance in Islamic, Confucian, Japanese, Hindu, Buddhist or Orthodox cultures. Western efforts to propagate such ideas produce instead a reaction against "human rights imperialism" and a reaffirmation of indigenous values, as can be seen in the support for religious fundamentalism by the younger generation in non-Western cultures. The very notion that there could be a "universal civilization" is a Western idea, directly at odds with the particularism of most Asian societies and their emphasis on what distinguishes one people from another. Indeed, the author of a review of 100 comparative studies of values in different societies concluded that "the values that are most important in the West are least important worldwide."* In the political realm, of course, these differences are most manifest in the efforts of the United States and other Western powers to induce other peoples to adopt Western ideas concerning democracy and human rights. Modern democratic government originated in the West. When it has developed in non-Western societies it has usually been the product of Western colonialism or imposition.

The central axis of world politics in the future is likely to be, in Kishore Mahbubani's phrase, the conflict between "the West and the Rest" and the responses of non-Western civilizations to Western power and values.† Those responses generally take one or a combination of three forms. At one extreme, non-Western states can, like Burma and North Korea, attempt to pursue a course of isolation, to insulate their societies from penetration or "corruption" by the West, and, in effect, to opt out of participation in the Western-dominated global community. The costs of this course, however, are high, and few states have pursued it exclusively. A second alternative, the equivalent of "band-wagoning" in international relations theory, is to attempt to join the West and accept its values and institutions. The third alternative is to attempt to "balance" the West by developing economic and military power and cooperating with other non-Western societies against the West, while preserving indigenous values and institutions; in short, to modernize but not to Westernize. . . .

---

* Harry C. Triandis, *The New York Times,* Dec. 25, 1990, p. 41, and "Cross-Cultural Studies of Individualism and Collectivism," Nebraska Symposium on Motivation, vol. 37, 1989, pp. 41–133.

† Kishore Mahbubani, "The West and the Rest," *The National Interest,* Summer 1992, pp. 3–13.

The Confucian-Islamic Connection

The obstacles to non-Western countries joining the West vary considerably. They are least for Latin American and East European countries. They are greater for the Orthodox countries of the former Soviet Union. They are still greater for Muslim, Confucian, Hindu and Buddhist societies. Japan has established a unique position for itself as an associate member of the West: it is in the West in some respects but clearly not of the West in important dimensions. Those countries that for reason of culture and power do not wish to, or cannot, join the West compete with the West by developing their own economic, military and political power. They do this by promoting their internal development and by cooperating with other non-Western countries. The most prominent form of this cooperation is the Confucian-Islamic connection that has emerged to challenge Western interests, values and power.

Almost without exception, Western countries are reducing their military power; under Yeltsin's leadership so also is Russia. China, North Korea and several Middle Eastern states, however, are significantly expanding their military capabilities. They are doing this by the import of arms from Western and non-Western sources and by the development of indigenous arms industries. One result is the emergence of what Charles Krauthammer has called "Weapon States," and the Weapon States are not Western states. Another result is the redefinition of arms control, which is a Western concept and a Western goal. During the Cold War the primary purpose of arms control was to establish a stable military balance between the United States and its allies and the Soviet Union and its allies. In the post-Cold War world the primary objective of arms control is to prevent the development by non-Western societies of military capabilities that could threaten Western interests. The West attempts to do this through international agreements, economic pressure and controls on the transfer of arms and weapons technologies.

The conflict between the West and the Confucian-Islamic states focuses largely, although not exclusively, on nuclear, chemical and biological weapons, ballistic missiles and other sophisticated means for delivering them, and the guidance, intelligence and other electronic capabilities for achieving that goal. The West promotes nonproliferation as a universal norm and nonproliferation treaties and inspections as means of realizing that norm. It also threatens a variety of sanctions against those who promote the spread of sophisticated weapons and proposes some benefits for those who do not. The attention of the West focuses, naturally, on nations that are actually or potentially hostile to the West.

The non-Western nations, on the other hand, assert their right to acquire and to deploy whatever weapons they think necessary for their security. They also have absorbed, to the full, the truth of the response of the Indian defense minister when asked what lesson he learned from the Gulf War: "Don't fight the United States unless you have nuclear weapons." Nuclear weapons, chemical weapons and missiles are viewed, probably erroneously, as the potential equalizer of superior Western conventional power. China, of course, already has nuclear weapons;

Pakistan and India have the capability to deploy them. North Korea, Iran, Iraq, Libya and Algeria appear to be attempting to acquire them. A top Iranian official has declared that all Muslim states should acquire nuclear weapons, and in 1988 the president of Iran reportedly issued a directive calling for development of "offensive and defensive chemical, biological and radiological weapons."

Centrally important to the development of counter-West military capabilities is the sustained expansion of China's military power and its means to create military power. Buoyed by spectacular economic development, China is rapidly increasing its military spending and vigorously moving forward with the modernization of its armed forces. It is purchasing weapons from the former Soviet states; it is developing long-range missiles; in 1992 it tested a one-megaton nuclear device. It is developing power-projection capabilities, acquiring aerial refueling technology, and trying to purchase an aircraft carrier. Its military buildup and assertion of sovereignty over the South China Sea are provoking a multilateral regional arms race in East Asia. China is also a major exporter of arms and weapons technology. It has exported materials to Libya and Iraq that could be used to manufacture nuclear weapons and nerve gas. It has helped Algeria build a reactor suitable for nuclear weapons research and production. China has sold to Iran nuclear technology that American officials believe could only be used to create weapons and apparently has shipped components of 300-mile-range missiles to Pakistan. North Korea has had a nuclear weapons program under way for some while and has sold advanced missiles and missile technology to Syria and Iran. The flow of weapons and weapons technology is generally from East Asia to the Middle East. There is, however, some movement in the reverse direction; China has received Stinger missiles from Pakistan.

A Confucian-Islamic military connection has thus come into being, designed to promote acquisition by its members of the weapons and weapons technologies needed to counter the military power of the West. It may or may not last. At present, however, it is, as Dave McCurdy has said, "a renegades' mutual support pact, run by the proliferators and their backers." A new form of arms competition is thus occurring between Islamic-Confucian states and the West. In an old-fashioned arms race, each side developed its own arms to balance or to achieve superiority against the other side. In this new form of arms competition, one side is developing its arms and the other side is attempting not to balance but to limit and prevent that arms build-up while at the same time reducing its own military capabilities.

Implications for the West

This article does not argue that civilization identities will replace all other identities, that nation states will disappear, that each civilization will become a single coherent political entity, that groups within a civilization will not conflict with and even fight each other. This paper does set forth the hypotheses that differences between civilizations are real and important; civilization-consciousness is increasing; conflict between civilizations will supplant ideological and other forms of conflict as the dominant global form of conflict; international relations, historically a game played out within Western civilization, will increasingly be de-Westernized and become a game in which non-Western civilizations are actors and not simply objects; successful political, security and economic international institutions are more likely to develop within civilizations than across civilizations; conflicts between groups in different civilizations will be more frequent, more sustained and more violent than conflicts between groups in the same civilization; violent conflicts between groups in different civilizations are the most likely and most dangerous source of escalation that could lead to global wars; the paramount axis of world politics will be the relations between "the West and the Rest"; the elites in some torn non-Western countries will try to make their countries part of the West, but in most cases face major obstacles to accomplishing this; a central focus of conflict for the immediate future will be between the West and several Islamic-Confucian states.

This is not to advocate the desirability of conflicts between civilizations. It is to set forth descriptive hypotheses as to what the future may be like. If these are plausible hypotheses, however, it is necessary to consider their implications for Western policy. These implications should be divided between short-term advantage and long-term accommodation. In the short term it is clearly in the interest of the West to promote greater cooperation and unity within its own civilization, particularly between its European and North American components; to incorporate into the West societies in Eastern Europe and Latin America whose cultures are close to those of the West; to promote and maintain cooperative relations with Russia and Japan; to prevent escalation of local inter-civilization conflicts into major inter-civilization wars; to limit the expansion of the military strength of Confucian and Islamic states; to moderate the reduction of Western military capabilities and maintain military superiority in East and Southwest Asia; to exploit differences and conflicts among Confucian and Islamic states; to support in other civilizations groups sympathetic to Western values and interests; to strengthen international institutions that reflect and legitimate Western interests and values and to promote the involvement of non-Western states in those institutions.

In the longer term other measures would be called for. Western civilization is both Western and modern. Non-Western civilizations have attempted to become modern without becoming Western. To date only Japan has fully succeeded in this quest. Non-Western civilizations will continue to attempt to acquire the wealth, technology, skills, machines and weapons that are part of being modern. They will also attempt to reconcile this modernity with their traditional culture and values. Their economic and military strength relative to the West will increase. Hence the West will increasingly have to accommodate these non-Western modern civilizations whose power approaches that of the West but whose values and interests differ significantly from those of the West. This will require the West to maintain the economic and military power necessary to protect its interests in relation to these civilizations. It will also, however, require the West to develop a more profound understanding of the basic religious and philosophical assumptions underlying other civilizations and the ways in which people in those civilizations see their interests. It will require an effort to identify elements of commonality between Western and other civilizations. For the relevant future, there will be no universal civilization, but instead a world of different civilizations, each of which will have to learn to coexist with the others.

 1.3

Jihad vs. McWorld

Benjamin Barber

According to Professor Barber, the most important political conflict in the world today pits Western-based capitalism, championed by multinational corporations that seek to extend markets throughout the world, against groups united by ethnic or religious ties that passionately oppose the values championed by capitalism of individualism, consumerism, and hedonism. Critics charge that the world is more complicated than Barber claims, that there are more alternatives than the two that he identifies (see the two other selections in Chapter 1). What is your position in this debate and why?

History is not over. Nor are we arrived in the wondrous land of techné promised by the futurologists. The collapse of state communism has not delivered people to a safe democratic haven, and the past, fratricide and civil discord perduring, still clouds the horizon just behind us. Those who look back see all of the horrors of the ancient slaughterbench reenacted in disintegral nations like Bosnia, Sri Lanka, Ossetia, and Rwanda and they declare that nothing has changed. Those who look forward prophesize commercial and technological interdependence—a virtual paradise made possible by spreading markets and global technology—and they proclaim that everything is or soon will be different. The rival observers seem to consult different almanacs drawn from the libraries of contrarian planets.

Yet anyone who reads the daily papers carefully, taking in the front page accounts of civil carnage as well as the business page stories on the mechanics of the information superhighway and the economics of communication mergers, anyone who turns deliberately to take in the whole 360-degree horizon, knows that our world and our lives are caught between what William Butler Yeats called the two eternities of race and soul: that of race reflecting the tribal past, that of soul anticipating the cosmopolitan future. Our secular eternities are corrupted, however, race reduced to an insignia of resentment, and soul sized down to fit the demanding body by which it now measures its needs. Neither race nor soul offers us a future that is other than bleak, neither promises a polity that is remotely democratic.

The first scenario rooted in race holds out the grim prospect of a retribalization of large swaths of humankind by war and bloodshed: a threatened balkanization of nation-states in which culture is pitted against culture, people against people, tribe against tribe, a Jihad in the name of a hundred narrowly conceived faiths against every kind of interdependence, every kind of artificial social cooperation and mutuality: against technology, against pop culture, and against integrated markets; against modernity itself as well as the future in which modernity issues. The second paints that future in shimmering pastels, a busy portrait of onrushing economic, technological, and ecological forces that demand integration and uniformity and that mesmerize peoples everywhere with fast music, fast computers, and fast food—MTV, Macintosh, and McDonald's—pressing nations into one homogenous global theme park, one McWorld tied together by communications, information, entertainment, and commerce. Caught between Babel and Disneyland, the planet is falling precipitously apart and coming reluctantly together at the very same moment.

Some stunned observers notice only Babel, complaining about the thousand newly sundered "peoples" who prefer to address their neighbors with sniper rifles and mortars; others—zealots in Disneyland—seize on futurological platitudes and the promise of virtuality, exclaiming "It's a small world after all!" Both are right, but how can that be?

We are compelled to choose between what passes as "the twilight of sovereignty" and an entropic end of all history;[1] or a return to the past's most fractious and demoralizing discord; to "the menace of global anarchy," to Milton's capital of hell, Pandaemonium; to a world totally "out of control."[2]

The apparent truth, which speaks to the paradox at the core of this book, is that the tendencies of both Jihad *and* McWorld are at work, both visible sometimes in the same country at the very same instant. Iranian zealots keep one ear tuned to the mullahs urging holy war and the other cocked to Rupert Murdoch's Star television beaming in *Dynasty*, *Donahue*, and *The Simpsons* from hovering satellites. Chinese entrepreneurs vie for the attention of party cadres in Beijing and simultaneously pursue KFC franchises in cities like Nanjing, Hangzhou, and Xian where twenty-eight outlets serve over 100,000 customers a day. The Russian Orthodox church, even as it struggles to renew the ancient faith, has entered a joint venture with California businessmen to bottle and sell natural waters under the rubric Saint Springs Water Company. Serbian assassins wear Adidas sneakers and listen to Madonna on Walkman headphones as they take aim through their gunscopes at scurrying Sarajevo civilians looking to fill family watercans. Orthodox Hasids and brooding neo-Nazis have both turned to rock music to get their traditional messages out to the new generation, while fundamentalists plot virtual conspiracies on the Internet.

Now neither Jihad nor McWorld is in itself novel. History ending in the triumph of science and reason or some monstrous perversion thereof (Mary Shelley's Doctor Frankenstein) has been the leitmotiv of every philosopher and poet who has regretted the Age of Reason since the Enlightenment. Yeats lamented "the center will not hold, mere anarchy is loosed upon the world," and observers of Jihad today have little but historical detail to add. The Christian parable of the Fall and of the possibilities of redemption that it makes possible captures the eighteenth-century ambivalence—and our own—about past and future. I want, however, to do more than dress up the central paradox of human history in modern clothes. It is not Jihad and McWorld but the relationship between them that most interests me. For, squeezed between their opposing forces, the world has been sent spinning out of control.[3] Can it be that what Jihad and McWorld have in common is anarchy: the absence of common will and that conscious and collective human control under the guidance of law we call democracy?

Progress moves in steps that sometimes lurch backwards; in history's twisting maze, Jihad not only revolts against but abets McWorld, while McWorld not only imperils but re-creates and reinforces Jihad. They produce their contraries and need one another. My object here then is not simply to offer sequential portraits of McWorld and Jihad, but while examining McWorld, to keep Jihad in my field of vision, and while dissecting Jihad, never to forget the context of McWorld. Call it a dialectic of McWorld: a study in the cunning of reason that does honor to the radical differences that distinguish Jihad and McWorld yet that acknowledges their powerful and paradoxical interdependence. . . .

What then does it mean in concrete terms to view Jihad and McWorld dialectically when the tendencies of the two sets of forces initially appear so intractably antithetical? After all, Jihad and McWorld operate with equal strength in opposite directions, the one driven by parochial hatreds, the other by universalizing markets, the one re-creating ancient subnational and ethnic borders from within, the other making national borders porous from without. Yet Jihad and McWorld have this in common: they both make war on the sovereign nation-state and thus undermine the nation-state's democratic institutions. Each eschews civil society and belittles democratic citizenship, neither seeks alternative democratic institutions. Their common thread is indifference to civil liberty. Jihad forges communities of blood rooted in exclusion and hatred, communities that slight democracy in favor of tyrannical paternalism or consensual tribalism. McWorld forges global markets rooted in consumption and profit, leaving to an untrustworthy, if not altogether fictitious, invisible hand issues of public interest and common good that once might have been nurtured by democratic citizenries and their watchful governments. Such governments, intimidated by market ideology, are actually pulling back at the very moment they ought to be aggressively intervening. What was once understood as protecting the public interest is now excoriated as heavy-handed regulatory browbeating.[4] Justice yields to markets, even though, as Felix Rohatyn has bluntly confessed, "there is a brutal Darwinian logic to these markets. They are nervous and greedy. They look for stability and transparency, but what they reward is not always our preferred form of democracy."[5] If the traditional conservators of freedom were democratic constitutions and Bills of Rights, "the new temples to liberty," George Steiner suggests, "will be McDonald's and Kentucky Fried Chicken."[6]

In being reduced to a choice between the market's universal church and a retribalizing politics of particularist identities, peoples around the globe are threatened with an atavistic return to medieval politics where local tribes and ambitious emperors together ruled the world entire, women and men united by the universal abstraction of Christianity even as they lived out isolated lives in warring fiefdoms defined by involuntary (ascriptive) forms of identity. This was a world in which princes and kings had little real power until they conceived the ideology of nationalism. Nationalism established government on a scale greater than the tribe yet less cosmopolitan than the universal church and in time gave birth to those intermediate, gradually more democratic institutions that would come to constitute the nation-state. Today, at the far end of this history, we seem intent on re-creating a world in which our only choices are the secular universalism of the cosmopolitan market and the everyday particularism of the fractious tribe.

In the tumult of the confrontation between global commerce and parochial ethnicity, the virtues of the democratic nation are lost and the instrumentalities by which it permitted peoples to transform themselves into nations and seize sovereign power in the name of liberty and the commonweal are put at risk. Neither Jihad nor McWorld aspires to resecure the civic virtues undermined by its denationalizing practices; neither global markets nor blood communities service public goods or pursue equality and justice. Impartial judiciaries and deliberative assemblies play no role in the roving killer bands that speak on behalf of newly liberated "peoples," and such democratic institutions have at best only marginal influence on the roving multinational corporations that speak on behalf of newly liberated markets. Jihad pursues a bloody politics of identity, McWorld a bloodless economics of profit. Belonging by default to McWorld, everyone is a consumer; seeking a repository for identity, everyone belongs to some tribe. But no one is a citizen. Without citizens, how can there be democracy?

From Self-Determination to Jihad

. . . In this tumultuous world, the real players are not nations at all but tribes, many of them at war with one another. Their aim is precisely to redraw boundaries in order to divide—say in Kurdish Iraq or Muslim Sudan or Serbian-populated sections of Croatia. Countries like Afghanistan, recently fighting a foreign invader in the name of its national independence, have been effectively dismembered: divided among Panthans, Hazaras, Uzbeks, and Tajiks. This is ethnic membership enhanced via national dismemberment—or by expulsion or expunction of unwanted contaminators, as has occurred in slaughter-happy Rwanda. Is this pandaemonium just an extension of benign efforts at multiculturalism? A natural consequence of a centuries-old impulse to self-determination? Or the appearance of a new disease that has corrupted integral nationalism and opened the way to ethnic and religious Jihad?

Jihad is, I recognize, a strong term. In its mildest form, it betokens religious struggle on behalf of faith, a kind of Islamic zeal. In its strongest political manifestation, it means bloody holy war on behalf of partisan identity that is metaphysically defined and fanatically defended. Thus, while for many Muslims it may signify only ardor in the name of a religion that can properly be regarded as universalizing (if not quite ecumenical), I borrow its meaning from those militants who make the slaughter of the "other" a higher duty.[7] I use the term in its militant construction to suggest dogmatic and violent particularism of a kind known to Christians no less than Muslims, to Germans and Hindis as well as to Arabs. The phenomena to which I apply the phrase have innocent enough beginnings: identity politics and multicultural diversity can represent strategies of a free society trying to give expression to its diversity. What ends as Jihad may begin as a simple search for a local identity, some set of common personal attributes to hold out against the numbing and neutering uniformities of industrial modernization and the colonizing culture of McWorld.

America is often taken as the model for this kind of benign multiculturalism, although we too have our critics like Arthur Schlesinger, Jr., for whom multiculturalism is never benign and for whom it signals the inaugural logic of a long-term disintegration.[8] . . . The startling fact is that less than 10 percent (about twenty) of the modern world's states are truly homogenous and thus, like Denmark or the Netherlands, can't get smaller unless they fracture into tribes or clans.[9] In only half is there a single ethnic group that comprises even 75 percent of the population.[10] As in the United States, multiculturalism is the rule, homogeneity the exception. Nations like Japan or Spain that appear to the outside world as integral turn out to be remarkably multicultural. And even if language alone, the nation's essential attribute, is made the condition for self-determination, a count of the number of languages spoken around the world suggests the community of nations could grow to over six thousand members.

The modern nation-state has actually acted as a cultural integrator and has adapted well to pluralist ideals: civic ideologies and constitutional faiths around which their many clans and tribes can rally. It has not been too difficult to contrive a civil religion for Americans or French or Swiss, since these "peoples" actually contain multitudes of subnational factions and ethnic tribes earnestly seeking common ground. But for Basques and Normans? What need have they for anything but blood and memory? And what of Alsatians, Bavarians, and East Prussians? Kurds, Ossetians, East Timorese, Quebecois, Abkhazians, Catalonians, Tamils, Inkatha Zulus, Kurile Islander Japanese—peoples without countries inhabiting nations they cannot call their own? Peoples trying to seal themselves off not just from others but from modernity? These are frightened tribes running not to but from civic faith in search of something more palpable and electrifying. How will peoples who define themselves by the slaughter of tribal neighbors be persuaded to subscribe to some flimsy artificial faith organized around abstract civic ideals or commercial markets? Can advertising divert warriors of blood from the genocide required by their ancient grievances? . . .

McWorld is a product of popular culture driven by expansionist commerce. Its template is American, its form style. Its goods are as much images as matériel, an aesthetic as well as a product line. It is about culture as commodity, apparel as ideology. Its symbols are Harley-Davidson motorcycles and Cadillac motorcars hoisted from the roadways, where they once represented a mode of transportation, to the marquees of global market cafés like Harley-Davidson's and the Hard Rock where they become icons of lifestyle. You don't drive them, you feel their vibes and rock to the images they conjure up from old movies and new celebrities, whose personal appearances are the key to the wildly popular international café chain Planet Hollywood. Music, video, theater, books, and theme parks—the new churches of a commercial civilization in which malls are the public squares and suburbs the neighborless neighborhoods—are all constructed as image exports creating a common world taste around common logos, advertising slogans, stars, songs, brand names, jingles, and trademarks. Hard power yields to soft, while ideology is transmuted into a kind of videology that works through sound bites and film clips. Videology is fuzzier and less dogmatic than traditional political ideology: it may as a consequence be far more successful in instilling the novel values required for global markets to succeed.

McWorld's videology remains Jihad's most formidable rival, and in the long run it may attenuate the force of Jihad's recidivist tribalisms.[11] Yet the information revolution's instrumentalities are also Jihad's favored weapons. Hutu or Bosnian Serb identity was less a matter of real historical memory than of media propaganda by a leadership set on liquidating rival clans. In both Rwanda and Bosnia, radio broadcasts whipped listeners into a killing frenzy. As *New York Times* rock critic Jon Pareles has noticed, "regionalism in pop music has become as trendy as microbrewery beer and narrowcasting cable channels, and for the same reasons."[12] The global culture is what gives the local culture its medium, its audience, and its aspirations. Fascist pop and Hasid rock are not oxymorons; rather they manifest the dialectics of McWorld in particularly dramatic ways. Belgrade's radio includes stations that broadcast Western pop music as a rebuke

to hard-liner Milosevic's supernationalist government and stations that broadcast native folk tunes laced with antiforeign and anti-Semitic sentiments. Even
the Internet has its neo-Nazi bulletin boards and Turk-trashing Armenian
"flamers" (who assail every use of the word *turkey*, fair and fowl alike, so to
speak), so that the abstractions of cyberspace too are infected with a peculiar
and rabid cultural territoriality all their own.

The dynamics of the Jihad-McWorld linkage are deeply dialectical. Japan has,
for example, become more culturally insistent on its own traditions in recent
years even as its people seek an ever greater purchase on McWorld. In 1992,
the number-one restaurant in Japan measured by volume of customers was
McDonald's, followed in the number-two spot by the Colonel's Kentucky Fried
Chicken.[13] In France, where cultural purists complain bitterly of a looming Six-
ième République ("la République Américaine"), the government attacks
"franglais" even as it funds EuroDisney park just outside of Paris. In the same
spirit, the cinema industry makes war on American film imports while it bestows
upon Sylvester Stallone one of France's highest honors, the Chevalier des arts et
lettres.[14] Ambivalence also stalks India. Just outside of Bombay, cheek by jowl
with villages still immersed in poverty and notorious for the informal execution
of unwanted female babies or, even, wives, can be found a new town known as
SCEEPZ—the Santa Cruz Electronic Export Processing Zone—where Hindi-,
Tamil-, and Mahratti-speaking computer programmers write software for Swiss-
air, AT&T, and other labor-cost-conscious multinationals. India is thus at once
a major exemplar of ancient ethnic and religious tensions and "an emerging
power in the international software industry."[15] To go to work at SCEEPZ, says
an employee, is "like crossing an international border." Not into another country,
but into the virtual nowhere-land of McWorld.

More dramatic even than in India, is the strange interplay of Jihad and
McWorld in the remnants of Yugoslavia. In an affecting *New Republic* report,
Slavenka Drakulic recently told the brief tragic love story of Admira and Bosko,
two young star-crossed lovers from Sarajevo: "They were born in the late
1960's," she writes. "They watched Spielberg movies; they listened to Iggy Pop;
they read John le Carré; they went to a disco every Saturday night and fantasized
about traveling to Paris or London."[16] Longing for safety, it seems they finally
negotiated with all sides for safe passage, and readied their departure from
Sarajevo. Before they could cross the magical border that separates their impoverished land from the seeming sanctuary of McWorld, Jihad caught up to them.
Their bodies lay along the riverbank, riddled with bullets from anonymous
snipers for whom safe passage signaled an invitation to target practice. The murdered young lovers, as befits émigrés to McWorld, were clothed in jeans and
sneakers. So too, one imagines, were their murderers.

Further east, tourists seeking a piece of old Russia that does not take them too
far from MTV can find traditional Matryoshka nesting dolls (that fit one inside
the other) featuring the nontraditional visages of (from largest to smallest)
Bruce Springsteen, Madonna, Boy George, Dave Stewart, and Annie Lennox.[17]

In Russia, in India, in Bosnia, in Japan, and in France too, modern history then leans both ways: toward the meretricious inevitability of McWorld, but also into Jihad's stiff winds, heaving to and fro and giving heart both to the Panglossians and the Pandoras, sometimes for the very same reasons. The Panglossians bank on Euro-Disney and Microsoft, while the Pandoras await nihilism and a world in Pandaemonium. Yet McWorld and Jihad do not really force a choice between such polarized scenarios. Together, they are likely to produce some stifling amalgam of the two suspended in chaos. Antithetical in every detail, Jihad and McWorld nonetheless conspire to undermine our hard-won (if only half-won) civil liberties and the possibility of a global democratic future. In the short run the forces of Jihad, noisier and more obviously nihilistic than those of McWorld, are likely to dominate the near future, etching small stories of local tragedy and regional genocide on the face of our times and creating a climate of instability marked by multimicrowars inimical to global integration. But in the long run, the forces of McWorld are the forces underlying the slow certain thrust of Western civilization and as such may be unstoppable. Jihad's microwars will hold the headlines well into the next century, making predictions of the end of history look terminally dumb. But McWorld's homogenization is likely to establish a macropeace that favors the triumph of commerce and its markets and to give to those who control information, communication, and entertainment ultimate (if inadvertent) control over human destiny. Unless we can offer an alternative to the struggle between Jihad and McWorld, the epoch on whose threshold we stand—postcommunist, postindustrial, postnational, yet sectarian, fearful, and bigoted—is likely also to be terminally postdemocratic.

Notes

1. Francis Fukuyama, in *The End of History and the Last Man* (New York: Free Press, 1992), although he is far less pleased by his prognosis in his book than he seemed in the original *National Interest* essay that occasioned all the controversy; and Walter B. Wriston, *Twilight of Sovereignty* (New York: Scribner's, 1992).

2. See Georgie Anne Geyer, "Our Disintegrating World: The Menace of Global Anarchy," *Encyclopaedia Britannica, Book of the Year, 1985* (Chicago: University of Chicago Press, 1985), pp. 11–25. Daniel Patrick Moynihan, *Pandaemonium: Ethnicity in International Politics* (New York: Oxford University Press, 1993); and Zbigniew Brzezinski, *Out of Control: Global Turmoil on the Eve of the Twenty-First Century* (New York: Scribner's, 1993). Also see Tony Judt, "The New Old Nationalisms," *The New York Review of Books*, May 26, 1994, pp. 44–51.

3. Two recent books, the one by Zbigniew Brzezinski cited above about the "global turmoil" of ethnic nationalism (Jihad), the other by Kevin Kelly about computers and "the rise of neo-biological civilization [McWorld]" both carry the title "Out of Control." See Brzezinski, *Out of Control;* and Kevin Kelly, *Out of Control: The Rise of Neo-Biological Civilization* (Reading, Mass.: Addison-Wesley, 1994). The metaphor is everywhere: for example, in Andrew Bard Schmookler's *The Illusion of Choice* (Albany: State University of New York at Albany Press, 1993), Part III on runaway markets is also entitled "Out of Control."

4. In its "new tack on technology," writes *New York Times* reporter Edmund L. Andrews, the Clinton administration wants only to avoid doing anything "to spook investors with heavy-handed regulatory

brow-beating," hoping rather to reduce "the regulatory barriers that have prevented competition." Edmund L. Andrews, "New Tack on Technology," *The New York Times*, January 12, 1994, p. A 1. At the end of the 1994 congressional session, a Communications Bill that would have imposed some controls on the information superhighway expired quietly.

5. Rohatyn cited by Thomas L. Friedman, "When Money Talks, Governments Listen," *The New York Times*, July 24, 1994, p. E 3.

6. Steiner writes that the new Eastern European democratic revolutions of recent years were not "inebriate with some abstract passion for freedom, for social justice." Consumer culture, "video cassettes, porno cassettes, American-style cosmetics and fast foods, not editions of Mill, Tocqueville or Solzhenitsyn, were the prizes snatched from every West[ern] shelf by the liberated." George Steiner, in *Granta*, cited by Anthony Lewis, "A Quake Hits the Summit," *International Herald Tribune*, June 2–3, 1990.

7. Muslim users at times intentionally obfuscate the difference between meanings; thus, speaking to an Arab audience in mid-1994 just as the accord over Jericho and Gaza went into effect, Yassar Arafat spoke militantly to a Palestinian audience of a Jihad to recapture Jerusalem—only to "explain" later to agitated Israelis and Westerners that he meant only to call for a peaceful struggle.

8. See Arthur Schlesinger, Jr., *Disuniting America* (New York: Norton, 1993).

9. A minimalist's list would include the Netherlands, Denmark, Iceland, Luxembourg, Norway, and Portugal representing less than 1 percent of the world's population. Japan is sometimes also included in the list, which brings the number to under 5 percent.

10. *The Washington Post*, National Weekly Edition, December 21–27, 1992, p. 28.

11. IRAN FIGHTS NEW FOE: WESTERN TELEVISION and FOR CLERICS, SATELLITES CARRYING MTV ARE DEADLIER THAN GUNS, scream *Wall Street Journal* headlines; *The Wall Street Journal*, August 8, 1994, above an article by Peter Waldman citing an Iranian cleric who complains that satellite dishes spread "the family-devastating diseases of the West," p. A 10.

12. Jon Pareles, "Striving to Become Rock's Next Seattle," *The New York Times*, July 17, 1994, Section 2, p. 1.

13. Of McDonald's nearly 15,000 restaurants, nearly forty-five hundred, or one-third, are abroad; there are over one thousand in Japan alone. Gary Hoover, *Hoover's Handbook of American Business* (Austin: Reference Press, 1994), pp. 746–747.

14. Jack Lang, the culture minister of the socialist government deposed in 1993, was especially ambivalent, personally leading the campaign on "franglais" and its mangling of authentic French and calling for legislation to protect the French language (passed under the successor conservative government) as well as the fight to protect the French film industry against Hollywood in the GATT round, yet also proclaiming his affection for Americans and their culture.

15. National Public Radio, *All Things Considered*, December 2, 1993, from the broadcast transcription.

16. Slavenka Drakulic, "Love Story: A True Tale from Sarajevo," *The New Republic*, October 26, 1993, pp. 14–16.

17. There is also a Michael Jackson babushka that gradually turns into a panther and a chimpanzee.

 Chapter 2

STATES AND REGIMES

Within a given country, the state is almost always the most powerful cluster of institutions. But just what is the state? The way the term is used in comparative politics is probably unfamiliar to many students. In the United States, it usually refers to the states in the federal system—Texas, California, and so on. But in the study of comparative politics, the "state" refers to the cluster of political institutions responsible for making, implementing, enforcing, and adjudicating important policies in a country. The most important state institutions are the national executive, notably, the president and/or prime minister and cabinet, along with the army, police, and administrative bureaucracy, as well as the legislature and courts.

The fact that states are the fundamental objects of analysis in comparative politics does not mean that all states are the same. Indeed, the organization of state institutions varies widely. The term "regime" highlights differences among the kinds of political institutions that comprise the state. Perhaps the most important distinction is whether regimes are democratic or authoritarian.

The term "regime" also highlights different forms of democratic and authoritarian institutions. For example, within democracies, an important contrast is between presidential and parliamentary regimes. (See the article by Stepan and Skach in Chapter 6, which compares these two sorts of regimes.)

States assert, usually with considerable success, the right to issue rules—notably, laws, administrative regulations, and court decisions—that are binding for people within the country. Even democratic regimes, in which top officials are chosen by procedures that permit all citizens to participate, can survive only if they can preserve enforcement (or coercive) powers both internally and with regard to other states. Many countries have highly undemocratic regimes, whose political survival depends on a heavy dose of repression. But even in such cases, long-term stability requires some measure of political legitimacy; that is, a significant segment of the citizenry must believe that the state is entitled to command. In the modern world, nearly all states claim to be democratic, even when, as the selection by Levitsky and Way describes, a democratic facade may obscure a heavy dose of authoritarian practices.

Political legitimacy is greatly affected by the state's ability to deliver the goods through satisfactory economic performance. Moreover, in the contemporary period legitimacy usually requires that states represent themselves as democratic in some fashion, whether or not they are in fact. Thus, *Readings in Comparative Politics* (RCP) examines closely both the state's role in governing the economy (Chapter 3) and the pressures exerted on states to be democratic (Chapter 4).

For several hundred years, states have been among the principal actors on the world stage. Of course, they were always forced to compete with other states and, in extreme cases (although one that has occurred countless times), fight wars to protect their position. Indeed, as the selection by Tilly describes, warmaking and statebuilding have been closely related.

The usual description of the world as neatly divided into independent states, however, was always misleading. Many regions, including most of Africa and Asia for much of the nineteenth and early twentieth centuries, were colonies of European powers. Furthermore, no state fully monopolizes power within its borders. This is true even for the most authoritarian states, such as Nazi Germany in the 1930s and 1940s, and the Soviet Union for the seventy years of its existence.

Recently, however, many scholars have asserted that globalization—defined as cross-border flows of people, capital, commodities, and ideas (culture)—has fundamentally undermined state supremacy. Publications with titles like *The Retreat of the State?,* "The Eclipse of the State?", and *Challenging the State** have analyzed how economic and technological developments—for example, the Internet and transnational corporate activity—have weakened states' ability to control activities within their borders. On the other hand, to adapt Mark Twain, when newspapers mistakenly announced his death, reports of the death of the state may be greatly exaggerated![†] The relationship of states to globalization is one of the most controversial topics in comparative politics today. (See the articles in this chapter by van Creveld, Rotberg, and Sassen.)

When you read the articles in this chapter, think about why it matters that states vary in time and place in terms of their regimes and the extent of their autonomy. What is the impact of differences in states and regimes for political and social life? The articles in this chapter will help you analyze this question. But states and regimes are so central to the study of comparative politics that many articles in other chapters of RCP will also consider this issue.

---

[*] Susan Strange, *The Retreat of the State?: The Diffusion of Power in the World Economy* (New York: Cambridge University Press, 1996); Peter Evans, "The Eclipse of the State? Reflections on Stateness in an Era of Globalization," *World Politics* 50, No. 1 (October 1997): 62–87; and Merilee S. Grindle, *Challenging the State: Crisis and Innovation in Latin America and Africa* (New York: Cambridge University Press, 1996).

[†] Robert Wade alludes to Twain's wry remark in the title of his fine essay suggesting the limits of globalization. See his essay, "Globalization and its Limits: Reports of the Death of the National Economy Are Greatly Exaggerated," in Suzanne Berger and Ronald Dore, eds., *National Diversity and Global Capitalism* (Ithaca: Cornell University Press, 1996), ch. 2.

▓ 2.1

War Making and State Making as Organized Crime

Charles Tilly

Charles Tilly makes a shocking claim—that state authority resembles organized crime, in that state authorities demand tribute (taxes and obedience) from citizens within their jurisdiction, in return for which they provide protection from . . . themselves! Tilly points out that protection also involves defending citizens from foreign threats. Thus, he claims, while states make war, wars make states. That is, in order to wage war effectively, he argues, states have been forced to develop the capacity to extract taxes, expand the country's economic base, and obtain the support of their citizens. In brief, waging war requires states to become larger, better organized, and more motivated to develop their country's economy. In reading this selection, think about what else besides the need to wage war might promote state development.

Warning

If protection rackets represent organized crime at its smoothest, then war making and state making—quintessential protection rackets with the advantage of legitimacy—qualify as our largest examples of organized crime. Without branding all generals and statesmen as murderers or thieves, I want to urge the value of that analogy. At least for the European experience of the past few centuries, a portrait of war makers and state makers as coercive and self-seeking entrepreneurs bears a far greater resemblance to the facts than do its chief alternatives: the idea of a social contract, the idea of an open market in which operators of armies and states offer services to willing consumers, the idea of a society whose shared norms and expectations call forth a certain kind of government.

The reflections that follow merely illustrate the analogy of war making and state making with organized crime from a few hundred years of European experience and offer tentative arguments concerning principles of change and variation underlying the experience. My reflections grow from contemporary concerns: worries about the increasing destructiveness of war, the expanding role of great powers as suppliers of arms and military organization to poor countries, and the growing importance of military rule in those same countries. They spring from the hope that the European experience, properly understood, will help us to grasp what is happening today, perhaps even to do something about it.

The Third World of the twentieth century does not greatly resemble Europe of the sixteenth or seventeenth century. In no simple sense can we read the future of Third World countries from the pasts of European countries. Yet a thoughtful exploration of European experience will serve us well. It will show us that coercive exploitation played a large part in the creation of the European states. It will show us that popular resistance to coercive exploitation forced would-be power holders to concede protection and constraints on their own action. It will therefore help us to eliminate faulty implicit comparisons between today's Third World and yesterday's Europe. That clarification will make it easier to understand exactly how today's world is different and what we therefore have to explain. It may even help us to explain the current looming presence of military organization and action throughout the world. Although that result would delight me, I do not promise anything so grand.

This essay, then, concerns the place of organized means of violence in the growth and change of those peculiar forms of government we call national states: relatively centralized, differentiated organizations the officials of which more or less successfully claim control over the chief concentrated means of violence within a population inhabiting a large, contiguous territory. The argument grows from historical work on the formation of national states in Western Europe, especially on the growth of the French state from 1600 onward. But it takes several deliberate steps away from that work, wheels, and stares hard at it from theoretical ground. The argument brings with it few illustrations and no evidence worthy of the name.

Just as one repacks a hastily filled rucksack after a few days on the trail—throwing out the waste, putting things in order of importance, and balancing the load—I have repacked my theoretical baggage for the climb to come; the real test of the new packing arrives only with the next stretch of the trail. The trimmed-down argument stresses the interdependence of war making and state making and the analogy between both of those processes and what, when less successful and smaller in scale, we call organized crime. War makes states, I shall claim. Banditry, piracy, gangland rivalry, policing, and war making all belong on the same continuum—that I shall claim as well. For the historically limited period in which national states were becoming the dominant organizations in

Western countries, I shall also claim that mercantile capitalism and state making reinforced each other.

Double-Edged Protection

In contemporary American parlance, the word "protection" sounds two contrasting tones. One is comforting, the other ominous. With one tone, "protection" calls up images of the shelter against danger provided by a powerful friend, a large insurance policy, or a sturdy roof. With the other, it evokes the racket in which a local strong man forces merchants to pay tribute in order to avoid damage—damage the strong man himself threatens to deliver. The difference, to be sure, is a matter of degree: A hell-and-damnation priest is likely to collect contributions from his parishioners only to the extent that they believe his predictions of brimstone for infidels; our neighborhood mobster may actually be, as he claims to be, a brothel's best guarantee of operation free of police interference.

Which image the word "protection" brings to mind depends mainly on our assessment of the reality and externality of the threat. Someone who produces both the danger and, at a price, the shield against it is a racketeer. Someone who provides a needed shield but has little control over the danger's appearance qualifies as a legitimate protector, especially if his price is no higher than his competitors'. Someone who supplies reliable, low-priced shielding both from local racketeers and from outside marauders makes the best offer of all.

Apologists for particular governments and for government in general commonly argue, precisely, that they offer protection from local and external violence. They claim that the prices they charge barely cover the costs of protection. They call people who complain about the price of protection "anarchists," "subversives," or both at once. But consider the definition of a racketeer as someone who creates a threat and then charges for its reduction. Governments' provision of protection, by this standard, often qualifies as racketeering. To the extent that the threats against which a given government protects its citizens are imaginary or are consequences of its own activities, the government has organized a protection racket. Since governments themselves commonly simulate, stimulate, or even fabricate threats of external war and since the repressive and extractive activities of governments often constitute the largest current threats to the livelihoods of their own citizens, many governments operate in essentially the same ways as racketeers. There is, of course, a difference: Racketeers, by the conventional definition, operate without the sanctity of governments.

How do racketeer governments themselves acquire authority? As a question of fact and of ethics, that is one of the oldest conundrums of political analysis. Back to Machiavelli and Hobbes, nevertheless, political observers have recognized that, whatever else they do, governments organize and, wherever possible, monopolize violence. It matters little whether we take violence in a narrow sense, such as damage to persons and objects, or in a broad sense, such as violation of people's desires and interests; by either criterion, governments stand out from other organizations by their tendency to monopolize the concentrated means of violence. The distinction between "legitimate" and "illegitimate" force, furthermore, makes no difference to the fact. If we take legitimacy to depend on conformity to an abstract principle or on the assent of the governed (or both at once), these conditions may serve to justify, perhaps even to explain, the tendency to monopolize force; they do not contradict the fact.

In any case, Arthur Stinchcombe's agreeably cynical treatment of legitimacy serves the purposes of political analysis much more efficiently. Legitimacy, according to Stinchcombe, depends rather little on abstract principle or assent of the governed: "The person *over whom power is exercised* is not usually as important as *other power-holders*."[1] Legitimacy is the probability that other authorities will act to confirm the decisions of a given authority. Other authorities, I would add, are much more likely to confirm the decisions of a challenged authority that controls substantial force; not only fear of retaliation, but also desire to maintain a stable environment recommend that general rule. The rule underscores the importance of the authority's monopoly of force. A tendency to monopolize the means of violence makes a government's claim to provide protection, in either the comforting or the ominous sense of the word, more credible and more difficult to resist.

Frank recognition of the central place of force in governmental activity does not require us to believe that governmental authority rests "only" or "ultimately" on the threat of violence. Nor does it entail the assumption that a government's only service is protection. Even when a government's use of force imposes a large cost, some people may well decide that the government's other services outbalance the costs of acceding to its monopoly of violence. Recognition of the centrality of force opens the way to an understanding of the growth and change of governmental forms.

Here is a preview of the most general argument: Power holders' pursuit of war involved them willy-nilly in the extraction of resources for war making from the populations over which they had control and in the promotion of capital accumulation by those who could help them borrow and buy. War making, extraction, and capital accumulation interacted to shape European state making. Power holders did not undertake those three momentous activities with the intention of creating national states—centralized, differentiated, autonomous, extensive political organizations. Nor did they ordinarily foresee that national states would emerge from war making, extraction, and capital accumulation.

Instead, the people who controlled European states and states in the making warred in order to check or overcome their competitors and thus to enjoy the advantages of power within a secure or expanding territory. To make more effective war, they attempted to locate more capital. In the short run, they might acquire that capital by conquest, by selling off their assets, or by coercing or dispossessing accumulators of capital. In the long run, the quest inevitably involved them in establishing regular access to capitalists who could supply and arrange credit and in imposing one form of regular taxation or another on the people and activities within their spheres of control.

As the process continued, state makers developed a durable interest in promoting the accumulation of capital, sometimes in the guise of direct return to their own enterprises. Variations in the difficulty of collecting taxes, in the expense of the particular kind of armed force adopted, in the amount of war making required to hold off competitors, and so on resulted in the principal variations in the forms of European states. It all began with the effort to monopolize the means of violence within a delimited territory adjacent to a power holder's base. . . .

What Do States Do?

. . . Under the general heading of organized violence, the agents of states characteristically carry on four different activities:

1. War making: Eliminating or neutralizing their own rivals outside the territories in which they have clear and continuous priority as wielders of force
2. State making: Eliminating or neutralizing their rivals inside those territories
3. Protection: Eliminating or neutralizing the enemies of their clients
4. Extraction: Acquiring the means of carrying out the first three activities—war making, state making, and protection

The third item corresponds to protection as analyzed by Lane, but the other three also involve the application of force. They overlap incompletely and to various degrees; for example, war making against the commercial rivals of the local bourgeoisie delivers protection to that bourgeoisie. To the extent that a population is divided into enemy classes and the state extends its favors partially to one class or another, state making actually reduces the protection given some classes.

War making, state making, protection, and extraction each take a number of forms. Extraction, for instance, ranges from outright plunder to regular tribute to bureaucratized taxation. Yet all four depend on the state's tendency to monopolize the concentrated means of coercion. From the perspectives of those who dominate the state, each of them—if carried on effectively—generally reinforces the others. Thus, a state that successfully eradicates its internal rivals strengthens its ability to extract resources, to wage war, and to protect its chief supporters. In the earlier European experience, broadly speaking, those supporters were typically landlords, armed retainers of the monarch, and churchmen.

Each of the major uses of violence produced characteristic forms of organization. War making yielded armies, navies, and supporting services. State making produced durable instruments of surveillance and control within the territory. Protection relied on the organization of war making and state making but added to it an apparatus by which the protected called forth the protection that was their due, notably through courts and representative assemblies. Extraction brought fiscal and accounting structures into being. The organization and deployment of violence themselves account for much of the characteristic structure of European states.

The general rule seems to have operated like this: The more costly the activity, all other things being equal, the greater was the organizational residue. To the extent, for example, that a given government invested in large standing armies—a very costly, if effective, means of war making—the bureaucracy created to service the army was likely to become bulky. Furthermore, a government building a standing army while controlling a small population was likely to incur greater costs, and therefore to build a bulkier structure, than a government within a populous country. Brandenburg–Prussia was the classic case of high cost for available resources. The Prussian effort to build an army matching those of its larger Continental neighbors created an immense structure; it militarized and bureaucratized much of German social life.

In the case of extraction, the smaller the pool of resources and the less commercialized the economy, other things being equal, the more difficult was the work of extracting resources to sustain war and other governmental activities; hence, the more extensive was the fiscal apparatus. England illustrated the corollary of that proposition, with a relatively large and commercialized pool of resources drawn on by a relatively small fiscal apparatus. As Gabriel Ardant has argued, the choice of fiscal strategy probably made an additional difference. On the whole, taxes on land were expensive to collect as compared with taxes on trade, especially large flows of trade past easily controlled checkpoints. Its position astride the entrance to the Baltic gave Denmark an extraordinary opportunity to profit from customs revenues.

With respect to state making (in the narrow sense of eliminating or neutralizing the local rivals of the people who controlled the state), a territory populated by great landlords or by distinct religious groups generally imposed larger costs on a conqueror than one of fragmented power or homogeneous culture. This time, fragmented and homogeneous Sweden, with its relatively small but effective apparatus of control, illustrates the corollary.

Finally, the cost of protection (in the sense of eliminating or neutralizing the enemies of the state makers' clients) mounted with the range over which that protection extended. Portugal's effort to bar the Mediterranean to its merchants' competitors in the spice trade provides a textbook case of an unsuccessful protection effort that nonetheless built up a massive structure.

Thus, the sheer size of the government varied directly with the effort devoted to extraction, state making, protection, and, especially, war making but inversely with the commercialization of the economy and the extent of the resource base. What is more, the relative bulk of different features of the government varied with the cost/resource ratios of extraction, state making, protection, and war making. In Spain we see hypertrophy of Court and courts as the outcome of centuries of effort at subduing internal enemies, whereas in Holland we are amazed to see how small a fiscal apparatus grows up with high taxes within a rich, commercialized economy.

Clearly, war making, extraction, state making, and protection were interdependent. Speaking very, very generally, the classic European statemaking experience followed this causal pattern:

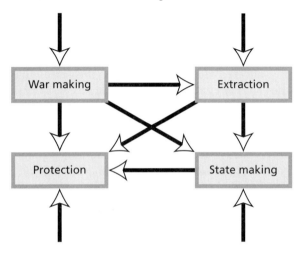

In an idealized sequence, a great lord made war so effectively as to become dominant in a substantial territory, but that war making led to increased extraction of the means of war—men, arms, food, lodging, transportation, supplies, and/or the money to buy them—from the population within that territory. The building up of war-making capacity likewise increased the capacity to extract. The very activity of extraction, if successful, entailed the elimination, neutralization, or cooptation of the great lord's local rivals; thus, it led to state making. As a by-product, it created organization in the form of tax-collection agencies, police forces, courts, exchequers, account keepers; thus it again led to state making. To a lesser extent, war making likewise led to state making through the expansion of military organization itself, as a standing army, war industries, supporting bureaucracies, and (rather later) schools grew up within the state apparatus. All of these structures checked potential rivals and opponents. In the course of making war, extracting resources, and building up the state apparatus, the managers of states formed alliances with specific social classes. The members of those classes loaned resources, provided technical services, or helped ensure the compliance of the rest of the population, all in return for a measure of protection against their own rivals and enemies. As a result of these multiple strategic choices, a distinctive state apparatus grew up within each major section of Europe.

How States Formed

This analysis, if correct, has two strong implications for the development of national states. First, popular resistance to war making and state making made a difference. When ordinary people resisted vigorously, authorities made concessions: guarantees of rights, representative institutions, courts of appeal. Those concessions, in their turn, constrained the later paths of war making and state making. To be sure, alliances with fragments of the ruling class greatly increased the effects of popular action; the broad mobilization of gentry against Charles I helped give the English Revolution of 1640 a far greater impact on political institutions than did any of the multiple rebellions during the Tudor era.

Second, the relative balance among war making, protection, extraction, and state making significantly affected the organization of the states that emerged from the four activities. To the extent that war making went on with relatively little extraction, protection, and state making, for example, military forces ended up playing a larger and more autonomous part in national politics. Spain is perhaps the best European example. To the extent that protection, as in Venice or Holland, prevailed over war making, extraction, and state making, oligarchies of the protected classes tended to dominate subsequent national politics. From the relative predominance of state making sprang the disproportionate elaboration of policing and surveillance; the Papal States illustrate that extreme. Before the twentieth century, the range of viable imbalances was fairly small. Any state that failed to put considerable effort into war making was likely to disappear. As the twentieth century wore on, however, it became increasingly common for one state to lend, give, or sell war-making means to another; in those cases, the recipient state could put a disproportionate effort into extraction, protection, and/or state making and yet survive. In our own time, clients of the United States and the Soviet Union provide numerous examples.

This simplified model, however, neglects the external relations that shaped every national state. Early in the process, the distinction between "internal" and "external" remained as unclear as the distinction between state power and the power accruing to lords allied with the state. Later, three interlocking influences connected any given national state to the European network of states. First, there were the flows of resources in the form of loans and supplies, especially loans and supplies devoted to war making. Second, there was the competition among states for hegemony in disputed territories, which stimulated war making and temporarily erased the distinctions among war making, state making, and extraction. Third, there was the intermittent creation of coalitions of states that temporarily combined their efforts to force a given state into a certain form and position within the international network. The war-making coalition is one example, but the peace-making coalition played an even more crucial part: From 1648, if not before, at the ends of wars all effective European states coalesced temporarily to bargain over the boundaries and rulers of the recent belligerents. From that point on, periods of major re-organization of the European state system came in spurts, at the settlement of widespread wars. From each large war, in general, emerged fewer national states than had entered it.

War as International Relations

In these circumstances, war became the normal condition of the international system of states and the normal means of defending or enhancing a position within the system. Why war? No simple answer will do; war as a potent means served more than one end. But surely part of the answer goes back to the central mechanisms of state making: The very logic by which a local lord extended or defended the perimeter within which he monopolized the means of violence, and thereby increased his return from tribute, continued on a larger scale into the logic of war. Early in the process, external and internal rivals overlapped to a large degree. Only the establishment of large perimeters of control within which great lords had checked their rivals sharpened the line between internal and external. George Modelski sums up the competitive logic cogently:

> Global power . . . strengthened those states that attained it relatively to all other polit-ical and other organizations. What is more, other states competing in the global power game developed similar organizational forms and similar hardiness: they too became nation-states—in a defensive reaction, because forced to take issue with or to confront a global power, as France confronted Spain and later Britain, or in imitation of its obvious success and effectiveness, as Germany followed the example of Britain in Weltmacht, or as earlier Peter the Great had rebuilt Russia on Dutch precepts and examples. Thus not only Portugal, the Netherlands, Britain and the United States became nation-states, but also Spain, France, Germany, Russia and Japan. The short, and the most parsimonious, answer to the question of why these succeeded where "most of the European efforts to build states failed" is that they were either global powers or successfully fought with or against them.[2]

This logic of international state making acts out on a large scale the logic of local aggrandizement. The external complements the internal.

If we allow that fragile distinction between "internal" and "external" state-making processes, then we might schematize the history of European state making as three stages: (a) The differential success of some power holders in "external" struggles establishes the difference between an "internal" and an "external" arena for the deployment of force; (b) "external" competition generates "internal" state making; (c) "external" compacts among states influence the form and locus of particular states ever more powerfully. In this perspective, state-certifying organizations such as the League of Nations and the United Nations simply extended the European-based process to the world as a whole. Whether forced or voluntary, bloody or peaceful, decolonization simply completed that process by which existing states leagued to create new ones.

The extension of the Europe-based state-making process to the rest of the world, however, did not result in the creation of states in the strict European image. Broadly speaking, internal struggles such as the checking of great regional lords and the imposition of taxation on peasant villages produced important organizational features of European states: the relative subordination of military power to civilian control, the extensive bureaucracy of fiscal surveillance, the representation of wronged interests via petition and parliament. On the whole, states elsewhere developed differently. The most telling feature of that difference appears in military organization. European states built up their military apparatuses through sustained struggles with their subject populations and by means of selective extension of protection to different classes within those populations. The agreements on protection constrained the rulers themselves, making them vulnerable to courts, to assemblies, to withdrawals of credit, services, and expertise.

To a larger degree, states that have come into being recently through decolonization or through reallocations of territory by dominant states have acquired their military organization from outside, without the same internal forging of mutual constraints between rulers and ruled. To the extent that outside states continue to supply military goods and expertise in return for commodities, military alliance or both, the new states harbor powerful, unconstrained organizations that easily overshadow all other organizations within their territories. To the extent that outside states guarantee their boundaries, the managers of those military organizations exercise extraordinary power within them. The advantages of military power become enormous, the incentives to seize power over the state as a whole by means of that advantage very strong. Despite the great place that war making occupied in the making of European states, the old national states of Europe almost never experienced the great disproportion between military organization and all other forms of organization that seems the fate of client states throughout the contemporary world. A century ago, Europeans might have congratulated themselves on the spread of civil government throughout the world. In our own time, the analogy between war making and state making, on the one hand, and organized crime, on the other, is becoming tragically apt.

Notes

1. Arthur L. Stinchcombe, *Constructing Social Theories* (New York: Harcourt, Brace & World, 1968), p. 150; italics in the original.
2. George Modelski, "The Long Cycle of Global Politics and the Nation State," *Comparative Studies in Society and History* 20 (1978): 231.

Bibliography

Ardent, Gabriel. "Financial Policy and Economic Infrastructure of Modern States and Nations." In *The Formation of National States in Western Europe*, edited by Charles Tilly. Princeton, N.J.: Princeton University Press, 1975.

2.2

Making Race and Nation: A Comparison of the United States, South Africa, and Brazil

Anthony W. Marx

On the basis of a comparison of the United States, South Africa, and Brazil, Anthony Marx describes why states in the first two countries played "the race card," whereas the Brazilian state did not. Marx suggests that there was more intense polarization between dominant white groups in South Africa and the United States than in Brazil during the period when the modern state was being constructed. White elites forged a compromise in South Africa and the United States by excluding black inhabitants (mostly, former slaves) from citizenship. In Brazil, on the other hand, there was not intense polarization among competing white groups, and therefore there was less need to compromise on the basis of a racially exclusionary formula. Can you apply Marx's argument to other countries? Does it help explain other forms of discrimination, for example, toward women?

◆ ◆ ◆ States are compulsory and continuous associations claiming control of society within a territory. They differ over time and place in their capacity to rule, in their autonomous power, and in their particular forms. But all states seek to contain challenges or instability threatening order and growth. To do so, ruling elites structure relations between states and civil society, shaping norms and reinforcing social and political identities accordingly.[1] The central identity encouraged by states is that of the nation, defined as the popular loyalty of a population held together in being obliged to serve and be served by the state.[2] By encouraging allegiance to the nation, states enhance their claimed monopoly of legitimacy.[3] Accordingly, state elites and others have been inspired by the goal of the nation-state, a coincidence of institutional rule and allegiance to it that would diminish internal conflict. As John Stuart Mill argued, "the boundaries of governments should coincide in the main with those of nationalities" or "fellow-feelings."[4] . . .

Anthony W. Marx, *Making Race and Nation: A Comparison of the United States, South Africa, and Brazil* (New York: Cambridge University Press, 1998), pp. 4–8, 11–13, 15–16, 280–285.

Citizenship is a key institutional mechanism for establishing boundaries of inclusion or exclusion in the nation-state.[5] It selectively allocates distinct civil, political, and economic rights, reinforcing a sense of commonality and loyalty among those included.[6] But by specifying to whom citizenship applies, states also define those outside the community of citizens, who then live within the state as objects of domination. Even in formal democracies, some are not included nor have their interests served. Such imposed exclusion inadvertently may serve as a unifying issue, mobilizing the excluded group to seek inclusion in the polity as a central popular aspiration.[7] Gradual expansion of citizenship is then gained through protracted contestation.[8] The goal of gaining citizenship rights, which were not originally universal, thus has often served as a frame for mobilization.[9] Extending a provocative analogy, groups use their voice to overcome their enduring and forced exit from the polity.[10]

The process of defining the nation with rules of citizenship is of obvious relevance for how racial categories are established and reinforced. Coercive powers have been used to define citizenship according to race—states bind the nation they claim to represent by institutionalizing identities of racial inclusion and exclusion. The extension of citizenship rights has been blocked by constructing racial boundaries. Barbara Fields has suggested that such official racial domination began at a particular historical moment, when the modern nation-state emerged.[11]

States then play a central role in imposing the terms of official domination, with unintended consequences. Official exclusion, as by race, legitimates these categories as a form of social identity, building upon and reshaping historical and cultural solidarities. In the short run, such exclusion benefits those included and hurts others. But in the longer run, institutionalized exclusion may further consolidate subordinate identity and encourages self-interested mobilization and protest. State-sanctioned racial categories impose real costs on their subjects but also offer oppressed populations both legal grounds for redress and bases for political mobilization. The reverse reasoning would also hold. Where and when a state does not impose categorical exclusion, potential subordinates are not so directly disadvantaged. But in the longer run, the preferable absence of such exclusion also may deprive informally subordinated peoples of an unavoidable demarcation unifying them as a group. Ironically, the lack of official racial domination then becomes an obstacle to effective collective action forcing redress of real inequality. In either case, state rule and solidarity from below continually interact.

Arguing that states have the capacity to establish racial boundaries of citizenship, provoking resistance accordingly, does not explain why a state does or does not enforce a racial cleavage. Such an explanation must be cognizant that the state is itself not unitary, but reflects divisions of the society in which it is embedded, and is itself often torn by competing global, national, and local pressures. For instance, does the state construct and use race because of international pressures, to preserve itself, to ensure revenues, to meet specific interests, to avoid class conflict, or to reflect popular racist beliefs? To proceed further, it is useful to turn to comparative historical analysis, looking both inside the state and outside to its social context. How autonomous was the state? How consequential were different state structures? The analytic category of "the state," though suggestive, must be broken down to explain the motives for particular forms of nation building and for specific official policies and outcomes.

Comparing and Excavating Historical Foundations

South Africa, the United States, and Brazil are the three most prominent cases in which European settlers dominated indigenous populations or slaves of African origin. In all three of these major regional powers, modern social and economic indicators demonstrate significant disparities between black and white. The legacies of slavery and of conquest established a common pattern of discrimination.[12] Indeed, there has been a rich tradition of comparison between two or three of these "big three" cases, the histories of which have often interacted.[13]

The common history of racial dynamics, so understood, makes the comparison of South Africa, the United States, and Brazil obvious. Their differences make comparison fruitful. Given earlier economic development in the United States and other significant variations of history, culture, state structures, and demography, the similarities in South African and U.S. rhetoric and practices of racial domination are striking, particularly in regard to segregation policies between the world wars.[14] There has also been remarkable comparability in the ideology and strategy of resistance challenging racial domination.[15] Yet a dichotomy of racial domination and conflict in South Africa and the United States, contrasted with Brazil's so-called racial democracy and relatively mild black protest, is too simple. Despite the commonality of early discrimination and maintained inequality, post abolition state policies encoded differing racial orders, with varying results. South African apartheid was more centrally imposed and pervasive than was Jim Crow segregation and exclusion in the more decentralized post-Reconstruction United States. And if South African race relations bark most loudly and the United States a bit more softly, why was Brazil the dog that didn't bark? These divergent outcomes present a useful puzzle.

Including Brazil is pivotal, reminding us that legal racial domination was not inevitable. While South Africa and the United States used earlier discrimination as the base for constructing continued racial domination, the connection between past and present in Brazil is more problematic. There, early prejudice and large-scale slavery seem oddly inconsistent with the later absence of legal segregation. . . . Brazil's distinctiveness did not then rest upon less historical discrimination, but rather in the country's purposeful denial of that legacy. What accounts for this divergence? . . .

Was there something similar about transitional moments in South Africa and the United States, but different for Brazil, that can account for the pattern of outcomes? One possible answer stands out immediately. Abolition and/or state consolidation in South Africa and the United States emerged out of the bloodiest conflicts in the histories of those countries, while Brazil suffered nothing remotely comparable to the Boer War or Civil War.[16] This divergence fits the general pattern of outcomes. But why would imperial conquest or internal wars and their aftereffects have produced apartheid and Jim Crow? Indeed, just the opposite might seem logical. It was the more liberal abolitionist British and Northerners who won those wars, yet later policies toward blacks were closer to those advocated by the defeated Afrikaners and Southerners. Something more than who won was at work. Furthermore, why would the lack of major internal war result in the absence of official racial domination in Brazil? Again this result is counterintuitive. The more peaceful process of abolition and state consolidation in Brazil left the earlier racial order and social hierarchy relatively undisturbed, yet in Brazil earlier racial discrimination was not codified in later state institutions.

Looking just at pivotal moments cannot fully account for the divergence in racial orders. Outcomes even ran counter to the victors' possible advantage. If the British had aligned themselves with and protected black South Africans, they could have forged a majority coalition to outvote Afrikaners. With the hubris of victory, the U.S. North assumed they could indeed forge such a coalition with blacks and impose reforms under Reconstruction, but this project was abandoned. Instead, the British and the North sought a coalition with the Afrikaners and the white South, respectively, because those defeated whites had earned a reputation in the prior conflict as being capable of violent disruption. Afrikaners and Southerners posed a viable threat of continuing disruption after the Boer War and during Reconstruction. Liberal interest in blacks was overshadowed by the stronger imperative to unify whites within the nation-state, in part because blacks themselves, divided by ethnicity in South Africa and outnumbered in the United States, were not seen as a comparably violent threat.[17] Earlier images of racial inferiority, shared by whites across ethnic or regional lines, reinforced the idea that blacks were not capable of organized and united disruption, and so could and should be subordinated. The strategic and ideological imperatives for a white coalition then set the terms of official racial domination. During the "moments of madness"[18] capping cataclysmic and violent change, official policies established the trajectory of racial order for close to a century.

South African and U.S. nation-state consolidation followed a similar logic. "Liberal" and industrializing forces defeated agrarian powers tied to coercive labor practices, with the victors then facing the challenge of reconciling divided loyalties reinforced by conflict. Ethnic tensions and sectionalism had to be diminished, even if they could not be altogether vanquished.[19] Afrikaners and Southerners demanding that citizenship not be extended to blacks were appeased. Intrawhite conflict was diminished by projecting white racial unity and domination. Blacks were sacrificed on the altar of white unity. In this sense, in the aftermath of the Civil and Boer Wars, further open conflict was contained by inscribing inequalities on which whites generally agreed into social institutions.[20] As Stinchcombe concludes, "the tragedy of social life is that every extension of solidarity . . . to nation, presents also the opportunity of organizing hatred at a larger scale."[21] Institutionalizing common prejudice against blacks reinforced white nationalism.[22] Both countries followed a "golden law . . . that every white bargain must be sealed by an

African sacrifice."[23] The pragmatic goal of conflict resolution and nation-state building consistently eclipsed liberal calls for racial justice.

Why did intrawhite conflict trigger the particular use of racial cleavage for domination and nation building? In South Africa and the United States, issues of race and the treatment of Africans were embedded in emerging ethnic or regional conflict, reinforcing existent racist ideologies. Issues of race exacerbating intrawhite conflict were then turned into an instrument for encouraging unity. And as elites victorious in war were more concerned with winning over their white rivals than blacks, constructing a racial order of white supremacy could and did diminish intrawhite conflict. Racial domination was embraced or allowed because it was potentially powerful enough to gradually integrate white populations in violent conflict with each other. Continuing ethnic or section conflicts would have exacerbated disruption. Neither capital nor labor could be so excluded because prosperity required the inclusion of both business and workers. And national unity could not be built on the exclusion of foreigners, who were needed as immigrant labor. . . .

Brazilian nation-state making and race making followed an altogether different linked trajectory. There was no competing European fragment akin to the Afrikaners in South Africa, so that the Portuguese were unchallenged in establishing central colonial authority.[24] In general, slavery was countrywide, producing little regional conflict over abolition, nor the elaboration of a programmatic racist ideology to defend slavery against such challenges.[25] A relative lack of early conflict was further preserved by Brazil's slow economic growth, contrasted with faster development producing more class conflict earlier among whites in South Africa and the United States. Brazilian unity had been preserved by compromise, and the continued rule of Portugal and Portuguese-descendant emperors ensured the persistence of an established order and religious-social hierarchy, with slaves at its bottom.[26] Brazil then modernized and peacefully transformed itself from colony to empire and to republic, and from slaveholding to free.[27] A "prefabricated" central state was in place when the winds of modernity hit. Abolition did raise the question of whether and how to incorporate blacks, but in the relative absence of major intrawhite conflict, there was little impetus to unify whites through racial exclusion. Whites were already relatively united; the nation was already bound up, at least among elites.

Brazilian elites found that they could maintain their long-established social order of white privilege without enforcing racial domination. Having experienced larger slave revolts, the Brazilian ruling class was more fearful of blacks than their U.S. or South African counterparts. They were eager to submerge potential racial conflict. Policies were debated and discrimination was evident in preferences for European immigrants and bars on Africans entering the country.[28] Racial categories were even encoded, but Brazil did not use these categories as a basis for domination. Inherited and continued racial inequality was denied or explained as reflecting unavoidable but fluid class distinctions. Some Afro-Brazilians were able to advance themselves, encouraging accommodation. Further miscegenation was promoted to "whiten" and unite the population. Seeking "the best of both worlds," such racial democracy maintains the structure of white privilege and non-white subordination, [and] avoids the constitution of race into a principle of collective identity and political action."[29] That prejudice was not legally instantiated had significant consequences. With no official segregation requiring strong state intervention, the republic decentralized power with little conflict or dissent.[30]

This analysis suggests a schematic pattern. For all three countries, racial discrimination was historically embedded, distinguishing blacks as blacks. But elites sharing this prejudice acted differently in response to the particular conflicts they faced or feared. In the United States and South Africa, nineteenth-century builders of the nation-state faced the threat of a potential triadic tension between two white groups and blacks. A coalition among whites was encouraged by enforcing an ideology and practice of racial domination, shifting the conflict to a more manageable dyadic form of white over black. Intrawhite conflict required reconciliation, and racial domination was imposed to unify white nationalism and allow for state centralization. In Brazil, with no comparably violent ethnic and less regional conflict standing in the way of unity, no reconciliation by exclusion was pursued. A more inclusive nationalism developed in place of a biracial divide. The earlier consolidated Brazilian state required no dyadic racial crutch to preserve the polity even as the form of rule repeatedly shifted. Thus, racial domination was constructed selectively and strategically as a tool for pursuing the goal of the nation-state, a twentieth-century preoccupation.

Notes

1. See Theda Skocpol, "Bringing the State Back In," in Peter Evans, Dietrich Rueschemeyer, and Theda Skocpol, eds., *Bringing the State Back In* (Cambridge: Cambridge University Press, 1985), pp. 7, 14; Katznelson, *Liberalism's Crooked Circle* (Princeton University Press, 1996), pp. 125, 178.
2. See Charles Tilly, "Reflections on the History of European Statemaking," in Charles Tilly, ed., *The Formation of National States in Western Europe* (Princeton: Princeton University Press, 1975), pp. 1–83. Tilly notes that such nationalism was encouraged with selection of personnel, control of groups, education, and other policies.
3. Bertrand Badie and Pierre Birnbaum, *The Sociology of the State* (Chicago: University of Chicago Press, 1983), p. 37.
4. Katznelson, p. 119.
5. Frank Parkin, *Max Weber* (London: Travistock, 1982), p. 100; Frank Parkin, *Marxism and Class Theory: A Bourgeois Critique* (New York: Columbia University Press, 1979), p. 95.
6. T. H. Marshall, *Citizenship and Social Class* (London: Pluto, 1992); and as quoted in Katznelson, *Liberalism's Crooked Circle*, p. 119.
7. Judith N. Shklar, *American Citizenship: The Quest for Inclusion* (Cambridge, Mass.: Harvard University Press, 1991), p. 3; Sidney Tarrow, *Power in Movement* (Cambridge: Cambridge University Press, 1994), p. 62.
8. Tarrow, *Power in Movement*, p. 76; Shklar, *American Citizenship*, p. 28; Charles Tilly, *Popular Contention in Great Britain, 1758–1834* (Cambridge, Mass.: Harvard University Press, 1995); Michael Lipsky, "Protest as a Political Resource," *American Political Science Review* 62 (1968), pp. 1144–58; Craig Calhoun, *Social Theory and the Politics of Identity* (Cambridge: Blackwell, 1994), p. 25; Margaret

R. Somers, "Citizenship and the Place of the Public Sphere," *American Sociological Review* 58.5 (October 1993), p. 589.

9. Aldon Morris and Carol McLurg Mueller, eds., *Frontiers in Social Movement Theory* (New Haven: Yale University Press, 1992), p. 189.

10. Albert O. Hirschman, *Exit, Voice and Loyalty* (Cambridge, Mass.: Harvard University Press, 1970).

11. Barbara Fields, "Slavery, Race and Ideology in the United States of America," *New Left Review* 181 (1990), p. 101. For a related discussion of racism as a "pitfall of nationalism," see Frantz Fanon, *The Wretched of the Earth* (New York: Grove, 1968), pp. 125–31.

12. Herbert S. Klein, *African Slavery in Latin America and the Caribbean* (New York: Oxford University Press, 1986), p. 10. Europe, with its absence of major domestic slaveholding, and history of ethnic exclusion, is not included in this comparative study.

13. See, for example, Pierre Van den Berghe, *Race and Racism* (New York: Wiley, 1967); Stanley B. Greenberg, *Race and State in Capitalist Development* (New Haven: Yale University Press, 1980); George M. Fredrickson, *White Supremacy* (Oxford: Oxford University Press, 1981); John W. Cell, *The Highest Stage of White Supremacy* (Cambridge: Cambridge University Press, 1982); Carl N. Degler, *Neither Black nor White* (Madison: University of Wisconsin Press, 1971).

14. C. Vann Woodward, *The Strange Career of Jim Crow* (New York: Oxford University Press, 1957), p. 97; George Reid Andrews, "Comparing the Comparers: White Supremacy in the United States and South Africa," *Journal of Social History* 20 (1987), p. 588; George M. Fredrickson, "Black–White Relations Since Emancipation: The Search for a Comparative Perspective," in Kees Gispen, ed., *What Made the South Different?* (Jackson: University Press of Mississippi, 1990), p. 141.

15. George M. Fredrickson, *Black Liberation: A Comparative History of Black Ideologies in the United States and South Africa* (New York: Oxford University Press, 1995).

16. Donald Pierson, *Negroes in Brazil* (Chicago: University of Chicago Press, 1942), p. 335.

17. See Andrews, "Comparing the Comparers," p. 589; A. Leon Higginbotham, Jr., "Racism in American and South African Courts: Similarities and Differences," *New York University Law Review* 65.3 (June 1990), p. 491; Richard M. Valelly, "Party, Coercion, and Inclusion: The Two Reconstructions of the South's Electoral Politics," *Politics and Society* 21.1 (March 1993), pp. 37–67.

18. Aristide Zolberg, "Moments of Madness," *Politics and Society* 2 (1978).

19. See V. O. Key, Jr., *Southern Politics in State and Nation* (New York: Knopf, 1949), p. 15.

20. See Michel Foucault, *Power/Knowledge*, ed. Colin Gordon (New York: Pantheon, 1980), p. 90.

21. Arthur Stinchcombe, "Social Structure and Politics," in Nelson W. Polsby and Fred Greenstein, eds., *Handbook of Political Science* (Reading: Addison-Wesley, 1975), vol. 3.

22. Kimberlie Crenshaw, "Race, Reform and Retrenchment," *Harvard Law Review* 101.7 (May 1988), p. 1360; William Julius Wilson, *Power, Racism and Privilege* (New York: Free Press, 1973), p. 35; George M. Fredrickson, *The Black Image in the White Mind* (Middletown, Conn.: Wesleyan University Press), p. 151; Connor, *Ethnonationalism*, p. 94.

23. Donald Denoon, *A Grand Illusion* (London: Longman, 1973), p. 158.

24. See Louis Hartz, *The Founding of New Societies* (San Diego: Harcourt Brace Jovanovich, 1964).

25. Fredrickson, *Black Liberation*, pp. 5, 8.

26. See Carlos Hasenbalg, "Race Relations in Post-Abolition Brazil," Ph.D. dissertation, University of California at Berkeley, 1978, p. 258; Carlos Hasenbalg, "Desigualdades Raciais no Brasil," *Dados* 14 (1977), p. 7; Roberto Da Matta, *Carnivals, Rogues and Heroes* (Notre Dame, Ind.: University of Notre Dame Press, 1991), pp. 139–40; Florestan Fernandes, *The Negro in Brazilian Society* (New York: Columbia University Press, 1969), pp. 180–1.

27. Scott, "Defining the Boundaries of Freedom," p. 96; Gilberto Freyre, *Brazil: An Interpretation* (New York: Knopf, 1945), pp. 120–1. See also Hartz, *Founding of New Societies*, pp. 78, 124.

28. Célia Marinho de Azevedo, *Onda Negra, Medo Branco* (Rio de Janeiro: Paz e Terra, 1987).

29. Hasenbalg, "Race Relations in Post-Abolition Brazil," p. 260.

30. Brazil's informal racial order is an example of what Foucault describes as the "effects of power which don't pass directly via the state apparatus yet often sustain the state more effectively than its own institutions, enlarging and maximizing its effectiveness." See Foucault, *Power/Knowledge*, p. 73.

2.3

The Rise of Competitive Authoritarianism

Steven Levitsky and Lucan A. Way

Most regimes throughout the world have been authoritarian. Some analysts have thought that authoritarian regimes would eventually crumble in face of popular demands for democracy. (Readings in Chapter 4 analyze this issue.) Levitsky and Way develop an opposite argument. They believe that new forms of authoritarian regimes have emerged that may display the trappings of democracy, especially elections, but not the substance. Rather than democracy being the inevitable wave of the future, then, Levitsky and Way believe that forms of authoritarian regimes will persist. In reading their article, think about why a state might adopt a democratic or authoritarian form of regime.

The post–Cold War world has been marked by the proliferation of hybrid political regimes. In different ways, and to varying degrees, polities across much of Africa (Ghana, Kenya, Mozambique, Zambia, Zimbabwe), post-communist Eurasia (Albania, Croatia, Russia, Serbia, Ukraine), Asia (Malaysia, Taiwan), and Latin America (Haiti, Mexico, Paraguay, Peru) combined democratic rules with authoritarian governance during the 1990s. Scholars often treated these regimes as incomplete or transitional forms of democracy. Yet in many cases these expectations (or hopes) proved overly optimistic. Particularly in Africa and the former Soviet Union, many regimes have either remained hybrid or moved in an authoritarian direction. It may therefore be time to stop thinking of these cases in terms of transitions to democracy and to begin thinking about the specific types of regimes they actually are.

In recent years, many scholars have pointed to the importance of hybrid regimes. Indeed, recent academic writings have produced a variety of labels for mixed cases, including not only "hybrid regime" but also "semidemocracy," "virtual democracy," "electoral democracy," "pseudodemocracy," "illiberal democracy," "semi-authoritarianism," "soft authoritarianism," "electoral authoritarianism," and Freedom House's "Partly Free."[1] . . .

Steven Levitsky and Lucan A. Way, "The Rise of Competitive Authoritarianism," *Journal of Democracy* 13, No. 2 (April 2002): 51–65 (excerpts). © National Endowment for Democracy and The Johns Hopkins University Press. Reprinted with permission of The Johns Hopkins University Press.

Defining Competitive Authoritarianism

This article examines one particular type of "hybrid" regime: *competitive authoritarianism*. In competitive authoritarian regimes, formal democratic institutions are widely viewed as the principal means of obtaining and exercising political authority. Incumbents violate those rules so often and to such an extent, however, that the regime fails to meet conventional minimum standards for democracy. Examples include Croatia under Franjo Tudjman, Serbia under Slobodan Milošević, Russia under Vladimir Putin, Ukraine under Leonid Kravchuk and Leonid Kuchma, Peru under Alberto Fujimori, and post-1995 Haiti, as well as Albania, Armenia, Ghana, Kenya, Malaysia, Mexico, and Zambia through much of the 1990s. Although scholars have characterized many of these regimes as partial or "diminished" forms of democracy, we agree with Juan Linz that they may be better described as a (diminished) form of authoritarianism.[2]

Competitive authoritarianism must be distinguished from democracy on the one hand and full-scale authoritarianism on the other. Modern democratic regimes all meet four minimum criteria: 1) Executives and legislatures are chosen through elections that are open, free, and fair; 2) virtually all adults possess the right to vote; 3) political rights and civil liberties, including freedom of the press, freedom of association, and freedom to criticize the government without reprisal, are broadly protected; and 4) elected authorities possess real authority to govern, in that they are not subject to the tutelary control of military or clerical leaders.[3] Although even fully democratic regimes may at times violate one or more of these criteria, such violations are not broad or systematic enough to seriously impede democratic challenges to incumbent governments. In other words, they do not fundamentally alter the playing field between government and opposition.[4]

In competitive authoritarian regimes, by contrast, violations of these criteria are both frequent enough and serious enough to create an uneven playing field between government and opposition. Although elections are regularly held and are generally free of massive fraud, incumbents routinely abuse state resources, deny the opposition adequate media coverage, harass opposition candidates and their supporters, and in some cases manipulate electoral results. Journalists, opposition politicians, and other government critics may be spied on, threatened, harassed, or arrested. Members of the opposition may be jailed, exiled, or—less frequently—even assaulted or murdered. Regimes characterized by such abuses cannot be called democratic.

Competitive authoritarianism must therefore be distinguished from unstable, ineffective, or otherwise flawed types of regimes that nevertheless meet basic standards of democracy, and this includes what Guillermo O'Donnell has called "delegative democracies."[5] According to O'Donnell, delegative democracies are characterized by low levels of horizontal accountability (checks and balances) and therefore exhibit powerful, plebiscitarian, and occasionally abusive executives. Yet such regimes meet minimum standards for democracy. Delegative democracy thus applies to such cases as Argentina and Brazil in the early 1990s, but not to Peru after Fujimori's 1992 presidential self-coup.

Yet if competitive authoritarian regimes fall short of democracy, they also fall short of full-scale authoritarianism. Although incumbents in competitive authoritarian regimes may routinely manipulate formal democratic rules, they are unable to eliminate them or reduce them to a mere façade. Rather than openly violating democratic rules (for example, by banning or repressing the opposition and the media), incumbents are more likely to use bribery, co-optation, and more subtle forms of persecution, such as the use of tax authorities, compliant judiciaries, and other state agencies to "legally" harass, persecute, or extort cooperative behavior from critics. Yet even if the cards are stacked in favor of autocratic incumbents, the persistence of meaningful democratic institutions creates arenas through which opposition forces may—and frequently do—pose significant challenges. As a result, even though democratic institutions may be badly flawed, both authoritarian incumbents and their opponents must take them seriously.

In this sense, competitive authoritarianism is distinct from what might be called "façade" electoral regimes—that is, regimes in which electoral institutions exist but yield no meaningful contestation for power (such as Egypt, Singapore, and Uzbekistan in the 1990s). Such regimes have been called "pseudodemocracies," "virtual democracies," and "electoral authoritarian" regimes. In our view, they are cases of full-scale authoritarianism.[6] The line between this type of regime and competitive authoritarianism can be hard to draw, and noncompetitive electoral institutions may one day become competitive (as occurred in Mexico). It is essential, however, to distinguish regimes in which democratic institutions offer an important channel through which the opposition may seek power from those regimes in which democratic rules simply serve as to legitimate an existing autocratic leadership.

Finally, competitive authoritarianism must be distinguished from other types of hybrid regimes. Regimes may mix authoritarian and democratic features in a variety of ways, and competitive authoritarianism should not be viewed as encompassing all of these regime forms. Other hybrid regime types include "exclusive republics"[7] (regimes with strong democratic institutions but highly restrictive citizenship laws) and "tutelary" or "guided" democracies—competitive regimes in which nondemocratic actors such as military or religious authorities wield veto power.

Four Arenas of Democratic Contestation

Due to the persistence of meaningful democratic institutions in competitive authoritarian regimes, arenas of contestation exist through which opposition forces may periodically challenge, weaken, and occasionally even defeat autocratic incumbents. Four such arenas are of particular importance: 1) the electoral arena; 2) the legislature; 3) the judiciary; and 4) the media.

1) The electoral arena. The first and most important arena of contestation is the electoral arena. In authoritarian regimes, elections either do not exist or are not seriously contested. Electoral competition is eliminated either de jure, as in Cuba and China, or de facto, as in Kazakhstan and Uzbekistan. In the latter, opposition parties are routinely banned or disqualified from electoral competition, and opposition leaders are often jailed. In addition, independent or outside observers are prevented from verifying results via parallel vote counts, which creates widespread opportunities for vote stealing. As a result, opposition forces do not present a serious electoral threat to incumbents, and elections are, for all intents and purposes, noncompetitive. Thus Kazakhstani president Nursultan Nazarbayev was reelected in 1999 with 80 percent of the vote, and in Uzbekistan, President Islam Karimov was reelected in 2000 with 92 percent of the vote. (As a rule of thumb, regimes in which presidents are reelected with more than 70 percent of the vote can generally be considered noncompetitive.) In such cases, the death or violent overthrow of the president is often viewed as a more likely means of succession than his electoral defeat.

In competitive authoritarian regimes, by contrast, elections are often bitterly fought. Although the electoral process may be characterized by large-scale abuses of state power, biased media coverage, (often violent) harassment of opposition candidates and activists,[8] and an overall lack of transparency, elections are regularly held, competitive (in that major opposition parties and candidates usually participate), and generally free of massive fraud. In many cases, the presence of international observers or the existence of parallel vote-counting procedures limits the capacity of incumbents to engage in large-scale fraud. As a result, elections may generate considerable uncertainty, and autocratic incumbents must therefore take them seriously. . . .

Although incumbents may manipulate election results, this often costs them dearly and can even bring them down. In Peru, for example, Fujimori was able to gain reelection in 2000 but was forced to resign amid scandal months later. Similarly, efforts by Milošević to falsify Serbian election results in 2000 led to a regime crisis and the president's removal. Regime crises resulting from electoral fraud also occurred in Mexico in 1988 and Armenia in 1996.

2) The legislative arena. A second arena of contestation is the legislature. In most full-scale authoritarian regimes, legislatures either do not exist or are so thoroughly controlled by the ruling party that conflict between the legislature and the executive branch is virtually unthinkable. In competitive authoritarian regimes, legislatures tend to be relatively weak, but they occasionally become focal points of opposition activity. This is particularly likely in cases in which incumbents lack strong majority parties. In both Ukraine and Russia in the 1990s, for example, presidents were faced with recalcitrant parliaments dominated by former communist and other left-wing parties. The Ukrainian parliament repeatedly blocked or watered down economic reform legislation proposed by President Kuchma, and in 2000–2001, despite Kuchma's threats to take "appropriate" measures if it did not cooperate, parliament blocked the president's effort to call a referendum aimed at reducing the powers of the legislature. Although incumbents may attempt to circumvent or even shut down the legislature (as in Peru in 1992 and Russia in 1993), such actions tend to be costly, particularly in the international arena. Thus both Fujimori and Yeltsin held new legislative elections within three years of their "self-coups," and Yeltsin continued to face opposition from the post-1993-coup parliament.

Even where incumbent executives enjoy large legislative majorities, opposition forces may use the legislature as a place for meeting and organizing and (to the extent that an independent media exists) as a public platform from which to denounce the regime. In Peru, despite the fact that opposition parties exerted little influence over the legislative process between 1995 and 2000, anti-Fujimori legislators used congress (and media coverage of it) as a place to air their views. In Ukraine in November 2000, opposition deputy Aleksandr Moroz used parliament to accuse the president of murder and to distribute damaging tapes of the president to the press.

3) *The judicial arena.* A third arena of potential contestation is the judiciary. Governments in competitive authoritarian regimes routinely attempt to subordinate the judiciary, often via impeachment, or, more subtly, through bribery, extortion, and other mechanisms of co-optation. In Peru, for example, scores of judges—including several Supreme Court justices—were entwined in the web of patronage, corruption, and black-mail constructed by Fujimori's intelligence chief, Vladimiro Montesinos. In Russia, when the Constitutional Court declared Yeltsin's 1993 decree disbanding parliament to be unconstitutional, Yeltsin cut off the Court's phone lines and took away its guards. In some cases, governments resort to threats and violence. In Zimbabwe, after the Supreme Court ruled that occupations of white-owned farmland—part of the Mugabe government's land-redistribution policy—were illegal, independent justices received a wave of violent threats from pro-government "war veterans." Four justices, including Chief Justice Anthony Gubbay, opted for early retirement in 2001 and were replaced by justices with closer ties to the government.

Yet the combination of formal judicial independence and incomplete control by the executive can give maverick judges an opening. In Ukraine, for example, the Constitutional Court stipulated that President Kuchma's referendum to reduce the powers of the legislature was not binding. In Slovakia, the Constitutional Court prevented Vladimír Mečiar's government from denying the opposition seats in parliament in 1994, and in Serbia, the courts legitimized local opposition electoral victories in 1996. Courts have also protected media and opposition figures from state persecution. In Croatia, the courts acquitted an opposition weekly that had been charged with falsely accusing President Tudjman of being a devotee of Spain's Francisco Franco. Similarly, in Malaysia in 2001, a High Court judge released two dissidents who had been jailed under the regime's Internal Security Act and publicly questioned the need for such a draconian law.[9]

Although competitive authoritarian governments may subsequently punish judges who rule against them, such acts against formally independent judiciaries may generate important costs in terms of domestic and international legitimacy. In Peru, for example, the pro-Fujimori congress sacked three members of the Constitutional Tribunal in 1997 after they attempted to block Fujimori's constitutionally dubious bid for a third presidential term. The move generated sharp criticism both domestically and abroad, however, and the case remained a thorn in the regime's side for the rest of the decade.

4) The media. Finally, the media are often a central point of contention in competitive authoritarian regimes. In most full-blown autocracies, the media are entirely state-owned, heavily censored, or systematically repressed. Leading television and radio stations are controlled by the government (or its close allies), and major independent newspapers and magazines are either prohibited by law (as in Cuba) or de facto eliminated (as in Uzbekistan and Turkmenistan). Journalists who provoke the ire of the government risk arrest, deportation, and even assassination. In competitive authoritarian regimes, by contrast, independent media outlets are not only legal but often quite influential, and journalists—though frequently threatened and periodically attacked—often emerge as important opposition figures. In Peru, for example, independent newspapers such as *La República* and *El Comercio* and weekly magazines such as *Sí* and *Caretas* operated freely throughout the 1990s. In Ukraine, newspapers such as *Zerkalo nedeli*, *Den*, and, more recently, *Vicherni visti* functioned as important sources of independent views on the Kuchma government.

Independent media outlets often play a critical watchdog role by investigating and exposing government malfeasance. The Peruvian media uncovered a range of government abuses, including the 1992 massacre of students at La Cantuta University and the forgery of the signatures needed for Fujimori's party to qualify for the 2000 elections. In Russia, Vladimir Gusinsky's Independent TV was an important source of criticism of the Yeltsin government, particularly with respect to its actions in Chechnya. In Zimbabwe, the *Daily News* played an important role in exposing the abuses of the Mugabe government. Media outlets may also serve as mouthpieces for opposition forces. In Serbia, the Belgrade radio station B-92 served as a key center of opposition to Milošević in the second half of the 1990s. Newspapers played an important role in supporting opposition forces in Panama and Nicaragua in the late 1980s.

Executives in competitive authoritarian regimes often actively seek to suppress the independent media, using more subtle mechanisms of repression than their counterparts in authoritarian regimes. These methods often include bribery, the selective allocation of state advertising, the manipulation of debts and taxes owed by media outlets, the fomentation of conflicts among stockholders, and restrictive press laws that facilitate the prosecution of independent and opposition journalists. In Russia, the government took advantage of Independent TV's debts to the main gas company, Gazprom, to engineer a takeover by government-friendly forces. In Peru, the Fujimori government gained de facto control over all of the country's privately owned television stations through a combination of bribery and legal shenanigans, such as the invalidation of Channel 2 owner Baruch Ivcher's citizenship. Governments also make extensive use of libel laws to harass or persecute independent newspapers "legally." In Ghana, for example, the Jerry Rawlings government used colonial-era libel statutes to imprison several newspaper editors and columnists in the 1990s, and in Croatia, the Open Society Institute reported in 1997 that major independent newspapers had been hit by more than 230 libel suits. Similarly, Armenia's government used libel suits to quiet press criticism after the country's controversial 1996 elections.[10]

Yet efforts to repress the media may be costly to incumbents in competitive authoritarian regimes. For example, when in 1996 the Tudjman government in Croatia tried to revoke the license of Radio 101, a popular independent station in the capital, the massive protests that broke out both galvanized the opposition and temporarily split the ruling party. In Ukraine in 2000, charges that President Kuchma had sought the killing of an opposition journalist led to large domestic protests and partial isolation from the West. In Peru, the persecution and exiling of Ivcher provoked substantial protest at home and became a focal point of criticism abroad.

Inherent Tensions

Authoritarian governments may coexist indefinitely with meaningful democratic institutions. As long as incumbents avoid egregious (and well-publicized) rights abuses and do not cancel or openly steal elections, the contradictions inherent in competitive authoritarianism may be manageable. Using bribery, co-optation, and various forms of "legal" persecution, governments may limit opposition challenges without provoking massive protest or international repudiation.

Yet the coexistence of democratic rules and autocratic methods aimed at keeping incumbents in power creates an inherent source of instability. The presence of elections, legislatures, courts, and an independent media creates periodic opportunities for challenges by opposition forces. Such challenges create a serious dilemma for autocratic incumbents. On the one hand, repressing them is costly, largely because the challenges tend to be both formally legal and widely perceived (domestically and internationally) as legitimate. On the other hand, incumbents could lose power if they let democratic challenges run their course.[11] Periods of serious democratic contestation thus bring out the contradictions inherent in competitive authoritarianism, forcing autocratic incumbents to choose between egregiously violating democratic rules, at the cost of international isolation and domestic conflict, and allowing the challenge to proceed, at the cost of possible defeat. The result is often some kind of regime crisis, as occurred in Mexico in 1988; Nicaragua in 1990; Zambia in 1991; Russia in 1993; Armenia in 1996; Albania in 1997; Ghana, Peru, Serbia, and Ukraine in 2000; and Zambia (again) in 2001. A similar crisis appears likely to emerge in Zimbabwe surrounding the March 2002 presidential election.

In some cases, such as those of Kenya, Malaysia, Russia, and Ukraine, autocratic incumbents weathered the storm. In several of these countries, the regime cracked down and dug in deeper. In other cases, such as Nicaragua in 1990, Zambia in 1991, and Ghana and Mexico in 2000, competitive authoritarian governments failed to crack down and lost power. In still other cases, including Peru and Serbia, autocrats attempted to crack down but, in doing so, were badly weakened and eventually fell.

But succession is not democratization. Although in many cases (Croatia, Nicaragua, Peru, Slovakia, Serbia) incumbent turnover resulted in democratic transitions, in other cases, including Albania, Zambia, Ukraine, and Belarus, newly elected leaders continued or even intensified many of the authoritarian practices of their predecessors. Hence, while the removal of autocratic elites creates an important *opportunity* for regime change and even democratization, it does not ensure such an outcome.

Although it is beyond the scope of this article to explain variations in the capacity of competitive authoritarian regimes to survive crises brought about by episodes of democratic contestation, one pattern is worth noting.[12] In regions with closer ties to the West, particularly Latin America and Central Europe, the removal of autocratic incumbents has generally resulted in democratization in the post–Cold War period. In Latin America, for example, four out of five competitive authoritarian regimes democratized after 1990 (the Dominican Republic, Mexico, Nicaragua, and Peru, but not Haiti). Similarly, during the same period four out of five competitive authoritarian regimes in Central Europe democratized (Croatia, Serbia, Slovakia, and Romania, but not Albania). By contrast, the record of competitive authoritarian regimes in Africa and the former Soviet Union is strikingly different. Among former Soviet republics, only one competitive authoritarian regime (Moldova) democratized in the 1990s.

This evidence suggests that proximity to the West may have been an important factor shaping the trajectory of competitive authoritarian regimes in the 1990s. Linkages to the West—in the form of cultural and media influence, elite networks, demonstration effects, and direct pressure from Western governments— appear to have raised the costs of authoritarian entrenchment, making the democratization of competitive authoritarian regimes more likely. Where Western linkages were weaker, or where alternative, nondemocratic hegemons (such as Russia or China) exerted substantial influence, competitive authoritarian regimes were more likely either to persist or to move in a more authoritarian direction. . . .

Conceptualizing Nondemocracies

We conclude by echoing Thomas Carothers' call to move beyond what he calls the "transition paradigm."[13] It is now clear that early hopes for democratization in much of the world were overly optimistic. Many authoritarian regimes have survived the "third wave" of democratization. In other cases, the collapse of one kind of authoritarianism yielded not democracy but a new form of nondemocratic rule. Indeed, a decade after the collapse of the Soviet Union, the majority of the world's independent states remained nondemocratic. Yet whereas an extensive literature has emerged concerning the causes and consequences of democratization, emerging types of democracy, and issues of democratic consolidation, remarkably little research has been undertaken on the emergence or persistence of nondemocratic regimes.

The post–Cold War Western liberal hegemony, global economic change, developments in media and communications technologies, and the growth of international networks aimed at promoting democracy and human rights all have contributed to reshaping the opportunities and constraints facing authoritarian elites. As a result, some forms of authoritarianism, such as totalitarianism and bureaucratic authoritarianism, have become more difficult to sustain. At the same time, however, several new (or partially new) nondemocratic regime types took on greater importance in the 1990s, including competitive authoritarianism. A range of other nondemocratic outcomes also gained in importance, including other types of hybrid regimes, postcommunist patrimonial dictatorships, and cases of sustained state collapse ("chaosocracy").[14] Research on these nondemocratic outcomes is critical to gaining a better understanding of the full (rather than hoped for) set of alternatives open to post–Cold War transitional regimes.

Notes

1. Terry Lynn Karl, "The Hybrid Regimes of Central America," *Journal of Democracy* 6 (July 1995): 72–87; William Case, "Can the 'Halfway House' Stand? Semidemocracy and Elite Theory in Three Southeast Asian Countries," *Comparative Politics* 28 (July 1996): 437–64; Richard A. Joseph, "Africa, 1990–1997: From *Abertura* to Closure," *Journal of Democracy* 9 (April 1998): 3–17; Larry Diamond, *Developing Democracy: Toward Consolidation* (Baltimore: Johns Hopkins University Press, 1999); Fareed Zakaria, "The Rise of Illiberal Democracy," *Foreign Affairs* 76 (November–December 1997): 22–41; Thomas Carothers, *Aiding Democracy Abroad: The Learning Curve* (Washington, D.C.: Carnegie Endowment for International Peace, 1999); Gordon P. Means, "Soft Authoritarianism in

Malaysia and Singapore," *Journal of Democracy* 7 (October 1996): 103–17; Andreas Schedler, "Mexico's Victory: The Democratic Revelation," *Journal of Democracy* 11 (October 2000): 5–19; and M. Steven Fish, "Authoritarianism Despite Elections: Russia in Light of Democratic Theory and Practice," paper prepared for delivery at the 2001 Annual Meeting of the American Political Science Association, San Francisco, 30 August–2 September 2001.

2. Juan J. Linz, *Totalitarian and Authoritarian Regimes* (Boulder, Colo.: Lynne Rienner, 2000), 34.

3. See Scott Mainwaring, Daniel Brinks, and Aníbal Pérez Linan, "Classifying Political Regimes in Latin America, 1945–1999," *Studies in Comparative International Development* 36 (Spring 2001). This definition is consistent with what Larry Diamond calls "mid-range" conceptions of democracy (Larry Diamond, *Developing Democracy*, 13–15).

4. Obviously, the exact point at which violations of civil and political rights begin to fundamentally alter the playing field is difficult to discern and will always be open to debate. However, the problem of scoring borderline cases is common to all regime conceptualizations.

5. Guillermo O'Donnell, "Delegative Democracy," *Journal of Democracy* 5 (January 1994): 55–69.

6. Larry Diamond, *Developing Democracy*, 15–16; Richard Joseph, "Africa, 1990–1997"; Jason Brownlee, "Double Edged Institutions: Electoral Authoritarianism in Egypt and Iran," paper presented at the 2001 Annual Meeting of the American Political Science Association, San Francisco, 30 August–2 September 2001.

7. Philip G. Roeder, "Varieties of Post-Soviet Authoritarian Regimes," *Post-Soviet Affairs* 10 (January–March 1994): 61–101.

8. In Kenya, government-backed death squads were responsible for large-scale violence, particularly in ethnic minority areas. See Joel Barkan and Njuguna Ng'ethe, "Kenya Tries Again," in Larry Diamond and Marc F. Plattner, eds., *Democratization in Africa* (Baltimore: Johns Hopkins University Press, 1999), 185. Substantial violence against opposition forces was also seen in Serbia and Zimbabwe in the 1990s.

9. *The Economist*, 14 July 2001, 37.

10. H. Kwasi Prempeh, "A New Jurisprudence for Africa," *Journal of Democracy* 10 (July 1999): 138; Nebojsa Bjelakovic and Sava Tatic, "Croatia: Another Year of Bleak Continuities," *Transitions-on-Line*, *http://archive.tol.cz/countries/croar97.html* (1997). Mikhail Diloyen, "Journalists Fall Through the Legal Cracks in Armenia," *Eurasia Insight* (June 2000).

11. These dilemmas are presented in an insightful way in Andreas Schedler, "The Nested Game of Democratization by Elections," *International Political Science Review* 23 (January 2002).

12. For a more developed explanation, see Steven Levitsky and Lucan A. Way, "Competitive Authoritarianism: Hybrid Regime Change in Peru and Ukraine in Comparative Perspective," Studies in Public Policy Working Paper No. 355 (Glasgow: University of Strathclyde Center for the Study of Public Policy, 2001).

13. Thomas Carothers, "The End of the Transition Paradigm," *Journal of Democracy* 13, no. 1 (January 2002): 5–21.

14. See Richard Snyder, "Does Lootable Wealth Breed Disorder? States, Regimes, and the Political Economy of Extraction," paper presented at the 2001 Annual Meeting of the American Political Science Association, San Francisco, 30 August–2 September 2001. See also Juan J. Linz, *Totalitarian and Authoritarian Regimes*, 37.

2.4

The Fate of the State

Martin van Creveld

This reading argues that, although states have been the dominant political institutions for several centuries, they are now losing power in key domains: military affairs, control over domestic economic and social matters, the technologies of communication (for example, the Internet), and the maintenance of public order. Van Creveld considers whether the results of declining state power are positive or negative. Good question to ponder! However, before assuming that van Creveld is correct that state power has declined, consider challenges to this position by scholars, such as Sassen (2.6), who argue that states continue to play a central role in world politics.

The State, which since the Treaty of Westphalia (1648) has been the most important and most characteristic of all modern institutions, is dying. Wherever we look, existing states are either combining into larger communities or falling apart; wherever we look, organizations that are not states are taking their place. On the international level, we are moving away from a system of separate, sovereign, states toward less distinct, more hierarchical, and in many ways more complex structures. Inside their borders, it seems that many states will soon no longer be able to protect the political, military, economic, social, and cultural life of their citizens. These developments may lead to upheavals as profound as those that took humanity out of the Middle Ages and into the Modern World. Whether the direction of change is desirable, as some hope, or undesirable, as others fear, remains to be seen.

In this article the state of the state will be discussed under five headings. Part I looks at the state's declining ability to fight other states. Part II outlines the rise and fall of the welfare state. Part III examines the effects of modern technology, economics, and the media. Part IV focuses on the state's ability to maintain public order. Finally, Part V is an attempt to tie all the threads together and to see where we are headed.

Martin van Creveld, "The Fate of the State," *Parameters,* Spring 1996: 4–17. Reprinted by permission of the author and the author's agent, Artellus Limited, London.

Part I. The Declining Ability to Fight

The principal function of the state, as that of all previous forms of government, has always been to fight other states, whether defensively in an attempt to defend its interests or offensively to extend them. Usually a state that was unable to do this was doomed to disappear. The best it could hope for was to lead a sort of shadowy existence under the protection of some other state, as Lebanon, for example, does under Syrian tutelage; even that existence was likely to be temporary.

Conversely, the need to fight other states has played a critical role in the development of the state's most important institutions. This includes the government bureaucracy, whose original function was to levy taxes for the purpose of waging war; the note-issuing state bank, an early 18th-century invention designed specifically to help pay for Britain's military effort during the wars against Louis XIV; and of course the regular armed forces. In most states, the latter continued to take up the lion's share of expenditure until well into the 19th century.

Driven largely by the need to fight other states, the power of the state expanded from 1700 on. The number of bureaucrats (the word itself is an 18th-century neologism) multiplied, and the amount of statistical information at their disposal increased, as did the share of GDP that was extracted by government. Technology drove war, and war, technology. International competition intensified until, during the second half of the 19th century, it reached the point where much of the world had been turned into an armed camp. Each of the so-called great powers was looking anxiously over its shoulder at all the rest to see which one was the most threatening, and which one, being less so for the moment, could be drawn into an alliance.

Most important of all, the French Revolution led to the nationalization of the masses and, with that, to a drastic change in the role of the state in the popular consciousness. Hobbes, Locke, and many of their 18th-century successors saw the state simply as an instrument for maintaining public order and permitting a civilized life; to quote a rhyme by Alexander Pope: "Over government fools contest/What is best administered is best." Now it became an end unto itself, an earthly god in whose honor festivals were celebrated, monuments erected, and hymns composed and sung. It was a vengeful god who, according to his greatest prophet, Georg Hegel, fed on blood and periodically demanded the sacrifice of hundreds of thousands if not millions—for their own highest good, needless to say. In retrospect, nothing in the history of the modern state is more astonishing than the willingness, occasionally even eagerness, of people to fight for it and lay down their lives for it.

The climax of these developments was reached during the years of total war between 1914 and 1945. Acting in the name of the need to protect or extend something known as the national interest, states conscripted their populations and fought each other on an unprecedented scale and with an unprecedented ferocity. Nor was it merely a question of soldiers killing each other in the field. At the grand strategic level, both 1914–18 and 1939–45 were conducted by attrition; this gave states time to mobilize not only troops but civilians (including women and children) as well, putting them to work in fields and factories. . . .

Thanks to the unprecedented mobilization of demographic, economic, industrial, technological, and scientific resources, the two world wars together, and each separately, dwarfed all the armed conflicts that had taken place in the past. More important to our purpose, mobilization warfare accelerated—if it did not create—technological progress. All through World War II in particular, tens of thousands of scientists were engaged in research and development, producing devices that ranged from radar to the electronic computer and from the jet engine to the first ballistic missiles. The climax arrived on 6 August 1945 when the first atomic bomb exploded over Hiroshima, killing an estimated 75,000 people.

At first, nuclear weapons were thought to have put unprecedented military power in the hands of the state; after a few years, though, it began to be realized that they did not so much serve the objectives of war as put an end to it. As the power of nuclear weapons grew—from 20,000 kilotons in 1945 to 58 megatons in 1961—and their numbers increased, wherever they made their appearance large-scale interstate war came to a halt. First the superpowers; then their close allies in NATO and the Warsaw Pact; then the U.S.S.R. and China; then China and India; then India and Pakistan; then Israel and its Arab neighbors. Much as they hated each other, they each in turn saw themselves with their horns locked and unable to fight each other in earnest.

Without exception, what large-scale interstate wars have taken place since 1945 have been waged either between or against third- and fourth-rate military powers. . . . Since 1945 no two first-rate states, meaning such as were armed with nuclear weapons, have fought each other; by some accounts they have not even come close to fighting each other.

Even more striking than the marginalization of the belligerents was the declining scale on which war was waged. Though the world's population has almost tripled since 1945, and though its ability to produce goods and services has increased many times over, both the size of armed forces and the number of the major weapon systems with which they are provided now amount to only a fraction of what they were in 1945. For example, the forces mobilized by the coalition in the Gulf were just one-seventh of the size of those deployed by Germany for its invasion of Russia in 1941. In most places the shrinking process is still under way. Not a day passes without some new cuts being announced. And in the face of the potential for nuclear destruction, there is not much chance of the mass forces of World War II being rebuilt in any kind of foreseeable future.

Part II. The Rise and Fall of the Welfare State

As the state lost its ability to expand at its neighbors' expense—a handicap confirmed by the Charter of the United Nations, which, as the most subscribed-to document in history, prohibits using force to annex territory—it turned its energies inward. It lies in the nature of a bureaucratic construct that it should seek to control and regulate everything; in so doing it created the welfare state.

The beginning of the story is in the period 1789 to 1830. First came the French Revolution, which, exported across the length and width of Europe, broke up the ancient feudal and ecclesiastic institutions; by atomizing society, it put the state in a much stronger position than ever before. Next came the industrial revolution. Starting in Britain, it brought with it economic freedom, unbridled capitalism (including its worst manifestations—a total lack of planning, widespread poverty, and inhumane exploitation), and the invisible hand. The influence of such figures as Adam Smith and Friedrich List caused one nation after another to dismantle internal and external economic controls and switch to free trade; with the Manchester School firmly in control, during the first half of the century the motto was *laissez faire*.

After 1850 or so, the prevailing mood began to change. One reason for this was a number of inquiries, some of them official, that were launched into the state of the working class and that brought to light the often shocking conditions in which working people lived. Another was the military competition mentioned in the previous section; with the most important states increasingly dependent on mass armies consisting of conscripts and reservists, their rulers felt they could no longer afford to neglect the populations that provided those armies. Finally there was the steady, if often stormy, movement toward democratization and the rise in many countries of socialist parties. The former made it necessary, in the words of one English parliamentarian, "to educate our masters." The latter attracted a growing number of voters and openly threatened violent revolution unless something was done to improve the lot of the masses.

Be the exact reasons what they may, the first Factory Acts were passed in Britain during the 1840s over howls of protests by the owners and their spokesmen. The laws' purpose was to put limits on working hours—initially those of women and children—and to institute at least some safety controls. Imitated by many countries, originally the new laws only applied to a few industries considered particularly dangerous, such as mining. Later they were extended to others such as textile and metalworking plants. Among the last to be reached were agriculture, domestic service, and small-scale light industry, particularly in the form of sweatshops. These were affected, to the extent that they were affected at all, only during the early years of the 20th century.

Once the state had begun to supervise the conditions of labor—including the establishment of labor exchanges, another early 20th-century development—it soon sought to do the same for education and public health. The pioneer in the former field was Prussia; following beginnings made in the reign of Frederick the Great, something like universal—although, as yet, not free—elementary education was achieved in the years after 1815 when Prussia became a much-imitated model and educators from all over the world flocked to see how it was done. In the rest of Europe the real push was provided by the war of 1870–71. The French in particular looked for an explanation; unable to agree on the causes of the defeat, in the end they pointed a finger at the schoolmaster. Around 1900 the "utopian vision"—the phrase used by the British Fabian socialist Beatrice Webb—of universal elementary education had been achieved in all the most advanced countries.

Advances in public health were made necessary by urban growth and were initially decentralized. In Britain, Germany, and to a growing extent the United States, laws were enacted that entrusted the task of providing better sanitation, better disease controls, to local authorities and municipalities; they also took over from the church and private charitable organizations by providing at least some hospitals for the indigenous ill. In the most advanced countries, ministries of health were established during the first two decades after 1900. Their task was to supervise those countries' entire health systems, including both medical practice and training; in addition, many of them also provided various programs, such as inoculation and prenatal care, that were compulsory, free, or both.

Like state-run education, state-run welfare was originally a German invention. The 1880s found Bismarck worried about the progress of the Social Democratic Party. This caused him to institute the so-called "Revolution from above" and the world's first schemes for unemployment, accident, sickness, and old age insurance. Between 1890 and 1914 his example was followed by others through much of Western Europe and Scandinavia. Seen from this point of view, the Bolshevik Revolution of 1917 was anything but an anomaly; instead it was simply an attempt to grab one particularly backward country by the neck, institute universal welfare at a single stroke, and extend state control to the point where civil society itself almost ceased to exist. Only the United States, with its tradition of free enterprise and rugged individualism, resisted the trend and, as a result, found itself lagging behind. In the land of the dollar it took the Great Depression and 13 million unemployed to make first the New Deal and then social security during the 1930s.

Still, what really made the modern welfare state was World War II. As had already been the case during World War I, governments took responsibility for running many aspects of their citizens' lives, including even the number of inches of hot water they were allowed to put in their tubs; but this time they did so with no intention of giving up their power after the war had ended. In one developed country after another, extensive health programs covering the entire population—as under the British National Health System which served as the model for many others—were established. To this were added a vast variety of ancillary programs, such as free or subsidized meals for children and the elderly, cheap housing, vocational training and retraining, and education. The latter often led to free education up to, and in some instances including, the university level.

These developments led to a huge increase in the number of bureaucrats per population and per square mile. By the end of the 1950s the number of ministries, which during the state's formative years in the 17th and 18th centuries had usually stood at four, had risen to something nearer 20 in most countries. . . .

To pay for these programs and these ministries, it became necessary to raise taxes—particularly direct ones—until, in countries such as Britain and Sweden, marginal rates of income tax could reach 90 percent and more. Taxation, though, was only part of the solution. The nationalization of industry had been demanded by socialist parties ever since the time of the *Communist Manifesto*. The way ahead had been shown in Britain by the creation of the Electricity Board in 1926; next, France during the premiership of León Blum (1936–37) nationalized its arms industry. Following World War II, in one European country after another entire sectors of the economy were taken out of private hands and put into those of the state. The exact identity of the industries in question varied. Often they included mass transportation such as sea, air, and rail; telecommunications, energy, banking, insurance, mining (particularly for coal and oil), and critical branches of manufacturing such as steel, shipbuilding, aviation, and military equipment. Initially it was hoped that the profits of these industries would be made to work for the community at large rather than for their shareholders alone. In practice it did not take long before many of them, run on electoral principles rather than business ones, turned into albatrosses that were grossly overstaffed, incurred enormous losses, demanded vast subsidies, and hung like chains around the state's neck.

In retrospect, the turning point in the history of nationalization and the welfare state came during the second half of the 1970s. Until then the trend toward greater state control had been increasing steadily. Even in the United States, always a latecomer in such matters, "big government" made its debut during the 1950s; in the 1960s the Kennedy and Johnson administrations declared "war on poverty" and presided over a vast expansion of various social programs. Then, in one country after another a reaction set in. It was motivated partly by the immense losses attributable to many nationalized industries; partly by the drastic increase in unemployment—and consequently in the cost of insuring against it—brought about by the oil crisis; and partly by the desire to cut the burden of taxes, which was regarded as stifling economic enterprise. On top of all this the welfare state had become a victim of its own success. The more it sought to help disadvantaged groups such as the aged or single parents, the larger the number of those who claimed the benefit of its services and the greater also the addition to the national debt.

By this time the naïve belief in the virtues of an "impartial" state bureaucracy that had inspired political scientists from Hegel to Max Weber was long since dead. Instead of representing rationality, bureaucracy was coming to be seen as its antithesis; instead of being an instrument of social progress, it was now perceived as an obstacle to change of any kind. During the late 1970s there emerged a number of political leaders such as Margaret Thatcher and Ronald Reagan whose goal, loudly professed, was to roll back the power of the state. "Standing on one's own feet" and "getting government off our backs" became the rallying cries under which some of the most important states set out to dismantle themselves; even though, in many places, progress—if that is the correct term—was greater in words than in deeds.

All through the 1980s the movement back to the 19th century gathered momentum. Late in the decade it was given a tremendous boost by the collapse of the U.S.S.R. For 70 years, communism had provided an alternative model in which the state, for all its manifold and perceived shortcomings, claimed to have eliminated the worst forms of poverty and promised security from the cradle to the grave; now the system's sudden demise left East Bloc states naked and their respective civil societies poorer than ever. Not only was laissez faire capitalism able to reemerge as the only way toward a better future, but it no longer felt obliged to apologize for its seamier sides, such as gross inequality, ever-present insecurity for both employers and employees, and the colossal waste resulting from the business cycle on the one hand and unplanned development on the other. To the contrary, many of the advocates of the new supply-side economics regarded those features as potentially useful tools toward the all-important goals of low inflation and steady economic growth.

As the last years of the century approached, not even those countries that were loudest in their praise of capitalism had made significant progress in reducing their bureaucracies, much less in cutting taxes as a percentage of GDP. On the other hand, in virtually all countries some of the juicier morsels of the economy had been sold off and others deregulated, to say nothing of the cuts that, with or without the aid of inflation, were effected in the real value of numerous social programs including, not least, the quality of education. The homeless people appearing on the streets of cities everywhere offered visible proof of the fact that the post–World War II trend toward a narrowing of social gaps had been reversed; it became a matter of policy for the state to take more and more but give less and less. No wonder that loyalty to it—as manifested most clearly in the willingness to do conscript service and fight if necessary—declined. In the United States under the Carter Administration, even the attempt to register young males for an eventual call-up met with opposition.

Part III. Modern Technology, Economics, and the Media

Meanwhile, and often going almost unnoticed, technology also had performed an about-face. The role played by print in the establishment of the state cannot be overestimated; after all, where would any government be without forms? Next, the telegraph and the railways enabled states to bring their populations under control and to cast their networks over entire countries, even continents. Nor were rulers satisfied when the time it took to travel from the capital to the provinces (for example, from Paris to Bordeaux or Toulouse) was reduced from weeks to days or hours. The role of technologies such as telephones, teleprinters, computers (first put to use in calculating the results of the U.S. census), highways, and other systems of transportation and communication was even greater than that of their predecessors. Without them it would have been impossible for the state to contemplate the task that it had undertaken since the beginning of the 19th century: to impose its control over every part of society from the highest to the lowest and almost regardless of distance and geographical location.

From the beginning, though, much of modern technology bore a Janus face. On the one hand it gave governments the tools with which to dominate their countries and populations as never before. On the other it tended to transcend national borders, crossing them and turning them into obstacles to domination. This was because, unlike its pre-1800 predecessors, much of modern technology can operate only when, and to the extent that, it is grouped into systems. A plough, a hammer, a musket, or a ship can do its job even in the absence of others of its kind; but an individual railway station—or a telegraph apparatus, or a telephone—is simply useless on its own. In such systems what matters is the network of tracks, or wires, or switchboards, that connects each unit with countless others. Even more crucial is the central directing hand which, sorting out routes and priorities, enables them to communicate with each other at will, in an orderly manner and without mutual interference.

As the history of both telegraphs and railways shows, most of the early technological systems were launched by private entrepreneurs. However, in most countries the demand for economic efficiency or military effectiveness soon caused them to be taken over by governments. Either this was done by way of outright ownership, through nationalization and the establishment of a state monopoly, or else by means of regulations designed to ensure that they would be available in wartime. Still, there were limits to the extent that governments could control this technology without at the same time reducing its cost-effectiveness. A railway net designed exclusively for meeting the needs of a single country—such as the broadgauged one constructed by Imperial Russia and later passed to the USSR—provided some protection against invasion but also acted as a barrier to Russian trade with other countries. The same applies to various attempts to build autonomous electricity grids, highway systems, or telephone networks, to say nothing of fax machines and computers.

In theory each state was free to exercise its sovereignty and build its own networks, ignoring those of its neighbors and refusing to integrate with them. In practice it could do so only by incurring a tremendous technological and economic cost. The current plight of North Korea is a perfect case in point; the price of isolation was inefficiency and an inability to maximize the benefits of precisely those technologies that have developed most rapidly since 1945—communication (including data processing) and transportation. Conversely, in order to enjoy those benefits, states had to integrate their networks with those of their neighbors. What is more, it was necessary for them to join the international bodies whose task was to regulate the new technologies on behalf of all. The first such body was the International Railway Committee, which traces its origins to the 1860s. A century later they numbered in the hundreds, and the only way for any state to avoid becoming entangled in their coils was to doom itself to something like a pre-industrial existence.

These technological developments brought about a decisive change in the nature of the global economy. The interwar period had been characterized by attempts to build self-contained empires; now, the most successful states were those which, like Germany and Japan and South Korea, were most integrated into the world market. By and large the more one exported and imported—in other words, maximized one's comparative advantage—the greater one's economic success. As more and more stock exchanges were opened to foreign investors and capital, a greater and greater percentage of a state's assets, and those of its citizens, was likely to be located beyond its borders. Conversely, inside those borders more and more wealth was likely to be controlled by persons and corporations based elsewhere. During the 1980s economic statistics began to recognize the change by separating GNP from GDP. Generally the gap between the two provided a good index for the economic performance of any particular country; for example, 40 percent of all Japanese goods are now being produced outside Japan.

Another blow to state control implicit in the shift toward a global economy was that governments gradually lost their grip over their own currencies. If a nation was to participate in international trade, its currency had to be convertible, as free as possible from administrative controls. But freedom from administrative controls put it at the mercy of the international market. Gone were the days when, as during the period 1914–39, most governments tried to create closed monetary systems and lay down the value of their currencies by fiat. Gone, too, were the Bretton Woods agreements which lasted from 1944 to 1971 and which pegged the various currencies to a U.S. dollar which was itself pegged to gold. Governments did not lose all influence over their currencies; they still controlled the money supply as well as interest rates. Nevertheless, the values of these currencies became subject to wild fluctuations that were often beyond the power of central banks, or even combinations of central banks, to regulate. Their inability to do so put a premium on hedging, on holding at least some of one's assets in foreign currency. The merry-go-round leading to less and less government control continued.

Finally, the unprecedented development of electronic information services seems to mark another step toward the coming collapse of the state. Traditionally no state has ever been able to completely control the thoughts of all its citizens; to the credit of the more liberally-minded among them, it must be added that they never even tried. Though the invention of print greatly increased the amount of information that could be produced, the ability to move that information across international borders remained limited by the need to physically transport paper, as well as by language barriers. The first of these problems was solved by the invention of radio. The introduction of television, which relies on pictures instead of words, to a large extent eliminated the second. During the 1980s cable and satellite TV, as well as videotape, became widely available and capable of providing near-instant coverage of events on a global scale. With the advent of computer networks and the consequent democratization of access to information, the battle between freedom and control was irretrievably lost by the latter, much to the regret of numerous governments. . . .

Part IV. Maintaining Public Order

As governments surrender or lose their hold over many aspects of the media, the economy, and technology, and as public ownership as well as welfare programs stagnate or retreat, one of the principal functions still remaining to the state is to protect its own integrity against internal disorder. Thus the question that must be asked is whether they have been successful in this task; is it being mastered, and can they be expected to accomplish it in the future?

So far this article has concentrated on the developed countries. However, at this point it is useful to invert the order, starting our survey with undeveloped ones. It is a characteristic of many traditional societies that the right to resort to violence, instead of being monopolized by an all-powerful state, is diffused in the hands of family heads, tribal chieftains, feudal noblemen, and the like, each of whom is responsible for policing his own subjects and for fighting off challenges by the rest. Conversely, the extent to which so-called Third World countries have succeeded in demolishing other organizations and concentrating violence in their own hands is one very good index of their progress toward modernization.

To look at many developing countries today, that progress has been either slow or nonexistent. . . . In much of sub-Saharan Africa the state has already collapsed, often before it was able to properly establish itself. Angola, Burundi, Ethiopia, Liberia, Nigeria, Rwanda, Somalia, the Sudan, and Zaire all have been torn by civil war or, at the very least, disorder on a scale that approximates it. On the Mediterranean littoral the position of Egypt and Algeria is scarcely better, confronted as those states are by the formidable challenge of Islamic fundamentalism, which in recent years has led to the deaths of thousands and which shows no sign of abating. Meanwhile, in the southern extremity of the continent, it is touch and go whether South Africa will be able to make progress toward a peaceful multiracial society or be torn apart by the war of all against all.

From Japan to Taiwan, South Korea, and Singapore, some Asian states have been enormously successful in maintaining internal order and protecting the lives and property of their residents. Not so others such as Afghanistan, Burma, Cambodia, India, Iran, Iraq, the Philippines, Sri Lanka, Turkey, and most recently, Pakistan; all of these are now confronted with a loss of control that ranges from riots and clashes between opposing gangs to full-scale civil war. China, too, is not immune. It is true that the coastal regions are making unprecedented economic progress; however, Beijing does not seem to be capable of dealing either with the 30-year-old Tibetan uprising or with the challenge of Muslim separatists in the undeveloped far west of the country. Against this background much of the Chinese leaders' opposition to liberalization may be attributed to the fear—which is certainly not unfounded—that the outcome may be anarchy of the kind that all but destroyed China between 1911 and 1949.

Finally, in Latin America the ability of the state to guarantee internal law and order has, given the lack of a proper technological infrastructure and the immense gaps between rich and poor, always been in doubt. While some parts of the continent, such as Chile, are making good progress toward modernization many others are clearly lagging behind and may be becoming less orderly rather than more. To adduce just two examples that have made headlines during the last few months, the government of Mexico has lost control over the southern part of the country, whereas that of Brazil is even now using the army in an attempt to reconquer its own former capital of Rio de Janeiro. In still other places it is the druglords who exercise de facto power. In countries where repeated assassinations of public officials take place, there can be no expectation for the rule of law or the kind of stability necessary for economic growth.

What makes these facts all the more disturbing is that, so far from remaining limited to Third World countries, the disorder seems to be spreading. The chaos that overtook Armenia, Azerbaijan, Chechnya, Georgia, Moldavia, Tajikistan, and Yugoslavia following the collapse of communist rule is well known; current conditions in these countries resemble those of the Hundred Years' War (1337–1453) more than they do anything that we would expect from a well-ordered modern state. Nor, to judge by the experience of Spain in the Basque country and of Britain in Northern Ireland (to say nothing of the recent Tokyo poison gas attack and the Oklahoma City bombing), does it appear that First World countries are in principle immune to threats of this kind. Many of them are challenged by organizations which, whatever their goals, are capable of commanding fanatical loyalties and unleashing them against the state; these organizations, incidentally, often take better care of their members than the state does.

Attempting to deal with nongovernmental organizations resorting to violence, many modern states have found themselves in a quandary. On the one hand their most important weapons and weapon systems—including not just nuclear ones but most conventional ones as well—are clearly too powerful and indiscriminate to be of much use against those groups. On the other hand, should they use the terrorists' own methods against them, there exists the clear danger that they will turn into terrorists themselves. Under these circumstances many First World governments have chosen to diddle. They counter the challenge without much resolution and pretend that since the number of casualties is often smaller than that which results from ordinary motor traffic, the problem is merely a nuisance. Others have given way and decentralized, as Spain did in the case of Catalonia; or else they are even now preparing to share control over some of their provinces with others, as are the British in Northern Ireland.

Meanwhile, from the White House to 10 Downing Street, the residences of presidents and prime ministers as well as entire government quarters have been transformed into fortresses. Private security has turned into a growth industry par excellence; in the United States alone it is said to employ 1.6 million people (as many as the number of active troops) and to cost $52 billion a year, far more than all U.S. police departments combined. Feeling themselves exposed, more and more individuals and corporations are either renting protection or setting up their own. While one does not want to exaggerate the problem, unquestionably all of this is symptomatic of the state's faltering ability to hold on to its monopoly over violence—or, in plain words, to protect its citizens' lives and property.

Part V. The Outlook

At a time when new states are being born almost daily, paradoxically the fate of the state appears sealed. The growth in numbers may itself be a sign of decay; what everybody has is worth little or nothing. Furthermore, far from safeguarding their hard-won sovereignty, most new states do not even wait until they have been properly established before they start looking for ways to integrate with their neighbors. A good example is provided by that unique political construct, the Commonwealth of Independent States. Another is the eventual Palestinian state. Its leaders are even now talking of cooperation with Israel, Jordan, and Egypt—in fact with anyone who can help them transcend the limits of their own people's small size.

Contrary to the fears of George Orwell in 1984, modern technology, in the form of nuclear weapons on the one hand and unprecedented means for communication and transportation on the other, has not resulted in the establishment of unshakable totalitarian dictatorships. Instead of thought control we have CNN and, which many regimes consider almost as dangerous, Aaron Spelling; instead of unpersons, Amnesty International. The net effect has been to make governments lose power in favor of organizations that are not sovereign and are not states.

Some of these organizations stand above the state—for example, the European Common Market, the West European Union, and, above all, the United Nations, which since the Gulf War has begun to play a role akin to that of the medieval popes in authorizing or prohibiting a state from waging international war. Others are of a completely different kind, such as international bodies, multinational corporations, the media, and various terrorist organizations some of which can barely be told apart from gangs of ordinary criminals. What they all have in common is that they either assume some of the functions of the state or manage to escape its control. All also have this in common: being either much larger than states or without geographical borders, they are better positioned to take advantage of recent developments in transportation and communications. The result is that their power seems to be growing while that of the state declines.

To sum up, the 300-year period that opened at Westphalia and during which the state was the most important organization in which people lived—first in Europe, then in other places—is coming to an end. Nobody knows the significance of the transition from a system of sovereign, territorial, legally equal states to one that takes greater cognizance of the new realities; it is likely to be eventual and, as is already the case in many places, quite possibly bloody. Still, it is worth recalling that the state's most remarkable products to date have been Hiroshima and Auschwitz; the former could never have been built by any organization but a state (and the most powerful one, at that), whereas the latter was above all an exercise in bureaucratic management. Whatever the future may bring, it cannot be much worse than the past. For those who regret and fear the passing away of the world with which we are familiar, let that be their consolation.

 2.5

Failed States in a World of Terror

Robert Rotberg

Even a rapid survey suggests that states in some regions of the world today are unable to carry out the basic requirements of a state: maintaining law and order in their territory; ensuring their citizens at least a minimum of food, shelter, and other material resources; and protecting the country from military threats. Failed states pose a danger to their own citizens and to their neighbors by engaging in violent activities in an attempt to increase their control. In rare cases, Professor Rotberg notes, failed states may collapse altogether, producing anarchy and chaos. Why does this happen? Why are failed states more likely to occur in some regions—above all, Africa?

The Road to Hell

In the wake of September 11, the threat of terrorism has given the problem of failed nation-states an immediacy and importance that transcends its previous humanitarian dimension. Since the early 1990s, wars in and among failed states have killed about eight million people, most of them civilians, and displaced another four million. The number of those impoverished, malnourished, and

---

Robert I. Rotberg, "Failed States in a World of Terror," *Foreign Affairs* 81, No. 4 (July–August 2002). Reprinted by permission of *Foreign Affairs*, 81, no. 4, July–August 2002. Copyright 2002 by the Council on Foreign Relations, Inc.

deprived of fundamental needs such as security, health care, and education has totaled in the hundreds of millions.

Although the phenomenon of state failure is not new, it has become much more relevant and worrying than ever before. In less interconnected eras, state weakness could be isolated and kept distant. Failure had fewer implications for peace and security. Now, these states pose dangers not only to themselves and their neighbors but also to peoples around the globe. Preventing states from failing, and resuscitating those that do fail, are thus strategic and moral imperatives.

But failed states are not homogeneous. The nature of state failure varies from place to place, sometimes dramatically. Failure and weakness can flow from a nation's geographical, physical, historical, and political circumstances, such as colonial errors and Cold War policy mistakes. More than structural or institutional weaknesses, human agency is also culpable, usually in a fatal way. Destructive decisions by individual leaders have almost always paved the way to state failure. President Mobutu Sese Seko's three-plus decades of kleptocratic rule sucked Zaire (now the Democratic Republic of Congo, or DRC) dry until he was deposed in 1997. In Sierra Leone, President Siaka Stevens (1967–85) systematically plundered his tiny country and instrumentalized disorder. President Mohamed Siad Barre (1969–91) did the same in Somalia. These rulers were personally greedy, but as predatory patrimonialists they also licensed and sponsored the avarice of others, thus preordaining the destruction of their states.

Today's failed states, such as Afghanistan, Sierra Leone, and Somalia, are incapable of projecting power and asserting authority within their own borders, leaving their territories governmentally empty. This outcome is troubling to world order, especially to an international system that demands—indeed, counts on—a state's capacity to govern its space. Failed states have come to be feared as "breeding grounds of instability, mass migration, and murder" (in the words of political scientist Stephen Walt), as well as reservoirs and exporters of terror. The existence of these kinds of countries, and the instability that they harbor, not only threatens the lives and livelihoods of their own peoples but endangers world peace.

Into the Abyss

The road to state failure is marked by several revealing signposts. On the economic side, living standards deteriorate rapidly as elites deliver financial rewards only to favored families, clans, or small groups. Foreign-exchange shortages provoke food and fuel scarcities and curtail government spending on essential services and political goods; accordingly, citizens see their medical, educational, and logistical entitlements melt away. Corruption flourishes as ruling cadres systematically skim the few resources available and stash their ill-gotten gains in hard-to-trace foreign bank accounts.

On the political side, leaders and their associates subvert prevailing democratic norms, coerce legislatures and bureaucracies into subservience, strangle judicial independence, block civil society, and gain control over security and defense forces. They usually patronize an ethnic group, clan, class, or kin. Other groups feel excluded or discriminated against, as was the case in Somalia and Sierra Leone in the 1970s and 1980s. Governments that once appeared to operate for the benefit of all the nation's citizens are perceived to have become partisan.

As these two paths converge, the state provides fewer and fewer services. Overall, ordinary citizens become poorer as their rulers become visibly wealthier. People feel preyed upon by the regime and its agents—often underpaid civil servants, police officers, and soldiers fending for themselves. Security, the most important political good, vanishes. Citizens, especially those who have known more prosperous and democratic times, increasingly feel that they exist solely to satisfy the power lust and financial greed of those in power. Meanwhile, corrupt despots drive grandly down city boulevards in motorcades, commandeer commercial aircraft for foreign excursions, and put their faces prominently on the local currency and on oversize photographs in public places. President Robert Mugabe of Zimbabwe, for example, purchased 19 expensively armored limousines for his own motorcade before his reelection earlier this year.

In the last phase of failure, the state's legitimacy crumbles. Lacking meaningful or realistic democratic means of redress, protesters take to the streets or mobilize along ethnic, religious, or linguistic lines. Because small arms and even more formidable weapons are cheap and easy to find, because historical grievances are readily remembered or manufactured, and because the spoils of separation, autonomy, or a total takeover are attractive, the potential for violent conflict grows exponentially as the state's power and legitimacy recede.

If preventive diplomacy, conflict resolution, or external intervention cannot arrest this process of disaffection and mutual antagonism, the state at risk can collapse completely (Somalia), break down and be sundered (Angola, the DRC, and Sudan), or plunge into civil war (Afghanistan and Liberia). The state may also lapse and then be restored to various degrees of health by the UN (Bosnia and Cambodia), a regional or subregional organization (Sierra Leone and Liberia), or a well-intentioned or hegemonic outside power (Syria in Lebanon, Russia in Tajikistan). A former colonial territory such as East Timor can be brought back to life by the efforts and cash infusions of a UN-run transitional administration.

Law and Order

State failure threatens global stability because national governments have become the primary building blocks of order. International security relies on states to protect against chaos at home and limit the cancerous spread of anarchy beyond their borders and throughout the world. States exist to deliver political (i.e., public) goods to their inhabitants. When they function as they ideally should, they mediate between the constraints and challenges of the international arena and the dynamic forces of their own internal economic, political, and social realities.

The new concern over state failure notwithstanding, strong, effective states are more numerous now than before 1914. This shift occurred after the collapse of the Ottoman and Austro-Hungarian empires, continued with the demise of colonialism in Africa and Asia, and concluded with the implosion of the Soviet Union. In 1914, 55 polities could be considered members of the global system; in 1960, there were 90 such states. After the Cold War, that number climbed to 192. But given the explosion in the number of states—so many of which are small, resource-deprived, geographically disadvantaged, and poor—it is no wonder that numerous states are at risk of failure.

States are not created equal. Their sizes and shapes, their human endowments, their capacity for delivering services, and their leadership capabilities vary enormously. More is required of the modern state, too, than ever before. Each is expected to provide good governance; to make its people secure, prosperous, healthy, and literate; and to instill a sense of national pride. States also exist to deliver political goods—i.e., services and benefits that the private sector is usually less able to provide. Foremost is the provision of national and individual security and public order. That promise includes security of property and inviolable contracts (both of which are grounded in an enforceable code of laws), an independent judiciary, and other methods of accountability. A second but vital political good is the provision, organization, and regulation of logistical and communications infrastructures. A nation without well-maintained arteries of commerce and information serves its citizens poorly. Finally, a state helps provide basic medical care and education, social services, a social safety net, regulation and supply of water and energy, and environmental protection. When governments refuse to or cannot provide such services to all of their citizens, failure looms.

But not all of the states that fit this general profile fail. Some rush to the brink of failure, totter at the abyss, remain fragile, but survive. Weakness is endemic in many developing nations—the halfway house between strength and failure. Some weak states, such as Chad and Kyrgyzstan (and even once-mighty Russia), exhibit several of the defining characteristics of failed states and yet do not fail. Others, such as Zimbabwe, may slide rapidly from comparative strength to the very edge of failure. A few, such as Sri Lanka and Colombia, may suffer from vicious, enduring civil wars without ever failing, while remaining weak and susceptible to failure. Some, such as Tajikistan, have retrieved themselves from possible collapse (sometimes with outside help) and remain shaky and vulnerable, but they no longer can be termed "failed." Thus it is important to ask what separates strong from weak states, and weak states from failed states. What defines the phenomenon of failure?

The Essence of Failure

Strong states control their territories and deliver a high order of political goods to their citizens. They perform well according to standard indicators such as per capita GDP, the UN's Human Development Index, Transparency International's Corruption Perception Index, and Freedom House's Freedom in the World report. Strong states offer high levels of security from political and criminal violence, ensure political freedom and civil liberties, and create environments conducive to the growth of economic opportunity. They are places of peace and order.

In contrast, failed states are tense, conflicted, and dangerous. They generally share the following characteristics: a rise in criminal and political violence; a loss of control over their borders; rising ethnic, religious, linguistic, and cultural hostilities; civil war; the use of terror against their own citizens; weak institutions; a deteriorated or insufficient infrastructure; an inability to collect taxes without undue coercion; high levels of corruption; a collapsed health system; rising levels of infant mortality and declining life expectancy; the end of regular schooling opportunities; declining levels of GDP per capita; escalating inflation; a widespread preference for non-national currencies; and basic food shortages, leading to starvation.

Failed states also face rising attacks on their fundamental legitimacy. As a state's capacity weakens and its rulers work exclusively for themselves, key interest groups show less and less loyalty to the state. The people's sense of political community vanishes and citizens feel disenfranchised and marginalized. The social contract that binds citizens and central structures is forfeit. Perhaps already divided by sectional differences and animosity, citizens transfer their allegiances to communal warlords. Domestic anarchy sets in. The rise of terrorist groups becomes more likely.

Seven failed states exist today: Afghanistan, Angola, Burundi, the DRC, Liberia, Sierra Leone, and Sudan. They each exhibit most, if not all, of the traits listed above. Internal hot wars are also a leading indicator of failure, but failure usually precedes the outbreak of war. Hence, the extent of internecine antagonisms and how they are handled are important predictors of failure. Likewise, the nature of the rulers' approach toward minorities, working classes, and other weak or marginalized peoples is indicative.

Among today's failed states, Angola and Sudan have oil wealth, and Angola, the DRC, and Sierra Leone boast diamonds and other mineral resources. But all four countries' governments, as well as those of Afghanistan, Burundi, and Liberia, share a common feature: they deliver security in limited quantities and across circumscribed areas. Moreover, their per capita GDP rates are very low, life expectancies are declining, and basic governmental services are lacking. In each case, the ruling regime projects little power. Each confronts ongoing civil strife, a proliferation of substate authorities, porous borders, high rates of civilian casualties, and a challenge to the regime's intrinsic legitimacy by competing internal forces. Utter collapse is possible in each case, as is dismemberment, out-side tutelage, or an interim assumption of UN control. All remain on the hu-manitarian watch list as potent sources of displaced persons and refugees. (Sierra Leone, however, has recently established a rudimentary government and has quieted its civil war with the assistance of 17,000 British and UN soldiers. But it was a collapsed state from the late 1990s until 2000.)

Total Collapse

Truly collapsed states, a rare and extreme version of a failed state, are typified by an absence of authority. Indeed, a collapsed state is a shell of a polity. Somalia is the model of a collapsed state: a geographical expression only, with borders but with no effective way to exert authority within those borders. Substate actors have taken over. The central government has been divided up, replaced by a functioning, unrecognized state called Somaliland in the north and a less well defined, putative state called Punt in the northeast. In the rump of the old Somalia, a transitional national government has emerged thanks to outside sup-port. But it has so far been unable to project its power even locally against the several warlords who control sections of Mogadishu and large swaths of the countryside. Private entrepreneurialism has displaced the central provision of political goods. Yet life somehow continues, even under conditions of unhealthy, dangerous chaos.

An example of a once-collapsed state is Lebanon, which had disintegrated before Syria's intervention in 1990 provided security and gave a sense of govern-mental legitimacy to the shell of the state. Lebanon today qualifies as a weak, rather than failed, polity because its government is credible, civil war is absent, and political goods are being provided in significant quantities and quality. Syria provides the security blanket, denies fractious warlords the freedom to aggran-dize themselves, and mandates that the usually antagonistic Muslim and Christian communities cooperate. The fear of being attacked preemptively by rivals, or of losing control of critical resources, is alleviated by Syria's imposed hegemony. Within that framework of security, the Lebanese people's traditional entrepreneurial spirit has transformed a failed state into a much stronger one.

The Art of Prevention

Experience suggests that the prevention of state failure depends almost entirely on a scarce commodity: international political will. In part, prevention relies on outsiders' recognizing early that a state's internal turmoil has the potential to be fatally destructive. That recognition should be accompanied by subregional, re-gional, and UN overtures, followed, if required, by private remonstrations—that is, quiet diplomacy. If such entreaties have little effect, there will be a need for public criticism by donor countries, international agencies, the UN, and regional groupings such as the European Union (EU) or the Association of Southeast Asian Nations. These entities should also cease economic assistance, impose "smart sanctions," ban international travel by miscreant leaders, and freeze their overseas accounts—much as the EU and the United States did to Mugabe and his cohort in February. Furthermore, misbehaving nations should be suspended from international organizations. In retrospect, if the international community had more effectively shunned Siad Barre, Mobutu, Idi Amin of Uganda, or Sani Abacha of Nigeria, it might have helped to minimize the destruction of their states. Ostracizing such strongmen and publicly criticizing their rogue states would also reduce the necessity for any subsequent UN peacekeeping and relief missions.

Zimbabwe is an instructive case. Two years ago, Mugabe began employing state-sponsored violence to harass opponents and intimidate voters during the runup to parliamentary elections. But South Africa and the other members of the Southern African Development Community (SADC) refrained from public criticism of Zimbabwe. The EU and the United States expressed displeasure at Mugabe's tactics of terror but likewise decided that constructive engagement would be more effective than an open rebuke. As brutally as Mugabe was acting, outsiders believed that Zimbabwe's despot could be persuaded to behave more responsibly.

Instead, Mugabe set about destroying the economic and political fabric of his country. Zimbabwe, once unquestionably secure, economically strong, socially advanced, and successfully modern, has plummeted rapidly toward failure—mimicking Afghanistan in the 1980s and 1990s, Burma from the 1960s onward, and the DRC, Liberia, Nigeria, and Sierra Leone in the 1990s. In the last several years, Zimbabwe's per capita GDP has fallen annually by 10 percent, while HIV infection rates have climbed to nearly 30 percent. Two thousand Zimbabweans die of AIDS each week. Life expectancy has dropped from 60 to 40 years, while annual inflation has increased from 40 to 116 percent. Corruption has become blatant. The central government no longer effectively provides fundamental political goods such as personal security, schooling, and medical facilities and treatment. Public order has broken down. This year many Zimbabweans may starve due to extremely serious food shortages, and fuel supplies are dwindling. Political institutions have ceased to function fully. Sizable sectional, ethnic, and linguistic fissures exist, and disaffection is everywhere. Even though the state remains intact, the government's legitimacy is now seriously challenged.

By the time of the presidential election in March, therefore, Mugabe had already driven his country to the very edge of failure. Observers, especially South Africa and its neighbors, focused on the election as a way to remove him, provided it were free and fair. But Mugabe persistently refused to play by the common rules of democratic contests. Ahead of the election, he escalated violence against his opponents and anyone who failed to obey him and his ruling party.

He unleashed a wave of thugs against the opposition and white farmers. He bombed independent newspapers and tried to jail their editors. He packed the nation's supreme court and refused to carry out its rulings when it still failed to toe the line. Meanwhile, Zimbabwe's neighbors, its major overseas friends and trading partners, and UN Secretary-General Kofi Annan continued to try to bring about change through quiet diplomacy. But Mugabe ignored New York, London, Washington, and Brussels. He thumbed his nose at President Thabo Mbeki of South Africa and President Olusegun Obasanjo of Nigeria, reneging on solemn promises about fair play, the rule of law, and respect for free speech and media freedom.

Very belatedly, on the eve of the election, the EU and the United States finally turned firm and imposed sanctions. But it was too late, well past the many opportunities for South Africa, the SADC, the United States, and the EU to isolate Mugabe. Ostracizing Mugabe and his close colleagues much earlier in 2001, through gradually escalating smart sanctions, might have led to freer and fairer elections in 2002 and helped to level the playing field. At the very least, international public criticism of Mugabe's tactics might have helped to encourage the growth of civil society in Zimbabwe. But Mbeki's trenchant criticisms were hesitant and muted. And South Africa, the regional superpower, did not threaten to cut off Zimbabwe's supplies of electric power and petroleum. No one in the West or in Africa effectively warned Mugabe that attacking one's own people, destroying a state, and stealing an election were impermissible.

 2.6

The State and Globalization

Saskia Sassen

Contrary to claims that the state's role has declined as a result of globalization (for example, see the article by van Creveld in this chapter), Professor Sassen suggests that the state continues to be fundamentally important. In her account, states are assuming an important new role, involving the passage of legislation, administrative regulations, and court decisions aiming to treat foreign-based and domestic business firms and banks equally. This represents an important contrast with the past, when domestically owned firms usually enjoyed a strong

preference over foreign firms, in terms of tax laws, government procurement policies, and so on. The result of what Sassen calls the "denationalization" of the
state fosters economic globalization by making it easier for companies to operate
across national borders. Compare Sassen's analysis with others, like that of van
Creveld (2.4), that see the state as becoming less important nowadays.

O ne of the roles of the state vis-à-vis today's global economy has been to
negotiate the intersection of national law and foreign actors—whether
firms, markets, or supranational organizations. This raises a question as
to whether there are particular conditions that make execution of this role in
the current phase distinctive and unlike what it may have been in earlier
phases of the world economy. We have, on the one hand, the existence of an
enormously elaborate body of law developed mostly over the past hundred
years, which secures the exclusive territorial authority of national states to an
extent not seen in earlier centuries, and, on the other, the considerable institutionalizing, especially in the 1990s, of the "rights" of non-national firms, the
deregulation of crossborder transactions, and the growing influence/power of
some of the supranational organizations. If securing these rights, options, and
powers entailed an even partial relinquishing of components of state authority
as constructed over the past century, then we can posit that this sets up the
conditions for a necessary engagement by national states in the process of
globalization.

We need to understand more about the nature of this engagement than is represented by concepts such as deregulation. It is becoming clear that the role of
the state in the process of deregulation involves the production of new types of
regulations, legislative items, court decisions—in brief, the production of a
whole series of new "legalities." The background condition here is that the state
remains as the ultimate guarantor of the "rights" of global capital, i.e., the protector of contracts and property rights, and, more generally, a major legitimator of
claims. In this regard the state can be seen as incorporating the global project
of its own shrinking role in regulating economic transactions and giving it operational effectiveness and legitimacy. The state here can be conceived of as representing a technical administrative capacity which cannot be replicated at this
time by any other institutional arrangement; although not in all cases, this is a
capacity backed by military power, with global power in the case of some states.
The objective for foreign firms and investors is to enjoy, transnationally, the

protections traditionally exercised by the state in the national realm of the economy for national firms, notably guaranteeing property rights and contracts. How this gets done may involve a range of options. To some extent this work of guaranteeing is becoming privatized, as is signaled by the growth of international commercial arbitration, and by key elements of the new privatized institutional order for governing the global economy.

It is in fact some states, particularly the United States and the UK, that are producing the design for these new legalities, i.e., items derived from Anglo-American commercial law and accounting standards, and are hence imposing these on other states given the interdependencies at the heart of the current phase of globalization. This creates and imposes a set of specific constraints on the other participating states. Legislative items, executive orders, adherence to new technical standards, and so on will have to be produced through the particular institutional and political structures of each of these states. In terms of research and theorization, this is a vast uncharted terrain: it would mean examining how that production takes place and gets legitimated in different countries. This signals the possibility of crossnational variations (which then would need to be established, measured, interpreted). The emergent, often imposed consensus in the community of states to further globalization is not merely a political decision: it entails specific types of work by a large number of distinct state institutions in each of these countries. Clearly, the role of the state will vary significantly depending on the power it may have both internally and internationally.

The US government as the hegemonic power of this period has led/forced other states to adopt these obligations toward global capital. And, in so doing, it has contributed to strengthening the forces that can challenge or destabilize what have historically been constructed as state powers.[1] In my reading this holds both for the United States and for other countries. One way in which this becomes evident is in the fact that, while the state continues to play a crucial, though no longer exclusive, role in the production of legality around new forms of economic activity, at least some of this production of legalities is increasingly feeding the power of a new emerging structure marked by denationalization or privatization of some of its components. . . .

In my reading, studies that emphasize deregulation and liberalization do not sufficiently recognize an important feature, one which matters for the analysis here: the global financial system has reached levels of complexity that require the existence of a crossborder network of financial centers to service the operations of global capital. Each actual financial center represents a massive and highly specialized concentration of resources and talent; and the network of these centers constitutes the operational architecture for the global capital market. . . .

Precisely because global processes need to be coordinated and serviced and because many of these functions materialize to a large extent in national territories, national states have had to become deeply involved in the implementation of the global economic system. In this process states have experienced transformations of various aspects of their institutional structure. This signals that the global economy and the national state are not mutually exclusive domains. Globalization leaves national territory basically unaltered but is having pronounced effects on the exclusive territoriality of the national state—that is, its effects are not on territory as such but on the institutional encasements of the geographic fact of national territory. But alongside and, in my reading, distinct from this diminished territorial authority of the state, there is the denationalizing of specific state agendas. The work of states in producing part of the technical and legal infrastructure for economic globalization has involved both a change in the exclusivity of state authority and in the composition of the work of states. Economic globalization entails a set of practices that destabilize another set of practices, i.e., some of the practices that came to constitute national state sovereignty.

Implementing today's global economic system in the context of national territorial sovereignty required multiple policy, analytic, and narrative negotiations. These negotiations have typically been summarized or coded as "deregulation." There is much more going on in these negotiations than the concept "deregulation" captures. The encounter of a global actor—firm or market—with one or another instantiation of the national state can be thought of as a new frontier. It is not merely a dividing line between the national economy and the global economy. It is a zone of politico-economic interactions that produce new institutional forms and alter some of the old ones. Nor is it just a matter of reducing regulations. For instance, in many countries, the necessity for autonomous central banks in the current global economic system has required a thickening of regulations in order to delink central banks from the influence of the executive branch of government and from deeply "national" political agendas.

Central banks illustrate this well. These are national institutions, concerned with national matters. Yet over the last decade they have become the institutional home within the national state for monetary policies that are necessary to further the development of a global capital market and indeed, more generally, a global economic system. The new conditionality of the global economic system—the requirements that need to be met for a country to become integrated into the global capital market—contains as one key element the autonomy of central banks. This facilitates the task of instituting a certain kind of monetary policy, e.g., one privileging low inflation over job growth even when a president may have preferred it the other way around, particularly at reelection time. While securing central bank autonomy has certainly eliminated a lot of corruption, it has also been the vehicle for one set of accommodations on the part of national states to the requirements of the global capital market. A parallel analysis can be made of ministries of finance (known as the Treasury in the United States and the UK) which have had to impose certain kinds of fiscal policies as part of the new conditionalities of economic globalization.

There is a set of strategic dynamics and institutional transformations at work here. They may incorporate a small number of state agencies and units within departments, a small number of legislative initiatives and of executive orders, and yet have the power to institute a new normativity at the heart of the state; this is especially so because these strategic sectors are operating in complex interactions with private, transnational, powerful actors. Much of the institutional apparatus of the state remains basically unchanged; the inertia of bureaucratic organizations, which creates its own version of path dependence, makes an enormous contribution to continuity. . . .

Further, the new types of crossborder collaborations among specialized government agencies concerned with a growing range of issues emerging from the globalization of capital markets and the new trade order are yet another aspect of this participation by the state in the implementation of a global economic system. A good example is the heightened interaction in the past three or four years among competition policy regulators from a large number of countries. This is a period of renewed concern about competition policy because economic globalization puts pressure on governments to work toward convergence given the crosscountry diversity of competition laws or enforcement practices. This convergence around specific competition policy issues can coexist with ongoing, often enormous differences among these countries when it comes to laws and regulations about those components of their economies that do not intersect with globalization. There are multiple other instances of this highly specialized type of convergence: regulatory issues concerning telecommunications, finance, the Internet, etc. It is, then, a very partial type of convergence among regulators of different countries who often begin to share more with each other than they do with colleagues in their home bureaucracies.

What is of particular concern here is that today we see a sharp increase in the work of establishing convergence.[2] We can clearly identify a new phase in the past ten years. In some of these sectors there has long been an often elementary convergence, or at least coordination, of standards. For instance, central bankers have long interacted with each other across borders, but today we see an intensification in these transactions, which becomes necessary in the effort to develop and extend a global capital market. The increase of crossborder trade has brought with it a sharpened need for convergence in standards, as is evident in the vast proliferation of International Organization for Standardization (ISO) items. Another example is the institutional and legal framework necessary for the operation of the crossborder commodity chains identified by Gereffi.[3]

One outcome of these various trends is the emergence of a strategic field of operations that represents a partial disembedding of specific state operations from the broader institutional world of the state that had been geared exclusively to national agendas. It is a field of crossborder transactions among government agencies and business sectors aimed at addressing the new conditions produced and demanded by economic globalization. In positing this I am rejecting the prevalent notion in much of the literature on globalization that the realm of the national and the realm of the global are two mutually exclusive zones. My argument is rather that globalization is partly endogenous to the national, and is in this regard produced through a dynamic of denationalizing what had been constructed as the national.[4]

It is also a field of particular types of transactions: they are strategic, cut across borders, and entail specific interactions with private actors. These transactions do not entail the state as such, as in international treaties, but rather consist of the operations and policies of specific subcomponents of the state—for instance, legislative initiatives, specialized technical regulatory agencies, or some of the agendas pursued by central banks. These are transactions that cut across borders in that they concern the standards and regulations imposed on firms and markets operating globally,[5] and hence produce a certain convergence at the level of national regulations and law in the creation of the requisite conditions for globalization. The result is a mix of new or strengthened forms of private authority and partly denationalized state authority, such as the instituting of private interests into state normativity.[6]

Notes

1. See, in this regard, Giovanni Arrighi, *The Long Twentieth Century: Money, Power, and the Origins of Our Times* (London: Verso, 1994); Diana E. Davis (ed.), "Chaos and Governance," *Political Power and Social Theory*, 13, Part IV: Scholarly Controversy (Stamford, Conn.: JAI Press, 1999).

2. I use the term convergence for expediency. In the larger project I posit that conceptualizing these outcomes as convergence is actually problematic and often incorrect. Rather than a dynamic whereby individual states wind up converging, what is at work is a global dynamic that gets filtered through the specifics of each "participating" state. Hence my central research concern is not so much the outcome, "convergence," but the work of producing this outcome.

3. Gary Gereffi,"Global Production Systems and Third World Development," in Barbara Stallings (ed.), *Global Change, Regional Response: The New International Context of Development* (New York: Cambridge University Press, 1995), pp. 100–42.

4. Further, insofar as it is partly embedded in national settings, e.g., global cities, the state has had to re-regulate specific aspects of its authority over national territory.

5. An important point, which is usually disregarded in much general commentary about the global economy, is that a firm can participate in the latter even if it operates inside a single country: the key is whether it participates in a market or a transaction that is part of the global "system." My concern in this regard has been to show that there is considerable institutional development of that which is called the global economy—it is not simply a matter of goods or money crossing borders. For a firm's operations to be part of the global economy, they need to be encased in this institutional framework. If they are not, they may constitute an informal crossborder transaction or part of the new transnational criminal economy. A simplified illustration of the point that the distinctiveness of participating in the global economy does not necessarily lie in the fact of crossing borders is, for example, a US-based firm (whether US or non-US) that invests in a non-US firm listed on the New York stock market. The point here is that there is a regime—a set of conditions and legalities—that governs the listing of foreign firms on a stock market that has been incorporated in the global system and that governs the conditions under which the investor can acquire stock in that firm. I see the key, determining issue to be whether the firms and investors involved are operating under the umbrella of this regime. This umbrella is partly constituted through national institutions and partly, perhaps increasingly so, through the new privatized institutional framework I discuss later. What comes together in this example in my reading are some of the specifications I summarize in the global city model and in

the notion of denationalization. On the other hand, the following would not be an instance of firms operating in the global economic system, even though it entails actual physical crossing of borders: two individuals residing in different countries making a deal informally for one of them to bring items, also informally—without following regulations, including WTO regulations—for the second individual to sell in the second country, with both individuals using informal accounting and trust systems to guarantee enforcement of the conditions of the agreement. This is an extreme contrast; there are many cases that are more ambiguous than this.

6. As I indicated earlier, I conceptualize denationalization as multivalent. Thus, in the case of human rights, matters which had been considered the prerogative of states—security and protection of its citizens—are universalized and in that sense denationalized (see Sassen, *Denationalization: Economy and Polity in a Global Digital Age* [Princeton: Princeton University Press, forthcoming]).

 Chapter 3

GOVERNING THE ECONOMY

As an intellectual discipline, political economy emerged in the eighteenth century as a broad inquiry into the goals and means of organizing economic life. The discipline considered how the production, exchange, and distribution of goods shaped life opportunities and how governments could (and should) influence economic outcomes. Today, political economy analyzes how governments affect economic performance—and how economic performance in turn affects a country's political processes. In this chapter of *Readings in Comparative Politics,* we include a set of contributions that address key questions and debates in comparative political economy.

How a country organizes production and intervenes to manage the economy is one of the key elements in its overall pattern of political as well as economic development. Whether in the developed or developing world, success in steering a national economy is an important goal. International competitiveness contributes to the political status of countries and influences their capacity to deliver the goods for their citizens. And, of course, all governments in the contemporary world are under intense pressure to achieve durable economic development—to design and implement successful strategies for governing the economy—or face the political consequences for failure.

The study of political economy is very contested terrain. Some political economists emphasize the distributive consequences of economic policy on the fate of broad collectivities—from regions of the world to nations, classes, genders, and ethnic groups. Others focus on individuals pursuing particular goals through the rational calculation of costs and benefits. In addition to these issues of methodology— differences in the unit of analysis and disputes about the importance of moral as distinct from scientific conclusions—the field is cluttered with other debates. Are the states that govern best those that systematically shape economic outcomes, those that leave the economy wherever possible to private actors and market forces, or those that strategically straddle the public-private divide? How far have cross-border economic transactions, multinational corporations, and the institutions of global economic governance (such as the World Trade Organization and the International Monetary Fund) overtaken states as the key players that shape political-economic outcomes? As the contributions in this chapter will make clear, political economy is a vital aspect of comparative politics, and an area of inquiry that is especially well suited to analyzing some of the most critical challenges facing nation-states—and transforming the global order—today.

3.1

Political Economy

Peter Gourevitch

In this contribution, Peter Gourevitch traces the evolution of political economy, the academic discipline that encompasses the selections in this chapter of *Readings in Comparative Politics*. As Gourevitch explains, political economy began as a broad and unified economic, political, and moral inquiry before subdividing into two distinct branches. One approach emphasizes the "interconnectedness" of politics, culture, social organization, and economics. The other approach focuses on "individual rationality" as the driving force behind the preferences and means-ends calculations that are thought to determine economic (as well as other social and political) outcomes. Gourevitch concludes that both theoretical and policy debates in political economy today reveal the origins as well as the bifurcated evolution of this robust intellectual tradition.

The discipline termed political economy examines the relationship of individuals to society, the economy, and the state. Having begun as an integrated field of moral, economic, and political inquiry, it has subsequently fragmented into the study of the economy as an autonomous system, the application of rational individualist reasoning to all aspects of society, and the debate over policy problems with an economic dimension.

Origins of the Concept—A Unified Theory

Emerging in the eighteenth century, political economy drew on the individualism of Hobbes and Locke, the pragmatism of Machiavelli, and the empiricism of Bacon. Its theorists desanctified social discourse. They thought of governments and all human institutions as instruments, as devices formed by human beings to solve problems, as "efficient institutions," not as divine creations nor the accretion of tradition. Political and social institutions were akin to machines: if broken, they were to be fixed, using standards of empiricism, pragmatism, and utility.

Political economy stressed purposive action by goal-seeking individuals. Adam Smith and David Ricardo used it to theorize about the market economy and to attack mercantilist policies. James Mill and Jeremy Bentham used it to integrate representative government with the calculus of utilitarianism, equating good policy with the aggregation of individual preferences: "the greatest good for the greatest number." Political economists wrote about everything: morals, prisons, freedom, wealth, art, goodness, virtue, constitutions, leadership, war, and peace. Over time, however, the concept of political economy fragmented into discrete components so varied that contemporary users of the label do not necessarily communicate with or know anything about each other. Still, we may identify two large limbs on the tree of political economy, each stressing a different postulate of the founders: one branch focuses on the postulate of individual rationality, the other on the postulate of interconnectedness, or the interaction between economics and other forces.

The Postulate of Individual Rationality

Methodological individualism can be applied to any branch of human behavior (or nonhuman, for that matter). In this approach, social analysis requires a secure "micro" foundation on individuals having a coherent goal (the maximization of welfare) and the capacity for ends-means calculations in pursuit of that goal. Preference functions are taken as given and human nature is held constant. What varies are incentives. Variance in human behavior derives from the rewards or punishments induced by alternative institutional arrangements.

These assumptions have led to various branches of work. At its most abstract, modern economics behaves like mathematics, drawing out the implications of a few key axioms as a deductive body of thought without any particular real-world reference. The ideas are tested solely by their internal logic, valued for beauty, elegance, coherence. In the more applied form, propositions about the economy are derived from theory and confronted with data from actual economies. The empirical debates have to do with such topics as monetarism, Keynesianism, inflation, market structure, rational expectations, and efficient institutions.

By and large, contemporary economics has been self-contained. It has not been interested in examining the influence upon economic behavior of variables that lie outside its logic: values, culture, history, politics, ideology. Prestige in research has gone to theory and to econometrics. Expertise specific to countries, historical periods, companies, and policy has had low prestige, as evidenced by the Nobel Prizes or appointments at leading universities. In recent years, however, applied topics and noneconomic influences on economic behavior have gained new favor as objects of theoretical attention.

Economic reasoning, the presumption of optimizing behavior by individuals, has been applied to many topics in fields other than economics. Social choice, public choice, and rational choice are all labels used for these efforts. . . .

The Postulate of Interconnectedness

This approach rejects the autonomy and self-sufficiency of neoclassical econom-ics. The economy is seen as a societal output. Economic performance derives from political choices, social organization, culture, circumstances, history. The economy is constructed, not somehow natural. Tocqueville, Marx, Saint-Simon, Comte, Durkheim, and Weber worked in this integrated manner in the nine-teenth century, as did Talcott Parsons in the twentieth century.

Contemporary social science links positivist research techniques to these kinds of systemic questions in modern political economy. . . .

Policy Debates

These differing intellectual approaches to the relationship between politics and economics are reflected in policy debates:

a) The role of public policy in shaping market efficiency. The analytic separation of market and society entails a quarrel over the role of the state and public pol-icy in producing growth and efficiency. The minimalist view sees least as best; the state need only be a "night watchman," keeping peace, preventing crime, al-lowing an autonomous economy to function. By contrast, the "developmental state view" sees the market as requiring substantial provision of public goods, that is, items whose diffuse benefits fail to elicit enough private rewards to be provided by the market. These include education, research, public health, phys-ical infrastructure, and uniform standards. Advocates of industrial policy argue that state policy can contribute to efficiency in the strategic promotion of se-lected industries. Theorists of regulation explore policies concerning market and firm structure to consider efficient institutions.

The policy disputes involve both highly advanced industrial economies and those at early stages of development. They arise from disagreement over the past, as well as the present. The minimalists claim that economic growth oc-curs when prices are right, a condition best achieved with little state action, for which they offer British and U.S. growth as proof. State intervention leads to "rent-seeking," an extraction of wealth by officials who contribute nothing to efficiency, or to interest group distortion of policy, favoring efficient sectors over potentially efficient ones (urban residents, for example, using political control to keep down food prices, thereby preventing farmers from earning income through exports).

The state activists dispute this interpretation of the U.S. and British past, not-ing state promotion of canal and railroad building and other infrastructure, and cite Alexander Hamilton and Adam Smith as advocates of this approach. They cite Germany and Japan as examples of state "involved" growth, a model now being taken up by the East Asian newly industrializing economies (NIEs), particularly the Republic of Korea (South Korea), Taiwan, Hong Kong, and

Singapore. The minimalists dispute this interpretation of those countries. Economists would see this as an argument over the volume and quality of public goods the state needs to supply; political scientists would see this as an argument over the political circumstances that produce growth-promoting policies, be they activist or minimalist; sociologists would see this as an argument about the determination of collective goals and social structures needed to sustain growth. . . .

The Asian financial crisis of 1997 provoked a sharp debate, still continuing, about the capacity of developmental states to surmount "crony capitalism," the adequacy of orthodox models of financial adjustment, and the role of international agencies in domestic policy.

b) Foreign economic policy. How should a nation relate to the international economy? The neoclassical argument hinges on free trade: the optimal policy for a country is to have open borders. This view has been challenged since the nineteenth century by conservative nationalists as well as by political radicals. Nationalists sought self-sufficiency and political military strength, radicals social transformation; neither thought that these goals could be reached by free trade within a capitalist economy. In their view, the market would act to favor those already strong, the first industrializers.

The debate continues for developing countries. Critics of dominance by the advanced industrial countries argued that the free market traps developing countries in a subordinate role in the international division of labor. In the Latin American view, the solution to the problem lay in state-directed import substitution industrialization (ISI) strategies. A few countries in East Asia opted for export-oriented industrialization (ESI) strategies instead: state intervention was extensive, but oriented toward promoting industries that would produce goods for export rather than toward replacing imports. In the event, ESI countries have developed more rapidly than those that chose ISI.

There is still much discussion regarding the political economy of development. The United States and international advisers have pressed governments to privatize, deregulate, and open their borders. Japan and some European advisers have argued that states need to invest in education, encourage research, and subsidize key growth industries. In the meantime, intellectual barriers that isolated regions of the world within specialized subfields have been surmounted. Comparisons between Latin America and Asia are now common. Similarly, there is comparison of deregulation in statist economies and transition problems in the former communist countries. Economic development has been revived as a field of economics; comparative political economy flourishes.

The advanced countries, meanwhile, have witnessed a revival of long-standing political tensions over the proper response to growing international trade. Can countries go their own way on domestic social services and economic policies, or does competition force convergence? The empirical side of this debate gives rise to research about the actual record of policy and outcomes. It largely finds that considerable differences remain in economic policy (the trade-offs among growth, equality, and stability) and in outcomes.

Trade requires international agreements that set forth the rules by which it will be conducted. The United States influenced those rules in 1945, but it then accounted for 50 percent of world GNP; although it is still the world's most dynamic economy, that figure is now closer to 20 percent. The world is economically multipolar. Can rules be established in the absence of a dominant power, a hegemon? In Europe economic integration has gone remarkably far, encompassing not only the integrated trade market and the concordance of regulatory standards but monetary union as well. In global terms, the shift from the General Agreement on Tariffs and Trade to the World Trade Organization testifies to a desire for stronger dispute resolution mechanisms, and thus for more free trade.

While countries have liberalized trade, disputes remain. Agricultural subsidies in the advanced industrial world harm the developing countries, for whom food exports would be a major instrument for launching a successful export-oriented growth strategy, propounded, indeed, by the very countries urging privatization and market strategies. Nontariff barriers remain potent and the subject of tension among the United States, Japan, and Europe. Regulation extends the debate over "improper" barriers to trade to include many aspects of society traditionally not on the international bargaining table. The United States and European countries accuse Japan of excluding products and investment through these instruments (leading to the "Structural Impediments Initiative"). Japan claims that the *keiretsu* and other forms of organization are simply efficient market instruments which are available to any country, and are therefore not valid elements of international regulation or dispute. Within countries, trade continues to generate political conflict over the degree of economic liberalization and the social support needed to manage the transitions involved. The political economy of trade and international economic relations is a highly developed area of research integrating economics and politics. . . .

Another arena of research explores the causes of efforts to remove central banks from political influence and the consequences of these steps.

c) Equality, social mobility, environment. A third category of policy disputes in political economy concerns the attainment of goals other than growth and efficiency. Arguments are made on behalf of equality of income, opportunity, and participation in public life; over notions of social justice, health, safety, housing, security, a safety "net" for each citizen; over the role of leisure, culture, and individual fulfillment; over gender, ethnicity, race, and other elements of social relationships; over environmental quality and preservation of resources; and finally, over values of national power, domination, attainment, glory, autonomy, and security. All of these goals have an economic component. At a minimum they involve resources and the allocation of resources. They involve the use of politics to interact with the economy in order to attain these goals. The political economy tradition approaches these questions with a set of distinctive tools. It asks cost-benefit questions and considers incentives, markets, and institutions. It proposes solutions that take account of collective action problems, monitoring, "agency," delegation of authority. It examines values, culture, and community in the context of institutions and interests. It is willing to put a price on pollution, for example, or on a type of medical operation, or on disease prevention, and to ask, "How much is saving a life worth?"—an approach which often enrages analysts not trained in this tradition.

The Field Today

Some students of political economy are interested in economics but not politics; as "pure economists" they study the properties of a model. Some are interested in politics but not economics; they study economic reasoning applied to political institutions. Still others explore the elements of interactive systems, as economics and economic reasoning interact with other social systems and influences.

Caveat lector.   Readers can [also] find trends in contemporary writing that evoke something of the historical linkage among morality, politics, economic reality, and economic reasoning with which political economy began more than two centuries ago. . . . In the hands of [the most able theorists,] political economy evokes the power and forcefulness of its ancestors.

 3.2

The Importance of Democracy

Amartya Sen

In this contribution, Amartya Sen applies what Peter Gourevitch called "the postulate of interconnectedness" to the vexing theme of the relationship between democracy and economic development. Sen argues firmly against those who suppose that democracy and political liberty are luxuries that citizens of poor countries cannot afford. On the contrary, suggests the author, even people who are suffering misery and economic deprivation would choose democracy if given the choice. In addition, according to Sen, democracy does better than authoritarianism in promoting economic growth and is the necessary condition for the

---

proper understanding of economic needs. Hence, democracy is the prerequisite for the design and effective implementation of public policies that can help society achieve economic development.

Bordering on the Bay of Bengal, at the southern edge of Bangladesh and of West Bengal in India, there is the Sundarban—which means "beautiful forest." That is the natural habitat of the famous Royal Bengal tiger, a magnificent animal with grace, speed, power, and some ferocity. Relatively few of them are left now, but the surviving tigers are protected by a hunting ban. The Sundarban is also famous for the honey it produces in large clusters of natural beehives. The people who live in the region, desperately poor as they are, go into the forests to collect the honey, which fetches quite a handsome price in the urban markets—maybe even the rupee equivalent of fifty U.S. cents per bottle. But the honey collectors also have to escape the tigers. In a good year, only about fifty or so honey gatherers are killed by tigers, but that number can be very much higher when things don't go so well. While the tigers are protected, nothing protects the miserable human beings who try to make a living by working in those woods, which are deep and lovely—and quite perilous.

This is just one illustration of the force of economic needs in many third world countries. It is not hard to feel that this force must outweigh other claims, including those of political liberty and civil rights. If poverty drives human beings to take such terrible risks—and perhaps to die terrible deaths—for a dollar or two of honey, it might well be odd to concentrate on their liberty and political freedoms. Habeas corpus may not seem like a communicable concept in that context. Priority must surely be given, so the argument runs, to fulfilling economic needs, even if it involves compromising political liberties. It is not hard to think that focusing on democracy and political liberty is a luxury that a poor country "cannot afford."

Economic Needs and Political Freedoms

Views such as these are presented with much frequency in international discussions. Why bother about the finesse of political freedoms given the overpowering grossness of intense economic needs? That question, and related ones reflecting doubts about the urgency of political liberty and civil rights, loomed large at the Vienna conference on human rights held in the spring of 1993, and delegates from several countries argued against general endorsement of basic political and civil rights across the globe, in particular in the third world. Rather, the focus would have to be, it was argued, on "economic rights" related to important material needs.

This is a well established line of analysis, and it was advocated forcefully in Vienna by the official delegations of a number of developing countries, led by

China, Singapore and other East Asian countries, but not opposed by India and the other South Asian and West Asian countries, nor by African governments. There is, in this line of analysis, the often repeated rhetoric: What should come first—removing poverty and misery, or guaranteeing political liberty and civil rights, for which poor people have little use anyway?

The Preeminence of Political Freedoms and Democracy

Is this a sensible way of approaching the problems of economic needs and political freedoms—in terms of a basic dichotomy that appears to undermine the relevance of political freedoms because the economic needs are so urgent? I would argue, no, this is altogether the wrong way to see the force of economic needs, or to understand the salience of political freedoms. The real issues that have to be addressed lie elsewhere, and they involve taking note of extensive interconnections between political freedoms and the understanding and fulfillment of economic needs. The connections are not only instrumental (political freedoms can have a major role in providing incentives and information in the solution of acute economic needs), but also constructive. Our conceptualization of economic needs depends crucially on open public debates and discussions, the guaranteeing of which requires insistence on basic political liberty and civil rights.

I shall argue that the intensity of economic needs *adds* to—rather than subtracts from—the urgency of political freedoms. There are three different considerations that take us in the direction of a general preeminence of basic political and liberal rights:

1. their *direct* importance in human living associated with basic capabilities (including that of political and social participation);
2. their *instrumental* role in enhancing the hearing that people get in expressing and supporting their claims to political attention (including the claims of economic needs);
3. their *constructive* role in the conceptualization of "needs" (including the understanding of "economic needs" in a social context).

These different considerations will be discussed presently, but first we have to examine the arguments presented by those who see a real conflict between political liberty and democratic rights, on the one hand, and the fulfillment of basic economic needs, on the other.

Arguments Against Political Freedoms and Civil Rights

The opposition to democracies and basic civil and political freedoms in developing countries comes from three different directions. First, there is the claim that these freedoms and rights hamper economic growth and development. This belief is called the Lee thesis (after Lee Kuan Yew, the former prime minister of Singapore, who formulated it succinctly).

Second, it has been argued that if poor people are given the choice between having political freedoms and fulfilling economic needs, they will invariably choose the latter. So there is, by this reasoning, a contradiction between the practice of democracy and its justification: to wit, the majority view would tend to reject democracy—given this choice. In a different but closely related variant of this argument, it is claimed that the real issue is not so much what people actually choose, but what they have *reason* to choose. Since people have reason to want to eliminate, first and foremost, economic deprivation and misery, they have reason enough for not insisting on political freedoms, which would get in the way of their real priorities. The presumed existence of a deep conflict between political freedoms and the fulfillment of economic needs provides an important premise in this syllogism, and in this sense, this variant of the second argument is parasitic on the first (that is, on the truth of the Lee thesis). . . .

Democracy and Economic Growth

Does authoritarianism really work so well? It is certainly true that some relatively authoritarian states (such as South Korea, Lee's own Singapore and post-reform China) have had faster rates of economic growth than many less authoritarian ones (including India, Costa Rica and Jamaica). But the Lee thesis is, in fact, based on very selective and limited information, rather than on any general statistical testing over the wide-ranging data that are available. We cannot really take the high economic growth of China or South Korea in Asia as a definitive proof that authoritarianism does better in promoting economic growth—any more than we can draw the opposite conclusion on the basis of the fact that the fastest-growing African country (and one of the fastest growers in the world), viz., Botswana, has been a oasis of democracy on that troubled continent. Much depends on the precise circumstances.

In fact, there is rather little general evidence that authoritarian governance and the suppression of political and civil rights are really beneficial in encouraging economic development. The statistical picture is much more complex. Systematic empirical studies give no real support to the claim that there is a general conflict between political freedoms and economic performance. The directional linkage seems to depend on many other circumstances, and while some statistical investigations note a weakly negative relation, others find a strongly positive one. On balance, the hypothesis that there is no relation between them in either direction is hard to reject. Since political liberty and freedom have importance of their own, the case for them remains unaffected.

In this context, it is also important to touch on a more basic issue of research methodology. We must not only look at statistical connections but, furthermore, examine and scrutinize the *causal* processes that are involved in economic growth and development. The economic policies and circumstances that led to the economic success of East Asian economies are by now reasonably well understood. While different empirical studies have varied in emphasis, there is by now a fairly agreed general list of "helpful policies" that includes openness to competition, the use of international markets, a high level of literacy and school education, successful land reforms and public provision of incentives for investment, exporting and industrialization. There is nothing whatsoever to indicate that any of these policies is inconsistent with greater democracy and actually had to be sustained by the elements of authoritarianism that happened to be present in South Korea or Singapore or China.

Furthermore, in judging economic development it is not adequate to look only at the growth of GNP or some other indicators of overall economic expansion. We have to look also at the impact of democracy and political freedoms on the lives and capabilities of the citizens. It is particularly important in this context to examine the connection between political and civil rights, on the one hand, and the prevention of major disasters (such as famines), on the other. Political and civil rights give people the opportunity to draw attention forcefully to general needs, and to demand appropriate public action. Governmental response to the acute suffering of people often depends on the pressure that is put on the government, and this is where the exercise of political rights (voting, criticizing, protesting and so on) can make a real difference. This is a part of the "instrumental" role of democracy and political freedoms. I shall have to come back to this important issue again, later on.

Do Poor People Care About Democracy and Political Rights?

I turn now to the second question. Are the citizens of third world countries indifferent to political and democratic rights? This claim, which is often made, is again based on too little empirical evidence (just as the Lee thesis is). The only way of verifying this would be to put the matter to democratic testing in free elections with freedom of opposition and expression—precisely the things that the supporters of authoritarianism do not allow to happen. It is not clear at all how this proposition can be checked when the ordinary citizens are given little political opportunity to express their views on this and even less to dispute the claims made by the authorities in office. The downgrading of these rights and freedoms is certainly part of the value system of the *government leaders* in many third world countries, but to take that to be the view of the people is to beg a very big question.

It is thus of some interest to note that when the Indian government, under Indira Gandhi's leadership, tried out a similar argument in India, to justify the "emergency" she had misguidedly declared in the mid-1970s, an election was called that divided the voters precisely on this issue. In that fateful election, fought largely on the acceptability of the "emergency," the suppression of basic political and civil rights was firmly rejected, and the Indian electorate—one of the poorest in the world—showed itself to be no less keen on protesting against the denial of basic liberties and rights than it was in complaining about economic poverty. To the extent that there has been any testing of the proposition that poor people in general do not care about civil and political rights, the evidence is entirely against that claim. Similar points can be made by observing the struggle for democratic freedoms in South Korea, Thailand, Bangladesh, Pakistan, Burma (or Myanmar) and elsewhere in Asia. Similarly, while political freedom is widely denied in Africa, there have been movements and protests about that fact whenever circumstances have permitted, even though military dictators have given few opportunities in this respect.

What about the other variant of this argument, to wit, that the poor have *reason* to forgo political and democratic rights in favor of economic needs? This argument, as was noted earlier, is parasitic on the Lee thesis. Since that thesis has little empirical support, the syllogism cannot sustain the argument.

Instrumental Importance of Political Freedom

I turn now from the negative criticisms of political rights to their positive value. The importance of political freedom as a part of basic capabilities has already been discussed. . . . We have reason to value liberty and freedom of expression and action in our lives, and it is not unreasonable for human beings—the social creatures that we are—to value unrestrained participation in political and social activities. Also, informed and unregimented *formation* of our values requires openness of communication and arguments, and political freedoms and civil rights can be central for this process. Furthermore, to express publicly what we value and to demand that attention be paid to it, we need free speech and democratic choice.

When we move from the direct importance of political freedom to its instrumental role, we have to consider the political incentives that operate on governments and on the persons and groups that are in office. The rulers have the incentive to listen to what people want if they have to face their criticism and seek their support in elections. [To take one example,] no substantial famine has ever occurred in any independent country with a democratic form of government and a relatively free press. Famines have occurred in ancient kingdoms and contemporary authoritarian societies, in primitive tribal communities and in modern technocratic dictatorships, in colonial economies run by imperialists from the north and in newly independent countries of the south run by despotic national leaders or by intolerant single parties. But they have never materialized in any country that is independent, that goes to elections regularly, that has opposition parties to voice criticisms and that permits newspapers to report freely and question the wisdom of government policies without extensive censorship. . . .

Constructive Role of Political Freedom

The instrumental roles of political freedoms and civil rights can be very substantial, but the connection between economic needs and political freedoms may have a *constructive* aspect as well. The exercise of basic political rights makes it more likely not only that there would be a policy response to economic needs, but also that the conceptualization—including comprehension—of "economic needs" itself may require the exercise of such rights. It can indeed be argued that a proper understanding of what economic needs are—their content and their force—requires discussion and exchange. Political and civil rights, especially those related to the guaranteeing of open discussion, debate, criticism, and dissent, are central to the processes of generating informed and reflected choices. These processes are crucial to the formation of values and priorities, and we cannot, in general, take preferences as given independently of public discussion, that is, irrespective of whether open debates and interchanges are permitted or not.

The reach and effectiveness of open dialogue are often underestimated in assessing social and political problems. For example, public discussion has an important role to play in reducing the high rates of fertility that characterize many developing countries. There is, in fact, much evidence that the sharp decline in fertility rates that has taken place in the more literate states in India has been much influenced by public discussion of the bad effects of high fertility rates especially on the lives of young women, and also on the community at large. If the view has emerged in, say, Kerala or Tamil Nadu that a happy family in the modern age is a small family, much discussion and debate have gone into the formation of these perspectives. Kerala now has a fertility rate of 1.7 (similar to that in Britain and France, and well below China's 1.9), and this has been achieved with no coercion, but mainly through the emergence of new values—a process in which political and social dialogues have played a major part. The high level of literacy of the Kerala population, especially female literacy, which is higher than that of every province of China, has greatly contributed to making such social and political dialogues possible. . . .

Miseries and deprivations can be of various kinds—some more amenable to social remedy than others. The totality of the human predicament would be a gross basis for identifying our "needs." For example, there are many things that we might have good reason to value if they were feasible—we could even want immortality, as Maitreyee did. But we don't see them as "needs." Our conception of needs relates to our ideas of the preventable nature of some depravations, and to our understanding of what can be done about them. In the formation of these understandings and beliefs, public discussions play a crucial role. Political rights, including freedom of expression and discussion, are not only pivotal in inducing social responses to economic needs, they are also central to the conceptualization of economic needs themselves.

Working of Democracy

The intrinsic relevance, the protective role and the constructive importance of democracy can indeed be very extensive. However, in presenting these arguments on the advantages of democracies, there is a danger of overselling their effectiveness. As was mentioned earlier, political freedoms and liberties are permissive advantages, and their effectiveness would depend on how they are exercised. Democracy has been especially successful in preventing those disasters that are easy to understand and where sympathy can take a particularly immediate form. Many other problems are not quite so accessible. For example, India's success in eradicating famines is not matched by that in eliminating regular undernutrition, or curing persistent illiteracy, or inequalities in gender relations. While the plight of famine victims is easy to politicize, these other deprivations call for deeper analysis and more effective use of communication and political participation—in short, fuller practice of democracy.

Inadequacy of practice applies also to some failings in more mature democracies as well. For example, the extraordinary deprivations in health care, education, and social environment of African Americans in the United States help to make their mortality rates exceptionally high, and this is evidently not prevented by the working of American democracy. Democracy has to be seen as creating a set of opportunities, and the use of these opportunities calls for analysis of a different kind, dealing with the *practice* of democratic and political rights. In this respect, the low percentage of voting in American elections, especially by African Americans, and other signs of apathy and alienation, cannot be ignored. Democracy does not serve as an automatic remedy of ailments as quinine works to remedy malaria. The opportunity it opens up has to be positively grabbed in order to achieve the desired effect. This is, of course, a basic feature of freedoms in general—much depends on how freedoms are actually exercised.

The Practice of Democracy and the Role of Opposition

The achievements of democracy depend not only on the rules and procedures that are adopted and safeguarded, but also on the way the opportunities are used by the citizens. Fidel Valdez Ramos, the former president of the Philippines, put the point with great clarity in a November 1998 speech at the Australian National University:

> Under dictatorial rule, people need not think—need not choose—need not make up their minds or give their consent. All they need to do is to follow. This has been a bitter lesson learned from Philippine political experience of not so long ago. By contrast, a democracy cannot survive without civic virtue. . . . The political challenge for people around the world today is not just to replace authoritarian regimes by democratic ones. Beyond this, it is to make democracy work for ordinary people.

Democracy does create this opportunity, which relates both to its "instrumental importance" and to its "constructive role." But with what strength such opportunities are seized depends on a variety of factors, including the vigor of multiparty politics as well as the dynamism of moral arguments and of value formation. For example, in India the priority of preventing starvation and famine was already fully grasped at the time of independence (as it had been in Ireland as well, with its own experience of famine under British rule). The activism of political participants was very effective in preventing famines and in sharply condemning governments for allowing open starvation to occur, and the quickness and force of this process made preventing such calamities an inescapable priority of every government. And yet successive opposition parties have been quite docile in not condemning widespread illiteracy, or the prevalence of non-extreme but serious undernourishment (especially among the children), or the failure to implement land reform programs legislated earlier. This docility of opposition has permitted successive governments to get away with unconscionable neglect of these vital matters of public policy.

In fact, the activism of opposition parties is an important force in nondemocratic societies as well as democratic ones. It can, for example, be argued that despite the lack of democratic guarantees, the vigor and persistence of opposition in pre-democratic South Korea and even in Pinochet's Chile (against heavy odds) were indirectly effective in those countries' governance even before democracy was restored. Many of the social programs that served these countries well were at least partly aimed at reducing the appeal of the opposition, and in this way, the opposition had some effectiveness even before coming to office.

Another such area is the persistence of gender inequality, which too requires forceful engagement, involving critique as well as pointers to reform. Indeed, as these neglected issues come into public debates and confrontations, the authorities have to provide some response. In a democracy, people tend to get what they demand, and more crucially, do not typically get what they do not demand. Two of the neglected areas of social opportunity in India—gender equity and elementary education—are now receiving more attention from the opposition parties, and as a result, from the legislative and executive authorities as well. While the final results will emerge only in the future, we cannot ignore the various moves that are already being made (including proposed legislation that would require that at least a third of the members of Indian parliament must be women, and a schooling program that would extend the right to elementary education to a substantially larger group of children).

In fact, it can be argued that the contribution of democracy in India has not, by any means, been confined to the prevention of economic disasters, such as famines. Despite the limits of its practice, democracy has given India some stability and security about which many people were very pessimistic as the country became independent in 1947. India had, then, an untried government, an undigested partition and unclear political alignments, combined with widespread communal violence and social disorder. It was hard to have faith in the future of a united and democratic India. And yet half a century later we find a democracy that has, taking the rough with the smooth, worked fairly well. Political differences have largely been tackled within the constitutional procedures. Governments have risen and fallen according to electoral and parliamentary rules. India, an ungainly, unlikely, inelegant combination of differences, survives and functions remarkably well as a political unit with a democratic system—indeed held together by its working democracy.

India has also survived the tremendous challenge of having a variety of major languages and a spectrum of religions—an extraordinary heterogeneity of religion and culture. Religious and communal differences are, of course, vulnerable to exploitation by sectarian politicians, and have indeed been so used on several occasions (including in recent years), causing much consternation in the country. But the fact that such consternation greets sectarian violence, and that most of the substantial sections of the nation condemn such deeds, provides ultimately the main democratic guarantee against the narrowly factional exploitation of sectarianism. This is essential for the survival and prosperity of a country as remarkably varied as India, which may have a Hindu majority, but which is also the third largest Muslim country in the world, in which millions of Christians, along with most of the world's Sikhs, Parsees, and Jains, live.

A Concluding Remark

Developing and strengthening a democratic system is an essential component of the process of development. The significance of democracy lies, I have argued, in three distinct virtues: (1) its *intrinsic importance*, (2) its *instrumental contributions*, and (3) its *constructive role* in the creation of values and norms. No evaluation of the democratic form of governance can be complete without considering each.

Despite their limitations, political freedoms and civil rights are used effectively often enough. Even in those fields in which they have not yet been very effective, the opportunity exists for making them effective. The permissive role of political and civil rights (in allowing—indeed in encouraging—open discussions and debates, participatory politics and unpersecuted opposition) applies over a very wide domain, even though it has been more effective in some areas than in others. Its demonstrated usefulness in preventing economic disasters is itself quite important. When things go fine and everything is routinely good, this role of democracy may not be badly missed. But it comes into its own when things get fouled up, for one reason or another (for example, the . . . financial crisis in East and Southeast Asia [from 1997 to 1999] that disrupted several economies and left many people destitute). The political incentives provided by democratic governance acquire great practical value at that time.

However, while we must acknowledge the importance of democratic institutions, they cannot be viewed as mechanical devices for development. Their use is conditioned by our values and priorities, and by the use we make of the available opportunities of articulation and participation. The role of organized opposition groups is particularly important in this context.

Public debates and discussions, permitted by political freedoms and civil rights, can also play a major part in the formation of values. Indeed, even the identification of needs cannot but be influenced by the nature of public participation and dialogue. Not only is the force of public discussion one of the correlates of democracy, with an extensive reach, but its cultivation can also make democracy itself function better. For example, more informed and less marginalized public discussion of environmental issues may not only be good for the environment; it could also be important to the health and functioning of the democratic system itself.

Just as it is important to emphasize the need for democracy, it is also crucial to safeguard the conditions and circumstances that ensure the range and reach of the democratic process. Valuable as democracy is as a major source of social opportunity (a recognition that may call for vigorous defense), there is also the need to examine ways and means of making it function well, to realize its potentials. The achievement of social justice depends not only on institutional forms (including democratic rules and regulations), but also on effective practice. I have presented reasons for taking the issue of practice to be of central importance in the contributions that can be expected from civil rights and political freedoms. This is a challenge that is faced both by well-established democracies such as the United States (especially with the differential participation of diverse racial groups) and by newer democracies. There are shared problems as well as disparate ones.

 3.3

Models of Capitalism in the New World Order

David Coates

How do we distinguish between different models of capitalism? On what grounds should we differentiate national economic models, assess their strengths and weaknesses, and predict the winners and losers in global competitiveness? As David Coates explains in this contribution, these questions have inspired a raging debate in comparative politics. Coates reviews the changing terms of the debate and then contributes to the debate with a comparison of market-led, state-led,

David Coates, revised excerpt of "Models of Capitalism in the New World Order," *Political Studies* 47, no. 4 (1999): 643–661, Blackwell Publishing. Reprinted by permission of the author and Blackwell Publishing.

and negotiated models of capitalism. He concludes that an integrated global economy will leave fewer spaces for social democratic models and raises an important note of caution about the social and economic consequences of the unregulated market-driven model.

The Nature of Capitalist Models

There is nothing particularly unusual about academics and political commentators differentiating types of capitalism. On the contrary, there is a long academic tradition of splitting capitalism into different stages. Marxists have been doing it for years: differentiating between "early capitalism" and "late," between "liberal capitalism," "monopoly capitalism" and "state monopoly capitalism" and between "organized" and "disorganized" capitalism. Mainstream scholarship has been equally active, differentiating "stages of economic growth" splitting early capitalism from the later "mixed economy" and even locating stages of competitive development (labelled, by Michael Porter for instance, as respectively "factor-driven," "investment driven," "innovation driven" and "wealth driven").[1]

In both Marxist and non-Marxist hands, the argument has been much the same: that capitalism as an economic form can be distinguished in different time periods by the qualitatively distinct mixes of technologies, forms of business organisation, characters of labor forces and state functions that come to predominate within it. In arguments of this kind, it is not so much that different models of capitalisms co-exist. They may, but that is not the main point. The main point is that over the lifecycle of capitalism as a whole, different forms of social organization and political structuring emerge as dominant for a period; and capitalism as a whole has, in consequence, to be understood as moving inexorably from one model to another over time. How are these models to be understood?

The key players and terms of debate have evolved over the years. The key players in the debates on models of capitalism today are the "new institutionalists": those economists, political scientists and comparative sociologists who are committed to the notion of the necessary social embeddedness of all economic institutions, and to the resulting path-dependent and socially specific nature of resulting economic trajectories. The new institutionalists have been very productive of late, generating a literature bedecked with an initially bewildering variety of different typologies, labels, and number of cases. So we have "the Scandinavian model," "Asian capitalism," "German social market capitalism," "American liberal capitalism," even Russian "mafia capitalism"; and we have typologies of welfare systems, of cultural networks, of forms of corporate organization, of systems of investment provision, of modes of labor market regulation, and of state-economy relations. We have "liberal," "corporatist" and "social democratic" welfare regimes; "individualistic" or "communitarian" value systems, among others. It is hardly surprising then, that the literature on models gives us not one, but several, listings of capitalist types, with a seemingly endless number of categories inside the various typologies. Capitalism comes in two forms for some writers, in three for some, in four for others, or in a infinite variety of internally differentiated national types for the really committed new institutionalists. But what it does not do is come in one form alone. On that much the new institutionalist scholarship is quite clear.

Putting order on all that complexity is difficult; but it is worth noting how—beneath all the differentiation—clear polar types of capitalist models regularly reappear. For this is a literature concerned with competitiveness; and competition is uniquely a practice that produces winners and losers. So literatures concerned with competitiveness tend ultimately to bifurcate or at most to map out only limited numbers of likely scenarios. For example, Lester Thurow played with a single distinction between Anglo-American and Japanese-German capitalisms, before eventually setting up his head-to-head as a three-way fight between the United States, Japan and Europe:

> America and Britain trumpet individualistic values: the brilliant entrepreneur, Nobel Prize winners, large wage differentials, individual responsibility for skills, easy to fire and easy to quit, profit maximisation, and hostile mergers and takeovers—their hero is the Lone Ranger. In contrast, Germany and Japan trumpet communitarian values: business groups, social responsibility for skills, teamwork, firm loyalty, industry strategies, and active industrial policies that promote growth. Anglo-Saxon firms are profit maximisers; Japanese business firms play a game that might better be known as "strategic conquest." Americans believe in "consumer economics"; Japanese believe in "producer economics."[2]

In fact, there are real dangers in setting up any simple two-case model of capitalist types. Certainly the great weakness of any modelling that collapses Japan and Germany into a similarly "communitarian" or "trust" based model (to be set against an Anglo-American individualistic one) is its failure to spot the very different role of labor movements in the Japanese and German cases, and therefore to see the very different sources of what, through liberal individualistic eyes, may initially seem to be a similar set of communitarian cultures. In Japan, the labor movement has historically been weak, and the main sources of cultural specificity have been broadly right-wing (conservative, religious and nationalist). In the European welfare capitalisms (especially post-war Sweden, but also to a lesser degree Germany) labor movements have been historically strong, and the sources of market-regulating cultures have been predominantly center-left, social democratic. The result has been that Japanese capital has had to deal with a very different set of welfare, worker, and trade union rights than has Western European capital; and has consolidated a very different set of institutional props for what are—on the surface—quite similar patterns of wage differentials, job security, labor turnover and training in the two systems. Those props in Europe have been largely public (state) props. In Japan, of course, they have been largely private (and corporate).

Moreover, any simple "U.S. versus the rest" tendency in the models literature can only obscure a much more variegated range of differences in who really are the key players (or stakeholders) in each particular capitalist model. Again, the

Anglo-Saxon version of stakeholding is reasonably straightforward. The shareholders are the key stakeholders in those capitalisms in which large corporations raise the bulk of their external capital in open financial markets, and where the level of short-term profit yield, executive salaries, and dividend distribution drive the whole system. And such a narrow base of stakeholding clearly differs from more bank-based systems of industrial finance, and from systems where interlocking sets of corporations sustain each other in long-term strategies of market capture and profit consolidation. Industrial companies, financial institutions, and public agencies, that is, interact differently in a variety of national contexts; and any modelling of capitalist types has to make space for that national differentiation.

This is why Thurow's differentiation of three geographical areas of future capitalist competition is probably a better guide to the basic choices here than any simple polarity would be. For the choices do seem to triangulate around a capital-labor-state set of overlapping polarities, a set which then allows a range of positioning within the parameters of the triangle as a whole. The three-way nature of the basic choices before us here can be isolated schematically in diagrammatic form. (See Figure 1.)

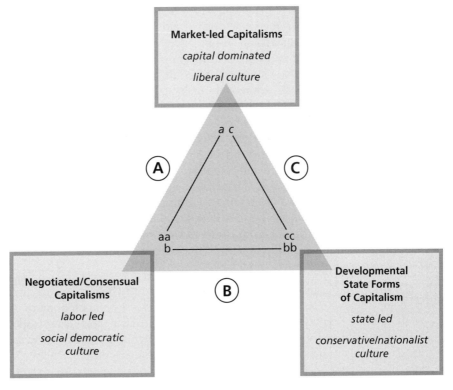

Figure 1 Models of Capitalism.

The diagram graphically depicts the recognition that the core institutional settlement that capitalism has taken (both temporally and spatially) varies around the central question of who/what decides how capital accumulation will be organized; and that that response can best be measured around two intersecting axes: one charting the degree of state regulation over private capital; the other recording the strength of labor rights in the face of the private ownership of the means of production. Is capital accumulation the private concern of individual entrepreneurs and firms—which it is in forms of capitalism that are predominantly market-led? Or is that accumulation a matter settled in some relationship between private firms and the state; or is it negotiated within industrial and political systems in which organized labor also has a voice?

The answers to these questions are invariably matters of degree, which is why a triangular representation of ideal types (allowing for a scaling of position along each dimension of the triangle) seems to work better than a simple set of boxes. Alongside dimension "A" in Figure 1, for example, particular models can be distinguished by the set of labor rights within which private capital is obliged to operate: very few such rights at point "a," very many at point "aa." Along dimension "B" in Figure 1, models can be differentiated by the political strength of labor movements (and by the associated provision of welfare rights and government policy on full employment): with labor movements strong at point "b," weak at point "bb." Along dimension "C" in Figure 1, models can be differentiated by the degree of autonomy of private firms from state regulation, direction, and control: with high levels of autonomy at point "c," and with high levels of state regulation at point "cc." Moreover, each of the defining points of the triangle tends to be associated with a particular cultural mix, and each face of the triangle tends to be associated with a particular distribution of power and rewards. So, as we rotate the triangle, different political ideologies and associated value systems come into view: (liberal political ideologies and values when we get to market-led capitalism, social democratic ideologies and values when we get to negotiated/consensual forms of capitalism, and conservative or nationalist ideologies and values when we reach state-led capitalisms). As we drop down the triangle from top to bottom, the number of stakeholders tends to widen and income inequalities tend to diminish; and as we move across the triangle from right to left, the distribution of social power tends to even out. And so on.

The diagram suggests the following ideal-typical form:

♦ In *market-led* capitalisms, accumulation decisions lie overwhelmingly with private companies, who are left free to pursue their own short-term profit motives and to raise their capital in open financial markets. In such capitalisms, workers enjoy only limited statutory industrial and social rights, and earn only what they can extract from their employers in largely unregulated labor markets. State involvement in economic management is limited largely to market-creating and protecting measures; and the dominant understandings of politics and morality in the society as a whole are individualistic and liberal in form.

- In *state-led* capitalisms by contrast, accumulation decisions are again primarily seen as the right and responsibility of private companies, but those decisions are invariably taken only after close liaison with public agencies, and are often indirectly determined through administrative guidance and bank leadership. In such capitalisms, labor movements tend still to lack strong political and social rights; but there is space for forms of labor relation which tie some workers to private corporations through company-based welfare provision. The dominant cultural forms in such capitalisms are likely to be conservative-nationalist in content.
- In *negotiated or consensual social* capitalisms the degree of direct state regulation of capital accumulation may still be small; but the political system entrenches a set of strong worker rights and welfare provision which gives organised labor a powerful market presence and the ability to participate directly in industrial decision-making. The dominant cultural networks in these capitalisms are invariably social democratic ones.

The triangle serves as a useful guide to the positioning of whole national economies. It does not seem unreasonable, as a first approximation, to position the United States towards the market-led end of the triangle, Japan nearer the state-led end, and Sweden and Germany along the axis linking market and social capitalism together.

The Viability of Capitalist Models

Recent center-left intellectual commentaries on capitalist models have developed a powerful critique of market-led capitalism and an associated defense of more consensual or negotiated forms of managed capitalism. That critique has been built around a number of linked themes.

One is that economies pursuing more negotiated/consensual forms of capitalist management achieve growth rates and levels of international competitiveness that are at least as good as those achieved by more market-led forms of capitalism; while at the same time attaining social targets (on welfare rights, job security, and income equality) that are distinctly superior. In their defense of organized labor as a key "social partner" in the regulation of economies dominated by privately owned companies, the advocates of Swedish corporatism and German social-market capitalism regularly cite the "beneficial constraints" imposed on capital accumulation by strong worker and trade union rights. By blocking off low wage sweat-shop routes to short-term profitability, such constraints are said to oblige local capitalists to prosper by investment and innovation; and by generating a strong sense of job security and corporate identification in the workforce, they are also said to enable organized labor to cooperate fully in the job changes and re-skilling processes necessarily associated with such high value-added production processes.

A parallel, though normally differently focused, argument from center-left intellectuals emphasizes the superiority of the "developmental state" model over the Anglo-Saxon one; and stresses in particular the superiority of the modes of industrial, social, and political organisation underpinning Japanese post-war economic success. In much of the center-left's comparative writings on Japan, emphasis is placed on the long-term nature of Japanese industrial planning (at both corporate and state levels), a long-termism that is supposedly rooted in the close (non–market-mediated) relationships that exist in Japan between financial and industrial capital, and between private firms and the state. This apparent Japanese propensity for "voice" rather than "exit" strategies in the management of economic life is also often related to the job security afforded to core workers by Japanese life-time employment policies; and to the nonconfrontational industrial relations that Confucian value systems are said to consolidate. Against market-led forms of capitalism, center-left enthusiasts for Asian models emphasize the competitive advantages of "trust-based" systems of economic regulation: and use the argument that "trust" is the missing ingredient in market-led capitalisms to link their enthusiasm for Japanese capitalism to that for the very different systems of European welfare-capitalism.

Both sets of arguments about the superiority of non–market-led models of capitalism share a common critique of neo-liberal economics, and a common reading of the economic weakness of the United Kingdom under Thatcher and Major and of the United States under Reagan and Bush. According to Will Hutton, for example, liberal economics is flawed in three ways: by its narrow view of economic rationality (and associated faith in the capacity of the price mechanism to trigger self-correcting market responses), its commitment to the law of diminishing returns and its belief in unregulated markets mechanisms as self-regulating optimizers.[3] In consequence, they are able to treat Anglo-Saxon ways of running capitalism as inherently outmoded and inappropriate to a modern world in which production has been transformed by more collaborative forms of labor, a tendency toward strategic alliances among firms, and a premium on quality-competitive rather than cost-competitive commodities. The cumulative impact of this embedded liberalism within Anglo-Saxon economies is—on this argument—a long-term loss of international competitiveness: a loss variously related by center-left intellectuals to the short-termism (and high dividend requirements) of stockmarket-led capital provision, and to the adversarial nature of industrial relations triggered by market-led personnel strategies.

According to center-left critics of market-led capitalisms, the absence of trust relationships along dimension "C" of Figure 1 leaves U.S. and U.K.-based private firms vulnerable to competition from East Asian and German multinationals who enjoy long-term relationships with their local banking systems and (in the Japanese case) with the planning agencies of the state; a weakness then compounded by the associated absence of trust relationships along dimension A of Figure 1, by what William Lazonick has called "the Achilles heel of US manufacturing. . . . [its] organisation of work on the shop-floor . . . and [its] dramatic weakening of the labour movement at precisely the time when unions needed to be brought into the investment decision-making process in both the private and the public sectors."[4]

Of late, such advocates of non–market-led capitalisms have been put on the defensive by the difficulties of first the European and then the East Asian economies. What looked in happier times like long-term relationships of trust between the suppliers and deployers of capital now stand condemned as inadequate financial regulation and systematically induced corruption; and the "beneficial constraints" are widely condemned as machines for the destruction of employment. In truth, center-left defenses of humane capitalism were always heavily challenged from both their left and their right. They were (and continue to be) challenged by a tradition of Marxist scholarship unimpressed by capitalist models of any kind: one concerned in particular with the degree of labor exploitation hidden behind the facade of capitalist trust-relationships, and with the fragility of class compacts and national corporatism in an age of expanding proletarianization and intensified global competition. And they were (and continue to be) challenged by a tradition of liberal scholarship committed to the very market forces that the center-left historically sought to control.

In fact the under-performance of certain capitalist models (the United Kingdom before 1979, European welfare capitalism since) has long been explained by liberal economists in exactly the reverse terms to those deployed by intellectuals of the center-left: as under-performance triggered by the *blunting* of market forces by political interference and labor-market regulation. Liberal scholarship on specific economies has long argued that innovation and change are made more difficult by strong trade unions, high welfare and tax regimes, and over-active governments; and that flexibility (particularly in labor markets) alone holds the key to competitiveness. Such arguments, as we know, held center-stage in the United Kingdom for two decades after 1979, where they shaped economic policy under the Conservatives and inspired the Labour Party to abandon its original commitments to public ownership, Keynesianism and full employment. They also were the standard intellectual tools of a whole series of international regulatory agencies throughout the same twenty-year period; and are now enshrined in the convergence criteria and the subsequent growth and stability pact of the Maastricht treaty on European monetary union (in effect suspended in November 2003 because France and Germany could not conform to the budgetary constraints). And, of course, current understandings (in both policy-making and academic circles) of the economic imperatives associated with intensified global competition are predominantly liberal in kind. Statism is out. Keynesianism is out. Welfare provision and trade union rights are heavily under siege. The current policy consensus in the corridors of power in advanced capitalism is steadily shifting back towards market-led solutions to rising unemployment and slow rates of economic growth.

Where the Marxist and neo-liberal critics of the new institutionalism converge is in their common recognition that this policy shift is not accidental. Where they differ is in their assessment of the likely viability of the convergence now under way. For certainly on a Marxist reading of the logics of contemporary capitalism, changes in the global economy are now squeezing the space for certain kinds of capitalist models. It is not just, as Zysman has it, that "national models of growth in the advanced countries are not collapsing, but are rather undergoing a common transition along distinct trajectories."[5] It is rather that the extensive industrialization of East Asia (and the associated proletarianization of the Asian rural poor) is qualitatively altering the balance of class forces on a world scale; and if that is not requiring a straightforward convergence in the relationships within capitalist classes (and between capital and the state), it *is* squeezing the space within which different relationships between capital and labor can be easily sustained. Globalization, understood in this sense of renewed industrialization on a global scale, has qualitatively altered the class parameters from those within which negotiated/consensual models of capitalism were initially created and sustained in Western Europe in what—for the western European labor movements—now does look as though it was capitalism's "golden age."

There may still be a space for the protection of existing (and construction of new) developmental state forms of capitalism; but those were never in the past (and will not be in the future) necessarily superior to Anglo-Saxon forms of capitalism as far as labor was concerned. But what is now becoming clear is that an increasingly integrated global economy will allow fewer and fewer spaces for social democratic models of capitalism.

If the future is Anglo-Saxon, what comfort are we to take from the progressive collapse of western European welfare capitalism as a viable capitalist model? Right-wing political forces might enjoy that victory, but left-wing ones should not. For if market-led capitalism is all that is left in its place, then the weaknesses of that model—as both a developmental engine and as a guarantor of minimum standards of welfare provision and worker rights, of the kind laid out by its critics in easier times—will simply become generalized through the world economy, and intensified there by the spread of world competition. Unregulated markets in an environment of extensive proletarianization and global capital mobility will generate an upward and permanent momentum in economic activity only if the central contradictions of a capitalist mode of production are suddenly and miraculously a thing of the past. But if they are not, we all face a long period of "ratcheting down" (of wages, job rights, employment, and welfare) and "ratcheting up" (of longer hours, intensified work routines, greater income inequality, and generalized economic insecurity). For, as Marx put it long before it became fashionable to talk of globalization and the convergence of capitalist models, we seem now at last to be approaching that point at which "the bourgeoisie . . . through its exploitation of the world market . . . compels all nations, on pain of extinction, to adopt the bourgeois mode of production. In one word, it creates a world after its own image": that point, moreover, where perhaps "man is at last compelled to face with sober senses his real conditions of life, and his relations with his kind."[6] It is 150 years since Marx wrote *The Communist Manifesto*. Contemporary developments suggest that, though its production was maybe a little premature, its central message has now at last found its time.

Notes

1. Michael Porter, *The Competitive Advantage of Nations* (New York: Free Press, 1990), pp. 545–560.
2. Lester Thurow, *Head to Head: The Coming Economic Battle among Japan, Europe, and America* (New York: William Morrow, 1992), p. 32.
3. Will Hutton, *The State We're In* (London: Cape, 1992), p. 236.
4. William Lazonick, *Business Organization and the Myth of the Market Economy* (Cambridge: Cambridge University Press, 1991), pp. 188, 189.
5. John Zysman, "The myth of the global economy: enduring national foundations and emerging regional realities," *New Political Economy*, 1(2) (July 1996): 159.
6. Karl Marx, *The Communist Manifesto*, reprinted in *Marx-Engels: Selected Works* (London: Lawrence and Wishart, 1968), pp. 38–39.

 3.4

Stabilization Tactics in Latin America: Menem, Cardoso, and the Politics of Low Inflation

Daniel Treisman

Why are some political leaders more able than others to implement controversial economic policies? This selection tries to understand why presidents Carlos Menem of Argentina and Fernando Henrique Cardoso of Brazil were much more successful than earlier presidents of the two countries in pursuing policies that brought down very high rates of inflation. Treisman makes a powerful case for the claim that what distinguished Menem and Cardoso from their predecessors was the importance of clever strategy. The key to their success was their ability to divide the coalition that benefited from high inflation and to redefine the interests of some groups formerly benefiting from inflation in a way that persuaded them

Daniel Treisman, "Stabilization Tactics in Latin America: Menem, Cardoso, and the Politics of Low Inflation," *Comparative Politics* 36, No. 4 (July 2004): 399–419 (excerpts). This article first appeared in *Comparative Politics* and is reprinted with their permission.

to support anti-inflationary policies. This selection demonstrates the close connection of politics and economics. Can you think of other cases where political leaders tried to gain support for their economic policies by adopting the strategy of "divide and conquer" and by shaping policies to "transform opponents into supporters"?

I n the 1990s presidents Carlos Menem of Argentina and Fernando Henrique Cardoso of Brazil both accomplished something of a macroeconomic miracle. They managed to bring their countries' chronically high inflation rates down close to zero and keep them very low for more than five years, after decades of price instability and unsuccessful attempts at stabilization.

Some of the shine has since come off both achievements. A currency crisis forced Brazil to devalue in 1998, and in 2002 fear of a left-wing victor in the presidential election roiled markets again. In Argentina Menem's successor, Fernando De la Rúa, struggled in vain to generate growth and fend off a debt default, currency crisis, and run on the banks. He left office in late 2001 amid street violence and a plummeting peso.

It is thus worth emphasizing just how historically unusual the reemergence of price stability in Brazil and Argentina in the 1990s was. As of 2002, Brazil's inflation had been under 10 percent for five years, and Argentina's had for eight. In each country, inflation for the first time in forty years stayed this low for more than one year. No equivalent eight-year spell of low inflation had occurred in Argentina since 1944. Brazil had not had a five-year period with such stable prices since before 1937. Argentina's commitment to stable money was so entrenched by the late 1990s that it survived a four-year recession and 18 percent unemployment. It took a major political crisis—and three presidents—to break the dollar peg. Even if this recession is taken into account, Argentine growth in the 1990s was higher than in any decade since the 1950s.

How did these political leaders stabilize prices when so many before them had failed? Political economists have offered a number of explanations. Some emphasize crisis, social "wars of attrition," or the electoral cycle. Others contend that Menem's left-wing Peronist credentials gave him greater credibility in demanding sacrifice from the working class. Although these factors may contribute to an answer, they do not provide a convincing account. Both achievements rested on a particularly effective political strategy that demobilized key beneficiaries of inflationary policies and created confidence in the durability of reforms.

While the specific tactics differed, they had many similarities. Both presidents split the labor movement, coopting parts in order to isolate the rest. Both wooed business leaders with tariff protection or privatization benefits and provided domestic banks short-run aid while ultimately weakening them relative to foreign competitors. Both offered state governors pork or cash in return for institutional changes. Perks, pork, and individual policy concessions coopted parliamentary leaders and helped assemble a legislative coalition of left-wingers, free market ideologues, and clientelistic regional bosses.

Although often labeled neoliberal, both economic programs were far from orthodox. Both leaders compromised their commitment to liberalization and fiscal balance—and to some extent their reputations—in order to create rents and buy support from opponents. The markets proved happy to forgive such departures from orthodoxy in return for the political credibility they generated. Leaders who tried harder to balance the budget (Collor, De la Rúa) panicked investors, because their commitments were not politically sustainable.

Argentina and Brazil offer inductive insights into the art of political tactics. How did these two politicians avoid the obstacles that defeated their predecessors? The goal is to illuminate the logic in the way a chess critic might compare famous games, identifying tactical combinations and examining why they work.[1] The analysis starts with the two classic tactics, divide and rule and cooptation. It proceeds to an additional technique, the deliberate introduction of a new player into the game to weaken preexisting opponents. It concludes with the advantages and disadvantages of two alternative means of cooptation—direct bargains and creation of vested interests—and the "cooptation currencies" usually associated with them.

Inflation and Stabilization

Brazil.   Between 1985 and 1993 Brazil's leaders tried to stabilize the macro-economy five times and adopted four new currencies. In 1985, when the military left power, inflation exceeded 200 percent a year. The Cruzado (1986–87), Bresser (June 1987), Summer (January 1989), Collor I (March 1990), and Collor II (1991) plans followed in quick succession. None reduced inflation below 100 percent a year. A series of presidents—Sarney, Collor, Franco—saw their political credibility sapped by their macroeconomic failures (and, in Collor's case, by charges of corruption). When, finally, the *Plano Real* introduced by finance minister Cardoso in 1993 stabilized prices, it won him the presidency in 1994. . . .

Under the Real Plan, inflation fell from more than 2,000 percent in 1994 to 66 percent in 1995 and 16 percent in 1996. Conventional wisdom assumes that stabilization attempts almost always fail unless government deficits are curtailed. They were not in Brazil. In fact, the operational public sector borrowing requirement—the public sector borrowing requirement corrected for the effect of inflation on government debt—averaged 4.25 percent of GDP in 1995–2000, compared to 0.3 percent of GDP in 1990–94. The most dramatic fiscal adjustment came under the unsuccessful Collor plans (1990–91), when the budget even yielded a surplus. Nor was this period one of strict adherence to monetary targets, many of which were missed and "quietly abandoned later."[2] In 1996–2000 M2 grew more than seven times as fast as prices. Since GDP increased during this period, the ratio of M2 to GDP grew moderately, from 17 percent in 1995 to 37 percent in 2000.

Argentina. Argentina's experience resembles Brazil's. In 1983 the military handed over an economy with inflation at 337 percent. For the next seven years, Presidents Alfonsín and then Menem struggled to reduce it. The Austral, Primavera, and Bunge and Born (BB) plans—along with less notable attempts— all achieved temporary drops, but prices quickly rebounded. Only when finance minister Domingo Cavallo introduced the Convertibility Plan in 1991 did inflation stay low.

Unlike in Brazil, the failures and ultimate success follow closely the record of fiscal adjustment. Alfonsín inherited a nonfinancial public sector deficit approaching 10 percent of GDP.[3] Attempts to lower price expectations by removing indexation were relatively effective in the short run. However, until the deficit was sharply reduced, successes were shortlived. . . .

Stakeholders and Stabilization Tactics

The outcomes of most games are not completely determined by the rules or goals of the players. They depend also on what strategies are chosen. Menem's and Cardoso's challenge was to identify which actors had the power and the motive to impede macroeconomic stabilization and to find ways to neutralize some while coopting others.

Brazil. In Brazil four groups benefited from inflationary spending and could obstruct change. First, public sector employees (along with pensioners and certain narrow interests) won expensive entitlements in the 1988 constitution. They could defend these by voting, demonstrating, striking, and lobbying through their unions. Second, politicians in parliament wanted to continue receiving the perquisites of office. Some also hoped to seek election in their states. They could block attempts to trim the federal budget or reform fiscal or banking laws. Third, state governors wanted to retain constitutionally decentralized revenues and extract additional funds, including bailouts for their state banks. Given weak party discipline, governors had authority over their state congressional delegations. They could provoke crises by refusing to remit federal taxes or restructure state banks.[4] Fourth, the business community feared the high interest rates needed to cure inflation. Big businesses could decline to buy federal bonds and lobby at all levels.

All these groups could mobilize politically to block spending cuts or other antiinflationary measures. In this context, reducing inflation temporarily was not difficult. A wage and price freeze or unilateral restructuring of state debt could accomplish this goal, as in 1986, 1990, and 1991.[5] But to keep inflation low investors had to be convinced to buy government bonds at moderate rates, and the distributive pressures from groups eager to grab a larger share of national income through price increases had to be restrained.

Previous presidents had failed in opposite ways. Sarney, starting out politically weak, sacrificed reform to please potential opponents. He increased nontax transfers to states and municipalities, raised central spending, and lavished patronage on parliament, all while trying to enforce a price freeze.[6] The plan collapsed amid suppressed inflation, soaring deficits, and business opposition. By contrast, Collor managed to unite all social forces against him by attacking all simultaneously. He froze 80 percent of the country's savings for eighteen months, raised taxes, reduced trade protection, canceled federal debt, fired 360,000 federal employees, prohibited state governments from rolling over their central bank debt, and tried to recentralize fiscal revenues.[7] His actions alienated business, the governors, parliamentary deputies, and the public. Collor was impeached for corruption in September 1992.

What made the Real Plan different was not a more effective fiscal adjustment or stricter monetary policy, but rather a more credible political strategy.[8] This strategy involved tactics for coopting or neutralizing each of the main stakeholders. Repeatedly, Cardoso played their "short-term interests off against their long-term goals," offering "patronage now in order to persuade politicians to accept state-building reforms that [sought] to limit patronage in the future."[9]

His approach to public employees was characteristic. Cardoso appeased them with short-term spending and higher salaries, while privatizing many of their workplaces. In late 1994 public sector salaries were raised, resulting in a 22 percent increase in federal personnel spending in 1995 and major additional payroll costs for the state governments.[10] The next year Cardoso set out to sell off state monopolies in electricity and gasoline. When the oil workers' union went on strike in May 1995, the government denounced the strikers as "enemies of the people" and sent the military to secure petroleum refineries.[11] Privatizations raised US$33.4 billion for the federal budget in 1994–98.[12]

Appeasing parliament entailed helping politicians please their local constituencies and not complaining too much about their perquisites.[13] One of Cardoso's first acts in office was to approve a 100 percent increase in legislative and executive salaries.[14] He did not insist on limiting the number of pensions a single public employee could draw, which would have hurt some major players.[15] While respecting parliamentarians' corporate perquisites, Cardoso sought to build a proreform coalition, forging an odd alliance with Sarney's PFL, a party of economic conservatives, clientelistic bosses, and former supporters of military rule, as well as with the centrist PMDB and several smaller conservative parties. The strength of the PFL and PMDB in the country's poorer, overrepresented North, Northeast, and Center-West helped push legislation through.[16] Northeastern deputies and senators were "strategically positioned on the key congressional committees" dealing with fiscal and infrastructure issues.[17] To woo rural deputies, Cardoso deferred some $1.8–5 billion in landowners' debt payments to the Banco do Brasil.[18]

To coopt the state governors, Cardoso offered them large financial benefits in return for ending their most inflationary practices—another trade of money (in this case, credit) for institutional reforms. The state banks' massive debts threatened the entire financial system; as of 1996, they held about half of all banking sector assets.[19] The state governments had little incentive to restructure or service their debts, since the senate let them continue to capitalize the interest.

Cardoso offered a simple exchange. First, in late 1995–96 states received R$2.5 billion in emergency funds in return for promising fiscal adjustment.[20] These promises were not all kept. Then, from December 1997 the government signed agreements with individual states committing them to close or restructure their banks and implement specific fiscal reforms. The federal government assumed much of the debt, exchanging federal for state bonds.[21] Up to August 2000 the total value of federal bonds issued was $R91.9 billion, or almost 10 percent of 1999 GDP.[22] One circumstance helped arrange these deals. Three of the biggest debtors—São Paulo, Rio de Janeiro, and Minas Geraís—had PSDB governors, elected on Cardoso's coattails in 1994; their future prospects depended on Cardoso's favor and continued success. Rio's state bank was successfully privatized in 1997, and Minas Geraís's was in 1998.[23] Other states found it that much harder to organize resistance to the refinancing scheme. . . .

Overall, Cardoso's administration is remarkable more for what it did not do than for what it did. It did not cut spending: public expenditure rose from 32.7 percent of GDP in 1994 to 38.2 percent in 1998. It did not balance the budget; operational deficits increased.[24] While denouncing overly generous social security provisions, it did not make the mistake of repealing them too soon. Stabilization relied on tight reserve requirements, high interest rates, import competition (except on protected goods), reform of state banks to restore investor confidence, privatization to raise cash and attract foreign capital, and fiscal and political payoffs to those threatened by aspects of this strategy. The relative political calm and high interest rates encouraged foreign investors to overlook large budget deficits and supply the funds on which the strategy depended. By contrast, Collor's administration had achieved a decisive fiscal adjustment and a budget surplus—scoring high marks for political will and neoliberalism—but failed to convince investors that these changes would be sustainable.

One should not exaggerate the coherence of Cardoso's strategy or the clairvoyance of its designer. In many ways it was improvised, and it could easily have collapsed. Credibility was won gradually and at moments seemed to be eroding, as in late 1996 when many thought the real was seriously overvalued and the business consultancy Standard and Poor's rated Brazil's banking system the riskiest in Latin America.[25] Debt accumulated rapidly, alarming many. Brazil's strategy, like that followed simultaneously by Russia's economic reformers, depended on the confidence of international financial markets. When it was lost, the currency failed and was devalued in January 1999. However, as in Russia, devaluation did not prompt more than a temporary burst of inflation. The coalitions and institutional changes that gave the Real Plan political credibility proved more important in the end than any particular exchange rate.

Argentina. Argentina's macroeconomic stakeholders resembled Brazil's. First, urban workers, especially public employees, hoped to use their unions to protect jobs and wages.[26] Second, two business subgroups could torpedo stabilization. A set of domestically oriented businessmen, the *capitanes de la industria*, benefited from state subsidies, contracts, and protection. Budget cuts, tax increases, and external liberalization would threaten their profits. Meanwhile, the relatively small internationally oriented sector in agroexports and banking would lose from real exchange rate appreciation. Both business sectors had friends in parliament and among provincial governors. Internationally oriented business had additional leverage. Given large fiscal deficits and low central bank reserves, its dollars were vital to sustain the currency and government bond markets. Third, despite Argentina's more centralized party system, provincial governors had influence over their provinces' congressional delegations. They wanted a large tax share and continued bailouts of their state banks. Fourth, parliamentary deputies sought to survive and prosper in office.[27] Navigating this obstacle course required the crafting of a sufficient coalition of stakeholders behind large tax increases and/or expenditure cuts, while avoiding an attack by currency speculators. Alfonsín failed, and Menem ultimately succeeded.

Alfonsín started out by alienating all interest groups simultaneously in a manner reminiscent of Collor. He offended agriculture by increasing its fiscal burden, business by ignoring its main confederations, labor leaders by seeking to democratize the unions, and the army by prosecuting officers for human rights violations while sharply cutting military spending.[28] Attempts to win popular support with salary increases and loose credit fueled runaway inflation. Alfonsín then tried to stabilize, but with no clear strategy to neutralize the main labor and business organizations. Wage freezes provoked militant protests; price controls prompted firms to withhold products from market. Agricultural exporters and large industrial firms speculated against the currency.[29] From late 1987 the government sought to coopt some domestically oriented businessmen and more conservative unionists. However, with a presidential election looming, these concessions proved insufficient. Labor pressed for higher wages. Draconian spending cuts failed to balance the budget since revenues also dropped. The agroexport and banking sectors again sold pesos. A run on the currency in February 1989 led to hyperinflation and later urban food riots.[30]

Alfonsín's failures suggest two points. First, unless a credible political coalition backed government policies, any budget cuts and dips in inflation would be viewed as temporary. A credible political coalition required the permanent weakening of some groups and cooptation of others. Second, given the difficulty of reducing deficits, the agroexport sector had to be in the coalition, at least initially. Because of the concentration of exports, the low level of foreign investment, and the central bank's meager reserves, a few major exporters could determine the exchange rate and thus the ability to finance deficits.

Menem's initial strategy looked as if it were designed to avoid Alfonsín's mistakes. Like his predecessor, he sought to coopt the *capitanes* and to side with mainstream labor leaders against the militants. But he also set out to neutralize the military, and, most important, the agroexport sector became the centerpiece of his coalition. For legislative and electoral support he relied on one of the two main subconstituencies of Peronism, political bosses from poorer, overrepresented, interior provinces. This support made it possible to marginalize the second constituency, the urban working class.[31]

Coalition partners were rewarded in the least inflationary currencies. Menem appeased the army with nonfinancial concessions—a sweeping pardon of soldiers accused or convicted of human rights abuses—while, like Alfonsín, reducing military spending.[32] He split the union movement, appointing some leaders to high positions (including his labor minister, Jorge Triaca) and driving the militants into opposition. When workers in the telephone, steel, and oil industries went on strike, Menem fired the ringleaders and threatened military force. To woo the agroexport sector, Menem appointed two successive economy ministers from the agrobusiness multinational Bunge and Born and let them design their own stabilization plan. He increased import duties for agrochemicals (a key line of Bunge and Born's business), while decreasing tariffs for other industrial products.[33] In return, the major grain companies promised to lend the central bank $2.5 billion.

Nevertheless, the plan collapsed in another *golpe de mercado*. Hoping to win lower export taxes, major agrobusinesses withheld an estimated $2 billion dollars from the exchange market.[34] As other speculators dumped australs, bond rates soared. Finally, the government surrendered, devaluing by 53 percent and unilaterally rescheduling its bonds. Certain vital members of the coalition had not yet been coopted. Those that had, most importantly the agrobusiness sector, won mostly symbolic benefits and did not withdraw their economic demands.[35] Since a bargain with agroexporters to support the currency would not in any case be enforceable, tactics were required to give holders of dollars a direct interest in currency stability.

The keystone of the successful strategy of 1990–92 was privatization. In a few months, utilities, petrochemical, iron, and steel firms, the post office, ports, and two television channels were offered for sale. Privatization had a direct fiscal purpose. It raised cash to finance the deficit—more than $10 billion in 1990–94—as well as to retire $5 billion of debt papers. It also reduced the need to fund insolvent public firms; in 1989 the losses of the thirteen largest came to almost $4 billion.[36] But privatization also had two political effects. First, it helped coopt leading *capitanes* and agroexport tycoons.[37] Early in Menem's term, the *capitanes* bitterly opposed privatization, which threatened their access to overpriced public contracts.[38] Within two years Menem won over their leaders by favoring them in public sales and sweetening the deals with debt cancellations, monopoly protections, or low prices. The *Wall Street Journal* accused Menem of selling Entel and the airline Aerolíneas Argentinas "for a fraction of their net worth."[39] Such sugar-coating overcame the business opposition that had blocked Alfonsín's attempts to privatize the same companies. Some leading agroexport conglomerates, such as Bunge and Born, also acquired stakes.[40]

By getting the titans of Argentine business to buy state enterprises, Menem changed their interests, at least temporarily. Such entrepreneurs now needed currency stability in order to sell their shares to foreign investors at a profit. Since many of the privatized firms produced nontradeables (telephone calls, airline flights, gas transportation), depreciation would lower the relative price of their output and the implicit dollar value of their assets.[41] An agroexporter whose grain became more competitive when the austral's value fell would, as an investor in a domestic gas distributor, suddenly have a lot to lose from devaluation. Firms accused of speculating against the currency in past crises would now have reason to prefer currency stability.[42] . . .

Privatization's second effect was to create a new stakeholder, foreign capital. Contest rules often required foreign involvement, and the foreign direct investment stock rose from $9 billion to $73 billion during the 1990s.[43] This inflow helped finance the balance of payments. It also had political effects. Foreign investors, concerned about the dollar value of their Argentine assets, had motive either to support the peso themselves, hedge risk with other investors (giving them reason to support it), or lobby their governments to provide financial aid at critical moments.[44] For instance, Spanish companies invested more than $30 billion in Argentina during privatization. By 2000 Spain's two largest banks, BBVA and SCH, controlled 20 percent of the Argentine banking system. Each invested heavily in government bonds and stood to lose billions in a devaluation.[45] In November 2001, as crisis loomed and most investors were exiting, SCH was planning an additional $670 million investment.[46] Earlier that year, the Spanish government pledged $170 million in aid to Argentina and was reportedly considering extending up to $1 billion.[47] Later, a former Spanish prime minister, Felipe Gonzalez, flew to Buenos Aires to lobby against devaluation.[48] Although ineffective against a total meltdown, such external efforts and pressures probably helped in smaller crises. A second effect of the influx of foreign dollars, which boosted the central bank's reserves, was to broaden the currency market and dilute the influence of Argentine exporters and banks over the peso's value. By creating a new stakeholder, Menem weakened an existing one.[49]

Financial liberalization, in particular, the increasing dollarization of bank lending, helped coopt the middle class and business community. Although Menem facilitated it, it may not have been a deliberate element of strategy. The proportion of loans to the Argentine nonfinancial private sector made in foreign currency increased from 41 to 62 percent in 1985–2000.[50] A home owner with mortgage payments in dollars or a small businessman with a dollar-denominated loan would have been devastated by a major devaluation. Indeed, they were in 2002. Even large businesses or banks that borrowed abroad would lose if the peso fell.

Long-term fiscal adjustment required reforms of the tax system, provincial banks, and social security. Despite opposition from within his own party, Menem managed to broaden the base of VAT, increasing federal tax revenues by three percent of GDP in 1989–93.[51] Provincial banks were gradually closed or privatized. Many provinces also accepted a federal takeover of their pension systems and agreed in 1992 to divert 15 percent of their coparticipation transfers to social security.

How did Menem do it? To pass fiscal legislation, he built a coalition of the overrepresented poorer provinces plus Buenos Aires province.[52] The poorer provinces stood to gain from larger federal collections, since a majority— seventeen of twenty-four in 1996—received more in estimated federal transfers and spending than their residents paid in federal taxes.[53] Discretionary transfers (ATN) to the poorer provinces rose from $68 million to $600 million in 1990–1995.[54] Where necessary, Menem bought support retail with targeted concessions. To wean provinces from central bank bailouts, he let them borrow privately using future federal transfers as collateral and offered cash incentives, partly funded by the World Bank, to those that surrendered their state banks. By mid 1998, twenty of the twenty-six provincial banks had been closed or privatized.[55] In a similar trade, the government assumed responsibility for provincial pension systems (eleven by 1996), at a cost that reached $1.5 billion in 1998 alone.[56] . . .

Concluding Remarks

Argentina and Brazil's recent struggles against inflation are hard to understand without examining the tactics of reformers. Each country's failures and achievements can not be traced straightforwardly to the extent of crisis, the electoral calendar, or the pattern of party control over veto points (although the last was probably important). Nor do the details fit interpretations of stabilization as the climax of a "war of attrition" or the result of left-wing leaders' greater credibility with labor.[57] . . .

Menem's and Cardoso's successes suggest lessons about the art of tactics. When confronted by opponents, reformers have two options. They can split their adversaries by coopting some. The challenge then is to drive a hard bargain, appeasing only as many stakeholders as are vital and paying as little as possible in inefficient currencies.[58] Or they can try to introduce a new player into the game who will divide the opposition or dilute its power. Both Menem and Cardoso managed to weaken domestic business by opening the economy to foreign investors, who became key allies supporting currency stability.

There are two ways to coopt allies. The first involves a direct bargain: the reformer promises some benefit in return for support. The problem with such a quid pro quo is that enforcement often lacks credibility. Had Menem promised the major exporters benefits if they did not dump australs, the anonymity of (black market) currency trades would have made his promise unenforceable. The second method is to create vested interests, to provide stakeholders with opportunities or assets whose value increases with success of the reform. The advantage of this technique is that it is self-enforcing. One example is the sale of enterprises producing nontradeables to the Argentine conglomerates, giving them a stake in currency stability. The difficulty is how to vest such interests; the conglomerates could sell privatized companies to other investors, restoring their freedom of action.

Allies can be paid off in three cooptation currencies. First, money might serve as part of a quid pro quo. Cardoso's assumption of state debts in return for the privatization of state banks or utilities is an example. In this case, the bargain was overt and easily enforceable. Second, the government might coopt stakeholders by giving or selling them property, for instance, Menem's sale of enterprises to the *capitanes*. The third cooptation currency is state-created market restrictions that generate rents, such as the 70 percent tariffs Cardoso placed on imported cars.

From the standpoint of efficiency, transferring property and cash are superior to introducing market distortions. Reformers can be judged on whether they used the least distorting cooptation currency. In the case of Brazilian car producers, a cash transfer might have worked as well (though it might have been harder to administer and justify). In the Argentine privatizations, lowering the price for key stakeholders would have been less distorting than guaranteeing monopoly power. Ironically, the more efficient options would probably have appeared more corrupt. They would also have cost the government more cash up front, at a time when cash was short.

Notes

1. Insightful previous analyses of political tactics include Paul Pierson, *Dismantling the Welfare State? Reagan, Thatcher, and the Politics of Retrenchment* (New York: Cambridge University Press, 1994); Javier Corrales, "Why Argentines Followed Cavallo: A Technocrat between Democracy and Economic Reform," in Jorge Domínguez, ed., *Technopols: Freeing Politics and Markets in Latin America in the 1990s* (University Park: Penn State Press, 1997), pp. 49–94; Javier Corrales, "Coalitions and Corporate Choices in Argentina, 1976–1994: The Recent Private Sector Support of Privatization," *Studies in Comparative International Development*, 32 (1998), 24–51; Hector Schamis, "Distributional Coalitions and the Politics of Economic Reform in Latin America," *World Politics*, 51 (1999), 236–68.

2. Alfredo Filho, *Currency Stabilisation under Conditions of International Capital Mobility: The Case of Brazil* (London: South Bank University, 1998), p. 6.

3. World Bank, *Argentina: The Convertibility Plan, Assessment and Potential Prospects* (Washington, D.C.: World Bank, 1996).

4. In 1998 the refusal of Governor Itamar Franco of Minas Geraís to pay his state's federal debt triggered a devaluation.

5. In 1990 Collor canceled almost half of Brazil's domestic treasury debt, worth about 10 percent of GDP.

6. Alfred Montero, "Devolving Democracy? Political Decentralization and the New Brazilian Federalism," in Peter Kingstone and Timothy Power, eds., *Democratic Brazil: Actors, Institutions, and Processes* (Pittsburgh: University of Pittsburgh Press, 2000), p. 64.

7. See Kurt Weyland, "The Brazilian State in the New Democracy," in Kingstone and Power, eds., pp. 36–57. For an excellent summary of Collor's tactics, see Peter Kingstone, *Crafting Coalitions for Reform: Business Preferences, Political Institutions, and Neoliberal Reform in Brazil* (University Park: Penn State Press, 1999), ch. 5.

8. The Real Plan also included a sophisticated method of coordinating expectations around a common index of value, the *unidade real de valor,* thus avoiding the need for a price freeze.

9. Weyland, p. 50.

10. IMF, *Brazil: Selected Issues and Statistical Appendix* (Washington, D.C.: IMF, 2001), p. 155.

11. Kingstone, p. 205.

12. Armando Pinheiro, *The Brazilian Privatization Experience: What's Next?* (Rio de Janeiro: BNDES, 2000).

13. Cardoso denounced congress's preoccupation with patronage but provided such patronage himself when necessary.

14. Kingstone, p. 202.

15. For instance, Sarney could draw separate pensions as a former president, governor, senator, and deputy. Fleischer, p. 131.

16. This alliance of Cardoso's social democratic party with clientelistic bosses from the poorer provinces recalls the "metropolitan" and "peripheral" subcoalitions in the Peronist movement under Menem and Perón himself and a similar cross-linkage in Mexico's PRI. The "peripheral" coalition in each case enabled a "left-wing" party to engage in neoliberal reform without damaging its electoral prospects. Edward Gibson, "The Populist Road to Market Reform: Policy and Electoral Coalitions in Mexico and Argentina," *World Politics,* 49 (1997).

17. Wayne Selcher, "The Politics of Decentralized Federalism, National Diversification, and Regionalism in Brazil," *Journal of Inter-American Studies and World Affairs,* 40 (1998), 25–50; Timothy Power, "Brazilian Politicians and Neoliberalism: Mapping Support for the Cardoso Reforms, 1995–97," *Journal of Inter-American Studies and World Affairs,* 40 (1998), 51–72.

18. Mainwaring, p. 317.

19. Wendy Dobson and Pierre Jacquet, *Financial Services Liberalization in the WTO* (Washington, D.C.: Institute for International Economics, 1998). The constitutional decentralization of revenues appeared impossible then to reverse; Cardoso concentrated instead on devolving matching spending responsibilities.

20. IMF, p. 156.

21. In part, the states' debts were written off; in part, states were to repay the federal government at subsidized interest rates.

22. IMF, p. 167.

23. Werner Baer, *The Brazilian Economy: Growth and Development* (Westport: Praeger, 2001), p. 313.

24. There was a significant fiscal adjustment in 1993–94, but in 1995 the operational public sector borrowing requirement jumped from −1.1 to 5.0 percent of GDP. Armando Pinheiro, Fabio Giambagi, and Joana Gostkorzewicz, "Brazil's Macroeconomic Performance in the 1990s" (Rio de Janeiro: BNDES, 2000), p. 19.

25. Kingstone, *Crafting Coalitions,* p. 218.

26. Victoria Murillo, "From Populism to Neoliberalism: Labor Unions and Market Reforms in Latin America," *World Politics,* 52 (2000), 135–74.

27. The military might be considered a fifth stakeholder. It wanted continued funding and could threaten coups.

28. See William Smith, "Hyperinflation, Macroeconomic Instability, and Neoliberal Restructuring in Democratic Argentina," and David Pion-Berlin and Ernesto López, "A House Divided: Crisis, Cleavage,

and Conflict in the Argentine Army," both in Edward Epstein, ed., *The New Argentine Democracy: The Search for a Successful Formula* (Westport: Praeger, 1992), pp. 20–60, 63–96. My point is not that these measures were undesirable, just that pursuing them simultaneously was bound to fail.

29. Increasing tensions with the army further complicated matters. Fearing they would be tried along with the junta leaders, junior officers rebelled three times. Alfonsín essentially conceded, raising military wages and passing a law presuming innocence for those who had committed crimes while following orders.

30. Edward Epstein, "Democracy in Argentina," in Epstein, ed., pp. 3–19.

31. Gibson.

32. Consolidated public sector spending on defense and security dropped from 2.4 percent of GDP in 1988 to 2.1 percent in 1993. IMF, *Argentina: Recent Economic Developments* (Washington, D.C.: IMF, 1998), p. 30.

33. Monica Peralta-Ramos, *The Political Economy of Argentina: Power and Class since 1930* (Boulder: Westview, 1992), p. 110.

34. Carlos Acuña, "Business Interests, Dictatorship, and Democracy in Argentina," in Ernest Bartell and Leigh Payne, eds., *Business and Democracy in Latin America* (Pittsburgh: University of Pittsburgh Press, 1995), p. 30.

35. In fact, the grain companies paid only $370 million of the promised $2.5 billion loan. Peralta-Ramos, p. 153.

36. Manuel Pastor, Jr. and Carol Wise, "Stabilization and Its Discontents: Argentina's Economic Restructuring in the 1990s," *World Development*, 27 (1999), 487.

37. Corrales, "Coalitions and Corporate Choices."

38. In 1989 private businesses overcharged the government by about $2.5 billion and received an additional $2.2 billion in tax breaks. Ibid., p. 34.

39. *Wall Street Journal*, Aug. 31, 1990, quoted in Peralta-Ramos, p. 117.

40. Juliana Bambaci, Tamara Saront, and Mariano Tommasi. "The Political Economy of Economic Reforms in Argentina" (Buenos Aires: CEDI, 2000), p. 35; Myrna Alexander and Carlos Corti, *Argentina's Privatization Program* (Washington, D.C.: World Bank, 1993), p. 2.

41. This was not true of some electricity companies, whose privatization contracts pegged prices to the dollar. But demand for electricity would have declined as the peso price rose, squeezing profits.

42. In December 1989 one Peronist congressman accused the engineering conglomerate Techint and the Banco General de Negocios of being among the leading speculators. *Latin American Weekly Report*, Dec. 7, 1989. The next year Techint became deeply involved in privatization, acquiring stakes in transportation companies and utilities. Banco General was among three chosen in 1991 to manage privatization of the electricity company SEGBA.

43. UNCTAD, *World Investment Report 2001* (New York: United Nations, 2001), p. 302.

44. I am not suggesting that investors would throw money away by betting on a falling currency or even that major investors engaged directly in currency trading. But their deep involvement in the market and interest in stability helped create confidence among other investors. In late 1996 international banks extended a $6.1 billion contingent repurchase facility to the Argentine central bank to provide emergency liquidity. IMF, *Argentina: Recent Economic Developments*, p. 6.

45. In late 2001 each held about $2 billion worth of Argentine government debt. Argentina's default in late 2001 was believed likely to cost SCH $4.6 billion and BBVA $3.6 billion. *The Economist*, Jan. 5, 2002, p. 64.

46. *Wall Street Journal*, Nov. 8, 2001, p. A16.

47. Morgan Stanley, *Global Economic Forum Briefing*, Aug. 8, 2001.

48. *The Economist*, Jan. 5, 2002, p. 64.

49. Menem initially coopted the domestic banking sector with continued protections; he began a more stringent liberalization after the 1994–95 Tequila crisis.

50. World Bank and Argentine Ministry of Economy.

51. IMF, *Government Finance Statistics Yearbooks*, various years.

52. William Dillinger and Steven Webb, *Fiscal Management in Federal Democracies: Argentina and Brazil* (Washington, D.C.: World Bank, 1999). Poor provinces, with 20 percent of the population, had

58 percent of senate seats. These provinces, along with Buenos Aires province, had a majority in the lower house. Bambaci, Saront, and Tommasi.

53. World Bank, *Argentina: The Fiscal Dimension of the Convertibility Plan: A Background Report,* vol. 1 (Washington: World Bank, 1998), pp. 53, 57.

54. World Bank, *Argentina: Provincial Finances Study,* vol. 1 (Washington, D.C.: World Bank, 1996), p. ii.

55. Juan Nicolini et al., "Decentralization, Fiscal Discipline in Sub-National Governments, and the Bailout Problem: The Case of Argentina" (Washington, D.C.: IADB, 2000), p. 8.

56. Ibid., p. 13.

57. Some commentators imply that the laws themselves, for example, the Argentine convertibility law or the 1992 central bank charter, entrenched the commitment to low inflation. However, parliament can repeal laws as well as pass them. In fact, it amended the central bank's charter in 1995 to permit it to provide discretionary advances to banks, precisely what the 1992 version prohibited. In any case, most of the money supply (for example, bank demand deposits) was not covered by hard currency reserve requirements, and up to 20 percent of the peso's backing could consist of the government's own bonds.

58. Sarney failed by making too many compromises that were not strategically useful. Menem may also have rewarded allies through privatization more generously than strictly necessary.

 3.5

From North-South to South-South

Robert J. S. Ross and Anita Chan

Many analyses of the global economy highlight inequalities between the affluent countries of the North and the less developed countries of the South. (See the articles by Stiglitz and McKibben.) Robert J. S. Ross and Anita Chan identify another important issue in contemporary political economy: competition among countries in the South to attract foreign investment. They argue that, in the absence of international treaties to protect labor standards (what is often called the social clause), competition among states of the South to attract foreign investment harms workers in these countries by lowering wages and promoting unsafe working conditions. Can you think of a reply to their argument?

Robert J. S. Ross and Anita Chan, "From North-South to South-South," *Foreign Affairs* 81, No. 5 (September–October 2002): 8–13. Reprinted by permission of *Foreign Affairs,* 81, no. 5, September–October 2002. Copyright 2002 by the Council on Foreign Relations, Inc.

As protesters battled the police in the streets of Seattle in 1999, calling on the World Trade Organization to include environmental and labor issues in its trade negotiations, government representatives in conference rooms were carrying on a battle of another sort. Many developing nations, particularly the Asian countries, were strongly resisting a U.S.-led proposal by developed countries to link trade to environmental and labor standards through a new "social clause" in WTO agreements. The clause, its opponents argued, was a protectionist ploy that rich nations would use to shelter their own workers' jobs from the competition in developing countries. This stance reflected a commonly held perception that the main competition in the production of goods is between the North and the South. But in truth, this competition—particularly in labor-intensive commodities—is not so much North versus South but South versus South. The absence of a mechanism establishing international labor standards is propelling the economies of the South in a race to the bottom in wages and labor conditions.

The social clause, in brief, refers to the proposed insertion of five core labor standards into trade agreements: freedom of association, freedom to organize and to bargain collectively, and freedom from forced labor, child labor, and job discrimination. Many poorer countries either lack the laws to protect these rights, which are enshrined in the conventions of the International Labor Organization (ILO), or they simply do not bother to enforce those laws in their export industries.

Trade Unions Divided

Governments do not necessarily reflect the interests of their country's workers, but labor unions are supposed to. So how do unions line up on the social-clause question? Although the issue at Seattle had united the government leaders of the South in opposition, the international trade-union movement holds diverse views. The International Confederation of Free Trade Unions, composed of 221 affiliated unions that represent 150 million workers in 148 countries, supports the social clause. But African backing for the clause has not always been uniform: trade unions in some countries, such as South Africa, are in favor, whereas those in others, such as Zimbabwe and Zambia, are opposed.

In Latin America, unions are more amenable to linking trade and labor rights, thanks in part to their strong relationships with their North American counterparts. Struggling unions in Guatemala, Honduras, El Salvador, and Nicaragua have strategically used the U.S. threat of trade sanctions (specifically, in response to violations of labor rights) to secure their own rights to organize. For example, Guatemalan workers formed an unrecognized union at a factory owned by the U.S. clothing giant Phillips–Van Heusen in the early 1990s. In a long and bitter campaign, their North American allies—including UNITE, the U.S. apparel-workers union—filed a lawsuit in the United States at their behest, alleging that Guatemala was ineligible for trade concessions because it denied workers the right to organize. This pressure finally led the firm and the Guatemalan government to recognize the union.

Other Latin American confederations of unions—for example, those in Argentina and Chile—support a social clause, too. The trade unions of several middle-income countries in Asia also approve. The Korean Confederation of Trade Unions believes the "social clause can be a significant and effective instrument to protect and achieve social rights and the basic trade union rights." Likewise, the Malaysian Trade Union Congress supports a linkage between labor standards and trade and exports—out of fear that its members' rights could be undermined by competition from the large number of Asian migrant workers working without labor protection in Malaysia's export zones.

But India's trade unions and China's quasi-governmental trade union federation take a different approach. The governments and trade unions of the two most populous countries in the world are determinedly against a social clause. And because of their dominant weight in the world's cheap-labor market, their positions have enormous repercussions on the wages of unskilled laborers throughout the underdeveloped world. This dominance may also explain the perception that the South is staunchly opposed to the social clause—even though the truth is more variegated.

Neck and Neck

In rejecting a regulated international labor regime, countries of the South lower their own labor standards to remain competitive and provide a "good" investment climate. This imperative gives businesses an excellent opportunity to exploit their work forces to the fullest; examples include the South Korean, Taiwanese, and Hong Kong firms that subcontract from brand-name corporations to do labor-intensive manufacturing in poor countries. The apparel industry aptly illustrates this type of globalized production. The work is highly labor intensive, and the industry continues to use a vast amount of unskilled labor supplied by the South, despite technological upgrading. This sector is also among the most footloose: production facilities can be moved easily from city to city or country to country. Apparel manufacturing employs a large number of workers in the South, mostly young women; in turn, this high volume of jobs affects the overall wage levels and labor standards of these countries.

Over the past four decades, the U.S. apparel industry has been overwhelmed by this global low-wage competition. Apparel imports rose from about 2 percent of U.S. domestic consumption in the early 1960s to more than 60 percent in the 1990s. In the largest categories of clothing imports—men's and women's tops— the $26 billion of imports furnishes more than 70 percent of the market by value and about 90 percent by quantity. Since 1980, imports have cut U.S. apparel-industry employment by half, a loss of more than 600,000 jobs. Many of the workers who remain in the U.S. garment industry, toiling as sweatshop workers or as underpaid home workers, suffer declining wages that today are often below the legal minimum. Even so, the North-South competition is basically over in this industry. The enormous difference in North-South wage levels ensures that those jobs lost will not return to the United States.

A Tale of Two Countries

In recent years, China and Mexico have become the lions of the U.S. clothing market, obtaining an equal market share since the 1993 signing of the North American Free Trade Agreement (NAFTA). By 2000, Mexico and China each supplied around 15 percent of all apparel imports to the United States. (The Chinese total includes Hong Kong's apparel manufacturing, which has relocated almost entirely to the mainland.) But Mexico enjoys two substantial advantages over China: close geography (hence a faster filling of orders) and the absence of quota restrictions, thanks to NAFTA. As a result, Asian investors—particularly South Koreans and Taiwanese—became increasingly active there in the 1990s, even moving apparel production out of Asia into Mexico.

The dramatic growth of apparel exports from Mexico and China to North America has created a surge of new jobs. In both countries, the export-oriented factories employ migrant workers from poor, rural areas. In China, the growth first began in the mid-1980s in Guangdong province (which neighbors Hong Kong) and picked up speed in the early 1990s. The entire Pearl River Delta in Guangdong, which 20 years ago was largely agricultural, is now a manufacturing powerhouse that churns out labor-intensive goods for the world market. Today, some 12 million migrant workers from poor parts of China's countryside staff these factories' production lines. A similar phenomenon emerged in Mexico in the 1990s. Along the U.S.-Mexican border, new investment created boomtowns where *maquiladoras* (assembly plants) have mushroomed. By 2000, these factories employed about one million workers—an increase of 150 percent since 1990—and production was spreading to other parts of the country.

Contrary to general wisdom, however, more jobs have not meant higher wages or rising labor standards for migrant workers, whether in Mexico or in China. On the contrary, wages have fallen as a result of intensified competition to attract factories that sell to the North's markets. This drop is reflected in both the low legal minimum wages set by the two countries and the real purchasing power of workers.

In China, the setting of a minimum wage is extremely decentralized. Any city, or even a city district, can set its own minimum wage based on a formula provided by Beijing. This formula takes into account such factors as the local cost of living, the prevailing wage, and the rate of inflation, and it is adjusted each year. In 2001, for example, the city of Shenzhen (just north of Hong Kong) had two standards. Inner Shenzhen, the city's commercialized sector, had the highest minimum wage in China at the equivalent of $72 per month, but the outer industrialized sector's minimum wage was only $55 per month. Elsewhere in China, legal minimum wages have been set even lower. Although these local governments comply on paper with Beijing's decrees on minimum wages, they attempt to attract investors by allowing them to pay workers below those rates. The legal minimum wage is set by the month and does not take into account that many migrant workers labor illegally for longer hours. (For example, our survey of China's footwear industry shows that the average number of hours worked each day is 11, and laborers often have no days off.) Furthermore, official statistics do not take into consideration the staggering amount of unpaid back wages. Some 40 percent of the 20,000 workers' complaints lodged with the Shenzhen authorities over nine months in 2001 were related to owed wages. Such abuse has become normal in southern China.

Official minimum wages also obscure other critical facts. They do not show the violence and physical abuses that have become pervasive in the factories in China owned by Taiwanese, Korean, and Hong Kong intermediaries; nor do they take into account the acute and chronic occupational health and safety hazards. These factories record a startlingly high incidence of severed limbs and fingers; Shenzhen alone certified more than 10,000 such accidents in 1999 among a migrant population of 4 million. In short, despite China's dramatic export growth, the benefits have not trickled down to the assembly-line workers who make the exported goods. Indeed, their situation has gotten even worse since the Asian financial crisis of 1997–98; the downturn intensified competition with Southeast Asian labor, which had become much cheaper in the wake of local currency devaluations. (Provincial surveys in China show that a downturn in migrant workers' pay started at that time.)

China's main challenge in apparel and other sectors, however, comes from Mexico. There, workers' conditions in the *maquiladoras* are also grim. But unlike in China, wage levels in Mexico are more regulated. Only three minimum-wage levels exist for the entire country, including one for the U.S.-Mexico border region (equivalent to $93 to $108 per month). These minimum wages, although low, are almost double those of Shenzhen, which are the highest in China. But Mexico's legal minimum wages fell by almost half during the 1990s, due in part to the peso's collapse in 1996. In addition, competition with countries such as China created a downward pressure on average real wages in Mexico. In the manufacturing sector, wages dropped in real purchasing power terms by 20 percent over the same period. And in the booming apparel sector, ILO data show that their wages shed 14 percent of their purchasing power from 1990 to 2000. Since 2000, wages have gained slightly, but that increase is threatened by the prospect of capital flight to regions with even lower labor costs.

In short, export workers in China and Mexico have not benefited from the economic boom. More workers are being employed, but over the course of the 1990s working conditions and wages deteriorated. These assembly workers are caught in an internationally competitive race to the bottom.

Intensifying Competition

In 2005, trade barriers on apparel are due to end under the 1975 Multi-Fiber Agreement (and its 1994 successor). Assuming that its wages remain low, China will then be poised to make more inroads into rich-country apparel markets, off-setting Mexico's advantage of proximity to the U.S. market. In other industries, the WTO's lowering of trade barriers will also tip the scales away from Mexico and toward China. Fearing this, Mexico sought to delay China's entry into the WTO; in fact, it was the last WTO member to sign last year the necessary bilateral agreement with China that paved the way for WTO accession.

Mexico is already feeling the increased competitive heat. Knowing that trade barriers will soon fall, intermediate firms have begun shifting their Mexican assembly lines back to Asia, particularly China. The number of *maquiladoras* swelled from 120 in the 1970s to 3,700 in 2000 but has dropped by 500 since then. Pressures are increasing on other Mexican factories to compete with China's long working hours and bargain-basement wages. These pressures may also threaten the incremental growth of an autonomous Mexican trade-union movement—a result of years of painstaking political and social change, supported by a solidarity movement in the United States and Canada. Employers who resist relocating to China or to other low-wage countries will be tempted to lower standards in Mexico by resisting the fledgling union movement.

Mexican President Vicente Fox has proposed the "Puebla to Panama Plan," which would build an investment corridor for more *maquiladoras* from southern Mexico through Central America—at wages even lower than those at the U.S.-Mexican border. In China, meanwhile, the government is encouraging foreign investors to go north and inland in pursuit of lower costs than can be found in southern China.

The examples of China and Mexico show just how much the international competition among nations of the South influences their workers' well-being. And this race to the bottom affects people elsewhere in the developing world who hold jobs in those sectors. Without regulations to protect labor, akin to rules that protect investors, poor-country workers will not share in the benefits of a growth in world trade. For that reason, labor standards ought to be as much a South-South issue as a North-South one.

Making Standards Stick

The debate over a WTO social clause has reached an impasse. Accordingly, there is no internationally binding enforcement mechanism to protect workers' rights in the South. Even the ILO, charged with this responsibility, has no means to enforce compliance with its conventions. It is doubtful that the Global Compact initiated in 1999 by UN Secretary-General Kofi Annan, which draws up guidelines for good corporate practices in the areas of human rights, labor rights, and the environment, will be useful, because it too lacks an enforcement mechanism. No competent global forum can enforce a verdict when a nation or its enterprises contravene fundamental labor rights.

Governments and trade unions of the South must confront this challenge. Their campaign against the North's protectionism has done little to improve the lot of their own work forces in export industries. They have to face the fact that they are competing among themselves—and that they themselves are partially responsible for the decline in wages and labor standards. The growing crisis in back wages (and wages simply never paid) owed to Chinese migrant workers shows that the bottom is continuing to fall. China is a key player in the South-South competition, and unless other countries can convince China to form or join a Southern consensus to put an international floor beneath wages, the scenario will only worsen. Only through enforceable minimum-wage standards can these countries prevent Northern corporations and intermediate suppliers from playing them off against each other. The possibility of WTO trade sanctions would deter abuses and give incentives to national labor-law enforcement. It would give all nations the right to complain about violations in an international forum. Picking up where President Bill Clinton and other developed-country leaders left off in Seattle, the WTO should devise a regulatory regime in line with a labor "social clause," so that violators, both governments and corporations, can be sanctioned if they contravene it. This scheme or something similar to it will be necessary before labor standards can be expected to improve—or even just stabilize. The globalization of capital has made the world smaller and safer for investors; now the question before the world community is whether it can do the same for workers.

 3.6

Globalism's Discontents

Joseph E. Stiglitz

In this selection, Joseph Stiglitz, who has served as chair of the Council of Economic Advisers and chief economist of the World Bank, and who is a Nobel prize winner in Economics, claims that economic globalization can produce great benefits. However, for this to occur, states must provide their citizens with adequate social safety nets, such as social assistance for those dislocated by economic change. States must also impose capital controls, that is, regulate the flow of foreign capital, to reduce the risk of instability and economic and financial crisis. Unfortunately, Stiglitz warns, these measures run counter to prevailing economic theory and the policies of many states and the International Monetary Fund (IMF), a powerful international financial institution. Stiglitz does not analyze that opposition to these policies has developed around the world. Do you think it has been influential?

Few subjects have polarized people throughout the world as much as globalization. Some see it as the way of the future, bringing unprecedented prosperity to everyone, everywhere. Others, symbolized by the Seattle protestors of December 1999, fault globalization as the source of untold problems, from the destruction of native cultures to increasing poverty and immiseration. In this article, I want to sort out the different meanings of globalization. In many countries, globalization has brought huge benefits to a few with few benefits to the many. But in the case of a few countries, it has brought enormous benefit to the many. Why have there been these huge differences in experiences? The answer is that globalization has meant different things in different places.

The countries that have managed globalization on their own, such as those in East Asia, have, by and large, ensured that they reaped huge benefits and that those benefits were equitably shared; they were able substantially to control the terms on which they engaged with the global economy. By contrast, the countries that have, by and large, had globalization managed for them by the International Monetary Fund and other international economic institutions have not done so well. The problem is thus not with globalization but with how it has been managed.

The international financial institutions have pushed a particular ideology—market fundamentalism—that is both bad economics and bad politics; it is based on premises concerning how markets work that do not hold even for developed countries, much less for developing countries. The IMF has pushed these economics policies without a broader vision of society or the role of economics within society. And it has pushed these policies in ways that have undermined emerging democracies.

More generally, globalization itself has been governed in ways that are undemocratic and have been disadvantageous to developing countries, especially the poor within those countries. The Seattle protestors pointed to the absence of democracy and of transparency, the governance of the international economic institutions by and for special corporate and financial interests, and the absence of countervailing democratic checks to ensure that these informal and public institutions serve a general interest. In these complaints, there is more than a grain of truth.

Beneficial Globalization

Of the countries of the world, those in East Asia have grown the fastest and done most to reduce poverty. And they have done so, emphatically, via "globalization." Their growth has been based on exports—by taking advantage of the global market for exports and by closing the technology gap. It was not just gaps in capital and other resources that separated the developed from the less-developed countries, but differences in knowledge. East Asian countries took advantage of the "globalization of knowledge" to reduce these disparities. But while some of the countries in the region grew by opening themselves up to multinational companies, others, such as Korea and Taiwan, grew by creating their own enterprises. Here is the key distinction: Each of the most successful globalizing countries determined its own pace of change; each made sure as it grew that the benefits were shared equitably; each rejected the basic tenets of the "Washington Consensus," which argued for a minimalist role for government and rapid privatization and liberalization.

In East Asia, government took an active role in managing the economy. The steel industry that the Korean government created was among the most efficient in the world—performing far better than its private-sector rivals in the United States (which, though private, are constantly turning to the government for protection and for subsidies). Financial markets were highly regulated. My research shows that those regulations promoted growth. It was only when these countries stripped away the regulations, under pressure from the U.S. Treasury and the IMF, that they encountered problems.

During the 1960s, 1970s, and 1980s, the East Asian economies not only grew rapidly but were remarkably stable. Two of the countries most touched by the 1997–1998 economic crisis had had in the preceding three decades not a single year of negative growth; two had only one year—a better performance than the United States or the other wealthy nations that make up the Organization for Economic Cooperation and Development (OECD). The single most important factor leading to the troubles that several of the East Asian countries encountered in the late 1990s—the East Asian crisis—was the rapid liberalization of financial and capital markets. In short, the countries of East Asia benefited from globalization because they made globalization work for them; it was when they succumbed to the pressures from the outside that they ran into problems that were beyond their own capacity to manage well.

Globalization can yield immense benefits. Elsewhere in the developing world, globalization of knowledge has brought improved health, with life spans increasing at a rapid pace. How can one put a price on these benefits of globalization? Globalization has brought still other benefits: Today there is the beginning of a globalized civil society that has begun to succeed with such reforms as the Mine Ban Treaty and debt forgiveness for the poorest highly indebted countries (the Jubilee movement). The globalization protest movement itself would not have been possible without globalization.

The Darker Side of Globalization

How then could a trend with the power to have so many benefits have produced such opposition? Simply because it has not only failed to live up to its potential but frequently has had very adverse effects. But this forces us to ask, why has it had such adverse effects? The answer can be seen by looking at each of the economic elements of globalization as pursued by the international financial institutions and especially by the IMF.

The most adverse effects have arisen from the liberalization of financial and capital markets—which has posed risks to developing countries without commensurate rewards. The liberalization has left them prey to hot money pouring into the country, an influx that has fueled speculative real-estate booms; just as suddenly, as investor sentiment changes, the money is pulled out, leaving in its wake economic devastation. Early on, the IMF said that these countries were being rightly punished for pursuing bad economic policies. But as the crisis spread from country to country, even those that the IMF had given high marks found themselves ravaged.

The IMF often speaks about the importance of the discipline provided by capital markets. In doing so, it exhibits a certain paternalism, a new form of the old colonial mentality: "We in the establishment, we in the North who run our capital markets, know best. Do what we tell you to do, and you will prosper." The arrogance is offensive, but the objection is more than just to style. The position is highly undemocratic: There is an implied assumption that democracy by itself does not provide sufficient discipline. But if one is to have an external disciplinarian, one should choose a good disciplinarian who knows what is good for growth, who shares one's values. One doesn't want an arbitrary and capricious taskmaster who one moment praises you for your virtues and the next screams at you for being rotten to the core. But capital markets are just such a fickle taskmaster; even ardent advocates talk about their bouts of irrational exuberance followed by equally irrational pessimism.

Lessons of Crisis

Nowhere was the fickleness more evident than in the last global financial crisis. Historically, most of the disturbances in capital flows into and out of a country are not the result of factors inside the country. Major disturbances arise, rather, from influences outside the country. When Argentina suddenly faced high interest rates in 1998, it wasn't because of what Argentina did but because of what happened in Russia. Argentina cannot be blamed for Russia's crisis.

Small developing countries find it virtually impossible to withstand this volatility. I have described capital-market liberalization with a simple metaphor: Small countries are like small boats. Liberalizing capital markets is like setting them loose on a rough sea. Even if the boats are well captained, even if the boats are sound, they are likely to be hit broadside by a big wave and capsize. But the IMF pushed for the boats to set forth into the roughest parts of the sea before they were seaworthy, with untrained captains and crews, and without life vests. No wonder matters turned out so badly!

To see why it is important to choose a disciplinarian who shares one's values, consider a world in which there were free mobility of skilled labor. Skilled labor would then provide discipline. Today, a country that does not treat capital well will find capital quickly withdrawing; in a world of free labor mobility if a country did not treat skilled labor well, it too would withdraw. Workers would worry about the quality of their children's education and their family's health care, the quality of their environment and of their own wages and working conditions. They would say to the government: If you fail to provide these essentials, we will move elsewhere. That is a far cry from the kind of discipline that free-flowing capital provides.

The liberalization of capital markets has not brought growth: How can one build factories or create jobs with money that can come in and out of a country overnight? And it gets worse: Prudential behavior requires countries to set aside reserves equal to the amount of short-term lending; so if a firm in a poor country borrows $100 million at, say, 20 percent interest rates short-term from a bank in the United States, the government must set aside a corresponding amount. The reserves are typically held in U.S. Treasury bills—a safe, liquid asset. In effect, the country is borrowing $100 million from the United States and lending $100 million to the United States. But when it borrows, it pays a high interest rate, 20 percent; when it lends, it receives a low interest rate, around 4 percent. This may be great for the United States, but it can hardly help the growth of the poor country. There is also a high opportunity cost of the reserves; the money could have been much better spent on building rural roads or constructing schools or health clinics. But instead, the country is, in effect, forced to lend money to the United States.

Thailand illustrates the true ironies of such policies: There, the free market led to investments in empty office buildings, starving other sectors—such as education and transportation—of badly needed resources. Until the IMF and the U.S. Treasury came along, Thailand had restricted bank lending for speculative real estate. The Thais had seen the record: Such lending is an essential part of the boom-bust cycle that has characterized capitalism for 200 years. It wanted to be sure that the scarce capital went to create jobs. But the IMF nixed this intervention in the free market. If the free market said, "Build empty office buildings," so be it! The market knew better than any government bureaucrat who mistakenly might have thought it wiser to build schools or factories.

The Costs of Volatility

Capital-market liberalization is inevitably accompanied by huge volatility, and this volatility impedes growth and increases poverty. It increases the risks of investing in the country, and thus investors demand a risk premium in the form of higher-than-normal profits. Not only is growth not enhanced but poverty is increased through several channels. The high volatility increases the likelihood of recessions—and the poor always bear the brunt of such downturns. Even in developed countries, safety nets are weak or nonexistent among the self-employed and in the rural sector. But these are the dominant sectors in developing countries. Without adequate safety nets, the recessions that follow from capital-market liberalization lead to impoverishment. In the name of imposing budget discipline and reassuring investors, the IMF invariably demands expenditure reductions, which almost inevitably result in cuts in outlays for safety nets that are already threadbare. Matters are even worse—for under the doctrines of the "discipline of the capital markets," if countries try to tax capital, capital flees. Thus, the IMF doctrines inevitably lead to an increase in tax burdens on the poor and the middle classes. Thus, while IMF bailouts enable the rich to take their money out of the country at more favorable terms (at the overvalued exchange rates), the burden of repaying the loans lies with the workers who remain behind.

The reason that I emphasize capital-market liberalization is that the case against it—and against the IMF's stance in pushing it—is so compelling. It illustrates what can go wrong with globalization. Even economists like Jagdish Bhagwati, strong advocates of free trade, see the folly in liberalizing capital markets. Belatedly, so too has the IMF—at least in its official rhetoric, though less so in its policy stances—but too late for all those countries that have suffered so much from following the IMF's prescriptions.

But while the case for trade liberalization—when properly done—is quite compelling, the way it has been pushed by the IMF has been far more problematic. The basic logic is simple: Trade liberalization is supposed to result in resources moving from inefficient protected sectors to more efficient export sectors. The problem is not only that job destruction comes before the job creation—so that unemployment and poverty result—but that the IMF's "structural adjustment programs" (designed in ways that allegedly would reassure global investors) make job creation almost impossible. For these programs are often accompanied by high interest rates that are often justified by a single-minded focus on inflation. Sometimes that concern is deserved; often, though, it is carried to an extreme. In the United States, we worry that small increases in the interest rate will discourage investment. The IMF has pushed for far higher interest rates in countries with a far less hospitable investment environment. The high interest rates mean that new jobs and enterprises are not created. What happens is that trade liberalization, rather than moving workers from low-productivity jobs to high-productivity ones, moves them from low-productivity jobs to unemployment. Rather than enhanced growth, the effect is increased poverty. To make matters even worse, the unfair trade-liberalization agenda forces poor countries to compete with highly subsidized American and European agriculture.

The Governance of Globalization

As the market economy has matured within countries, there has been increasing recognition of the importance of having rules to govern it. One hundred fifty years ago, in many parts of the world, there was a domestic process that was in some ways analogous to globalization. In the United States, government promoted the formation of the national economy, the building of the railroads, and the development of the telegraph—all of which reduced transportation and communication costs within the United States. As that process occurred, the democratically elected national government provided oversight: supervising and regulating, balancing interests, tempering crises, and limiting adverse consequences of this very large change in economic structure. So, for instance, in 1863 the U.S. government established the first financial banking regulatory authority—the Office of the Comptroller of Currency—because it was important to have strong national banks, and that requires strong regulation.

The United States, among the least statist of the industrial democracies, adopted other policies. Agriculture, the central industry of the United States in the mid-nineteenth century, was supported by the 1862 Morrill Act, which established research, extension, and teaching programs. That system worked extremely well and is widely credited with playing a central role in the enormous increases in agricultural productivity over the last century and a half. We established an industrial policy for other fledgling industries, including radio and civil aviation. The beginning of the telecommunications industry, with the first telegraph line between Baltimore and Washington, D.C., was funded by the federal government. And it is a tradition that has continued, with the U.S. government's founding of the Internet.

By contrast, in the current process of globalization we have a system of what I call global governance without global government. International institutions like the World Trade Organization, the IMF, the World Bank, and others provide an ad hoc system of global governance, but it is a far cry from global government and lacks democratic accountability. Although it is perhaps better than not having any system of global governance, the system is structured not to serve general interests or assure equitable results. This not only raises issues of whether broader values are given short shrift; it does not even promote growth as much as an alternative might.

Governance Through Ideology

Consider the contrast between how economic decisions are made inside the United States and how they are made in the international economic institutions. In this country, economic decisions within the administration are undertaken largely by the National Economic Council, which includes the secretary of labor, the secretary of commerce, the chairman of the Council of Economic

Advisers, the treasury secretary, the assistant attorney general for antitrust, and the U.S. trade representative. The Treasury is only one vote and often gets voted down. All of these officials, of course, are part of an administration that must face Congress and the democratic electorate. But in the international arena, only the voices of the financial community are heard. The IMF reports to the ministers of finance and the governors of the central banks, and one of the important items on its agenda is to make these central banks more independent—and less democratically accountable. It might make little difference if the IMF dealt only with matters of concern to the financial community, such as the clearance of checks; but in fact, its policies affect every aspect of life. It forces countries to have tight monetary and fiscal policies: It evaluates the trade-off between inflation and unemployment, and in that trade-off it always puts far more weight on inflation than on jobs.

The problem with having the rules of the game dictated by the IMF—and thus by the financial community—is not just a question of values (though that is important) but also a question of ideology. The financial community's view of the world predominates—even when there is little evidence in its support. Indeed, beliefs on key issues are held so strongly that theoretical and empirical support of the positions is viewed as hardly necessary.

Recall again the IMF's position on liberalizing capital markets. As noted, the IMF pushed a set of policies that exposed countries to serious risk. One might have thought, given the evidence of the costs, that the IMF could offer plenty of evidence that the policies also did some good. In fact, there was no such evidence; the evidence that was available suggested that there was little if any positive effect on growth. Ideology enabled IMF officials not only to ignore the absence of benefits but also to overlook the evidence of the huge costs imposed on countries.

An Unfair Trade Agenda

The trade-liberalization agenda has been set by the North, or more accurately, by special interests in the North. Consequently, a disproportionate part of the gains has accrued to the advanced industrial countries, and in some cases the less-developed countries have actually been worse off. After the last round of trade negotiations, the Uruguay Round that ended in 1994, the World Bank calculated the gains and losses to each of the regions of the world. The United States and Europe gained enormously. But sub-Saharan Africa, the poorest region of the world, lost by about 2 percent because of terms-of-trade effects: The trade negotiations opened their markets to manufactured goods produced by the industrialized countries but did not open up the markets of Europe and the United States to the agricultural goods in which poor countries often have a comparative advantage. Nor did the trade agreements eliminate the subsidies to agriculture that make it so hard for the developing countries to compete.

The U.S. negotiations with China over its membership in the WTO displayed a double standard bordering on the surreal. The U.S. trade representative, the chief negotiator for the United States, began by insisting that China was a developed country. Under WTO rules, developing countries are allowed longer transition periods in which state subsidies and other departures from the WTO strictures are permitted. China certainly wishes it were a developed country, with Western-style per capita incomes. And since China has a lot of "capitas," it's possible to multiply a huge number of people by very small average incomes and conclude that the People's Republic is a big economy. But China is not only a developing economy; it is a low-income developing country. Yet the United States insisted that China be treated like a developed country! China went along with the fiction; the negotiations dragged on so long that China got some extra time to adjust. But the true hypocrisy was shown when U.S. negotiators asked, in effect, for developing-country status for the United States to get extra time to shelter the American textile industry.

Trade negotiations in the service industries also illustrate the unlevel nature of the playing field. Which service industries did the United States say were very important? Financial services—industries in which Wall Street has a comparative advantage. Construction industries and maritime services were not on the agenda, because the developing countries would have a comparative advantage in these sectors.

Consider also intellectual-property rights, which are important if innovators are to have incentives to innovate (though many of the corporate advocates of intellectual property exaggerate its importance and fail to note that much of the most important research, as in basic science and mathematics, is not patentable). Intellectual-property rights, such as patents and trademarks, need to balance the interests of producers with those of users—not only users in developing countries, but researchers in developed countries. If we underprice the profitability of innovation to the inventor, we deter invention. If we overprice its cost to the research community and the end user, we retard its diffusion and beneficial effects on living standards.

In the final stages of the Uruguay negotiations, both the White House Office of Science and Technology Policy and the Council of Economic Advisers worried that we had not got the balance right—that the agreement put producers' interests over users'. We worried that, with this imbalance, the rate of progress and innovation might actually be impeded. After all, knowledge is the most important input into research, and overly strong intellectual-property rights can, in effect, increase the price of this input. We were also concerned about the consequences of denying lifesaving medicines to the poor. This issue subsequently gained international attention in the context of the provision of AIDS medicines in South Africa. The international outrage forced the drug companies to back down—and it appears that, going forward, the most adverse consequences will be circumscribed. But it is worth noting that initially, even the Democratic U.S. administration supported the pharmaceutical companies.

What we were not fully aware of was another danger—what has come to be called "biopiracy," which involves international drug companies patenting traditional medicines. Not only do they seek to make money from "resources" and knowledge that rightfully belong to the developing countries, but in doing so they squelch domestic firms who long provided these traditional medicines. While it is not clear whether these patents would hold up in court if they were effectively challenged, it is clear that the less-developed countries may not have the legal and financial resources required to mount such a challenge. The issue has become the source of enormous emotional, and potentially economic, concern throughout the developing world. This fall, while I was in Ecuador visiting a village in the high Andes, the Indian mayor railed against how globalization had led to biopiracy.

Globalization and September 11

September 11 brought home a still darker side of globalization—it provided a global arena for terrorists. But the ensuing events and discussions highlighted broader aspects of the globalization debate. It made clear how untenable American unilateralist positions were. President Bush, who had unilaterally rejected the international agreement to address one of the long-term global risks perceived by countries around the world—global warming, in which the United States is the largest culprit—called for a global alliance against terrorism. The administration realized that success would require concerted action by all.

One of the ways to fight terrorists, Washington soon discovered, was to cut off their sources of funding. Ever since the East Asian crisis, global attention had focused on the secretive offshore banking centers. Discussions following that crisis focused on the importance of good information—transparency, or openness—but this was intended for the developing countries. As international discussions turned to the lack of transparency shown by IMF and the offshore banking centers, the U.S. Treasury changed its tune. It is not because these secretive banking havens provide better services than those provided by banks in New York or London that billions have been put there; the secrecy serves a variety of nefarious purposes—including avoiding taxation and money laundering. These institutions could be shut down overnight—or forced to comply with international norms—if the United States and the other leading countries wanted. They continue to exist because they serve the interests of the financial community and the wealthy. Their continuing existence is no accident. Indeed, the OECD drafted an agreement to limit their scope—and before September 11, the Bush administration unilaterally walked away from this agreement too. How foolish this looks now in retrospect! Had it been embraced, we would have been further along the road to controlling the flow of money into the hands of the terrorists.

There is one more aspect to the aftermath of September 11 worth noting here. The United States was already in recession, but the attack made matters worse. It used to be said that when the United States sneezed, Mexico caught a cold. With globalization, when the United States sneezes, much of the rest of the world risks catching pneumonia. And the United States now has a bad case of the flu. With globalization, mismanaged macroeconomic policy in the United States—the failure to design an effective stimulus package—has global consequences. But around the world, anger at the traditional IMF policies is growing. The developing countries are saying to the industrialized nations: "When you face a slowdown, you follow the precepts that we are all taught in our economic courses: You adopt expansionary monetary and fiscal policies. But when we face a slowdown, you insist on contractionary policies. For you, deficits are okay; for us, they are impermissible—even if we can raise the funds through 'selling forward,' say, some natural resources." A heightened sense of inequity prevails, partly because the consequences of maintaining contractionary policies are so great.

Global Social Justice

Today, in much of the developing world, globalization is being questioned. For instance, in Latin America, after a short burst of growth in the early 1990s, stagnation and recession have set in. The growth was not sustained—some might say, was not sustainable. Indeed, at this juncture, the growth record of the so-called post-reform era looks no better, and in some countries much worse, than in the widely criticized import-substitution period of the 1950s and 1960s when Latin countries tried to industrialize by discouraging imports. Indeed, reform critics point out that the burst of growth in the early 1990s was little more than a "catch-up" that did not even make up for the lost decade of the 1980s.

Throughout the region, people are asking: "Has reform failed or has globalization failed?" The distinction is perhaps artificial, for globalization was at the center of the reforms. Even in those countries that have managed to grow, such as Mexico, the benefits have accrued largely to the upper 30 percent and have been even more concentrated in the top 10 percent. Those at the bottom have gained little; many are even worse off. The reforms have exposed countries to greater risk, and the risks have been borne disproportionately by those least able to cope with them. Just as in many countries where the pacing and sequencing of reforms has resulted in job destruction outmatching job creation, so too has the exposure to risk outmatched the ability to create institutions for coping with risk, including effective safety nets.

In this bleak landscape, there are some positive signs. Those in the North have become more aware of the inequities of the global economic architecture. The agreement at Doha to hold a new round of trade negotiations—the "Development Round"—promises to rectify some of the imbalances of the past.

There has been a marked change in the rhetoric of the international economic institutions—at least they talk about poverty. At the World Bank, there have been some real reforms; there has been some progress in translating the rhetoric into reality—in ensuring that the voices of the poor are heard and the concerns of the developing countries are listened to. But elsewhere, there is often a gap between the rhetoric and the reality. Serious reforms in governance, in who makes decisions and how they are made, are not on the table. If one of the problems at the IMF has been that the ideology, interests, and perspectives of the financial community in the advanced industrialized countries have been given disproportionate weight (in matters whose effects go well beyond finance), then the prospects for success in the current discussions of reform, in which the same parties continue to predominate, are bleak. They are more likely to result in slight changes in the shape of the table, not changes in who is at the table or what is on the agenda.

September 11 has resulted in a global alliance against terrorism. What we now need is not just an alliance against evil, but an alliance for something positive—a global alliance for reducing poverty and for creating a better environment, an alliance for creating a global society with more social justice.

Chapter 4

THE CHALLENGE OF DEMOCRACY

Few concepts in comparative politics have provoked as much scholarly research and debate as democracy. The concept taps into intense emotions, in which the empirical ("what is") and the normative ("what ought to be") are often closely linked. The fact that democracy is universally popular—it ranks with parenthood and apple pie!—explains why virtually all political leaders claim that their regimes are democratic. (The selection by Sen claims that democracy is a universal value, whose core elements are the same across all cultures.) But what are the standards that must be met for a regime to qualify as democratic? Many answers have been given to this apparently simple question. One influential book, for example, describes six models of democracy!*

One way to begin is to distinguish between two influential approaches. The first emphasizes the importance of *procedures*. It defines democratic regimes as those in which all citizens have an equal right to participate in the selection of governmental leaders. The second emphasizes the importance of *outcomes,* that is, the distribution of benefits. It defines democratic regimes as those that distribute power, material benefits, and other important resources equally among all citizens.

The procedural understanding of democracy has been dominant in the current era. The selections by Dahl, and Schmitter and Karl, describe major elements of this approach. Linz and Stepan describe what is necessary for regimes that have undergone democratic reforms to become consolidated or stable democracies. But how do undemocratic, that is, authoritarian regimes, become democratic? The selections by Bunce, O'Donnell, and Carothers summarize—and criticize—an influential approach that focused on explaining transitions to democracy in the 1970s and 1980s. Bunce describes why the model, developed on the basis of transitions in Southern Europe and Latin America, failed to explain the experience of states that abandoned communism in the former Soviet Union and East-Central Europe in the late 1980s and 1990s. Carothers asserts that political upheavals in the present day suggest that the basic underpinnings of the transition model should be abandoned altogether.

---

*David Held, *Models of Democracy,* 2nd ed. (Cambridge: Polity Press, 1996). Also see David Collier and Steven Levitsky, "Democracy with Adjectives: Conceptual Innovation in Comparative Research," *World Politics* 49, No. 3 (1997): 430–451.

The selection by O'Donnell analyzes how, in recently established democracies, there can be a yawning gulf between the appearance and reality of democracy. (Also see 2.3, by Levitsky and Way.) But even the most durable democracies exhibit immense concentrations of wealth and private power. In George Orwell's satirical novel *Animal Farm,* although everyone is equal, some are more equal than others! In the United States, for example, when affluent citizens make lavish campaign contributions, the chances that government policy will represent their interests sharply increase. Readings in this chapter explore variations in the character, desirability, and durability of democracy. They provide rich testimony to the fact that democracy remains a terrain of vigorous contestation!

▦ 4.1

Polyarchy: Participation and Opposition

Robert Dahl

Robert Dahl, among the most distinguished political scientists of the past century, provides in this selection seven criteria that he considers essential for a regime to be considered democratic. Dahl further suggests that no regime qualifies as fully democratic, judged by this standard. He proposes that the less demanding term "polyarchy" be used to describe regimes that are moderately successful in meeting the standards of democracy.

Over thirty years after it was published, Dahl's account continues to be highly influential. Many scholarly studies, including several articles in this chapter, refer to it. Dahl's argument has generated extensive debate. Some critics argue that he set the bar for a regime to qualify as a democracy too low; others think that he set it too high. What do you think?

G iven a regime in which the opponents of the government cannot openly and legally organize into political parties in order to oppose the government in free and fair elections, what conditions favor or impede a transformation into a regime in which they can? That is the question with which this [discussion] is concerned.

Concepts

Since the development of a political system that allows for opposition, rivalry, or competition between a government and its opponents is an important aspect of democratization, this [discussion] is necessarily about one aspect of democratization. But the two processes—democratization and the development of public opposition—are not, in my view, identical. A full description of the differences could lead us into a tedious exploration of a semantic bog. To avoid this detour, I hope I may be allowed to indicate rather summarily some of my assumptions without much in the way of defense or elaboration.

I assume that a key characteristic of a democracy is the continuing responsiveness of the government to the preferences of its citizens, considered as political equals. What other characteristics might be required for a system to be strictly democratic, I do not intend to consider here. In this [discussion] I should like to reserve the term "democracy" for a political system one of the characteristics of which is the quality of being completely or almost completely responsive to all its citizens. Whether such a system actually exists, has existed, or can exist need not concern us for the moment. Surely one can conceive a hypothetical system of this kind; such a conception has served as an ideal, or part of an ideal, for many people. As a hypothetical system, one end of a scale, or a limiting state of affairs, it can (like a perfect vacuum) serve as a basis for estimating the degree to which various systems approach this theoretical limit.

I assume further that in order for a government to continue over a period of time to be responsive to the preferences of its citizens, considered as political equals, all full citizens must have unimpaired opportunities:

1. To formulate their preferences
2. To signify their preferences to their fellow citizens and the government by individual and collective action
3. To have their preferences weighed equally in the conduct of the government, that is, weighted with no discrimination because of the content or source of the preference

These, then, appear to me to be three necessary conditions for a democracy, though they are probably not sufficient. Next, I assume that for these three opportunities to exist among a large number of people, such as the number of people who comprise most nation-states at the present time, the institutions of the society must provide at least eight guarantees. These are indicated in Table 1.

I am going to make the further assumption that the connections between the guarantees and the three fundamental opportunities are sufficiently evident to need no further elaboration here.[1]

Now from examination of the list of eight institutional guarantees, it appears that they might provide us with a theoretical scale along which it would be possible to order different political systems. Upon closer examination, however, it appears that the eight guarantees might be fruitfully interpreted as constituting two somewhat different theoretical dimensions of democratization.

1. Both historically and at the present time, regimes vary enormously in the extent to which the eight institutional conditions are openly available, publicly employed, and fully guaranteed to at least some members of the political system who wish to contest the conduct of the government. Thus a scale reflecting these eight conditions would enable us to compare different regimes according to the extent of permissible opposition, public contestation, or political competition.[2] However, since a regime might permit opposition to a

Table 1

Some Requirements for a Democracy Among a Large Number of People

For the opportunity to:	The following institutional guarantees are required:
I. Formulate preferences	1. Freedom to form and join organizations 2. Freedom of expression 3. Right to vote 4. Right of political leaders to compete for support 5. Alternative sources of information
II. Signify preferences	1. Freedom to form and join organizations 2. Freedom of expression 3. Right to vote 4. Eligibility for public office 5. Right of political leaders to compete for support 6. Alternative sources of information 7. Free and fair elections
III. Have preferences weighted equally in conduct of government	1. Freedom to form and join organizations 2. Freedom of expression 3. Right to vote 4. Eligibility for public office 5. Right of political leaders to compete for support 5a. Right of political leaders to compete for votes 6. Alternative sources of information 7. Free and fair elections 8. Institutions for making government policies depend on votes and other expressions of preference

very small or a very large proportion of the population, clearly we need a second dimension.

2. Both historically and contemporaneously, regimes also vary in the proportion of the population entitled to participate on a more or less equal plane in controlling and contesting the conduct of the government: to participate, so to speak, in the system of public contestation. A scale reflecting the breadth of the right to participate in public contestation would enable us to compare different regimes according to their inclusiveness.

The right to vote in free and fair elections, for example, partakes of both dimensions. When a regime grants this right to some of its citizens, it moves toward greater public contestation. But the larger the proportion of citizens who enjoy the right, the more inclusive the regime.

Public contestation and inclusiveness vary somewhat independently. Britain had a highly developed system of public contestation by the end of the eighteenth century, but only a miniscule fraction of the population was fully included in it until after the expansion of the suffrage in 1867 and 1884.

Switzerland has one of the most fully developed systems of public contestation in the world. Probably few people would challenge the view that the Swiss regime is highly "democratic." Yet the feminine half of the Swiss population is still excluded from national elections. By contrast, the USSR still has almost no system of public contestation, though it does have universal suffrage. In fact one of the most striking changes during this century has been the virtual disappearance of an outright denial of the legitimacy of popular participation in government. Only a handful of countries have failed to grant at least a ritualistic vote to their citizens and to hold at least nominal elections; even the most repressive dictators usually pay some lip service today to the legitimate right of the people to participate in the government, that is, to participate in "governing" though not in public contestation.

Needless to say, in the absence of the right to oppose the right to "participate" is stripped of a very large part of the significance it has in a country where public contestation exists. A country with universal suffrage and a completely repressive government would provide fewer opportunities for oppositions, surely, than a country with a narrow suffrage but a highly tolerant government. Consequently, when countries are ranked solely according to their inclusiveness, not taking into account the surrounding circumstances, the results are anomalous. Nonetheless, as long as we keep clearly in mind the fact that the extent of the "suffrage" or, more generally, the right to participate indicates only *one* characteristic of systems, a characteristic that cannot be interpreted except in the context of other characteristics, it is useful to distinguish between regimes according to their inclusiveness.

Suppose, then, that we think of democratization as made up of at least two dimensions: public contestation and the right to participate (Figure 1). Doubtless most readers believe that democratization involves more than these two dimensions; in a moment I shall discuss a third dimension. But I propose to limit the discussion here to these two. For the point has already emerged, I think: developing a system of public contestation is not necessarily equivalent to full democratization.

To display the relationship between public contestation and democratization more clearly, let us now lay out the two dimensions as in Figure 2. Since a regime may be located, theoretically, anywhere in the space bounded by the two dimensions, it is at once obvious that our terminology for regimes is almost hopelessly inadequate, for it is a terminology invariably based upon classifying rather than ranking. The space enclosed by our two dimensions could of course be cut up into any number of cells, each of which might be given a name. But the purposes of this [discussion] make an elaborate typology redundant. Let me instead provide a small vocabulary—a reasonable one, I hope—that will enable me to speak precisely enough about the kinds of changes in regimes that I want to discuss.

Let me call a regime near the lower left corner of Figure 2 a closed hegemony. If a hegemonic regime shifts upward, as along path I, then it is moving toward greater public contestation. Without stretching language too far, one

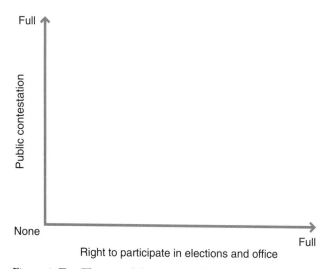

Figure 1 Two Theoretical Dimensions of Democratization.

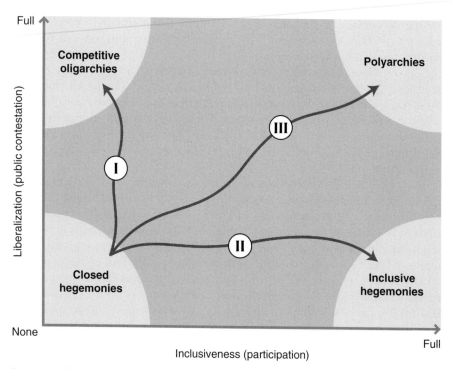

Figure 2 Liberalization, Inclusiveness, and Democratization.

could say that a change in this direction involves the liberalization of a regime; alternatively one might say that the regime becomes more competitive. If a regime changes to provide greater participation, as along path II, it might be said to change toward greater popularization, or that it is becoming inclusive. A regime might change along one dimension and not the other. If we call a regime near the upper left corner a competitive oligarchy, then path I represents a change from a closed hegemony to a competitive oligarchy. But a closed hegemony might also become more inclusive without liberalizing, i.e., without increasing the opportunities for public contestation, as along path II. In this case the regime changes from a closed to an inclusive hegemony.

Democracy might be conceived of as lying at the upper right corner. But since democracy may involve more dimensions than the two in Figure 2, and since (in my view) no large system in the real world is fully democratized, I prefer to call real world systems that are closest to the upper right corner polyarchies. Any change in a regime that moves it upward and to the right, for example along path III, may be said to represent some degree of democratization. Polyarchies, then, may be thought of as relatively (but incompletely) democratized regimes, or, to put it in another way, polyarchies are regimes that have been substantially popularized and liberalized, that is, highly inclusive and extensively open to public contestation.

You will notice that although I have given names to regimes lying near the four corners, the large space in the middle of the figure is not named, nor is it subdivided. The absence of names partly reflects the historic tendency to classify regimes in terms of extreme types; it also reflects my own desire to avoid redundant terminology. The lack of nomenclature does not mean a lack of regimes; in fact, perhaps the preponderant number of national regimes in the world today would fall into the mid-area. Many significant changes in regimes, then, involve shifts within, into, or out of this important central area, as these regimes become more (or less) inclusive and increase (or reduce) opportunities for public contestation. In order to refer to regimes in this large middle area, I shall sometimes resort to the terms near or nearly: a nearly hegemonic regime has somewhat more opportunities for public contestation than a hegemonic regime; a near-polyarchy could be quite inclusive but would have more severe restrictions on public contestation than a full polyarchy, or it might provide opportunities for public contestation comparable to those of a full polyarchy and yet be somewhat less inclusive.[3]

Notes

1. Some of the relationships are discussed in my A Preface to Democratic Theory (Chicago: University of Chicago Press, 1956), pp. 63–81, and in Robert A. Dahl and Charles E. Lindblom, Politics, Economics and Welfare (New York: Harper, 1953), chaps. 10 and 11.

2. Throughout this [discussion] the terms liberalization, political competition, competitive politics, public contestation, and public opposition are used interchangeably to refer to this dimension, and regimes relatively high on this dimension are frequently referred to as competitive regimes.

3. The problem of terminology is formidable, since it seems impossible to find terms already in use that do not carry with them a large freight of ambiguity and surplus meaning. The reader should remind himself that the terms used here are employed throughout [this discussion], to the best of my ability, only with the meanings indicated in the preceding paragraphs. Some readers will doubtless resist the term polyarchy as an alternative to the word democracy, but it is important to maintain the distinction between democracy as an ideal system and the institutional arrangements that have come to be regarded as a kind of imperfect approximation of an ideal, and experience shows, I believe, that when the same term is used for both, needless confusion and essentially irrelevant semantic arguments get in the way of the analysis. At the opposite corner, hegemony is not altogether satisfactory; yet given the meaning I have indicated, the term hegemonic seems to me more appropriate than hierarchical, monocratic, absolutist, autocratic, despotic, authoritarian, totalitarian, etc. My use of the term "contestation" in "public contestation" is well within normal (if infrequent) English usage; in English contestation means to contest, which means to make something the subject of dispute, contention, or litigation, and its most immediate synonyms are to dispute, challenge, or vie. The utility of the term was, however, first suggested to me by Bertrand de Jouvenel's "The Means of Contestation," *Government and Opposition* 1 (January 1966): 155–74. Jouvenel's usage is similar to my own, as is the identical French term he used in the original, meaning: *débat, objection, conflit, opposition*. In the same issue of this journal, however, Ghita Ionescu ("Control and Contestation in Some One-Party States" pp. 240–50) uses the term in its narrower but currently quite common meaning as "the anti-system, basic and permanent postulates of any opposition on the grounds of fundamental, dichotomic differences of opinion and ideologies" (p. 241). Clearly this is a more restricted definition of the concept than the one I use here and that, I believe, Jouvenel uses in his essay.

 4.2

What Democracy Is . . . and Is Not

Philippe C. Schmitter and Terry Lynn Karl

Schmitter and Karl believe that the seven criteria that Robert Dahl provides for evaluating democracy or polyarchy (see 4.1) are insufficient. In order for polyarchy to exist, they assert, political institutions must be autonomous; that is, they must not be under the control of extra-constitutional or foreign forces. Schmitter and Karl thus propose setting the bar higher than Dahl specified. On the other

Philippe C. Schmitter and Terry Lynn Karl, "What Democracy Is . . . and Is Not," *Journal of Democracy* 2 (Summer 1991), 75–87; reprinted in Larry Diamond and Marc F. Plattner, eds., *The Global Resurgence of Democracy,* 2nd ed. (Baltimore: The Johns Hopkins University Press, 1996): 49–62. © National Endowment for Democracy and The Johns Hopkins University Press. Reprinted with permission of The Johns Hopkins University Press.

hand, Schmitter and Karl warn that, even when democracy functions effectively, it is not a recipe for producing ideal policies.

What ways can you suggest to improve the quality of democratic institutions and policies?

For some time, the word democracy has been circulating as a debased currency in the political marketplace. Politicians with a wide range of convictions and practices strove to appropriate the label and attach it to their actions. Scholars, conversely, hesitated to use it—without adding qualifying adjectives—because of the ambiguity that surrounds it. The distinguished American political theorist Robert Dahl even tried to introduce a new term, "polyarchy," in its stead in the (vain) hope of gaining a greater measure of conceptual precision. But for better or worse, we are "stuck" with democracy as the catchword of contemporary political discourse. It is the word that resonates in people's minds and springs from their lips as they struggle for freedom and a better way of life; it is the word whose meaning we must discern if it is to be of any use in guiding political analysis and practice.

The wave of transitions away from autocratic rule that began with Portugal's "Revolution of the Carnations" in 1974 and seems to have crested with the collapse of communist regimes across Eastern Europe in 1989 has produced a welcome convergence towards a common definition of democracy.[1] Everywhere there has been a silent abandonment of dubious adjectives like "popular," "guided," "bourgeois," and "formal" to modify "democracy." At the same time, a remarkable consensus has emerged concerning the minimal conditions that polities must meet in order to merit the prestigious appellation of "democratic." Moreover, a number of international organizations now monitor how well these standards are met; indeed, some countries even consider them when formulating foreign policy.[2]

What Democracy Is

Let us begin by broadly defining democracy and the generic *concepts* that distinguish it as a unique system for organizing relations between rulers and the ruled. We will then briefly review *procedures*, the rules and arrangements that are needed if democracy is to endure. Finally, we will discuss two operative *principles* that make democracy work. They are not expressly included among the generic concepts or formal procedures, but the prospect for democracy is grim if their underlying conditioning effects are not present.

One of the major themes of this essay is that democracy does not consist of a single unique set of institutions. There are many types of democracy, and their diverse practices produce a similarly varied set of effects. The specific form democracy takes is contingent upon a country's socioeconomic conditions as well as its entrenched state structures and policy practices.

Modern political democracy is a system of governance in which rulers are held accountable for their actions in the public realm by citizens, acting indirectly through the competition and cooperation of their elected representatives.[3]

A *regime or system of governance* is an ensemble of patterns that determines the methods of access to the principal public offices; the characteristics of the actors admitted to or excluded from such access; the strategies that actors may use to gain access; and the rules that are followed in the making of publicly binding decisions. To work properly, the ensemble must be institutionalized—that is to say, the various patterns must be habitually known, practiced, and accepted by most, if not all, actors. Increasingly, the preferred mechanism of institutionalization is a written body of laws undergirded by a written constitution, though many enduring political norms can have an informal, prudential, or traditional basis.[4]

For the sake of economy and comparison, these forms, characteristics, and rules are usually bundled together and given a generic label. Democratic is one; others are autocratic, authoritarian, despotic, dictatorial, tyrannical, totalitarian, absolutist, traditional, monarchic, oligarchic, plutocratic, aristocratic, and sultanistic.[5] Each of these regime forms may in turn be broken down into subtypes.

Like all regimes, democracies depend upon the presence of *rulers*, persons who occupy specialized authority roles and can give legitimate commands to others. What distinguishes democratic rulers from nondemocratic ones are the norms that condition how the former come to power and the practices that hold them accountable for their actions.

The *public realm* encompasses the making of collective norms and choices that are binding on the society and backed by state coercion. Its content can vary a great deal across democracies, depending upon preexisting distinctions between the public and the private, state and society, legitimate coercion and voluntary exchange, and collective needs and individual preferences. The liberal conception of democracy advocates circumscribing the public realm as narrowly as possible, while the socialist or social-democratic approach would extend that realm through regulation, subsidization, and, in some cases, collective ownership of property. Neither is intrinsically more democratic than the other—just *differently* democratic. This implies that measures aimed at "developing the private sector" are no more democratic than those aimed at "developing the public sector." Both, if carried to extremes, could undermine the practice of democracy, the former by destroying the basis for satisfying collective needs and exercising legitimate authority; the latter by destroying the basis for satisfying individual preferences and controlling illegitimate government actions. Differences of opinion over the optimal mix of the two provide much of the substantive content of political conflict within established democracies.

Citizens are the most distinctive element in democracies. All regimes have rulers and a public realm, but only to the extent that they are democratic do they have citizens. Historically, severe restrictions on citizenship were imposed in most emerging or partial democracies according to criteria of age, gender, class, race, literacy, property ownership, tax-paying status, and so on. Only a small part of the total population was eligible to vote or run for office. Only restricted social categories were allowed to form, join, or support political associations. After protracted struggle—in some cases involving violent domestic upheaval or international war—most of these restrictions were lifted. Today, the criteria for inclusion are fairly standard. All native-born adults are eligible, although somewhat higher age limits may still be imposed upon candidates for certain offices. Unlike the early American and European democracies of the nineteenth century, none of the recent democracies in southern Europe, Latin America, Asia, or Eastern Europe has even attempted to impose formal restrictions on the franchise or eligibility to office. When it comes to informal restrictions on the effective exercise of citizenship rights, however, the story can be quite different. This explains the central importance (discussed below) of procedures.

Competition has not always been considered an essential defining condition of democracy. "Classic" democracies presumed decision making based on direct participation leading to consensus. The assembled citizenry was expected to agree on a common course of action after listening to the alternatives and weighing their respective merits and demerits. A tradition of hostility to "faction," and "particular interests" persists in democratic thought, but at least since *The Federalist Papers* it has become widely accepted that competition among factions is a necessary evil in democracies that operate on a more-than-local scale. Since, as James Madison argued, "the latent causes of faction are sown in the nature of man," and the possible remedies for "the mischief of faction" are worse than the disease, the best course is to recognize them and to attempt to control their effects.[6] Yet while democrats may agree on the inevitability of factions, they tend to disagree about the best forms and rules for governing factional competition. Indeed, differences over the preferred modes and boundaries of competition contribute most to distinguishing one subtype of democracy from another.

The most popular definition of democracy equates it with regular *elections*, fairly conducted and honestly counted. Some even consider the mere fact of elections—even ones from which specific parties or candidates are excluded, or in which substantial portions of the population cannot freely participate—as a sufficient condition for the existence of democracy. This fallacy has been called "electoralism" or "the faith that merely holding elections will channel political action into peaceful contests among elites and accord public legitimacy to the winners"—no matter how they are conducted or what else constrains those who win them.[7] However central to democracy, elections occur intermittently and only allow citizens to choose between the highly aggregated alternatives offered by political parties, which can, especially in the early stages of a democratic transition, proliferate in a bewildering variety. During the intervals between elections, citizens can seek to influence public policy through a wide variety of other intermediaries: interest associations, social movements, locality groupings, clientelistic arrangements, and so forth. *Modern democracy, in other words, offers a variety of competitive processes and channels for the expression of interests and values—associational as well as partisan, functional as well as territorial, collective as well as individual. All are integral to its practice.*

Another commonly accepted image of democracy identifies it with *majority rule*. Any governing body that makes decisions by combining the votes of more than half of those eligible and present is said to be democratic, whether that majority emerges within an electorate, a parliament, a committee, a city council, or a party caucus. For exceptional purposes (e.g., amending the constitution or expelling a member), "qualified majorities" of more than 50 percent may be required, but few would deny that democracy must involve some means of aggregating the equal preferences of individuals.

A problem arises, however, when *numbers* meet *intensities*. What happens when a properly assembled majority (especially a stable, self-perpetuating one) regularly makes decisions that harm some minority (especially a threatened cultural or ethnic group)? In these circumstances, successful democracies tend to qualify the central principle of majority rule in order to protect minority rights. Such qualifications can take the form of constitutional provisions that place certain matters beyond the reach of majorities (bills of rights); requirements for concurrent majorities in several different constituencies (confederalism); guarantees securing the autonomy of local or regional governments against the demands of the central authority (federalism); grand coalition governments that incorporate all parties (consociationalism); or the negotiation of social pacts between major social groups like business and labor (neocorporatism). The most common and effective way of protecting minorities, however, lies in the everyday operation of interest associations and social movements. These reflect (some would say, amplify) the different intensities of preference that exist in the population and bring them to bear on democratically elected decision makers. Another way of putting this intrinsic tension between numbers and intensities would be to say that "in modern democracies, votes may be counted, but influences alone are weighted."

Cooperation has always been a central feature of democracy. Actors must voluntarily make collective decisions binding on the polity as a whole. They must cooperate in order to compete. They must be capable of acting collectively through parties, associations, and movements in order to select candidates, articulate preferences, petition authorities, and influence policies.

But democracy's freedoms should also encourage citizens to deliberate among themselves, to discover their common needs, and to resolve their differences without relying on some supreme central authority. Classical democracy emphasized these qualities, and they are by no means extinct, despite repeated efforts by contemporary theorists to stress the analogy with behavior in the economic marketplace and to reduce all of democracy's operations to competitive interest maximization. Alexis de Tocqueville best described the importance of independent groups for democracy in his *Democracy in America*, a work which remains a major source of inspiration for all those who persist in viewing democracy as something more than a struggle for election and re-election among competing candidates.[8]

In contemporary political discourse, this phenomenon of cooperation and deliberation via autonomous group activity goes under the rubric of "civil society." The diverse units of social identity and interest, by remaining independent of the state (and perhaps even of parties), not only can restrain the arbitrary actions of rulers, but can also contribute to forming better citizens who are more aware of the preferences of others, more self-confident in their actions, and more civic-minded in their willingness to sacrifice for the common good. At its best, civil society provides an intermediate layer of governance between the individual and the state that is capable of resolving conflicts and controlling the behavior of members without public coercion. Rather than overloading decision makers with increased demands and making the system ungovernable,[9] a viable civil society can mitigate conflicts and improve the quality of citizenship—without relying exclusively on the privatism of the marketplace.

Representatives—whether directly or indirectly elected—do most of the real work in modern democracies. Most are professional politicians who orient their careers around the desire to fill key offices. It is doubtful that any democracy could survive without such people. The central question, therefore, is not whether or not there will be a political elite or even a professional political class, but how these representatives are chosen and then held accountable for their actions.

As noted above, there are many channels of representation in modern democracy. The electoral one, based on territorial constituencies, is the most visible and public. It culminates in a parliament or a presidency that is periodically accountable to the citizenry as a whole. Yet the sheer growth of government (in large part as a byproduct of popular demand) has increased the number, variety, and power of agencies charged with making public decisions and not subject to elections. Around these agencies there has developed a vast apparatus of specialized representation based largely on functional interests, not territorial constituencies. These interest associations, and not political parties, have become the primary expression of civil society in most stable democracies, supplemented by the more sporadic interventions of social movements.

The new and fragile democracies that have sprung up since 1974 must live in "compressed time." They will not resemble the European democracies of the nineteenth and early twentieth centuries, and they cannot expect to acquire the multiple channels of representation in gradual historical progression as did most of their predecessors. A bewildering array of parties, interests, and movements will all simultaneously seek political influence in them, creating challenges to the polity that did not exist in earlier processes of democratization.

Procedures That Make Democracy Possible

The defining components of democracy are necessarily abstract, and may give rise to a considerable variety of institutions and subtypes of democracy. For democracy to thrive, however, specific procedural norms must be followed and civic rights must be respected. Any polity that fails to impose such restrictions upon itself, that fails to follow the "rule of law" with regard to its own proce-dures, should not be considered democratic. These procedures alone do not de-fine democracy, but their presence is indispensable to its persistence. In essence, they are necessary but not sufficient conditions for its existence.

Robert Dahl has offered the most generally accepted listing of what he terms the "procedural minimal" conditions that must be present for modern political democracy (or as he puts it, "polyarchy") to exist:

1. Control over government decisions about policy is constitutionally vested in elected officials.
2. Elected officials are chosen in frequent and fairly conducted elections in which coercion is comparatively uncommon.
3. Practically all adults have the right to vote in the election of officials.
4. Practically all adults have the right to run for elective offices in the govern-ment. . . .
5. Citizens have a right to express themselves without the danger of severe pun-ishment on political matters broadly defined. . . .
6. Citizens have a right to seek out alternative sources of information. More-over, alternative sources of information exist and are protected by law.
7. . . . Citizens also have the right to form relatively independent associations or organizations, including independent political parties and interest groups.[10]

These seven conditions seem to capture the essence of procedural democracy for many theorists, but we propose to add two others. The first might be thought of as a further refinement of item 1, while the second might be called an implicit prior condition to all seven of the above.

8. Popularly elected officials must be able to exercise their constitutional pow-ers without being subjected to overriding (albeit informal) opposition from unelected officials. Democracy is in jeopardy if military officers, entrenched civil servants, or state managers retain the capacity to act independently of elected civilians or even veto decisions made by the people's representatives. Without this additional caveat, the militarized polities of contemporary Central America, where civilian control over the military does not exist, might be classified by many scholars as democracies, just as they have been (with the exception of Sandinista Nicaragua) by U.S. policy makers. The caveat thus guards against what we earlier called "electoralism"—the ten-dency to focus on the holding of elections while ignoring other political realities.
9. The polity must be self-governing; it must be able to act independently of constraints imposed by some other overarching political system. Dahl and other contemporary democratic theorists probably took this condition for

granted since they referred to formally sovereign nation-states. However, with the development of blocs, alliances, spheres of influence, and a variety of "neocolonial" arrangements, the question of autonomy has been a salient one. Is a system really democratic if its elected officials are unable to make binding decisions without the approval of actors outside their territorial domain? This is significant even if the outsiders are themselves democratically constituted and if the insiders are relatively free to alter or even end the encompassing arrangement (as in Puerto Rico), but it becomes especially critical if neither condition obtains (as in the Baltic states).

Principles That Make Democracy Feasible

Lists of component processes and procedural norms help us to specify what democracy is, but they do not tell us much about how it actually functions. The simplest answer is "by the consent of the people"; the more complex one is "by the contingent consent of politicians acting under conditions of bounded uncertainty."

In a democracy, representatives must at least informally agree that those who win greater electoral support or influence over policy will not use their temporary superiority to bar the losers from taking office or exerting influence in the future, and that in exchange for this opportunity to keep competing for power and place, momentary losers will respect the winners' right to make binding decisions. Citizens are expected to obey the decisions ensuing from such a process of competition, provided its outcome remains contingent upon their collective preferences as expressed through fair and regular elections or open and repeated negotiations.

The challenge is not so much to find a set of goals that command widespread consensus as to find a set of rules that embody contingent consent. The precise shape of this "democratic bargain," to use Dahl's expression,[11] can vary a good deal from society to society. It depends on social cleavages and such subjective factors as mutual trust, the standard of fairness, and the willingness to compromise. It may even be compatible with a great deal of dissensus on substantive policy issues.

All democracies involve a degree of uncertainty about who will be elected and what policies they will pursue. Even in those polities where one party persists in winning elections or one policy is consistently implemented, the possibility of change through independent collective action still exists, as in Italy, Japan, and the Scandinavian social democracies. If it does not, the system is not democratic, as in Mexico, Senegal, or Indonesia.

But the uncertainty embedded in the core of all democracies is bounded. Not just any actor can get into the competition and raise any issue he or she pleases—there are previously established rules that must be respected. Not just any policy can be adopted—there are conditions that must be met. Democracy institutionalizes "normal," limited political uncertainty. These boundaries vary from country to country. Constitutional guarantees of property, privacy, expression, and other rights are a part of this, but the most effective boundaries are generated by competition among interest groups and cooperation within civil society. Whatever the rhetoric (and some polities appear to offer their citizens more dramatic alternatives than others), once the rules of contingent consent have been agreed upon, the actual variation is likely to stay within a predictable and generally accepted range.

This emphasis on operative guidelines contrasts with a highly persistent, but misleading theme in recent literature on democracy—namely, the emphasis upon "civic culture." The principles we have suggested here rest on rules of prudence, not on deeply ingrained habits of tolerance, moderation, mutual respect, fair play, readiness to compromise, or trust in public authorities. Waiting for such habits to sink deep and lasting roots implies a very slow process of regime consolidation—one that takes generations—and it would probably condemn most contemporary experiences *ex hypothesi* to failure. Our assertion is that contingent consent and bounded uncertainty can emerge from the interaction between antagonistic and mutually suspicious actors and that the far more benevolent and ingrained norms of a civic culture are better thought of as a *product* and not a producer of democracy. . . .

What Democracy Is Not

We have attempted to convey the general meaning of modern democracy without identifying it with some particular set of rules and institutions or restricting it to some specific culture or level of development. We have also argued that it cannot be reduced to the regular holding of elections or equated with a particular notion of the role of the state, but we have not said much more about what democracy is not or about what democracy may not be capable of producing.

There is an understandable temptation to load too many expectations on this concept and to imagine that by attaining democracy, a society will have resolved all of its political, social, economic, administrative, and cultural problems. Unfortunately, "all good things do not necessarily go together."

First, democracies are not necessarily more efficient economically than other forms of government. Their rates of aggregate growth, savings, and investment may be no better than those of nondemocracies. This is especially likely during the transition, when propertied groups and administrative elites may respond to real or imagined threats to the "rights" they enjoyed under authoritarian rule by initiating capital flight, disinvestment, or sabotage. In time, depending upon the type of democracy, benevolent long-term effects upon income distribution, aggregate demand, education, productivity, and creativity may eventually combine to improve economic and social performance, but it is certainly too much to expect that these improvements will occur immediately—much less that they will be defining characteristics of democratization.

Second, democracies are not necessarily more efficient administratively. Their capacity to make decisions may even be slower than that of the regimes they replace, if only because more actors must be consulted. The costs of getting things done may be higher, if only because "payoffs" have to be made to a wider and more resourceful set of clients (although one should never underestimate the degree of corruption to be found within autocracies). Popular satisfaction with the new democratic government's performance may not even seem greater, if only because necessary compromises often please no one completely, and because the losers are free to complain.

Third, democracies are not likely to appear more orderly, consensual, stable, or governable than the autocracies they replace. This is partly a byproduct of democratic freedom of expression, but it is also a reflection of the likelihood of continuing disagreement over new rules and institutions. These products of imposition or compromise are often initially quite ambiguous in nature and uncertain in effect until actors have learned how to use them. What is more, they come in the aftermath of serious struggles motivated by high ideals. Groups and individuals with recently acquired autonomy will test certain rules, protest against the actions of certain institutions, and insist on renegotiating their part of the bargain. Thus the presence of antisystem parties should be neither surprising nor seen as a failure of democratic consolidation. What counts is whether such parties are willing, however reluctantly, to play by the general rules of bounded uncertainty and contingent consent.

Governability is a challenge for all regimes, not just democratic ones. Given the political exhaustion and loss of legitimacy that have befallen autocracies from sultanistic Paraguay to totalitarian Albania, it may seem that only democracies can now be expected to govern effectively and legitimately. Experience has shown, however, that democracies too can lose the ability to govern. Mass publics can become disenchanted with their performance. Even more threatening is the temptation for leaders to fiddle with procedures and ultimately undermine the principles of contingent consent and bounded uncertainty. Perhaps the most critical moment comes once the politicians begin to settle into the more predictable roles and relations of a consolidated democracy. Many will find their expectations frustrated; some will discover that the new rules of competition put them at a disadvantage; a few may even feel that their vital interests are threatened by popular majorities.

Finally, democracies will have more open societies and polities than the autocracies they replace, but not necessarily more open economies. Many of today's most successful and well-established democracies have historically resorted to protectionism and closed borders, and have relied extensively upon public institutions to promote economic development. While the long-term compatibility between democracy and capitalism does not seem to be in doubt, despite their continuous tension, it is not clear whether the promotion of such liberal economic goals as the right of individuals to own property and retain profits, the clearing function of markets, the private settlement of disputes, the freedom to produce without government regulation, or the privatization of state-owned enterprises necessarily furthers the consolidation of democracy. After all, democracies do need to levy taxes and regulate certain transactions, especially where private monopolies and oligopolies exist. Citizens or their representatives may decide that it is desirable to protect the rights of collectivities from encroachment by individuals, especially propertied ones, and they may choose to set aside certain forms of property for public or cooperative ownership. In short, notions of economic liberty that are currently put forward in neoliberal economic models are not synonymous with political freedom—and may even impede it.

Democratization will not necessarily bring in its wake economic growth, social peace, administrative efficiency, political harmony, free markets, or "the end of ideology." Least of all will it bring about "the end of history." No doubt some of these qualities could make the consolidation of democracy easier, but they are neither prerequisites for it nor immediate products of it. Instead, what we should be hoping for is the emergence of political institutions that can peacefully compete to form governments and influence public policy, that can channel social and economic conflicts through regular procedures, and that have sufficient linkages to civil society to represent their constituencies and commit them to collective courses of action. Some types of democracies, especially in developing countries, have been unable to fulfill this promise, perhaps due to the circumstances of their transition from authoritarian rule.[12] The democratic wager is that such a regime, once established, will not only persist by reproducing itself within its initial confining conditions, but will eventually expand beyond them.[13] Unlike authoritarian regimes, democracies have the capacity to modify their rules and institutions consensually in response to changing circumstances. They may not immediately produce all the goods mentioned above, but they stand a better chance of eventually doing so than do autocracies.

Notes

1. For a comparative analysis of the recent regime changes in southern Europe and Latin America, see Guillermo O'Donnell, Philippe C. Schmitter, and Laurence Whitehead, eds., *Transitions from Authoritarian Rule*, 4 vols. (Baltimore: Johns Hopkins University Press, 1986). For another compilation that adopts a more structural approach see Larry Diamond, Juan Linz, and Seymour Martin Lipset, eds., *Democracy in Developing Countries*, vols. 2, 3, and 4 (Boulder, Colo.: Lynne Rienner, 1989).

2. Numerous attempts have been made to codify and quantify the existence of democracy across political systems. The best known is probably Freedom House's *Freedom in the World: Political Rights and Civil Liberties*, published since 1973 by Greenwood Press and since 1988 by University Press of America. Also see Charles Humana, *World Human Rights Guide* (New York: Facts on File, 1986).

3. The definition most commonly used by American social scientists is that of Joseph Schumpeter: "that institutional arrangement for arriving at political decisions in which individuals acquire the power to decide by means of a competitive struggle for the people's vote." *Capitalism, Socialism and Democracy* (London: George Allen and Unwin, 1943), 269. We accept certain aspects of the classical procedural approach to modern democracy, but differ primarily in our emphasis on the accountability of rulers to citizens and the relevance of mechanisms of competition other than elections.

4. Not only do some countries practice a stable form of democracy without a formal constitution (e.g., Great Britain and Israel), but even more countries have constitutions and legal codes that offer no guarantee of reliable practice. On paper, Stalin's 1936 constitution for the USSR was a virtual model of democratic rights and entitlements.

5. For the most valiant attempt to make some sense out of this thicket of distinctions, see Juan Linz, "Totalitarian and Authoritarian Regimes" in *Handbook of Political Science*, eds. Fred I. Greenstein and Nelson W. Polsby (Reading, Mass.: Addison-Wesley, 1975), 175–411.

6. "Publius" (Alexander Hamilton, John Jay, and James Madison), *The Federalist Papers* (New York: Anchor Books, 1961). The quote is from Number 10.

7. See Terry Karl, "Imposing Consent? Electoralism versus Democratization in El Salvador," in *Elections and Democratization in Latin America, 1980–1985*, eds. Paul Drake and Eduardo Silva (San Diego: Center for Iberian and Latin American Studies, Center for US/Mexican Studies, University of California, San Diego, 1986), 9–36.

8. Alexis de Tocqueville, *Democracy in America*, 2 vols. (New York: Vintage Books, 1945).

9. This fear of overloaded government and the imminent collapse of democracy is well reflected in the work of Samuel P. Huntington during the 1970s. See especially Michel Crozier, Samuel P. Huntington, and Joji Watanuki, *The Crisis of Democracy* (New York: New York University Press, 1975). For Huntington's (revised) thoughts about the prospects for democracy, see his "Will More Countries Become Democratic?," *Political Science Quarterly* 99 (Summer 1984): 193–218.

10. Robert Dahl, *Dilemmas of Pluralist Democracy* (New Haven: Yale University Press, 1982), 11.

11. Robert Dahl, *After the Revolution: Authority in a Good Society* (New Haven: Yale University Press, 1970).

12. Terry Lynn Karl, "Dilemmas of Democratization in Latin America," *Comparative Politics* 23 (October 1990): 1–23.

13. Otto Kirchheimer, "Confining Conditions and Revolutionary Breakthroughs," *American Political Science Review* 59 (1965): 964–974.

 4.3

Democracy as a Universal Value

Amartya Sen

Nobel prize winner Amartya Sen challenges the argument, put forward by some scholars and political leaders, that democracy is appropriate only for Western societies. Instead, he claims that democracy reflects universally shared values and that it provides a variety of benefits to people of all cultures and regions.

Amartya Sen, "Democracy as a Universal Value," *Journal of Democracy* 10, No. 3 (July 1999): 3–17. © National Endowment for Democracy and The Johns Hopkins University Press. Reprinted with permission of The Johns Hopkins University Press.

If democracy is a universal value, why are not all regimes democratic? In reading this selection, consider what forces might oppose democracy.

I n the summer of 1997, I was asked by a leading Japanese newspaper what I
     thought was the most important thing that had happened in the twentieth
     century. I found this to be an unusually thought-provoking question, since so
many things of gravity have happened over the last hundred years. The European
empires, especially the British and French ones that had so dominated the nineteenth century, came to an end. We witnessed two world wars. We saw the
rise and fall of fascism and Nazism. The century witnessed the rise of communism, and its fall (as in the former Soviet bloc) or radical transformation (as in
China). We also saw a shift from the economic dominance of the West to a new
economic balance much more dominated by Japan and East and Southeast Asia.
Even though that region is going through some financial and economic problems right now, this is not going to nullify the shift in the balance of the world
economy that has occurred over many decades (in the case of Japan, through
nearly the entire century). The past hundred years are not lacking in important
events.

The Nevertheless, among the great variety of developments that have occurred in
the twentieth century, I did not, ultimately, have any difficulty in choosing one
as the preeminent development of the period: the rise of democracy. This is not
to deny that other occurrences have also been important, but I would argue that
in the distant future, when people look back at what happened in this century,
they will find it difficult not to accord primacy to the emergence of democracy
as the preeminently acceptable form of governance.

The idea of democracy originated, of course, in ancient Greece, more than
two millennia ago. Piecemeal efforts at democratization were attempted elsewhere as well, including in India.[1] But it is really in ancient Greece that the idea
of democracy took shape and was seriously put into practice (albeit on a limited
scale), before it collapsed and was replaced by more authoritarian and asymmet-
ric forms of government. There were no other kinds anywhere else.

Thereafter, democracy as we know it took a long time to emerge. Its gradual—
and ultimately triumphant—emergence as a working system of governance was
bolstered by many developments, from the signing of the Magna Carta in 1215,
to the French and the American Revolutions in the eighteenth century, to the
widening of the franchise in Europe and North America in the nineteenth century. It was in the twentieth century, however, that the idea of democracy
became established as the "normal" form of government to which any nation is
entitled—whether in Europe, America, Asia, or Africa. . . .

I do not deny that there are challenges to democracy's claim to universality.
These challenges come in many shapes and forms—and from different directions. Indeed, that is part of the subject of this essay. I have to examine the claim

of democracy as a universal value and the disputes that surround that claim. Before I begin that exercise, however, it is necessary to grasp clearly the sense in which democracy has become a dominant belief in the contemporary world.

In any age and social climate, there are some sweeping beliefs that seem to command respect as a kind of general rule—like a "default" setting in a computer program; they are considered right *unless* their claim is somehow precisely negated. While democracy is not yet universally practiced, nor indeed uniformly accepted, in the general climate of world opinion, democratic governance has now achieved the status of being taken to be generally right. The ball is very much in the court of those who want to rubbish democracy to provide justification for that rejection.

This is a historic change from not very long ago, when the advocates of democracy for Asia or Africa had to argue for democracy with their backs to the wall. While we still have reason enough to dispute those who, implicitly or explicitly, reject the need for democracy, we must also note clearly how the general climate of opinion has shifted from what it was in previous centuries. We do not have to establish afresh, each time, whether such and such a country (South Africa, or Cambodia, or Chile) is "fit for democracy" (a question that was prominent in the discourse of the nineteenth century); we now take that for granted. This recognition of democracy as a universally relevant system, which moves in the direction of its acceptance as a universal value, is a major revolution in thinking, and one of the main contributions of the twentieth century. It is in this context that we have to examine the question of democracy as a universal value. . . .

Democracy and Economic Development

. . . There is, in fact, no convincing general evidence that authoritarian governance and the suppression of political and civil rights are really beneficial to economic development. Indeed, the general statistical picture does not permit any such induction. Systematic empirical studies . . . give no real support to the claim that there is a general conflict between political rights and economic performance. The directional linkage seems to depend on many other circumstances, and while some statistical investigations note a weakly negative relation, others find a strongly positive one. If all the comparative studies are viewed together, the hypothesis that there is no clear relation between economic growth and democracy in *either* direction remains extremely plausible. Since democracy and political liberty have importance in themselves, the case for them therefore remains untarnished.[2]

The question also involves a fundamental issue of methods of economic research. We must not only look at statistical connections, but also examine and scrutinize the *causal* processes that are involved in economic growth and development. The economic policies and circumstances that led to the economic success of countries in East Asia are by now reasonably well understood. While different empirical studies have varied in emphasis, there is by now broad consensus on a list of "helpful policies" that includes openness to competition, the use of international markets, public provision of incentives for investment and export, a high level of literacy and schooling, successful land reforms, and other social opportunities that widen participation in the process of economic expansion. There is no reason at all to assume that any of these policies is inconsistent with greater democracy and had to be forcibly sustained by the elements of authoritarianism that happened to be present in South Korea or Singapore or China. Indeed, there is overwhelming evidence to show that what is needed for generating faster economic growth is a friendlier economic climate rather than a harsher political system.

To complete this examination, we must go beyond the narrow confines of economic growth and scrutinize the broader demands of economic development, including the need for economic and social security. In that context, we have to look at the connection between political and civil rights, on the one hand, and the prevention of major economic disasters, on the other. Political and civil rights give people the opportunity to draw attention forcefully to general needs and to demand appropriate public action. The response of a government to the acute suffering of its people often depends on the pressure that is put on it. The exercise of political rights (such as voting, criticizing, protesting, and the like) can make a real difference to the political incentives that operate on a government. . . .

There is, I believe, an important lesson here. Many economic technocrats recommend the use of economic incentives (which the market system provides) while ignoring political incentives (which democratic systems could guarantee). This is to opt for a deeply unbalanced set of ground rules. The protective power of democracy may not be missed much when a country is lucky enough to be facing no serious calamity, when everything is going quite smoothly. Yet the danger of insecurity, arising from changed economic or other circumstances, or from uncorrected mistakes of policy, can lurk behind what looks like a healthy state. . . .

The Functions of Democracy

I have so far allowed the agenda of this essay to be determined by the critics of democracy, especially the economic critics. I shall return to criticisms again, taking up the arguments of the cultural critics in particular, but the time has come for me to pursue further the positive analysis of what democracy does and what may lie at the base of its claim to be a universal value.

What exactly is democracy? We must not identify democracy with majority rule. Democracy has complex demands, which certainly include voting and respect for election results, but it also requires the protection of liberties and freedoms, respect for legal entitlements, and the guaranteeing of free discussion and uncensored distribution of news and fair comment. Even elections can be deeply defective if they occur without the different sides getting an adequate opportunity to present their respective cases, or without the electorate enjoying the freedom to obtain news and to consider the views of the competing protagonists. Democracy is a demanding system, and not just a mechanical condition (like majority rule) taken in isolation.

Viewed in this light, the merits of democracy and its claim as a universal value can be related to certain distinct virtues that go with its unfettered practice. Indeed, we can distinguish three different ways in which democracy enriches the lives of the citizens. First, political freedom is a part of human freedom in general, and exercising civil and political rights is a crucial part of good lives of individuals as social beings. Political and social participation has *intrinsic value* for human life and well-being. To be prevented from participation in the political life of the community is a major deprivation.

Second, as I have just discussed (in disputing the claim that democracy is in tension with economic development), democracy has an important *instrumental value* in enhancing the hearing that people get in expressing and supporting their claims to political attention (including claims of economic needs). Third—and this is a point to be explored further—the practice of democracy gives citizens an opportunity to learn from one another, and helps society to form its values and priorities. Even the idea of "needs," including the understanding of "economic needs," requires public discussion and exchange of information, views, and analyses. In this sense, democracy has *constructive* importance, in addition to its intrinsic value for the lives of the citizens and its instrumental importance in political decisions. The claims of democracy as a universal value have to take note of this diversity of considerations.

The conceptualization—even comprehension—of what are to count as "needs," including "economic needs," may itself require the exercise of political and civil rights. A proper understanding of what economic needs are—their content and their force—may require discussion and exchange. Political and civil rights, especially those related to the guaranteeing of open discussion, debate, criticism, and dissent, are central to the process of generating informed and considered choices. These processes are crucial to the formation of values and priorities, and we cannot, in general, take preferences as given independently of public discussion, that is, irrespective of whether open interchange and debate are permitted or not.

In fact, the reach and effectiveness of open dialogue are often underestimated in assessing social and political problems. For example, public discussion has an important role to play in reducing the high rates of fertility that characterize many developing countries. There is substantial evidence that the sharp decline in fertility rates in India's more literate states has been much influenced by public discussion of the bad effects of high fertility rates on the community at large, and especially on the lives of young women. If the view has emerged in, say, the Indian state of Kerala or of Tamil Nadu that a happy family in the modern age is a small family, much discussion and debate have gone into the formation of these perspectives. Kerala now has a fertility rate of 1.7 (similar to that of Britain and France, and well below China's 1.9), and this has been achieved with no coercion, but mainly through the emergence of new values—a process in which political and social dialogue has played a major part. Kerala's high literacy rate (it ranks higher in literacy than any province in China), especially among women, has greatly contributed to making such social and political dialogue possible.

Miseries and deprivations can be of various kinds, some more amenable to social remedies than others. The totality of the human predicament would be a gross basis for identifying our "needs." For example, there are many things that we might have good reason to value and thus could be taken as "needs" if they were feasible. We could even want immortality, as Maitreyee, that remarkable inquiring mind in the *Upanishads*, famously did in her 3000-year old conversation with Yajnvalkya. But we do not see immortality as a "need" because it is clearly unfeasible. Our conception of needs relates to our ideas of the preventable nature of some deprivations and to our understanding of what can be done about them. In the formation of understandings and beliefs about feasibility (particularly, *social* feasibility), public discussions play a crucial role. Political rights, including freedom of expression and discussion, are not only pivotal in inducing social responses to economic needs, they are also central to the conceptualization of economic needs themselves.

Universality of Values

If the above analysis is correct, then democracy's claim to be valuable does not rest on just one particular merit. There is a plurality of virtues here, including, first, the *intrinsic* importance of political participation and freedom in human life; second, the *instrumental* importance of political incentives in keeping governments responsible and accountable; and third, the *constructive* role of democracy in the formation of values and in the understanding of needs, rights, and duties. In the light of this diagnosis, we may now address the motivating question of this essay, namely the case for seeing democracy as a universal value.

In disputing this claim, it is sometimes argued that not everyone agrees on the decisive importance of democracy, particularly when it competes with other desirable things for our attention and loyalty. This is indeed so, and there is no unanimity here. This lack of unanimity is seen by some as sufficient evidence that democracy is not a universal value.

Clearly, we must begin by dealing with a methodological question: What is a universal value? For a value to be considered universal, must it have the consent of everyone? If that were indeed necessary, then the category of universal values might well be empty. I know of no value—not even motherhood (I think of *Mommie Dearest*)—to which no one has ever objected. I would argue that universal consent is not required for something to be a universal value. Rather, the claim of a universal value is that people anywhere may have reason to see it as valuable.

When Mahatma Gandhi argued for the universal value of non-violence, he was not arguing that people everywhere already acted according to this value, but rather that they had good reason to see it as valuable. Similarly, when Rabindranath Tagore argued for "the freedom of the mind" as a universal value, he was not saying that this claim is accepted by all, but that all do have reason enough to accept it—a reason that he did much to explore, present, and propagate.[3] Understood in this way, any claim that something is a universal value involves some counterfactual analysis—in particular, whether people might see some value in a claim that they have not yet considered adequately. All claims to universal value—not just that of democracy—have this implicit presumption.

I would argue that it is with regard to this often *implicit* presumption that the biggest attitudinal shift toward democracy has occurred in the twentieth century. In considering democracy for a country that does not have it and where many people may not yet have had the opportunity to consider it for actual practice, it is now presumed that the people involved would approve of it once it becomes a reality in their lives. In the nineteenth century this assumption typically would have not been made, but the presumption that is taken to be natural (what I earlier called the "default" position) has changed radically during the twentieth century.

It must also be noted that this change is, to a great extent, based on observing the history of the twentieth century. As democracy has spread, its adherents have grown, not shrunk. Starting off from Europe and America, democracy as a system has reached very many distant shores, where it has been met with willing participation and acceptance. Moreover, when an existing democracy has been overthrown, there have been widespread protests, even though these protests have often been brutally suppressed. Many people have been willing to risk their lives in the fight to bring back democracy.

Some who dispute the status of democracy as a universal value base their argument not on the absence of unanimity, but on the presence of regional contrasts. These alleged contrasts are sometimes related to the poverty of some nations. According to this argument, poor people are interested, and have reason to be interested, in bread, not in democracy. This oft-repeated argument is fallacious at two different levels.

First, as discussed above, the protective role of democracy may be particularly important for the poor. This obviously applies to potential famine victims who face starvation. It also applies to the destitute thrown off the economic ladder in a financial crisis. People in economic need also need a political voice. Democracy is not a luxury that can await the arrival of general prosperity.

Second, there is very little evidence that poor people, given the choice, prefer to reject democracy. It is thus of some interest to note that when an erstwhile Indian government in the mid-1970s tried out a similar argument to justify the alleged "emergency" (and the suppression of various political and civil rights) that it had declared, an election was called that divided the voters precisely on this issue. In that fateful election, fought largely on this one overriding theme, the suppression of basic political and civil rights was firmly rejected, and the Indian electorate—one of the poorest in the world—showed itself to be no less keen on protesting against the denial of basic liberties and rights than on complaining about economic deprivation.

To the extent that there has been any testing of the proposition that the poor do not care about civil and political rights, the evidence is entirely against that claim. Similar points can be made by observing the struggle for democratic freedoms in South Korea, Thailand, Bangladesh, Pakistan, Burma, Indonesia, and elsewhere in Asia. Similarly, while political freedom is widely denied in Africa, there have been movements and protests against such repression whenever circumstances have permitted them.

The Argument from Cultural Differences

There is also another argument in defense of an allegedly fundamental regional contrast, one related not to economic circumstances but to cultural differences. Perhaps the most famous of these claims relates to what have been called "Asian values." It has been claimed that Asians traditionally value discipline, not political freedom, and thus the attitude to democracy must inevitably be much more skeptical in these countries. . . .

It is very hard to find any real basis for this intellectual claim in the history of Asian cultures, especially if we look at the classical traditions of India, the Middle East, Iran, and other parts of Asia. For example, one of the earliest and most emphatic statements advocating the tolerance of pluralism and the duty of the state to protect minorities can be found in the inscriptions of the Indian emperor Ashoka in the third century B.C.

Asia is, of course, a very large area, containing 60 percent of the world's population, and generalizations about such a vast set of peoples is not easy. Sometimes the advocates of "Asian values" have tended to look primarily at East Asia as the region of particular applicability. The general thesis of a contrast between the West and Asia often concentrates on the lands to the east of Thailand, even though there is also a more ambitious claim that the rest of Asia is rather "similar." . . .

Even East Asia itself, however, is remarkably diverse, with many variations to be found not only among Japan, China, Korea, and other countries of the region, but also *within* each country. Confucius is the standard author quoted in interpreting Asian values, but he is not the only intellectual influence in these countries (in Japan, China, and Korea for example, there are very old and very widespread Buddhist traditions, powerful for over a millennium and a half, and there are also other influences, including a considerable Christian presence). There is no homogeneous worship of order over freedom in any of these cultures.

Furthermore, Confucius himself did not recommend blind allegiance to the state. When Zilu asks him "how to serve a prince," Confucius replies (in a statement that the censors of authoritarian regimes may want to ponder), "Tell him the truth even if it offends him."[4] Confucius is not averse to practical caution and tact, but does not forgo the recommendation to oppose a bad government (tactfully, if necessary): "When the [good] way prevails in the state, speak boldly and act boldly. When the state has lost the way, act boldly and speak softly."[5]

Indeed, Confucius provides a clear pointer to the fact that the two pillars of the imagined edifice of Asian values, loyalty to family and obedience to the state, can be in severe conflict with each other. Many advocates of the power of "Asian values" see the role of the state as an extension of the role of the family, but as Confucius noted, there can be tension between the two. The Governor of She told Confucius, "Among my people, there is a man of unbending integrity: when his father stole a sheep, he denounced him." To this Confucius replied, "Among my people, men of integrity do things differently: a father covers up for his son, a son covers up for his father—and there is integrity in what they do."[6]

The monolithic interpretation of Asian values as hostile to democracy and political rights does not bear critical scrutiny. I should not, I suppose, be too critical of the lack of scholarship supporting these beliefs, since those who have made these claims are not scholars but political leaders, often official or unofficial spokesmen for authoritarian governments. It is, however, interesting to see that while we academics can be impractical about practical politics, practical politicians can, in turn, be rather impractical about scholarship.

It is not hard, of course, to find authoritarian writings within the Asian traditions. But neither is it hard to find them in Western classics: One has only to reflect on the writings of Plato or Aquinas to see that devotion to discipline is not a special Asian taste. To dismiss the plausibility of democracy as a universal value because of the presence of some Asian writings on discipline and order would be similar to rejecting the plausibility of democracy as a natural form of government in Europe or America today on the basis of the writings of Plato or Aquinas (not to mention the substantial medieval literature in support of the Inquisitions).

Due to the experience of contemporary political battles, especially in the Middle East, Islam is often portrayed as fundamentally intolerant of and hostile to individual freedom. But the presence of diversity and variety *within* a tradition applies very much to Islam as well. In India, Akbar and most of the other Moghul emperors (with the notable exception of Aurangzeb) provide good examples of both the theory and practice of political and religious tolerance. The Turkish emperors were often more tolerant than their European contemporaries. Abundant examples can also be found among rulers in Cairo and Baghdad. Indeed, in the twelfth century, the great Jewish scholar Maimonides had to run away from an intolerant Europe (where he was born), and from its persecution of Jews, to the security of a tolerant and urbane Cairo and the patronage of Sultan Saladin.

Diversity is a feature of most cultures in the world. Western civilization is no exception. The practice of democracy that has won out in the *modern* West is largely a result of a consensus that has emerged since the Enlightenment and the Industrial Revolution, and particularly in the last century or so. To read in this a historical commitment of the West—over the millennia—to democracy, and then to contrast it with non-Western traditions (treating each as monolithic) would be a great mistake. This tendency toward oversimplification can be seen not only in the writings of some governmental spokesmen in Asia, but also in the theories of some of the finest Western scholars themselves.

As an example from the writings of a major scholar whose works, in many other ways, have been totally impressive, let me cite Samuel Huntington's thesis on the clash of civilizations, where the heterogeneities *within* each culture get quite inadequate recognition. His study comes to the clear conclusion that "a sense of individualism and a tradition of rights and liberties" can be found in the West that are "unique among civilized societies."[7] Huntington also argues that "the central characteristics of the West, those which distinguish it from other civilizations, antedate the modernization of the West." In his view, "The West was West long before it was modern."[8] It is this thesis that—I have argued—does not survive historical scrutiny.

For every attempt by an Asian government spokesman to contrast alleged "Asian values" with alleged Western ones, there is, it seems, an attempt by a Western intellectual to make a similar contrast from the other side. But even though every Asian pull may be matched by a Western push, the two together do not really manage to dent democracy's claim to be a universal value.

Where the Debate Belongs

I have tried to cover a number of issues related to the claim that democracy is a universal value. The value of democracy includes its *intrinsic importance* in human life, its *instrumental role* in generating political incentives, and its *constructive function* in the formation of values (and in understanding the force and feasibility of claims of needs, rights, and duties). These merits are not regional in character. Nor is the advocacy of discipline or order. Heterogeneity of values seems to characterize most, perhaps all, major cultures. The cultural argument does not foreclose, nor indeed deeply constrain, the choices we can make today.

Those choices have to be made here and now, taking note of the functional roles of democracy, on which the case for democracy in the contemporary world depends. I have argued that this case is indeed strong and not regionally contingent. The force of the claim that democracy is a universal value lies, ultimately, in that strength. That is where the debate belongs. It cannot be disposed of by imagined cultural taboos or assumed civilizational predispositions imposed by our various pasts.

Notes

1. In Aldous Huxley's novel *Point Counter Point*, this was enough to give an adequate excuse to a cheating husband, who tells his wife that he must go to London to study democracy in ancient India in the library of the British Museum, while in reality he goes to see his mistress.
2. I have examined the empirical evidence and causal connections in some detail in my book *Development as Freedom*, forthcoming from Knopf in 1999.
3. See my "Tagore and His India," *New York Review of Books*, 26 June 1997.
4. *The Analects of Confucius*, Simon Leys, trans. (New York: Norton, 1997), 14.22, 70.
5. *The Analects of Confucius*, 14.3, 66.
6. *The Analects of Confucius*, 13.18, 63.
7. Samuel P. Huntington, *The Clash of Civilizations and the Remaking of World Order* (New York: Simon and Schuster, 1996), 71.
8. Huntington, *The Clash of Civilizations*, 69.

 4.4

Toward Consolidated Democracies

Juan J. Linz and Alfred Stepan

Linz and Stepan assert that for an authoritarian regime to become a stable democracy, it is not sufficient to eliminate autocratic rulers. The authors distinguish between democratic *transitions* and democratic *consolidation*. Transitions involve toppling an authoritarian regime; consolidation involves the development of a durable democratic regime. Linz and Stepan identify additional changes that they consider necessary for a transition to democracy to become consolidated.

Linz and Stepan do not claim that these additional changes will inevitably occur. Can you think of why they might or might not? What affects the prospects that a regime that has experienced a democratic transition will be consolidated?

I n most cases after a democratic transition is completed, there are still many tasks that need to be accomplished, conditions that must be established, and attitudes and habits that must be cultivated before democracy can be

Juan J. Linz and Alfred Stepan, "Toward Consolidated Democracies," ch. 2 in Larry Diamond, Mark F. Plattner, Yun-han Chu, and Hung-mao Tien, eds., *Consolidating the Third Wave Democracies: Themes and Perspectives* (Baltimore: The Johns Hopkins University Press, 1997). Pp. 15–23, 30–33. © 1977 The Johns Hopkins University Press. Reprinted with permission of The Johns Hopkins University Press.

regarded as consolidated. What, then, are the characteristics of a consolidated democracy? Many scholars, in advancing definitions of consolidated democracy, enumerate all the regime characteristics that would improve the overall quality of democracy. We favor, instead, a narrower definition of democratic consolidation, but one that nonetheless combines behavioral, attitudinal, and constitutional dimensions. Essentially, by a "consolidated democracy" we mean a political regime in which democracy as a complex system of institutions, rules, and patterned incentives and disincentives has become, in a phrase, "the only game in town."[1]

Behaviorally, democracy becomes the only game in town when no significant political group seriously attempts to overthrow the democratic regime or to promote domestic or international violence in order to secede from the state. When this situation obtains, the behavior of the newly elected government that has emerged from the democratic transition is no longer dominated by the problem of how to avoid democratic breakdown. (Exceptionally, the democratic process can be used to achieve secession, creating separate states that can be democracies.) Attitudinally, democracy becomes the only game in town when, even in the face of severe political and economic crises, the overwhelming majority of the people believe that any further political change must emerge from within the parameters of democratic procedures. Constitutionally, democracy becomes the only game in town when all of the actors in the polity become habituated to the fact that political conflict within the state will be resolved according to established norms, and that violations of these norms are likely to be both ineffective and costly. In short, with consolidation, democracy becomes routinized and deeply internalized in social, institutional, and even psychological life, as well as in political calculations for achieving success.

Our working definition of a consolidated democracy is then as follows: *Behaviorally*, a democratic regime in a territory is consolidated when no significant national, social, economic, political, or institutional actors spend significant resources attempting to achieve their objectives by creating a nondemocratic regime or by seceding from the state. *Attitudinally*, a democratic regime is consolidated when a strong majority of public opinion, even in the midst of major economic problems and deep dissatisfaction with incumbents, holds the belief that democratic procedures and institutions are the most appropriate way to govern collective life, and when support for antisystem alternatives is quite small or is more-or-less isolated from prodemocratic forces. *Constitutionally*, a democratic regime is consolidated when governmental and nongovernmental forces alike become subject to, as well as habituated to, the resolution of conflict within the bounds of the specific laws, procedures, and institutions that are sanctioned by the new democratic process.

We must add two important caveats. First, when we say a regime is a consolidated democracy, we do not preclude the possibility that at some future time it could break down. Such a breakdown, however, would be related not to weaknesses or problems specific to the historic process of democratic consolidation, but to a new dynamic in which the democratic regime cannot solve a set of problems, a nondemocratic alternative gains significant supporters, and former democratic regime loyalists begin to behave in a constitutionally disloyal or semiloyal manner.[2]

Our second caveat is that we do not want to imply that there is only one type of consolidated democracy. An exciting new area of research is concerned with precisely this issue—the varieties of consolidated democracies. We also do not want to imply that consolidated democracies could not continue to improve their quality by raising the minimal economic plateau upon which all citizens stand, and by deepening popular participation in the political and social life of the country. Within the category of consolidated democracies, there is a continuum from low-quality to high-quality democracies. Improving the quality of consolidated democracies is an urgent political and intellectual task, but our goal in this essay, though related, is a different one. As we are living in a period in which an unprecedented number of countries have completed democratic transitions and are attempting to consolidate democracies, it is both politically and conceptually important that we understand the specific tasks in "crafting" democratic consolidation. Unfortunately, too much of the discussion of the current "wave" of democratization focuses almost solely on elections or on the presumed democratizing potential of market mechanisms. Democratic consolidation, however, requires much more than elections and markets.

Crafting and Conditions

In addition to a functioning state, five other interconnected and mutually reinforcing conditions must be present, or be crafted, in order for a democracy to be consolidated. First, the conditions must exist for the development of a free and lively *civil society*. Second, there must be a relatively autonomous *political society*. Third, throughout the territory of the state all major political actors, especially the government and the state apparatus, must be effectively subjected to a *rule of law* that protects individual freedoms and associational life. Fourth, there must be a *state bureaucracy* that is usable by the new democratic government. Fifth, there must be an institutionalized *economic society*. Let us explain what is involved in crafting this interrelated set of conditions.

By "civil society," we refer to that arena of the polity where self-organizing and relatively autonomous groups, movements, and individuals attempt to articulate values, to create associations and solidarities, and to advance their interests. Civil society can include manifold social movements (e.g., women's groups, neighborhood associations, religious groupings, and intellectual organizations), as well as associations from all social strata (such as trade unions, entrepreneurial groups, and professional associations).

By "political society," we mean that arena in which political actors compete for the legitimate right to exercise control over public power and the state apparatus. Civil society by itself can destroy a nondemocratic regime, but democratic consolidation (or even a full democratic transition) must involve political society. Democratic consolidation requires that citizens develop an appreciation for the core institutions of a democratic political society—political parties, legislatures, elections, electoral rules, political leadership, and interparty alliances.

It is important to stress not only the difference between civil society and political society, but also their complementarity, which is not always recognized. One of these two arenas is frequently neglected in favor of the other. Worse, within the democratic community, champions of either civil society or political society all too often adopt a discourse and a set of practices that are implicitly inimical to the normal development of the other.

In the recent struggles against the nondemocratic regimes of Eastern Europe and Latin America, a discourse was constructed that emphasized "civil society versus the state"—a dichotomy that has a long philosophical genealogy. More importantly for our purposes, it was also politically useful to those democratic movements emerging in states where explicitly political organizations were forbidden or extremely weak. In many countries, civil society was rightly considered to be the hero of democratic resistance and transition.

The problem arises at the moment of democratic transition. Democratic leaders of political society quite often argue that civil society, having played its historic role, should be demobilized so as to allow for the development of normal democratic politics. Such an argument is not only bad democratic theory, it is also bad democratic politics. A robust civil society, with the capacity to generate political alternatives and to monitor government and state, can help start transitions, help resist reversals, help push transitions to their completion, and help consolidate and deepen democracy. At all stages of the democratization process, therefore, a lively and independent civil society is invaluable.

But we should also consider how to recognize (and thus help overcome) the false opposition sometimes drawn between civil society and political society. The danger posed for the development of political society by civil society is that normative preferences and styles of organization perfectly appropriate to civil society might be taken to be the desirable—or indeed the only legitimate—style of organization for political society. For example, many civil society leaders view "internal conflict" and "division" within the democratic forces with moral antipathy. "Institutional routinization," "intermediaries," and "compromise" within politics are often spoken of pejoratively. But each of the above terms refers to an indispensable practice of political society in a consolidated democracy. Democratic consolidation requires political parties, one of whose primary tasks is precisely to aggregate and represent differences between democrats. Consolidation requires that habituation to the norms and procedures of democratic conflict-regulation be developed. A high degree of institutional routinization is a key part of such a process. Intermediation between the state and civil society, and the structuring of compromise, are likewise legitimate and necessary tasks of political society. In short, political society—informed, pressured, and periodically renewed by civil society—must somehow achieve a workable agreement on the myriad ways in which democratic power will be crafted and exercised.

The Need for a *Rechtsstaat*

To achieve a consolidated democracy, the necessary degree of autonomy of civil and political society must be embedded in, and supported by, our third arena, the rule of law. All significant actors—especially the democratic government and the state apparatus—must be held accountable to, and become habituated to, the rule of law. For the types of civil society and political society we have just described, a rule of law animated by a spirit of constitutionalism is an indispensable condition. Constitutionalism, which should not be confused with majoritarianism, entails a relatively strong consensus regarding the constitution, and especially a commitment to "self-binding" procedures of governance that can be altered only by exceptional majorities. It also requires a clear hierarchy of laws, interpreted by an independent judicial system and supported by a strong legal culture in civil society.[3]

The emergence of a *Rechtsstaat*—a state of law, or perhaps more accurately a state subject to law—was one of the major accomplishments of nineteenth-century liberalism (long before full democratization) in continental Europe and to some extent in Japan. A *Rechtsstaat* meant that the government and the state apparatus would be subject to the law, that areas of discretionary power would be defined and increasingly limited, and that citizens could turn to courts to defend themselves against the state and its officials. The modern *Rechtsstaat* is fundamental in making democratization possible, since without it citizens would not be able to exercise their political rights with full freedom and independence.

A state of law is particularly crucial for the consolidation of democracy. It is the most important continuous and routine way in which the elected government and the state administration are subjected to a network of laws, courts, semiautonomous review and control agencies, and civil-society norms that not only check the state's illegal tendencies but also embed it in an interconnecting web of mechanisms requiring transparency and accountability. Freely elected governments can, but do not necessarily, create such a state of law. The consolidation of democracy, however, requires such a law-bound, constraint-embedded state. Indeed, the more that all the institutions of the state function according to the principle of the state of law, the higher the quality of democracy and the better the society.

Constitutionalism and the rule of law must determine the offices to be filled by election, the procedures to elect those officeholders, and the definition of and limits to their power in order for people to be willing to participate in, and to accept the outcomes of, the democratic game. This may pose a problem if the rules, even if enacted by a majority, are so unfair or poorly crafted and so difficult to change democratically that they are unacceptable to a large number of citizens. For example, an electoral law that gives 80 percent of the seats in parliament to a party that wins less than 50 percent of the vote, or an ideologically loaded constitution that is extremely difficult to amend, is not likely to be conducive to democratic consolidation.

Finally, a democracy in which a single leader enjoys, or thinks he or she enjoys, a "democratic" legitimacy that allows him or her to ignore, dismiss, or alter other institutions—the legislature, the courts, the constitutional limits of power—does not fit our conception of rule of law in a democratic regime. The formal or informal institutionalization of such a system is not likely to result in a consolidated democracy unless such discretion is checked.

Some presidential democracies—with their tendency toward populist, plebiscitarian, "delegative" characteristics, together with a fixed term of office and a "no-reelection" rule that excludes accountability before the electorate—encourage nonconstitutional or anticonstitutional behavior that threatens the rule of law, often democracy itself, and certainly democratic consolidation. A prime minister who develops similar tendencies toward abuse of power is more likely than a president to be checked by other institutions: votes of no confidence by the opposition, or the loss of support by members of his own party. Early elections are a legal vehicle available in parliamentarianism—but unavailable in presidentialism—to help solve crises generated by such abusive leadership.

A Usable Bureaucracy

These three conditions—a lively and independent civil society, a political society with sufficient autonomy and a working consensus about procedures of governance, and constitutionalism and a rule of law—are virtually definitional prerequisites of a consolidated democracy. However, these conditions are much more likely to be satisfied where there are also found a bureaucracy usable by democratic leaders and an institutionalized economic society.

Democracy is a form of governance in which the rights of citizens are guaranteed and protected. To protect the rights of its citizens and to deliver other basic services that citizens demand, a democratic government needs to be able to exercise effectively its claim to a monopoly of the legitimate use of force in its territory. Even if the state had no other functions than these, it would have to tax compulsorily in order to pay for police officers, judges, and basic services. A modern democracy, therefore, needs the effective capacity to command, to regulate, and to extract tax revenues. For this, it needs a functioning state with a bureaucracy considered usable by the new democratic government.

In many territories of the world today—especially in parts of the former Soviet Union—no adequately functioning state exists. Insufficient taxing capacity on the part of the state or a weak normative and bureaucratic "presence" in much of its territory, such that citizens cannot effectively demand that their rights be respected or receive any basic entitlements, is also a great problem in many countries in Latin America, including Brazil. The question of the usability of the state bureaucracy by the new democratic regime also emerges in countries such as Chile, where the outgoing nondemocratic regime was able to give tenure to many key members of the state bureaucracy in politically sensitive areas such as justice and education. Important questions about the usability of the state bureaucracy by new democrats inevitably emerge in cases where the distinction between the communist party and the state had been virtually obliterated (as in much of postcommunist Europe), and the party is now out of power.

Economic Society

The final supportive condition for a consolidated democracy concerns the economy, an arena that we believe should be called "economic society." We use this phrase to call attention to two claims that we believe are theoretically and empirically sound. First, there has never been, and there cannot be, a consolidated democracy that has a command economy (except perhaps in wartime). Second, there has never been, and almost certainly will never be, a modern consolidated democracy with a pure market economy. Modern consolidated democracies require a set of sociopolitically crafted and accepted norms, institutions, and regulations—what we call "economic society"—that mediate between the state and the market.

No empirical evidence has ever been adduced to indicate that a polity meeting our definition of a consolidated democracy has ever existed with a command economy. Is there a theoretical reason to explain such a universal empirical outcome? We think so. On theoretical grounds, our assumption is that at least a nontrivial degree of market autonomy and of ownership diversity in the economy is necessary to produce the independence and liveliness of civil society that allow it to make its contribution to a democracy. Similarly, if all property is in the hands of the state, along with all decisions about pricing, labor, supply, and distribution, the relative autonomy of political society required for a consolidated democracy could not exist.[4]

But why are completely free markets unable to coexist with modern consolidated democracies? Empirically, serious studies of modern polities repeatedly verify the existence of significant degrees of market intervention and state ownership in all consolidated democracies.[5] Theoretically, there are at least three reasons why this should be so. First, notwithstanding certain ideologically extreme but surprisingly prevalent neoliberal claims about the self-sufficiency of the market, pure market economies could neither come into being nor be maintained without a degree of state regulation. Markets require legally enforced contracts, the issuance of money, regulated standards for weights and measures, and the protection of property, both public and private. These requirements dictate a role for the state in the economy. Second, even the best of markets experience "market failures" that must be corrected if the market is to function well.[6] No less an advocate of the "invisible hand" of the market than Adam

Smith acknowledged that the state is necessary to perform certain functions. In a crucial but neglected passage in the *Wealth of Nations*, Adam Smith identified three important tasks of the state:

> First, the duty of protecting the society from the violence and invasion of other independent societies; secondly, the duty of protecting, as far as possible, every member of the society from the injustice or oppression of every other member of it, or the duty of establishing an exact administration of justice; and, thirdly, the duty of erecting and maintaining certain public works and certain public institutions which it can never be for the interest of any individual, or small number of individuals, to erect and maintain; because the profit could never repay the expense to any individual or small number of individuals, though it may frequently do much more than repay it to a great society.[7]

Finally, and most importantly, democracy entails free public contestation concerning governmental priorities and policies. If a democracy never produced policies that generated government-mandated public goods in the areas of education, health, and transportation, and never provided some economic safety net for its citizens and some alleviation of gross economic inequality, democracy would not be sustainable. Theoretically, of course, it would be antidemocratic to take such public policies off the agenda of legitimate public contestation. Thus, even in the extreme hypothetical case of a democracy that began with a pure market economy, the very working of a modern democracy (and a modern advanced capitalist economy) would lead to the transformation of that pure market economy into a mixed economy, or that set of norms, regulations, policies, and institutions which we call "economic society."[8]

Any way we analyze the problem, democratic consolidation requires the institutionalization of a politically regulated market. This requires an economic society, which in turn requires an effective state. Even a goal such as narrowing the scope of public ownership (i.e., privatization) in an orderly and legal way is almost certainly carried out more effectively by a stronger state than by a weaker one. Economic deterioration due to the state's inability to carry out needed regulatory functions greatly compounds the problems of economic reform and democratization.[9]

In summary, a modern consolidated democracy can be conceived of as comprising five major interrelated arenas, each of which, to function properly, must have its own primary organizing principle. Rightly understood, democracy is more than a regime; it is an interacting system. No single arena in such a system can function properly without some support from another arena, or often from all of the remaining arenas. For example, civil society in a democracy needs the support of a rule of law that guarantees to people their right of association, and needs the support of a state apparatus that will effectively impose legal sanctions on those who would illegally attempt to deny others that right. Furthermore, each arena in the democratic system has an impact on other arenas. For example, political society manages the governmental bureaucracy and produces the overall regulatory framework that guides and contains economic society. In a consolidated democracy, therefore, there are constant mediations among the five principal arenas, each of which is influenced by the others. . . .

Democracy and the Quality of Life

While we believe that it is a good thing for democracies to be consolidated, we should make it clear that consolidation does not necessarily entail either a high-quality democracy or a high-quality society. Democratic institutions—however important—are only one set of public institutions affecting citizens' lives. The courts, the central bank, the police, the armed forces, certain independent regulatory agencies, public-service agencies, and public hospitals are not governed democratically, and their officials are not elected by the citizens. Even in established democracies, not all of these institutions are controlled by elected officials, although many are overseen by them. These institutions operate, however, in a legal framework created by elected bodies and thereby derive their authority from them.

In view of all this, the quality of public life is in great measure a reflection not simply of the democratic or nondemocratic character of the regime, but of the quality of those other institutions.

Policy decisions by democratic governments and legislators certainly affect the quality of life, particularly in the long run, but no democracy can assure the presence of reputable bankers, entrepreneurs with initiative, physicians devoted to their patients, competent professors, creative scholars and artists, or even honest judges. The overall quality of a society is only in small part a function of democracy (or, for that matter, a function of nondemocratic regimes). Yet all of those dimensions of society affect the satisfaction of its citizens, including their satisfaction with the government and even with democracy itself. The feeling that democracy is to blame for all sorts of other problems is likely to be particularly acute in societies in which the distinctive contributions of democracy to the quality of life are not well understood and perhaps not highly valued. The more that democrats suggest that the achievement of democratic politics will bring the attainment of all those other goods, the greater will be the eventual disenchantment.

There are problems specific to the functioning of the state, and particularly to democratic institutions and political processes, that allow us to speak of the quality of democracy separately from the quality of society. Our assumption is that the quality of democracy can contribute positively or negatively to the quality of society, but that the two should not be confused. We as scholars should, in our research, explore both dimensions of the overall quality of life.

Notes

This essay is largely drawn from our book *Problems of Democratic Transition and Consolidation: Southern Europe, South America, and Post-Communist Europe* (Baltimore: Johns Hopkins University Press, 1996). Interested readers can find more detailed documentation, analysis, and references there. We thank the Ford Foundation and the Carnegie Corporation of New York for help in our research.

1. For other discussions about the concept of democratic consolidation, see Scott Mainwaring, Guillermo O'Donnell, and J. Samuel Valenzuela, eds., *Issues in Democratic Consolidation: The New South American Democracies in Comparative Perspective* (Notre Dame, Ind.: University of Notre Dame Press, 1992).

2. In essence, this means that the literature on democratic breakdown, such as that found in Juan J. Linz and Alfred Stepan, eds., *The Breakdown of Democratic Regimes* (Baltimore: Johns Hopkins University Press, 1978), would be much more directly relevant to analyzing such a phenomenon than this essay or related books on democratic transition and consolidation. This is not a criticism of the transition literature; rather, our point is that the democratic-transition and democratic-breakdown literatures need to be integrated into the overall literature on modern democratic theory. From the perspective of such an integrated theory, the "breakdown of a consolidated democracy" is not an oxymoron.

3. On the relationships between constitutionalism, democracy, legal culture, and "self-bindingness," see Jon Elster and Rune Slagstad, eds., *Constitutionalism and Democracy* (Cambridge: Cambridge University Press, 1988), 1–18.

4. Robert A. Dahl, in a similar argument, talks about two arrows of causation that produce this result; see his "Why All Democratic Countries Have Mixed Economies," in John Chapman and Ian Shapiro, eds., *Democratic Community, Nomos XXXV* (New York: New York University Press, 1993), 259–82.

5. See, for example, John R. Freeman, *Democracies and Market: The Politics of Mixed Economies* (Ithaca, N.Y.: Cornell University Press, 1989).

6. For an excellent analysis of inevitable market failures, see Peter Murrell, "Can Neoclassical Economics Underpin the Reform of Centrally Planned Economies?" *Journal of Economic Perspectives* 5 (1991): 59–76.

7. Adam Smith, *The Wealth of Nations,* 2 vols. (London: J.M. Dent and Sons, Everyman's Library, 1910), 2:180–81.

8. Robert A. Dahl's line of reasoning follows a similar development. See his "Why All Democratic Countries Have Mixed Economies," 259–82.

9. In postcommunist Europe, the Czech Republic and Hungary are well on the way to becoming institutionalized economic societies. In sharp contrast, in Ukraine and Russia the writ of the state does not extend far enough for us to speak of an economic society. The consequences of the lack of an economic society are manifest everywhere. For example, Russia, with a population 15 times larger than Hungary's and with vastly more raw materials, received only 3.6 billion dollars of direct foreign investment in 1992–93, whereas Hungary received 9 billion dollars of direct foreign investment in the same two years.

 4.5

Rethinking Democratization: Lessons from the Postcommunist Experience

Valerie Bunce

Most theorizing about how countries became democratic in the 1970s and 1980s was based on countries in Latin America and Southern Europe. Valerie Bunce suggests that democracy developed out of Communist regimes in the former

Valerie Bunce, "Rethinking Democratization: Lessons from the Postcommunist Experience," *World Politics* 55, No. 2 (Jan. 2003): 170–189. © The Johns Hopkins University Press. Reprinted with permission of The Johns Hopkins University Press.

Soviet Union and East-Central Europe in a very different manner. In particular, she claims, popular or mass mobilization played a much more important role in toppling Communist regimes. She thus warns against generalizing beyond the cases on which a theory (in this case, a theory of democratic transitions) is originally based.

More generally, Bunce's article invites us to think about the respective role of grassroots pressure versus the strategies of political leaders in understanding why large-scale change occurs. Does Bunce's analysis help us think about why change occurs in other settings?

Comparing New Democracies

This article aims to use the postcommunist experience in East-Central Europe and the former Soviet Union—twenty-seven cases in all—to rethink our understanding of recent democratization. It does so by conducting a conversation between two bodies of research: (1) studies of Latin America and southern Europe, which collectively have constituted the reigning wisdom in the field, and (2) research on postcommunist politics. The discussion will focus on two relationships central to discussions in the field—between transitional politics and subsequent regime trajectories and between the consolidation and the sustainability of democracy. We will see that the postcommunist experience challenges the way both issues have been understood.

In particular, I argue the following. First, the degree of uncertainty in democratic transitions varies considerably. This in turn affects the strategies of transition and their payoffs. Second, mass mobilization can contribute to both the founding and the consolidation of democracy. Third, under certain conditions the democratic project is furthered by transitions that involve both nationalist protest and changes in state boundaries. Fourth, while rapid progress in democratic consolidation improves the prospects for democratic survival in the future, it does not follow that unconsolidated democracies are necessarily less sustainable. Indeed, compromising democracy (and the state) may *contribute* to democratic survival. Finally, while comparisons among new democracies can identify the optimal *conditions* for democratization, they may have less to say about optimal *strategies* for democratization.

Transitions to Democracy: Assumptions and Arguments

The analysis of recent democratization has been premised on some core assumptions about transitions from dictatorship to democracy—with the transitional period understood as beginning with an evident weakening of authoritarian rule and ending with the first competitive elections. These assumptions include the following: (1) that immediate influences are more important than historical considerations in shaping transitional dynamics; (2) that transitions are inherently quite uncertain; (3) that the central dynamic in a transition is bargaining between authoritarian leaders and leaders of the democratic opposition, with outcomes a function of their relative power; and (4) that the key issues on the table during the transition are breaking with authoritarian rule, building democratic institutions, and eliciting the cooperation of authoritarians.[1]

These assumptions, coupled with comparative studies of Latin America and southern Europe, have produced several generalizations about what constitutes the ideal approach to transition. First, as Dankwart Rustow argued more than thirty years ago, successful democratization seems to require at the very least a prior settlement of the national and state questions.[2] Second, bargaining about the rules of the transition and the new political order should be limited to a small group of authoritarian elites and representatives of the democratic opposition. Finally, given the uncertainty of transitions, it is useful to forge compromises that promote political stability during the construction of a democratic order. In practice, this means pacting; reducing the range of issues on the bargaining table (for example, avoiding reforms of the state and, if possible, major and inherently destabilizing economic reforms); demobilizing publics (which also limits the issues on the table, while depriving the authoritarians of a rationale for sabotaging democratization); forming interim governments with leaders agreeable to both sides; giving the military some room for political maneuver in the constitution; and holding a competitive election that produces a government broadly representative of both authoritarians and democrats.[3]

Mass Mobilization

The postcommunist experience seems to challenge many of these assumptions about transitional strategies. Let us begin by addressing the role of mass publics in the transition. It is widely agreed among specialists and confirmed by the rankings over time by Freedom House that the most successful transitions to democracy in the postcommunist region have been in the Czech Republic, Estonia, Hungary, Latvia, Lithuania, Poland, and Slovenia. The transition to democracy in every one of these cases, except Hungary, began with mass protests.[4] Moreover, if we restrict our focus to those countries that show significant improvement in their democratic performance over time, or Bulgaria and Romania, we see the same pattern: mass mobilization at the beginning of the transition.

Why was mass mobilization so often helpful to the democratic transition in the postcommunist context? The answer is that political protests performed a number of valuable functions. They signaled the breakdown of the authoritarian order; created a widespread sense that there were alternatives to that order; pushed authoritarian leaders (and sometimes even leaders of the opposition, as with Wałesa in Poland) to the bargaining table; created (and sometimes restored) a large opposition united by its rejection of the incumbent regime; and gave opposition leaders a resource advantage when bargaining with authoritarian elites. Finally, mass mobilization created a mandate for radical change that subsequently translated into a large victory for the democratic forces in the first competitive elections and, following that, led to the introduction of far-reaching economic and political reforms.

Uncertainty

If we accept that mass mobilization during the transition can further the democratic project, then we necessarily confront additional challenges to the received wisdom about recent democratization. First, it can be argued that in many cases such mobilization in the postcommunist region reduced the uncertainty of the transition—by providing a clear reading of mass sentiments, by strengthening the bargaining power of opposition leaders, and by forcing the communists to give up their defense of the old order, either stepping aside quickly (as in Czechoslovakia) or, when thinking prospectively, joining the movement for democracy (as in Poland, Slovenia, and the Baltic states).[5] At the same time, mass mobilization promised—and delivered—a popular mandate for democracy in the first competitive elections.

Most of the transitions to democracy in the postcommunist world were, of course, highly uncertain. This is evidenced by the fact that the first competitive election in most of the countries in the region led to a communist victory. Indeed, the larger the victory, the more likely that authoritarian rule continued. Moreover, even ten years after the transition began, only one-third of the postcommunist regimes were ranked fully free. Although this is the highest number since state socialism fell, it is a percentage much lower than what one finds at a comparable point in the Latin American and southern European transitions. When combined with the earlier observations, these patterns suggest that the uncertainty surrounding postcommunist political trajectories varied significantly.[6] In some cases, a democratic outcome was relatively predictable; in most others, the political options after communism were far more open-ended.

Strategic Implications of Uncertainty

The existence of a more certain political environment in some countries calls into question both the necessity and the logic, outlined earlier, of safeguarding the new democracy by forging compromises between authoritarians and democrats. It is precisely the absence of pressure to do so in the Polish, the Czech, and the other highly successful transitions that explains another contrast between the "East" and the "South." It is true that many of the most successful transitions in the postcommunist area included pacting (though rarely as elaborate as the

Spanish experience) and that some also evidenced for a brief time broadly representative interim governments.[7] It is also true, however, that the transitions in the postcommunist region that combined pacting with demobilized publics—or what has been asserted to be the preferred approach in the South—were precisely the transitions that were most likely to continue authoritarian rule in the postcommunist region.[8] Moreover, the other compromises that were deemed so beneficial for the southern European and Latin American transitions were rejected by opposition leaders in Poland, Hungary, Slovenia, and the like. Instead, they were strongly positioned to favor an immediate and sharp break with the authoritarian past. Thus, in every highly successful case of democratization in the region, the military was excluded from political influence from the start; the first elections involved a radical break with the political leadership of the past; and major changes in the economy were introduced quickly. Just as important was the commitment in each of these cases to reforming the state, including in most of them its very boundaries. For the Czech Republic, Hungary, Poland, Slovenia, and the Baltic states, then, the agenda of transition was unusually ambitious.

Postcommunist transition dynamics therefore ask us to amend the familiar formulation drawn from the South. It was precisely because mass mobilization was so threatening to authoritarians that leaders of the opposition in some of these countries were free to carry out radical political and economic reforms. Put differently: because of popular mobilization or, in the Hungarian case, reform communism and collaboration between democrats and authoritarians, opposition leaders in what became the most sustainable and full-scale democracies in the East could proceed quickly in breaking with authoritarian rule and building democratic (and, for that matter, capitalist) institutions without worrying as much as their counterparts elsewhere about appeasing authoritarian interests.

This, in turn, altered the strategies of transition and their payoffs. While bridging between the old and the new order constituted by all accounts the most successful approach to democratization in Latin America and southern Europe, the most successful strategy in the postcommunist region was the opposite—severing ties.

The Role of the Military

Also contributing to these interregional contrasts in the optimal strategies of transition was the very different role of the military in Latin America and southern Europe, on the one hand, and in the communist area, on the other hand. Specialists in the South have argued with essentially one voice that the biggest threat to democracy today, as in the past, is the military. One has only to recall, for example, the long history of military interventions in Latin American politics, most of which terminated democracy (though some of them oversaw a return to democratic governance, as also occurred in unusually circuitous fashion, in the Portuguese transition). There is, in addition, the attempted military coup d'état in Spain in

1982. Indeed, precisely because of its long importance in politics, the military has been awarded remarkable powers in many Latin American constitutions, their democratic claims notwithstanding.[9] When combined, these examples carry an obvious message: the military in these contexts can make or break regimes. It is precisely this capacity that contributed to the uncertainty of the transitions in the South and that necessitated compromises with authoritarian forces.

In much of the postcommunist world, by contrast, there is a long tradition of civilian control over the military—a tradition that goes far back in Russian history and that, following the Bolshevik Revolution and the demilitarization after the Civil War, was maintained at home and then after World War II was projected outward to the members of the Soviet bloc.[10] Civil-military relations, in short, constituted one area where the authoritarian past proved to be beneficial, rather than a burden, for democratization after state socialism.[11]

With the military less threatening in the postcommunist context and with mass publics in some cases mobilized in support of democracy, authoritarian elites in the postcommunist region were indeed under siege. This was particularly the case in East-Central Europe, where domestic control over the military (and the secret police)—except in Yugoslavia, Romania, and Albania—had been ceded to the Soviet Union after 1968. All this left the opposition in what came to be the most successful democracies in the region with unusual freedom of maneuver—a freedom enhanced by public support in the streets. As a result, both the effects of mass mobilization *and* the most successful strategies of transition were different in the postcommunist context from what they had been in Latin America and southern Europe.

Nationalist Mobilization

The analysis thus far has sidestepped an issue of considerable importance in the transitions from state socialism: the distinction between protests against the regime and protests against the state. Here, the postcommunist region exhibits another surprising pattern. While popular protest in both the Czech lands and Poland targeted the regime, the Baltic and Slovene demonstrations are better understood as both liberal and nationalist. In the latter cases, then, nationalism supported democratic governance, even when nationalist concerns grew out of and were in part responsible for the disintegration of a state.

There also seems to be another positive linkage between nationalist mobilization and successful, sustained democratization. The republics that made up the Soviet Union, Yugoslavia, and Czechoslovakia varied considerably from each other with respect to whether publics protested, whether the opposition was strong and united, and whether publics, the opposition, and, indeed, even the communists were committed to democratization. With the breakup of these three ethnofederal states along republican lines, those republics with the best conditions for democratic governance were liberated from a political and economic context that made such an outcome unlikely, if not impossible. Thus, not just Slovenia and the Baltic republics, but also Macedonia, Moldova, Russia, and Ukraine were better positioned to pursue a democratic course following state disintegration.[12]

How can we reconcile these observations with the familiar argument that nationalist mobilization poses a threat to democracy on the grounds that the logics of state building and democratization are contradictory? This argument, moreover, has empirical support in the postcommunist world, given the deleterious effects of nationalism on political developments after state socialism in Bosnia, Croatia, Georgia, Serbia and Montenegro (and Kosovo), and Slovakia. In each of these cases the nationalist movement excluded minorities residing within the republic; transformed some communists into nationalists, who then used nationalism to maintain authoritarian control; and constructed illiberal successor regimes while deconstructing successor states.[13] What explains these divergent consequences of nationalism?

When nationalism enters the discussion, parsimonious arguments often give way to thick explanations. In this instance, however, there seems to be a relatively simple distinction: *when* nationalist demonstrations began in the republics. Late nationalist mobilization—or nationalist demonstrations that first appeared when the communist regime and state were disintegrating—is associated in virtually every instance with a rapid transition to democracy and progress since that time in building a stable—or at least increasingly stable—democratic order. This describes, in particular, not just the cases of Estonia, Latvia, Lithuania, and Slovenia, but also the far more flawed, but nonetheless durable democracies of Moldova, Russia, and Ukraine.

By contrast, nationalist demonstrations that first occurred before the regime and state began to unravel are associated with very different political pathways after state socialism—either democratic breakdown or a delayed transition to democracy. There were five republics and one autonomous province that experienced such demonstrations by their titular nation during the 1970s or at the beginning of the 1980s: Armenia, Croatia, Georgia, Kosovo, Slovakia, and, to a more limited extent, Serbia.[14] In every one of these cases the subsequent transition to democracy was undermined, as was the successor state in most cases.

Why is timing so important? The key seems to be differences in regime context. In the "early" cases, nationalist mobilization arose in response to two conditions: a strong sense of identity on the part of members and especially the self-appointed leaders of the republic's titular nation (reflecting earlier developments, such as the experience of statehood prior to communist party rule) coupled with republican political dynamics that featured domination by the titular nation along with significant autonomy from the center. Once demonstrations began, three developments followed: minorities within these republics (except homogeneous Armenia) defended themselves from titular domination by building countermovements while allying with the center; the center, fearing that nationalist protests would spread and thereby challenge both the regime and the state, suppressed the titular national protesters, purged the republican party, and empowered minorities as a counterweight to the titular nation; and the republican party fissured in the face of irreconcilable demands from local nationalists versus central communists.

As a result, by the time state socialism began to dissolve, the stage was already set for an unusually problematic transition to both democratic rule and independent statehood. Two insurmountable divides were in place. The first was between nationalists, who dominated the political scene, and liberals, who had been demobilized. The second was between leaders of the majority nation and leaders of minority communities. The national identities of these groups were well defined and exclusivist, and their competing identities were joined with competing interests, political alliances, and preferences for the future. Moreover, the communist leaders of these republics, facing the loss of both their institutional and their ideological bases for ruling, did not have the option their Slovenian counterparts had, of defecting to an opposition that embraced both independent statehood and liberal democracy. Instead, they could either become nationalists or, if adopting a liberal position, face political marginalization.

By contrast, when nationalist mobilization began only later, in response to the weakening of the regime and the state, all these conditions were absent—or at least less well defined. This meant that the majority and the minorities were free to coalesce around the issues of republican sovereignty and liberal democracy. Thus, in these contexts a liberal agenda combined with a nationalist agenda; and not only opposition forces but even many communists embraced that agenda.

We can now conclude our discussion of transitions in the South versus the East. The experiences of the latter region suggest the following, all running counter to the received wisdom about Latin America and southern Europe. First, historical factors are critical in shaping the resources and especially the preferences of elites during the transition, as well as, more generally, transition trajectories. Second, one proximate and positive influence, lying outside the high politics of the transition, is mass mobilization. Third, transitions seem to vary in their degree of uncertainty, and this affects what constitutes the most successful path. In the postcommunist world, where some transitions were less uncertain, the most successful approach was one that moved quickly on both political and economic fronts. Fourth, democratization can be successful when it is combined with nationalist mobilization and the founding of a new state. This is particularly so when such mobilization first begins with the weakening of the state and the regime. . . .

Conclusions

Research on democratization, particularly the founding and performance of new democracies, is largely a literature about the choices political leaders have made and the consequences of those choices. It is also largely a literature based on the return to democracy in Latin America and southern Europe. The purpose of this article has been both to question and to complicate the focus on elites and the generalizations that have been made about transitions to democracy, democratic consolidation, and democratic sustainability. I have done so by adding an additional region to the empirical equation—the twenty-seven countries that make up the Eurasian postcommunist region.

Several conclusions emerged. First, transitions to democracy seem to vary considerably with respect to the uncertainty surrounding the process. This variance in turn affects the strategies of transition and their payoffs. In the postcommunist region it was widely assumed that the uncertainty surrounding these transitions was unusually high, given, for example, the absence in most cases of a democratic past together, the extraordinary economic and political penetration of state socialism, and the seeming tensions among democratization, state building, the construction of a capitalist economy, and the radically changed relationship of the state to the international system. It turns out, however, that for a number of countries in the region the transition to democracy was in fact not so uncertain, for two reasons. First, the military was eliminated from the transition. Second, there was present a powerful opposition that gained strength from popular mobilization against the regime (often also against the state) (as with the Baltic, Slovenian, Czech, and Polish cases) and/or reform communists who collaborated with an opposition committed to democracy (as with the Baltic countries, Slovenia, Poland, and Hungary).

Because uncertainty was lower, moreover, the transition in all of these cases produced a sharp break with the state socialist past—for example, through founding elections that gave the opposition a large mandate, rapid progress in constructing democratic institutions, quick introduction of far-reaching economic reforms, and, in most of the cases, the construction of a new state. By contrast, transition was far more uncertain where the military was engaged in the transition, where mass mobilization focused on leaving the state but not building democracy, and/or where the communists were able to command considerable support in the first election. As a result, the break with the authoritarian past was less definitive—in terms of both political leadership and public policy.

These contrasts have several implications. One is that, while the most successful transitions in the South involved bridging, the most successful transitions in the East involved breakage. Indeed, it is precisely the bridging approach in the East that produced the most fragile democracies. The other is that the contrast between bridging and breakage—and the costs and benefits of each approach—in large measure reflected differences in uncertainty.

Another conclusion is that mass mobilization can play a very positive role in the transition, as it did, for example, in the Baltic, Polish, Czech, and Slovenian cases and, most recently, in Serbia and Montenegro. This is largely because mass mobilization can reduce uncertainty, thereby influencing the preferences of the communists, as well as the division of power between them and the opposition.

Nationalist mobilization and the disintegration of the state can also influence the democratic project. Whether this occurs seems to reflect a key distinction: whether such protests first arose when the regime and state were unraveling or whether the demonstrations at that time were the culmination of a longer history of such protests. In the first case, which describes Slovenia, the Baltic countries, Russia, Ukraine, and Moldova, the transition produced sustainable democratic orders, albeit of varying quality. By contrast, in every transition where nationalist protest had a longer lineage, both the old and the new state, as well as the democratic project, experienced continuing contestation.

Notes

1. Guillermo O'Donnell, Philippe C. Schmitter, and Laurence Whitehead, *Transitions from Authoritarian Rule*, vols. 1–4 (Baltimore: Johns Hopkins University Press, 1986); Terry Lynn Karl, "Dilemmas of Democratization in Latin America," *Comparative Politics* 23 (Spring 1990); Guiseppe Di Palma, *To Craft Democracy* (Berkeley: University of California Press, 1990).
2. Dankwart Rustow, "Transitions to Democracy: Toward a Dynamic Model," *Comparative Politics* 2 (April 1970).
3. O'Donnell, Schmitter, and Whitehead; Richard Gunther, "Spain: The Very Model of a Modern Elite Settlement," in John Higley and Richard Gunther, eds., *Elites and Democratic Consolidation in Latin America and Southern Europe* (Baltimore: Johns Hopkins University Press, 1992); Robert M. Fishman, "Rethinking State and Regime: Southern Europe's Transition to Democracy," *World Politics* 42 (April 1990); Stephen Haggard and Robert Kaufman, *The Political Economy of Democratic Transitions* (Princeton: Princeton University Press, 1995); Jose Maria Maravall, "Politics and Policy: Economic Reforms in Southern Europe," in Luiz Carlos Bresser Pereira, Jose Maria Maravall, and Adam Przeworski, eds., *Economic Reforms in New Democracies: A Social Democratic Approach* (Cambridge: Cambridge University Press, 1993). Moderate policies, however, do not imply the absence of political conflict. See Nancy Bermeo, "Myths of Moderation," *Comparative Politics* 29 (April 1997).
4. In Hungary mass mobilization was understood to be politically risky (and turned out ultimately to be unnecessary), given the brutal suppression of the Hungarian Revolution in 1956, on the one hand, and the willingness of the reform communists, even before the roundtable, to jump on the democratic bandwagon, on the other hand. See Patrick H. O'Neil, "Revolution from Within: Institutional Analysis, Transitions from Authoritarianism, and the Case of Hungary," *World Politics* 48 (July 1996).
5. See Anna M. Grzymala-Busse, *Redeeming the Communist Past: The Regeneration of Communist Parties in East-Central Europe* (Cambridge: Cambridge University Press, 2002).
6. Because Poland was the first country in the region to break with communist party rule, its transition was somewhat more uncertain. Given the character of the Soviet bloc, however, developments in Poland during the first half of 1989 lowered the risks of transition for other members of the bloc.
7. Jon Elster, ed., *The Roundtable Talks and the Breakdown of Communism* (Chicago: University of Chicago Press, 1996).
8. Pauline Jones Luong, *Institutional Change and Political Continuity in Post-Soviet Central Asia: Power, Perceptions and Pacts* (Cambridge: Cambridge University Press, 2002).
9. Brian Loveman, "Protected Democracies and Military Guardianship: Political Transitions in Latin America, 1978–1993," *Journal of Inter-American Studies and World Affairs* 36 (Summer 1994).
10. The key phrase is "members of the Soviet bloc." For those communist regimes outside the bloc or mavericks within the bloc (Albania, Romania, and Yugoslavia), party control over the military was compromised. It was precisely in these cases that the exit from state socialism was violent. Variations in civil-military relations also account in part for the violent disintegration of the Yugoslav state, in contrast to the peaceful dissolution of both the Soviet Union and Czechoslovakia.

11. See Bela Greskovits, "Rival Views of Postcommunist Market Society: The Path Dependence of Transitology," in Michel Dobry, ed., *Democratic and Capitalist Transitions in Eastern Europe: Lessons for the Social Sciences* (Dordrecht: Kluwer Academic Publishers, 2000).

12. For a parallel situation, see Michael Bernhard, "Democratization in Germany: A Reappraisal," *Comparative Politics* 33, no. 4 (2001).

13. See Zsuzsa Czergo, "Language and Democracy: A Comparative Study of Contestations over Language Use in Romania and Slovakia" (Ph.D. diss., George Washington University, 2000); Georgi Derluguian, "The Tale of Two Resorts: Abkhazia and Adjaria before and since the Soviet Collapse," in Beverly Crawford and Ronnie D. Lipschutz, eds., *The "Myth" of Ethnic Conflict: Politics, Economics and Cultural Violence*, Research Monograph, no. 98. (Berkeley: University of California International and Area Studies, 1998); Ronald Suny, *The Making of the Georgian Nation*, 2d ed. (Bloomington: Indiana University Press, 1994); Valerie Bunce and Stephen Watts, "Managing Diversity and Sustaining Democracy: Ethnofederal versus Unitary States in the Postsocialist World" (Paper presented at the workshop on Power-Sharing and Peace-Making, San Diego, December 10–11, 2001).

14. See . . . Besnik Pula, "Contested Sovereignty and State Disintegration: The Rise of the Albanian Secessionist Movement in Kosovo" (Master's Thesis, Georgetown University, 2001). On the Serbian case, see Valere P. Gagnon, "Liberalism and Minorities: Serbs as Agents and Victims of Liberal Conceptions of Space" (Paper presented at the workshop on Citizenship in Multicultural States: Comparing the Former Yugoslavia and Israel, Austrian Institute of International Affairs, Vienna, April 20–21, 2001).

 4.6

Illusions About Consolidation

Guillermo O'Donnell

Professor O'Donnell challenges what he considers illusions about the character of democracy. Basing his argument on analysis of Latin American and other newly democratic regimes, he claims that although regimes may exhibit the formal characteristics of a democracy or polyarchy (see the readings by Dahl, and Schmitter and Karl), this appearance can be deceptive. The reason is that informal practices, what O'Donnell terms "particularism," often undermine democratic institutions. Examples of particularism include nepotism (when public officials give family members jobs and other favors) and outright corruption, when public officials accept bribes in exchange for illegal actions. (Beyond a certain point, as Levitsky and Way argue in 2.3, such regimes can more accurately be described as authoritarian.)

Guillermo O'Donnell, "Illusions About Consolidation," *Journal of Democracy* 7, No. 2 (April 1996): 34–51. © National Endowment for Democracy and The Johns Hopkins University Press. Reprinted with permission of The Johns Hopkins University Press.

O'Donnell's article focuses on young democracies. How applicable is it to long-established democracies?

Democracies used to be few in number, and most were located in the northwestern quarter of the world. Over the last two decades, however, many countries have rid themselves of authoritarian regimes. There are many variations among these countries. Some of them have reverted to new brands of authoritarianism (even if from time to time they hold elections), while others have clearly embraced democracy. Still others seem to inhabit a gray area; they bear a family resemblance to the old established democracies, but either lack or only precariously possess some of their key attributes. The bulk of the contemporary scholarly literature tells us that these "incomplete" democracies are failing to become consolidated, or institutionalized.

This poses two tasks. One is to establish a cutoff point that separates all democracies from all nondemocracies. This point's location depends on the questions we ask, and so is always arbitrary. Many different definitions of democracy have been offered.[1] The one that I find particularly useful is Robert Dahl's concept of "polyarchy." Once a reasonably well delimited set of democracies is obtained, the second task is to examine the criteria that a given stream of the literature uses for comparing cases within this set. If the criteria are found wanting, the next step is to propose alternative concepts for these comparisons. This is what I attempt in this essay, albeit in preliminary and schematic fashion.

Contemporary Latin America is my empirical referent, although my discussion probably also applies to various newly democratized countries in other parts of the world. The main argument is that, contrary to what most current scholarship holds, the problem with many new polyarchies is not that they lack institutionalization. Rather, the way in which political scientists usually conceptualize some institutions prevents us from recognizing that these polyarchies actually have two extremely important institutions. One is highly formalized, but intermittent: elections. The other is informal, permanent, and pervasive: particularism (or clientelism, broadly defined). An important fact is that, in contrast to previous periods of authoritarian rule, particularism now exists in uneasy tension with the formal rules and institutions of what I call the "full institutional package" of polyarchy. These arguments open up a series of issues that in future publications I will analyze with the detail and nuance they deserve. My purpose at present is to furnish some elements of what I believe are needed revisions in the conceptual and comparative agenda for the study of all existing polyarchies, especially those that are *informally institutionalized*.[2]

Polyarchy, as defined by Dahl, has seven attributes: 1) elected officials; 2) free and fair elections; 3) inclusive suffrage; 4) the right to run for office; 5) freedom of expression; 6) alternative information; and 7) associational autonomy.[3] Attributes 1 to 4 tell us that a basic aspect of polyarchy is that elections are inclusive, fair, and competitive. Attributes 5 to 7 refer to political and social freedoms that are minimally necessary not only during but also between elections as a condition for elections to be fair and competitive. According to these criteria, some countries of Latin America currently are not polyarchies: the Dominican Republic, Haiti, and Mexico have recently held elections, but these were marred by serious irregularities before, during, and after the voting.

Other attributes need to be added to Dahl's list. One is that elected (and some appointed) officials should not be arbitrarily terminated before the end of their constitutionally mandated terms (Peru's Alberto Fujimori and Russia's Boris Yeltsin may have been elected in fair elections, but they abolished polyarchy when they forcefully closed their countries' congresses and fired their supreme courts). A second addition is that the elected authorities should not be subject to severe constraints, vetoes, or exclusion from certain policy domains by other, nonelected actors, especially the armed forces.[4] In this sense, Guatemala and Paraguay, as well as probably El Salvador and Honduras, do not qualify as polyarchies.[5] Chile is an odd case, where restrictions of this sort are part of a constitution inherited from the authoritarian regime. But Chile clearly meets Dahl's seven criteria of polyarchy. Peru is another doubtful case, since the 1995 presidential elections were not untarnished, and the armed forces retain tutelary powers over various policy areas. Third, there should be an uncontested national territory that clearly defines the voting population.[6] Finally, an appropriate definition of polyarchy should also include an intertemporal dimension: the generalized expectation that a fair electoral process and its surrounding freedoms will continue into an indefinite future.

These criteria leave us with the three polyarchies—Colombia, Costa Rica, and Venezuela—whose origins date from before the wave of democratization that began in the mid-1970s, and with nine others that resulted from this wave: Argentina, Bolivia, Brazil, Ecuador, Nicaragua, Panama, Uruguay and, with the caveats noted, Chile and Peru. Only in the oldest Latin American polyarchy (Costa Rica) and in two cases of redemocratization (Chile and Uruguay) do the executive branch, congress, parties, and the judiciary function in a manner that is reasonably close to their formal institutional rules, making them effective institutional knots in the flow of political power and policy. Colombia and Venezuela used to function like this, but do so no longer. These two countries, jointly with Argentina, Bolivia, Brazil, Ecuador, Nicaragua, Panama, and Peru—a set that includes a large majority of the Latin American population and GNP—function in ways that current democratic theory has ill prepared us to understand.

We must go back to the definition of polyarchy. This definition, precise in regard to elections (attributes 1 to 4) and rather generic about contextual freedoms (attributes 5 to 7), is mute with respect to institutional features such as parliamentarism or presidentialism, centralism or federalism, majoritarianism or consensualism, and the presence or absence of a written constitution and judicial review. Also, the definition of polyarchy is silent about important but elusive themes such as if, how, and to what degree governments are responsive or accountable to citizens between elections, and the degree to which the rule of law extends over the country's geographic and social terrain.[7] These silences are appropriate: the definition of polyarchy, let us recall, establishes a crucial cutoff point—one that separates cases where there exist inclusive, fair, and competitive elections and basic accompanying freedoms from all others, including not only unabashed authoritarian regimes but also countries that hold elections but lack some of the characteristics that jointly define polyarchy.

Among polyarchies, however, there are many variations. These differences are empirical, but they can also be normatively evaluated, and their likely effect on the survival prospects of each polyarchy may eventually be assessed. These are important issues that merit some conceptual clarification.

By definition, all the Latin American cases that I have labeled polyarchies are such because of a simple but crucial fact: elections are institutionalized. By an institution I mean a regularized pattern of interaction that is known, practiced, and accepted (if not necessarily approved) by actors who expect to continue interacting under the rules sanctioned and backed by that pattern.[8] Institutions are typically taken for granted, in their existence and continuity, by the actors who interact with and through them. Institutions are "there," usually unquestioned regulators of expectations and behavior. Sometimes, institutions become complex organizations: they are supposed to operate under highly formalized and explicit rules, and materialize in buildings, rituals, and officials. These are the institutions on which both "prebehavioral" and most of contemporary neo-institutionalist political science focus. An unusual characteristic of elections *qua* institutions is that they are highly formalized by detailed and explicit rules, but function intermittently and do not always have a permanent organizational embodiment.

In all polyarchies, old and new, elections are institutionalized, both in themselves and in the reasonable[9] effectiveness of the surrounding conditions of freedom of expression, access to alternative information, and associational autonomy. Leaders and voters take for granted that in the future inclusive, fair, and competitive elections will take place as legally scheduled, voters will be properly registered and free from physical coercion, and their votes will be counted fairly. It is also taken for granted that the winners will take office, and will not have their terms arbitrarily terminated. Furthermore, for this electoral process to exist, freedom of opinion and of association (including the freedom to form political parties) and an uncensored media must also exist. Countries where elections do not have these characteristics do not qualify as polyarchies.[10]

Most students of democratization agree that many of the new polyarchies are at best poorly institutionalized. Few seem to have institutionalized anything but elections, at least in terms of what one would expect from looking at older polyarchies. But appearances can be misleading, since other institutions may exist, even though they may not be the ones that most of us would prefer or easily recognize.

Theories of "Consolidation"

When elections and their surrounding freedoms are institutionalized, it might be said that polyarchy (or political democracy) is "consolidated," that is, likely to endure. This, jointly with the proviso of absence of veto powers over elected authorities, is the influential definition of "democratic consolidation" offered by Juan J. Linz, who calls it a state of affairs "in which none of the major political actors, parties, or organized interests, forces, or institutions consider that there is any alternative to democratic processes to gain power, and . . . no political institution or group has a claim to veto the action of democratically elected decision makers. . . . To put it simply, democracy must be seen as the 'only game in town.'"[11] This minimalist definition has important advantages. Still, I see little analytical gain in attaching the term "consolidated" to something that will probably though not certainly endure—"democracy" and "consolidation" are terms too polysemic to make a good pair.

Other authors offer more expanded definitions of democratic consolidation, many of them centered on the achievement of a high degree of "institutionalization."[12] Usually these definitions do not see elections as an institution.[13] They focus on complex organizations, basically the executive, parties, congress, and sometimes the judiciary. Many valuable studies have been conducted from this point of view. By the very logic of their assessment of many new polyarchies as noninstitutionalized, however, these studies presuppose, as their comparative yardstick, a generic and somewhat idealized view of the old polyarchies. The meaning of such a yardstick perplexes me: often it is unclear whether it is something like an average of characteristics observed within the set of old polyarchies, or an ideal type generated from some of these characteristics, or a generalization to the whole set of the characteristics of some of its members, or a normative statement of preferred traits. Furthermore, this mode of reasoning carries a strong teleological flavor. Cases that have not "arrived" at full institutionalization, or that do not seem to be moving in this direction, are seen as stunted, frozen, protractedly unconsolidated, and the like. Such a view presupposes that there are, or should be, factors working in favor of increased consolidation or institutionalization, but that countervailing "obstacles" stymie a process of change that otherwise would operate unfettered.[14] That some of these polyarchies have been in a state of "protracted unconsolidation"[15] for some 20 years suggests that there is something extremely odd about this kind of thinking. . . .

One way or the other polyarchies that are seen as unconsolidated, noninstitutionalized, or poorly institutionalized are defined negatively, for what they lack: the type and degree of institutionalization presumably achieved by old polyarchies. Yet negative definitions shift attention away from building typologies of polyarchies on the basis of the specific, positively described traits of each type.[16] Such typologies are needed, among other purposes, for assessing each type's likelihood of endurance, for exploring its patterns of change, and for clarifying the various dimensions on which issues of quality and performance of polyarchy may be discussed and researched.

There is no theory that would tell us why and how the new polyarchies that have institutionalized elections will "complete" their institutional set, or otherwise become "consolidated." All we can say at present is that, as long as elections are institutionalized, polyarchies are likely to endure. We can add the hypothesis that this likelihood is greater for polyarchies that are formally institutionalized. But this proposition is not terribly interesting unless we take into account other factors that most likely have strong independent effects on the survival chances of polyarchies.[17] Consequently, calling some polyarchies "consolidated" or "highly institutionalized" may be no more than saying that they are institutionalized in ways that one expects and of which one approves. Without a theory of how and why this may happen, it is at best premature to expect that newer polyarchies will or should become "consolidated" or "highly institutionalized." In any event, such a theory can only be elaborated on the basis of a positive description of the main traits of the pertinent cases.

The Importance of Informal Rules

Polyarchy is the happy result of centuries-long processes, mostly in countries in the global Northwest. In spite of many variations among these countries, polyarchy is embodied in an institutional package: a set of rules and institutions (many of them complex organizations) that is explicitly formalized in constitutions and auxiliary legislation. Rules are supposed to guide how individuals in institutions, and individuals interacting with institutions, behave. The extent to which behavior and expectations hew to or deviate from formal rules is difficult to gauge empirically. But when the fit is reasonably close, formal rules simplify our task; they are good predictors of behavior and expectations. In this case, one may conclude that all or most of the formal rules and institutions of polyarchy are fully, or close to fully, institutionalized.[18] When the fit is loose or practically nonexistent, we are confronted with the double task of describing actual behavior and discovering the (usually informal) rules that behavior and expectations do follow. Actors are as rational in these settings as in highly formalized ones, but the contours of their rationality cannot be traced without knowing the actual rules, and the common knowledge of these rules, that they follow. One may define this situation negatively, emphasizing the lack of fit between formal rules and observed behavior. As anthropologists have long known, however, this is no substitute for studying the actual rules that are being followed; nor does it authorize the assumption that somehow there is a tendency toward increasing compliance with formal rules. This is especially true when informal rules are widely shared and deeply rooted; in this case, it may be said that these rules (rather than the formal ones) are highly institutionalized.[19]

To some extent this also happens in the old polyarchies. The various laments, from all parts of the ideological spectrum, about the decay of democracy in these countries are largely a consequence of the visible and apparently increasing gap between formal rules and the behavior of all sorts of political actors. But the gap is even larger in many new polyarchies, where the formal rules about how political institutions are supposed to work are often poor guides to what actually happens.

Many new polyarchies do not lack institutionalization, but a fixation on highly formalized and complex organizations prevents us from seeing an extremely influential, informal, and sometimes concealed institution: clientelism and, more generally, particularism. For brevity's sake, I will put details and nuances aside[20] and use these terms to refer broadly to various sorts of nonuniversalistic relationships, ranging from hierarchical particularistic exchanges, patronage, nepotism, and favors to actions that, under the formal rules of the institutional package of polyarchy, would be considered corrupt.[21]

Particularism—like its counterparts, neopatrimonial[22] and delegative conceptions and practices of rule—is antagonistic to one of the main aspects of the full institutional package of polyarchy: the behavioral, legal, and normative distinction between a public and a private sphere. This distinction is an important aspect of the formal institutionalization of polyarchy. Individuals performing roles in political and state institutions are supposed to be guided not by particularistic motives but by universalistic orientations to some version of the public good. The boundaries between the public and the private are often blurred in the old polyarchies, but the very notion of the boundary is broadly accepted and, often, vigorously asserted when it seems breached by public officials acting from particularistic motives. Where particularism is pervasive, this notion is weaker, less widely held, and seldom enforced.

But polyarchy matters, even in the institutional spheres that, against their formal rules, are dominated by particularism. In congress, the judiciary, and some actions of the executive, rituals and discourses are performed as if the formal rules were the main guides of behavior. The consequences are twofold. On one side, by paying tribute to the formal rules, these rituals and discourses encourage demands that these rules be truly followed and that public-oriented governmental behavior prevail. On the other side, the blatant hypocrisy of many of these rituals and discourses breeds cynicism about the institutions of polyarchy, their incumbents, and "politicians" in general. As long as this second consequence is highly visible, particularism is taken for granted, and practiced as the main way of gaining and wielding political power. In such polyarchies, particularism is an important part of the regime.[23] Polyarchies are regimes, but not all polyarchies are the same kind of regime.

Here we see the ambiguity of the assertion made by Juan J. Linz, Adam Przeworski,[24] and others who argue that consolidation occurs when democracy becomes "the only game in town." It is clear that these authors are referring to the formal rules of polyarchy. More generally, even though they may not refer to "institutionalization," authors who limit themselves to the term "consolidation" also assert, more or less implicitly, the same close fit between formal rules and actual behavior.[25] For example, Przeworski argues that democratic consolidation occurs "when no one can imagine acting outside the democratic institutions." But this does not preclude the possibility that the games played "inside" the democratic institutions are different from the ones dictated by their formal rules. Przeworski also states: "To put it somewhat more technically, democracy is consolidated when compliance—acting within the institutional framework—constitutes the equilibrium of the decentralized strategies of all the relevant forces."[26] Clearly, Przeworski is assuming that there is only one equilibrium, the one generated by a close fit between formal rules and behavior. Yet however inferior they may be in terms of performances and outcomes that we value, the situations that I am describing may constitute an equilibrium, too.[27]

A Theoretical Limbo

If the main criterion for democratic consolidation or institutionalization is more or less explicitly a reasonably close fit between formal rules and actual behavior, then what of countries such as Italy, Japan, and India? These are long-enduring polyarchies where, by all indications, various forms of particularism are rampant. Yet these cases do not appear problematic in the literature I am discussing. That they are listed as "consolidated" (or, at least, not listed as "unconsolidated") suggests the strength—and the inconsistency—of this view. It attaches the label "consolidated" to cases that clearly do not fit its arguments but that have endured for a significantly longer period than the new polyarchies have so far. This is a typical paradigmatic anomaly. It deals with these cases by relegating them to a theoretical limbo,[28] as if, because they are somehow considered to be "consolidated," the big gaps between their formal rules and behavior were irrelevant. This is a pity, because variations that are theoretically and empirically important for the study of the whole set of existing polyarchies are thereby obscured.

Another confusing issue is raised by the requirement of "legitimacy" that some definitions of consolidation add. Who must accept formal democratic rules, and how deep must this acceptance run? Here, the literature oscillates between holding that only certain leaders need adhere to democratic principles and arguing that most of the country's people should be democrats, and between requiring normative acceptance of these principles and resting content with a mere perception that there is no feasible alternative to democracy. The scope of this adherence is also problematic: Is it enough that it refers to the formal institutions of the regime, or should it extend to other areas, such as a broadly shared democratic political culture?

Given these conceptual quandaries, it is not surprising that it is impossible clearly to specify when a democracy has become "consolidated." To illustrate this point, consider the "tests" of democratic consolidation that Gunther, Diamandouros, and Puhle propose. These tests supposedly help them to differentiate the consolidated

Southern European cases from the unconsolidated Latin American, as well as East European and Asian, ones. The indicators that "may constitute evidence that a regime is consolidated" are: 1) "alternation in power between former rivals";[29] 2) "continued widespread support and stability during times of extreme economic hardship"; 3) "successful defeat and punishment of a handful of strategically placed rebels"; 4) "regime stability in the face of a radical restructuring of the party system"; and 5) "the absence of a politically significant antisystem party or social movement."

With respect to Latin America, it bears commenting in relation to each of these points that: 1) alternations in government through peaceful electoral processes have occurred in Latin America as frequently as in Southern Europe; 2) in the former, support for regime stability has persisted—in Argentina, Brazil, and Bolivia, among other countries—even in the face of far more acute recessions than Southern Europe has seen, and in the midst of quadruple-digit inflation; 3) the record of punishment is poor, albeit with important exceptions in both regions; 4) even when thinking about Italy today, it is hard to imagine party-system restructurings more radical than the ones that occurred in Bolivia, Brazil, and Ecuador; and 5) "antisystem" political parties are as absent from the Latin American as from the Southern European polyarchies. The indicators of democratic consolidation invoked by these authors (and shared by many others) suffer from extreme ambiguity.[30] Finally, one might note that their argument points toward a *reductio ad absurdum*, for one could in following its logic argue that Latin America's polyarchies are actually "more consolidated" because they have endured more "severe tests" than their Southern European counterparts.

Polyarchies, Particularism, and Accountability

It almost goes without saying that all actual cases exhibit various combinations of universalism and particularism across various relevant dimensions. This observation, however, should not lead to the Procrustean solution of lumping all cases together; differences in the degree to which each case approximates either pole may justify their separate classification and analysis. Of course, one may for various reasons prefer a political process that adheres quite closely to the formal rules of the full institutional package of polyarchy. Yet there exist polyarchies— some of them as old as Italy, India, and Japan, or in Latin America, Colombia, and Venezuela—that endure even though they do not function as their formal rules dictate. To understand these cases we need to know what games are really being played, and under what rules.

In many countries of the global East and South, there is an old and deep split between the *pays réel* and the *pays légal*. Today, with many of these countries claiming to be democracies and adopting a constitutional framework, the persistence and high visibility of this split may not threaten the survival of their polyarchies—but neither does it facilitate overcoming the split. Institutions are resilient, especially when they have deep historical roots; particularism is no exception. Particularism is a permanent feature of human society; only recently, and only in some places and institutional sites, has it been tempered by universalistic norms and rules. In many new polyarchies, particularism vigorously inhabits most formal political institutions, yet the incumbency of top government posts is decided by the universalistic process of fairly counting each vote as one. This may sound paradoxical but it is not; it means that these are polyarchies, but they are neither the ones that the theory of democracy had in mind as it grew out of reflection on the political regimes of the global Northwest, nor what many studies of democratization assume that a democracy should be or become.

That some polyarchies are informally institutionalized has important consequences. Here I want to stress one that is closely related to the blurring of the boundary between the private and the public spheres: accountability, a crucial aspect of formally institutionalized polyarchy, is seriously hindered. To be sure, the institutionalization of elections means that retrospective electoral accountability exists, and a reasonably free press and various active segments of society see to it that some egregiously unlawful acts of government are exposed (if seldom punished). Polyarchy, even if not formally institutionalized, marks a huge improvement over authoritarian regimes of all kinds. What is largely lacking, however, is another dimension of accountability, which I call "horizontal." By this I mean the controls that state agencies are supposed to exercise over other state agencies. All formally institutionalized polyarchies include various agencies endowed with legally defined authority to sanction unlawful or otherwise inappropriate actions by other state agents. This is an often-overlooked expression of the rule of law in one of the areas where it is hardest to implant, that is, over state agents, especially high-ranking officials. The basic idea is that formal institutions have well-defined, legally established boundaries that delimit the proper exercise of their authority, and that there are state agencies empowered to control and redress trespasses of these boundaries by any official or agency. These boundaries are closely related to the private-public boundary, in that those who perform public roles are supposed to follow universalistic and public-oriented rules, rather than their own particular interests. Even though its actual functioning is far from perfect, this network of boundaries and accountabilities is an important part of the formal institutionalization of the full package of polyarchy.[31]

By contrast, little horizontal accountability exists in most new polyarchies. Furthermore, in many of them the executive makes strenuous, and often successful, efforts to erode whatever horizontal accountability does exist. The combination of institutionalized elections, particularism as a dominant political institution, and a big gap between the formal rules and the way most political institutions actually work makes for a strong affinity with delegative, not representative, notions of political authority. By this I mean a caesaristic, plebiscitarian executive that once elected sees itself as empowered to govern the country as it deems fit. Reinforced by the urgencies of severe socioeconomic crises and consonant with old *volkisch*, nonindividualistic conceptions of politics, delegative practices strive headlong against formal political institutionalization; congress, the judiciary, and various state agencies of control are seen as hindrances placed in the way of the proper discharge of the tasks that the voters have delegated to the executive. The executive's efforts to weaken these institutions, invade their legal authority, and lower their prestige are a logical corollary of this view.[32] On the other hand, as Max Weber warned, institutions deprived of real power and responsibility tend to act in ways that seem to confirm the reasons adduced for this deprivation. In the cases that concern us here, particularism becomes even more rampant in congress and parties, courts ostensibly fail to administer justice, and agencies of control are eliminated or reduced to passivity. This context encourages the further erosion of legally established authority, renders the boundary between public and private even more tenuous, and creates enormous temptations for corruption.

In this sea of particularism and blurred boundaries, why does the universalistic process of fair and competitive elections survive? Governments willing to tamper with laws are hardly solid guarantors of the integrity of electoral processes. Part of the answer, at least with respect to elections to top national positions, is close international attention and wide reporting abroad of electoral irregularities. Fair elections are the main, if not the only, characteristic that certifies countries as democratic before other governments and international opinion. Nowadays this certification has important advantages for countries and for those who govern them. Within the country, elections are a moment when something similar to horizontal accountability operates: parties other than the one in government are present at the polling places, sharing an interest in preventing fraud. Elections create a sharp focus on political matters and on the symbols and rituals that surround the act of voting. At this moment, the citizens' sense of basic fairness manifests itself with special intensity. Violations are likely to be immediately reported. Faced with the protests that might ensue and their repercussions in the international media, and considering the further damage that would come from trying to impose obviously tainted results, most governments are willing to run the risks inherent in fair and competitive elections.

Pervasive particularism, delegative rule, and weak horizontal accountability have at least two serious drawbacks. The first is that the generalized lack of control enables old authoritarian practices to reassert themselves.[33] The second is that, in countries that inaugurated polyarchy under conditions of sharp and increasing inequality, the making and implementation of policy becomes further biased in favor of highly organized and economically powerful interests.

In the countries that occupy us here, the more properly political, *democratic* freedoms are effective: uncoerced voting; freedom of opinion, movement, and association; and others already listed. But for large sections of the population, basic *liberal* freedoms are denied or recurrently trampled. The rights of battered women to sue their husbands and of peasants to obtain a fair trial against their landlords, the inviolability of domiciles in poor neighborhoods, and in general the right of the poor and various minorities to decent treatment and fair access to public agencies and courts are often denied. The effectiveness of the whole ensemble of rights, democratic and liberal, makes for full civil and political citizenship. In many of the new polyarchies, individuals are citizens only in relation to the one institution that functions in a manner close to what its formal rules prescribe—elections. As for full citizenship, only the members of a privileged minority enjoy it.[34] Formally institutionalized polyarchies exhibit various mixes of democracy, liberalism, and republicanism (understood as a view that concurs with liberalism in tracing a clear public-private distinction, but that adds an ennobling and personally demanding conception of participation in the public sphere). Informally institutionalized polyarchies are democratic, in the sense just defined; when they add, as they often do, the plebiscitarian component of delegative rule, they are also strongly majoritarian. But their liberal and republican components are extremely weak.

Notes

For their comments on an earlier version of this text, I am grateful to Michael Coppedge, Gabriela Ippolito-O'Donnell, Scott Mainwaring, Sebastián Mazzuca, Peter Moody, Gerardo Munck, and Adam Przeworski.

1. Reflecting the lack of clearly established criteria in the literature, David Collier and Steven Levitsky have inventoried and interestingly discussed the more than one hundred qualifiers that have been attached to the term "democracy." Many such qualifiers are intended to indicate that the respective cases are in some sense lacking the full attributes of democracy as defined by each author. See Collier and Levitsky, "Democracy 'With Adjectives': Finding Conceptual Order in Recent Comparative Research" (unpubl. ms., University of California–Berkeley, Political Science Department, 1995).

2. I have tried unsuccessfully to find terms appropriate to what the literature refers to as highly institutionalized versus noninstitutionalized (or poorly institutionalized), or as consolidated versus unconsolidated democracies, with most of the old polyarchies belonging to the first terms of these pairs, and most of the new ones to the second. For reasons that will be clear below, I have opted for labeling the first group "formally institutionalized" and the second "informally institutionalized," but not without misgivings: in the first set of countries, many things happen outside formally prescribed institutional rules, while the second set includes one highly formalized institution, elections.

3. This list is from Robert Dahl, *Democracy and Its Critics* (New Haven: Yale University Press, 1989), 221; the reader may want to examine further details of these attributes, discussed by Dahl in this book.

4. See especially J. Samuel Valenzuela, "Democratic Consolidation in Post-Transitional Settings: Notion, Process, and Facilitating Conditions," in Scott Mainwaring, Guillermo O'Donnell, and J. Samuel Valenzuela, eds., *Issues in Democratic Consolidation: The New South American Democracies in Comparative Perspective* (Notre Dame, Ind.: University of Notre Dame Press, 1992), 57–104; and Philippe C. Schmitter and Terry Lynn Karl, "What Democracy Is . . . and Is Not," *Journal of Democracy* 2 (Summer 1991): 75–88.

5. See Terry Lynn Karl, "The Hybrid Regimes of Central America," *Journal of Democracy* 6 (July 1995): 73–86; and "Imposing Consent? Electoralism vs. Democratization in El Salvador," in Paul Drake and Eduardo Silva, eds., *Elections and Democratization in Latin America, 1980–85* (San Diego: Center for Iberian and Latin American Studies, 1986), 9–36.

6. See especially Juan J. Linz and Alfred Stepan, *Problems of Democratic Transition and Consolidation: Southern Europe, South America, and Post-Communist Europe* (Baltimore: Johns Hopkins University Press, 1996); and Philippe Schmitter, "Dangers and Dilemmas of Democracy," *Journal of Democracy* 5 (April 1994): 57–74.

7. For a useful listing of these institutional variations, see Schmitter and Karl, "What Democracy Is . . . and Is Not."

8. For a more detailed discussion of institutions, see my "Delegative Democracy," *Journal of Democracy* 5 (January 1994): 56–69.

9. The term "reasonable" is admittedly ambiguous. Nowhere are these freedoms completely uncurtailed, if by nothing else than the political consequences of social inequality. By "reasonable" I mean that there are neither de jure prohibitions on these freedoms nor systematic and usually successful efforts by the government or private actors to annul them.

10. On the other hand, elections can be made more authentically competitive by, say, measures that diminish the advantages of incumbents or of economically powerful parties. These are, of course, important issues. But the point I want to make at the moment is that these differences obtain among countries that already qualify as polyarchies.

11. Juan J. Linz, "Transitions to Democracy," *Washington Quarterly* 13 (1990): 156. The assertion about "the only game in town" entails some ambiguities that I discuss below.

12. Even though most definitions of democratic consolidation are centered around "institutionalization" (whether explicitly or implicitly, by asserting acceptance or approval of democratic institutions and their formal rules), they offer a wide variety of additional criteria. My own count in a recent review of the literature is twelve; see Doh Chull Shin, "On the Third Wave of Democratization: A Synthesis and Evaluation of Recent Theory and Research," *World Politics* 47 (October 1994): 135–70.

13. Even though he does not use this language, an exception is the definition of democratic consolidation offered by J. Samuel Valenzuela, which is centered in what I call here the institutionalization of elections and the absence of veto powers; see his "Democratic Consolidation in Post-Transitional Settings," 69.

14. It is high time for self-criticism. The term "stunted" I used jointly with Scott Mainwaring and J. Samuel Valenzuela in the introduction to our *Issues in Democratic Consolidation*, 11. Furthermore, in my chapter in the same volume (pp. 17–56), I offer a nonminimalist definition of democratic consolidation, and propose the concept of a "second transition," from a democratically elected government to a consolidated democratic regime. These concepts partake of the teleology I criticize here. This teleological view is homologous to the one used by many modernization studies in the 1950s and 1960s; it was abundantly, but evidently not decisively, criticized at the time. For a critique of the concept of "democratic consolidation" that is convergent with mine, see Ben Ross Schneider, "Democratic Consolidations: Some Broad Comparisons and Sweeping Arguments," *Latin American Research Review* 30 (1995): 215–34; Schneider concludes by warning against "the fallacy of excessive universalism" (p. 231).

15. Philippe C. Schmitter with Terry Lynn Karl, "The Conceptual Travels of Transitologists and Consolidologists: How Far to the East Should They Attempt to Go?" *Slavic Review* 63 (Spring 1994): 173–85.

16. We should remember that several typologies have been proposed for formally institutionalized polyarchies; see especially Arend Lijphart, *Democracies: Patterns of Majoritarian and Consensus Government in Twenty-one Countries* (New Haven: Yale University Press, 1984). This work has been extremely useful in advancing knowledge about these polyarchies, which underscores the need for similar efforts on the now greatly expanded whole set of polyarchies. For an attempt in this direction see Carlos Acuña and William Smith, "Future Politico-Economic Scenarios for Latin America," in William Smith, Carlos Acuña, and Eduardo Gamarra, eds., *Democracy, Markets, and Structural Reform in Latin America* (New Brunswick, N.J.: Transaction, 1993), 1–28.

17. Adam Przeworski and his collaborators found that higher economic development and a parliamentary regime increase the average survival rate of polyarchies. These are important findings, but the authors have not tested the impacts of socioeconomic inequality and of the kind of informal institutionalization that I discuss below. Pending further research, it is impossible to assess the causal direction and weight of all these variables. I suspect that high socioeconomic inequality has a close relationship with informal institutionalization. But we do not know if either or both, directly or indirectly, affect the chances of survival of polyarchy, or if they might cancel the effect of economic development that Przeworski et al. found. See Adam Przeworski and Fernando Limongi, "Modernization: Theories and Facts" (Working Paper No. 4, Chicago Center for Democracy, University of Chicago, November 1994).

18. A topic that does not concern me here is the extent to which formal rules are institutionalized across various old polyarchies and, within them, across various issue areas, though the variations seem quite important on both counts.

19. The lore of many countries is filled with jokes about the naive foreigner or the native "sucker" who gets into trouble by following the formal rules of a given situation. I have explored some of these issues with reference to Brazil and Argentina in "Democracia en la Argentina: Micro y macro" (Working Paper No. 2, Helen Kellogg Institute for International Studies, Notre Dame, Ind., 1983); "Y a mí qué me importa? Notas sobre sociabilidad y política en Argentina y Brasil" (Working Paper No. 9, Helen Kellogg Institute for International Studies, Notre Dame, Ind., 1984); and "Micro-escenas de la privatización de lo público en Brasil" (Working Paper No. 21, with commentaries by Roberto DaMatta and J. Samuel Valenzuela, Helen Kellogg Institute for International Studies, Notre Dame, Ind., 1989).

20. For the purposes of the generic argument presented in this essay, and not without hesitation because of its vagueness, from now on I will use the term "particularism" to refer to these phenomena. On the contemporary relevance of clientelism, see Luis Roniger and Ayse Gunes-Ayata, eds., *Democracy, Clientelism, and Civil Society* (Boulder, Colo.: Lynne Rienner, 1994). For studies focused on Latin America that are germane to my argument, see especially Roberto DaMatta, *A Case e a rua: Espaco, cidadania, mulher e morte no Brasil* (São Paulo: Editora Brasiliense, 1985); Jonathan Fox, "The Difficult Transition from Clientelism to Citizenship," *World Politics* 46 (January 1994): 151–84; Francis Hagopian, "The Compromised Transition: The Political Class in the Brazilian Transition," in Mainwaring et al., *Issues in Democratic Consolidation*, 243–93; and Scott Mainwaring, "Brazilian Party Underdevelopment in Comparative Perspective," *Political Science Quarterly* 107 (Winter 1992–93): 677–707. These and other studies show that particularism and its concomitants are not ignored by good field researchers. But, attesting to the paradigmatic force of the prevalent views on democratization, in this literature the rich data and findings emerging from such case studies are not conceptually processed as an intrinsic part of the *problématique* of democratization, or are seen as just "obstacles" interposed in the way of its presumed direction of change.

21. Particularistic relationships can be found in formally institutionalized polyarchies, of course. I am pointing here to differences of degree that seem large enough to require conceptual recognition. One important indication of these differences is the extraordinary leniency with which, in informally institutionalized polyarchies, political leaders, most of public opinion, and even courts treat situations that in the other polyarchies would be considered as entailing very severe conflicts of interest.

22. For a discussion of neopatrimonialism, see my "Transitions, Continuities, and Paradoxes," in Mainwaring et al., *Issues in Democratic Consolidation*, 17–56. An interesting recent discussion of neopatrimonialism is Jonathan Hartlyn's "Crisis-Ridden Elections (Again) in the Dominican Republic: Neopatrimonialism, Presidentialism, and Weak Electoral Oversight," *Journal of Interamerican and World Affairs* 34 (Winter 1994): 91–144.

23. By "regime" I mean "the set of effectively prevailing patterns (not necessarily legally formalized) that establish the modalities of recruitment and access to governmental roles, and the permissible resources that form the basis for expectations of access to such roles," as defined in my *Bureaucratic Authoritarianism: Argentina, 1966–1973, in Comparative Perspective* (Berkeley: University of California Press, 1988), 6.

24. Adam Przeworski, *Democracy and the Market: Political and Economic Reforms in Eastern Europe and Latin America* (Cambridge: Cambridge University Press, 1991).

25. See, among many others that could be cited (some transcribed in Shin, "On the Third Wave of Democratization"), the definition of democratic consolidation proposed by Richard Gunther, P. Nikiforos Diamandouros, and Hans-Jürgen Puhle, eds., *The Politics of Democratic Consolidation: Southern Europe in Comparative Perspective* (Baltimore: Johns Hopkins University Press, 1995), 3: "the achievement of substantial attitudinal support for and behavioral compliance with the new democratic institutions and the rules which they establish." A broader but equivalent definition is offered four pages later.

26. Przeworski, *Democracy and the Market*, 26.

27. In another influential discussion, Philippe C. Schmitter, although he does not use this language, expresses a similar view of democratic consolidation; see his "Dangers and Dilemmas of Democracy," *Journal of Democracy* 5 (April 1994): 56–74. Schmitter begins by asserting, "In South America, Eastern Europe, and Asia the specter haunting the transition is . . . nonconsolidation. . . . These countries are 'doomed' to remain democratic almost by default." He acknowledges that the attributes of polyarchy may hold in these countries—but these "patterns never quite crystallize" (pp. 60–61). To say that democracy exists "almost by default" (i.e., is negatively defined) and is not "crystallized" (i.e., not formally institutionalized) is another way of stating the generalized view that I am discussing.

28. An exception is Gunther et al., *Politics of Democratic Consolidation*, where Italy is one of the four cases studied. But the way they deal with recent events in Italy is exemplary of the conceptual problems I am discussing. They assert that in Italy "several important partial regimes . . . were challenged, became deconsolidated, and entered into a significant process of restructuring beginning in 1991" (p. 19). On the same page, the reader learns that these partial regimes include nothing less than "the electoral system, the party system, and the structure of the state itself." (Added to this list later on is "the basic nature of executive-legislative relations" [p. 394].) Yet the "Italian democracy remains strong and resilient"—after practically every important aspect of its regime, and even of the state, became "deconsolidated" (p. 412). If the authors mean that, in spite of a severe crisis, the Italian polyarchy is likely to endure, I agree.

29. Actually, the authors are ambiguous about this first "test." Just before articulating their list of tests with this one at its head, they assert that they "reject [peaceful alternation in government between parties that were once bitterly opposed] as a *prerequisite* for regarding a regime as consolidated" (emphasis added). See Gunther et al., *Politics of Democratic Consolidation*, 12.

30. In the text on which I am commenting, the problem is further compounded by the use of categories such as "partial consolidation" and "sufficient consolidation" (which the authors say preceded "full consolidation" in some Southern European cases). They even speak of a stage of "democratic persistence" that is supposed to follow the achievement of "full [democratic] consolidation."

31. I may have sounded naive in my earlier comments about how individuals performing public roles are supposed to be guided by universalistic orientations to some version of the public good. Now I can add that, as the authors of the *Federalist Papers* knew, this is not only, or even mostly, a matter of the subjective intentions of these individuals. It is to a large extent contingent on institutional arrangements of control and accountability, and on expectations built around these arrangements, that furnish incentives (including the threats of severe sanctions and public discredit) for that kind of behavior. That these incentives are often insufficient should not be allowed to blur the difference with cases where the institutional arrangements are nonexistent or ineffective; these situations freely invite the enormous temptations that always come with holding political power. I wish to thank Adam Przeworski and Michael Coppedge for raising this point in private communications.

32. The reader has surely noticed that I am referring to countries that have presidentialist regimes and that, consequently, I am glossing over the arguments, initiated by Juan J. Linz and followed up by a number of other scholars, about the advantages of parliamentarism over the presidentialist regimes that characterize Latin America. Although these arguments convince me in the abstract, because of the very characteristics I am depicting I am skeptical about the practical consequences of attempting to implant parliamentarism in these countries.

33. For analyses of some of these situations, see Paulo Sérgio Pinheiro, "The Legacy of Authoritarianism in Democratic Brazil," in Stuart S. Nagel, ed., *Latin American Development and Public Policy* (New York: St. Martin's, 1995), 237–53; and Martha K. Huggins, ed., *Vigilantism and the State in Modern Latin America: Essays on Extralegal Violence* (New York: Praeger, 1991). See also the worrisome analysis, based on Freedom House data, that Larry Diamond presents in his "Democracy in Latin America: Degrees, Illusions, and Directions for Consolidation," in Tom Farer, ed., *Beyond Sovereignty: Collectively Defending Democracy in the Americas* (Baltimore: Johns Hopkins University Press, 1996). In recent years, the Freedom House indices reveal, more Latin American countries have regressed rather than advanced. For a discussion of various aspects of the resulting obliteration of the rule of law and

weakening of citizenship, see Guillermo O'Donnell, "On the State, Democratization, and Some Conceptual Problems: A Latin American View with Glances at Some Post-Communist Countries," *World Development* 21 (1993): 1355–69.

34. There is a huge adjacent theme that I will not discuss here: the linkage of these problems with widespread poverty and, even more, with deep inequalities of various sorts.

 4.7

The End of the Transition Paradigm

Thomas Carothers

In the 1970s and 1980s, it was widely believed that more and more regimes around the world were becoming democratic. (For an influential claim along these lines, see the selection by Fukuyama, 1.1.) In the 1990s, however, scholars began to express doubts about this trend. (See O'Donnell, 4.6., and Levitsky and Way, 2.3.) In the present selection, Carothers proposes that we should abandon the claim that democracy will be the wave of the future.

What accounts for the increasing doubts about the spread of democracy? Could a trend to democracy recur? What might produce such a trend in the future?

In the last quarter of the twentieth century, trends in seven different regions converged to change the political landscape of the world: 1) the fall of right-wing authoritarian regimes in Southern Europe in the mid-1970s; 2) the replacement of military dictatorships by elected civilian governments across Latin America from the late 1970s through the late 1980s; 3) the decline of authoritarian rule in parts of East and South Asia starting in the mid-1980s; 4) the collapse of communist regimes in Eastern Europe at the end of the 1980s; 5) the breakup of the Soviet Union and the establishment of 15 post-Soviet republics in 1991; 6) the decline of one-party regimes in many parts of sub-Saharan Africa

Thomas Carothers, "The End of the Transition Paradigm," *Journal of Democracy* 13, No. 1 (Jan. 2002), pp. 5–12, 13–18. © National Endowment for Democracy and The Johns Hopkins University Press. Reprinted with permission of The Johns Hopkins University Press.

in the first half of the 1990s; and 7) a weak but recognizable liberalizing trend in some Middle Eastern countries in the 1990s.

The causes, shape, and pace of these different trends varied considerably. But they shared a dominant characteristic—simultaneous movement in at least several countries in each region away from dictatorial rule toward more liberal and often more democratic governance. And though differing in many ways, these trends influenced and to some extent built on one another. As a result, they were considered by many observers, especially in the West, as component parts of a larger whole, a global democratic trend that thanks to Samuel Huntington has widely come to be known as the "third wave" of democracy.[1]

This striking tide of political change was seized upon with enthusiasm by the U.S. government and the broader U.S. foreign policy community. As early as the mid-1980s, President Ronald Reagan, Secretary of State George Shultz, and other high-level U.S. officials were referring regularly to "the worldwide democratic revolution." During the 1980s, an active array of governmental, quasi-governmental, and nongovernmental organizations devoted to promoting democracy abroad sprang into being. This new democracy-promotion community had a pressing need for an analytic framework to conceptualize and respond to the ongoing political events. Confronted with the initial parts of the third wave—democratization in Southern Europe, Latin America, and a few countries in Asia (especially the Philippines)—the U.S. democracy community rapidly embraced an analytic model of democratic transition. It was derived principally from their own interpretation of the patterns of democratic change taking place, but also to a lesser extent from the early works of the emergent academic field of "transitology," above all the seminal work of Guillermo O'Donnell and Philippe Schmitter.[2]

As the third wave spread to Eastern Europe, the Soviet Union, sub-Saharan Africa, and elsewhere in the 1990s, democracy promoters extended this model as a universal paradigm for understanding democratization. It became ubiquitous in U.S. policy circles as a way of talking about, thinking about, and designing interventions in processes of political change around the world. And it stayed remarkably constant despite many variations in those patterns of political change and a stream of increasingly diverse scholarly views about the course and nature of democratic transitions.[3]

The transition paradigm has been somewhat useful during a time of momentous and often surprising political upheaval in the world. But it is increasingly clear that reality is no longer conforming to the model. Many countries that policy makers and aid practitioners persist in calling "transitional" are not in transition to democracy, and of the democratic transitions that are under way, more than a few are not following the model. Sticking with the paradigm beyond its useful life is retarding evolution in the field of democratic assistance and is leading policy makers astray in other ways. It is time to recognize that the transition paradigm has outlived its usefulness and to look for a better lens.

Core Assumptions

Five core assumptions define the transition paradigm. The first, which is an umbrella for all the others, is that any country moving *away* from dictatorial rule can be considered a country in transition *toward* democracy. Especially in the first half of the 1990s, when political change accelerated in many regions, numerous policy makers and aid practitioners reflexively labeled any formerly authoritarian country that was attempting some political liberalization as a "transitional country." The set of "transitional countries" swelled dramatically, and nearly 100 countries (approximately 20 in Latin America, 25 in Eastern Europe and the former Soviet Union, 30 in sub-Saharan Africa, 10 in Asia, and 5 in the Middle East) were thrown into the conceptual pot of the transition paradigm. Once so labeled, their political life was automatically analyzed in terms of their movement toward or away from democracy, and they were held up to the implicit expectations of the paradigm, as detailed below. . . .

The second assumption is that democratization tends to unfold in a set sequence of stages. First there occurs the *opening,* a period of democratic ferment and political liberalization in which cracks appear in the ruling dictatorial regime, with the most prominent fault line being that between hardliners and softliners. There follows the *breakthrough*—the collapse of the regime and the rapid emergence of a new, democratic system, with the coming to power of a new government through national elections and the establishment of a democratic institutional structure, often through the promulgation of a new constitution. After the transition comes *consolidation,* a slow but purposeful process in which democratic forms are transformed into democratic substance through the reform of state institutions, the regularization of elections, the strengthening of civil society, and the overall habituation of the society to the new democratic "rules of the game."

Democracy activists admit that it is not inevitable that transitional countries will move steadily on this assumed path from opening and breakthrough to consolidation. Transitional countries, they say, can and do go backward or stagnate as well as move forward along the path. Yet even the deviations from the assumed sequence that they are willing to acknowledge are defined in terms of the path itself. The options are all cast in terms of the speed and direction with which countries move on the path, not in terms of movement that does not conform with the path at all. And at least in the peak years of the third wave, many democracy enthusiasts clearly believed that, while the success of the dozens of new transitions was not assured, democratization was in some important sense a natural process, one that was likely to flourish once the initial breakthrough occurred. . . .

Related to the idea of a core sequence of democratization is the third assumption—the belief in the determinative importance of elections. Democracy promoters have not been guilty—as critics often charge—of believing that elections equal democracy. For years they have advocated and pursued a much broader range of assistance programs than just elections-focused efforts. Nevertheless, they have tended to hold very high expectations for what the establishment of regular, genuine elections will do for democratization. Not only will elections give new postdictatorial governments democratic legitimacy, they believe, but the elections will serve to broaden and deepen political participation and the democratic accountability of the state to its citizens. In other words, it has been assumed that in attempted transitions to democracy, elections will be not just a foundation stone but a key generator over time of further democratic reforms.

A fourth assumption is that the underlying conditions in transitional countries—their economic level, political history, institutional legacies, ethnic make-up, sociocultural traditions, or other "structural" features—will not be major factors in either the onset or the outcome of the transition process. A remarkable characteristic of the early period of the third wave was that democracy seemed to be breaking out in the most unlikely and unexpected places, whether Mongolia, Albania, or Mauritania. All that seemed to be necessary for democratization was a decision by a country's political elites to move toward democracy and an ability on the part of those elites to fend off the contrary actions of remaining antidemocratic forces. . . .

Fifth, the transition paradigm rests on the assumption that the democratic transitions making up the third wave are being built on coherent, functioning states. The process of democratization is assumed to include some redesign of state institutions—such as the creation of new electoral institutions, parliamentary reform, and judicial reform—but as a modification of already functioning states. As they arrived at their frameworks for understanding democratization, democracy aid practitioners did not give significant attention to the challenge of a society trying to democratize while it is grappling with the reality of building a state from scratch or coping with an existent but largely nonfunctional state. This did not appear to be an issue in Southern Europe or Latin America, the two regions that served as the experiential basis for the formation of the transition paradigm. To the extent that democracy promoters did consider the possibility of state-building as part of the transition process, they assumed that democracy-building and state-building would be mutually reinforcing endeavors or even two sides of the same coin.

Into the Gray Zone

We turn then from the underlying assumptions of the paradigm to the record of experience. . . .

Of the nearly 100 countries considered as "transitional" in recent years, only a relatively small number—probably fewer than 20—are clearly en route to becoming successful, well-functioning democracies or at least have made some democratic progress and still enjoy a positive dynamic of democratization.[4] The leaders of the group are found primarily in Central Europe and the Baltic region—Poland, Hungary, the Czech Republic, Estonia, and Slovenia—though there are a few in South America and East Asia, notably Chile, Uruguay, and Taiwan. Those that have made somewhat less progress but appear to be still advancing include Slovakia, Romania, Bulgaria, Mexico, Brazil, Ghana, the Philippines, and South Korea.

By far the majority of third-wave countries have not achieved relatively well-functioning democracy or do not seem to be deepening or advancing whatever democratic progress they have made. In a small number of countries, initial political openings have clearly failed and authoritarian regimes have resolidified, as in Uzbekistan, Turkmenistan, Belarus, and Togo. Most of the "transitional countries," however, are neither dictatorial nor clearly headed toward democracy. They have entered a political gray zone.[5] They have some attributes of democratic political life, including at least limited political space for opposition parties and independent civil society, as well as regular elections and democratic constitutions. Yet they suffer from serious democratic deficits, often including poor representation of citizens' interests, low levels of political participation beyond voting, frequent abuse of the law by government officials, elections of uncertain legitimacy, very low levels of public confidence in state institutions, and persistently poor institutional performance by the state.

As the number of countries falling in between outright dictatorship and well-established liberal democracy has swollen, political analysts have proffered an array of "qualified democracy" terms to characterize them, including semi-democracy, formal democracy, electoral democracy, façade democracy, pseudo-democracy, weak democracy, partial democracy, illiberal democracy, and virtual democracy.[6] Some of these terms, such as "façade democracy" and "pseudo-democracy," apply only to a fairly specific subset of gray-zone cases. Other terms, such as "weak democracy" and "partial democracy," are intended to have much broader applicability. Useful though these terms can be, especially when rooted in probing analysis such as O'Donnell's work on "delegative democracy," they share a significant liability: By describing countries in the gray zone as types of democracies, analysts are in effect trying to apply the transition paradigm to the very countries whose political evolution is calling that paradigm into question.[7] Most of the "qualified democracy" terms are used to characterize countries as being stuck somewhere on the assumed democratization sequence, usually at the start of the consolidation phase. . . .

The Crash of Assumptions

Taken together, the political trajectories of most third-wave countries call into serious doubt the transition paradigm. This is apparent if we revisit the major assumptions underlying the paradigm in light of the above analysis.

First, the almost automatic assumption of democracy promoters during the peak years of the third wave that any country moving away from dictatorship was "in transition to democracy" has often been inaccurate and misleading. Some of those countries have hardly democratized at all. Many have taken on a smattering of democratic features but show few signs of democratizing much further and are certainly not following any predictable democratization script. The most common political patterns to date among the "transitional countries"— feckless pluralism and dominant-power politics—include elements of democracy but should be understood as alternative directions, not way stations to liberal democracy. The persistence in official U.S. democracy-promotion circles of using transitional language to characterize countries that in no way conform to any democratization paradigm borders in some case on the surreal—including not just the case of Congo cited above but many others, such as Moldova ("Moldova's democratic transition continues to progress steadily"), Zambia ("Zambia is . . . moving steadily toward . . . the creation of a viable multiparty democracy"), Cambodia ("policy successes in Cambodia towards democracy and improved governance within the past 18 months are numerous"), and Guinea ("Guinea has made significant strides toward building a democratic society").[8] The continued use of the transition paradigm constitutes a dangerous habit of trying to impose a simplistic and often incorrect conceptual order on an empirical tableau of considerable complexity.

Second, not only is the general label and concept of "transitional country" unhelpful, but the assumed sequence of stages of democratization is defied by the record of experience. Some of the most encouraging cases of democratization in recent years—such as Taiwan, South Korea, and Mexico—did not go through the paradigmatic process of democratic breakthrough followed rapidly by national elections and a new democratic institutional framework. Their political evolutions were defined by an almost opposite phenomenon—extremely gradual, incremental processes of liberalization with an organized political opposition (not softliners in the regime) pushing for change across successive elections and finally winning. And in many of the countries that did go through some version of what appeared to be a democratic breakthrough, the assumed sequence of changes—first settling constitutive issues then working through second-order reforms—has not held. Constitutive issues have reemerged at unpredictable times, upending what are supposed to be later stages of transition, as in the recent political crises in Ecuador, the Central African Republic, and Chad.

Moreover, the various assumed component processes of consolidation—political party development, civil society strengthening, judicial reform, and media development—almost never conform to the technocratic ideal of rational sequences on which the indicator frameworks and strategic objectives of democracy promoters are built. Instead they are chaotic processes of change that go backwards and sideways as much as forward, and do not do so in any regular manner.

The third assumption of the transition paradigm—the notion that achieving regular, genuine elections will not only confer democratic legitimacy on new governments but continuously deepen political participation and democratic accountability—has often come up short. In many "transitional countries," reasonably regular, genuine elections are held but political participation beyond voting remains shallow and governmental accountability is weak. The wide gulf between political elites and citizens in many of these countries turns out to be rooted in structural conditions, such as the concentration of wealth or certain sociocultural traditions, that elections themselves do not overcome. It is also striking how often electoral competition does little to stimulate the renovation or development of political parties in many gray-zone countries. Such profound pathologies as highly personalistic parties, transient and shifting parties, or stagnant patronage-based politics appear to be able to coexist for sustained periods with at least somewhat legitimate processes of political pluralism and competition. . . .

Fourth, ever since "preconditions for democracy" were enthusiastically banished in the heady early days of the third wave, a contrary reality—the fact that various structural conditions clearly weigh heavily in shaping political outcomes—has been working its way back in. Looking at the more successful recent cases of democratization, for example, which tend to be found in Central Europe, the Southern Cone, or East Asia, it is clear that relative economic wealth, as well as past experience with political pluralism, contributes to the chances for democratic success. And looking comparatively within regions, whether in the former communist world or sub-Saharan Africa, it is evident that the specific institutional legacies from predecessor regimes strongly affect the outcomes of attempted transitions. . . .

Fifth, state-building has been a much larger and more problematic issue than originally envisaged in the transition paradigm. Contrary to the early assumptions of democracy-aid practitioners, many third-wave countries have faced fundamental state-building challenges. Approximately 20 countries in the former Soviet Union and former Yugoslavia have had to build national state institutions where none existed before. Throughout much of sub-Saharan Africa, the liberalizing political wave of the 1990s ran squarely into the sobering reality of devastatingly weak states. In many parts of Latin America, the Middle East, and Asia, political change was carried out in the context of stable state structures, but the erratic performance of those states complicated every step.

Where state-building from scratch had to be carried out, the core impulses and interests of powerholders—such as locking in access to power and resources as quickly as possible—ran directly contrary to what democracy-building would have required. In countries with existing but extremely weak states, the democracy-building efforts funded by donors usually neglected the issue of state-building. With their frequent emphasis on diffusing power and weakening the relative power of the executive branch—by strengthening the legislative and judicial branches of government, encouraging decentralization, and building civil society—they were more about the redistribution of state power than about state-building. The programs that democracy promoters have directed at governance have tended to be minor technocratic efforts, such as training ministerial staff or aiding cabinet offices, rather than major efforts at bolstering state capacity.

Letting Go

It is time for the democracy-promotion community to discard the transition paradigm. Analyzing the record of experience in the many countries that democracy activists have been labeling "transitional countries," it is evident that it is no longer appropriate to assume:

◆ that most of these countries are actually in a transition to democracy;
◆ that countries moving away from authoritarianism tend to follow a three-part process of democratization consisting of opening, breakthrough, and consolidation;
◆ that the establishment of regular, genuine elections will not only give new governments democratic legitimacy but foster a longer term deepening of democratic participation and accountability;
◆ that a country's chances for successfully democratizing depend primarily on the political intentions and actions of its political elites without significant influence from underlying economic, social, and institutional conditions and legacies;
◆ that state-building is a secondary challenge to democracy-building and largely compatible with it.

It is hard to let go of the transitional paradigm, both for the conceptual order and for the hopeful vision it provides. Giving it up constitutes a major break, but not a total one. It does not mean denying that important democratic reforms have occurred in many countries in the past two decades. It does not mean that countries in the gray zone are doomed never to achieve well-functioning liberal democracy. It does not mean that free and fair elections in "transitional countries" are futile or not worth supporting. It does not mean that the United States and other international actors should abandon efforts to promote democracy in the world (if anything, it implies that, given how difficult democratization is, efforts to promote it should be redoubled).

It does mean, however, that democracy promoters should approach their work with some very different assumptions. They should start by assuming that what is often thought of as an uneasy, precarious middle ground between full-fledged democracy and outright dictatorship is actually the most common political condition today of countries in the developing world and the postcommunist world. It is not an exceptional category to be defined only in terms of its not being one thing or the other; it is a state of normality for many societies, for better or worse. The seemingly continual surprise and disappointment that Western political analysts express over the very frequent falling short of democracy in "transitional countries" should be replaced with realistic expectations about the likely patterns of political life in these countries.

Aid practitioners and policy makers looking at politics in a country that has recently moved away from authoritarianism should not start by asking, "How is its democratic transition going?" They should instead formulate a more open-ended query, "What is happening politically?" Insisting on the former approach leads to optimistic assumptions that often shunt the analysis down a blind alley. . . .

A whole generation of democracy aid is based on the transition paradigm, above all the typical emphasis on an institutional "checklist" as a basis for creating programs, and the creation of nearly standard portfolios of aid projects consisting of the same diffuse set of efforts all over—some judicial reform, parliamentary strengthening, civil society assistance, media work, political party development, civic education, and electoral programs. Much of the democracy aid based on this paradigm is exhausted. Where the paradigm fits well—in the small number of clearly successful transitions—the aid is not much needed. Where democracy aid is needed most, in many of the gray-zone countries, the paradigm fits poorly.

Notes

The author would like to thank Jeffrey Krutz for his research assistance relating to this article and Daniel Brumberg, Charles King, Michael McFaul, Marina Ottaway, Chris Sabatini, and Michael Shifter for their comments on the first draft.

1. Samuel P. Huntington, *The Third Wave: Democratization in the Late Twentieth Century* (Norman: University of Oklahoma Press, 1991).
2. Guillermo O'Donnell and Philippe C. Schmitter, *Transitions from Authoritarian Rule: Tentative Conclusions About Uncertain Democracies* (Baltimore: Johns Hopkins University Press, 1986).
3. Ruth Collier argues that a similar transition paradigm has prevailed in the scholarly writing on democratization. "The 'transitions literature,' as this current work has come to be known, has as its best representative the founding essay by O'Donnell and Schmitter (1986), which established a framework that is implicitly or explicitly followed in most other contributions." Ruth Berins Collier, *Paths Toward Democracy: The Working Class and Elites in Western Europe and South America* (Cambridge: Cambridge University Press, 1999), 5.
4. An insightful account of the state of the third wave is found in Larry Diamond, "Is the Third Wave Over?" *Journal of Democracy* 7 (July 1996): 20–37.
5. Larry Diamond uses the term "twilight zone" to refer to a sizeable but smaller set of countries—electoral democracies that are in a zone of "persistence without legitimation or institutionalization," in *Developing Democracy: Toward Consolidation* (Baltimore: Johns Hopkins University Press, 1999), 22.
6. David Collier and Steven Levitsky, "Democracy with Adjectives: Conceptual Innovation in Comparative Research," *World Politics* 49 (April 1997): 430–51.
7. Guillermo O'Donnell, "Delegative Democracy," *Journal of Democracy* 5 (January 1994): 55–69.
8. These quotes are all taken from the country descriptions in the democracy-building section of the USAID website, *www.usaid.gov/democracy.html*.

# Chapter 5

COLLECTIVE IDENTITIES

The movement of peoples across borders and between continents—searching for jobs and better lives, fleeing war or repressive regimes, migrating in cross-generational cycles of colonial and post-colonial encounters—affects politics in profound ways. Today, it is difficult to find any pure cases of a culturally, linguistically, and ethnically homogeneous population (the nation) corresponding exactly to the territorial-juridical limits of sovereign control (the state). Thus, all countries encompass multinational, multiethnic societies, a reality with powerful political reverberations.

How do individuals understand who they are in political terms—in other words, how do they view their collective political identities? And how do they come together and mobilize to advance common political interests and aspirations? Comparativists once thought that social class—solidarities based on the shared experience of work or, more broadly, economic position—had become the most important source of collective identity. We now know that the formation of group attachments and the interplay of politically relevant collective identities are far more complex and uncertain, and that politics is shaped in significant ways by a range of group attachments, such as those associated with class, race, ethnicity, nationality, religion, and gender.

Can liberal democracy, with its emphasis on individual rights, representative assemblies, and the principle of a limited state, be reconciled with the demands by identity groups for rights, the political recognition of their needs and distinctive contributions, and the allocation of scarce resources to meet those needs? How do the requirements of multiethnic, multicultural societies—as well as concerns that women achieve full equality—shape our understandings of citizenship, representation, political rights, and community? Can the increasingly urgent and often violent conflict between religious and secular worldviews be contained—or resolved? Nearly every country faces the challenge of reconciling cultural differences with the aspirations of national unity. The politics of collective identities is one of the most challenging aspects of governance today—and an increasingly significant dimension of the study of comparative politics.

▦ 5.1

Cultural Obstacles to Equal Representation

Pippa Norris and Ronald Inglehart

In explaining gender inequality in political representation, how important are structural factors such as levels of socioeconomic development or the percentage of women in professional and managerial positions? How significant are political factors such as the nature of electoral systems? How important are cultural factors such as traditional attitudes about gender roles? In this contribution, Pippa Norris and Ronald Inglehart examine the worldwide phenomenon of the under-representation of women in political leadership. The authors note that both political and institutional arguments produce important insights, yet they do not satisfactorily explain the patterns of cross-national variation in women's leadership. Norris and Inglehart conclude that disparate historical legacies continue to influence cultural attitudes and that egalitarian attitudes toward women leaders correlate strongly with the presence of more women in national parliaments.

A fundamental problem facing the worldwide process of democratization is the continued lack of gender equality in political leadership. The basic facts are not in dispute: Today women represent only one in seven parliamentarians, one in ten cabinet ministers, and, at the apex of power, one in 20 heads of state or government. Multiple factors have contributed to this situation, including structural and institutional barriers. But what is the influence of political culture? Are attitudes toward women as political leaders a significant barrier to their empowerment? In particular, how important is culture as compared with structural and institutional factors? These are the questions that our study seeks to address.

Despite moves toward gender equality in many spheres, barriers to the entry of women into elected office persist. . . .

. . . Despite the success of some redoubtable and well-known figures, such as Margaret Thatcher, Gro Harlem Bruntland, and Golda Meir, only 39 states have *ever* elected a woman president or prime minister. According to [a] UN report [*The World's Women 2000: Trends and Statistics*] women today comprise less than

Pippa Norris and Ronald Inglehart, "Cultural Obstacles to Equal Representation," *Journal of Democracy* 12, No. 3 (July 2001): 126–140. © National Endowment for Democracy and The Johns Hopkins University Press. Reprinted with permission of The Johns Hopkins University Press.

one-tenth of the world's cabinet ministers and one-fifth of all subministerial positions. The Inter-Parliamentary Union (IPU) estimates that worldwide there were about 5,400 women in parliaments in Spring 2001, representing 13.8 percent of all members, up from 9 percent in 1987. If growth at this level is maintained (0.36 percent per year), a simple linear projection predicts that women parliamentarians will not achieve parity with men until the beginning of the twenty-second century.

Although worldwide progress has been slow, the proportion of women elected to the legislative branch is much greater in some regions than in others. Women have not achieved equal representation with men in any country. The most gender-balanced parliaments are in the Nordic nations, where on average 38.8 percent of lower-house members are women. Sweden leads the world: Women comprise half of the ministers in Prime Minister Goran Persson's cabinet and 43 percent of the Riksdag, up from 10 percent in 1950. The proportion of women members of parliament is much lower in other regions, including the Americas (15.7 percent), Asia (14.3 percent), non-Nordic Europe (14.0 percent), sub-Saharan Africa (12.5 percent), and the Pacific (11.8 percent). The worst record for women's representation is the Arab countries, where women constitute less than 5 percent of elected representatives and continue to be barred by law from standing for parliament in Kuwait, Qatar, Saudi Arabia, Oman, and the United Arab Emirates. Despite official declarations by many countries of the intent to establish conditions of gender equality in the public sphere, in practice major barriers continue to restrict women's advancement in public life.

Several explanations have been offered to account for the continuing dearth of women in political leadership: *structural factors*, including levels of socioeconomic development and the proportion of women in professional and managerial occupations; the impact of *political institutions*, such as electoral systems based on proportional-representation; and *cultural factors*, like the predominance of traditional attitudes toward gender roles.

Social Structures and Political Institutions

Early sociological accounts commonly assigned a critical role in determining the eligibility pool for elected office to a country's social system, including the occupational, educational, and socioeconomic status of women. In developing societies, women may find it difficult to break into electoral office because they are generally disadvantaged by poor childcare, low literacy, inadequate health care, and poverty. A country's level of socioeconomic development is significantly related to its proportion of women parliamentarians. Comparative studies of established democracies have long emphasized the importance of the pool of women in the professional, administrative, and managerial occupations that typically lead to political careers. Jobs in such fields as law and journalism commonly provide the flexibility, financial resources, experience, and social networks that facilitate running for elected office. In recent decades, women in many postindustrial societies have forged ahead in the private and public sectors and greatly increased their enrollment in higher education.

This study suggests that modernization creates systematic, predictable changes in gender roles, observable in two phases. First, industrialization brings women into the paid workforce and dramatically reduces fertility rates. During this stage, women make substantial gains in educational opportunities and literacy. Women are enfranchised and begin to participate in representative government, but they still have far less power than men. The second, postindustrial phase brings a shift toward greater gender equality, as women move into higher-status economic roles and gain greater political influence within elected and appointed bodies. Over half the world has not yet begun this process, however, and even the most advanced industrial societies are still undergoing it.

Yet in many ways structural explanations fail to account for the barriers facing women who seek elected office. These accounts cannot explain major disparities between relatively similar societies in the proportion of women in national parliaments, such as the contrasts between Canada (where 20 percent of parliamentarians are women) and the United States (13 percent), between the Netherlands (36 percent) and Italy (11 percent), or between South Africa (30 percent) and Niger (1 percent). A worldwide comparison of the proportion of women elected to lower houses of the legislature confirms that a high level of socioeconomic development is not a necessary condition for the success of women. For example, female representation is far greater today in some poorer societies—like Mozambique (ranking 9th in the world), South Africa (10th), and Venezuela (11th)—than in some of the most affluent, including the United States (50th), France (59th), and Japan (94th).

In many postindustrial societies, despite the transformations of women's and men's lifestyles, electoral success has continued to elude women. This pattern is exemplified by the United States: Although almost one-third of all U.S. lawyers are now female and law remains the most common training ground for legislative office in America, only 11 out of 100 U.S. senators are women. This suggests that while improvements in women's educational and professional status serve as *facilitating* conditions for women's empowerment, structural changes by themselves may be insufficient for women to achieve greater success in winning elected office. Indeed, something more than the size of the eligibility pool is at work.

One alternative explanation is provided by *institutional* accounts, which emphasize the type of political system and some of its specific features, like proportional representation in elections and gender quotas in party recruitment processes. This increasingly popular approach is probably the mainstream perspective among scholars today. Institutional accounts suggest that the political rules of the game are the primary explanation for systematic differences in women's representation among relatively similar societies, and that changing those rules is the most effective way to promote women's political leadership.

Among institutional factors, the *level of democratization* has the broadest effects. In general, the transition and consolidation of democratic societies can be expected to promote widespread political and civil liberties, including the right of women to vote and to stand for elected office. Yet the role of democracy in promoting women's role in public life remains in dispute: Andrew Reynolds finds no significant relationship between the level of democratization and that of women's parliamentary representation.[1] . . .

Since the 1955 publication of Maurice Duverger's seminal *The Political Role of Women*, the type of *electoral system* has been regarded as an important factor affecting women's political presence. Many studies have demonstrated that far more women are elected under proportional party-list systems than under majoritarian single-member-district systems. The level of *party competition*, in terms of the number of parties and their degree of ideological polarization, is another factor that may influence women's opportunities for candidacy. Greater party competition may increase the access points for female candidacies, although this in itself does not necessarily lead to more women being elected.

The fact that we can test these propositions—whether the proportion of women in parliaments is significantly related to the level of democratization, the type of electoral system, and the level of party competition—enables institutional accounts to provide many important insights into why women politicians have advanced further and faster in some countries than in others. Yet several puzzles remain. Why do apparently similar institutional reforms turn out to have diverse and often unanticipated consequences, even among relatively similar political and social systems? Why should national-list proportional representation have a very different impact on women's electoral fortunes in Israel than in the Netherlands? Why should the use of gender quotas for candidacies seem to work better in Argentina than in Ecuador? As the failure of Westminster-style parliaments in many African states in the 1960s demonstrated, transplanted institutions do not necessarily flourish in alien environments.

Cultural Barriers

Structural and institutional explanations need to be supplemented by accounts emphasizing the importance of political culture. It has long been assumed that traditional anti-egalitarian attitudes toward gender slow down the political advancement of women, though little systematic crossnational evidence has been available to verify this proposition. Theories of socialization have long emphasized the importance of gender roles—especially the predominance of either egalitarian or traditional attitudes toward women in the private and public spheres. Studies of political recruitment processes in established democracies like Britain, Finland, and the Netherlands have found that these attitudes influence both whether women are prepared to come forward as candidates for office (the supply side of the equation) and the criteria that are used by political gatekeepers when evaluating candidates (the demand side). In cultures with traditional attitudes toward the role of women in the home and family, many women may be reluctant to run and, if they seek office, may fail to attract sufficient support to win. A recent study by the [Inter-Parliamentary Union (IPU)] found that female politicians in many countries cited hostile attitudes toward political participation by women as one of the most important barriers to running for parliament.[2]

Cultural explanations provide a plausible reason why women have made much greater advances in parliaments within the Nordic region than in socially and institutionally comparable European societies like Switzerland, Italy, or Belgium. In Scandinavia, a long tradition of government intervention to promote social equality may have made the public more receptive to the idea of positive actions (such as gender quotas) designed to achieve equality for women in public life. Culture also appears to be an important reason why many nations with strict Islamic traditions have often ranked at the bottom of the list in terms of women in parliament, despite a few notable women in top leadership positions.

In spite of these apparent effects of culture, little systematic crossnational evidence has been available on the subject, and most comparative studies have been forced to adopt proxy indicators of culture, such as religion. An early comparison found that there was less political activism among women in West European Catholic countries than in Protestant ones and suggested that this was because the Catholic Church was associated with a more hierarchical and authoritarian culture. A more recent worldwide comparison of women in politics in 180 countries reveals that the greatest contrasts are between predominantly Christian countries (both Protestant and Catholic) and countries of other religions, including Islam, Buddhism, Judaism, Confucianism, and Hinduism, all of which had lower proportions of women in legislatures and in cabinet offices.[3] An alternative approach has compared attitudes within Western Europe toward the women's movement, feminism, and equality in the home and workplace; while this provides insights into support for feminism within that region, it does not necessarily reveal attitudes toward women in political leadership positions, and there are no comparable results for societies in other regions.

Our own study uses survey and aggregate evidence to compare how political culture is systematically related to the advancement of women in elected office in a wide range of countries with varying political systems and levels of economic development.[4] We focus on four related propositions: 1) There are substantial differences in attitudes toward women's leadership in postindustrial, postcommunist, and developing societies; 2) traditional attitudes are a major barrier to the election of women to parliament; 3) culture continues to be a significant influence on the proportion of women parliamentarians, even with the introduction of prior structural and institutional controls; and 4) as a result of the process of modernization and value change, these cultural barriers have been fading most rapidly among younger generations in postindustrial societies.

Attitudes Toward Women's Political Leadership

First, how does the public regard women as political leaders and how do these attitudes vary systematically between postindustrial, postcommunist, and developing societies? The World Values Survey measures support for gender equality in political leadership with a question asking respondents how far they agreed or disagreed (on a 4-point scale) with the following statement: "On the whole, men make better political leaders than women do." A comparison of responses shows that there are substantial crossnational differences. The countries that are most positive toward women's leadership include the Nordic nations and other postindustrial societies such as New Zealand, Australia, the United States, and Spain; the countries that are most traditional include many of the poorer developing societies, including Egypt, Jordan, Iran, and Nigeria.

Regression analysis, without any prior controls, demonstrates a striking link between socioeconomic development and support for egalitarian gender roles in politics. The simple correlation between these factors is strong and significant ($r = .456$; sig. $= .01$);[5] more affluent nations are by far the most egalitarian. Nonetheless, despite the role of socioeconomic development, diverse historical legacies in different world regions continue to affect cultural attitudes. A few postindustrial societies like Norway, West Germany, and Finland express higher than expected support for women's political leadership, while Spain, Australia, and (to a lesser extent) the United States are close behind. Among richer nations, the Asian societies of Japan, Taiwan, and South Korea show lower support for women in politics than would be predicted by their levels of socioeconomic development alone. Middle-income countries in Latin America tend to have the moderately egalitarian attitudes that might be expected. Many postcommunist societies display more traditional attitudes favoring male leadership (with the important exception of East Germany, which is close to West Germany). Finally, Nigeria, Iran, Jordan, and Egypt, all poorer countries with sizeable Muslim populations, evince very traditional attitudes. Therefore, socioeconomic development does appear to be significantly related to the global distribution of egalitarian attitudes toward women's political leadership. Yet the dramatic contrasts between developing nations with similar levels of GNP (India and China are surprisingly egalitarian, while Nigeria and Egypt are quite traditional) indicate that much more is at work than simply differences between rich and poor societies.

To explore the extent to which attitudes toward women as political leaders tap into and reflect deeper cultural values, these responses have been compared with a 24-item scale reflecting a much broader range of traditional versus "rational" values.[6] This scale includes items reflecting belief in the importance of religion and in adherence to traditional moral standards on issues like divorce, euthanasia, and the family. Correlation analysis shows that Scandinavian and West European societies are consistently the most rational in their moral and ethical values, as well as the most favorable toward gender equality in politics. In contrast, Nigeria, Jordan, and Egypt emerge as the most traditional on

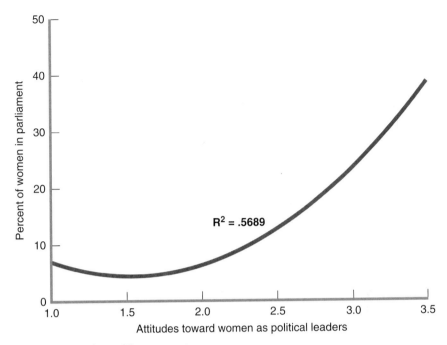

Figure 1 Attitudes and Representation.

Sources: For women's representation, see Inter-Parliamentary Union, "Women in National Parliaments," *www.ipu.org/wmn-e/classif.htm*; for attitudes, responses to: "On the whole, men make better political leaders than women do," on a 4-point scale (1 = strongly disagree; 2 = disagree; 3 = agree; 4 = strongly agree) in the World Values Survey conducted in 1995–99; see *http://wvs.isr.umich.edu*.

both dimensions, along with Iran and Azerbaijan. Attitudes toward women and men as political leaders therefore do appear to be related to broader ideological values on a wide range of ethical and moral issues.

Women in Parliaments

Now that we have established the existence of cultural patterns in attitudes toward women's political leadership, we must ask: Do they matter in practice? In particular, do more egalitarian attitudes toward women leaders influence the proportion of women actually elected to office? There is striking evidence that they do (see Figure 1 above). Egalitarian attitudes toward women leaders are strongly related to the proportion of women elected to the lower houses of national parliaments (r = .57; sig. = .01). Simply put, countries with a more egalitarian culture have more women in power. The Scandinavian countries are at the forefront of both indicators, while Jordan, Egypt, Pakistan, and many of the Central Asian postcommunist states are low on both scales.

Yet there are some striking outliers to this general pattern that deserve attention. Some established democracies—including Australia, Spain, and the
United States—display more egalitarian attitudes than might be expected given
the proportion of women elected to their parliaments. In these countries, public
opinion may have run ahead of the opportunities that women actually have for
pursuing public office. On the other hand, Bosnia-Herzegovina, South Africa,
and China all have more women parliamentarians than would be expected from
their cultural attitudes alone, suggesting that proactive strategies adopted to
boost women's leadership, like the use of gender quotas in South Africa and
China, may be ahead of public opinion.

Of course, a pattern of causation cannot be determined from any simple correlation, and we cannot rule out an interaction effect. It could well be that the
experience of having many women involved in political life shifts public opinion in a more egalitarian direction, dispelling traditional views that men make
better political leaders than women. Nevertheless, it seems equally plausible to
assume that the causal direction flows primarily from political culture to the success of women in elected office, since increasingly egalitarian attitudes could
persuade more women to seek elected office and could simultaneously influence
the political gatekeepers' evaluations of suitable candidates.

One way that this can be tested further is by examining the relationship
between the proportion of women in parliament and the broader scale of
traditional versus rational values. The results show that there is a strong and
significant correlation between these factors ($r = .408$; sig. $= .004$). Since these
broader moral values should not be greatly affected by an increase of women
in leadership, this strongly suggests that culture drives the success of women in
elected office, rather than vice versa.

So far we have demonstrated that culture matters, but not *how much* it matters
relative to other factors associated with gender equality in politics. The relationship could, after all, prove spurious if some social or institutional dynamic is
simultaneously promoting both egalitarian attitudes and the political success of
women. Multivariate analysis is required to test whether the relationship
remains significant even with controls. Accordingly, regression models were run
to estimate the relative impacts of cultural, structural, and institutional factors
on women's representation in parliaments worldwide. Ultimately, the relationship between political culture and women's empowerment survives unscathed
our best attempts to explain it away with prior controls.

Generational Shifts

Finally, given the importance of culture, is there evidence that views about
women's suitability for political office are changing? The measure of attitudes
toward women's political leadership was only included in the third wave of the
World Values Survey, so we are unable to compare directly trends over time. But

by using cohort analysis, which groups the population by date of birth, we can analyze the distribution of attitudes among generations within each type of society. Many theories of socialization suggest that people's attitudes are shaped by formative experiences in their early years and that their basic values are largely fixed by adulthood. In postindustrial societies, the formative experiences of younger generations of women and men have differed significantly from those of older generations. In the twentieth century, gender roles were affected by a long series of developments, including the extension of suffrage and full citizenship rights to women; the entry of more women into higher education and the paid labor force; the rise of the Second Wave women's movement and radical shifts in sexual mores and lifestyles in the mid-1960s; dramatic changes in the family, marriage, and the division of labor within the home; and the experience of seeing more women as leaders in public life. All these factors can be expected to have altered norms regarding the appropriate role of women in the public sphere and the suitability of women for elected office.

Outside the postindustrial societies, social change has followed different paths. In the postcommunist countries, the experience of women in the workforce, the widespread use of quotas in parliaments under communism and their subsequent abandonment, and the role of the organized women's movement in Central and Eastern Europe have all affected the development of gender-related norms. As a result, we would expect that, while some generational shifts in attitudes will be evident, the pace of change will be slower in these countries.

The evidence confirms these expectations. The traditional belief that men make better leaders than women shows a substantial generational decline in postindustrial societies, with younger postwar generations far more egalitarian than their parents or grandparents. Yet in postcommunist and developing societies, attitudes among younger and older generations are almost identical, with at most a modest shift toward less traditional views among the young. Moreover, when we disaggregate the cohort analysis for women and men in all types of society, the most striking pattern is the substantial widening of a "gender gap" on this issue among younger generations. In prewar generations, there is no difference by sex: Women are as traditional in their attitudes as men, or even slightly more so. Yet with each successive cohort, the gap widens between women's increasingly egalitarian attitudes and men's more traditional ones, until by the youngest generation the disparity has become considerable (see Figure 2).

This analysis suggests that, through the gradual process of demographic turnover, attitudes toward women in public leadership roles are likely to become more egalitarian, especially among women themselves. The effects of modernization will proceed in the broader political culture, even if no proactive strategies or institutional reforms are adopted to hasten the election of more women to public office. Nevertheless, there is little evidence that a similar process has yet begun to transform public opinion in postcommunist and developing countries, where traditional values are prevalent among younger as well as older citizens.

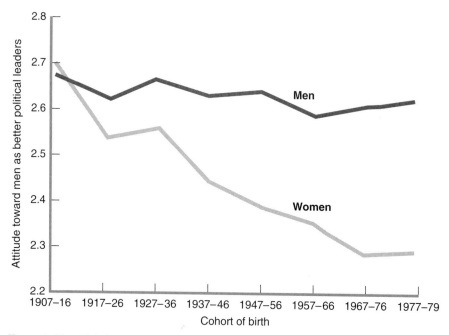

Figure 2 The Global Gender Gap in Attitudes Toward Women's Political Leadership.
Source: Responses to: "On the whole, men make better political leaders than women do," on a 4-point
scale (1 = strongly disagree; 2 = disagree; 3 = agree; 4 = strongly agree), in the World Values Survey
conducted in 1995–99; see *http://wvs.isr.umich.edu.*

The Implications for Change

The idea that the values prevailing in the broader political culture affect the
success of women in gaining elected office has always been assumed but rarely, if
ever, proved in a convincing fashion using systematic comparative evidence.
We have long suspected that culture is the unknown factor that accounts for the
striking political achievements of women in Scandinavia as compared to their
counterparts in Mediterranean Europe, let alone Latin America, Asia, sub-
Saharan Africa, and the Arab states. Yet that factor has proved difficult to
capture on the basis of existing aggregate data.

This study demonstrates that egalitarian attitudes toward women in office are
more widespread in postindustrial societies, reflecting broad patterns of socioeconomic development and cultural modernization. Such attitudes are not simply
interesting for their own sake but are significantly associated with the political
success of women. In short, culture matters. Moreover, the more egalitarian attitudes evident among younger generations in postindustrial societies, especially
among younger women, suggest that we can expect to see continued progress in

female representation in these societies. Yet the empowerment of women remains a complex process. As the cases of Australia, the United States, and Spain demonstrate, favorable attitudes toward women's leadership are not sufficient by themselves to produce breakthroughs, since some social structures and institutions continue to act as barriers. Nor can we expect the overnight transformation of the deep-rooted traditional beliefs about gender roles prevalent in many developing and postcommunist societies. . . .

Trying to alter deep-seated attitudes toward gender roles in public life may prove to be a frustrating exercise in the short term, even with extensive educational and public-awareness campaigns. In the longer term, however, the secular trends in value change associated with modernization, especially among younger generations, are likely to facilitate the process of getting more women into power. Indeed, the combination of cultural shifts in attitudes and institutional reforms of recruitment processes offers considerable promise that women may achieve political parity well before the dawn of the twenty-second century.

Notes

1. Andrew Reynolds, "Women in the Legislatures and Executives of the World: Knocking at the Highest Glass Ceiling," *World Politics* 51 (July 1999): 547–72.
2. Inter-Parliamentary Union, *Politics: Women's Insight*, IPU Reports and Documents No. 36 (Geneva: IPU, 2000).
3. Andrew Reynolds, "Women in the Legislatures and Executives of the World."
4. Data are drawn from the third wave of the World Values Survey, conducted in 1995–99 and covering 55 societies worldwide, including 11 postindustrial, 23 postcommunist, and 21 developing societies. Full information about the nations, fieldwork, methodology, and questionnaire for the survey is available online at *http://wvs.isr.umich.edu*.
5. Socioeconomic development is measured here by logged per-capita income in terms of purchasing power parity. R can vary from − 1 (a perfect inverse association) to 0 (no relationship at all) to 1, meaning a perfect association between the two variables. A significance level of .01 means that the statistical finding would happen by chance only one time in a hundred.
6. Ronald Inglehart and Wayne E. Baker, "Modernization, Cultural Change and the Persistence of Traditional Values," *American Sociological Review* 65 (February 2000): 19–51.

5.2

The Claims of Culture

Seyla Benhabib

In December 2003, France inspired a passionate and often anguished debate across Europe about ethnic identity and inclusion, when President Jacques Chirac endorsed the proposal from a presidential commission that would ban the wearing of "conspicuously religious" symbols in schools. Although written to apply equally to diverse religious and ethnic traditions, the draft law that followed reignited a long-standing dispute over the right of Islamic girls to wear head-scarves to public schools. Seyla Benhabib's contribution traces the history and explains the importance of this dispute in France. The selection also examines the famous case of Shah Bano in India that raised similar issues about the role of women in society and the challenges of religious tolerance and coexistence in countries where national unity is a highly prized and rather elusive goal. Benhabib argues that there is no simple recipe for accommodating difference and protecting the rights of individuals within a minority group, especially when it comes to the treatment of women.

For as long as human societies and cultures have interacted and compared themselves with another, the status of women and children and the rituals of sex, marriage, and death have occupied a special place in intercultural understandings. . . .

In his comprehensive treatment of the puzzles of multicultural coexistence, Bhikhu Parekh lists twelve practices that most frequently lead to clashes of intercultural evaluation: female circumcision; polygamy; Muslim and Jewish methods of animal slaughter; arranged marriages; marriages within prohibited degrees of relationships; scarring children's cheeks or other parts of the body; Muslim withdrawal of girls from coeducational practices such as sports and swimming lessons; Muslim insistence that girls wear the *hijab*, or headscarf; Sikh insistence on wearing or taking off the traditional turbans; Gypsy and Amish refusal to send their children to public schools either altogether or after a certain age; Hindu requests to be allowed to cremate their deceased; the subordinate

---

status of women and all that entails (2000, 264–65). Of the twelve practices listed by Parekh, seven concern the status of women in distinct cultural communities; two bear on dress codes pertaining to both sexes (the wearing of the turban and the *hijab*); two are about the lines separating private from public jurisdictional authority in the education of children; and one each concerns dietary codes and funeral rites. How can we account for the preponderance of cultural practices concerning the status of women, girls, marriage, and sexuality that lead to intercultural conflict? . . .

These interconnections between psychic identity, the practices of the private sphere, and cultural difference assume a new configuration in modern liberal democracies. These societies demarcate the private from the public along the following lines: the political sphere, together with the economy and certain domains of civil society, is considered "public" in multiple senses: accessible to all; shared by all; and in the interests of all. The household is considered private, in the sense that it strictly regulates access through kinship and marriage, and does not concern itself with the interest of all. In liberal societies, institutional patterns of regulating the private and the public spheres are undergirded by other assumptions as well. Liberalism is based on the conviction that privacy extends to those most deeply held beliefs pertaining to religion, culture, aesthetics, and lifestyle. Liberalism not only respects "the privacy" of the familial-domestic sphere; it also requires that the state not regulate matters of religious, cultural, and aesthetic belief. . . . Of course, matters are never that simple, and the line between the public and the private is always contested. From the standpoint of the liberal state, the family is a public institution in which practices governing marriage and divorce are defined and regulated by political as well as legal norms. The state confers fiscal and economic status upon the family in that it defines the tax status of those who are considered family members; in not recognizing same-sex unions as marriages, the state also upholds a specific conception of the family. Viewed as an institution within the modern state, then, the family has nothing "private" about it. Likewise, the lines separating religion from the state, aesthetics from politics, are always hotly contested.

In this [discussion] I focus on a number of highly publicized multicultural disputes regarding . . . family law, in the course of which traditional distinctions between the public and the private were contested and resignified. I then revisit the debate in feminist theory initiated by Susan Moller Okin's provocative question, "Is multiculturalism bad for women?" (1999). I argue that this manner of posing the question has led to an unnecessary impasse and polarization, because both opponents and proponents of multiculturalism, despite disclaimers to the contrary, continue to defend a faulty understanding of cultures as unified, holistic, and self-consistent wholes. Therefore cultural processes of resignification and reinterpretation, which women in minority ethnic communities engaged in, are ignored. A deliberative democratic multicultural politics does not confine women and children to their communities of origin against their will, but encourages them to develop their autonomous agency vis-à-vis their ascribed identities. . . .

Multiculturalism and Personal and Family Law

A divorced Muslim woman, Shah Bano Begum, filed an application for maintenance under section 125 of the Indian Code of Criminal Procedure against her
husband, the advocate Mohammad Ahmad Khan. Married to Ahmad Khan in
1932, Shah Bano was driven out of the matrimonial home in 1975. In April
1978, she filed an application against her husband in the court of the judicial
magistrate, Indore, asking for maintenance at the rate of 500 rupees. On
November 6, 1978 the apellant (Khan) divorced the respondent (Shah Bano)
by an irrevocable *talaq* (divorce), permitted under Muslim personal law.
Mohammad Ahmad Khan filed a criminal appeal against Shah Bano Begum and
others in the Supreme Court of India in 1985. His claim was that Shah Bano
had ceased to be his wife after his second marriage, and that in accordance with
Muslim law, he had paid a maintenance allowance for two years prior to the date
at which Shah Bano filed her claim, as well as depositing 3,000 rupees by way of
a dower. The principal legal dispute centered on whether section 125 of the
Code of Criminal Procedure was applicable to Muslims in India.

The judgment of the Indian Supreme Court, which decided that the Code of
Criminal Procedure was indeed applicable to Muslims, ordered the appellant to
raise his maintenance to Shah Bano from 70 to 130 rupees. But the court's decision went much further than this. Chief Justice Chandrachud commented on
the injustice done to women of all religions, on the desirability of evolving a
common civil code as envisaged by paragraph 44 of the Indian Federal Constitution, and on the provisions in the Shariat (Muslim religious law) regarding the
obligation of a husband to his divorced wife. According to most interpreters,
the Supreme Court of India thus opened the floodgates to a series of debates between the Muslim and Indian communities, and within the Muslim community
itself—between "progressives" and "fundamentalists," between women's groups
and Muslim leaders, and so forth. The political debates, pressures, and counter-
pressures led to the passage of the Muslim Women (Protection of Rights and
Divorce) Bill of 1986. Clearly, the Shah Bano controversy raised issues that
went far beyond the case at hand, into the very heart of the practice of legal
pluralism, of religious coexistence and tolerance, and of the meaning of Indian
national unity and identity. . . .

The Muslim community was forced to rework distinctions and modalities of
coexistence in view of growing demands for the recognition of women's equality
on the one hand and changing family lives and economic patterns on the other.
A movement for the passing of the Muslim Women's Bill developed. As passed
in 1986, this bill stipulated that a divorced woman was to be supported by relatives, such as brothers and sons, who were in the category of heirs, and when
such relatives were unable to support the woman, then it was the responsibility
of the community to support her through its *waqf* (obligatory charitable organizations) boards. Clearly, the purpose of even this supposed reform bill was to anchor the dependency of women upon a male-dominated, hierarchical structure,

either the natal family or the community board. The possibility of assuring the divorced woman's independence through integrating her into a larger civil society and making her to some extent financially autonomous was totally blocked. . . . Under pressure from the Muslim community, Shah Bano eventually withdrew her claim and accepted the earlier alimony settlement. Multiculturalist juggling, in this case as well, produced the defeat of women. . . .

Multiculturalism, Laicité, and the Scarf Affair in France

Consider now what has been referred to as *l'affaire foulard*—the scarf affair—in France. Whereas in the cases of "cultural defense" and Shah Bano, we have encountered the liberal-democratic state and its institutions reinscribing women's identities within their natal communities of faith and culture, in the foulard affair we encounter public officials and institutions that supposedly champion women's emancipation from these communities by suppressing the practice of veiling. The state here acts as the champion of women's emancipation from their communities of birth. Yet, as we shall see, some women resisted the state not to affirm their religious and sexual subordination as much as to assert a quasi-personal identity independent of the dominant French culture.

The practice of veiling among Muslim women is a complex institution that exhibits great variety across many Muslim countries. The terms *chador, hijab, niqab,* and *foulard* refer to distinct items of clothing worn by women from different Muslim communities: for example, the chador is essentially Iranian and refers to the long black robe and head scarf worn in a rectangular manner around the face; the niqab is a veil that covers the eyes and the mouth and leaves only the nose exposed; it may or may not be worn in conjunction with the chador. Most Muslim women from Turkey are likely to wear either long overcoats and a foulard (a head scarf) or a *carsaf* (a black garment that most resembles the chador). These items of clothing have a symbolic function within the Muslim community itself: women from different countries signal to one another their ethnic and national origins through their clothing, as well as their distance or proximity to tradition. The brighter the colors of their overcoats and scarves— bright blue, green, beige, lilac, as opposed to brown, gray, navy, and, of course, black—and the more fashionable their cuts and material by Western standards, the more we can assume the distance from Islamic orthodoxy of the women who wear them. Seen from the outside, however, this complex semiotic of dress codes is reduced to one or two items of clothing that then assume the function of crucial symbols of complex negotiations between Muslim religious and cultural identities and Western cultures.

L'affaire foulard refers to a long and drawn-out set of public confrontations that began in France in 1989 with the expulsions from their school in Creil (Oise) of three scarf-wearing Muslim girls and continued to the mass exclusion of twenty-three Muslim girls from their schools in November 1996 upon the decision of the Conseil d'Etat. The affair, referred to as a "national drama" or even a "national trauma," occurred in the wake of France's celebration of the second centennial of the French Revolution and seemed to question the foundations of the French educational system and its philosophical principle, *laicité*. This concept is difficult to translate in terms like the "separation of Church and State" or even secularization: at its best, it can be understood as the public and manifest neutrality of the state toward all kinds of religious practices, institutionalized through a vigilant removal of sectarian religious symbols, signs, icons, and items of clothing from official public spheres. Yet within the French Republic the balance between respecting the individual's right to freedom of conscience and religion, on the one hand, and maintaining a public sphere devoid of all religious symbolisms, on the other, was so fragile that it took only the actions of a handful of teenagers to expose this fragility. The ensuing debate went far beyond the original dispute and touched upon the self-understanding of French republicanism for the left as well as the right, on the meaning of social and sexual equality, and liberalism versus republicanism versus multiculturalism in French life.

The affair began when on October 19, 1989, Ernest Chenière, headmaster of the college Gabriel-Havez of Creil, forbade three girls—Fatima, Leila, and Samira—to attend classes with their heads covered. Each had appeared in class that morning wearing her scarf, despite a compromise reached between their headmasters and their parents encouraging them to go unscarfed. The three girls had apparently decided to wear the scarf once more upon the advice of Daniel Youssouf Leclerq, the head of an organization called Integrité and the former president of the National Federation of Muslims in France (FNMF). Although hardly noted in the press, the fact that the girls had been in touch with Leclerq indicates that wearing the scarf was a conscious political gesture on their part, a complex act of identification and defiance. In doing so, Fatima, Leila, and Samira on the one hand claimed to exercise their freedom of religion as French citizens; on the other hand they exhibited their Muslim and North African origins in a context that sought to envelop them, as students of the nation, within an egalitarian, secularist ideal of republican citizenship. In the years to come, their followers and supporters forced what the French state wanted to view as a private symbol—an individual item of clothing—into the shared public sphere, thus challenging the boundaries between the public and the private. Ironically, they used the freedom given to them by French society and French political traditions, not the least of which is the availability of free and compulsory public education for all children on French soil, to juxtapose an aspect of their private identity onto the public sphere. In doing so, they problematized the school as well as the home: they no longer treated the school as a neutral space of French acculturation, but openly manifested their cultural and religious differences. They used the symbol of the home in the public sphere, retaining the modesty required of them by Islam in covering their heads; yet at the same time, they left the home to become public actors in a civil public space, in which they defied the state. Those who saw in the girls' actions simply an indication of their oppression were just as blind to the symbolic meaning of their deeds as were those who defended their rights simply on the basis of freedom of religion. . . .

The complexity of the social and cultural negotiations hidden behind the simple act of veiling elicited an equally ambiguous and complex decision by the French Conseil d'Etat. On November 4, 1989, the French minister of education, Lionel Jospin, took the matter to the Conseil d'Etat (the French Supreme Court). The Conseil rendered a notoriously ambiguous decision. The minister of education asked three questions, two of which were related to the administrative handling of the answer, which would result from an answer to the first question: "If, in view of the principles of the Constitution and the laws of the Republic and with respect to the totality of rules pertaining to the organization and functioning of the public school, the wearing of signs of belonging to a religious community is or is not compatible with the principle of laïcité" (cited in Brun-Rovet 2000, 28). The court responded by citing France's adherence to constitutional and legislative texts and to international conventions, and invoked from the outset the necessity of doing justice to two principles: that the laïcité and neutrality of the state be retained in the rendering of public services and that the liberty of conscience of the students be respected. All discrimination based upon the religious convictions or beliefs of the students would be inadmissable. . . .

. . . Yet instead of articulating some clear guidelines, the court left the proper interpretation of the meaning of these signs to the judgment of the school authorities. The decisive factors in curtailing the students' freedom of religion was not the individual students' beliefs about what a religious scarf (or for that matter yarmulke) meant to them, but how the school authorities interpreted the scarf's meaning, and whether or not it could be seen as a means of provocation, confrontation, or remonstration. It is not difficult to see why this judgment encouraged both sides to the conflict to pursue their goals further and led to additional repression through the promulgation on September 10, 1994, of the Bayrou Guidelines, issued by Minister of Education François Bayrou. Lamenting the ambiguities of the judgment of the court for conveying an impression of "weaknesses" vis-à-vis Islamicist movements, the minister declared that students had the right to wear discrete religious symbols, but that the veil was not among them.

The Bayrou declaration further hardened the fronts of various political actors: intellectuals, teachers' unions, various Islamic organizations, antiimmigrant groups, and the like. The French population was already highly polarized on the issues of Islam, immigration, and national security. In the summer of 1994, a bomb planted by Muslim fundamentalist groups exploded in the metro in Paris; thus it seemed that France, despite herself, was sucked into the vortex of violence coming from fundamentalist Islamic groups, and that its traditions of tolerance and pluralism were misused by these groups to further their own sectarian political goals.

The evolution of SOS-Racisme's attitudes in view of these developments is quite telling. During the Creil episode in 1989, SOS-Racisme—one of the most militant antiracist groups, drawing its membership particularly from among the young—led large sections of the French left into defending laïcité and protesting the exclusion of the Muslim girls. But by 1994, the new president of the association called for a ban on all religious symbols; many had now come to see the recurrence of the wearing of the scarfs not as isolated incidents, but as a provocation on the part of an organized Islam that had to be confronted clearly and unequivocally (Brun-Rovet 2000). L'affaire foulard eventually came to stand for all dilemmas of French national identity in the age of globalization and multiculturalism: how to retain French traditions of laïcité, republican equality, and democratic citizenship in view of France's integration into the European Union, on the one hand, and the pressures of multiculturalism generated through the presence of second- and third-generation immigrants from Muslim countries on French soil, on the other hand. Would the practices and institutions of French citizenship be flexible and generous enough to encompass multicultural differences within an ideal of republican equality? Clearly, this affair is by no means over. As European integration and multiculturalist pressures continue, France, just like India and the United States, will have to discover new models of legal, pedagogical, social, and cultural institutions to deal with the dual imperatives of liberal democracies to preserve freedom of religious expression and the principles of secularism.

Is Multiculturalism Bad for Women?

These [two] cases suggest that multicultural institutional arrangements and legal compromises very often work to the detriment of women. Either they imprison them in arcane arrangements of dependency upon their husbands and male relatives—as was the case with Shah Bano—. . . or they make women and girls objects of state regulation and punishment in order to teach the nation a lesson, as in the case of the scarf affair in France. . . .

Yet the standpoint of the feminist critic, in this respect, is not all that different from the standpoint of the legislator. . . . The Indian courts are obliged to accept the jurisdictional division of labor between a unified criminal code and separate private and family law for India's Muslim and Hindu communities. The French Conseil d'État tries to do justice to the principles of laïcité as well as the freedom of conscience and religion, but delivers the girls with the head scarves to the intensified scrutiny and authority of their school supervisors and disregards the students' own understanding of their actions.

The cases discussed in this [contribution] illustrate what Ayelet Shachar has named "the paradox of multicultural vulnerability" (2000, 386). "Well-meaning accommodation policies by the state, aimed at leveling the playing field between minority communities and the wider society," argues Shachar, "may unwittingly allow systematic maltreatment of individuals within the accommodated minority group—an impact, in certain cases, so severe that it nullifies these individuals' rights as citizens" (386). The tension and, in many cases, the moral dilemma between accommodating difference and doing justice to all members of a minority group propels contemporary discussions of multiculturalism into a new phase.

References

Brun-Rovet, Marianne. 2000. "A Perspective on the Multiculturalism Debate: 'L'affaire foulard' and *laïcité* in France, 1989–1999." Seminar paper submitted to Professor Benhabib's class "Nations, States, and Citizens," Harvard University, Department of Government. On file with the author.

Okin, Susan Moller. 1999. "Is Multiculturalism Bad for Women?" In *Is Multiculturalism Bad for Women?* by Susan Moller Okin, edited by Joshua Cohen, Matthew Howard, and Martha C. Nussbaum. Princeton: Princeton University Press.

Parekh, Bhikhu. 2000. *Rethinking Multiculturalism: Cultural Diversity and Political Theory.* Cambridge: Harvard University Press.

Shachar, Ayelet. 2000. "The Puzzle of Interlocking Power Hierarchies: Sharing the Pieces of Jurisdictional Authority." *Harvard Civil Rights—Civil Liberties Law Review* 35, no. 2 (Summer 2000): 387–426.

 5.3

Race in the Twenty-First Century

Howard Winant

In this selection, Howard Winant brings a historical and comparative perspective to the theme of racial politics. At the start of the twenty-first century, Winant argues, racial politics has been reinvented along seemingly nonracist lines, yet racial inequality and injustice persist as defining features of the contemporary global order. Drawing on the national cases of the United States, South Africa, and Brazil, as well as the regional experience of the European Union countries, Winant concludes that racism remains a crucial component of contemporary social and political life. More optimistically, he suggests that the world still has a chance not to "move beyond" race, but rather to break the association between racial politics and injustice.

As the world lurches forward into the twenty-first century, there is widespread confusion and anxiety about the political significance, and even the meaning, of race. The future of democracy itself depends on the outcomes of racial politics and policies, as they develop both in various national societies and in the world at large. This means that the future of democracy also depends on the concept of race, the meaning that is attached to race. Contemporary threats to human rights and social well-being—including the resurgent

---

Howard Winant, "Race in the Twenty-First Century," *Tikkun* (Jan.–Feb., 2002). Reprinted from *Tikkun: A Bimonthly Interfaith Critique of Politics, Culture & Society.*

dangers of fascism, increasing impoverishment, and massive social polarization—cannot be managed or even understood without paying new and better attention to issues of race. We need a set of conceptual tools that can facilitate this task.

The present moment is unique in the history of race. Starting during World War II and culminating in the 1960s, there was a global shift, a "break," in the worldwide racial system that had endured for centuries. The shift occurred because many challenges to the old forms of racial hierarchy converged after the war: anti-colonialism, anti-apartheid, worldwide revulsion at fascism, and perhaps most important, the U.S. civil rights movement and U.S.–USSR competition in the world's South. All called white supremacy into question to an extent unparalleled in modern history. These events and conflicts linked anti-racism to democratic political development more strongly than ever before. As a result, for the first time in modern history, there is widespread, indeed worldwide, support for what had until recently been a "dream," Dr. King's dream let us say, of racial equality.

Yet white supremacy is hardly dead. It has proven itself capable of absorbing and adapting much of the "dream," repackaging itself as "colorblind," nonracialist, and meritocratic. In our post-imperial, post–Cold War world, a new racial politics is developing, one which has tried to reinvent itself along overtly nonracist lines. In fact, its capacity to present itself as "beyond race" is in many ways the crucial index of its stability. Paradoxically, however, in this reformed version racial inequality can live on, still battening on all sorts of stereotypes and fears, still resorting to exclusionism and scapegoating when politically necessary, still invoking the supposed superiority of "mainstream" (a.k.a. white) values, and cheerfully maintaining that equality has been largely achieved. Despite all the political reforms, despite the real amelioration of the most degrading features of the old-world racial system, the centuries-old and deeply entrenched system of racial inequality and injustice has hardly been eliminated. Rather, this new "colorblind" racial system may be more effective in containing the challenges posed over the past few decades by movements for racial justice than any intransigent, overtly racist "backlash" could possibly have been.

Although the reformed and officially nonracial version of white supremacy has succeeded in curtailing progress toward the "dream" in many dubious battles—over immigration and citizenship, income redistribution and poverty, and above all in respect to the compensatory programs commonly called "affirmative action"—the new racial politics has hardly won the day. It has certainly not eliminated the movement for racial justice that spawned it. Rather, the racial politics that results from this synthesis of challenge and incorporation, racial conflict and racial reform, has proved neither stable nor certain. It is a strange brew, often appearing more inclusive, more pluralistic than ever before, yet also filled with threats: of "ethnic cleansing," resurgent neofascism, and perhaps equally insidious, a renewed racial complacency.

No longer unabashedly white supremacist, the new racial politics is, so to speak, abashedly white supremacist.

The Modern World Racial System

Popular culture tends to represent racism as an archaic phenomenon, an out-growth of pre-modern slave-based societies. But modernity has to be acknowl-edged as a racial phenomenon in its own right. The Enlightenment's recognition of a unified, intelligible world, the construction of an international economy, the rise of democracy and popular sovereignty, and the emergence of a global culture were all deeply racialized processes. To understand how race was funda-mental to the construction of modernity is of more than historical interest: it also explains much about the present. Notably, it demolishes the commonly-held belief that racism is largely a thing of the past, the idea that after the bad old days of white supremacism and colonial rule, there has occurred in our own time a belated resolution to the "race problem."

The tension between slavery on the one hand, and nascent democracy on the other, structured the lengthy transition to the modern world. Resistance against slavery contributed crucially to the broader redefinition of political rights for which early advocates of democracy yearned and fought. Indeed, the violence and genocide of earlier racial phenomena prefigured contemporary atrocities like the Holocaust, "ethnic cleansing," and totalitarianism.

The abolition of African slavery was the great rehearsal for the "break" with white supremacy that took place in our own time. Abolition was not completed with the triumph of the Union in the American Civil War and the passage of the Reconstruction amendments to the Constitution. Only when Brazil, the last country to free its slaves, did so in 1888, did the first crucial battle in the centuries-long war against white supremacy draw to a close. Abolition, that is, was not the result of one war in one country, but was made possible by three momen-tous social changes: the triumph of industrial capitalism, the upsurge of democra-tic movements, and the mobilization of slaves themselves in search of freedom.

But abolition left many emancipatory tasks unfinished. New forms of racial inequality succeeded slavery. Even after slavery had been ended, democracy was still partial. Racialization—for example the U.S. laws and social practices known as "Jim Crow"—continued to define the mechanisms of authoritarian rule and to distribute resources, not only in the U.S. but on a global scale. Racial thought and practices continued to associate subordinated status almost irrevo-cably with distinct types of human bodies, thus enabling and justifying world systemic rule. Generalized processes of racial stratification continued to support enormous and oppressive systems of commercial agriculture and mining. Through the mid-twentieth century, the unfulfilled dreams of human rights and equality were still tied up with the logic of race.

Although there was always resistance to racist rule, it was only in the period after World War II that opposition to racial stratification and racial exclusion once again turned into major political conflicts. Civil rights and anti-racist movements, as well as nationalist and indigenous ones, fiercely contested the racial limitations on democracy. These movements challenged the conditions under which racialized labor was available for exploitation in the former colonies as well as the metropoles. Picking up the anti-fascist legacy of World War II, they also took advantage of the geopolitical conflicts of the Cold War. They rendered old forms of political exclusion problematic, and revealed the inherent racist bias in many mainstream cultural icons—artistic, linguistic, scientific, and of course political—that had long been considered unproblematic. To cite some U.S. examples: many of the "founding fathers," for example, were newly recognized as committed slaveholders; corporate complicity with slavery and imperialism was rediscovered. Familiar writers such as Hemingway were reread with racial issues in mind. And popular culture, the "material culture" with its Aunt Jemima pancakes and Cream of Wheat cereal boxes, suddenly appeared surprising (to whites at least).

Drawing on the experience of millions who had undergone military mobilization followed by an embittering return to a segregated or colonized homeland, the anti-racist movements were able to recognize anew their international character, as massive postwar labor demand sparked international migration from the world's South to its North, from areas of peasant agriculture to industrial areas. These enormous transformations manifested themselves in a vast demand to complete the work begun a century before with slavery's abolition. They sparked the worldwide "break" with the tradition of white supremacy.

As the tumultuous 1960s drew to a close, the descendants of slaves and ex-colonials had forced at least the partial dismantling of most official forms of discrimination and empire. But with these developments—the enactment of a new series of civil rights laws, decolonization, and the adoption of cultural policies of a universalistic character—the global racial system entered a new period of instability and tension. The immediate result of the "break" was an uneven series of racial reforms that had the general effect of ameliorating racial injustice and inequality, but also worked to contain social protest. Thus the widespread demands of the racially subordinated and their supporters were at best answered in a limited fashion; in this way a new period of racial instability and uncertainty was inaugurated.

Some National Cases

The "break" was a worldwide phenomenon, but it obviously took very different forms in particular national settings. Racial conditions are generally understood to vary dramatically in distinct political, economic, and cultural contexts. Here I'd like to focus, however briefly, on four national case studies: the United States, South Africa, Brazil, and the European Union (considered as a whole). I chose these four cases, because they are crucial variants, important laboratories in which new racial dynamics are being developed.

These comparative case studies demonstrate that the post–World War II "break" is a global backdrop, an economic, political, and cultural context in which national racial conflicts are being worked out. They give us a context for understanding the developing nature of the new racial politics.

The United States

How permanent is the "color line"? The activities of the civil rights movement and related anti-racist initiatives achieved substantial, if partial, democratic reforms in earlier postwar decades. These innovations continue to coexist, however, with a weighty legacy of white supremacy whose origins lie in the colonial and slavery era. How do these two currents combine and conflict today?

Massive migration, both internal and international, has reshaped the U.S. population, both numerically and geographically. A multipolar racial pattern has largely supplanted the old racial system, which was often (and somewhat erroneously) viewed as a bipolar white-black hierarchy. In the contemporary United States, new varieties of inter-minority competition, as well as new awareness of the international "embeddedness" of racial identity, have greater prominence. Racial stratification varies substantially by class, region, and indeed among groups, although comprehensive racial inequality certainly endures. Racial reform policies are under attack in many spheres of social policy and law, where the claim is forcefully made that the demands of the civil rights movement have largely been met, and that the United States has entered a "postracial" stage of its history.

The racial "break" in the United States was a partial democratization, produced by the moderate coalition that dominated the political landscape in the post–World War II years. The partial victory of the civil rights movement was achieved by a synthesis of mass mobilization on the one hand, and a tactical alliance with U.S. national interests on the other. This alliance was brokered by racial "moderates": political centrists largely affiliated with the Democratic Party, who perceived the need to ameliorate racial conflict and end outright racial dictatorship, but who also understood and feared the radical potential of the black movement.

There was a price to be paid for civil rights reform. It could take place only in a suitably deradicalized fashion, only if its key provisions were articulated (legislatively, juridicially) in terms compatible with the core values of U.S. politics and culture: individualism, equality, competition, opportunity, and the accessibility of "the American dream," etc. This price was to be paid by the movement's radicals: revolutionaries, socialists, and political nationalists—black, brown, red, yellow, and white—who were required to forego their vision of major social transformation or to face marginalization, repression, or death if they would not.

The radical vision was an alternative "dream," Dr. King's dream let us call it, a dream in which racial justice played the central part. To be "free at last" meant something deeper than symbolic reforms and palliation of the worst excesses of white supremacy. It meant substantive social reorganization that would be manifested in egalitarian economic and democratizing political consequences. It meant something like social democracy, human rights, and social citizenship for blacks and other "minorities."

But it was precisely here that the "moderate" custodians of racial reform drew their boundary line, both in practical terms and in theoretical ones. To strike down officially sanctioned racial inequality was permissible; to create racial equality through positive state action was not. The danger of redistribution—of acceding to demands to make substantive redress for the unjustified expropriation and restriction of black economic and political resources, both historically and in the present—was to be avoided at all costs.

Civil rights reform thus became the agenda of the political center, which moved "from domination to hegemony." The key component of modern political rule, of "hegemony" as theorized by Gramsci most profoundly, is the capacity to *incorporate opposition*. By adopting many of the movement's demands, by developing a comprehensive and coherent program of "racial democracy" that hewed to a centrist political logic and reinforced key dimensions of U.S. nationalist ideology, racial "moderates" were able to define a new racial "common sense." Thus they divided the movement, reasserted a certain stability, and defused a great deal of political opposition. This was accomplished not all at once, but over a prolonged period from about the mid-1960s to the mid-1980s.

This partial reconfiguration of the U.S. racial order was based on real concessions but left major issues unresolved, notably the endurance of significant patterns of inequality and discrimination. Still, the reform that did occur was sufficient to reduce the political challenge posed by antiracist movements. Certainly it has been more successful than the intransigent strategy of diehard segregationists—based in the slogan of "massive resistance" to even minimal integration—would have been.

Yet the fundamental problems of racial injustice and inequality, of white supremacy, of course remain: moderated perhaps, but hardly resolved.

So in the U.S. context, race not only retains its significance as a social structural phenomenon, but also continues to define North American identities and life chances, well after the supposed triumph of the "civil rights revolution." Indeed "the American dilemma" may be more problematic than ever as the twenty-first century commences. For achieving a "moderate" race policy agenda has required that the civil rights vision be drawn and quartered, beginning in the late 1960s and with ever-greater success in the following two decades.

The tugging and hauling, the escalating contestation over the meaning of race, has resulted in ever more disrupted and contradictory notions of racial identity. The significance of race ("declining" or increasing?), the interpretation of racial equality ("colorblind" or color-conscious?), the institutionalization of racial justice ("reverse discrimination" or affirmative action?), and the very categories—black, white, Latino/Hispanic, Asian American, and Native American—employed to classify racial groups . . . all these were called into question as they emerged from the civil rights "victory" of the mid-1960s.

Despite this continuous degradation of the dream of equality, the view that racial injustice has largely been surpassed in a post–civil rights era has become the new national "common sense." This view has acquired not only elite and academic spokespeople, but also widespread mass adherence, especially among whites. As a result, the already limited racial reform policies ("affirmative action") and the relatively powerless state agencies charged with enforcing civil rights laws (Equal Employment Opportunity Commission) developed in the 1960s are undergoing new and severe attack.

The argument is now made that the demands of the civil rights movement have largely been met, and that the United States has entered a "post-racial" stage of its history. Advocates of such positions—usually classified as "neoconservative" (but sometimes also found on the left)—ceaselessly instruct racially-defined minorities to "pull themselves up by their own bootstraps," and, in callous distortion of Martin Luther King Jr.'s message, exhort them to accept the "content of their character" (rather than "the color of their skin") as the basic social value of the country. . . .

After the dust had settled from the titanic confrontation between the movement's radical propensities and the "establishment's" tremendous capacity for incorporative "moderate" reform, a great deal remained unresolved. The ambiguous and contradictory racial conditions in the United States today result from decades-long attempts to simultaneously ameliorate racial opposition and to placate the *ancien regime raciale*. The unending reiteration of these opposite gestures, these contradictory practices, itself testifies to the limitations of democracy and the continuing significance of race in the United States.

South Africa

In the mid-1990s, South Africa—the most explicitly racialized society in the late twentieth century—entered a difficult but promising transition. The apartheid state had of course been committed to a racialized framework of citizenship, civic inclusion, and law in general; the post-apartheid constitution incorporates the principles of nonracialism originally articulated in the ANC-based Freedom Charter of 1955. Yet the country still bears the terrible burden of apartheid's sequelae: persistent racial inequality across every level of society. The legacies of segregated residential areas, combined with a highly racialized distribution of resources of every sort, combine to urge moderation on political leadership. White fears must be placated in order to sustain the country's economic base and to minimize capital flight. Whites continue to hold controlling positions throughout the economy; the handful of blacks who have made their way into the corporate and state elites understand very well the price the country would pay for a radical turn in policy.

Yet this is a state committed to racial equality, and to promoting black advancement, individually and collectively. Can the post-apartheid state stabilize the process of political, social, and economic integration of the black majority? Can it maintain an official nonracialism in the face of such comprehensive racial inequality? How can the vast majority of citizens—excluded until so recently from access to land, education, clean water, and decent shelter; debarred from Africa's wealthiest economy; and denied the most elementary civic and political rights—garner the economic access they so desperately need, without reinforcing white paranoia and fear? How can the post-apartheid state facilitate the reform of racial attitudes and practices, challenging inequality, white supremacism, and the legacy of racial separatism, without engendering white flight and subversion?

Both the anti-apartheid movement and the new government's policies were shaped by global concerns as well as by local ones. Internal political debates reflect changing global discussions around race and politics. Just as the South African Black Consciousness Movement drew on the speeches of Malcolm X and Aimé Cesaire in its understanding of racial oppression, just as the anti-apartheid movement used international anti-racist sentiment to build momentum for sanctions on the old regime, so too the current government is both guided and constrained by international pressures and issues.

Moreover, internal politics bring international resources to bear: through the post-war era, the anti-apartheid movement drew much of its resources and ideas from an international anti-racist movement, largely linked to an international trend to support decolonization. Since the 1994 election, however, international constraints have limited the sphere of action of the new democratic government. Critics of affirmative action policies, for example, emphasize the danger of undermining efficiency in the name of redistribution, much as critics of redistributive policies deploy neoliberal economic arguments to reject nationalization. In each case, they invoke international discourses that are nonracial in form, yet have racial implications in practice. The South African state continues to face considerable challenges from both left and right: will it be possible to reconstruct South Africa by building not only a democracy but a greater degree of consensus, of citizenship and belonging? To what degree can a policy of "class compromise" forestall the dangers of social upheaval and capital flight?

Understanding these processes requires viewing South African racial debates in global perspective, and exploring the ways in which local actors seek to change the rules of engagement as they restructure national politics. The 1994 elections changed the racial character of the state, although many white civil servants remain in place; affirmative action policies, to which the ANC-led government is committed, could reorganize racial distribution of incomes, if not wealth. Yet in the context of a global debate over affirmative action, and in the face of the threat of the flight of white capital and skills, the process of reform has been far slower than many South Africans, white and black, expected. This dilemma remains unresolved: how can democratic nonracial institutions be constructed in a society where most attributes of socioeconomic position and identity remain highly racialized?

Brazil

Brazil presents significant parallels, both historical and contemporary, to other American nations, including the United States. These similarities include Brazil's history of slavery and black inequality, its displacement and neglect of a large indigenous population, its intermittent and ambiguous commitment to immigration, its incomplete democracy, and its vast, increasingly urban, and disproportionately black underclass. Brazilian racial dynamics have traditionally received little attention, either from scholars or policy makers, despite the fact that the country has the second largest black population in the world (after Nigeria). Its post-emancipation adoption of a policy of "whitening," which was to be achieved by concerted recruitment of European immigrants, owed much to the U.S. example, and also drew on nineteenth century French racial theorizing.

Amazingly, the "myth of racial democracy" still flourishes in Brazil, even though it has been amply demonstrated to be little more than a fig leaf covering widespread racial inequality, injustice, and prejudice. The Brazilian racial system, with its "color continuum" (as opposed to the more familiar "color line" of North America), tends to dilute democratic demands. Indeed, Brazilian racial dynamics have made it difficult to promote policies that might address racial inequality. Public discourse resolutely discourages any attempt to define inequality along racial lines; the [former] President, Fernando Henrique Cardoso, [was] the first even to broach the subject seriously, although vociferous denials both official and informal persist. If politicians do point out racial inequalities, they challenge the myth of racial democracy, and are subject to charges that they are themselves provoking racial discrimination by stressing difference. . . .

The emergence of the *Movimento Negro Unificado* as a force to be reckoned with—though by no means as strong as the 1960s U.S. civil rights movement—represents a new development. The MNU used the 1988 centennial of the abolition of Brazilian slavery, as well as the 1990–91 census, to dramatize persistent racial inequalities. As in South Africa, this phase of the black movement takes its reference points partly from international anti-racist struggles, often drawing on examples, symbols, and images from the civil rights and anti-apartheid movements.

In the 1990s, a range of racial reforms were proposed in Brazil—largely in response to the increasingly visible *Movimento Negro*. To enact these reforms, to prompt the state to adopt anti-racist policies, however, will require far greater support for change than presently exists. The political dilemma is familiar. Blacks need organized allies: in the party system, among other impoverished and disenfranchised groups, and on the international scene. Yet in order to mobilize, they must also begin to assert a racialized political identity, or there will be little collective support for racial reforms. How can blacks address this dualistic, if not contradictory, situation? How can Afro-Brazilians assert claims on the basis of group solidarity, without simultaneously undermining the fragile democratic consensus that has begun to emerge across many constituencies? How can democratic institutions be built alongside policies designed to address racial inequalities, without undermining a vision of common citizenship and equality?

The European Union

The last few decades have established that, indeed, "the empire strikes back." Racially plural societies are in place throughout Europe, especially in former imperial powers like the United Kingdom, the Netherlands, France, and Spain, but also in Germany, Italy, the Scandinavian countries, and to some extent in the East. The influx of substantial numbers of nonwhites during the post-colonial period has deeply altered a dynamic in which the racial system and the imperial order had been one, and in which the "other" was by and large kept outside the walls of the "mother country." As a stroll around London, Frankfurt, Paris, or Madrid quickly reveals, those days are now gone forever. Yet the response to the new situation too often takes repressive and anti-democratic forms, focusing attention on the "immigrant problem" (or the "Islamic problem"), seeking not only to shut the gates to Maghrebines or sub-Saharan Africans, Turks, or Slavs (including Balkan refugees), but often also to define those "others" who are already present as enemies of the national culture and threats to the "ordinary German" (or English, or French, etc.) way of life. This rationale for racial exclusion and restriction in Europe has been analyzed as "differentialist": its distinction from the meritocratic logic of discrimination in the United States has been linked to a generally lower European interest in issues of individual equality, and a relatively greater concern with the integrity of national cultures.

Thus the particular racial issue that must be confronted in Europe is the newly heterogeneous situation, the multiplication of group identities. Currently, anti-democratic tendencies are widely visible: new right-wing and neofascist groups are widespread. At both the state and regional levels the agenda of restriction is gaining adherence, jeopardizing mobility of employment or residence, and sometimes stigmatizing religious or other cultural practices. Conflicts over immigration and citizenship have taken on new intensity, with crucial implications for the character of democracy.

The dynamics of integration raise a wide range of questions about future European racial logics. Conflicting principles of citizenship should it be based on principles of descent or on those of territory, *jus sanguinis* or *jus soli?*—are deeply imbedded in the distinct European national makeups, and their resolution in a common cultural/political framework will not come easily. Relations with ex-colonies vary, raising serious questions not only of immigrant access and economic ties between the old empires and the new Europe, but also giving rise to serious anxieties about "security" and "terrorism." Popular anti-racist sentiments stimulated the formation of many multiculturalist and pluralist organizations, particularly in the early 1980s. But over the past decade they have largely ceased to function as mass mobilization initiatives in support of democracy. So, while the slogan *"Touche pas mon pôte"* ("Hands off my buddy") no longer summons tens of thousands into the street in defense of the democratic rights of racially-defined minorities, the transition to racial pluralism is still very much underway.

Toward New Racial Dynamics

To understand the changing significance of race in the aftermath of the twenti-eth century—the century whose central malady was diagnosed by W. E. B. Du Bois as "the problem of the color-line"—we must reconsider where the racialized world came from, and where it is going. In the settings I've discussed, the "break" that began with movement activity after World War II, and that was contained from the late 1960s onward by political reforms, has not been consolidated. At the end of the century the world as a whole, and our national cases as well, are far from overcoming the tenacious legacies of colonial rule, apartheid, and seg-regation. All still experience continuing confusion, anxiety, and contention about race. Yet the legacies of epochal struggles for freedom, democracy, and human rights persist as well. To evaluate the transition to a new world racial system in comparative and historical perspective requires keeping in view the continuing tension that characterizes the present.

It is impossible to address worldwide dilemmas of race and racism by ignoring or "transcending" this situation, for example by adopting so-called "colorblind" policies. In the past, the centrality of race deeply determined the economic, political, and cultural configuration of the modern world; although recent decades have seen a tremendous efflorescence of movements for racial equality and justice, the legacies of centuries of racial oppression have not been over-come. Nor is a vision of racial justice fully worked out. Certainly the idea that such justice has already been largely achieved—as seen in the "colorblind" paradigm in the United States, the "nonracialist" rhetoric of the South African Freedom Charter, the Brazilian rhetoric of "racial democracy," the emerging "racial differentialism" of the European Union—remains problematic.

What would a more credible vision entail? The pressing task today is not to jettison the concept of race, but instead to come to terms with it as a form of flexible human variety.

What does this mean in respect to racism? Racism has been a crucial compo-nent of modernity, a key pillar of the global capitalist system, for 500 years. So it remains today. Yet it has been changed, damaged, and forced to reorganize by the massive social movements which have taken place in recent decades. In the past these movements were international in scope and influence. They were deeply linked to democratizing and egalitarian trends, such as labor politics and femi-nism. They were able both to mobilize around the injustices and exclusion expe-rienced by racially subordinated groups, and simultaneously to sustain alliances across racial lines. This is background; such experiences cannot simply recur.

Still, the massive mobilizations which created the global "break" that fol-lowed World War II have certainly reshaped our world. Were these movements fated to be the last popular upsurges, the last egalitarian challenges to elite supremacy, to racial hierarchy? Surely not. In the countries I have discussed, and in transnational anti-racist networks as well, these earlier precedents still wield their influence. They still spark new attempts to challenge racism.

Will race ever be "transcended"? Will the world ever "get beyond" race? Probably not. But the entire world still has a chance of overcoming the stratification, the hierarchy, the taken-for-granted injustice and inhumanity that so often accompanies the "race concept." Like religion or language, race can be accepted as part of the spectrum of the human condition, while it is simultaneously and categorically resisted as a means of stratifying national or global societies. Nothing is more essential in the effort to reinforce democratic commitments, not to mention global survival and prosperity, as we enter a new millennium.

 5.4

Migration and Politics: Explaining Variation Among Rich Democracies in Recent Nativist Protest

Harold L. Wilensky[1]

In this selection, Harold Wilensky argues that rich democracies display significant convergence in their cultural and social diversity as well as in their experiences of immigration. Although there are variations over time and place, the economic impact of immigrants tends to be positive. In the United States, for example, immigrants contribute more to tax revenues than they receive in welfare state benefits. What then explains anti-immigrant violence and the popular support for anti-immigrant (nativist) movements and parties? In a wide-ranging comparative analysis, Wilensky concludes that public policies toward immigration shape both voting and violence, and offers the intriguing observation that these two expressions of anti-immigrant sentiment may be inversely correlated.

Rich democracies evidence convergent trends in immigration experience (cf. Gary P. Freeman, 1994, pp. 17–30; Collinson, 1993, pp. 57–59; and Hollifield, 1992, pp. 32–33, 84–85, 204–213):

◆ Increasing effort and capacity to regulate migration flows, especially absolute numbers.

Harold L. Wilensky, "Migration and Politics: Explaining variation among rich democracies in recent nativist protest," Paper presented at the 14th World Conference of Sociology, Montreal, Canada, July 26–August 1, 1998. Institute of Industrial Relations Working Paper Series (University of California, Berkeley). Copyright 1998 by Harold L. Wilensky. Reprinted by permission of the author.

- The increased moral resonance of family unification as a major criterion for admission, accounting for an increasing percentage of total immigration and decreasing state control of the social characteristics (education, skills) of the immigrants.
- An hour-glass shape of the education and skills of the recent immigration population. Although there are some national differences here, the central tendency is toward some overrepresentation of college graduates and a very big overrepresentation of the least educated and least skilled. [It is estimated] that American immigrants are 30 percent highly skilled, 20 percent in the middle, and 50 percent unskilled.
- The transformation of temporary work programs into permanent immigration. (Like The Man Who Came to Dinner and stayed for several months, the guest workers of Europe increasingly settled down in the host countries for long periods, even their whole working lives.) Movements for expanding immigrant rights were a natural outcome.
- The uneven spread of migrants in Western Europe 1950–93. The explanation: variation in (1) the demand for and recruitment of "temporary" labor; (2) the openness to the rising tide of political refugees, East to West and increasingly South to North.[2]
- As legal entry routes are restricted in response to xenophobic political pressure, illegal entrants and visa overstayers have increased, although nations vary in their capacity to police their borders and control illegal immigration.[3]

Economic Effects of Immigration

The economic impact of immigration, considering all costs and benefits over the long run, is very likely positive. This reality, however, is not what plays out in politics, where immigrants are used as scapegoats for a wide range of troubles. Complicating any assessment, the real economic effects vary over time and place.

Studies of the U.S. using data from before 1980 show that ". . . immigrants have been absorbed into the American labor market with little adverse effect on natives." In fact, in areas of greatest immigrant concentration—e.g. Miami, Los Angeles, New York, San Francisco—employment of natives increased with rising immigration, except for New York. The reasons: immigrants purchase goods and services where they work, thereby raising demand for labor; immigrant skills complement the skills of many native workers, raising demand for them; even with their concentration in gateway cities, if immigrants had not taken the low-skilled jobs there, similarly young, uneducated Americans would have filled the gap via migration from other areas; and natives attenuate the negative earnings effects of recent immigration by moving to other localities while at least 20 to 30 percent of the foreign born in the U.S., probably the least self-supporting, return to their birthplace or migrate elsewhere within a decade or two, thereby relieving pressure on the labor market.

But as the percentage of uneducated, unskilled immigrant labor rose in the 1980s when the U.S. job market for the least educated was deteriorating, studies of that decade concluded that immigration was depressing the earnings of natives, especially the relative earnings of high-school dropouts, including young Blacks and earlier-arriving Hispanics. An oversupply of cheap immigrant labor was competing with an oversupply of cheap native labor.

It is a popular idea that immigrants are a disproportionate burden on the welfare state. This is largely a myth. In the United States, immigrants are probably ripped off by American taxpayers. The reasons: First, they are overwhelmingly young workers who pay Social Security and Medicare taxes (not the native aged who use most of the expensive pension, disability, and health-care services) whose fertility rates are as low as the comparable young natives (no disproportionate use of schools). The very youth of the immigrant population is a boon for the U.S.; the immigrants will help pay for the babyboomers' retirement and medical care, partially offsetting the looming mismatch of pensioners and workers. Second, they pay state sales taxes, local property taxes, and gasoline taxes; their employers pay unemployment insurance and worker's compensation taxes. Third, if they are legal, their use of social welfare benefits in earlier decades was less than that of natives. Although such use is now slightly above the natives' (because of higher unemployment rates of the young and because the aged among them use means-tested SSI), these are the smallest parts of welfare-state burdens and have deteriorated in real value. Finally, if they are illegals they are by law denied almost all welfare benefits and are afraid to use *any* services for fear of being deported. . . .

National experiences differ depending on institutions and policies. In Germany, for instance, although foreigners are increasingly overrepresented among the recipients of social assistance (which is only 5 percent of the Federal Republic's social expenditures), the aggregate impact of foreigners on the entire German system of taxes and transfers is positive—e.g. a fiscal gain of about 14 billion DM in 1991. A similar finding of net gain is reported from studies of France. Regarding the labor market, both Australia and Germany evidence much less negative earnings impact than the U.S. because their occupational wage differentials are smaller than those of the U.S. and their unionization rates are much higher. Germany also invests more in training, job creation, and job placement. And Australia from the 1970s through the early 1980s used education and skills as criteria for admission so the differences between natives and immigrants did not grow so much. On the other hand, countries that match Sweden's generosity in social programs for immigrants may find that the costs exceed the benefits even in the long run.

Whatever the European political economies do about the welfare state, labor-market and social policies, and whatever the real economic effects of immigration, I suspect that they will all experience a moderate increase in ethnic-racial-religious conflict, hardly unknown to the Continent in the past, only this time without major war.

Explaining Variation in Nativist Protest

Insofar as rich democracies converge in the number of immigrants as a fraction of the labor force, they are likely to experience cycles of nativist, xenophobic protest, some of it parliamentary, some violent, as in the history of the older immigrant nations, the U.S., Australia, and Canada. The cycles of protest are driven by the convergence of economic downturns (unemployment, downward mobility, declines in income), immigrant population numbers and concentration, and the social distance between immigrants and natives. How anti-immigrant sentiments are channeled, however, is another matter.[4] National and local mobilizing structures—political parties, legislatures, prime ministers, interest groups— can either legitimize or oppose xenophobic expression, exploit mass fears and prejudices in a search for scapegoats or try to contain them.

We can see the interaction of strong economic deprivation, much immigrant concentration, big social distance, and nativist political mobilization at work in the U.S. and Germany in the early 1990s. In the Los Angeles riots of 1992 much of the violence of blacks was targeted at Koreans and Chinese; the locations were areas of high unemployment of young males. In the 1994 election in California and in most closely-contested Congressional districts in many states the Republicans used the problems of crime, welfare mothers, and illegal Mexican or Caribbean immigrants as negative symbols in a successful campaign to direct a frenzy of anger at their Democratic opponents. Media "talk-shows" poured oil on that fire. White men of the middle mass (high school or part-college educated) from the West and South who said that their family's economic situation had worsened in the last four years were especially attracted to those appeals (based on exit polls, New York Times 2002, pp. 46–47, 375–378 on the revolt of the middle mass).

Anti-immigrant violence and voting in Germany has similar roots. Since 1961 the percentage of foreigners in the German population rose from 1.2 percent to over 8 percent—about the same as the 8.7 percent of the United States in 1994. As Alber shows bursts of nativist violence (acts/1000 asylum seekers) occurred in 1983–84, a time of accelerating unemployment, and 1991–1993 (combining recession, the economic strain of reunification, and rising immigration). He reports an average of nearly 6 violent acts per 1000 asylum seekers every day, including several arson fires during 1991–1993. Regarding social distance, although Germany's proportion of resident foreigners is not as large as Belgium's, its percentage of immigrants from non-European countries (6%) puts it first among countries of the European Union. Regarding mobilization, in the 1990 election male East German voters below the age of 25, whose unemployment was greatest, gave the extreme right nativist Republican Party its best election result of 7 percent. The party broke through first in Bremen, a port city with a declining industrial center, a high rate of unemployment and a heavy concentration of Turks, Poles and other immigrants. The combination of youth unemployment and social distance is also captured in Solingen, where the killers of a Turkish girl in May 1993 were members of a youth gang who had been kicked out of a Turkish restaurant; five other Turkish females, long-term residents, were killed in a single gruesome arson fire in the same city that month.

That public policies toward immigration shape the intensity of anti-immigrant violence and voting is suggested by a comparison of two countries with substantial recent immigration, generous social policies, and low rates of poverty and inequality, but contrasting immigration policies: Germany, where the principle of *jus sanguinis* is dominant and nationality is conferred mainly by blood ties, and Sweden, where the principle of *jus soli* is dominant and nationality is conferred mainly by place of birth. In 1992 Germany accepted 5.3 times as many asylum seekers as Sweden but experienced 29 times as many acts of anti-foreign arson or bombing attacks. In a rough comparison of nativist violence in the early 1990s in five European countries (France, Britain, Switzerland, Sweden, and Germany), Alber suggests that while Britain, Switzerland, Sweden, and Germany all experienced an increase in violent incidents, the number and intensity of anti-foreign violence is highest in Germany. An explanation of Sweden's much lower rate of violence is its policy of assimilating immigrants by aggressive education, training, and integrative social programs and by giving immigrants the right to vote and run for office in community and regional elections after three years of residence. Sweden is also first among 12 European countries in its naturalization rate.[5]

Voting vs. Violence

Comparing Germany and France yields a hint of an inverse relationship between anti-immigration voting and anti-immigrant violence.[6] It also validates the idea that integration policies reduce the rate of violence even where perceived economic deprivation and social distance are similar.

First, the similarities. The supporters of anti-immigrant, populist-right groups and parties in both countries are concentrated in areas of exceptional immigrant concentration and economic instability or at least perceived instability. These groups draw support from both the losers and winners of structural readjustment. It is not only economic deterioration alone that provokes protest; it is any major economic change, up or down, that heightens the sense of insecurity. For instance, among the German winners are Baden-Württemberg and Bavaria; among the French winners are Paris and the Ile-de-France and Alsace. German losers include Schleswig-Holstein and Bremen; French losers include Marseilles and Bouche du Rhône. All of these areas are either strongholds of protest voting or evidence above-average support for anti-immigrant politicians.

The core supporters of Le Pen in France and the Republikaner in Germany are not especially marginal. They are citizens of the middle mass (lower white collar, upper working class, self-employed). In both countries, most are males with vocational training or high school but no higher education. Whether they are employed or not they have a strong sense of insecurity—economic and physical—that is much more intense and widespread than among voters for other more established parties. They rank insecurity, law-and-order and crime at the top of their concerns. Even the lawless skinheads in Germany identify their biggest worry as Zukunftssicherheit or "future security." Responding to political demagogues, they blame their job insecurities and other troubles on immigrants.

In both countries the targets of protest voters and violent gangs are distant in language and appearance; they are typically Islamic—e.g. "guestworker" Turks and Balkan refugees in Germany, Arabs from North Africa and the Sub-Sahara in France. In both countries ethnic segregation in substandard housing and poor neighborhoods is common. Both include immigrants in universal welfare-state benefits, whose alleged drain on the taxpayer-citizen is a centerpiece of political propaganda. All this should sound familiar to television viewers in the United States who were exposed to saturation advertising on crime, immigrants and welfare during the poisonous Congressional campaign of 1994.

With all these French-German similarities it is striking that Germany has much more anti-immigrant violence than France while France has much higher populist right anti-immigrant voting than Germany. For instance, per capita acts of extreme right xenophobic violence in Germany after 1990 were at least 2.5 times higher than in France. But electoral support shows the reverse pattern: Le Pen's *Front National* received between 26 and 28 percent of the vote in 1988 Presidential elections in areas of high immigrant concentration in Southwest France—Marseilles, Toulon, and Nice; in February 1997, the *Front National* won its first absolute majority of the vote in a municipal election in the Marseilles suburb of Vitrolles. In contrast, from 1973 to 1989 German support for similar extreme right-wing parties at its peak in the 1989 Euro-elections was only 7.1 percent (excluding Bavaria and Baden-Württemberg the other Länder ranged between 4 and 6 percent of the vote going to the REPs). At its peak in national elections since unification that vote was less than 5 percent. In fact, in the 1994 national election the Republikaner got only 1.9 percent of the vote.

Contrasts in public policy and politics as well as rates of immigration provide a reasonable explanation. The German policy of ethnic exclusion based on descent and combined with wide open access to refugees up to 1993 (perhaps driven by historical guilt) makes the cultural and social integration of minorities difficult, no matter how long they stay (some of the Turks are third-generation workers).[7] Sheer numbers add to nativist resentment and violence.[8] In contrast, French policy, while not as assimilative as that of the U.S. or Canada, is inclusive. French official administrative classifications from the first have been socio-professional or "national"; from the Third Republic on, the French forbade all Census questions about ethnic, religious, and linguistic origins. The French version of the melting pot myth is that the fusion of peoples came to an end with the Revolution and no redefinition of "French" can come from subsequent waves of immigration. French universalism has had a paradoxical result: it exaggerates the social distance between nation-conscious Frenchmen and foreigners; at the same time it shapes the law of immigration in more liberal directions. Encouragement of assimilation may reduce violence but still permit political expression of nativist sentiments. As an added explanation of Le Pen's strength, France has run a much higher rate of unemployment than Germany for many years. Vitrolles, where LePen's party reached its first majority, has not only a large concentration of North African immigrants; it also has an abundance of alienated French workers hard hit by 19 percent unemployment.

A final piece of this puzzle is the role of electoral laws as they shape protest voting. Both France and Germany have mixed proportional-plurality electoral systems with two-stage voting. But the two ballots in the French case are cast a week or two apart; only the second is decisive. The two ballots of the Germans— one for the candidate, one for the party—are simultaneous and both ballots shape the final political composition of the government. French voters can therefore indulge their xenophobic sentiments in a first-ballot protest against the political establishment with little consequence in most cases; German voters are denied any second thoughts. In short, the German combination of much higher numbers of socially-distant strangers, an exclusionary naturalization policy, and an electoral system that discourages pure protest voting (and incidentally makes neo-Nazi parties illegal) encourages violence; the French combination of lower numbers of immigrants, universalistic ideology and assimilative policies, greater unemployment but electoral laws and traditions favorable to protest voting minimizes violence and provides xenophobic movements with an abundance of voters.

Nativism and Tax-Welfare Backlash Go Together[9]

[W]e also analyzed tax-welfare backlash in 19 rich democracies—the universe of democracies in the upper one-sixth of GNP per capita with a million or more population. By tax-welfare backlash I mean strong social-political movements and/or parties that emphasize anti-tax, anti-social spending, anti-bureaucratic ideological themes and achieve electoral success for substantial periods. . . .

What is most interesting for our understanding of nativism is that when we analyzed tax-welfare backlash, it proved impossible to separate anti-tax, anti-social spending, anti-bureaucratic protest movements and parties from nativist, xenophobic or racist protests; these two themes appear together in all the high-scoring countries except Denmark in the 1970s. (Even in Denmark the Progress Party began to complain about immigrants in the 1980s.) When Hollywood-actor Ronald Reagan swept California in the 1966 gubernatorial election he sounded not only the familiar anti-tax, anti-social spending, anti-bureaucratic themes but at the same time baited welfare mothers. He brought the house down when he asserted that welfare recipients (code words for black welfare poor) are on a "prepaid lifetime vacation plan." In 1970, after four years in office, with taxes rising, welfare costs soaring, and campus disruption recurring (all of which he vowed to stop), Governor Reagan ran and won on the same slogans: "We are fighting the big-spending politicians who advocate a welfare state, the welfare bureaucrats whose jobs depend on expanding the welfare system, and the cadres of professional poor who have adopted welfare as a way of life." That movement culminated in eight years of the Reagan Presidency, and ultimately a Republican takeover of Congress in 1994 with identical campaign themes—anti-tax, anti-spend, anti-bureaucracy combined with the complaint that immigrants and other poor racial and linguistic minorities were creating immense burdens of welfare and crime. For backlash politicians the slogan "no welfare for immigrants" is a "two-fer": it encapsulates two unpopular targets, recipients of social assistance (the undeserving poor) and despised minority groups. As President, Reagan repeatedly referred to mythical "welfare queens" as symbols of welfare fraud and abuse.[10]

Similarly, in the U.K. in the early 1970s, Conservative Enoch Powell, the Cambridge-educated establishment version of George Wallace or Ronald Reagan, became the charismatic hero of the middle mass. He not only targeted social spending and taxing as a drag on the British economy; he also railed against the hordes of West Indian blacks and other immigrants who were un-English and would undermine the British way of life. Although Powell failed to become top man of the Tories—they were embarrassed by his racism—Margaret Thatcher managed to become their top person articulating all of Powell's arguments except the overt complaints about racial minorities. Switzerland, too, has blended tax-welfare backlash with nativism. James Schwarzenbach in 1970 reached his peak of 46 percent of the total vote in a national referendum which proposed to limit the admission of foreign workers, a measure that his party claimed essential not only to preserve the Swiss way of life but to avoid an ultimately staggering burden of social services. In the late 1970s, a Schwarzenbach-type movement was still operating—various right-wing populist parties rose in votes in the late 1970s and early 1980s and remained strong in the 1991 election. They include the Swiss Democrats, especially strong in Berne, Zurich and Graubünden; the Lega Ticinese (anti-tax, anti-spend, anti-bureaucratic, anti-corruption) in Italian-speaking Ticino; and more recently the Motorist Party ("Parti des Automobilistes") who favor privatization of transportation, denial of social benefits to foreign workers, and are generally anti-government and anti-Green. In the 1990s, the populist, charismatic leader of the right, Christopher Blocher of Zurich, was orchestrating the themes of these disparate parties and groups. Although small right-wing parties lost votes in the 1995 election, Blocher's People's Party was a winner (up 3 percent); the total backlash vote remained steady. Finally, Canada, with an above-average backlash score based largely on the populist tax revolts confined to Alberta and British Columbia, evidences the same merging of anti-tax, anti-social spending, anti-bureaucratic sentiments with a rising Western resentment of the Francophones of Quebec and the politicians in Ottawa who coddle them. (The Social Credit Party, in

office in Alberta from 1935 to 1971, also appealed to anti-Semites.) More recently, the Reform Party, emerging in Alberta, then BC, rose to third in popular
vote nationally in 1993; it even more clearly combined tax-welfare backlash
with hostility to Francophones and all foreigners.[11] And in June 1997 it became
the official opposition to the ruling Liberals in Parliament.

In short, while nativism is widespread among all rich democracies, only a few
rank high on tax-welfare backlash; these few cases almost always combine hostility to taxing, spending, and government bureaucracy with hostility to socially-
distant minority groups. Facilitating the merger of tax-welfare backlash and
nativism is the social locus of both in the middle mass. Politicians mobilizing
lower-middle class and upper working-class people who feel economically-
squeezed between the privileged top and the competing bottom can easily add
racial-ethnic resentments prevalent in the same population.

Summary and Conclusion

Migration from poor areas to rich is new neither in its rate nor in its consequences. Rich democracies are now converging in their cultural and social diversity and in their conflict focused on immigration. They differ, however, in
their openness to political and economic refugees, their policies toward immigrant integration, and the intensity of anti-immigrant mobilization. Anti-immigrant sentiments are most intense where the number and concentration of immigrants are heavy, the social distance between natives and strangers (in
education, religion, language, ethnicity, and race) is great, and the economic instability of industrial readjustment is most widely experienced. Most important,
industrial democracies differ in their ways of channeling mass prejudices and
populist-right movements. A country that makes a serious effort to minimize
illegal immigration, and to assimilate immigrants via inclusionary naturalization
policies, job creation, training, and placement, and language and citizenship education will minimize nativist violence. It may ultimately reduce the electoral
appeal of political demagogues who intensify mass fears and hatreds to achieve
power.

Finally, I doubt that European democracies and Japan, as they experience increased immigration, must necessarily produce an alienated underclass, the target
of a middle-mass revolt, American style. Only if they abandon the public policies
that encouraged labor peace and kept their poverty rates low—family policies, an
active labor-market policy, an accommodative framework for industrial relations,
a universalistic welfare state—will they drift into the Anglo-American pattern.
Some may choose that road; but the choice is there.

There is no tidal wave of immigrants to the affluent democracies. In relation
to world population international migration is a rare event. In general, the negative economic effects of increased migration are exaggerated and the political
effects can be contained.

Notes

1. Paper presented at the 14th World Congress of Sociology, Montreal, Canada, July 26–August 1, 1998. Based on parts of chapters 1, 5, 10, and 18 of H. L. Wilensky, *Rich Democracies: Political Economy, Public Policy, and Performance* (2002) and Wilensky (1993). I am grateful to Karen Adelberger and Fred Schaffer for research assistance and to the Institute of Governmental Studies, the Center for German and European Studies, and the Institute of Industrial Relations for support.

2. According to Heinz Fassman and Rainer Münz (1994), of an estimated 14,160,000 migrants from East to West (including those from the GDR, ex-Yugoslavia, Poland, Soviet Union and the Balkans) from 1950 to 1993, 68.1 percent landed in Germany, 8.1 percent in Israel, 6.6 percent in Turkey, 4.8 percent in the U.S. and 12.8 percent in other countries (Austria, Scandinavia, France, U.K., Canada, etc.) Of these 14 million about three in four can be classified as "ethnic" migrants, often the product of bilateral agreements between sender and receiver. Less than 15 percent can be classified as regular or irregular labor migrants or as dependent family of labor migrants. For much of the postwar period, the political and economic split of East and West prevented much movement of labor (or capital), except for more than half a million Yugoslavs. About ten percent can be classified as political refugees and asylum seekers escaping persecution (Hungarians 1956–57, Czechoslovaks 1968–69, Poles 1980–81, Albanians 1990–91, former Yugoslavs 1991–93). Fassman and Muenz's category of "ethnic" migrants doubtless includes some political and economic migrants.

3. Employer sanctions, used by almost all our 19 countries (Britain is an exception) vary in their effectiveness: Vital to their success are adequate resources for enforcement, a secure identification system, links to broader strategies for controlling illegal migration and enforcing labor standards, and steps to prevent employer discrimination. The U.S. fails on all counts. Several European countries—Germany, France, Switzerland—approximate them. (M. J. Miller 1987.)

    Openness to refugees also varies. In 1992 Germany took in two-thirds of the 572,000 asylum-seekers entering Europe as it struggled to get other countries to share the burden. On July 1, 1993 it changed its open asylum policy to accept refugees only from regimes that were persecuting them. It made it difficult for persons who passed through "presumably safe countries"—including Romania, Bulgaria, Gambia, Ghana, and Poland—to apply for asylum. Germany worked out arrangements with each adjacent country to help police its borders, giving money to Czechoslovakia and Poland for that purpose. All this sharply cut the number of applicants. The German Bundestag later approved an expansion of the number and power of the border police and raised penalties on illegal alien smugglers. Again, it is far from impossible to regulate immigration. (*Migration News*, vol. 1, #7). Of course it is a beggar-thy-neighbor policy—one country's successful border control is often another country's headache, a powerful reason for international agreements on burden-sharing.

4. These three forces that encourage nativist protest action—economic deprivation, large numbers and concentration of immigrants, and great social distance between immigrants and natives (Wilensky, 1975, pp. 57–59)—are the same as the forces that foster prejudice and the perception of group threat. See Lincoln Quillian (1995), an analysis of Eurobarometer Survey #30 results on attitudes toward immigrants and racial minorities in 12 EEC countries, Fall 1988. Individual characteristics had little impact on prejudice and explained none of the country differences. Economic conditions of the country, the size of the minority group and its social composition (e.g. non-EEC immigration) are the important variables shaping both levels of prejudice and the militancy of protest movements discussed below.

5. In the most recent year available (circa 1991) naturalizations as a percentage of the stock of foreign population in the year before was 5.4 percent in Sweden, 2.7 percent in Germany (Guimezanes, 1994, p. 25).

6. The next six paragraphs draw on data developed in a 1993 paper by my assistant, Karen Adelberger, from French and German surveys and recent literature. See also Wilensky (1975, p. 57–59 and 1976, pp. 12–34).

7. For an account of recent German immigration debates, policies, and administrative practices, see Halfmann, 1995. Brubaker (1992) describes the evolution of French and German citizenship policies.

8. Alber (1994), using Eurobarometer surveys and data from Wiegand and Fuchs, Gerhards and Roller, devises an index of "rejection of foreigners" (respondents who say that there are too many foreigners in their country, that the presence of foreigners is disturbing, that the rights of foreigners should be restricted, and that asylum seekers should no longer be accepted). For 11 EC countries this index of xenophobia correlates .82 with the percentage of foreigners from non-EC countries in each nation, underscoring the importance of numbers.

9. This section is based on chapter 10, "Tax-Welfare Backlash: How to Tax, Spend, and Yet Keep Cool" of my *Rich Democracies: Political Economy, Public Policy, and Performance* (2002) and Wilensky (1976).

10. Chapter 8 of Wilensky's *Rich Democracies* discusses why "welfare"—means-tested public assistance, a small fraction of public expenditures—became a political obsession in the United States.

11. A careful analysis of the 1993 election showed that the defectors from the Progressive Conservatives who went in droves to the Reform Party, while they shared the Reform Party's protest against taxing and spending, were virulently anti-immigrant and anti-Quebec—more xenophobic than other Tory voters (Nevitte et al., 1995). With the victory of the Conservative party of Ontario in June 1995, a third provincial backlash movement with explicit inspiration from the campaigns of Ronald Reagan and Margaret Thatcher, came to power (*Wall Street Journal*, June 12, 1995 and October 3, 1995). Thus, developments in the 1990s might justify a score for Canada of 3.5 rather than 3, which would strengthen the results reported in my earlier analysis (1976). (Interviews with politicians and journalists confirm this.) In my update I note that recent developments in Norway and Finland would move their above-average scores of 3 toward Sweden's 2, strengthening the idea that corporatist consensus insulates a democracy against backlash. Similarly, a study of 16 of the most threatening ethno-regional parties in five West European democracies (Britain, Italy, Spain, Belgium, Finland) shows that their electoral success from 1980 to 1992 is related to the degree of centralized corporatist bargaining. These parties had less success in corporatist Belgium and Finland, more where such structures are non-existent (Britain) or weak (Italy) (Müller-Rommel, 1994, p. 194 and Table 2.) Müller-Rommel (1994) confines analysis to ethno-regional parties that contested at least two national and regional elections from 1980 to 1992, polled at least 3 percent of the regional vote, and actually gained seats in the national parliament—a fair test of serious challenges to established parties. In the United Kingdom these include separatists such as the Ulster Unionists and Loyalists and United Ireland/Sinn Fein, as well as the left-libertarian federalists, the Scottish National Party and the Social Democratic Labour Party. In Belgium, it includes parties that demand autonomy and language rights within the nation-state—the Christeijk Vlaame Volksunie and the Front Démocratique des Bruxellois Francophoners. In Finland, it includes the Svenska Folkpartiet, which aims to defend the interests of a linguistic community without secession or a major restructuring of the state. In Italy, the Union Valdotaine fought for linguistic rights and regional decentralization; today the Northern League advocates federalism, threatens secession, and expresses great hostility to the backward, corrupt South as well as all immigrants (see chapter 8). The secessionist Parti Québécois in Canada, like the Basques in Spain, would fit the more-militant secessionists in the Müller-Rommel study.

    Finally, a study of the radical right in Europe similarly concludes that its greatest electoral successes occur when it couples a fierce commitment to free markets with equally-fierce xenophobia or racism (Kitschelt, 1995).

References

Abowd, John M. and Richard B. Freeman. "Introduction and Summary." In *Immigration, Trade and the Labor Market*, ed. John M. Abowd and Richard B. Freeman. 1–25. Chicago: University of Chicago Press, 1991.

Abowd, John M. and Richard J. Freeman, ed. *Immigration, Trade and the Labor Market*. Chicago: University of Chicago Press, 1991.

Alber, Jens. "Towards Explaining Anti-Foreign Violence in Germany." Unpublished lecture at the Center for European Studies, Harvard University, March 17, 1994.

Borjas, George J. *Friends of Strangers: The Impact of Immigrants on the U.S. Economy*. New York: Basic Books, 1990.

Borjas, George J., Richard B. Freeman, and Kevin Lang. "Undocumented Mexican-born Workers in the United States: How Many, How Permanent?" In *Immigration, Trade and the Labor Market*, ed. John M. Abowd and Richard B. Freeman. 77–100. Chicago: University of Chicago Press, 1991.

Borjas, George J., Richard B. Freeman, and Lawrence F. Katz. "On the Labor Market Effects of Immigration and Trade." In *Immigration and the Work Force: Economic Consequences for the United States and Souce Areas*, ed. George J. Borjas and Richard B. Freeman. 213–244. Chicago: University of Chicago Press, 1992.

Borjas, George J. and Richard B. Freeman. "Introduction and Summary." In *Immigration and the Work Force: Economic Consequences for the United States and the Source Areas*, ed. Geroge J. Borjas and Richard B. Freeman. 1–15. Chicago: University of Chicago Press, 1992.

Borjas, George J. "National Origin and Skills of Immigrants in the Postwar Period." In *Immigration and the Work Force: Economic Consequences for the United States and Source Areas*, ed. George J. Borjas and Richard B. Freeman. 17–47. Chicago: University of Chicago Press, 1992.

Brubaker, Rogers. *Citizenship and Nationhood in France and Germany*. Cambridge, Mass.: Harvard University Press, 1992.

Clark, Rebecca L. and Jeffrey S. Passel. *How Much Do Immigrants Pay in Taxes? Evidence from Los Angeles County*. Program for Research on Immigration Policy, Washington, D.C.: The Urban Institute, 1993.

Esman, Milton J. "The Political Fallout of International Migration." *Diaspora* 2 (1 1992): 3–41.

Fassmann, Heinz and Rainer Münz, "European East-West Migration 1945–1992." *International Migration Review* 28 (1994): 520–538.

Fix, Michael and Jeffrey S. Passel. *Immigration and Immigrants: Setting the Record Straight*. Washington, D.C.: The Urban Institute, 1994.

Freeman, Gary P. "Can Liberal States Control Unwanted Migration?" *Annals of the American Academy of Political and Social Science* 534 (1994): 17–30.

Guimezanes, Nicole. "What Laws for Naturalization?" *OECD Observer* 188 (1994): 24–26.

Halfmann, Jost. "Two Discourses of Citizenship in Germany: The Difference Between Public Debate and Administrative Practice." In *The Postwar Transformation of Germany: Democracy, Prosperity and Nationhood*. Center for German and European Studies, University of California, Berkeley, Berkeley CA, 1995.

Hollifield, James F. *Immigrants, Markets, and States: The Political Economy of Postwar Europe*. Cambridge, MA: Harvard University Press, 1992.

Huddle, Donald. *The Costs of Immigration: Executive Summary*. Carrying Capacity Network, 1993.

Kitschelt, Herbert, in collaboration with Anthony J. McGann. *The Radical Right in Western Europe: A Comparative Analysis*. Ann Arbor: University of Michigan Press, 1995.

Nee, Victor, Jimy M. Sanders, and Scott Sernau. "Job Transitions in an Immigrant Metropolis: Ethnic Boundaries and the Mixed Economy." *American Sociological Review* 59 (1994): 849–872.

Noiriel, Gérard. "Difficulties in French Historical Research on Immigration." In *Immigrants in Two Democracies: French and American Experience*, ed. Donald L. Horowitz and Gérard Noiriel. New York: New York University Press, 1992.

Passel, Jeffrey S. *Immigrants and Taxes: A Reappraisal of Huddle's "The Cost of Immigrants."* Program for Research on Immigration Policy, Washington, D.C.: The Urban Institute, 1994.

Quillian, Lincoln. "Prejudice as a Response to Perceived Group Threat: Population Composition and Anti-Immigrant and Racial Prejudice in Europe." *American Sociological Review* 60 (1995): 586–611.

Wilensky, Harold L. *The Welfare State and Equality: Structural and Ideological Roots of Public Expenditures*. Berkeley, CA: University of California Press, 1975.

Wilensky, Harold L. *The 'New Corporatism,' Centralization and the Welfare State*. London and Beverly Hills: Sage Publications, 1976.

Wilensky, Harold L. "The Nation-State, Social Policy, and Economic Performance." In *Globaliz-zazione e sistemi di welfare*, ed. M. Ferrara. 41–63. Torino, Italy: Edzioni della Fondazione G. Agnelli, 1993.

Wilensky, Harold L. *Rich Democracies: Political Economy, Public Policy, and Performance.* Berkeley: University of California Press, 2002.

 5.5

A Nation Is a Nation, Is a State, Is an Ethnic Group, Is a . . .

Walker Connor

Why is the key institution of global governance and international diplomacy called the "United Nations" when membership is really based on statehood? As Walker Connor explains in this selection, the terms "nation" and "state" are used almost interchangeably, but there are important differences between the two concepts. In fact, the expression "nation-state" (what in common usage is termed a "country") can be very misleading. The one-to-one correspondence between a nation or people and the exclusive political organization of a given territory by a state is usually considered the one best way to divide the world into stable units. Yet Connor concludes that nation-states are very much the exception. Thirty-five years ago scholars thought that perhaps 10 percent or fewer states could properly be called nation-states. Today, in this era of immigration and cultural diffusion, it is difficult to think of any pure cases of a culturally, ethnically, and linguistically homogeneous people (the nation) corresponding perfectly to the sovereign territory of political control represented at the United Nations (the state).

One of the most common manifestations of terminological license is the interutilization of the words *state* and *nation*. This tendency is perplexing because at one level of consciousness most scholars are clearly well aware of the vital distinctions between the two concepts. The state is the major

From Walker Connor, "A Nation Is a Nation, Is a State, Is an Ethnic Group, Is a . . . ," *Ethnic and Racial Studies* 1/4 (1978), pp. 379–388. Reprinted by permission of Taylor & Francis Ltd. <http://www.tandf.co.uk/journals>.

political subdivision of the globe. As such, it is readily defined and, what is of greater moment to the present discussion, is easily conceptualized in quantitative terms. Peru, for illustration, can be defined in an easily conceptualized manner as the territorial–political unit consisting of the sixteen million inhabitants of the 514,060 square miles located on the west coast of South America between 69° and 80° West, and 2° and 18°, 21° South.

Defining and conceptualizing the nation is much more difficult because the essence of a nation is intangible. This essence is a psychological bond that joins a people and differentiates it, in the subconscious conviction of its members, from all other people in a most vital way. The nature of that bond and its wellspring remain shadowy and elusive, and the consequent difficulty of defining the nation is usually acknowledged by those who attempt this task. Thus, a popular dictionary of International Relations defines a nation as follows:

> A social group which shares a common ideology, common institutions and customs, and a *sense* of homogenetry. "Nation" is difficult to define so precisely as to differentiate the term from such other groups as religious sects, which exhibit some of the same characteristics. In the nation, however, there is also present a strong group *sense* of belonging associated with a particular territory considered to be peculiarly its own.

Whereas the key word in this particular definition is *sense*, other authorities may substitute *feeling* or *intuition*, but proper appreciation of the abstract essence of the nation is customary *in definitions*. But after focusing attention upon that essential psychological bond, little probing of its nature follows. Indeed, having defined the nation as an essentially psychological phenomenon, authorities [. . .] then regularly proceed to treat it as fully synonymous with the very different and totally tangible concept of the state.

Even when one restricts *nation* to its proper, non-political meaning of a human collectivity, the ambiguity surrounding its nature is not thereby evaporated. How does one differentiate the nation from other human collectivities? The above cited definition spoke of "a sense of homogeneity." Others speak of a feeling of sameness, of oneness, of belonging, or of consciousness of kind. But all such definitions appear a bit timid, and thereby fail to distinguish the nation from numerous other types of groups. Thus, one can conceive of the Amish, Appalachian hill people, or "down Mainers" as all fitting rather neatly within any of the preceding standards.

With but very few exceptions, authorities have shied away from describing the nation as a kinship group and have usually explicitly denied that the notion of shared blood is a factor. Such denials are supported by data illustrating that most groups claiming nationhood do in fact incorporate several genetic strains. But such an approach ignores the wisdom of the old saw that when analysing sociopolitical situations, what ultimately matters is not *what is* but *what people believe is*. And a subconscious belief in the group's separate origin and evolution is an important ingredient of national psychology. When one avers that he is Chinese, he is identifying himself not just with the Chinese people and culture of today, but with the Chinese people and their activities throughout time. The Chinese Communist Party was appealing to just such a sense of separate origin and evolution in 1937:

> [W]e know that in order to transform the glorious future into a new China, independent, free, and happy, all our fellow countrymen, every single, zealous descendant of Huang-ti [the legendary first emperor of China] must determinedly and relentlessly participate in the concerted struggle.
> . . . Our great Chinese nation, with its long history is inconquerable.

Bismarck's famous exhortation to the German people, over the heads of their particular political leaders, to "think with your blood" was a similar attempt to activate a mass psychological vibration predicated upon an intuitive sense of consanguinity. An unstated presumption of a Chinese (or German) nation is that there existed in some hazy, prerecorded era a Chinese (or German) Adam and Eve, and that the couple's progeny has evolved in essentially unadulterated form down to the present. It was recognition of this dimension of the nation that caused numerous writers of the nineteenth and early twentieth centuries to employ *race* as a synonym for *nation*, references to a German race or to the English race being quite common.

Since the nation is a self-defined rather than an other-defined grouping, the broadly held conviction concerning the group's singular origin need not and seldom will accord with factual data. Thus, the anthropologist may prove to his own satisfaction that there are several genetic strains within the Pushtun people who populate the Afghani-Pakistani border-region and conclude therefrom that the group represents the variegated offspring of several peoples who have moved through the region. The important fact, however, is that the Pushtuns themselves are convinced that all Pushtuns are evolved from a single source and have remained essentially unadulterated. This is a matter which is *known* intuitively and unquestionably, a matter of attitude and not of fact. It is a matter, the underlying conviction of which is not apt to be disturbed substantially even by the rational acceptance of anthropological or other evidence to the contrary. Depending upon the sophistication of the treatise, this type of sensory knowledge may be described as "a priori," "an emotional rather than a rational conviction," "primordial," "thinking with the heart (or with the blood) rather than with the mind," or "a 'gut' or 'knee-jerk' response." Regardless of the nomenclature, it is an extremely important adjunct of the national idea. It is the intuitive conviction which can give to nations a psychological dimension approximating that of the extended family, i.e. a feeling of common blood lineage.

The word *nation* comes from the Latin and, when first coined, clearly conveyed the idea of common blood ties. It was derived from the past participle of the verb *nasci*, meaning to be born. And hence the Latin noun, *nationem*, connoting *breed* or *race*. Unfortunately, terms used to describe human collectivities (terms such as race and class) invite an unusual degree of literary license, and *nation* certainly proved to be no exception. Thus, at some medieval universities, a student's *nationem* designated the sector of the country from whence he came. But when introduced into the English language in the late thirteenth century, it was with its primary connotation of a blood related group. One etymologist notes, however, that by the early seventeenth century, *nation* was also being used to describe the inhabitants of a country, regardless of that population's ethnonational composition, thereby becoming a substitute for less specific human categories such as *the people* or *the citizenry*. This infelicitous practice continues to the present day, and accounts for often encountered references to the American citizenry as the American nation. Whatever the American people are (and they may well be *sui generis*), they are not a nation in the pristine sense of the word. However, the unfortunate habit of calling them a nation, and thus verbally equating American with German, Chinese, English, and the like, has seduced scholars into erroneous analogies. Indeed, while proud of being "a nation of immigrants" with a "melting pot" tradition, the absence of a common origin may well make it more difficult, and conceivably impossible, for the American to appreciate instinctively the idea of the nation in the same dimension and with the same poignant clarity as do the Japanese, the Bengali, or the Kikuyu. It is difficult for an American to appreciate what it means for a German to be German or for a Frenchman to be French, because the psychological effect of being American is not precisely equatable. Some of the associations are missing and others may be quite different.

Far more detrimental to the study of nationalism, however, has been the propensity to employ the term nation as a substitute for that territorial juridical unit, the state. How this practice developed is unclear, though it seems to have become a relatively common practice in the late seventeenth century. Two possible explanations for this development present themselves. One involves the rapid spread of the doctrine of popular sovereignty that was precipitated about this time by the writings of men such as Locke. In identifying *the people* as the font of all political power, this revolutionary doctrine made the people and the state almost synonymous. *L'état c'est moi* became *l'état c'est le peuple*. And therefore the nation and the state had become near synonyms, for we have already noted the tendency to equate nation with the entire people or citizenry. Thus, the French *Declaration of Rights of Man and Citizen* would proclaim that "the source of all sovereignty resides essentially in the nation; no group, no individual may exercise authority not emanating expressly therefrom." Though the drafters of the Declaration may not have been aware, "the nation" to which they referred contained Alsatians, Basques, Bretons, Catalans, Corsicans, Flemings, and Occitanians, as well as Frenchmen.

It is also probable that the habit of interutilizing *nation* and *state* developed as alternative abbreviations for the expression *nation-state*. The very coining of this hyphenate illustrated an appreciation of the vital differences between *nation* and *state*. It was designed to describe a territorial–political unit (a state) whose borders coincided or nearly coincided with the territorial distribution of a national group. More concisely, it described a situation in which a nation had its own state. Unfortunately, however, *nation-state* has come to be applied indiscriminately to all states. Thus one authority has stated that "a prime fact about the world is that it is largely composed of nation-states." The statement should read that "a prime fact about the world is that it is *not* largely composed of nation-states." A survey of the 132 entities generally considered to be states as of 1971, produced the following breakdown:

1. Only 12 states (9.1%) can justifiably be described as nation-states.
2. Twenty-five (18.9%) contain a nation or potential nation accounting for more than 90% of the state's total population but also contain an important minority.
3. Another 25 (18.9%) contain a nation or potential nation accounting for between 75% and 89% of the population.
4. In 31 (23.5%), the largest ethnic element accounts for 50% to 74% of the population.
5. In 39 (29.5%), the largest nation or potential nation accounts for less than half of the population.

Were all states nation-states, no great harm would result from referring to them as nations, and people who insisted that the distinction between *nation* and *state* be maintained could be dismissed as linguistic purists or semantic nit-pickers. Where *nation* and *state* essentially coincide, their verbal interutilization is inconsequential because the two are indistinguishably merged in popular perception. The state is perceived as the political extension of the nation, and appeals to one trigger the identical, positive psychological responses as appeals to the other. To ask a Japanese *kamikaze* pilot or a banzai-charge participant whether he was about to die for *Nippon* or for the Nipponese people would be an incomprehensible query since the two blurred into an inseparable whole. Hitler could variously make his appeals to the German people in the name of state (Deutsches Reich), nation (Volksdeutsch), or homeland (Deutschland), because all triggered the same emotional associations. Similar responses can be elicited from members of a nation that is clearly predominant within a state. But the invoking of such symbols has quite a different impact upon minorities. Thus, "Mother Russia" evokes one type of response from a Russian and something quite different from a Ukrainian. De Gaulle's emotional evocations of *La France* met quite different audiences within the Île de France and within Brittany or Corsica.

Whatever the original reason for the interutilization of *nation* and *state*, even the briefest reflection suffices to establish the all-pervasive effect that this careless use of terminology has had upon the intellectual–cultural milieu within which the study of nationalism is perforce conducted. The League of Nations and the United Nations are obvious misnomers. The discipline called International Relations should be designated *Interstate* Relations. One listing of contemporary organizations contains sixty-six entries beginning with the word

International (e.g. the International Court of Justice and the International Monetary Fund), none of which, either in its membership or in its function, reflects any relationship to nations. International Law and International Organization are still other significant illustrations of the common but improper tendency to equate state and nation. National income, national wealth, national interest, and the like, refer in fact to statal concerns. A recently coined malapropism, *transnational* (and even *transnationalism*) is used to describe interstate, extragovernmental relations. *Nationalization* is still another of the numerous misnomers that muddy understanding of the national phenomenon.

With the concepts of the nation and the state thus hopelessly confused, it is perhaps not too surprising that *nationalism* should come to mean identification with the state rather than loyalty to the nation. Even the same International Relations Dictionary whose definition of the *nation* we cited for its proper appreciation of the psychological essence of the nation, makes this error. After carefully noting that "a nation may comprise part of a state, or extend beyond the borders of a single state," it elsewhere says of *nationalism* that "it makes the state the ultimate focus of the individual's loyalty." It also says of nationalism that "as a mass emotion it is the most powerful political force operative in the world." Few would disagree with this assessment of the power of nationalism, *and this is precisely the problem. Impressed with the force of nationalism, and assuming it to be in the service of the state, the scholar of political development has been pre-programmed to assume that the new states of Africa and Asia would naturally become the foci of their inhabitants' loyalties.* Nationalism, here as elsewhere, would prove irresistible, and alternative foci of loyalty would therefore lose the competition to that political structure alternately called the nation, the state, or the nation-state. This syndrome of assumptions and terminological confusion which has generally characterized the political development school is reflected in the early self-description of its endeavors as "nation-building." Contrary to its nomenclature, the "nation-building" school has in fact been dedicated to building viable states. And with a very few exceptions, the greatest barrier to state unity has been the fact that the states each contain more than one nation, and sometimes hundreds. Yet, a review of the literature will uncover little reflection on how the psychological bonds that presently tie segments of the state's population are to be destroyed. One searches the literature in vain for techniques by which group-ties predicated upon such things as a sense of separate origin, development, and destiny are to be supplanted by loyalty to a state-structure, whose population has never shared such common feelings. The nature and power of those abstract ties that identify the true nation remain almost unmentioned, to say nothing of unprobed. The assumption that the powerful force called nationalism is in the service of the state makes the difficult investigation of such abstractions unnecessary.

As in the case of substituting the word *nation* for *state*, it is difficult to pinpoint the origin of the tendency to equate nationalism with loyalty to the state. It is unquestionably a very recent development, for the word *nationalism* is itself of very recent creation. G. de Bertier de Sauvigny believes it first appeared in literature in 1798 and did not reappear until 1830. Moreover, its absence from lexicographies until the late nineteenth and early twentieth centuries suggests that its use was not extensive until much more recently. Furthermore, all of the examples of its early use convey the idea of identification *not* with the state, but with the nation as properly understood. While unable to pinpoint nationalism's subsequent association with the state, it indubitably followed and flowed from the tendency to equate state and nation. It also unquestionably received a strong impetus from the great body of literature occasioned by the growth of militant nationalism in Germany and Japan during the 1930s and early 1940s.

As outstanding illustrations of the fanatical responses that nationalism can engender, German and Japanese nationalism of this period have come to occupy an important place in all subsequent scholarship on nationalism. And, unfortunately, these manifestations of extreme nationalism have been firmly identified with the loyalty to the state. The most common word applied to them has been *fascism,* a doctrine postulating unswerving obedience to an organic, corporate state. The most popular alternative descriptive phrase, *totalitarianism,* perhaps even more strongly conveys the idea of the complete (total) identification of the individual with the state.

The linking of the state to these examples *par excellence* of extreme nationalism suggests the likelihood that other states will also become the object of mass devotion. If some states could elicit such fanatical devotion, why not others? Granted, few would wish to see such extreme and perverted dedication to the state arise elsewhere. But if the concept of a Japanese state could, during World War II, motivate "banzai charges," kamikaze missions, and numerous decisions of suicide rather than surrender (as well as the many post-war illustrations of people enduring for years an animal-like existence in caves on Pacific islands) because of a loyalty to the Japanese state that was so unassailable as to place that state's defeat beyond comprehension, then surely the states of the Third World should at least be able to evoke a sufficiently strong loyalty from their inhabitants so as to prevail against any competing group-allegiances. If a loyalty to a German state could motivate Germans to carry on a war long after it became evident that the cause was hopeless and that perseverance could only entail more deprivation, destruction, and death, then surely other states could at least elicit a sense of common cause and identity from their populations that would prove more powerful than any counter-tendencies to draw distinctions among segments of the populace. If the German and Japanese experiences were pertinent elsewhere, then optimism concerning the stability of present state structures would be justified.

But what has been too readily ignored is the fact that Germany and Japan were among the handful of states that clearly qualify as nation-states. As earlier noted, in such cases the state and the nation are indistinguishably linked in popular perception. Japan to the Japanese, just as Germany to the Germans, was something far more personal and profound than a territorial–political structure termed a state; it was an embodiment of the nation-idea and therefore an extension of self. As postulated by fascist doctrine, these states were indeed popularly conceived as corporate organisms, for they were equated with the Japanese and German nations. As Hitler wrote in *Mein Kampf*: "We as Aryans, are therefore able to imagine a State only to be the living organism of a nationality which not only safeguards the preservation of that nationality, but which, by further training of its spiritual and ideal abilities, leads it to its highest freedom."

But could such an emotion-laden conception of the state take root where the nation and the state were not popularly equated? The single rubric of fascism was applied to Hitler's Germany, Tojo's Japan, Mussolini's Italy, Franco's Spain, and Peron's Argentina. It is evident, however, that appeals in the name of Spain have not elicited any great emotion from the Basques, Catalans, and Galicians. In polygenetic Argentina, Peron's message was not a unifying appeal to all Argentinians, but was in fact a divisive call in the name of socioeconomic class. Within Italy, a sense of loyalty to the state proved woefully and surprisingly inadequate in the face of its first major test, the invasion by Allied forces. The reason appears to be that the concept of a single people (national awareness) has not yet permeated the subconsciousness of the Italians to the same measure as a similar concept had permeated the German and Japanese people. In equating nationalism with loyalty to the state, scholars had failed to inquire how many cases there have been where fanatical devotion to a state has arisen in the absence of a popular conception of the state as the state of one's particular nation. Rather than suggesting certain victory on the part of new states in the competition for loyalty, the experiences of Germany and Japan exemplify the potential strength of those emotional ties to one's nation with which the multiethnic state must contend. German and Japanese nationalism were more prophetic auguries of the growth of concepts such as, *inter alia*, Ibo, Bengali, Kikuyu, Naga, Karen, Lao, Bahutu, Kurd, and Baganda, than they were auguries of the growth of concepts such as Nigeria, Pakistan, Kenya, India, Burma, Thailand, Rwanda, Iraq and Uganda.

Mistakenly equating nationalism with loyalty to the state has further contributed to terminological confusion by leading to the introduction of still other confusing terms. With nationalism preempted, authorities have had difficulty agreeing on a term to describe the loyalty of segments of a state's population to their particular nation. Ethnicity, primordialism, pluralism, tribalism, regionalism, communalism, and parochialism are among the most commonly encountered. This varied vocabulary further impedes an understanding of nationalism by creating the impression that each is describing a separate phenomenon. Moreover, reserving nationalism to convey loyalty to the state (or, more commonly, to the word *nation* when the latter is improperly substituted for state), while using words with different roots and fundamentally different connotations to refer to loyalty to the nation, adds immeasurably to the confusion. Each of the above terms has exercised its own particular negative impact upon the study of nationalism.

Ethnicity

Ethnicity (identity with one's ethnic group) is, if anything, more definitionally chameleonic than *nation*. It is derived from *Ethnos*, the Greek word for *nation* in the latter's pristine sense of a group characterized by common descent. Consonant with this derivation, there developed a general agreement that an ethnic group referred to a basic human category (i.e. not a subgroup). Unfortunately, however, American sociologists came to employ *ethnic group* to refer to "a group with a common cultural tradition and a sense of identity which exists as a subgroup of a larger society." This definition makes ethnic group synonymous with minority, and, indeed, with regard to group relations within the United States, it has been used in reference to nearly any discernible minority, religious, linguistic, or otherwise.

The definition of ethnic group by American sociologists violates its original meaning with regard to at least two important particulars. In the traditional sense of an ancestrally related unit, it is evident that an ethnic group need not be a subordinate part of a larger political society but may be the dominant element within a state (the Chinese, English, or French, for example) or may extend across several states, as do the Arabs. Secondly, the indiscriminate application of ethnic group to numerous types of groups, obscures vital distinctions between various forms of identity. In a stimulating and often cited introduction to a volume entitled *Ethnicity*, Nathan Glazer and Daniel Patrick Moynihan, while rejecting the notion that ethnicity refers only to minorities, defended the incorporation of several forms of identity under this single rubric.

> Thus, there is some legitimacy to finding that forms of identification based on social realities as different as religion, language, and national origin all have something in common, such that a new term is coined to refer to all of them: "ethnicity." What they have in common is that they have all become effective foci for group mobilization for concrete political ends . . .

However, despite the usefulness that such a categorization possesses for the study of the politics of special interest groups, there is little question but that it has exerted a damaging influence upon the study of nationalism. One result is that the researcher, when struggling through thousands of entries in union catalogs, indices to periodicals, and the like cannot be sure whether a so-called ethnic study will prove germane to the study of nationalism. Sometimes the unit under examination does constitute a national or potential national group. Other times it is a transnational (inter- or intrastate) group such as the Amerindians. And, in most instances, it is a group related only marginally, if at all, to the nation, as properly understood (e.g. the Catholic community within the Netherlands). Moreover, a review of the indices and bibliographies found in those ethnic studies that do deal with a national or potential national group, illustrate all too often that the author is unaware of the relationship of his work to nationalism. The student of nationalism and the student of ethnicity seldom cross-fertilize. The

American journal, *Ethnicity*, and the *Canadian Review of Studies in Nationalism*, for example, are remarkably free of overlap with regard to (1) the academic background of their contributors and (2) footnoted materials.

Even if the author uses the term *ethnicity* solely in relation to national groups, his equating of nationalism with loyalty to the state will predispose him to underestimate the comparative magnetism of the former. But the much more common practice of employing ethnicity as a cloak for several different types of identity exerts a more baneful effect. Such a single grouping presumes that all of the identities are of the same order. We shall reserve further comment on the adverse consequences of this presumption to a later discussion of *primordialism* and *pluralism*, noting here only that this presumption circumvents raising the key question as to which of a person's several identities is apt to win out in a test of loyalties.

Anthropologists, ethnologists, and scholars concerned with global comparisons have been more prone to use *ethnicity* and *ethnic group* in their pristine sense of involving a sense of common ancestry. Max Weber, for example, noted:

> We shall call "ethnic groups" those human groups that entertain a subjective belief in their common descent . . . , this belief must be important for the propagation of group formation; conversely, it does not matter whether or not an objective blood relationship exists. Ethnic membership (*Gemeinsamkeit*) differs from the kinship group precisely by being a presumed identity . . .

This definition would appear to equate *ethnic group* and *nation* and [. . .] Weber did indeed link the two notions. However, elsewhere Weber made an important and useful distinction between the two:

> [T]he idea of the nation is apt to include the notions of common descent and of an essential though frequently indefinite homogeneity. The "nation" has these notions in common with the sentiment of solidarity of ethnic communities, which is also nourished from various sources, as we have seen before. *But the sentiment of ethnic solidarity does not by itself make a "nation."* Undoubtedly, even the White Russians in the face of the Great Russians have always had a sentiment of ethnic solidarity, yet even at the present time they would hardly claim to qualify as a separate "nation." The Poles of Upper Silesia, until recently, had hardly any feeling of solidarity with the "Polish nation." They felt themselves to be a separate ethnic group in the face of the Germans, but for the rest they were Prussian subjects and nothing else.

Weber is here clearly speaking of pre-national peoples or [. . .] potential nations. His illustrations are of peoples not yet cognizant of belonging to a larger ethnic element. The group consciousness to which he refers—that rather low level of ethnic solidarity that a segment of the ethnic element feels when confronted with a foreign element—need not be very important politically and comes closer to xenophobia than to nationalism. To the degree that it represents a step in the process of nation-formation, it testifies that a group of people must know ethnically what they *are not* before they know what they *are*. Thus, to Weber's illustrations, we can add the Slovaks, Croats, and Slovenes who, under the Habsburg Empire, were aware that they were neither German nor Magyar, long before they possessed positive opinions concerning their ethnic or national identity. In such cases, meaningful identity of a positive nature remains limited to locale, region, clan, or tribe. Thus, members need not be conscious of belonging to the ethnic group. Ernest Barker made this same point with regard to all peoples prior to the nineteenth century:

> The self-consciousness of nations is a product of the nineteenth century. This is a matter of the first importance. Nations were already there; they had indeed been there for centuries. But it is not the things which are simply "there" that matter in human life. What really and finally matters is the thing which is apprehended as an idea, and, as an idea, is vested with emotion until it becomes a cause and a spring of action. In the world of action apprehended ideas are alone electrical; and a nation must be an idea as well as a fact before it can become a dynamic force.

To refine Barker's wording only slightly, and his meaning not at all, a nation is a self-aware ethnic group. An ethnic group may be readily discerned by an anthropologist or other outside observer, but until the members are themselves aware of the group's uniqueness, it is merely an ethnic group and not a nation. While an ethnic group *may*, therefore, be other-defined, the nation *must* be self-defined. Employing ethnic group or ethnicity in relationship to several types of identities therefore beclouds the relationship between the *ethnic group* and the *nation* and also deprives scholarship of an excellent term for referring to both nations and potential nations.

 5.6

Lessons from the Muslim World

Vali Nasr

In recent decades, fundamentalism in all its varieties—Christian, Islamic, Hindu, and Jewish among others—has inspired profound challenges to secular societies in both the developed and the developing world. Particularly since 9/11, the violent and destabilizing role of fundamentalism in the Muslim world has attracted

---

Vali Nasr, "Lessons from the Muslim World," *Daedalus*, Vol. 132, No. 3 (Summer 2003): 67–72.

tremendous interest. In this contribution, Vali Nasr explains that the raging conflict between religious and secular worldviews may lead to a distinctive homegrown model of government in the Muslim world. Can a moderate fundamentalism open to compromise engage secular forces to help advance development and modernization in Muslim states?

Secularism has come under assault over the course of the last two decades, in developing as well as industrialized societies, in democracies as well as dictatorships. Christian, Hindu, Islamic, and Jewish fundamentalisms, with different political aspirations representing diverse constituencies, have spearheaded the resurgence of religious values, institutions, and organizations. On a global scale, the fundamentalist juggernaut has eroded the place of secularism in politics, policy-making, law, and social relations, and has posed a profound challenge to old ways of thinking about modernity, its prerequisites, directives, and institutions. . . .

. . . To understand the shape of things to come we have to take stock of the changes that have taken place over the past few decades and also look closely at changes that are currently unfolding. This we should do not through the lens of old paradigms, but with a view to identifying emerging trends.

Nowhere is the scope of change produced by fundamentalism more evident than in the Muslim world. It was here that fundamentalism found its most vociferous and disruptive expression and mounted its most direct and poignant challenge to secularism and its institutions. It is also here that the intensity of the struggle between religion and secularism is producing new paradigms and institutions that will shape our world for years to come.

In the Muslim Middle East and Asia, secularism was not a product of socio-economic, technological, or cultural change—it was not associated with any internal social dynamic. In fact, it was not even an indigenous force. Secularism was first and foremost a project of the state—first the colonial state, and later the postcolonial state. It was a Western import, meant to support the state's aim of long-run development. As a result, from the outset a religious-secular divide came to reflect the increasingly contentious relations between the society and the colonial state.

The postcolonial state in the Muslim world reproduced these tensions in a voluntary effort to emulate the Western state, which it understood to be inherently secular. The Turkish Republic established after World War I serves as the most lucid example here. It was militantly secular and adopted nationalism in lieu of religion to forge a modern nation. The Turkish state soon became a model for state formation in much of the Muslim world; Iran during the Pahlavi period, Arab nationalist regimes, Indonesia, Pakistan—all to varying degrees emulated the Turkish model.

In the Muslim world, the postcolonial state thus sought to drive religion out of politics and public life—just as Atatürk had done in Turkey. Attempting to use nationalism or socialism or both to mold citizens into a secular whole, the state showed a great concern for regulating the daily lives and cultural outlook of its subjects. Social engineering went hand in hand with the conscious secularization of the judiciary and the educational system, and with the nationalization of religious endowments, thus truncating the sociopolitical role of religion.

Still, the process of secularization was problematic in the Muslim world, insofar as it did not seek to separate religion from politics, but rather to subjugate religion to political control. This had the effect of politicizing religion as Muslim institutions struggled with the state, often in an effort to loosen the state's control over society. Though forcibly marginalized, religion thus remained relevant: in the struggle between state and society, religion in some cases became a focus for resisting authoritarian forms of secularism. In Egypt for instance, Gamal Abd al-Nasser's imposition of reforms on the al-Azhar Islamic educational institution to bring its values into alignment with the goals of the state had the effect of imparting political attitudes on religious leaders and institutions, which eventually culminated in the growing influence of fundamentalism and parties dedicated to a "re-Islamization" of Egyptian society after 1980.

Secularism in the Muslim world never overcame its colonial origins and never lost its association with the postcolonial state's continuous struggle to dominate society. Its fortunes became tied to those of the state: the more the state's ideology came into question, and the more its actions alienated social forces, the more secularism was rejected in favor of indigenous worldviews and social institutions—which were for the most part tied to Islam. As such, the decline of secularism was a reflection of the decline of the postcolonial state in the Muslim world.

The crisis facing states from Malaysia to Morocco in the latter part of the twentieth century fostered an Islamic challenge to secularism and the postcolonial state. The emerging trend became most spectacularly evident with the Iranian revolution of 1979. The revolution was the first instance of a fundamentalist movement replacing a secular state, and it inspired similar challenges to state authority and its secular underpinnings across the Muslim world.

Since 1979, revolutionary movements in Algeria, Lebanon, Egypt, Palestine, Afghanistan, Pakistan, and Indonesia, as well as international umbrella groups such as Al Qaeda, have harkened to the Iranian model. But in Iran itself fundamentalism is no longer the revolutionary force that it once was; the Islamic Republic of Iran has failed to produce a viable model for Islamic government and is today facing a crisis that will likely end the political dominance of religion there. Equally important, elsewhere in the Muslim world fundamentalism has proved to be neither as successful nor as intractable and uncompromising as the example of revolutionary Iran suggests. It has interacted with secularism and the state to produce new approaches to modern society and politics and the role of religion therein.

In the process, fundamentalism has by and large matured. Although it still inspires extremism, that tendency is no longer the dominant force in many Muslim societies. Indeed, fundamentalism has developed new perspectives on society and politics, compromised on its narrow ideals, and become an ingredient in the broader movement toward the modernization and development of Muslim states. And what comes out of this process will inevitably determine the relation between religion and secularism in the Muslim world and beyond.

Islamic fundamentalism was not successful in its assault on secularism and the state in the wake of the Iranian revolution—but it was able to institutionalize a role for Islam in society and politics. In so doing, it both gave impetus to a greater popular role for Islam in the public sphere and made Islam a legitimate—and in many cases attractive—tool with which to achieve political goals, thus encouraging many more social and political actors to use Islam in a largely secular public arena. Though unable to achieve its own avowed goal of replacing the postcolonial state, fundamentalism was able to make Islam a critical force in society and politics.

The advocates of a return to Islam have been able to make religious values, however rigid, seem relevant to modern society. They have been able to bridge traditional and modern segments of society. At the same time, fundamentalists have done much to politicize Islamic symbols and to formulate new Islamic concepts of relevance to politics—such as "Islamic economics," "Islamic education," "Islamization of knowledge," and the "Islamic state." They have both articulated the manner in which these symbols should serve political ends and convinced large numbers of citizens that "Islamization" is a necessary and beneficial process. Despite their opposition to secularism, many fundamentalists have supported extensive state intervention in the economy and society, and, in some countries, have given fresh legitimacy to the idea of a domineering state.

As a result, fundamentalists have been able to redefine the concept of politics in much of the Muslim world, shaping how politicians, state institutions, dissident groups, even how educated youth and segments of the intelligentsia define their goals.

Islamic fundamentalism became ensconced in the politics of Muslim societies at a time when the secular conception of the state and its nationalist underpinning were losing legitimacy and, hence, political efficacy. Still, because fundamentalism was not able to completely replace existing political and social structures, it has set the stage for an ongoing and intense struggle over the proper balance between religion and secularism in Muslim societies.

Many secular states have responded to the fundamentalist challenge by appropriating aspects of its discourse, to bolster their legitimacy and thus augment their power. Malaysia and Pakistan exemplify this trend. In both countries, the leadership has successfully confounded its fundamentalist opposition while reaping the fruits of its propaganda. By introducing "fundamentalism from above," they have been able to exploit the fundamentalist challenge from below, while strengthening their control over politics and society.

Faced with the staying power of the secular state, still other fundamentalist forces in other countries have opted to change. By compromising, they have been able to gain a foothold in the political process. Here it is Islamic forces rather than the state that have been at the forefront of political change, defining the ways in which Islam and secular politics could blend to produce new models for state and society to follow.

Turkey is perhaps the best example in this regard. Faced with the uncompromising secularism of the state, Turkish Islamic forces have abandoned their narrow fundamentalist views in favor of an inclusive and pragmatic approach to the role of religion in politics: they have dropped their demands for strict adherence to Islamic law, they support Turkey's relations with the West, and they even accept the need to maintain relations with Israel. The pragmatism of Turkey's Islamic forces has produced a model for the rest of the Muslim world to follow, one in which modern state and social institutions that are secular in nature also reflect Islamic values.

Iran—a secular state that fell to an Islamic revolution that now faces a secular backlash—represents a very different model of what the future may hold. Through the crucible of revolution, and the rise and fall of popular support for creating an Islamic republic, Iran has been experimenting with a unique combination of religion and secularism. There the state is now the repository of Islam and the society is pushing for secularization—the obverse of what is happening in the rest of the Muslim world.

Iran's Islamic Republic enjoyed only temporary success in implementing its vision. Its theocratic ideal quickly became a facade behind which religious and political authorities stood increasingly apart from one another. The state was never able to completely control its sizable secular social stratum, which has become a primary source of secular resistance to the Islamic Republic. So in time the Republic had to bow to other pressures that, for one, have necessitated the use of elections to settle struggles for power. And the practice of voting has, in turn, inadvertently produced a certain degree of pluralism and also a distinct political momentum for institutionalizing more democratic practices and modes of political behavior.

This dialectic—a growing secularism in society reinforced by a gradual opening of the Islamic state—is peculiar to Iran. It represents a unique model in which secularism and the sociopolitical institutions associated with it are not merely imported ideals imposed from above, but homegrown trends that have emerged to curtail the power of the Islamic state. As a result, Iran promises to produce a religio-secular model whose point of origin is Islamic rather than secular—and quite different from what one finds elsewhere in the Muslim Middle East and Asia.

As the example of Iran suggests, the Muslim world is in the midst of a process of change, experimenting with models that, by balancing the competing demands of religion and secularism, can create viable ways for these societies to modernize. What is likely to emerge at the end is nation-states that strike a very different balance between religion and secularism from that drawn in the West. These states will call upon the cultural resources of religion to address their social and economic needs—but not necessarily in the manner that European history suggests.

 Chapter 6

POLITICAL INSTITUTIONS
AND PUBLIC POLICIES

An important topic of research in comparative politics these days involves the study of political institutions and public policies. Why? Because political institutions and policies have a critical impact on citizens' lives and political and social life—often in ways that are subtle and possibly unintended. When it comes to political institutions and public policies, the devil is often in the details.

What, then, are institutions? One of the most frequently quoted definitions of institutions has been suggested by Peter Hall: "The concept of institutions . . . refer[s] to the formal rules, compliance procedures, and standard operating practices that structure the relationship between individuals in various units of the polity and economy."* Note that this definition is very broad: Hall defines institutions both as formal rules and procedures—what are commonly described as organizations—and what he calls "standard operating procedures," that is, informal understandings. Formal rules and procedures are enumerated in constitutions and law books. Although it is more difficult to define and identify informal institutions, they may be extremely influential. For example, there is no law that dictates that senators from a given state who share the president's party affiliation have a veto power over the selection of federal judges from that state. But this time-honored custom has such force that it can be considered an institution. Comparativists engage in extensive research to understand how institutions originate, the impact they have, and how they change. The selections in this chapter all analyze why the design of institutions affects political outcomes. Stepan claims that parliamentary forms of government are more likely than presidential regimes to promote political compromise and stability. Mansfield and Snyder assert that when institutions concentrate power in the hands of political leaders, they are less likely to resort to war to consolidate their control. Reilly suggests that electoral procedures can either unite or polarize ethnically divided societies. Katzenstein suggests that the design of institutions affects the possibilities and character of protest that may occur within these institutions. And Weldon

---

* Peter A. Hall, *Governing the Economy: The Politics of State Intervention in Britain and France* (New York: Oxford University Press, 1986), p. 19.

documents that a particular combination of governmental institutions and grass-roots women's movements is most likely to be associated with low rates of violence against women.

Public policy can be considered the output or activity of political institutions. It is the mechanism by which institutions influence society, economy, and polity—both home and abroad. Policies are reflected in laws, for example, those that specify the level of taxes and the rates that citizens and business firms are expected to pay; or laws that specify who is entitled to marry (note the intense controversy these days about whether same-sex couples shall be entitled to marry); or laws that create programs providing citizens with unemployment insurance, pensions, and medical care (that is, social policy).

Policies are also the product of administrative action. Bureaucratic agencies issue policies on infinitely diverse aspects of social, economic, cultural, and political life. Furthermore, policies may be a result of political institutions *not* acting.

All policies distribute costs and benefits unequally. And policies reflect values or preferences—which rarely command unanimity. When we study policy, therefore, we are studying not only what is, but what should be. Sanderson's article suggests that the possibility for promoting conservation increases when it is linked to economic development. Most of the other articles in this chapter are also rich with policy implications. Thus, debates over policy are a key feature of political life and involve the most far-reaching questions within the study of politics.

Constitutional Frameworks and Democratic Consolidation: Parliamentarianism versus Presidentialism

Alfred Stepan, with Cindy Skach

Alfred Stepan seeks to demonstrate that the design of political institutions influences the chances that newly established democratic regimes will endure. In particular, he compares the impact of presidential and parliamentary systems. According to Stepan, the fact that the executive and legislature are elected separately in a presidential system, and are independent of each other, increases the chance of political stalemate. In a parliamentary system, the executive is chosen by the legislature (parliament), and the two branches are mutually dependent. The fact that they must sink or swim (together) induces the two branches to cooperate and reach accommodation.

More generally, this selection suggests how the design of institutions influences political action. Can you think of other examples of how institutional design affects political activity?

Introduction

The struggle to consolidate the new democracies—especially those in Eastern Europe, Latin America, and Asia—has given rise to a wide-ranging debate about the hard choices concerning economic restructuring, economic institutions, and economic markets.[1] A similar debate has focused on democratic *political* institutions and *political* markets. This literature has produced provocative hypotheses about the effects of institutions on democracy. It forms part of the "new institutionalism" literature in comparative politics that holds as a premise that "political democracy depends not only on economic and social conditions but also on the design of political institutions."[2]

One fundamental political-institutional question that has only recently received serious scholarly attention concerns the impact of different constitutional

Alfred Stepan, with Cindy Skach, "Constitutional Frameworks and Democratic Consolidation: Parliamentarianism versus Presidentialism," *World Politics* 46:1 (1993), 1–22. © The Johns Hopkins University Press. Reprinted with permission of The Johns Hopkins University Press.

frameworks on democratic consolidation.[3] Although the topic has been increasingly debated and discussed, little systematic cross-regional evidence has been brought to bear on it. This is unfortunate, because constitutions are essentially "institutional frameworks" that in functioning democracies provide the basic decision rules and incentive systems concerning government formation, the conditions under which governments can continue to rule, and the conditions by which they can be terminated democratically. More than simply one of the many dimensions of a democratic system,[4] constitutions create much of the overall system of incentives and organizations within which the other institutions and dimensions found in the many types of democracy are structured and processed.

Study shows that the range of existing constitutional frameworks in the world's long-standing democracies is narrower than one would think.[5] With one exception (Switzerland), every existing democracy today is either presidential (as in the United States), parliamentary (as in most of Western Europe), or a semipresidential hybrid of the two (as in France and Portugal, where there is a directly elected president and a prime minister who must have a majority in the legislature).[6] In this essay we pay particular attention to contrasting what we call "pure parliamentarianism" with "pure presidentialism."[7] Each type has only two fundamental characteristics, and for our purposes of classification these characteristics are necessary and sufficient.

A pure parliamentary regime in a democracy is a system of mutual dependence:

1. The chief executive power must be supported by a majority in the legislature and can fall if it receives a vote of no confidence.
2. The executive power (normally in conjunction with the head of state) has the capacity to dissolve the legislature and call for elections.

A pure presidential regime in a democracy is a system of mutual independence:

1. The legislative power has a fixed electoral mandate that is its own source of legitimacy.
2. The chief executive power has a fixed electoral mandate that is its own source of legitimacy.

These necessary and sufficient characteristics are more than classificatory. They are also the constraining conditions within which the vast majority of aspiring democracies must somehow attempt simultaneously to produce major socioeconomic changes and to strengthen democratic institutions.[8]

Pure parliamentarianism, as defined here, had been the norm in the democratic world following World War II.[9] However, so far, in the 1980s and 1990s, all the new aspirant democracies in Latin America and Asia (Korea and the Philippines) have chosen pure presidentialism. And to date, of the approximately twenty-five countries that now constitute Eastern Europe and the former Soviet Union, only three—Hungary, the new Czech Republic, and Slovakia—have chosen pure parliamentarianism.[10]

We question the wisdom of this virtual dismissal of the pure parliamentary model by most new democracies and believe that the hasty embrace of presidential models should be reconsidered. In this article we bring evidence in support of the theoretical argument that parliamentary democracies tend to increase the degrees of freedom that facilitate the momentous tasks of economic and social restructuring facing new democracies as they simultaneously attempt to consolidate their democratic institutions.

It is not our purpose in this article to weigh the benefits and the drawbacks of parliamentarianism and presidentialism. Our intention is to report and analyze numerous different sources of data, all of which point in the direction of a much stronger correlation between democratic consolidation and pure parliamentarianism than between democratic consolidation and pure presidentialism. We believe our findings are sufficiently strong to warrant long-range studies that test the probabilistic propositions we indicate.[11] . . .

The Contrasting Logics of Pure Parliamentarianism and Pure Presidentialism

Let us step back from the data for a brief note about the type of statements that can be made about political institutions and democratic consolidation. The status of statements about the impact of institutions is not causally determinative (A causes B) but probabilistic (A tends to be associated with B). For example, Maurice Duverger's well-known observation about electoral systems is a probabilistic proposition: it holds that systems with single-member districts and where a simple plurality wins the seat tend to produce two-party systems, whereas electoral systems with multimember districts and proportional representation tend to produce multiparty systems.[12] The fact that Austria and Canada are exceptions to his proposition is less important than the fact that nineteen of the twenty-one cases of uninterrupted democracy in postwar industrialized countries conform to his proposition.[13]

A probabilistic proposition in politics is more than a statistical assertion. It entails the identification and explanation of the specific political processes that tend to produce the probabilistic results. And to establish even greater confidence in the proposition, one should examine case studies to explain whether and how the important hypothesized institutional characteristics actually came into play in individual cases.[14]

Whatever the constitutional framework, consolidating democracy outside of the industrialized core of the world is difficult and perilous. The quantitative evidence we have brought to bear on presidentialism and parliamentarianism would assume greater theoretical and political significance if a strong case could be made that the empirically evident propensities we have documented are the logical, indeed the predictable, result of the constitutional frameworks themselves. We believe that such a case can be made.

The essence of pure parliamentarianism is mutual dependence. From this defining condition a series of incentives and decision rules for creating and maintaining single-party or coalitional majorities, minimizing legislative impasses, inhibiting the executive from flouting the constitution, and discouraging political society's support for military coups predictably flows. The essence of pure presidentialism is mutual independence. From this defining (and confining) condition a series of incentives and decision rules for encouraging the emergence of minority governments, discouraging the formation of durable coalitions, maximizing legislative impasses, motivating executives to flout the constitution, and stimulating political society to call periodically for military coups predictably flows. Presidents and legislatures are directly elected and have their own fixed mandates. This mutual independence creates the possibility of a political impasse between the chief executive and the legislative body for which there is no constitutionally available impasse-breaking device.

Here, then, is a paradox. Many new democracies select presidentialism because they believe it to be a strong form of executive government. Yet our data show that between 1973 and 1987 presidential democracies enjoyed legislative majorities less than half of the time. With this relatively low percentage of "supported time" and the fixed mandates of the presidential framework, executives and legislatures in these countries were "stuck" with one another, and executives were condemned to serve out their terms. How often did these executives find it necessary to govern by decree-law—at the edge of constitutionalism—in order to implement the economic restructuring and austerity plans they considered necessary for their development projects?

Our evidence shows that, in contrast to presidentialism, the executive's party in parliamentary democracies enjoyed a majority of seats in the legislature over 83 percent of the time period under study. For the remaining 17 percent of the years, parliamentary executives, motivated by the necessity to survive votes of confidence, formed coalition governments and party alliances in order to attract necessary support. When they were unable to do this, the absence of fixed mandates and the safety devices of the parliamentary institutional framework allowed for calling rapid new elections, the constitutional removal of unpopular, unsupported governments through the vote of no confidence, or simply the withdrawal from the government of a vital coalition partner.

Parliamentarianism entails mutual dependence. The prime minister and his or her government cannot survive without at least the passive support of a legislative majority. The inherent mechanisms of parliamentarianism involved in the mutual dependency relationship—the executive's right to dissolve parliament and the legislature's right to pass a vote of no confidence—are deadlock-breaking devices. These decision rules do not assure that any particular government will be efficient in formulating policies; nor do they assure government stability. But the decision mechanisms available in the parliamentary framework do provide constitutional means for removing deadlocked or inefficient governments (executives and parliaments). The danger that a government without a majority will rule by decree is sharply curtailed by the decision rule that allows the parliamentary majority (or the prime minister's coalition allies or even his or her own party) to call for government reformation.

Why is it logical and predictable that military coups are much more likely in pure presidential constitutional frameworks than in pure parliamentary frameworks? Because, as we discussed above, parliamentary democracies have two decision rules that help resolve crises of the government before they become crises of the regime. First, a government cannot form unless it has acquired at least a "supported minority" in the legislature; second, a government that is perceived to have lost the confidence of the legislature can be voted out of office by the simple political vote of no confidence (or in Germany and Spain by a positive legislative vote for an alternative government). Presidentialism, in sharp contrast, systematically contributes to impasses and democratic breakdown. Because the president and the legislature have separate and fixed mandates, and because presidents more than half of the time find themselves frustrated in the exercise of their power due to their lack of a legislative majority, presidents may often be tempted to bypass the legislature and rule by decree-law. It is extremely difficult to remove even a president who has virtually no consensual support in the country or who is acting unconstitutionally; it usually requires a political–legal–criminal trial (impeachment), whose successful execution requires exceptional majorities.[15] Thus, even when the socioeconomic crises are identical in two countries, the country with the presidential system is more likely to find itself in a crisis of governance and will find it more difficult to solve the crisis before it becomes a regime crisis.[16] Such situations often cause both the president and the opposition to seek military involvement to resolve the crisis in their favor.

Guillermo O'Donnell documented a phenomenon observed in the new Latin American democracies in his extremely interesting (and alarming) article on "delegative democracy," a conceptual opposite of representative democracy.[17] Key characteristics of delegative democracy include (1) presidents who present themselves as being "above" parties, (2) institutions such as congress and the judiciary that are viewed as "a nuisance," with accountability to them considered an unnecessary impediment, (3) a president and his staff who are the alpha and omega of politics, and (4) a president who insulates himself from most existing political institutions and organized interactions and becomes the sole person responsible for "his" policies. We suggest that these characteristics of O'Donnell's delegative democracy are some of the predictable pathologies produced by the multiple logics of the presidential framework. Consider the following: Presidential democracy, due to the logic of its framework, always produces (1) presidents who are directly elected and (2) presidents with fixed terms. Presidential democracy often produces (1) presidents who feel they have a personal mandate and (2) presidents who do not have legislative majorities. Thus, the logic of presidentialism has a strong tendency to produce (1) presidents who adopt a discourse that attacks a key part of political society (the legislature and parties) and (2) presidents who increasingly attempt to rely upon a "state-people" political style and discourse that marginalizes organized groups in political society and civil society. Delegative democracy can no doubt exist in the other constitutional frameworks; however, the multiple logics of pure parliamentarianism seem to work against delegative democracy.

Why are there many enduring multiparty parliamentary democracies but no long-standing presidential ones? In a parliamentary system, the junior political parties that participate in the ruling coalition are institutional members of the government and are often able to negotiate not only the ministers they will receive, but who will be appointed to them. All members of the coalition have an incentive to cooperate if they do not want the government of the day to fall. In these circumstances, democracies with four, five, or six political parties in the legislature can function quite well.

There are far fewer incentives for coalitional cooperation in presidentialism. The office of the presidency is nondivisible. The president may select members of the political parties other than his own to serve in the cabinet, but they are selected as individuals, not as members of an enduring and disciplined coalition. Thus, if the president's party (as in President Collor's party in Brazil) has less than 10 percent of the seats in the legislature, he rules with a permanent minority and with weak coalitional incentives. On a vote-by-vote basis, the president may cajole or buy a majority, but repeated purchases of majorities are absolutely inconsistent with the principled austerity plans of restructuring that face most East European and Latin American democracies.

East European or Latin American political leaders who believe that their countries, for historical reasons, are inevitably multiparty in political representation are playing against great odds if they select a presidential system, as the existing evidence demonstrates. Brazil's high party fragmentation, for example, has contributed to a presidential-legislative deadlock that has frozen the lawmaking process in an already fragile democracy. Party fragmentation, the lack of party discipline, and general party underdevelopment in Brazil have been exacerbated by its electoral system, which combines proportional representation with an open list. The 1990 elections yielded 8.5 effective parties in the Brazilian Chamber of Deputies and 6.0 in the Senate.[18] These numbers seem alarmingly high considering that all the long-standing, pure presidential democracies . . . had fewer than 2.6 effective political parties.

Moreover, the closer a country approaches the ideal types of "sultanship," "totalitarianism," or early "posttotalitarianism," the "flatter" are their civil and political societies.[19] In these circumstances, adopting the constitutional framework of presidentialism in the period of transition from sultanship, totalitarianism, or early posttotalitarianism reduces the degrees of freedom for an emerging civil and political society to make a midcourse correction, because heads of government have been elected for fixed terms (as in Georgia). In contrast, the Bulgarian transition had significant parliamentary features, which allowed an emerging political society to change the prime minister (and the indirectly elected president) so as to accommodate new demands.

In Poland, where constitutional reformers are flirting with the idea of strengthening the role of the president, party fragmentation is even greater than in Brazil; the effective number of parties in the Polish Sejm after the 1991 legislative elections was 10.8.[20] Most of these parties in the Polish legislature, like those in Brazil, lack clear programs and exist as mere labels for politicians to use for election into office.[21] Our data suggest that Poland would be playing against the odds were it to move toward a purely presidential system.

Also flowing from the logic of the constitutional framework are the questions of why ministers serve short terms in presidential democracies and why they are rarely reappointed in their lifetime. Because presidents do not normally enjoy majorities in the legislature, they resort to rapid ministerial rotation as a device in their perpetual search for support on key issues. In parliamentary systems, by contrast, coalitional majorities make such rapid turnover unnecessary. Furthermore, key ministers usually have long and strong associations with their political parties and are often reappointed as government coalitions form and re-form during the life of their careers. In presidential democracies, ministers are strongly associated with a particular president, leave office when the president does, and normally never serve as a minister again in their life.

Conclusion

Let us consider the question that follows from the data. Why does pure parliamentarianism seem to present a more supportive evolutionary framework for consolidating democracy than pure presidentialism? We believe we are now in a position to say that the explanation of why parliamentarianism is a more supportive constitutional framework lies in the following theoretically predictable and empirically observable tendencies: its greater propensity for governments to have majorities to implement their programs; its greater ability to rule in a multiparty setting; its lower propensity for executives to rule at the edge of the constitution and its greater facility at removing a chief executive who does so; its lower susceptibility to military coup; and its greater tendency to provide long party-government careers, which add loyalty and experience to political society.

The analytically separable propensities of parliamentarianism interact to form a mutually supporting system. This system, qua system, increases the degrees of freedom politicians have as they attempt to consolidate democracy. The analytically separable propensities of presidentialism also form a highly interactive system, but they work to impede democratic consolidation.

Notes

1. See, e.g., Stephan Haggard and Robert R. Kaufman, eds., *The Politics of Economic Adjustment* (Princeton: Princeton University Press, 1992); Adam Przeworski, *Democracy and the Market: Political and Economic Reforms in Eastern Europe and Latin America* (Cambridge: Cambridge University Press, 1991); and Christopher Clague and Gordon C. Rausser, eds., *The Emergence of Market Economies in Eastern Europe* (Cambridge: Blackwell Press, 1992).

2. James G. March and Johan P. Olsen, "The New Institutionalism: Organizational Factors in Political Life," *American Political Science Review* 78 (September 1984), 738. For a pioneering early work exemplifying this approach, see Maurice Duverger, *Political Parties* (New York: Wiley, 1954). Other important works that explore the causal relationship between institutions such as electoral systems and political parties, and democratic stability include Giovanni Sartori, *Parties and Party Systems: A Framework for Analysis* (Cambridge: Cambridge University Press, 1976); Douglas Rae, *The Political Consequences of Electoral Laws* (New Haven: Yale University Press, 1967); William H. Riker, *The Theory of Political Coalitions* (New Haven: Yale University Press, 1962); Bernard Grofman and Arend Lijphart, eds., *Electoral Laws and Their Political Consequences* (New York: Agathon, 1986); Rein Taagepera and Matthew Soberg Shugart, *Seats and Votes* (New Haven: Yale University Press, 1989); and Matthew Soberg Shugart and John Carey, *Presidents and Assemblies* (Cambridge: Cambridge University Press, 1992). An important work in the neoinstitutionalist literature that focuses on legislatures and structure-induced equilibrium is Kenneth Shepsle, "Institutional Equilibrium and Equilibrium Institutions," in Herbert F. Weisberg, ed., *Political Science: The Science of Politics* (New York: Agathon, 1986). See also Mathew D. McCubbins and Terry Sullivan, eds., *Congress: Structure and Policy* (Cambridge: Cambridge University Press, 1987).

3. There is a growing literature on this question. Much of it is brought together in Juan J. Linz and Arturo Valenzuela, eds., *Presidentialism and Parliamentarianism: Does It Make a Difference?* (Baltimore: Johns Hopkins University Press, forthcoming). However, no article in this valuable collection attempts to gather systematic global quantitative data to address directly the question raised in the title of the book and by Przeworski. Linz first appeared in print on this subject in a brief "Excursus on Presidential and Parliamentary Democracy," in Linz and Alfred Stepan, eds., *The Breakdown of Democratic Regimes* (Baltimore: Johns Hopkins University Press, 1978). His much-cited seminal "underground" paper with the same title as his forthcoming book was first presented at the workshop on "Political Parties in the Southern Cone," Woodrow Wilson International Center, Washington, D.C., 1984; see also idem, "The Perils of Presidentialism," *Journal of Democracy* 1 (Winter 1990). See also Scott Mainwaring, "Presidentialism, Multiparty Systems, and Democracy: The Difficult Equation," *Kellogg Institute Working Paper,* no. 144 (Notre Dame, Ind.: University of Notre Dame, September 1990).

4. We agree with Philippe C. Schmitter's argument that there are many types of democracies and that "consolidation includes a mix of institutions." See Schmitter, "The Consolidation of Democracy and the Choice of Institutions," *East-South System Transformations Working Paper,* no. 7 (Chicago: Department of Political Science, University of Chicago, September 1991), 7. See also Schmitter and Terry Karl, "What Democracy Is . . . and Is Not," *Journal of Democracy* (Summer 1991). The authors list eleven important dimensions that provide a matrix of potential combinations by which political systems can be differently democratic.

5. We realize that any effort to operationalize the concept of "democracy" so that it can be used for purposes of classification of all the countries of the world is inherently difficult. Fortunately there have been two independently designed efforts that attempt this task. One, by Michael Coppedge and Wolfgang Reinicke, attempted to operationalize the eight "institutional guarantees" that Robert Dahl argued were required for a polyarchy. The authors assigned values to 137 countries on a polyarchy scale, based on their assessment of political conditions as of mid-1985. The results are available in Coppedge and Reinicke, "A Measure of Polyarchy" (Paper presented at the Conference on Measuring Democracy, Hoover Institution, Stanford University, May 27–8, 1988); and in idem, "A Scale of Polyarchy," in Raymond D. Gastil, ed., *Freedom in the World: Political Rights and Civil Liberties, 1987–1988* (New York: Freedom House, 1990), 101–28. Robert A. Dahl's seminal discussion of the institutional guarantees needed for polyarchy is found in his *Polyarchy: Participation and Opposition* (New Haven: Yale University Press, 1971), 1–16.

The other effort to operationalize a scale of democracy is the annual Freedom House evaluation of virtually all the countries of the world. The advisory panel in recent years has included such scholars as Seymour Martin Lipset, Giovanni Sartori, and Lucian W. Pye. The value assigned for each year 1973 to 1987 can be found in the above-cited Gastil, 54–65. In this essay, we will call a country a "continuous democracy" if it has received no higher than a scale score of 3 on the Coppedge–Reinicke Polyarchy Scale for 1985 and no higher than a 2.5 averaged score of the ratings for "political rights" and "civil liberties" on the Gastil Democracy Scale, for the 1980–9 period.

6. On the defining characteristics of semipresidentialism, see the seminal article by Maurice Duverger, "A New Political System Model: Semi-Presidential Government," *European Journal of Political Research* 8 (June 1980). See also idem, *Echec au Roi* (Paris: Albin Michel, 1978); and idem, *La monarchie républicaine* (Paris: R. Laffont, 1974).

7. For a discussion of the semipresidential constitutional framework, its inherent problem of "executive dualism," and the exceptional circumstances that allowed France to manage these problems, see Alfred Stepan and Ezra N. Suleiman, "The French Fifth Republic: A Model for Import? Reflections on Poland and Brazil," in H. E. Chehabi and Alfred Stepan, eds., *Politics, Society and Democracy: Comparative Studies* (Boulder, Colo.: Westview Press, forthcoming).

8. Alfred Stepan will develop this argument in greater detail in a book he is writing entitled *Democratic Capacities/Democratic Institutions*.

9. For example, in Arend Lijphart's list of the twenty-one continuous democracies of the world since World War II, seventeen were pure parliamentary democracies, two were mixed, one was semipresidential, and only one, the United States, was pure presidential. See Lijphart, *Democracies: Patterns of Majoritarian and Consensus Government in Twenty-one Countries* (New Haven: Yale University Press, 1984), 38.

10. The norm is a directly elected president with very strong *de jure* and *de facto* prerogatives coexisting with a prime minister who needs the support of parliament. As of this writing (April 1993), only Hungary and the newly created Czech Republic and Slovakia had opted for the pure parliamentary constitutional framework. Despite having directly elected presidents, Slovenia, Estonia, and Bulgaria have strong parliamentary features. In Slovakia and Estonia presidents will now be selected by parliament. Bulgaria, however, has moved from an indirectly to a directly elected president. For political, legal, and sociological analyses of constitution making in East European transitions, see the quarterly publication *East European Constitutional Review*, which is part of the Center for the Study of Constitutionalism in Eastern Europe at the University of Chicago. The center was established in 1990 in partnership with the Central European University.

11. Duration analysis would be particularly appropriate because it estimates the *conditional* probability of an event taking place (for example, of a democracy "dying," by undergoing military coup), given that the regime has survived for a given period of time as a democracy. This conditional probability is in turn parameterized as a function of exogenous explanatory variables (such as constitutional frameworks). The sign of an estimated coefficient then indicates the direction of the effect of the explanatory variable on the conditional probability of a democracy dying at a given time. Such models allow us to estimate whether democracies exhibit positive or negative "duration dependence": specifically, whether the probability of a democracy dying increases or decreases, respectively, with increases in the duration of the spell. Mike Alvarez, a Ph.D. candidate in political science at the University of Chicago, is creating the data and the appropriate statistical techniques and then implementing this duration analysis as part of his dissertation. Adam Przeworski, too, has embarked on such research. See also Nicholas M. Kiefer, "Economic Duration Data and Hazard Functions," *Journal of Economic Literature* 26 (June 1988).

12. See Duverger (n. 2).

13. For a discussion of Duverger's proposition in the context of modern industrialized democracies, see Arend Lijphart, *Democracies: Patterns of Majoritarian and Consensus Government in Twenty-one Countries* (New Haven: Yale University Press, 1984), 156–9.

14. There is a growing literature of case studies examining the influence of constitutional frameworks on stability and/or breakdown in developing countries. See, e.g., David M. Lipset, "Papua New Guinea: The Melanesian Ethic and the Spirit of Capitalism, 1975–1986," in Larry Diamond, Juan J. Linz, and Seymour Martin Lipset, eds., *Democracy in Developing Countries: Asia* (Boulder, Colo: Lynne Rienner, 1989), esp. 413. Lipset discusses how the constitutional framework came into play to prevent regime breakdown in Papua New Guinea.

15. Schmitter and Karl (n. 4) quite correctly build into their definition of democracy the concept of accountability. But with the exception of the U.S. where a president can be directly reelected only once, no president in any other long-standing democracy in the world, once in office, can be held politically accountable by a vote of the citizens' representatives. The accountability mechanism is so

extreme and difficult—with the political-legal-criminal trial that needs exceptional majorities (impeachment)—that the accountability principle in presidentialism is weaker than in parliamentarianism.

16. For theoretical differentiation between crises of government and crises of regime, see Juan J. Linz and Alfred Stepan, eds., *The Breakdown of Democratic Regimes* (Baltimore: Johns Hopkins University Press, 1978), esp. 74.

17. See O'Donnell, "Democracia Delegativa?" *Novos Estudos* CEBRAP, no. 31 (October 1991).

18. These numbers were calculated using the Laakso–Taagepera formula and the data reported in *Keesings Record of World Events* (1990); and Arthur S. Banks, ed., *Political Handbook of the World* (Binghamton: csa Publishers, State University of New York, 1991).

19. This argument is developed in Juan J. Linz and Alfred Stepan, "Problems of Democratic Transition and Consolidation: Eastern Europe, Southern Europe and South America" (Book manuscript), pt. 1.

20. This is developed in Stepan and Suleiman (n. 7).

21. For a discussion of how both the political culture and the institutional structure in Brazil contributed to the country's weak party system, see Scott Mainwaring, "Dilemmas of Multiparty Presidential Democracy: The Case of Brazil," *Kellogg Institute Working Paper* no. 174 (Notre Dame, Ind.: University of Notre Dame, 1992). See also idem, "Politicians, Parties, and Electoral Systems: Brazil in Comparative Perspective," *Comparative Politics* 24 (October 1991); and his forthcoming book on Brazilian political parties.

 6.2

Democratic Transitions, Institutional Strength, and War

Edward D. Mansfield and Jack Snyder

Professors Mansfield and Snyder reported in previous research that regimes that had recently become democratic were especially likely to engage in foreign war. In the present selection, they analyze which features of the institutional design of new democracies increase the chances of initiating war. They find that political institutions that fragment and reduce the power of rulers, such as federalism, may tempt rulers to initiate war to increase their power.

On the other hand, Mansfield and Snyder don't consider that federalism may have other advantages. For example, some scholars have suggested that it provides ethnic minorities with a share of power that they wouldn't have in more centralized systems. Can you think of a way to resolve this problem?

Edward D. Mansfield and Jack Snyder, "Democratic Transitions, Institutional Strength, and War," *International Organization* 56, No. 2 (Spring 2002): 297–304. © 2002 by the IO Foundation and the Massachusetts Institute of Technology.

The centerpiece of U.S. foreign policy in the 1990s was the claim that promoting democracy would foster peace. Noting that no two democracies have ever fought a war against each other, President Bill Clinton argued that support for democratization would be an antidote to international war and civil strife.[1] Yet the 1990s turned out to be a decade of both democratization and chronic nationalist conflict, both within and between some transitional states.

While the world would probably be more peaceful if all states were mature democracies, Clinton's conventional wisdom failed to anticipate the dangers of getting from here to there. Prominent critics have pointed out that newly democratizing states are often neither liberal nor peaceful.[2] Since the French Revolution, the earliest phases of democratization have triggered some of the world's bloodiest nationalist struggles. Similarly, during the 1990s, intense armed violence broke out in a number of regions that had just begun to experiment with electoral democracy and more pluralist public discourse. In some cases, such as the former Yugoslavia, the Caucasus, and Indonesia, transitions from dictatorship to more pluralistic political systems coincided with the rise of national independence movements, spurring separatist warfare that often spilled across international borders.[3] In other cases, transitional regimes clashed in interstate warfare. Ethiopia and Eritrea, both moving toward more pluralistic forms of government in the 1990s, fought a bloody border war from 1998 to 2000.[4] The elected regimes of India and Pakistan battled during 1999 in the mountainous borderlands of Kashmir. Peru and Ecuador, democratizing in fits and starts during the 1980s and 1990s, culminated a series of armed clashes with a small war in the upper Amazon in 1995.[5]

In previous research, we reported that states undergoing democratic transitions were substantially more likely to participate in external wars than were states whose regimes remained unchanged or changed in an autocratic direction.[6] We argued that elites in newly democratizing states often use nationalist appeals to attract mass support without submitting to full democratic accountability and that the institutional weakness of transitional states creates the opportunity for such war-causing strategies to succeed. However, these earlier studies did not fully address the circumstances under which transitions are most likely to precipitate war, and they did not take into account various important causes of war. Equally, some critics worried that the time periods over which we measured the effects of democratization were sometimes so long that events occurring at the beginning of a period would be unlikely to influence foreign policy at its end.[7]

Employing a more refined research design than in our prior work, we aim here to identify more precisely the conditions under which democratization stimulates hostilities. We find that the heightened danger of war grows primarily out of the transition from an autocratic regime to one that is partly democratic. The specter of war during this phase of democratization looms especially large when governmental institutions, including those regulating political participation, are especially weak. Under these conditions, elites commonly employ nationalist rhetoric to mobilize mass support but then become drawn into the belligerent foreign policies unleashed by this process. We find, in contrast, that transitions that quickly culminate in a fully coherent democracy are much less perilous.[8] Further, our results refute the view that transitional democracies are simply inviting targets of attack because of their temporary weakness. In fact, they tend to be the initiators of war. We also refute the view that any regime change is likely to precipitate the outbreak of war. We find that transitions toward democracy are significantly more likely to generate hostilities than transitions toward autocracy.

Weak Institutions, Incomplete Democratic Transitions, and War

The early stages of democratization unleash intense competition among myriad social groups and interests. Many transitional democracies lack state institutions that are sufficiently strong and coherent to effectively regulate this mass political competition. To use Samuel Huntington's terminology, such countries frequently suffer from a gap between high levels of political participation and weak political institutions.[9] The weaker these institutions, the greater the likelihood that war-provoking nationalism will emerge in democratizing countries.[10]

Belligerent nationalism is likely to arise in this setting for two related reasons. The first and more general reason is that political leaders try to use nationalism as an ideological motivator of national collective action in the absence of effective political institutions. Leaders of various stripes find that appeals to national sentiment are essential for mobilizing popular support when more routine instruments of legitimacy and governance—parties, legislatures, courts, and independent news media—are in their infancy. Both old and new elites share this incentive to play the nationalist card. Often such appeals depend for their success on exaggerating foreign threats. Allegations that internal foes have treasonous ties to these external enemies of the nation help the regime hold on to power despite the weakness of governmental institutions. At the outset of the French Revolution, for example, mass nationalism was weak, but soon the leaders of various republican factions found that the rhetoric of war and treason was indispensable to their political survival in the revolutionary institutional wasteland.[11] Newspapers tied to political factions inflamed public opinion with the paired themes of war and treason.

A second reason democratization often fosters belligerent nationalism is that the breakup of authoritarian regimes threatens powerful interests, including military bureaucracies and economic actors that derive a parochial benefit from war and empire. To salvage their position, threatened interests frequently try to recruit mass support, typically by resorting to nationalist appeals that allow them to claim to rule in the name of the people, but without instituting full democratic accountability to the average voter. Exploiting what remains of their governmental, economic, and media power, these elites may succeed in establishing terms of inclusion in politics that force opposition groups to accept nationalism as the common currency of public discourse. For example, Bismarck and his successors in Prussia and Germany used nationalist, military, and colonial issues to rally middle class and rural voters against the working classes while perpetuating a system of rule that kept the power to name government ministers in the hands of the hereditary Kaiser rather than the elected legislature.[12]

Competition to rally popular support around elite interests has different consequences when democratic institutions are weak and highly imperfect than when they are better developed. In mature democracies, the average voter who would suffer from reckless, nationalist policies has more chance to obtain accurate information about those risks and punish reckless politicians through the ballot box. This greater accountability and better information helps to explain not only the absence of war between mature democracies but also their more prudent policies toward states of any regime type. Although democracies are about as likely as nondemocratic regimes to become embroiled in wars,[13] democracies choose their wars more wisely,[14] tend to win them and suffer fewer casualties,[15] are less likely to initiate crises,[16] rarely fight preventive wars,[17] and are more adept at signaling the credibility of their commitments.[18] Moreover, democratic great powers pull back more astutely from imperial overstretch than their nondemocratic counterparts.[19] . . .

The happy outcomes of the democratic peace, however, emerge only after a transition to democracy is well consolidated. Establishing effective democratic institutions takes time. Where powerful groups feel threatened by democracy, they seek to keep its institutions weak and malleable. Thus the practices of many newly democratizing states are only loose approximations of those that characterize mature democracies. Limited suffrage, unfair constraints on electoral competition, disorganized political parties, corrupt bureaucracies, or partial media monopolies may skew political outcomes in newly democratizing states away from the patterns that coherent democracies generally produce. Although elites in newly democratizing states need to solicit mass support, the weakness of democratic institutions allows them to avoid full public accountability. Nationalist ideas help perpetuate this semidemocratic condition by justifying the exclusion of opponents from political participation on the grounds that they are enemies of the nation. Such claims are harder to refute in newly democratizing states, where partial media monopolies prevent a complete airing of evidence and argument. In Weimar Germany, for example, the monopoly wire-service feeding nationalist-slanted news to most smaller cities and towns was owned by a former director of Krupp Steel who was the head of the largest nationalist party. These readers became a central part of the constituency that voted for Hitler.[20]

Moreover, while federalism may generate certain benefits for mature democracies, the decentralization and fragmentation of power in newly democratizing regimes is likely to exacerbate the problems attendant to democratic transitions. As the bloody breakups of Yugoslavia and the Soviet Union show, divisive nationalism is especially likely when the state's power is dispersed among ethnically defined federal regions. Hence, none of the mechanisms that produce the democratic peace among mature democracies operate in the same fashion in newly democratizing states. Indeed, in their imperfect condition, these mechanisms have the opposite effect.

In short, newly democratizing countries often experience a weakening of central state institutions because their old institutions have eroded and their new ones are only partially developed. Autocratic power is in decline vis-à-vis both elite interest groups and mass groups, and democratic institutions lack the strength to integrate these contending interests and views. Not all newly democratizing states suffer from institutional weakness, but for those that do the resulting political dynamic creates conditions that encourage hostilities. In the face of this institutional deficit, political leaders rely on expedient strategies to cope with the political impasse of democratization. Such tactics, which often include the appeasement of nationalist veto groups or competition among factions in nationalist bidding wars (or both), can breed reckless foreign policies and the resort to war.

Nationalist Veto Groups and Logrolling

The power of central authorities is typically reduced in newly democratizing states. The old authoritarian state has broken up, leaving behind the vestiges of its ruling class as still-powerful interest groups. Some of these groups, including the military bureaucracy and dominant economic interests, may have self-serving reasons to lobby for military expansion or the exclusion of foreign economic competition, policies that could cause tensions with other states. At the same time, dissatisfied ethnic elites or rising proponents of commercial expansion may press their demands on the weakened state. These elite groups and the political parties aligned with them may become even further committed to nationalism, foreign expansion, or economic protectionism as a result of their rhetorical appeals for popular support. Consequently, political coalitions in newly democratizing states are especially likely to be beholden to veto groups, at least some of which have a stake in assertive foreign policies and nationalist political rhetoric.

One form that such veto-group politics may take is "logrolling," that is, mutual back-scratching among narrowly self-serving interests. In forging a logrolled bargain, each group in the coalition agrees to support the others on the issue that each cares about most. For example, the ruling coalition in Germany before World War I was the nationalist "marriage of iron and rye," in which aristocratic landowners supported a fleet-building program that industrial interests desired; in exchange, big business supported high agricultural tariffs.[21]

To some degree, logrolling and other forms of veto-group politics occur in all political systems; but they tend to be especially pervasive in partially democratized states, such as pre-1914 Germany. Since mature democracies have strong mechanisms of accountability to the average voter, logrolls that impose huge costs and risks on the citizenry are likely to provoke strong and effective opposition. Democracy, when it works correctly, confers power on the taxpayers, consumers, and military conscripts who would have to pay the diffuse costs that are side effects of the logroll. In newly democratizing states, however, the power of elite groups is likely to be strengthened vis-à-vis the weakened autocratic center, though the power of mass groups is not yet institutionalized in the manner of a mature democracy. Thus democratizing states are especially at risk for unchecked logrolling among elite interest groups, and this can fuel violent nationalist conflicts.

Furthermore, partially democratizing countries with weak political institutions often lack the governmental coherence and predictability to send clear and credible signals of commitment to allies and enemies alike. With multiple centers of authority and uncertain tenure of office, leaders in transitional states may have difficulty making credible deterrent commitments or believable promises to refrain from attacking in the future. One faction may signal willingness to compromise, whereas another may signal an inclination for preventive war. As the puzzled Austrian chief of staff asked about strategic authority in semidemocratic Germany in July 1914, "Who rules in Berlin, [Chancellor] Bethmann or [Chief of Staff] Moltke?"[22] Whereas the superior signaling and bargaining ability of mature democracies may be a factor underpinning the democratic peace,[23] the signaling handicaps of newly democratizing states may hinder their ability to negotiate the settlement of disputes.

Popular Nationalist Bidding Wars

Even if elite coalitions worry that the costs and risks of their belligerent foreign policies are beginning to get out of hand, they can find themselves locked into these policies by the tactics they have used to recruit mass support. To survive in an era of democratization, these elite interests must attract a degree of popular support, often through the use of nationalist rhetoric. Elite control over a dependent, unprofessional news media may provide a ready vehicle for this campaign of persuasion. However, rising alternative elites may seize on this rhetoric and try to turn it against the old elites, triggering a nationalist bidding war. Prior to World War I, for instance, German middle-class nationalist groups such as the Navy League argued that if Germany was really encircled by national enemies, as the ruling elites claimed, then the government's ineffectual policies were endangering the nation. The old elite should step aside, they argued, and let the more vigorous middle classes reform Germany's army, toughen its foreign policy, and use coercion to break up the encircling alliance of France, Russia, and England. The "iron and rye" government felt compelled to outbid these nationalist critics. In an attempt to gain nationalist prestige in the eyes of the domestic audience, the German government trumped up a series of international crises, such as the showdowns with France over control of Morocco in 1905 and 1911. This reckless and counterproductive strategy served only to tighten the noose around the neck of the German elites and pushed them toward a decision to launch a preventive war in 1914.[24]

This argument has some points in common with so-called diversionary theories of war, which contend that regimes sometimes attempt to use rivalry abroad to strengthen their shaky position at home. Such theories invoke two rather different causal mechanisms. The first asserts a psychological propensity for out-group conflict to increase in-group cohesion. If such a mechanism exists, however, research shows that it is likely to come into play only if the group demonstrates considerable cohesion before the conflict breaks out, the external threat is seen as endangering the in-group as a whole, and the instigators of the conflict are seen to be the outsiders rather than the leadership of the in-group.[25] Our argument suggests how these conditions might be created in newly democratizing states through the development of a nationalist ideology, which constitutes a set of ideas for interpreting conflict with out-groups. . . .

A second set of causal mechanisms is rationalistic. Alastair Smith speculates that international assertiveness helps domestically hard-pressed regimes to demonstrate their competence by achieving foreign policy successes.[26] Unlike mature democracies, however, newly democratizing states are not particularly good at choosing wars that are easy to win and cheap to fight. A more plausible rationalistic argument for their wars is that elites in transitional states are "gambling for resurrection," that is, taking a risk at long odds that foreign policy confrontations will help them avoid losing power. Deductive arguments of this type propose that elites' informational advantages relative to their mass audience help them carry out such gambles.[27] Empirical research suggests that the strength of the incentive for downwardly mobile elites to gamble depends on the regime type and on the elites' ability to use their influence over the media to make the reckless strategy seem plausible to their constituents.[28] Our argument explains why the motive and opportunity to use this strategy are especially likely to be present when incomplete transitions to democracy occur in states with weak institutions.

In short, elites in newly democratizing states typically face the difficult political task of cobbling together a heterogeneous coalition of elite and popular supporters in a context of weakly developed democratic institutions. Many of the expedients that they adopt, such as logrolled overcommitments and nationalist outbidding strategies, heighten the risk of external conflict. These outcomes are most likely when threatened elites' interests cannot be easily adapted to a fully democratic setting and when mass political participation increases before the basic foundation for democratic institutions is firmly in place. Under such conditions, political entrepreneurs have both the incentive and the opportunity to promote conflict-causing nationalist myths.

Notes

1. See transcript of Clinton's 1994 State of the Union address, *New York Times*, 26 January 1994, A17.
2. Zakaria 1997.
3. Snyder 2000.
4. Gurr codes Ethiopia as making a transition to a regime with both democratic and autocratic characteristics in 1994. Gurr 2000, 293. Eritrea adopted a democratic constitution in 1997 in a process involving nationwide grassroots meetings, but the war precluded holding elections. Tronvoll argues that the war reflected the Eritrean regime's need to use a violent policy of border demarcation to solidify its territorial form of popular nationalism in a multiethnic state. See Iyob 1997; and Tronvoll 1999.
5. Mares 2001.
6. Mansfield and Snyder 1995a,b.
7. On the latter point, see Maoz 1998.
8. Similarly, Gurr finds that since the late 1980s, the likelihood of ethnic conflict has increased in the initial phase of transitions to democracy, especially in new states, but that democratic consolidation reduced this likelihood. Gurr 2000, 153–54.
9. Huntington 1968.
10. We define nationalism as the doctrine that a people who see themselves as distinctive in their culture, history, institutions, or principles should rule themselves in a political system that expresses and protects those distinctive characteristics.
11. Furet 1981.
12. See Fairbairn 1997; and Wehler 1985.
13. Russett and Oneal 2001, 47–50. However, some observers challenge this claim and argue that, in monadic terms, democracies are less prone to conflict than nondemocracies. See, for example, Ray 2000.
14. Reiter and Stam 1998.
15. See Bennett and Stam 1998; Lake 1992; and Siverson 1995.
16. Rousseau et al. 1996.
17. Schweller 1992.
18. Fearon 1994.
19. Snyder 1991.
20. Eksteins 1975, 78–81.
21. Snyder 1991.
22. Quoted in Ritter 1969, 257–63. See also Davis 2000.
23. Schultz 1998.
24. See Eley 1980; and Retallack 1993.
25. See Levy 1989; and Stein 1976.
26. Smith 1996.
27. See Downs and Rocke 1993; and Smith 1996.
28. See Goemans 2000; Levy 1989, 277–79; Levy and Vakili 1992; and Snyder 2000.

References

Bennett, D. Scott, and Allan C. Stam. 1998. The Declining Advantages of Democracy: A Combined Model of War Outcomes and Duration. *Journal of Conflict Resolution* 42 (3):344–66.

Davis, James W., Jr. 2000. *Threats and Promises: The Pursuit of International Influence*. Baltimore, Md.: Johns Hopkins University Press.

Downs, George W., and David M. Rocke. 1993. Conflict, Agency, and Gambling for Resurrection: The Principal-Agent Problem Goes to War. *American Journal of Political Science* 38 (2):362–80.

Eksteins, Modris. 1975. *The Limits of Reason: The German Democratic Press and the Collapse of Weimar Democracy*. London: Oxford University Press.

Eley, Geoff. 1980. *Reshaping the German Right*. New Haven, Conn.: Yale University Press.

Enterline, Andrew. 1996. Driving While Democratizing. *International Security* 20 (4):183–96.

Fairbain, Brett. 1997. *Democracy in the Undemocratic State: The German Reichstag Elections of 1898 and 1903*. Toronto: University of Toronto Press.

Fearon, James. 1994. Domestic Political Audiences and the Escalation of International Disputes. *American Political Science Review* 88 (3):577–92.

Furet, François. 1981. *Interpreting the French Revolution*. Cambridge: Cambridge University Press.

Gurr, Ted Robert. 2000. *Peoples Versus States*. Washington, D.C.: United States Institute of Peace.

Huntington, Samuel P. 1968. *Political Order in Changing Societies*. New Haven, Conn.: Yale University Press.

Iyob, Ruth. 1997. The Eritrean Experiment: A Cautious Pragmatism? *Journal of Modern African Studies* 35 (4):647–73.

Lake, David A. 1992. Powerful Pacifists: Democratic States and War. *American Political Science Review* 86 (1):24–37.

Levy, Jack S. 1989. The Causes of War: A Review of Theories and Evidence. In *Behavior, Society, and Nuclear War*. Vol. 1, edited by Philip E. Tetlock, Jo L. Husbands, Robert Jervis, Paul C. Stern, and Charles Tilly, 209–313. New York: Oxford University Press.

Levy, Jack S., and Lily Vakili. 1992. Diversionary Action by Authoritarian Regimes. In *The Internationalization of Communal Strife*, edited by Manus Midlarsky, 118–46. London: Routledge.

Mansfield, Edward D., and Jack Snyder. 1995a. Democratization and the Danger of War. *International Security* 20 (1):5–38.

———. 1995b. Democratization and War. *Foreign Affairs* 74 (3):79–97.

———. Forthcoming. *Democratization and War*. Cambridge, Mass.: MIT Press.

Maoz, Zeev. 1998. Realist and Cultural Critiques of the Democratic Peace: A Theoretical and Empirical Re-assessment. *International Interactions* 24 (1):3–89.

Mares, David R. 2001. *Violent Peace: Militarized Interstate Bargaining in Latin America*. New York: Columbia University Press.

Ray, James Lee. 2000. Democracy: On the Level(s), Does Democracy Correlate with Peace? In *What Do We Know About War?*, edited by John A. Vasquez, 299–316. Lanham, Md.: Rowman and Littlefield.

Reiter, Dan, and Allan C. Stam. 1998. Democracy, War Initiation, and Victory. *American Political Science Review* 92 (2):377–90.

Retallack, James. 1993. The Road to Philippi: The Conservative Party and Bethmann Hollweg's "Politics of the Diagonal," 1909–1914. In *Between Reform, Reaction, and Resistance: Studies in the History of German Conservatism from 1789 to 1945*, edited by Larry Eugene Jones and James Retallack, 261–98. Providence, R.I.: Berg.

Ritter, Gerhard. 1969. *The Sword and the Sceptre: The Problem of Militarism in Germany*, Vol. 2. Coral Gables, Fla.: University of Miami Press.

Russett, Bruce, and John R. Oneal. 2001. *Triangulating Peace: Democracy, Interdependence, and International Organizations*. New York: Norton.

Sater, William F. 1986. *Chile and the War of the Pacific*. Lincoln: University of Nebraska Press.

Schultz, Kenneth. 1998. Domestic Opposition and Signaling in International Crises. *American Political Science Review* 92 (4):829–44.

Schweller, Randall. 1992. Domestic Structure and Preventive War: Are Democracies More Pacific? *World Politics* 44 (2):235–69.

Siverson, Randolph M. 1995. Democracies and War Participation: In Defense of the Institutional Constraints Argument. *European Journal of International Relations* 1 (4):481–89.

Smith, Alastair. 1996. Diversionary Foreign Policy in Democratic Systems. *International Studies Quarterly* 40 (1):133–53.

Snyder, Jack. 1991. *Myths of Empire: Domestic Politics and International Ambition*. Ithaca, N.Y.: Cornell University Press.

———. 2000. *From Voting to Violence: Democratization and Nationalist Conflict*. New York: Norton.

Stein, Arthur A. 1976. Conflict and Cohesion: A Review of the Literature. *Journal of Conflict Resolution* 20 (1):143–72.

Tronvoll, Kjetil. 1999. Borders of Violence—Boundaries of Identity: Demarcating the Eritrean Nation-State. *Ethnic and Racial Studies* 22 (6):1037–60.

Wehler, Hans-Ulrich. 1985. *The German Empire: 1871–1918*. Dover, N.H.: Berg.

Zakaria, Fareed. 1997. The Rise of Illiberal Democracy. *Foreign Affairs* 76 (6):22–43.

 6.3

Electoral Systems for Divided Societies

Benjamin Reilly

As other selections in RCP have demonstrated (see selections 2.2, by Marx, and 6.2, by Mansfield and Snyder), ethnic differences are an important political cleavage in many countries. At the extreme, ethnic conflicts have involved violence and even genocide (notably, since the 1990s, in Rwanda, Sudan, and the former Yugoslavia during the 1990s). This selection analyzes the possibility that electoral procedures for choosing legislators may affect the extent of ethnic conflicts. Reilly finds that the voting procedure known as preferential voting reduces the likelihood of ethnic separatism. In his view, preferential voting (a procedure that he defines in the article) encourages political leaders to cooperate across the ethnic divide.

Can you think of other kinds of institutional procedures that might persuade political leaders from different ethnic groups to cooperate?

What kinds of electoral systems can help democracy survive in countries split by deep cleavages of race, religion, language, or ethnicity? As is well-known, politicians in such "divided societies" often have strong incentives to "play the ethnic card" at election time, using communal appeals to mobilize voters. "Outbidding"—increasingly extreme rhetoric and demands—can offer rewards greater than those of moderation. In such circumstances, politics can quickly turn centrifugal, as the center is pulled apart by extremist

Benjamin Reilly, "Electoral Systems for Divided Societies," *Journal of Democracy* 13, No. 2 (April 2002), pp. 155–159, 161–162. © National Endowment for Democracy and The Johns Hopkins University Press. Reprinted with permission of The Johns Hopkins University Press.

forces and "winner-take-all" rules the day. The failure of democracy is often the result.[1]

Any strategy for building sustainable democracy in divided societies must place a premium on avoiding this depressingly familiar pattern and must instead find ways to promote interethnic accommodation, multiethnic political parties, and moderate, centrist politics. Because elections help shape broader norms of political behavior, scholars and practitioners alike agree that electoral systems can play a powerful role in promoting both democracy and successful conflict management. For example, by changing the incentives and payoffs available to political actors in their search for electoral victory, astutely crafted electoral rules can make some types of behavior more politically rewarding than others. Over the past two decades, such "electoral engineering" has become increasingly attractive for those attempting to build democracy in divided societies.[2]

While political scientists agree broadly that electoral systems do much to shape the wider political arena, they disagree deeply about which electoral systems are most appropriate for divided societies.

Two schools of thought predominate. The scholarly orthodoxy has long argued that some form of proportional representation (PR) is needed in cases of deep-rooted ethnic divisions. PR is a key element of *consociational* approaches, which emphasize the need to develop mechanisms for elite power-sharing if democracy is to survive ethnic or other conflicts. Arend Lijphart, the scholar most associated with the consociational model, developed this prescription from a detailed examination of the features of power-sharing democracy in some continental European countries (the Netherlands, Belgium, and Switzerland), and there is disagreement over how well these measures can work (if at all) when applied to ethnic conflict in developing countries.[3] Yet there is little doubt that among scholars consociationalism represents the dominant model of democracy for divided societies. In terms of electoral systems, consociationalists argue that party-list PR is the best choice, as it enables all significant ethnic groups, including minorities, to "define themselves" into ethnically based parties and thereby gain representation in the parliament in proportion to their numbers in the community as a whole.[4]

The "Preferential" Option

In contrast to this orthodoxy, some critics argue that the best way to mitigate the destructive patterns of divided societies is not to encourage the formation of ethnic parties, thereby replicating existing ethnic divisions in the legislature, but rather to utilize electoral systems that encourage cooperation and accommodation among rival groups, and therefore work to reduce the salience of ethnicity. One core strategy, advocated by Donald Horowitz, is to design electoral rules that promote reciprocal vote-pooling, bargaining, and accommodation across group lines.[5] Presidential elections in Nigeria, for example, require the winning candidate to gain support from different regions, thus helping to diminish claims of narrow parochialism or regionalism. Lebanon's electoral system attempts to defuse the importance of ethnicity by pre-assigning ethnic proportions in each constituency, thus requiring parties to present ethnically mixed slates of candidates for election and making voters base their choices on issues other than ethnicity.

Yet the most powerful electoral systems for encouraging accommodation are those that make politicians reciprocally dependent on votes from groups other than their own. This essay examines the empirical record of one such electoral innovation as a tool of conflict management: the use of "preferential" electoral systems that enable voters to rank-order their choices among different parties or candidates on the ballot paper. All preferential electoral systems share a common, distinguishing feature: They enable electors to indicate how they would vote if their favored candidate was defeated and they had to choose among those remaining. Such systems include the "alternative vote" (AV) and the "single transferable vote" (STV).

AV is a majoritarian system used in single-member electoral districts that requires the winning candidate to gain not just a plurality but an absolute majority of votes. If no candidate has an absolute majority of first preferences, the candidate with the lowest number of first-preference votes is eliminated and his or her ballots are redistributed to the remaining candidates according to the lower preferences marked. This process of sequential elimination and transfer of votes continues until a majority winner emerges.

STV, by contrast, is a proportional system based around multimember districts that, depending on the number of members elected in each district, can allow even small minorities access to representation. Voters rank candidates in order of preference on the ballot in the same manner as AV. The count begins by determining the "quota" of votes required to elect a single candidate.[6] Any candidate who has more first preferences than the quota is immediately elected. If no one has achieved the quota, the candidate with the lowest number of first preferences is eliminated, and his or her second and later preferences are redistributed to the candidates left in the race. At the same time, the "surplus" votes of elected candidates (that is, their votes above the quota) are redistributed at a reduced value according to the lower preferences on the ballots, until all seats for the constituency are filled.

Because they enable electors to rank candidates in their order of preference, such systems can encourage politicians in divided societies to campaign not just for first-preference votes from their own community, but for "second-choice" votes from other groups as well—thus providing parties and candidates with an incentive to "pool votes" across ethnic lines. To attract second-level support, candidates may need to make crossethnic appeals and demonstrate their capacity to represent groups other than their own. Alternately, where a moderate or nonethnic "middle" part of the electorate exists, candidates may need to move to the center on policy issues to attract these voters.

Either way, negotiations between rival candidates and their supporters for reciprocal vote transfers can greatly increase the chances that votes will shift from ethnic parties to nonethnic ones—thus encouraging, even in deeply divided societies, the formation and strengthening of a core of "moderate middle" sentiment within the electorate as a whole. Such negotiations can also stimulate the development of alliances between parties and aid the development of multiethnic parties or coalitions of parties. Scholars have increasingly found that aggregative party systems can help new or transitional democracies achieve stability.

This broad approach to conflict management has been dubbed "centripetalism" because "the explicit aim is to engineer a centripetal spin to the political system—to pull the parties toward moderate, compromising policies and to discover and reinforce the center of a deeply divided political spectrum."[7] A centripetal political system or strategy is designed to focus competition at the moderate center rather than the extremes by making politicians do more than just shop for votes in their own community.

Accordingly, I use the term centripetalism as a shorthand for three related but distinct phenomena: 1) the provision of *electoral incentives* for campaigning politicians to reach out to and attract votes from ethnic groups other than their own, thus encouraging candidates to moderate their political rhetoric on potentially divisive issues and forcing them to broaden their policy positions; 2) the presence of an *arena of bargaining,* in which political actors from different groups have an incentive to come together and cut deals on reciprocal electoral support, and hence perhaps on other more substantial issues as well; and 3) the development of *centrist, aggregative, and multiethnic political parties* or coalitions of parties that are capable of making crossethnic appeals and presenting a complex and diverse range of policy options to the electorate. . . .

Evaluating the Evidence

All of these cases provide important empirical evidence for evaluating claims that preferential electoral systems can, under certain circumstances, promote cooperation among competing groups in divided societies. This in itself is an important conclusion, as a recurring criticism of centripetal theories in general, and of the case for preferential voting in particular, has been a perceived lack of real-world examples. Apparently similar institutional designs, however, also appear to have had markedly different impacts in different countries. In Northern Ireland, for example, it is clear that vote transfers assisted the process of moderation in the breakthrough 1998 election. But the evidence from elections held under similar rules in 1973 or 1982—or, for that matter, from Estonia's 1990 election—is much more ambiguous. Similarly, Papua New Guinea's experience with AV in the 1960s and 1970s was markedly more successful than that of its Pacific neighbor, Fiji, more recently. Why?

A key facilitating condition appears to be the presence of a core group of *moderates*, both among the political leadership and in the electorate at large. Centripetal strategies for conflict management assume that there is sufficient moderate sentiment within a community for crossethnic voting to be possible. In some circumstances, the presence of vote-pooling institutions may even encourage the development of this type of moderate core, via repeated interelite interaction within bargaining arenas. But it cannot invent moderation where none exists. It is likely that a major factor in the success or failure of centripetalism in Northern Ireland was the lack of a moderate core in earlier elections and its clear presence in 1998. This is reflected in part by the fact that, in the 1998 election, far more votes were transferred from sectarian to nonsectarian "middle" parties than across the ethnic divide per se.[8]

The argument that preferential election rules induce moderation rests on the assumption that politicians are rational actors who will do what needs to be done to gain election. Under different types of preferential voting rules, however, "what needs to be done" varies considerably, depending on the electoral formula in place and the social makeup of the electorate. For example, if candidates are confident of achieving an absolute majority or winning the required quota of first preferences, they need only focus on maximizing votes from their own supporters in order to win the seat. In cases where no candidate has outright majority support, however, the role of second and later preferences becomes crucial to gaining an overall majority. Thus some scholars such as Horowitz favor majoritarian forms of preferential voting like AV over the proportional variant of STV, since the former's threshold for immediate victory is higher. In addition, Horowitz's case for "vote pooling" is based on the purported possibility of cross-ethnic voting—that is, the assumption that even in deeply divided societies some electors will be prepared to give some votes, even if only lower-order ones, to members of another ethnic group. In Northern Ireland, however, while vote transfers played an important role in promoting accommodation, these ran predominantly from anti-agreement to pro-agreement parties on the same side of the sectarian divide, or from sectarian to nonsectarian "middle" parties, rather than across the communal cleavage between unionists and nationalists.

Second, *continuity of experience* appears to be a critical variable. The evidence suggests that successive elections held under the same rules encourage a gradual process of political learning. Structural incentives need to be kept constant over several elections before the effects of any electoral package can be judged— particularly with preferential systems, where the routines of deal-making and preference-swapping by politicians, and the understanding of these devices by voters, take time to emerge. In the world's two longest-running cases of preferential voting—Australia and Ireland—it took many years for the full strategic potential of vote-transfers to became clear to politicians and voters alike (in fact, rates of preference-swapping in Australian elections have increased steadily over recent decades), while Estonia's preferential system may have been so short-lived that voters and politicians never became adjusted to it.

Third, the *social context* in which elections are held appears all-important. Countries like Northern Ireland and Estonia feature "bipolar" splits between two large and relatively cohesive ethnic groups, both of which were effectively guaranteed representation under STV's proportional election rules. But in 1998, Northern Ireland also had a third group: the middle, nonsectarian parties that were not clearly bound to either community. By advantaging the representation of this group, STV promoted outcomes that would not have been likely under AV or other majority systems, or under party-list PR. In other cases, however, where there is greater ethnic heterogeneity or a much smaller nonethnic center, STV may not work so well—indeed, it did not work well in Northern Ireland's previous elections. All this suggests that a key element of any electoral-engineering prescription must be a careful understanding of the prevailing social and demographic conditions—particularly the size, number, and dispersion of ethnic groups.

The importance of ethnic demography is highlighted by the cases of Fiji and Papua New Guinea. In Fiji, most open electoral districts—which are supposed to encapsulate a "good proportion" of members of both major communities—are drawn in such a way as to become the exclusive preserve of one ethnic group or the other. Thus genuine opportunities for interethnic cooperation at the constituency level are rare, and most contests provide no opportunity at all for crossethnic campaigns, appeals, or outcomes. Indeed, only six seats were genuinely competitive between ethnic groups in the 1999 election, while in the rest clear Indian or Fijian majorities prevailed.[9]

Contrast this with the situation in Papua New Guinea, where the extreme fragmentation of traditional society means that most districts feature dozens of small tribal ethnopolities. To be elected under a preferential majority system like AV, candidates had no option but to amass votes from a range of groups beyond their own. Under such conditions, candidates had a strong incentive to behave accommodatingly toward rival groups. Not surprisingly, electoral violence was much rarer under the AV system than under the more recent plurality rules, which lacks such incentives.

Such cases remind us that divided societies, like Tolstoy's unhappy families, tend to be divided in different ways. Yet it is surprising how many "one-size-fits-all" conflict-management packages have been recommended for divided societies without sufficient understanding of the structure of the society itself. Differences in ethnic demography need to be matched by differences in constitutional designs across different regions. African minorities, for example, have been found to be more highly concentrated in contiguous geographical areas than minorities in other regions, making it difficult to create ethnically heterogenous electorates.[10] Contrast this with the highly intermixed patterns of ethnic settlement found in many parts of Europe (the Baltics), Asia (India, Singapore, Malaysia), and the Caribbean (Guyana, Suriname, Trinidad and Tobago), in which members of various ethnic groups tend to have more day-to-day contact with one another. In such contexts, electoral districts are likely to be ethnically heterogeneous, and ethnic identities will often be mitigated by other crosscutting cleavages, so that centripetal designs which encourage parties to seek the support of various ethnic groups may very well break down interethnic antagonisms and promote the development of broad, multiethnic parties. Such prosaic details can determine the success of centripetal approaches to the management of ethnic conflict.

Notes

1. For good discussions of the interaction between ethnicity and electoral politics, see Donald L. Horowitz, *Ethnic Groups in Conflict* (Berkeley: University of California Press, 1985); Larry Diamond and Marc F. Plattner, eds., *Nationalism, Ethnic Conflict, and Democracy* (Baltimore: Johns Hopkins University Press, 1994); and Timothy D. Sisk, *Power Sharing and International Mediation in Ethnic Conflicts* (Washington, D.C.: U.S. Institute of Peace Press, 1996).
2. See, for example, Arend Lijphart, *Democracy in Plural Societies: A Comparative Exploration* (New Haven: Yale University Press, 1977); Donald L. Horowitz, *A Democratic South Africa? Constitutional Engineering in a Divided Society* (Berkeley: University of California Press, 1991); Giovanni Sartori, *Comparative Constitutional Engineering: An Inquiry into Structures, Incentives and Outcomes* (London: Macmillan, 1994); and Benjamin Reilly and Andrew Reynolds, *Electoral Systems and Conflict in Divided Societies* (Washington, D.C.: National Research Council, 1999).
3. See Arend Lijphart, *Democracy in Plural Societies;* and Timothy D. Sisk, *Power Sharing and International Mediation in Ethnic Conflicts,* 27–45. See also Donald L. Horowitz, "Making Moderation Pay: The Comparative Politics of Ethnic Conflict Management," in Joseph V. Montville, ed., *Conflict and Peacemaking in Multiethnic Societies* (New York: Lexington Books, 1991), 451–76.
4. Arend Lijphart, "Electoral Systems, Party Systems and Conflict Management in Segmented Societies," in R.A. Schrire, ed., *Critical Choices for South Africa: An Agenda for the 1990s* (Cape Town: Oxford University Press, 1990), 10–13.
5. See Donald L. Horowitz, *Ethnic Groups in Conflict;* and Donald L. Horowitz, "Making Moderation Pay."
6. The formula used divides the total number of votes in the count by one more than the number of seats to be elected, and then adds one to the result. For example, if there are 6,000 votes and five members to be elected, the quota for election is 6,000/(5 + 1) + 1, or 1,001 votes.
7. Timothy D. Sisk, *Democratization in South Africa: The Elusive Social Contract* (Princeton: Princeton University Press, 1995), 19.
8. See Richard Simmott, "Centrist politics makes modest but significant progress: cross-community transfers were low," *Irish Times* (Dublin), 29 June 1998.
9. See Nigel Roberts, "Living up to Expectations? The New Fijian Electoral System and the 1999 General Election," paper presented to Citizens Constitutional Forum, Suva, Fiji, 18 July 1999.
10. James R. Scarritt, "Communal Conflict and Contention for Power in Africa South of the Sahara," in Ted Robert Gurr, ed., *Minorities at Risk: A Global View of Ethnopolitical Conflicts* (Washington, D.C.: U.S. Institute of Peace Press, 1993).

6.4

Stepsisters: Feminist Movement Activism in Different Institutional Spaces

Mary Fainsod Katzenstein

Mary Katzenstein claims that protest can occur not only in the streets, that is, by dramatic disruption, but also within institutions. Although protest within institutions is less public, it can nonetheless be highly influential. Katzenstein further suggests that the design of institutions affects the character of protest activity that takes place. She illustrates her argument by comparing women's protest activity within the U.S. military and the Catholic Church.

Can you think of how the design of other institutions, for example, colleges or corporations, can influence the extent and character of protest that occurs in these sites?

Students of social movements commonly associate institutionalization with demobilization (Piven and Cloward 1971; Kriesi et al. 1992, p. 250; Tarrow 1989, pp. 330–34).[1] Social movements, in this view, are necessarily extrainstitutional: claims voiced by social movements, when incorporated within institutional settings, are thought to be both routinized and depoliticized. Institutional actors (lawyers, judges, politicians, employers, journalists) are definitionally precluded from being social movement activists—except after hours. In the social movement literature, those who wield influence inside institutions are generally denoted as "third parties" called on as allies of, rather than parties to, a movement's effort to effect change (Lipsky 1968).

This presumed inconsistency between movement politics and institutional politics is based on a frequently drawn linkage of location, form, and content. When social movement actors doing street politics (location) opt for or ally themselves with those who use conventional modes (form) of political activism such as lobbying or voting, a social movement is generally deemed to have crossed the threshold separating protest politics from institutional politics, and the result is presumed to be deradicalizing (content).

Mary Fainsod Katzenstein, "Stepsisters: Feminist Movement Activism in Different Institutional Spaces," in David S. Meyer and Sidney Tarrow, eds., *The Social Movement Society: Contentious Politics for a New Century* (Lanham, MD: Rowman & Littlefield, 1998), ch. 9, pp. 199–216. Reprinted by permission of Rowman and Littlefield Publishers.

This location-form-content distinction between movement and institutions invites judgments that are too readily overdrawn. It is too easy to presume that what occurs on the streets is disruptive and what occurs within institutional contexts is accommodative. But what does "disruption" really mean? Is a demonstration outside the White House or a snake dance around the Pentagon that causes security to be deployed and that may temporarily interrupt traffic and block the entry of people trying to reach their place of employment more disruptive than the presence of self-acknowledged feminists at the workplace who make known their expectations about changes in language, sexual behavior, and office hierarchies? Disruption needs to be distinguished from "interruption." Disruption is about challenges to power that have the potential of compelling change. . . .

The 1990s provide an ideal moment to study the intersection of movement and institution. Their encounter (the marriage of movement and institution) has by now produced a generation of offspring who are no longer toddlers, or even adolescents, but old enough to have developed identities of their own. This is a study of two stepsisters: born of a common feminist mother (the women's movement), the institutionalization of feminist protest in two organizational environments imparts a tale of siblings whose lives are both different and the same. Feminist activism in the military is well behaved—behavior that belies its sometimes defiant character. Feminist activism in the Catholic Church is openly rebellious but not in the short run, I think, any more threatening to the institution. . . .

Pressure Group Activism in the U.S. Military

Law and Opportunity.   To tell the "story" of feminist activism in the military over the last several decades is to relate a three-part narrative about how (1) women's claims making has been institutionalized; (2) how the law has instigated activism by providing opportunities for feminist pressure politics; and (3) how the law has contained this activism by shaping the ways activists see themselves (their political identities), thus influencing what activists think to want politically.

Now in her forties and recently a mother, Rosemary Mariner became in 1990 the United States Navy's first female jet squadron commander. She spent the initial twenty years of her career "operational"—not behind a desk but behind the controls of anything she was allowed to fly, from helicopters to high-performance jets, racking up over 3,500 flight hours. Flying was a childhood dream for Mariner, a dream she announced early on to the principal of her Catholic girls school. Along with becoming a crackerjack aviator (testing planes and training male aviators for combat missions that she was not by law permitted to perform herself), Mariner became an activist promoting gender equality in Navy aviation. She hadn't always been outspoken. In the mid-1970s, Mariner was asked to join in the *Owens v. Brown* class action suit in which women were suing the service to open up Navy ships to uniformed women. At the time, Mariner was establishing herself as an up-and-coming young aviator in a fighter community. Going it on her own seemed smarter than calling attention to herself as part of a cadre of discontented women. "I basically wimped out. Because I had it good, I didn't want to get in trouble with the Navy. And I consider that moral cowardice on my part" (Zimmerman 1995, p. 121).

By the late 1980s, however, the military had changed and so had Mariner. Equality of opportunity was official institutional orthodoxy, at least at the level of rhetoric. A Southern Californian product of parochial schools and Orange County Republicanism, Mariner had become a feminist. This was a shifting of identity if not a metamorphosis. Losing none of her dyed-in-the-wool patriotic love of country, Mariner, nonetheless, became an unrelenting advocate of women's career advancement. As squadron command leader, Mariner worked self-consciously to support women seeking training and promotion. In the late 1980s, Mariner became the head of Women Military Aviators, an organization of six hundred that networked in support of equal opportunity. As with most women activists in the military, this was not a feminism Mariner brought with her into the armed forces. It was a commitment to gender equality that Mariner discovered and made her own *in* the military, itself.

The Women Military Aviators arrived on the scene later than several other groups that sought to support women's equality in the armed forces. Other habitats also existed that supported women activists: WOPA (the Women's Officers' Professional Association) began as an informal network of Navy women in 1978, incorporating in 1984. Both organizations brought women officers together to network, to attend talks, and in informal ways to create a sense of mutuality and strength in numbers. Other civilian organizations "worked the issues." The Defense Advisory Committee on Women in the Services, founded in the early 1950s as a public relations arm to facilitate military recruitment, was by the late 1970s an active lobbying force for military women operating from an office in the Pentagon, pressuring decision makers to reconsider a range of discriminatory policies. The Ford Foundation–funded Women and Military Project housed in the Women's Equity Action League was directed in the early 1980s by an ex-army officer, Carolyn Becraft, a woman who was to become for the next ten years a one-person social movement, monitoring the services, networking, strategizing, coordinating, and ultimately leading the lobbying efforts to change discriminatory practices and law. These civilian groups were a crucial lifeline to the uniformed women who wanted to be active but could not assume all the burden of speaking out themselves.

Even more important to the survival of feminism within the institution was the legitimation that came in the 1970s from the courts. Given the pressures on military women (and on all members of the military) to support the "party line," or at least to seek redress for any grievances they might harbor but without making waves, it is astonishing that even some military women chose to identify themselves as advocates for women. They could afford to do so, however, because throughout the 1970s, coinciding with the early days of the all-volunteer force, the courts sided with women who sued the military for sex discrimination. This judicial sponsorship—despite its reversal in the 1980s—was vital in supporting uniformed women together with their allies in nonprofit and lobbying organizations who entered the fray to struggle for equal opportunity. Although the courts pulled back from equality of opportunity norms in the 1980s, by that time, military women and their lobbyist confederates were already invested in the promises of equal opportunity.

The 1970s tell a remarkable tale. Time after time the courts, which had generally allowed the military broad leeway to set its own standards of conduct, refused to allow the services the autonomy to practice sex discrimination. During this decade the court was prepared to instruct the military to begin to make good on the transgressions of sex discrimination even as, in *other* arenas, the court demonstrated consistent deference to military sovereignty. . . .

Feminism in the military, then, played by the rules. Far from taking to the streets, they formed organizations to try to influence policy in the services and when that seemed to fail, they took to the courts. The law created opportunities for feminist activism in two ways. First, it provided direct authorization for military women who felt compelled to take their charges of discrimination outside the chain of command and outside the institution. When uniformed women did so, at least in the 1970s, the courts listened. Although the courts went on to play a more restrictive role in subsequent years, following the Court's determination to hold the line on all-male conscription with *Rostker* (1981), the courts' reversion was in some senses too late.[2] By 1980, the courts had transmitted the message to women that in certain basic respects, under the Constitution, they were entitled to equal treatment. Second, not only did the law directly affirm women's claims by providing a hearing outside the perimeters of the military, but the law also invested women with ammunition for their battles inside. The courts' endorsement of equal opportunity, although less than wholehearted, spawned a shift in institutional norms. As the belief in equality of opportunity spread, it provided women with an ideological resource to use in their internal efforts to argue for policy change. As Brigadier General Evelyn P. Foote (1993), one of the most forceful advocates for military women, put it, "It is simply far easier to challenge a policy that has a basis in law." . . .

Discursive Activism in the Catholic Church

. . . To tell the story of feminist activism in the American Catholic Church is to relate a very different three-part narrative: (1) As with the military, feminist claims making in the Church has been institutionalized. (2) Unlike the military, in which the law affirmed the legitimacy of activism, the absence of such legal legitimation for women activists in the Church means that the sources of affirmation or condemnation of feminism in the Church are largely institutional. (3) The opportunity- and identity-forming power of the Church, in contrast to the military, has radicalized feminism within the Church.

The habitats which came to house feminist activism in the Catholic Church were of several types. Religious congregations themselves constituted one such space where women who were rethinking their lives in relationship to the Church came together, debated, reflected, explored, and refashioned their life and spiritual missions.[3]

Church renewal and social justice organizations provided a second habitat for the development of a feminist voice within the Church. One of the first organizations to be established was the National Assembly of Women Religious (NAWR), later to change its name to the National Assembly of Religious Women (NARW) to reflect the participation of laywomen. Founded in 1968, NARW endeavored to give voice to a more grassroots expression of views by religious women than was at that time possible in the Leadership Conference of Women Religious, and it remained until its demise in 1995 one of the groups most actively involved in tackling class and race issues within the movement of Catholic feminism.[4] The National Coalition of American Nuns was formed in 1969 with the intent of speaking out on a range of social justice and human rights issues.[5] Also in 1971, Las Hermanas, an organization of Hispanic sisters and laywomen engaged in the struggle against poverty and discrimination, was also founded. Numerous other organizations were founded throughout the decade that addressed issues about ordination, reproductive rights, homosexuality, and a range of poverty and antiracist concerns.[6]

A third habitat for feminism within the church has been academic institutions housing feminist scholars. By the 1980s, feminist theologians, historians, and sociologists had secured, in fairly significant numbers, tenured places in American universities.[7] These positions have provided sometimes safe and sometimes highly contentious (as with Mary Daly's tenure fight at Boston College) spaces from which feminist scholars have been able to produce hundreds of volumes about church teachings and church history. It was of no small importance to feminism's institutionalization that feminist theological writings found outlets in prominent commercial presses (Harper and Row, Simon and Schuster, Beacon) in addition to the presses that carry largely religious publications.[8] It is also telling that by the late 1980s, women were one-quarter of all students enrolled in American Roman Catholic theological schools (Baumgaertner 1989, pp. 90–92, as quoted in Wallace 1992, p. 5).

Many feminist organizations within the Church gained a visibility surprising in light of their tiny staffs and limited budgets. Skilled in the arts of communications and media, all the renewal organizations, no matter how small, ran workshops, organized conferences, and produced quantities of literature—newsletters,[9] resources for workshops, liturgies, and press releases, not to mention fiction, poetry, plays, posters, tapes, and extensive dramaturgy of all sorts. The spokespersons for the organizations were also spending large amounts of time on the road, interacting with others in projects, meetings, and educational endeavors. Feminism in the Church was above all discursive, engaged as it was in a project of reinterpretation and meaning making (Katzenstein 1995).

The agenda of these groups was both discursive and radical. Feminists worked at knowledge producing that questioned some of the basic precepts of the contemporary institutional Church. Substantial numbers of feminists, for instance, have argued against women's ordination as merely underwriting the hierarchy of the Church itself. Many have questioned the structural basis of inequity and injustice in state, in society, and in the Church. Activist nuns and laywomen have worked in prisons, in shelters, with refugees from Central and Latin America, with babies (often born drug addicted) and children of poor mothers. A number have worked on issues about homosexuality within the Church. A few, supported by outside funding (principally the Ford Foundation), have worked on issues about reproductive rights. The agenda is not monolithic—with important debates recurrently flaring up over Christology in a renewed Church, Catholic feminism's own racism/classism, and the accountability of women to their orders and to the hierarchy. In comparison with feminism in other institutional contexts, women activists in the Church stand out as overtly, vocally committed to a restructuring of the society according to principles of equity and inclusiveness.

Opportunity and Identity

The explanation for the rise and endurance of this spirit of insurgency is found within the history of the institution itself. Unlike women activists in the military, women religious could not turn to the law. But in certain ways they were able to turn to the Church itself. Not all would-be activists were ready to do this. In the face of Vatican intransigence, some chose conformity and silence. Others chose to leave the Church. But many stayed within the Church and opted to challenge its hierarchy, making abundant use of the discursive resources of print, speech, and song.

What activist women found in the Church was both opportunity and identity. The opportunity came with the declarations of Vatican II. By asking what role the Church should assume in the modern world and by inviting the active participation of the laity in the construction of a lived faith, Pope John XXIII and Pope Paul VI catalyzed vast changes. The call for renewal invited all religious orders to examine their constitution, directories, ceremonies, and prayers—indeed, their entire mission and self-understanding (see Ware 1985; Curb and Manahan 1985). When, in response to Vatican II, nuns rewrote their orders' constitutions and recomposed their rituals, they exchanged the old standardization of behavior based on rigid rules of obedience and conformity for new rules that provided at once for greater community and greater individual autonomy. Gone were the requirements to ask the mother superior for permission to take a bath, to use a needle and thread, to read the newspaper, to go outside, to consult a book other than the Bible. No longer were letters between the eighteen-year-old postulant and her mother or father or erstwhile boyfriend opened, read, and maybe not delivered. Gone were the ban on "particular friendships" and the arbitrary assignments to jobs and locations arrived at through closed deliberations to which the nun assignee was not privy.

The opportunity Vatican II provided, then, came in the form of the injunction: that the church was to be understood as the people. But in the successor years in which Pope John Paul II reasserted strict centralized control over Church affairs, Vatican II was reinterpreted by many increasingly exasperated feminist sisters and laywomen to mean "If the church is the people, and we are the people, then the church is us—womenchurch." . . .

As an institution, the Catholic Church in some ways nurtures the possibility of defining oneself as in dissent. One word that is often used to legitimize dissent within the Church is *prophetic*. One cannot exactly be "prophetic" in the military—disagreeing with those higher in the chain of command. In the Church, there is at least the possibility of appeal to the tradition of prophets and to the call of moral conscience. But this would not explain a readier tendency to insurgency among American religious than among their female counterparts in many other parts of the world. To understand the American "exceptionalism" means turning to the way American women in the Church came to be influenced not only by the social movements of the time (the civil rights, peace, and women's movements) but by the specific migration of ideas to North America from the ecclesial neighbors to the south.

Beginning in the 1960s, Latin American liberation theology exerted a powerful influence over many women religious in North America. At least some of this influence was transmitted through the presence of United States sisters who were sent to work throughout Latin America. Already by 1961, the Church hierarchy had appealed to religious communities in the United States to send 10 percent of their community members to missions in Latin America (Prevallet 1995, p. 91). . . .

By the 1980s, many sisters were traveling to Central and South America. Many worked as teachers and health workers in El Salvador, Nicaragua, and elsewhere in Latin America.[10] The 1980 rape and murder of two Maryknoll and one Ursuline sister and a laywoman who had been working with local communities in El Salvador by members of the National Guard sent shock waves through the religious communities of North America and undoubtedly intensified further the attention that religious groups were directing to events in Latin America (Neal 1990, p. 39; Ferraro and Hussey 1990, p. 197). In the 1980s, Sister Marjorie Tuite, much revered by activist sisters, established the Women's Coalition against United States Intervention in Latin America and the Carribean. She made continuous trips to Central America and Cuba, taking groups of women religious with her to be "present in the struggle."[11] The National Assembly of Religious Women (NARW), which Tuite founded, shared offices with an organization working with Guatemalan women and continued to work in alliance with women like Renny Golden who were active in the sanctuary movement. Network, the Catholic lobbying group in Washington run by sisters, made U.S. policy in Central America one of its central issues. Deeply committed to a common struggle for social justice, the entire Loretto order's assembly voted to spend significant amounts of money on Latin American projects: $30,000 in humanitarian aid to Nicaragua in 1979, $20,000 for two projects in 1980 in El Salvador, $23,500 for aid to refugees from "repressive Central American countries" in 1981 (Ware 1995, p. 75). But even for those women who had no direct experience in Latin America, the writings of Paulo Freire and the practices of *conscientiazation*[12] were present in the methodologies of discussion and reflection used in meetings of women religious. "Speak outs," breaking up into small groups—methods of deliberation incorporated into the assemblies of many religious orders during the 1970s—were all at least partly a result of teachings that had come to the United States through liberation theology.

Vatican II created the opportunity for nuns to rethink their vocation. But the Vatican call for renewal did not dictate the character of that vocation. Nuns and many laywomen came to see themselves in distinctly radical terms, to redefine their identities, strongly influenced by the social movements outside the Church and by the powerful might of liberation theology whose teachings were transported from Latin American missions to the meeting rooms of American religious.

Conclusion

To see the social movements of the 1990s through the lenses of the 1960s may invite a misreading of the 1990s. The 1960s held out what seemed to be, at least then, a clearer definition of who was (in the language of the time) "inside the system" and who was out. A 1960s student protester could readily define someone inside the system as an adult living in a world the student had not yet had chronological reason to enter. An African American might have readily seen an insider as necessarily white given the near-absence of persons of color in government, in universities, on the television set, running local businesses, or in the courthouse. The boundaries separating protest on the outside and business as usual on the inside seemed clearer than they do today. The distinction between movement politics and institutional life seemed unmistakeable.

The inside/outside of feminism in the 1990s is, in two ways, less distinct. First, in the 1960s, the energy of protest movements could be sapped by young activists opting to enter business, enter politics, become a lawyer, or get a government job. In the 1990s, feminist activists in the Church and military did not leave the movement for the institution; feminists, in particular, came *to* the movement *from within* the institution. Second, by the 1990s, there was protest drama inside and outside institutions. Partly because of the exposé-hungry culture of the media, the public has come to witness theatrical "episodes" in once-private spaces—the suites of the Las Vegas Hilton, the living rooms of army drill instructors. The reasons for taking protest into the institution are now vivid and compelling.

But do we see in the 1990s what the 1960s activists feared—that claims voiced from within an institutional milieu must face an inevitable routinization and deradicalization in the face of the controlling rules of institutional life? If the experiences of the military and the Church provide any single answer to this question, it is that feminism runs a different course depending on its institutional location.

On first take, feminism's encounter with the military appears in some ways to be a straightforward exemplification of the deradicalization thesis. After twenty years of equal opportunity, women's numbers in the academies and in the services are nowhere above 20 percent and mostly well below; uniformed women activists are careful to keep their political struggles out of the press and to contain their issues to "women-focused" concerns. Only recently have women's organizations in the military begun exploring the commonalities of race and gender, and, for the most part, they continue to segment their cause from any tarnishing it might suffer by linking issues of gender inequality to the bigotry of heterosexist policy and culture in the armed services.

At the same time, such a narrative, if it is not to be reductionist, must acknowledge additional realities. Military feminists were hardly radicals to begin with. If the institution plays a role in containing protest, it is not to subdue what was there before, as much as to divert what might be there in some future time. Clearly military elites fear change: At each turn military feminists face vehement resistance from within (with the integration of the academies, with their efforts to seek institutional resolutions to problems of sexual harassment, with their insistence on women's inclusion in the combat specialties of military aviation and the naval services). If the opposition women activists encounter at virtually every turn is any indication, what they seek to change is not easily dismissable as matters that are marginal to the definition of the institution. Reformist, perhaps, but words like *depoliticization* and *deradicalization* are inadequate to describe institutionalized feminism in the military.

Relative to their counterparts in the military, feminism in the Catholic Church is a far more insurgent enterprise. Feminist habitats in the Church are some of the few places, in the 1990s, where a 1960s activist can feel at home. In the face of a Church that excludes women from its hierarchy, that condemns the sin of homosexuality, and in the face of a society that dismisses any defense of affirmative action and welfare rights as evidence of extremism, the words of activist laywomen and women religious in the Catholic Church produce texts in which radicals still "talk the talk."

. . . If the politics of activism inside institutions is to be understood in *both* its radical and more moderate forms, the character of its particular institutional location must be carefully specified. Feminist habitats in the Church and military are nested in very different institutional environments (Aggarwal 1986; Tsebelis 1990; Meyer and Whittier 1994).[13] Situated in a transnational church and insulated from the law, the Vatican has been able to repudiate the demands of

American religious women, paradoxically inviting a rebelliousness born out of foreclosed political options. Military activists, by contrast, occupied habitats in an institution that was situated in a national context that bound institutional leadership to the law and that promised activists at least some rewards for moderately voiced claims. The question for today's activists is perhaps less about whether you are outside or inside institutions than it is about the systems of authority the institution is nested within.

Notes

1. Frances Fox Piven and Richard A. Cloward (1971, p. 456) write, "Protest movements have always been the resort of those who lacked institutionalized forms of political access and influence." In their introductory essay in David S. Meyer and Sidney Tarrow, eds., *The Social Movement Society: Contentious Politics for a New Century* (Lanham, MD: Rowman & Littlefield, 1998), Meyer and Tarrow speak of institutionalization as transporting movement actors into a realm of more routinized and established political practices. They do not see institutional actors as abandoning political goals, a perspective that I share. They describe institutionalization, however, as defined partially by the occurrence of cooptation, meaning that "challengers alter their claims and tactics to ones that can be pursued without disrupting the normal practice of politics." I argue, by contrast, that institutionalized activism may or may not be cooptative and can be, under particular circumstances, quite disruptive.

2. In *Rostker v. Goldberg*, the Court was confronted with the issue of women in combat—touching, as Bill Brundage terms it, "the defining nucleus" of the military mission: it drew back. This shift occurred as the Court moved ever-closer to the self-defined essence of the military—the combat issue. Moving from dependency allowances, to the pregnancy issue, to the matter of women's service on ships, the Court began to approach what many saw as the core definition of a masculinist military—the composition of a fighting force. Justice Rehnquist, writing for a six-justice majority, claimed that draft registration directly related to conscription and thereby to combat. The dissenting judges claimed that women could be registered or drafted without necessarily implicating them in combat duties. And in language that was significant in its absence from earlier sex discrimination cases brought against the military, Justice Rehnquist affirmed the importance of a "healthy deference to legislative and executive judgments in the area of military affairs."

3. Throughout the late 1960s and continuing to this day, many religious orders have held discussions in their regular assembly meetings about gender and race issues. These discussions raised both spiritual and secular issues. They considered the meaning of religious renewal and such specific matters as whether the congregation should support the ERA. What does racism mean in the everyday lives of sisters? What does an inclusive liturgy mean? Should a particular resolution on sanctuaries be adopted? In the case of particular orders (the Sisters of Mercy), there were discussions, for instance, about the responsibilities of Sister-run hospitals for women's gynecological and reproductive health care. Smaller networks were also formed within a congregation. When particular subgroups within an order wished to address themselves to an issue not necessarily involving the whole congregation, measures were taken to constitute community-connected associations. Loretto Women's Network, formed by a group within the Loretto Sisters, and the Network's newspaper, *couRAGE*, are examples; see the essays in Ware (1995), particularly the chapter by Virginia Williams, "Loretto and the Women's Movement: From 'Sister' to 'Sister,'" especially pp. 245–46 on the origins of the Loretto Women's Network. The Adrian Dominicans also have a commission for women. Similarly, the Sisters of Charity of the blessed Virgin Mary have a network for Women's Issues—loosely held together through small group discussions, personal contact, and a newsletter.

4. See the final issue of *Probe* for a history of NARW. Vol. XXIII, No. 2. Summer, 1995.

5. For a history of NCAN, see "If Anyone Can, NCAN: Twenty Years of Speaking Out," edited by Margaret Traxler and Ann Patrick Ware and available from NCAN, 7315 S. Yale, Chicago, Ill 60621.

6. The Women's Ordination Conference (WOC) was founded in 1974, the same year that Chicago Catholic Women (CCW) was established. In 1974, Catholics for a Free Choice (CFFC), directed by Frances Kissling, was founded to support the right to legal reproductive health care including family planning and abortion, later to be declared by the Vatican as not an official voice of the Catholic Church. Other multiple-issue groups also date from this period (the Quixote Center, the Eighth Day Center for Justice, Call to Action), all of which work toward the advancement of gender equality as part of their broad agendas. In 1977, Sister Jeannine Gramick and Father Robert Nugent founded the New Ways ministry to work toward reconciliation of Church teachings and gay/lesbian issues. In 1982, Mary Hunt and Diann Neu founded the Women's Alliance for Theology, Ethics, and Religion, which organizes workshops and resources for an ecumenical constituency. In 1987, Mary's Pence was established to raise and distribute money for women's causes. Peter's Pence collections raise money for the papacy. The feast of Teresa of Avila, October 15, has been selected as Mary's Pence Day, but because many of the fund's donors are not churchgoers, much of the fundraising occurs through other avenues. In 1995, the fund distributed $60,000—a surprisingly high sum given that Mary's Pence has not been approved for entry in the Kennedy Book that lists sanctioned Catholic charities.

7. The writings of feminist historians, sociologists, and political scientists throughout the 1980s were also very important in the creation of an epistemic community. Some prominent examples from the roster of names of present/former women religious include Sister Marie Augusta Neal, SND de Namur, Department of Sociology, Emmanuel College; Helen Rose Ebaugh, Department of Sociology, University of Houston; Ruth Wallace, Department of Sociology, George Washington University, but the literature produced by the vast numbers of women religious with M.A.'s and Ph.D.'s documenting, reanalyzing, and reconstructing (in the 1970s and 1980s) the history of women in the Church is far too great and too important to represent in an endnote. Part of what is extraordinary about some of that literature, which is highly scholarly, is that it was done by women who had neither the salary nor the free time provided by academic institutions. Lay academics have also been significant contributors to this community of scholars, including historians (e.g., Mary Jo Weaver, professor of religion at Indiana University; Margaret Thompson, Syracuse University); and political scientists (e.g., Mary Segers, Rutgers University; Joann Formicola, Seton Hall University).

8. From this early stage in which feminist theologians came to be recognized and widely read (1970s and 1980s), I include only a sampling of the theological writings or the regular reviews in such publications as the *National Catholic Reporter* (which in one of the September and February issues regularly reviews writings on women and theology). More complete writings are easily traced through such bibliographical sources as the *Catholic Religion and Periodical Index*. See, for instance, Daly (1973, 1975, 1984); Ruether (1974, 1975, 1983 and 1988); Ruether and McLaughlin (1979); Schussler Fiorenza (1983, 1984); Carr (1988); and Swidler and Swidler (1977). For an analysis of some of these writings from this period, see Weaver (1986). See also Weaver's (1993) own more recent and very interesting theological explorations and also Graff (1993). Note the importance to this process of institutionalization of such presses as Harper and Row, Simon and Schuster, and, of course, Beacon Press, which has long specialized in the writings of feminist theologians and feminists writing about spirituality.

9. Some examples: NARW's bimonthly was *Probe*; WOC's *New Women, New Church* is a quarterly with four thousand readers. WATER publishes *WATER-wheel*; the sisters of Loretto network puts out *courRAGE*; Las Hermanas produces *Informes*. The National Coalition of American Nuns has a regular newsletter; Chicago Catholic Women regularly produces information, calendars, and announcement sheets; CFFC produces numerous working papers, brochures, and the newsletter/journal *Conscience*.

10. See the very moving story of friendship and love between two Loretto sisters depicted in Crawley (1995). Ann Manganaro taught barefoot doctor techniques in El Salvador in the late 1980s until her death in 1993.

11. Ferraro and Hussey (1990, p. 196). See the National Assembly of Religious Women's newsletter, *Probe*, of which Tuite was the first editor, for a sense of the deep involvement of some women religious in working on Latin American social justice issues, combatting U.S. imperialism, and assisting with the sanctuary movement.

12. A Brazilian educator, Freire (1970) laid out methods of consciousness raising that could be incorporated within literary classes.

13. I am grateful to David Meyer for suggesting this framing years back when I first undertook this comparison.

References

Aggarwal, Vinod K. 1986. *Liberal Protectionism: The International Politics of the Organized Textile Trade*. Berkeley: University of California Press.

Baumgaertner, William L., ed. 1989. *Fact Book on Theological Education: 1987–88*. Vandalia, OH: Association of Theological Schools in the United States and Canada.

Carr, Anne E. 1988. *Transforming Grace: Christian Tradition and Women's Experience*. San Francisco: Harper & Row.

Crawley, Martha. 1995. "Salvador: Land of Love, Land of War." Pp. 115–37 in Ann Patrick Ware, ed., *Naming Our Truths: Stories of Loretto Women*. Inverness, CA: Chardon.

Curb, Rosemary, and Nancy Manahan. 1985. *Lesbian Nuns: Breaking Silence*. Tallahassee, FL: Naiad.

Daly, Mary. 1973. *Beyond God the Father*. Boston: Beacon.

——. 1975. *The Church and the Second Sex: With a New Feminist Post-Christian Introduction*. New York: Harper Colophon.

——. 1984. *Pure Lust*. Boston: Beacon.

Ferraro, Barbara, and Patricia Hussey with Jane O'Reilly. 1990. *No Turning Back: Two Nuns Battle with the Vatican over Women's Rights to Choose*. New York: Poseidon.

Foote, Evelyn P. 1993, November. "Institutional Change and the U.S. Military: The Changing Role of Women." Discussion during Peace Studies Workshop, Cornell University, Ithaca, NY.

Freire, Paulo. 1970. *Pedagogy of the Oppressed*. New York: Continuum.

Graff, Ann O'Hara. 1993. "Catholic Feminist Theologians on Catholic Women in the Church." *New Theology Review* 6 (May): 2.

Katzenstein, Mary Fainsod. 1995. "Discursive Politics and Feminist Activism in the Catholic Church." Pp. 35–52 in Myra Marx Ferree and Patricia Yancey Martin, eds., *Feminist Organizations*. Philadelphia: Temple University Press.

Kriesi, Hanspeter, Ruud Koopmans, Jan W. Duyvendak, and Marco G. Giugni. 1992. "New Social Movements and Political Opportunities in Western Europe." *European Journal of Political Research* 22 (2): 219–44.

Lipsky, Michael. 1968. "Protest as a Political Resource." *American Political Science Review* 62: 1144–58.

Meyer, David S., and Nancy Whittier. 1994. "Social Movement Spillover." *Social Problems* 41: 277–98.

Neal, Marie Augusta, SND de Namur. 1990. *From Nuns to Sisters: An Expanding Vocation*. Mystic, CT: Twenty Third Publications.

Piven, Frances Fox, and Richard Cloward. 1971. *Regulating the Poor: The Functions of Public Welfare*. New York: Vintage.

Prevallet, Elaine. 1995. "Testing the Roots: The Story of *Colegio Loreto* in La Paz." Pp. 91–113 in Ann Patrick Ware, ed., *Naming Our Truths: Stories of Loretto Women*. Inverness, CA: Chardon.

Rostker v. Goldberg. 1981. 101 S. Ct. 2646.

Ruether, Rosemary Radford. 1974. *Religion and Sexism: Images of Women in the Jewish and Christian Traditions*. New York: Simon & Schuster.

——. 1975. *New Woman, New Earth: Sexist Ideologies and Human Liberation*. New York: Seabury.

——. 1983. *Sexism and God-Talk: Toward a Feminist Theology*. Boston: Beacon.

——. 1988. *Women-Church: Theology and Practice*. San Francisco: Harper & Row.

Ruether, Rosemary Radford, with Eleanor McLaughlin, eds. 1979. *Women of Spirit: Female Leadership in the Jewish and Christian Traditions*. New York: Simon & Schuster.

Schussler Fiorenza, Elisabeth. 1983. *In Memory of Her: A Feminist Theological Reconstruction of Christian Origins*. New York: Crossroad.

——. 1984. *Bread Not Stone: The Challenge of Feminist Biblical Interpretation*. Boston: Beacon.

Scott, W. Richard, and John W. Meyer. 1994. *Institutional Environments and Organizations.* Thousand Oaks, CA: Sage.

Swidler, Leonard, and Arlene Swidler. 1977. *Women Priests: A Commentary on the Vatican Declaration.* New York: Paulist.

Tarrow, Sidney. 1989. *Democracy and Disorder: Protest and Politics in Italy, 1965–1975.* Oxford: Clarendon.

Tsebelis, George. 1990. *Nested Games: Rational Choice in Comparative Politics.* Berkeley: University of California Press.

Wallace, Ruth A. 1992. *They Call Her Pastor: A New Role for Catholic Women.* Albany: State University of New York.

Ware, Ann Patrick. 1985. *Midwives of the Future: American Sisters Tell Their Story.* Kansas City, MO: Leavan.

——. 1995. "Loretto's Hispanic Tradition: Lights and Shadows," in Ann Patrick Ware, ed., *Naming Our Truth: Stories of Loretto Women.* Inverness, CA: Chardon.

Weaver, Mary Jo. 1986. *New Catholic Women: A Contemporary Challenge to Traditional Religious Authority.* New York: Harper and Row. (Reprinted 1995.)

——. 1993. *Springs of Water in a Dry Land: Spiritual Survival for Catholic Women Today.* Boston: Beacon.

Zimmerman, Jean. 1995. *Tailspin: Women at War in the Wake of Tailhook.* New York: Doubleday.

 6.5

The Future of Conservation

Steven Sanderson

In this selection, Steven Sanderson claims that public policies designed to promote conservation and policies designed to promote economic development need to be combined. Typically, the two policies are pursued separately—with the result that they often conflict. However, Sanderson does not suggest how to forge a synthesis. This is a challenge worth considering!

Don't Blink

If you want to see wild nature, your options are declining. Within a few decades, orangutans, Asian elephants, Sumatran tigers, Chilean flamingos, Amur leopards, and many other well-known species will likely disappear from the wild. The problems are not limited to large, charismatic animals.

Steven Sanderson, "The Future of Conservation," Reprinted by permission of *Foreign Affairs*, 81, No. 5 (September–October 2002): 162–173. Copyright 2002 by the Council on Foreign Relations, Inc.

Untouched wild places have now shrunk to one-sixth of the Earth's land surface. Virtually all of the world's fisheries are distressed, and oceans have been depleted of predator fish, marine mammals, and birds. Tropical forests may still be dense with trees, but thanks to excessive hunting they no longer contain all the key animals needed to sustain their value to the Earth.

Wild nature is in deep distress, and whatever their occasional protestations, the international institutions charged with Earth's care are not managing it with an eye on "sustainability." Rising to that challenge will test the limits of diplomacy and development. It will also demand strategies in the private sector to rescue conservation from development and poverty alleviation from ecological degradation.

Global losses in biodiversity and wild places are not the stuff of environmental alarmism; they describe our world today, as detailed in volumes of hard scientific evidence. The long-term impact can be calculated in economic terms, but in truth, it represents much more. In the foreseeable future, most of the world's population will not know nature in any direct way. The cultural traditions and languages of peoples dependent on large natural ecosystems will disappear. Great animal assemblages and unique ecological events like those that have inspired humanity through the ages will vanish. As the world grows economically richer, it is becoming biologically poorer.

All these impending losses have a human origin. Economic expansion, population growth, urbanization, and development lead to greater consumption. In turn, growing consumer demand fires competition for fresh water, energy, arable land, forest products, and fish. And globalized production permits the harvesting of nature at ever more rapid rates.

Untrammeled development has resulted in increased demand for flood control and urban water availability at the expense of wild rivers and the rural poor. Hydroelectric projects, energy exploitation, and road, rail, and port development have stripped natural systems of their biological resilience and geographic integrity, delivering instead modern agriculture, dams, mills, factories, and aquaculture. Economic progress has spent down our natural endowment, and few have paid any heed to the long-term resource costs of growth.

Conservation in a world of use is hardly a new challenge. European and American industrialization depended on the exploitation of natural resources for growth, and later developing countries joined the modern ethic of consumption. Today many call for even more development at an even quicker pace, not least to alleviate the grinding poverty of the billion-plus people who try to survive on incomes of less than a dollar a day. Poverty reduction is a noble cause and legitimate priority. But unless the mechanisms of development in the twenty-first century incorporate a greater regard for conservation than did their predecessors, the habitability and natural variety of the world we live in will increasingly be put at risk.

The Road from Rio

If development has ignored conservation, conservation has paid too little attention to development. Economic policymakers have concentrated on growth, developmentalists on the distribution of the benefits of growth, and conservationists on the costs and consequences of growth for nature and the environment. The result has been an agreement to disagree, with the growth, development, and conservation communities proceeding down separate paths. In practice, the concept of "sustainable development" has proven less a viable middle ground than an empty rhetorical vessel.

Conservation science falls into two basic categories: threat assessment and the analysis of small populations of animals. The former has led to familiar alarms about the disappearance of the wild, the latter to attempts at protecting its remnants. Together they have inspired the creation of various kinds of protected areas, the success of which has been a principal calling card of international conservation organizations. The focus of the conservation community has been on setting aside ecologically important marine and terrestrial areas, reducing the overharvesting of wildlife, lessening the pollution of fragile lands and waters, and protecting long-term ecological processes.

Fitful cooperation between scientists and intergovernmental organizations has yielded some important conservation-related achievements over the years, including the Ramsar Convention on Wetlands, the Atmospheric Nuclear Test Ban, the partial ban on the use of the insecticide DDT, the Biosafety Protocol, the Convention on International Trade in Endangered Species of Wild Fauna and Flora (CITES), and the creation of a list of World Heritage Sites. But these occasional victories have not added up to broader success, and over the last decade conservation has maintained only a tenuous grip on the global political agenda. As the World Summit on Sustainable Development convenes in Johannesburg, South Africa, in late August, conservationists struggle to hang on to the little ground they have gained rather than advancing toward major new accomplishments.

The anemic official conservation agenda has been shaped by international political and economic institutions designed for other purposes. Debate over economic development, financial stabilization and adjustment, the global commons, global climate change, and the protection of biodiversity has been controlled by national governments, the UN, and the World Bank and the International Monetary Fund. Three decades of Earth summitry—from Stockholm in 1972, to Rio in 1992, to Johannesburg in 2002—have been produced, directed, and attended principally by official government delegations. Private nonprofit organizations—which generate much of the innovation, human capital, and advocacy on behalf of global conservation—carry on in the shadows without full standing in international political forums. So the nongovernmental organizations (NGOs) that work on conservation issues serve as sherpas and pro bono advisers to global environmental summitry, but never as full participants.

The costs of this public-private separation have been high. Ten years ago, as the 1992 UN Conference on Environment and Development ended, many thought the prospects for conservation were bright. The Rio summit yielded a Convention on Biodiversity (COB), principles for sustainable forestry, a Framework Convention on Climate Change, and a generous if overblown set of goals called "Agenda 21." Some global business leaders came forward to advocate profit-enhancing "green" technologies and responsible global citizenship. The Montreal Protocol on Ozone Depleting Substances emerged as a model for future efforts, based as it was on strong science, globally agreed-upon standards, and aggressive action by relevant industries. With the Cold War over, new green leadership in Europe, and an environmentalist U.S. vice president, speculation turned to the possibility of a peace dividend, a development dividend, and even an environmental dividend in the new world order. Conservationists hoped for a new set of regimes covering global ocean fisheries management, climate change, and biodiversity, and perhaps even a real global dialogue about what "sustainability" means and requires.

But the 1990s proved to be difficult and disappointing. Protectionists invoked a cartoonish environmentalism to justify their objections to free trade, reducing the environment to a nontariff trade barrier. Nationalists diverted the COB away from conservation toward a generally fruitless dispute over private-property claims to nature; still without the United States as a party, it remains underfunded and torpid. And even in older, well-established, government-to-government environmental bodies, decision-making continued to be hindered by the need for an unreasonably high level of consensus (e.g., the three-quarters majority required to change the International Whaling Commission's regulations), with the result being paralysis rather than good governance.

Whose fault has it been? Practically everyone can claim a share of the blame. Developing countries have shied away from their post-Rio obligations, even though collectively they will contribute much future growth in global fossil-fuel consumption and natural resource use. Countries with tropical forests have been reluctant to strengthen agreements on tropical deforestation. Some African countries regularly try to end the ban on trade in elephant ivory, and some have joined Japan in its dissent from the international whaling regime. Trade in endangered species continues to horrify, even with CITES in place. Logging companies, global energy interests, and wildlife-product markets are but a few of the self-interested actors that stand in the way of effective collective action. And the multilateral development assistance community, pressed by global poverty, has not accepted the burden of adjustment to sustainability.

Private Actors, Public Goods

So long as national governments and the intergovernmental system are solely responsible for global conservation policy leadership, better results cannot be expected. Private society—individuals, companies, civic institutions, and con-servation NGOs—must share in the design of a sustainable future. Conserva-tionists must embrace a new agenda, led by a coalition of actors in civil society, including leaders from the global corporate community.

Conservation politics has always been problematic. The international system depends on strong principles of national sovereignty and voluntary cooperation, but nature and science do not fit within political boundaries. Sovereign actors and their designated international representatives debate how to manage the Earth's future in bilateral relationships, alliance regimes, the UN, and the mul-tilateral development and finance system. Sometimes this architecture promotes conservation—such as through the International Council of Scientific Unions and the World Conservation Union, whose forte is networking and convening scientific specialists—but often it does not.

Private conservation organizations that operate within and around such global networks, meanwhile, are engaged as only one of many stakeholders in the debate over global resource allocation. Their claims to standing are weak because they are independent of any real process of political legitimation, and opponents scoff at their professed devotion to the public good. Yet the global commons is nothing if not transnational, and the NGOs can speak for planetary collective interests in ways that other actors cannot.

Conservation organizations deliver social services and resource manage-ment capability at the fragile ecological frontier, such as in the upper Amazon, the Congo basin, and central Sulawesi. They demand transparency in the public policy debate and help provide scientific legwork and publicity for global biodiversity assessments. They maintain communication with the most isolated nations (such as Myanmar and North Korea) when conven-tional diplomacy does not. And they engage the private sector on behalf of preserving the natural endowment all people depend on for long-term survival.

Relying on the formal international system alone to defend the environment risks a tragedy of the global commons: collective inaction because no country has much of an incentive to favor conservation except when national interests coincide. Losses in coral reefs, ocean fisheries, and transboundary habitats all testify to the limits of a system driven by national prerogative and resistant to strong global regimes. Even World Heritage Sites and regionally or globally im-portant biological and cultural phenomena, such as the North American migra-tion of Monarch butterflies or the unique seasonal transformation of Cambodia's Tonle Sap, the largest freshwater lake in Southeast Asia, are defended mainly in the breach, except by NGOs. China and the smaller Mekong Delta countries will not speak up for Tonle Sap; Canada, Mexico, and the United States will not defend the Monarch butterfly.

The resulting drama features an interstate system that does not adequately defend the integrity of global biodiversity and a bevy of NGOs willing to fill the gap but unable to find political traction or adequate funding to do so. The official global conservation funds that do exist—such as the Global Environ-mental Facility, administered by the World Bank, the UN Development Program, and the UN Environment Program—are disbursed state-to-state, or occasionally through small grants. National governments are naturally reluctant to cede con-trol over such a transnational mechanism to actors in civil society, and they are especially wary of international environmental organizations whose sense of diplomacy and tact is often lacking.

Yet precisely because of their differences, NGOs and governments can play complementary roles. The conservation community can contribute to global political economy and society and enrich the intergovernmental system's effort to design a platform for sustainable development. Before this can happen, however, certain issues have to be faced squarely—poverty foremost among them.

The Johannesburg script reads like the North-South dialogue of a generation ago, with international equity, development assistance, technology transfer, and concessional trade dominating the conversation. In preparation for the summit, advocates of poverty alleviation denied the tradeoff between economic growth and environmental protection. Reprising the "growth with equity" and "basic human needs" perspectives of the 1970s, they focused on the need to alter the distribution of existing resources and future increments of growth.

Developmentalists promise that this approach will provide environmental dividends in passing, because poor people will grow more concerned with long-term sustainability issues once they are less concerned with their immediate livelihood. From this perspective, in fact, poverty alleviation and sustainability end up looking like much the same thing.

This focus on development leaves the conservation community in the role of Cassandra, pointing out unpleasantly that not all natural resource use is conser-vation and good things do not necessarily go together. Without careful planning and revised goals, economic growth will end up having a negative impact on conservation. Freeing the tropics from infectious diseases will also free fragile lands for human settlement and lead to environmental degradation. Develop-ment will produce few environmental dividends early on, and if we wait too much longer, much of what needs to be protected will already have been destroyed.

Still, if conservationists simply criticize development and poverty alleviation without offering realistic alternatives, they will consign themselves to perpetual irrelevance. If they cannot connect short-term human betterment with conser-vation for long-term sustainability, they will lose the opportunity to influence the future of global public policy. The challenge for conservationists is to show how poverty can be alleviated with minimal additional damage to wild places and wild creatures. Conservationists are well positioned to make such a case, al-though it will require a focus on the rural poor and more realistic expectations about dramatic changes in aggregate economic performance on the ecological frontier.

A New Conservation Agenda

Rather than becoming unthinking enemies or simple fellow travelers of development, conservationists must identify specific places and modes of poverty alleviation where sustainability can be defended. In practice this will mean supporting well-designed development-assistance programs targeted at out-of-the-way rural places, especially where poverty and conservation collide. Such programs will end up helping individuals and small communities rather than triggering major shifts in global poverty indicators. Moreover, they will often have to be routed around governments rather than through them, since state capacity in the hinterland is quite small and often rigid.

Conservationists need not walk away from current partnerships with national governments and the interstate system. Nor can they pretend to represent the poor in general or offer a panacea for the future. What conservationists can do is take the challenge and promise of global civil society seriously and propose their own agenda, convergent with but not dependent on the international system of governance, development assistance, and economic growth. The new conservation agenda will be private, scientific, and grounded at the site of conservation needs; it is likely to revolve around elements such as the following.

The politics of place. Conservation happens in the field, not in the corridors of power. It is not a public relations campaign, and neither poverty alleviation nor conservation can be conquered in Washington, New York, or Brussels. Sustainability requires impact on the wild and the people who live and work there. The acid test of a conservation organization should therefore be its connection to the field and its long-term commitment to working in partnership with those who need sustainability most: the long-forgotten rural poor of the fragile frontier.

Moreover, efforts need to be focused on the principal areas of conservation importance. Thanks to more than a decade of analysis of "biodiversity hotspots," "critical ecoregions" and "the last wild places," the conservation community's threat assessments are pretty comprehensive. But only some of the principal sites of conservation importance coincide with large or growing human habitation and poverty. These are concentrated in South Asia, Southeast Asia, equatorial Africa, the Russian Far East, and the tropical Andean hinterland. Marrying rural poverty alleviation with conservation at the local level in these areas can yield true sustainability while providing an important source of foreign exchange to hard-pressed locales.

Wildlife health surveillance. The globalization cliché that we are all connected should not be dismissed. Scientists warn that vast clouds of dust and pathogens transported across continents may link the future of the Sahel to such costly problems as citrus canker and red tide in Florida. Phytophthora, a family of pathogens responsible for the nineteenth-century Irish potato famine, is reappearing in California as Sudden Oak Death Syndrome thanks to international trade in nursery plants. Other invasive plants and animals transported through trade threaten the $8 billion restoration of the Everglades ecosystem. Cruise ships around the world flush ballast water with unknown "hitchhiker" organisms that can cross national borders without approval or known impact.

Field conservationists today provide a biodiversity surveillance system essential to protecting a changing and highly connected Earth and its inhabitants. If it had not been for the scientific wildlife surveillance capability at the Bronx Zoo, for example, the recent outbreak of the West Nile virus in the United States would have escaped early detection and correct diagnosis. The same conservation surveillance capability will likely provide any signals that chronic wasting disease among elk and deer or brucellosis in bison might jump to beef cattle, and in general provide an early warning system to catch future crossings of the wildlife-human disease frontier.

Tracking the state of the wild. Beyond keeping an eye on the disease frontier, conservationists must help identify and quantify such important but difficult concepts as the growing "extinction debt," whereby the biotic capital of the planet is depleted without immediately obvious consequences. Increasing evidence points to the danger of our fishing down the food web, harvesting lower forms of prey fish, and impoverishing the seas by diminishing the prey necessary to ocean biodiversity. Similar extinction debts appear to be deepening in the terrestrial biosphere. Global ecological surveillance cannot depend entirely on the vicissitudes of publicly funded science; the conservation movement must inform society regularly and rigorously about the state of the wild.

Scientific sustainability audits. A new concept of "sustainability science" is on the horizon, whereby the international community will benefit from clear scientific assessment of various human possibilities in an increasingly fragile biosphere. The conservation community can contribute mightily to this idea by conducting concrete conservation audits of projects and programs undertaken by the development community.

The protection of global heritage. Cultural and ecological sites of global importance have struggled with inadequate funding and the reliance on national agencies for protection. Conservationists can help address this problem by explaining why protection should extend not only to grand architectural sites but also to unique ecological phenomena of great value to human society. They can explain why in Cambodia, for example, it is important to preserve both Angkor Wat and Tonle Sap. During monsoon season, the drainage of Tonle Sap reverses and its volume expands fourfold; it symbolizes sustainability and culture and is both a biodiversity wellspring and the breadbasket of Cambodia. Other ecologically and culturally unique sites abound. By supporting and embracing the World Heritage Site concept, conservationists can add value by working in sites that demonstrate long-term human sustainability in action, such as the ancient rice terraces of Asia, Balinese water temples, and the traditional monsoon water-harvesting systems of southern India.

Endowing conservation rather than governments. Last year in *Science*, conservation scientists wrote that "nature's decline" could be halted in coming years with an estimated annual global investment of about $30 billion. Providing substantial stewardship of additional protected areas would cost an order of magnitude less. Even if this estimate is slightly off, it mocks the idea that long-term conservation is too expensive to implement or so costly as not to be worth the candle. Raising a private endowment fund on this scale and disbursing it globally through an independent foundation and a prestigious science board would allow the conservation community to escape the sometimes crippling constraints of government-to-government mechanisms. Even more could be achieved if private sources of conservation financing were paired with public funding, through bilateral and multilateral assistance.

Mainstreaming the Convention on Biodiversity. The private conservation community has assisted the COB with ideas, management planning, writing national COB plans, implementation, and support. But the scale and scope of this support has been limited, because funding for it has depended on public entities. Conservation organizations must secure funding for national biodiversity assessments through regional development plans and private support for national academies of science. The conservation community, moreover, can and should help mainstream the COB in international agencies and in countries where conservation activity occurs.

Creating global conservation alliances. Sometimes the conservation community works together, but not often enough. Conservation organizations are starting to collaborate more effectively, but they need a strong agenda and a higher degree of mutual trust. A collaborative global agenda could include a worldwide conservation mapping-and-action exercise that establishes various organizations' relative strengths and brands the activity of conservation itself rather than individual organizations.

A conservation code of conduct. The Sullivan principles, a private code of conduct for firms wishing to adhere to progressive human and civil rights standards, made a real difference in the ethics of investment in South Africa during the late apartheid era. Today, numerous business and industry leaders and associations are already engaged in an interesting dialogue on corporate social responsibility. To take advantage of this beginning the conservation community needs to work with the private sector to develop a stronger statement of corporate conservation ethics. The UN Global Compact and other multilateral efforts on corporate governance are insufficient, and a pragmatic partnership between leading conservation organizations and the private corporate world could make a dramatic impact on the behavioral canons of economic growth and development.

Deliverance

In sum, the public agenda cannot be surrendered entirely to public institutions. Conservation opportunities exist beyond the Johannesburg summit and the constraints of the interstate system. But if global civil society is to contribute more to a sustainable future, it must come together in a more organized and decisive way.

It is high time for NGOs to claim a greater role in the conservation debate by forging novel pragmatic alliances among themselves and with the corporate sector. Just as government can deliver what private society cannot—public safety, national defense, the rules of the international system—the conservation community can deliver what government cannot: science-based conservation along with poverty alleviation at the furthest redoubts of the human-nature frontier.

 6.6

Protest, Policy, and the Problem of Violence Against Women: A Cross-National Comparison

S. Laurel Weldon

S. Laurel Weldon seeks to explain why the extent of violence against women varies considerably among countries that are all stable democracies. Her answer, based on analyzing a large sample of countries, is that violence against women is significantly lower in countries with both powerful grassroots women's movements in society and government agencies specifically charged with promoting women's interests. Either one alone is insufficient; it is the combination of the two that is associated with reduced violence against women.

Weldon does not ask what factors promote the existence of powerful women's movements. Any suggestions?

The Limits of Effective Women's Policy Machineries

When they provide access to activists and have sufficient resources, women's policy agencies can improve government responsiveness to violence against women. But sometimes, it appears, these agencies and offices have little or no effect on government responsiveness. Although eight national governments among the thirty-six stable democracies considered

S. Laurel Weldon, *Protest, Policy, and the Problem of Violence Against Women: A Cross-National Comparison* (Pittsburgh: University of Pittsburgh Press, 2002): 139–143, 163–164.

Table 1
Responsiveness of Eight National Governments with Effective Policy Machineries, 1994

Country	Strong, Autonomous Women's Movement	Percent of Women in Cabinet	No. of Policy Areas Addressed
Australia	Yes	12.9	7
Belgium	Yes	11.1	4
Canada	Yes	13.6	7
Costa Rica	Yes (after 1984)	9.5	5
Germany	No	5.2	2
Netherlands	Yes	10.3	3
Portugal	No	5.1	2
Venezuela	No	0.0	0

Source: Data provided by the United Nations.

here have a women's policy machinery that meets the criteria for institutional effectiveness, only three of these (Canada, Australia, and Costa Rica) are among the most responsive countries, that is, those addressing five or more areas of policy (see Table 1). Moreover, some national governments with effective women's institutions (such as Portugal and Germany) are addressing only two of seven areas of policy. Venezuela had not undertaken any action to address violence against women by 1994.

Venezuela, Germany, and Portugal are also characterized by the absence of a strong, autonomous women's movement. We know that women's movements are important for articulating the issue of violence against women but are, on their own, unlikely to produce a broad, multifaceted government response. We also know that the presence of an effective women's policy machinery is strongly related to the scope of government response. This suggests that the relationship between institutional structure and policy outcome may be an interactive one, that is, it may depend on the *interaction* between women's movements and institutional structure.

The Interaction of Institutions and Women's Movements

Women's movements and effective women's policy machineries interact to improve government responsiveness to violence against women. Understanding the interaction between these elements is key to understanding the effect of each on violence-against-women policy, and to understanding their joint effect.

An effective women's policy machinery can strengthen a women's movement. By providing research support and opportunities for input on policy development, women's policy machineries can greatly increase the effectiveness of women's movement activists. In addition, by giving financial support for organizing and for independent research, women's policy machineries provide additional resources to women's organizations. These agencies also offer continuity over time for women's movement activists—sort of institutional memory. Instead of having to spend their energies reeducating each new policymaker about past efforts, activists can work to improve existing policies.

Duerst-Lahti (1989) has shown that the state commissions on the status of women in the United States played a very important role in the development of the women's movement, providing research, funding, and other organizational resources. The state commissions thereby strengthened the nascent women's movement, and they were especially critical in its transition from a loose collection of dispersed local movements to a national movement.

Conversely, strong, autonomous women's movements improve the institutional capabilities of government to address women's issues. When the women's movement is a significant political force, the women's policy machinery has more leverage over other government departments. Government departments will want to avoid conflict with activists and will want to be able to show that their policies take women's concerns into account; and bureaucrats inside the women's policy machinery can point to demands from the women's movement when asking for increased funding and other resources.

Increased leverage on the part of the women's policy machinery improves the institutional capability to coordinate policy action across departments and to revise departmental agendas to reflect women's priorities. Women's policy machineries can also provide the research support and analytic focus required for sound policy design and evaluation. A strong women's movement therefore improves the capacity of a set of political institutions to respond to women's concerns, when that set includes a women's policy agency.

Thus, strong, autonomous women's movements and effective women's policy agencies reinforce one another. This effect is not purely additive; it is interactive. Each factor magnifies the effect of the other.

Policy Development in the Most Responsive Governments

Does the account developed above seem to explain the process of policy development in the most responsive countries? I focus on the most responsive countries as a form of plausibility probe: if the development of policy in these eight countries cannot be explained by the account I have developed, then it is possible that I am not accurately interpreting the relationships I have discovered, or that they are an artifact of the measurements I am using, or of the year on which I have chosen to focus. After establishing the plausibility of the theoretical account, I examine whether the statistical analysis supports the account.

I consider those governments addressing five or more areas to be the most responsive. There are eight governments in this category: Australia, Canada, the United States, France, Costa Rica, Israel, New Zealand, and Ireland. I focus both on explaining why these countries were more responsive and on accounting for the variation in responsiveness across these eight governments. Why are they more responsive than the other democratic governments identified in this study? Furthermore, why are Canada and Australia even more responsive than the others?

The process of policy development in these eight governments appears to conform to the hypothesized pattern. In every case, it was the women's movement that first articulated the issue of violence against women and pressed for government action. And every country had a strong, autonomous women's movement.

In all eight countries, powerful insiders who took up the demands of the women's movement placed violence against women on the government agenda. Strategically placed allies of the women's movement were also important in retaining the feminist content of legislation despite pressure to the contrary. In Ireland in 1987, for example, a submission by a rape crisis center to a nonpartisan committee of legislators resulted in a public report recommending policy reforms. Feminist bureaucrats inside the Irish government helped ensure that there was such a committee in the first place and that the final policy recommendations reflected the original ones from the rape crisis center (Mahon 1995). Following this report, there was a significant expansion in the Irish government's response to this problem. The government began addressing more areas after the publication of the report (with these new measures taking effect in 1990) and continues to improve its response (Ireland, Office of the Tanaiste, 1997). Similarly, the response by the Costa Rican government appears to be a product of cooperation between feminists in a government agency (the Center for the Development of Women and the Family) and a variety of women's organizations. In the United States, the proposals of organized women's groups were taken up by sympathetic legislators both in the early policy initiatives of the 1970s and in the case of the Violence Against Women Act, passed in 1994. Although male legislators played an important role in the passage of the act, it appears that a feminist in the office of Senator Joseph Biden was key to retaining the feminist content of the bill despite pressure from Senator Orrin Hatch to the contrary. The women's caucus also seems to have played a role (Gelb 1998).

These examples illustrate the general pattern of policy development in this area: independent women's movements partner with feminist insiders to achieve policy change. This explains why some democracies with strong, autonomous women's movements have been able to procure government action on violence while others have not. I stress that it is feminist allies in influential positions, rather than simply women in government, who provide the window of opportunity.

In order to explain policy development in the two most responsive countries, however, we must examine the interaction of the institutional structure—the women's policy machinery—with the women's movement. Why did the government response in Canada and Australia not remain limited to a primarily criminal justice response, as it did in the United States? Why was the response not restricted to a focus on domestic violence, as it was in New Zealand and Ireland? Why did it go beyond the partial response of France and Costa Rica? In Canada and Australia, the relationship between women's movements and their internal allies was particularly effective because of the presence of an effective women's policy machinery. Feminist bureaucrats working inside the government worked with women's movements and with the resources of the women's policy machinery to get violence on the government agenda and to ensure feminist input into the policymaking process.

The national governments of Australia and Canada first began addressing the issue of violence against women in 1975. Since that time, there has been a proliferation of institutions designed to improve the status of women in both countries. This institutionalization has provided a permanent point of contact and an institutional memory that has strengthened both the women's movement and its allies within government. The institutionalization has made the difference between the fleeting window of opportunity provided by the election of legislative allies and the more long-term possibility of the ongoing development of government response with critiques and suggestions from the women's movement. It has also provided the institutional framework needed for a comprehensive, cross-sectoral response to violence against women. . . .

Conclusion

In summary, women's movements are always necessary for the initial articulation of violence against women as an issue. The initiative to address violence against women is always a response on the part of government to a demand that originates outside political institutions. However, women's movements alone almost never put the issue on the government agenda. Hence, a women's movement alone is not sufficient to produce a government response. Allies inside government are critical: when there are policymakers sympathetic to the women's movement, or even part of it, the issue of violence against women is more likely to be adopted as part of the decision agenda. Most policies to address violence against women are thus products of partnerships between women's movements and sympathetic insiders.

Such partnerships are much less effective in the absence of a women's policy machinery. In that case, the insider-outsider partnerships tend to produce partial, fragmented responses. In the presence of an effective women's policy machinery, they are more likely to result in broad, multifaceted policies to address violence against women.

A women's policy machinery, however, is not necessary for putting violence on the public agenda. It should also be noted that a women's policy machinery without a strong, autonomous women's movement will not articulate the issue of violence against women, so it is not sufficient, on its own, to produce a government response. It is only in the context of a strong, autonomous women's movement articulating the issue and pressing for government action that women's policy machineries have such a strong effect.

An effective women's policy machinery can strengthen a women's movement. Conversely, a strong women's movement improves the capacity of a set of political institutions to respond to women's concerns when that set includes a women's policy agency. Thus, strong, autonomous women's movements and effective women's policy agencies reinforce one another. This effect is not purely additive; it is interactive, meaning that each factor magnifies the effect of the other.

This argument also appears to hold for marginalized subgroups of women: policy responsiveness to the distinct needs of minority women is enhanced by independent organization combined with some degree of solidarity from the broader women's movement. When minority women are organized independently of organizations dominated by white women or minority men, the existence of government offices for women seems to improve policy response to minority women as well as to women in general. It also seems that offices for multiculturalism or Aboriginal affairs may increase policy responsiveness to women of color.

These findings have important implications for theories of democratic policymaking, as well as for feminist theory. They also suggest some concrete ways of improving government responsiveness to violence against women and to marginalized groups in general.

References

Duerst-Lahti, Georgia. 1989. "The Government's Role in Building the Women's Movement." *Political Science Quarterly* 104, no. 3:249–68.

Gelb, Joyce. 1998. "Legislating Against Violence: The Violence Against Women Act of 1994." Paper presented at the Annual Meeting of the American Political Science Association, Boston, September 3–6.

Ireland. Office of the Tanaiste. 1997. *Report of the Task Force on Violence Against Women*. Dublin: Government of Ireland.

Mahon, Evelyn. 1995. "Ireland's Policy Machinery: The Ministry of State for Women's Affairs and Joint Oireachtas Committees for Women's Rights." In *Comparative State Feminism*, edited by Dorothy McBride Stetson and Amy G. Mazur. Thousand Oaks, Calif.: Sage.

 Chapter 7

POLITICAL CHALLENGES AND CHANGING AGENDAS

We conclude *Readings in Comparative Politics* with a selection of readings that highlight political challenges and proposals for change. But in one sense this entire book has focused on political challenges and reform proposals, for we live in a turbulent, unsettled world. Even the most stable democratic countries are buffeted by challenges from within their borders and external attacks (see the selections by Howard, Tarrow, and Putnam).

The concluding chapter of *Readings in Comparative Politics* focuses on proposals for change. Of course, there is rarely agreement on the character and causes of political, economic, and social problems, much less what should be done about them. Thus, this chapter will highlight diversity and debates. One of the major reasons for providing this chapter is to urge students to apply their best thinking to honing ideas for change.

We have sampled a range of problems and proposals to convey the notion that politics involves choice. (See, in particular, the selections by Przeworski, Zakaria, and McKibben.) Some proposals may strike you as foolish, utopian, and even dangerous—or all of the above! Others may strike you as overly timid. Fine! We hope that you will provide good reasons why you think so. We recommend that you apply the same standards of rigor to evaluate reform proposals as you do to assessing the validity and value of empirically focused research. But the fact that vigorous debate exists about what should be done is no reason to avoid entering the debate. As Rosa Luxemburg, a revolutionary thinker, warned long ago, the most naive utopianism is that which claims that the present can be preserved unchanged. We would add that too much cries out for improvement to believe that this is the best of all possible worlds.

After September 11th: Chances for a Left Foreign Policy

Dick Howard

In the aftermath of the terror attacks on the World Trade Center and the Pentagon, the Social Science Research Council invited several U.S. and international scholars to reflect on the meaning and significance of September 11, 2001. Dick Howard's contribution to the forum invites Americans to move beyond the familiar frames of reference that have defined U.S. foreign policy—isolationism, multilateralism, and unilateralism—to consider a more historical framework. Howard suggests that such a "back to the future" approach creates the possibility for more accurate and potentially more progressive foreign policy choices in today's post–cold war and post-9/11 global order.

A leftist (or "progressive") American intellectual is expected to criticize his government. That seems to be the reason that many Europeans were astonished, for example, to find the name of a Socialist intellectual like Michael Walzer co-existing peacefully with people of rather different convictions on petitions supporting the Bush administration response to September 11th. And when the progressive American speaks foreign tongues, it is expected that he will go on to deplore American isolationism—or unilateralism, or both, as sins of equal evil. He will be expected, in short, to be more European than the Europeans. Hence, let me say at the outset, in French, that "tout comprendre n'est pas tout pardoner." [to understand is not to forgive.] And let me explain myself by adding, in German, [an extrapolation from] Marx's famous 11th Thesis: "Die Politiker haben die Welt nur verändern wollen, es kommt aber darauf an, sie zu verstehen." [The politicians have only sought to change the world; what is crucial, rather, is to understand it.]

I will propose here some ideas toward elaborating a leftist approach (which is not simply an alternative) to current American foreign policy choices. But to do

Dick Howard, "After September 11th: Chances for a Left Foreign Policy," *Social Science Research Council*, http://www.ssrc.org/sept11/essays/howard_text_only.htm.

Dick Howard is Distinguished Professor of Political Philosophy at the State University of New York, Stony Brook. This article develops arguments from his *The Specter of Democracy* (2002). Reprinted by permission of the author.

so, I must first criticize some interpretations of those policies because they use categories that describe foreign policy choices as they existed during the Cold War but are only apparently relevant today. I will then sketch an historical framework for understanding some constants in American foreign policy choices as part of a *democratic* political dynamic. In this context, the task of the intellectual changes; criticism no longer suffices. The difference between the left and the right is replaced by an opposition between democratic and anti-democratic politics. The progressive intellectual—and the Europeans who worry about the American hegemon without thinking about their own "democratic deficit"—have to imagine forms of political intervention that encourage the openness of democratic debate while avoiding the anti-political temptations that are particularly strong in the sphere of foreign policy.

1. Are the Old Categories Still Useful?

The first reactions to September 11th were that nothing would remain the same, that the old political clichés had lost their meaning, and that Leftist intellectuals could not simply repeat their hardy stance of opposition and the pacifist opposition to power. Yet that cannot be true; change does not occur overnight. Geo-political relations remain over the long term; political cultures do not change in the blink of an eye nor do national habits. . . .

    The political response of the Bush administration seemed to reflect the weight of habit. This was the unilateralist government that had refused to sign the Kyoto accords, denounced the ABM treaty that interfered with their dream of a missile defense, and were determined to eliminate Saddam Hussein regardless of the opinion of its allies. Those allies' invocation of Article 5 of the NATO treaty as an expression of solidarity was briefly noted and quickly forgotten as the Bush team took its own initiatives in Afghanistan, accepting token offerings from the allies while giving them no voice in return. Its attitude was summed up in Secretary of Defense Rumsfeld's pithy remark that this time (as opposed to the haggling that almost crippled the intervention in Kosovo) the mission would determine the coalition rather than the coalition determining the mission. The fact that Rumsfeld referred to a coalition, not an alliance, is significant: an alliance implies a shared global vision elaborated by consultation and deliberation among equals; a coalition is heteroclite, uses its members as expendable "spare parts" to fill temporary needs. Similar disdain for multilateral cooperation was starkly evident in the . . . decision by Washington to "un-sign" (rather than simply not send to the Senate for ratification) the Rome treaty creating an international court; at a time when the "war" on terrorism would seem to call for such a trans-national institution, the Bush administration defiantly insisted that it would go its own way. . . .

    Those who want to see an incremental learning process rather than immobility suggest that a President who had barely traveled outside the country, and a

Congress whose majority leadership takes pride in its provincialism, have abandoned the historical American politics of *isolationism*. Insofar as foreign policy played a role in the 2000 campaign, it was epitomized in Bush's denunciation of so-called "nation-building" and multi-lateral interventions into the affairs of others.[1] Thus, on taking office, the not-quite legitimate president broke with tradition by ostentatiously reserving his first visit for Canada, and his next for Mexico (neglecting England, and Europe). . . .

In this context, it appears that the Bush administration has moved from isolationism toward a recognition of a multi-facetted world whose complexity it could not master. As a result, it has now sought to reduce this complexity by exerting unilateral control. Not for nothing does the US spend more on national defense than the next 15 nations *together,* not for nothing do the Americans tell their European allies: *modernize or be marginalized*. And whereas the Europeans protest and demand to be treated as equals, the . . . signing of a new (475 word, ignoring among other things tactical weapons) missile treaty as well as acceptance of American withdrawal from the ABM treaty suggests that the Russia of Mr. Putin has understood the hard realities of a new American century. Europe, on the other hand, seems to be fulfilling the (low) expectations of Defense Secretary Rumsfeld, who recalls bitterly his period as US Ambassador to NATO a quarter century ago, in 1973–4.

But are these categories—isolationism, multilateralism and unilateralism—still useful for a characterization of American foreign policy? Isolationism has a long tradition; but it stands opposed to *both* multilateralism and unilateralism, which are themselves opposites. This duality leads to confusion; it conceals differences that, particularly in the new post–Cold War era, are politically important. Think of some recent examples. Unilateralism need not be the action of an imperial power snuffing out freedom as it works its will; it may be necessary when the wrangling of coalition partners prevents action at times when human rights (or lives) are in peril, as in Bosnia, Kosovo or recent cases in Africa. Multilateralism can be functional for the creation of a world of mutual interdependence whose members will reciprocally civilize each other's behavior; but it can also be a formula for pious words that make impossible practical deeds—as in the cases just mentioned. Even isolationism can have different meanings. It need not be the stance that wishes to hear or see no evil which is condemned to pay the price of its good-natured naiveté; non-action denounced as isolationism may be the recognition that not every problem can be solved immediately and that simple solutions cannot be imposed upon people unwilling or unable to admit them—indeed, there are problems that can only be solved after they fester until the times are ripe.

2. Categorizing Democratic Dynamics

There are good reasons, both geographical and historical, to repeat the usual description of US foreign policy as congenitally isolationist. One of the founding moments of American democracy, George Washington's "Farewell Address," marks not only a recognition of the limits of political power in a pluralist society but contains also the warning to his countrymen to avoid "entangling alliances." This phrase, learned by every American school child, has become what Walter Russell Mead calls "the foreign policy equivalent of the Bill of Rights . . ."[2] One of the goals of Mead's remarkable new book, *Special Providence: American Foreign Policy and How it Changed the World*, is to show that, even before the creation of the new nation—indeed, as a political condition of its creation, which depended on French, Dutch and Spanish alliances—Americans knew, and practiced skillfully, the art of foreign policy. More than that, Mead's claim is that—as opposed to the contemporary stereotype—foreign policy has been one of the chief issues dividing the contesting political parties, at least until the achievement of a certain "mythical" modus vivendi with the outbreak of the Cold War.

As opposed to the now-ambivalent categories inherited from the Cold War, Mead analyzes historically and illustrates pragmatically four currents associated with historical figures of the American past. The result goes beyond the dichotomy with which Henry Kissinger introduced his *Diplomacy*, when he distinguished the naïve idealism of Wilson from the hardened balance-of-power realism of Theodore Roosevelt.[3] Mead's first category reflects the primacy of business and commerce throughout American foreign relations: *Hamiltonians* stress the alliance of government and business to insure stability at home and integration into the world economy. *Wilsonians* then introduce a moral dimension that wants to spread American values in order to create a peaceful world under the rule of law. *Jeffersonians* strive above all to protect democracy at home, and therefore avoid unsavory alliances by Hamiltonians and risks of war run by Wilsonians. Finally, populist *Jacksonians* insist that domestic and foreign policy must insure the security and well-being of the people; while they don't seek foreign quarrels, when war becomes necessary, these Jacksonians demand that it be fought to the finish.

Because of their historical specificity, Mead's categories are able to take into account the dynamics of political competition because, in order to remain the same, each of them must mutate as political conditions change. This flexibility is double: it takes into account changed socio-economic conditions as well as the contending political parties. For example, the original Hamiltonian vision of the way to achieve the primacy of trade and commerce was formulated in Hamilton's "Report on Industries," which defended the protection of "infant industries" by means of a high tariff. Such protectionist policies could only be maintained at the end of the 19th century because protected industries still paid good wages and guaranteed secure jobs. By the middle of the 20th century, however, American economic power meant that lower tariffs (i.e., free trade) would benefit the economy—but now wages and jobs came under pressure. If a new Hamiltonian policy was to be enacted, it would have to find new allies, perhaps among the (nationalist) Jacksonians, since its former supporters had gone either to the Wilsonians (the NGOs opposing exploitation) or to the Jeffersonians (attacking business power as a threat to democracy). Hamiltonian politics would, in other words, have to change in order to remain the same. . . .

Leaving aside the historian's question of the accuracy of these classifications, they do seem to offer a recognizable picture of America. What is significant is that they do not coincide with actual party lines; they point rather to the ingredients of shifting coalitions, and they can reflect different policy goals—or lead participants to change their policies (or to compromise) in order to maintain their original intentions. Mead attributes the success of American foreign policy to the competition among these basic categories; and he recognizes that the domination of one or the other would be harmful (which is why he dismisses at the outset the "myth" of the Cold War and a unified America for which only one policy is possible or just). His critics deplore this flexibility because it lacks predictive power; his thesis seems non-falsifiable because he can always explain *post festum* new combinations or splits and realignments.[4] For example, Hamiltonians among the Clinton administration appealed to the civilizing effects of Montesquieu's "doux commerce" while Hamiltonians in the Bush camp are more crudely pro-business. Wilsonians might well ally themselves with the former, who are making the world safe for their own (modern forms of) missionary work; but other Wilsonians would insist that globalization destroys the dignity of indigenous cultures. This second group could in turn find allies among those Jeffersonians whose fear for the fragility of democracy leads them toward isolationism. But the historical fact that Jeffersonian fear of big government led many of them to oppose US entry into World War I, to reject the League of Nations and above all to appease the new totalitarians in the 1930s discredited this orientation. What remained of their influence depended on an alliance with the Jacksonians, which disintegrated with the Vietnam war. Both tendencies were appalled by the effects of the war at home and by the corrupt Vietnamese government it defended; but the Jeffersonians wanted to cut-and-run which, to the Jacksonians, was a violation of a code of honor that cut more deeply than the fear for the safety of domestic democracy.

Mead draws two conclusions from his analysis. The first is that the interplay of these four political tendencies accounts for the unquestionable successes of American foreign policy, including the victory in the Cold War. He wants his readers to learn from this history, and to recognize that foreign policy has been fundamental to the history of American democracy. The second conclusion is more contemporary and pragmatic. He suggests that the Hamiltonian and Wilsonian came together after 1989 to provide the basis of the New World Order, whose "the rise and retreat" he chronicles. Free trade plus globalization joined with increasingly powerful NGOs to pursue the creation of rule of law and the spread of democracy while protecting human rights. But this coalition was short lived; the other two tendencies affirmed themselves, and history did not come to an end, after all. What then of "the future of American foreign policy"? "I believe," says Mead, "[that] I owe it to readers to declare my preference among the schools." His carefully hedged adhesion is to Jeffersonianism, whose "caution," and "conservation of . . . liberty and lives, and . . . passion for limits" is said, finally, to be the ideal that motivated John Quincy Adams and James Monroe in 1823.[5]

I want to propose a different conclusion from Mead's stimulating account. The constant interplay among the four categories that he describes means that none of them can uphold the claim that it has a monopoly on wisdom, that it expresses the unique national interest, or even that it expresses the *vox populi*. Mead's analysis suggests that foreign policy success, particularly in the post–Cold War world, is not predicated on such (real or imagined) national unity; indeed, the totalitarian disasters of the 20th century in the Soviet, German (and Japanese) cases resulted from just such unitary presuppositions. The task of the democratic intellectual is not to propose another vision of unity that claims to be superior to those failed attempts. That was the project of the progressive intellectuals who rallied to Jack Kennedy, only to find themselves unable to escape from their Vietnam nightmare because their politics was defined by the moral imperatives of Cold War anti-communism. But their equally moralist left wing critics could only adopt an "anti-anti-communist" stance which had nothing political to offer, especially in the domain of foreign policy. Mead's account suggests the direction in which to search for a new politics; although he doesn't say it in so many words, democracy for him is not simply a means; it can also be an end to be sought in the post–Cold War world.

3. Political Dynamics in the Post–Cold War World

The end of the Cold War appeared to leave the US alone on a world stage that had no overarching structure. Omnipotence was coupled uneasily with impotence, in the Balkans, in Rwanda, in the pious words and absent deeds of the Clinton years. In 1994, Henry Kissinger argued in *Diplomacy* that the ethical basis of the unity of American Cold War politics was useless in the emerging political-strategic world; American power was in fact limited and could be exercised only if it rediscovered the principles of diplomatic realism of which Kissinger claimed to be a master. Seven years later, in *Does America Need a Foreign Policy?*, in his first chapter, Kissinger posed the question: "America at the Apex: Empire or Leader?" Empire, he argued, is not a policy; it confuses strategy with economics, while ignoring the political, cultural and spiritual impact of the new technological world. Leadership is exercised through alliances, such as NATO. An alliance differs from a guarantee of collective security, which is merely a juridical promise that, like a UN resolution, will not be carried out if major participants fail to act. . . .[6]

Kissinger's rejection of the old political concept of empire may be too facile (and self-interested); after all, the power and reach of 21st century America has no historical parallels. Recall the time when optimism about a Soviet revival under Gorbachev's *perestroika* was widespread; historian Paul Kennedy's best-seller, *The Rise and Fall of the Great Powers: Economic Change and Military Conflict from 1500 to 2000* (1987), convinced many that the result of America's "imperial over-reach" would be an inevitable decline. Today, Paul Kennedy has to admit that while Rome was limited by the Persian and Chinese empires, and the size of the British navy was equal only to the next two navies, the US stands alone. More aggressively, the *Wall Street Journal* editorialist, Max Boot, writing in the conservative *The Weekly Standard,* suggests that September 11th resulted not from foreign resentment at America's action in the world but from the insufficient involvement of the US in its true mission. In the same vein, Robert D. Kaplan, whose *Balkan Ghosts* (1993) was said to have dissuaded Clinton from his aggressive "lift and strike" option for Bosnia, drew a similarly amoral lesson in *Warrior Politics: Why Leadership Demands a Pagan Ethos* (2001). If order is to be imposed in an anarchic world, the American cop will have to do the job—and he will be applauded for his work by willing masses already seduced by the pleasures promised by America's vaunted "soft power."

What theorists of empire forget is that America acquired its hegemony without any specific political project other than its moral righteousness—the end of the Cold War was more a Soviet defeat than an American victory (an arms-race-to-the-death . . . rather than a duel of utopias). Indeed, Bush's national security advisor Condoleezza Rice wrote in *Foreign Affairs* in 2000 that since the end of the Cold War American foreign policy seemed to have lost its direction.[7] She was not alone in that analysis. But she is not alone either, today, in her revision of that analysis, whose new premise is that the post–September 11th period is "analogous to 1945–47," when the doctrine of containment was elaborated and made operational.

The proposed post–Cold War imperial policy is often associated with the names of deputy Defense Secretary Paul Wolfowitz and Vice-President Cheney. Its academic label was provided by Zalmay Khalizad (now American proconsul in Afghanistan): it is the passage from "containment to global leadership." This project, or vision, seems to have only become truly possible with the shedding of American blood on September 11th. However America acquired its hegemonic position, its rulers now intend to keep it, by all means necessary. And those means include pre-emptive strikes (possibly even nuclear), the redrawing of regional maps, and the intervention needed to create what is called euphemistically a "democratic zone of peace." Another, less euphemistic label for this project is proposed by Colin Powell's chief intellectual advisor, Richard Haass, who occupies the office first held by George Kennan, the father of containment theory. In an interview with Lemann, the State Department's Richard Haass suggests that there are "limits of sovereignty" that prevent governments from abusing the rights of their citizens; and there are legitimate interventions that prevent them from doing so. More important, such limits also prevent governments from supporting terrorism or from the production of weapons of mass destruction—whose possession legitimates "preventive, or peremptory, self-defense." Obviously, such a policy would have its first application in Iraq, permitting the son to fulfill the task left for him by his father.

But, are the proponents of such a policy right in thinking that September 11th will permit them to gain public support? The cynic might reply that the manner in which this administration has used the metaphor of the war-on-terror to prevent not just dissent but even the questioning of its policies by members of the opposition (or by Republicans like Richard Shelby or Dan Burton) will insure public support by its manipulations. What can the progressive intellectual do in the face of this onslaught? What can Europe do?

Turning first to the intellectual, from whose position I began this discussion, he is assumed to be a critic of the American policy. The stance of the intellectual as critic is an old one. During the Cold War, the progressive intellectual could only be a critic of one of the competing world systems, without reflecting on the manner in which his critique implied at least tacit support of the other system. In the American context, this meant that the left was "*anti*-anti-communist," with the result that it had nothing positive to defend, no ideals to realize, no project for the future. Typical of this attitude was the oldest existing weekly journal of the left, *The Nation*. To put the matter differently, the leftist intellectual acquired the habit of finding all glasses to be half-empty; there was never any question of finding it to be half-full . . . and in need of further positive measures. As a result, at the end of the Cold War (if not before, which is another debate), the left made no contributions to ongoing political debates, and was blind to its Eastern compagnons.

But "the" left was and is (and should not be) so unified, as these last remarks imply. There was an anti-totalitarian left too, one that contributed to the overcoming of the Soviet order. It was not so strong in the US as for example in France. Learning from Eastern European dissidents who recognized the need to insure rights and freedoms, this new left recognized the radical political implications of democracy—which is not simply another justification of capitalist economic exploitation. Although it was a minority among the left, this new direction (and its Eastern friends) seized upon Basket III of the 1975 Helsinki Accords, which conservatives denounced as a sell-out in which the West recognized the legitimacy of the Soviet imperium. Despite Henry Kissinger's attempt to reclaim this achievement for himself, there is no reason for a progressive left to let him take the credit and play the democrat. Why should the left not claim that the glass is half-full? There is no reason, for example, for a critical left not to agree with the State Department's Richard Haass about the limits of sovereignty (although it might dissent from the possible pre-emptive nuclear strikes suggested by Paul Wolfowitz). The left should favor interventions to encourage democracy.

In this same context, one sees how the categorial framework of Walter Russell Mead offers a possible guideline for European political action as well. Two points in particular seem promising. If it is true that the democratic nature of American foreign policy depends on the constant interaction—call it checks-and-balances—of the four political tendencies, then Europeans should be on guard to insure that their words and actions do not favor the domination of one or the other tendency. Democracy in US foreign policy is good for Europe as well.

Second, the lability of the flexible categories, which can enter into various alliances at different historical conjunctures, suggests that European reaction to American actions needs to bear in mind that these policies are not the result of a single unified will expressing itself in the one and only form it can possibly take. American actions result from multiple interactions; the imposition of a tariff on steel, or the decision to intervene in Iraq, are not pre-ordained; they result from political coalition building, and there is no reason only to criticize when the fact that coalitions are built by partners means that the temporary alliances can also be drawn apart and reconfigured by sufficiently subtle approaches. In a word, as with the intellectual, Europe has to remember that, despite appearances, America remains a republican democracy, plural in its values and open to the future. It is a glass that only appears half-empty; if we understand that it is also half-full, we are on our way to realizing what Marx should have intended when he wrote the 11th Feuerbach Thesis, with which I proposed to begin this discussion of intellectuals and foreign policy.

Notes

1. There is a long and honorable precedent for this attitude, which is perhaps best articulated by John Quincy Adams, the theoretical force behind the creation of the Monroe Doctrine which long-guided American foreign policy after 1821. Sounding perhaps like the "compassionate conservative" that Bush wanted to represent, Adams wrote that "[w]herever the standard of freedom and independence has been or shall be unfurled, there will be America's heart, her benedictions and her prayers. But she goes not abroad in search of monsters to destroy. She is the well-wisher to the freedom and independence of all. She is the champion and vindicator only of her own . . . She well knows that by once enlisting under other banners than her own . . . she would involve herself beyond the power of extrication . . . She might become the dictatress of the world. She would no longer be the ruler of her own spirit." It is worth noting that I am citing this passage from Henry Kissinger's *Does America Need a Foreign Policy?* (New York: Simon & Schuster, 2001), p. 238.
2. Isolationism can also take an aggressive form, as in the previously mentioned case of Chomsky, for whom whatever the US does is harmful; or it can be adopted by his right-wing political opposite, Patrick Buchanan, whose recent book is called *America, A Republic Not an Empire*.
3. Walter Russell Mead, *Special Providence: American Foreign Policy and How it Changed the World* (New York: Knopf, 2001), p. 59. I will make use of Mead's categories, but do so in a different context. Mead's concern, as his subtitle indicates, is to vindicate the success of a democratic foreign policy; mine is to look at the dynamic underlying that politics. Mead is a diplomatic historian who uses his framework to re-tell a coherent story, but his categories are too general to deal adequately with contemporary politics, as is clear in former Assistant Secretary of State for Public Affairs James P. Rubin's review in *The New Republic* (March 18, 2002, pp. 29–33).
4. Henry Kissinger, *Diplomacy* (New York: Simon & Schuster, 1994).
5. Mead, *op. cit.*, pp. 331, 334.
6. Henry Kissinger, *Does America Need a Foreign Policy?* (New York: Simon & Schuster, 2001).
7. Condoleezza Rice, "Promoting the National Interest," *Foreign Affairs,* January/February 2000, pp. 45–62.

7.2

Democratic Capitalism at the Crossroads

Adam Przeworski and Michael Wallerstein

In this selection, Przeworski and Wallerstein explore the dilemmas of social democracy (the project of center-left parties, particularly in Europe, to parlay working-class support into electoral victory and the opportunity to implement a set of policies to guarantee employment, improve wages, and deliver robust social protections). The authors examine the "Keynesian Revolution" as the ideological and political foundation of social democracy and conclude that since the later 1970s the Right has waged a counterrevolution against social democracy with far reaching consequences for democracy.

The Keynesian Revolution as a Compromise

The combination of democracy and capitalism constitutes a compromise: those who do not own instruments of production consent to the institution of the private ownership of capital stock while those who own productive instruments consent to political institutions that permit other groups to effectively press their claims to the allocation of resources and the distribution of output. It may be worth recalling that this compromise was deemed unfeasible by Marx, who claims that the "bourgeois republic" is based on a contradiction that renders it inherently unstable as a form of social organization. A combination of private ownership of the means of production with universal suffrage, Marx argued, must lead either to "social emancipation" of the oppressed classes utilizing their political power or to "political restoration" of the oppressing class utilizing its economic power. Hence, Marx held, capitalist democracy is "only the political form of revolution of bourgeois society and not its conservative form of life," "only a spasmodic, exceptional state of things . . . impossible as the normal form of society."

Adam Przeworski, *Capitalism and Social Democracy* (Cambridge: Cambridge University Press, 1985), ch. 6, pp. 207–211; 218–221. © Maison de Sciences de l'homme and Cambridge University Press 1985. Reprinted with the permission of Cambridge University Press.

It was Keynesianism that provided the ideological and political foundations for the compromise of capitalist democracy. Keynesianism held out the prospect that the state could reconcile the private ownership of the means of production with democratic management of the economy. As Keynes himself put it: "It is not the ownership of the instruments of production which it is important for the state to assume. If the state is able to determine the aggregate amount of resources devoted to augmenting the instruments and the basic reward to those who own them, it will have accomplished all that is necessary." Democratic control over the level of unemployment and the distribution of income became the terms of the compromise that made democratic capitalism possible.

The problem of the 1930s was that resources lay fallow: machines stood idle while men were out of work. At no time in history was the irrationality of the capitalist system more blatant. As families starved, food—already produced food—was destroyed. Coffee was burned, pigs were killed, inventories rotted, machines rusted. Unemployment was the central political problem of society.

According to the economic orthodoxy of the time, this state of affairs was simply a given and the only recourse was to cut the costs of production, which meant cutting wages and transfers. Some relief measures to assist the employed were obviously urgently required, but whether such measures were advisable from an economic point of view was at best controversial. In Great Britain the Labour government in fact proposed to reduce unemployment compensations: this was the condition for being bailed out by the I.M.F. of the time, where "M." stood for the Morgan Bank. But in Sweden the Social Democratic Party, having won the election of 1932, broke the shell of the orthodox monetary policy. As unemployment climbed sharply with the onset of the Great Depression, they stumbled upon an idea that was truly new: instead of assisting the unemployed, the Swedish Social Democrats employed them. It was the beginning of the marriage of the Left and Keynesian economics.

Keynesianism provided the foundation for class compromise by supplying those political parties representing workers with a justification for holding office within capitalist societies. And such a justification was desperately needed. Ever since the 1890s, social democrats had thought that their irreversible electoral progress would culminate in an electoral majority that would allow them one day to enter into office and legislate their societies into socialism. They were completely unprepared for what ensued: in several countries social democratic, labor, and socialist parties were invited to form governments by default, without winning the majority that would have been necessary to pursue the program of nationalization, because the bourgeois parties were too divided to continue their traditional coalitions. Indeed, the first elected socialist government in the world was formed by the Swedish Social Democrats in 1920 just as they suffered their first electoral reversal. And once in office, socialists found themselves in the embarrassing situation of not being able to pursue the program of nationalization and not having any other program that would distinguish them from their bourgeois opponents. They could and did pursue ad-hoc measures designed to improve conditions for their electoral constituency: the development of public housing, the institution of unemployment relief, the introduction of minimum wages, income and inheritance taxes, and old age pensions. But such measures did not differ from the tradition of conservative reforms associated with Bismarck, Disraeli, or Giolitti. Socialists behaved like all other parties: with some distributional bias toward their own constituency but full of respect for the golden principles of the balanced budget, deflation, gold standard, etc.

Keynesianism suddenly provided working-class political parties with a reason to be in office. It appeared that there was something to be done, that the economy was not moving according to natural laws, that economic crises could be attenuated and the waste of resources and the suffering alleviated if the state pursued anticyclical policies of demand management. If the economy was producing at a level below its capacity, given the existing stock of capital and labor, a proper government policy could increase output until it approached the economy's full potential. The government had the capacity to close the "full-employment gap," to insure that there would be no unemployment of men and machines. Full employment became a realistic goal that could be pursued at all times.

How was this to be done? Here again Keynesian economics provided a technical justification for class compromise. The answer it provided was to increase consumption. In the Keynesian diagnosis, the cause of unemployment was the insufficiency of demand. Hence any redistribution of income downwards to people who consume most of it and any expansion of government spending will stimulate production and reduce unemployment. Given the existing capital stock, the actual output can always be raised by increasing wages, transfers to the poor, and government spending, or by reducing taxes. Since raising output means augmenting the rate of utilization of resources, the same policies will diminish unemployment. Thus the distributional bias of the Left toward their electoral constituency found a rationalization in a technical economic theory. As Léon Blum put it, "a better distribution . . . would revive production at the same time that it would satisfy justice."

But more was at stake. In the orthodox thinking, any demands by workers or the unemployed for higher consumption appeared as a particularistic interest, inimical to future national development. To increase wages or social services was to raise costs of production and to divert resources from the investment necessary for growth, accumulation of capital, and improved productivity. The welfare of the poor was a matter of private charity, not of economics. But in the Keynesian framework it is consumption that provides the motor force for production, and suddenly workers and the poor turned out to be the representatives of the universal interest. Their particularistic interest in consumption coincided with the general interest in production. The "people" became the hegemonic force in society. . . . The terms of discourse became transformed.

Not all "Keynesian" positions are the same. One policy direction—warmly embraced by the radical Left—focused on the redistribution of income toward wages and transfers. This is what happened in France in 1936. A more cautious and more successful, policy consisted of manipulating government spending, taxation, and the money supply. The Swedish policy of 1932 was exclusively an "employment policy": it consisted of productive public employment financed by deficits and increased taxation. Wage rates did not increase in Sweden until 1938, well after the economy was out of the slump. In fact, the simple formal framework of Keynesian economics, as is found in modern macro-economic textbooks, favors government spending over redistribution of income: the "multiplier" for government spending is greater than unity, while for wages and transfers it is less than unity. Hence, at least in principle, government spending more than pays for itself in increased production, while distribution of income partially hurts other components of demand.

In all of its forms, the Keynesian compromise consisted of a dual program: "full employment and equality," where the first term meant regulation of the level of employment via the management of demand, particularly government spending, and the latter consisted of the net of social services that constituted the "welfare state." The Keynesian compromise, therefore, came to consist of more than an active role for the government in macro-economic management. As the provider of social services and regulator of the market, the state acted in multiple social realms. Governments developed manpower programs, family policies, housing schemes, income assistance nets, health systems, etc. They attempted to regulate the labor force by mixing incentives and deterrents to participation in the labor market. They sought to alter patterns of racial and regional disparities. The result is that social relations are mediated through democratic political institutions rather than remaining private.

At the same time, the Keynesian compromise became increasingly dependent upon economic concessions granted to groups of people organized as nonmarket actors. Politics turned into an interplay of coalitions among such groups, giving rise to corporatist tendencies of direct negotiation, either between organized groups—particularly labor and capital—under the tutelage of the government or between each group and the government. The allocation of economic resources became increasingly dominated by relations of political forces.

The compromise was tenable as long as it could provide employment and material security. Indeed, by most criteria of economic progress the Keynesian era was a success. Whether or not this was due to the efficacy of Keynesian economic policies or was merely fortuitous is a matter of debate. Nevertheless, output grew, unemployment was low, social services were extended, and social peace reigned. Until the late 1960s, Keynesianism was the established ideology of class compromise, under which different groups could conflict within the confines of a capitalist and democratic system. And, with the possible exception of Karl Rehn's 1951 program in Sweden and the Italian Communist Party's short-lived austerity policy of the mid-1970s, Keynesianism provided the only framework for such a compromise. The crisis of Keynesianism is a crisis of democratic capitalism. . . .

Market Economics as a Political Project

In any society some decisions have a public impact while others have a private, or limited, effect. And in any society some decisions are made by the public while others are restricted to the private realm. Investment decisions—decisions to withhold a part of society's resources from current consumption and to allocate them to replace or augment the instruments of production—have an impact that is both general and long-lasting, that is, public. Yet the very institution of private property implies that they are a private prerogative. Control over investment is the central political issue under capitalism precisely because no other privately made decisions have such a profound public impact.

The program of the Right is to let the type and quantity of investment be determined by the market. The market, after all, is an institution that coordinates private decisions and aggregates preferences. If the market is undistorted by monopolies, externalities, etc., and consumers are sovereign, the market aggregates private decisions in a way that corresponds to preferences of individuals as consumers. The decisions made by profit-maximizing investors will respond to the preference of consumers concerning the atemporal and intertemporal allocation of resources. But the preferences to which the market responds are weighted by the amount of resources each individual controls. That an idealized "perfect" market matches aggregated consumer preferences for private goods efficiently is the first lesson of welfare economics. That aggregated consumer preferences reflect the distribution of income and wealth is an often neglected corollary.

A democratic political system constitutes another mechanism by which individual preferences are aggregated. If political competition is free of coercion and if voters are sovereign, then government policies will reflect the aggregated preferences of individuals as citizens. But as citizens individuals are weighted equally. Hence, the same set of individual preferences, for private as well as public goods, will normally yield a demand for a different allocation of resources when they are aggregated by political institutions rather than by the market.

Further, the market provides no guarantee that those whose consumption is most restrained in the present will reap the rewards of investment in the future. In any society some part of the current output must be withheld from consumption if production is to continue and consumption is to increase. What distinguishes capitalism is that investment is financed mostly out of profits, the part of the product withheld from wage-earners. It is upon profits that the renewal and enlargement of the capital stock depend. Hence, under capitalism, the presence of profits is a necessary condition for the improvement of material conditions of any group within the society. But it is not sufficient. Profits may be hoarded, consumed, exported, or invested badly. Even if capitalists are abstemious, efficient, and prescient, their market relation with workers ends as the cycle of production is completed and the wages are paid, and there is nothing in the structure of the capitalist system of production that would guarantee that wage-earners would be the ones to benefit from the fact that a part of the product is currently withheld from them as profit.

Any class compromise must, therefore, have at least two aspects: one concerning the distribution of income and the second concerning investment. If those who do not own capital are to consent voluntarily to the private property of the instruments of production, they must have a reasonable certainty that their material conditions would improve in the future as the result of current appropriation of profit by capitalists. Until recently, this compromise was rarely stated explicitly, for it is basically institutional: workers consent to the institution of private property of the instruments of production and owners of these instruments consent to political institutions through which other groups can effectively process their demands. Today, as trust in the compromise is eroding, workers are demanding more explicit commitments. . . .

The current period, however, is the first moment since the 1920s in which owners of capital have openly rejected a compromise that involves public influence over investment and the distribution of income. For the first time in several decades, the Right has an historical project of its own: to free accumulation from all the fetters imposed upon it by democracy. For the bourgeoisie never completed its revolution.

Just as it freed accumulation from the restraint of the feudal order, the bourgeoisie was forced to subject it to the constraint of popular control exercised through universal suffrage. The combination of private property of the means of production with universal suffrage is a compromise, and this compromise implies that the logic of accumulation is not exclusively the logic of private actors.

What is involved in the current offensive of the Right is not simply a question of taxes, government spending, or even the distribution of income. The plans for relaxing taxation of profits, abolishing environmental controls, eliminating welfare programs, removing government control over product safety and conditions of work, and weakening the labor unions add up to more than reorientation of the economic policy. They constitute a project for a new society, a bourgeois revolution.

It is thus necessary to consider the following question: what kind of a society would it be in which accumulation would be free from any form of political control, free from constraints of income distribution, from considerations of employment, environment, health of workers, and safety of consumers? Such hypothetical questions have no ready-made answers, but let us speculate.

It would be a society composed of households and firms, related to each other exclusively through the market. Social relations would become coextensive with market relations and the role of the political authority would be reduced to defending the market from attempts by any group organized as nonmarket actors (i.e. other than households and firms) to alter the rationality of market allocations. Since social and political relations would be depoliticized, demands by nonmarket actors would find no audience. The tension between accumulation and legitimation would be overcome: accumulation would be self-legitimizing for those who benefit from it and no other legitimacy would be sought. As it has been said, "the government does not owe anybody anything."

Household income would depend solely upon the market value of the labor performed. Reproduction of the labor force would be reprivatized and the traditional division of labor within the household—between earners and nurturers—would be restored. Persons excluded from participation in gainful activities would have no institutional guarantee of survival. They might be isolated on "reservations," whether inner cities or depressed regions, where they could be forgotten or ignored.

Workers would be disorganized as a class. If wage bargaining is decentralized by law to the level of the firm (as it is now in Chile) and if the process of internationalization of production continues, the monopoly power of unions would be effectively broken. Workers would be controlled by a combination of decentralized co-optation by some firms, by repression oriented against monopoly power, and—most importantly—by the threat of unemployment.

All of these changes would represent a reversal of trends that we are accustomed to see as irreversible. Indeed, the picture we drew can be easily obtained by combining the trends of contemporary capitalism described by, say, E. H. Carr or Jürgen Habermas, and reversing them. Economic relations would be depoliticized. Government economic planning would be abandoned. Legitimation would be left to the market. The "economic whip" would be reinstated as the central mechanism of political control.

Is such a society feasible? . . .

Where electoral participation has traditionally been high, where working-class parties enjoy electoral support, and where access to the electoral system is relatively open—in most Western European countries—the project of the Right seems doomed to failure under democratic conditions. But in the United States, where about 40 percent of adults never vote, where parties of notables have a duopolistic control over the electoral system, and where the barriers to entry are prohibitive, one must be less sanguine about the prospects. For suppose that the project is economically successful, even if for purely fortuitous reasons, and beneficial for a sizeable part of the electorate, that the Right captures both parties, and the offensive enjoys the support of the mass media. . . . Such a prospect is not totally far-fetched.

7.3

A Movement Society?

Sidney Tarrow

In this selection, the concluding chapter of his path-breaking work on the elusive but often formidable power of social movements, Sidney Tarrow provides a fascinating retrospective on two hundred years of social movements. He argues that in many ways the transnational rebellion of 1989, which marked the unraveling of the Communist world, reflected a set of trends in cycles and forms of protest that began with the French Revolution of 1789. At the same time, argues Tarrow, the movement of 1989 reveals a set of cumulative changes in social movements. Above all, Tarrow suggests that movements today are increasingly transnational and they spread far more rapidly than ever before. As a result, have we entered a state of perpetual disorder and violence?

In 1789, as word of France's revolution reached England, abolitionist Thomas Clarkson crossed the Channel to urge his French colleagues to join his country's antislavery agitation. Clarkson took the same route again in 1814, following a second wave of agitation in Britain. But "twice," writes the leading American student of antislavery, "he failed utterly." Although the French abolished slavery in their colonies in 1794, this was no more than "a desperate response to wartime contingencies," writes Drescher (1991: 712), and was reversed when Napoleon came to power. Only when it coincided with greater political earthquakes did antislavery cross the channel (pp. 719–20).

Two hundred years later, diffused by word of mouth, printed page and television, collective action spread rapidly across the internal boundaries of the Soviet bloc. As the French were commemorating—and burying!—the bicentennial of their Revolution,[1] a new wave of revolution swept over the Communist world. Centered on Eastern and Central Europe, enjoying a brief, tragic echo in China, the movement eventually gave way to savage confrontations in Romania, in the Caucasus and ultimately in Yugoslavia. Not only in semi-Stalinized Poland and in the restive Baltic states, but in ironfisted East Germany and subjugated

---

Sidney Tarrow, *Power in Movement: Social Movements, Collective Action and Politics* (Cambridge: Cambridge University Press, 1994), ch. 11, pp. 187–199. © Cambridge University Press 1994. Reprinted with the permission of Cambridge University Press.

Czechoslovakia, within a year communism was gone. By 1991, even the Soviet Union, heartland of proletarian internationalism, had collapsed, giving way to a galaxy of semi-democratic, semi-market, deeply conflicted societies.

When we compare the rapid diffusion of the movements of 1989 to Clarkson's inability to bring abolitionism across 30 miles of water, we can begin to understand the progress of the social movement over the past two hundred years. For not only did Eastern Europeans rebel *en masse* in 1989: They did so against similar targets, at virtually the same time and in the name of goals that varied only in their details. In 1789 antislavery advocates had difficulty crossing the English Channel. But in 1989 the democracy movement spread from Berlin to Beijing in a matter of weeks.

The significance of this change is still emerging, and its implications for democracy are mixed—to say the least. But its implications for the nature of social movements were profound. For not only did these changes close the door on the most important revolutionary movement of the twentieth century; by the end of 1989, not only in Eastern Europe, but all over the Communist bloc, the movement against state socialism had become general and its modalities modular. Even in Italy, so far from the periphery of world communism that its Communist Party was barely recognizable by 1989, party leaders rejected their historic identity and changed their flag.

But the heart of the movement was in Eastern Europe. There, with little prior organization, people who had never met (or who knew each other in the apolitical networks of what Eastern Europeans were calling "civil society"), were employing similar forms of organization and action, and in the name of similar frames of meaning, rose up against authorities. If the Communist Party elites gave in practically without a fight, it was not only because they had lost heart, but because they could see what forces were arrayed against them and knew what it would take to suppress them. Not only this movement, but *the* social movement triumphed in 1989.

The rapid spread and dramatic success of the movement of 1989 was a reflection of the powers of movement. . . . But it also raises some troubling questions for social movement theory and about the emerging world order; about the increase of violence, the recrudescence of ethnic conflicts, the possible transcendence of the national state and the internationalization of conflict. In this [discussion], I will first [offer some reflections about] the power in movement before turning to the questions raised by the cataclysm of 1989 and its violent aftermath.

Two Hundred Years of Movement

Since collective action is the common denominator of all kinds of social movements, we began with the theory of collective action. Twenty years ago, political scientists and sociologists interested in social movements began to look at their subject not from the standpoint of actions taken, but as a puzzle; based on the assumption that collective action is difficult to bring about. I argue . . . that this puzzle *is* only a puzzle (and not a sociological law), because in so many situations and against so many odds, collective action *does* occur, often instigated by people with few resources and little inherent power.

The "solution" to that puzzle was first sought by collective action theorists building on economist Mancur Olson's theory that "large groups" mobilize members through selective incentives and constraints. While the Olsonian theory worked well for interest groups, it was inadequate for social movements for the simple reason that they are multipolar actors in sustained conflict with opponents and have few incentives or constraints to deploy. Unlike voluntary associations, movements are not organizations, and those who try to lead them have little or no control over those they hope will follow them.

The central task for movement organizers is to resolve what I called the "social transaction costs of collective action"; creating focal points for people who have no sources of compulsory coordination, who often lack direct connections with one another and have few, if any, internal resources. While large firms and interest groups solve their transaction cost problem by internalizing their assets, movements seldom have this option. Indeed, organizers who try to turn their "base" into disciplined cadres squander much of their energy on achieving internal control. How movements become the focal points for collective action and sustain it against opponents and the state [remains] the central question. . . .

I argued, in response to this question, that the main incentives for movement creation and diffusion are found in the structure of political opportunities. Increasing access to power, realignments in the political system, conflicts among elites and the availability of allies give early challengers the incentives to assault the power structure and create opportunities for others. The diffusion of movements takes place by many mechanisms and draws on a variety of resources; but the major incentive for new groups to join a movement are the political opportunities that are exposed by the actions of "early risers" and exploited by others.

In response to political opportunities, movements use different forms of collective action singly and in combination to link people to one another and with opponents, supporters and third parties. They take advantage of both the familiarity of these forms of action . . . innovating around their edges to inspire the imagination of supporters and create fear and uncertainty among opponents. Collective action is best seen not as a simple cost, but as both a cost and a benefit for social movements.

The balance between the costs and benefits helps determine the dynamics of the movement. As the benefits of a particular form of collective action decline, organizers have incentives to develop new actions, increase the numbers of participants or radicalize their interaction with opponents. The conflicts and defections within social movements, as well as their confrontations with the state, are, in part, the result of the attempt to maintain the movement's momentum through the use of new and more daring collective actions.

But in the formation of a social movement, there is more than a "pull" toward particular forms of action; there must also be a "push" from solidarity and collective identity. Solidarity has much to do with interest, but it produces a sustained movement only when consensus is built around common meanings and values. These meanings and values are partly inherited and partly constructed in the act of confronting opponents. They are also constituted by the interactions within movements. One of the main factors distinguishing successful movements from failures is their capacity to link inherited understandings to the imperative for activism.

Collective action is often led by movement organizations, but these are sometimes beneficiaries, sometimes inciters and at other times destroyers of popular politics. The recurring controversy about whether organizations produce movements or suppress them can be resolved only if we examine the less formal structures that they draw upon—the social networks at the base of society, and the mobilizing structures that link them to the focal points of conflict. Sustaining a movement is the result of a delicate balance between suffocating the power in movement by providing too much organization and leaving it to spin off uselessly away through the tyranny of decentralization.

Opportunities, Cycles and the Consumption of Movement

But collective action repertoires, cultural frames and organization are only the potential sources of power; they can be employed just as easily for social control as for insurgency. [R]ecurring protest cycles . . . are the products of the diffusion of political opportunities that transform the potential for mobilization into action. In these crucibles of conflict and innovation, movements not only take advantage of available opportunities; they create them for others by producing new forms of action, hammering out new "master frames," activating social networks and making coalitions that force the state to respond to the disorder around it.

That response is often repressive, but even repression is often mixed with reform. Particularly when counterelites within the system see the opportunity to aggrandize themselves in alliance with challengers, rulers are placed in a vulnerable position to which reform is a frequent response. As conflict collapses and militants retire to lick their wounds, many of their advances are reversed, but they leave behind incremental expansions in participation, changes in popular culture and residual movement networks. Movement cycles are a season for sowing, but the reaping is often done during the periods of demobilization that follow, by latecomers to the cause.

If cycles of protest are opened up by expanding opportunities, how do they decline as they inevitably do? Is it simply because people tire of agitation, because enervating factional struggles develop within their movements, because organizations become oppressive or because elites repress and placate challengers? All of these are contributory causes of cyclical decline, but there is a more systemic cause as well: Since the power in movement depends on the mobilization of external opportunities, when opportunities expand from challengers to other groups and shift to elites and authorities, movements lose their primary source of power. For brief periods of history the power in movement seems irresistible; but it disperses rapidly and passes inexorably into more institutional forms of politics. Let us turn to how the power in movement has changed.

1789/1989

If each new social movement had to create anew its forms of collective action, its frames of meaning and its mobilizing structures, then the collective action problem would be insuperable and the world would be a much quieter place than it has become. If there is a central message . . . it is that the power in movement is cumulative. Social theorists are forever discovering waves of "new" social movements; but the claim of "the new" fades when we contemplate the larger historical picture. For new movements not only repeat many of the themes of their predecessors, like identity, autonomy and injustice, but build on the practices and institutions of the past.

It was the consolidation of the national state in the eighteenth century that created the framework in which national social movements developed. They resulted both from statebuilders' penetration of society and from their creation of common frameworks for citizenship. Although expanding states sought to repress opposition and reduce the periphery to obedience, they also created national categories of identity, standard relationships and offered a fulcrum on which people could fight out their social conflicts with others.

This creation of a central state target and fulcrum for conflict transformed how people made claims. Using the central state to seek a benefit or attack an opponent meant using the repertoire of collective action that state elites recognized. In democratic states, the mass, modular and largely peaceful repertoire of the twentieth century was the result. The novelty of this new repertoire was not that it existed, but that it had the capacity to bring broad coalitions of challengers together in sustained interactions with national states, and to mount general claims against them.

Why did this capacity develop when it did in the West? It was the rise of modern states and an international capitalist economy that provided the targets and the resources that helped movements to flourish and that laid the bases for today's social movements. Movements began in the West because that was where the consolidated national state first appeared. When western states and expanding capitalism moved outward to colonize the rest of the world, they brought the preconditions and the practices of the social movement with them.

In the process of movement development, two major structural changes were critical: regular associations which provided legal and conventional forms that more contentious actors could employ; and new and expanded means of communication which diffused models of collective action and new cognitive frames from one sector or country to another. Though early analysts insisted on the importance of class in galvanizing these movements, it was through the interclass and translocal coalitions created through print and association that the first successful movements took shape. The nationalist movements that spread across Europe and America and throughout the world had the capacity to cross class lines and form such interclass coalitions.

These were not random processes. Repeated confrontations linked specific social actors with their antagonists through forms of collective action that became recurring routines: the strike between workers and employers; the demonstration between protesters and opponents; the insurrection between insurgents and the state. The national social movement developed as a sequence of sustained challenges to elites, authorities or opponents by people with collective purposes and solidarity, or by those who claimed to represent them.

Once these opportunities, conventions and resources became available to ordinary people, the problem of social transaction costs could be solved and movements could spread to entire societies, producing the periods of turbulence and realignment that I have called cycles of protest. Such periods had repercussions that sometimes resulted in repression, sometimes in reform, often in both. They were the major watersheds for the innovations in collective action we see today, for changes in political culture, for increased political involvements and for the creation of future networks of militants and supporters.

The first major cycle of protest occurred in 1789, but its diffusion across the borders of France was carried mainly on the tips of French bayonets. The first major international cycle occurred during the 1848 Revolution. The most recent ones before 1989 were the anticolonial movements of the post–World War II period, and the 1960s movements in Europe and the United States. These latter movements were, in the main, nonviolent. While 1848 ended in armed strife and foreign intervention, both anticolonial nationalism and the movements of the 1960s brought the tools of nonviolent direct action to new heights of refinement and effectiveness.

The movements of Eastern Europe in 1989 were in many ways the culmination of these trends. Like these earlier movements, they were not class movements; they were, at first, remarkably nonviolent; and they spread rapidly across the region. Both new and old forms of collective action were employed; new frames of meaning like anticorruption and participation joined the themes of injustice and liberation; the organizations used were weak but collective action and consent spread through social networks at the base. As in the past, the major incentives that turned underlying discontents into movements were political opportunities.

Of these opportunities, the most important were transnational: the openings, the realignments, the splits between reform and orthodox Communists and the encouragement to dissidents produced by Gorbachev's domestic reforms and by his policies towards Eastern Europe. As each country in the region experienced the weakening of its elites and the crumbling of their resistance, newer and wider opportunities were created. The movement spread much as the 1848 Revolution had done, by a process of imitation, diffusion, reaction and transformation of scattered movements, culminating in elite negotiations and the attempt to build new institutions out of struggle.

But like 1848, as the movement wound through Eastern Europe, the mood shifted from liberalism and representative government to ethnic particularism and national assertiveness. If crowds of Czechs and Slovaks turned out to demonstrate for freedom in Prague and Bratislava in 1989, by 1992 these cities had become the capitals of a country split in two; if thousands of Hungarians demonstrated at the tomb of Imre Najy in 1988, by the early 1990s, the parties that liberated their country from communism were having difficulty attracting a plurality of voters. If West and East Germans joined in an ode to freedom on the Berlin Wall in 1989, by 1991 "Ossies" and "Wessies" were watching each other with suspicion, In Poland, the Solidarity leaders who had started the process a decade earlier split into rival political parties. And in Russia the democratic movement of the late 1980s gave way to a range of semi-parties, some of them holdovers from the recent regime and others reviving forms of xenophobia from the Czarist past.

Immediately after the ebullience of 1989, some observers foresaw old elites being rapidly swept off the public scene, state-run economies rapidly privatized and a new democratic politics emerging in the image of the West. But by the early 1990s, not only were old elites still active in many parts of the former Communist world—some of them transformed from *apparachniks* into *entrepreneurniks*—but the privatization of their economies was making heavy weather. Under the strain, the opportunities and the uncertainties of the post-1989 years provided space for a variety of players, not all of whom had democracy or the market as their goals. Just as the Springtime of Freedom of 1848 was closed by Napoleon's coup of 1851, the Ode to Freedom at the Berlin Wall was the prelude to the ethnic conflicts of the 1990s and the carnage at Sarajevo.

A Movement Society: Transnational and Violent?

How representative was the movement of 1989? It certainly had peculiarities due to the nearly unique nature of the Soviet bloc. For example, it was the first movement in history to destroy a powerful multistate empire in one blow. It was also—at least at first—predominantly handled through peaceful negotiation, with the menace of mass violence held in abeyance in almost every country of the region until state socialism was gone. But despite its particularity, the 1989 cycle can help us to see some of the ways in which the national social movement has changed in its two-hundred-year history. If these changes are substantial and cumulative, then the world may be moving from a logic of alternation between periods of movement and periods of quiescence into a permanent movement society. At this stage, all we can do is guess at the possibilities and speculate about their implications.

Transnational Movements

When we return to the comparison between Clarkson's failure in 1789 and the success of 1989, we see one major difference; that movements spread far more rapidly now than they did in the past—even in the absence of formal organizations. This is, in part, an expression of the universality of the repertoire of collective action, in part, due to the rapidity of global communication, and, in part, because of the appearance of transnational movements. The contrast between antislavery in 1789 and the movements of 1989 will illustrate all three points.

In contrast to Clarkson's inability to bring abolitionism across a mere thirty miles of water in 1789, the knowledge of how to mount a social movement had become so general by 1989 that the liberation from state socialism took remarkably similar form across a continent and a half. For example, the human chain that protestors stretched across the Baltics in 1989 was the same tactic that had been used a few years earlier by the European peace movement. The "round table" that was used to outline the future division of power in Poland was adopted in many other countries of the region. "What is remarkable," write Valerie Bunce and Dennis Chong, "is the speed with which the masses in each country converged on particular strategies, coordinated its actions, and successfully executed its plans" (1990: 3).

Second, the appearance of global television had a great influence in the diffusion of the movement, and this is not limited to Eastern Europe in 1989. In the eighteenth century, movements were still diffused by word of mouth, by print and association or by people like Clarkson who acted as missionaries of movement. But in 1989, the spread of the democratic movement in Eastern Europe—not to mention its tragic echo in China—left little doubt that collective action can spread by global communication. Not only do potential protestors learn about political opportunities through the mass media; when they see people not very different from themselves acting in contentious ways succeeding, it is easy for them to imagine themselves doing the same. And just as they learn *from* television, they have become skilled at using it to project word of their movements to international centers of power.

Third, because of the centrality of the national state, movements like antislavery spread slowly and took different forms in different parts of Europe; so did the democratic movement of the late eighteenth century. In the nineteenth century, both radical democracy and socialism were diffused more quickly, but it still took fifty years for social democracy to reach Russia—and it arrived in very different form than in the West.

The most recent cycles of protest have been inherently—and perhaps increasingly—transnational and thus have diffused more rapidly. The decolonization movements in the former British and French empires; the European and American New Left of the 1960s; the peace movements of the 1980s; global environmental movements like Greenpeace: These are no longer cases of simple imitation and diffusion, but expressions of the same movement acting against similar targets. The movements of 1989 in Eastern Europe were extreme in this respect, but in their interdependence and mutual dependence on international trends, they were not so different than these other recent movements.

The archetypical case of a transnational movement in recent years has been militant, fundamentalist Islam. Its spread from Iran to Afghanistan, to the Bekaa Valley and the Gaza Strip, and more recently to North Africa bridges institutional religion and guerilla warfare. In between these extremes of violence and institutionalization, its organizers have employed an array of similar tactics everywhere: the mobilization of slum dwellers, the intimidation of women, the extortion of funds from small businessmen—even elections, when this has been convenient. One deeply rooted secular movement—the Palestinian Liberation Organization—has been severely challenged by Islamic competition; the Soviet army was forced out of Afghanistan by another; while the Sudanese government was overthrown by a third. The Algerian government was only saved from Islamic domination by a military takeover. And by 1992, even secular Egypt was under attack from internationally supported fundamentalists.

The spread of such transnational movements as militant Islam leads to a larger and more portentous question. Since we seem to be living in an increasingly interdependent world, are we becoming a single movement society? And if we are, will movements lose the cyclical and national rhythms of the past and take on the character of continual turbulence spreading across national boundaries out of the control of national states? A movement society may be an increasingly violent society. What is the evidence for such a claim?

Ex-Prisoners of the State?[2]

In his book *Turbulence in World Politics*, James Rosenau argues that we are becoming a single, more turbulent world. Rosenau sees the entire period since the end of World War II as the beginning of a new era of "global turbulence." Among the factors that convince him that ours is an era of turbulence is "a marked increase in the number of spontaneous collective actions" and their rapid spread around the world (1990: 369). If Rosenau is right, then the implications for the future of civil politics is troubling.

The national social movement grew out of the efforts of states to consolidate power, integrate their peripheries and standardize discourse among groups of citizens and between them and their rulers. Many of the characteristics of the social movements we have seen in this [discussion] grew out of that relationship—including the conventionalization of collective action, the channeling of movements into national opportunity structures and the institution of citizenship itself. If movements are becoming transnational, they may be freeing themselves of state structures and thence of the constraining influence of state-mediated contention.

Three kinds of arguments can be made on behalf of this thesis. First, the dominant economic trends of the late twentieth century have been towards greater international interdependence. "The increasing fluidity of capital, labor, commodities, money, and cultural practices," argues Charles Tilly in a recent paper, "undermines the capacity of any particular state to control events within its boundaries" (1991: 1). One result is that strikes that used to be mounted against domestic capitalists must now be risked against multinational corporations whose capital can be moved elsewhere. The interdependent global economy may be producing transnational collective action.[3]

Second, the economic growth of the 1970s and 1980s increased the imbalance of wealth and poverty between the North and West and the East and South, while bringing their citizens cognitively and physically closer to one another. This is not only the result of faster communication and cheaper transportation, but because, since the end of World War II, Third World countries have attempted to mimic the economic success of the West. . . .

Interdependence and the international gap in income both contribute to a third factor: a continued stream of migration that takes different forms than in the past. In the nineteenth century, much of the international movement of population went from core to periphery, with migrants permanently leaving their homes behind. The current wave of migration overwhelmingly favors the industrial countries of the West and immigrants seldom lose touch with their country of origin. "The Filipino maid in Milan and the Tamil busdriver in Toronto," observes Benedict Anderson, "are only a few sky hours away" from their homeland and seconds away by satellite telephone communication (1992: 8).

While mass population movements have become one of the major sources of domestic conflict in the contemporary world, citizenship—the expected outcome of immigration in the nineteenth century—has become an impossible dream for most immigrants. A major cultural cleavage pits immigrant groups with restricted citizenship rights against increasingly restive indigenous populations in states whose governments, from Paris to California, are under pressure to reduce the rights of resident immigrants and to cut them off from further entry. All over the West, from the eastern border of Germany to the southern border of the United States, doors are being shut to immigrants, and—just as important—earlier arrivals are being sealed off into immigrant ghettos.

One result—the rise of racist movements in Western Europe—we have already seen. But another is the rise of what Anderson calls "long-distance nationalism." For every nineteenth-century Mazzini and Garibaldi who fomented revolution at a great distance from their home country, there are thousands of Palestinians in New York, Punjabis in Toronto, Croats in Australia, Tamils in Britain, Irish in Massachusetts, Algerians in France and Cubans in

Miami whose ties to their countries of origin are kept alive through transnational social networks (Anderson 1992: 12).

Most of these meekly accept their subaltern status and hope for an affluent return to their homelands. But others use the ease of international communication and transportation to support movements at home. By more-or-less covert financial contributions, by fax and E-mail, by letter bombs and discrete arms purchases, these long-distance nationalists are disturbing the neat symmetry between national states and national social movements that the world has inherited from the last century.

Not only nationalist migrants, but transnational ecologists, developmentalists and fighters for the rights of minorities increasingly aim their actions at other people's governments. We live in an age when rubber tappers in Brazil can enjoy the assistance of American nongovernmental organizations; when U.N.-supported technical teams teach Indian ecologists to use video cameras that they can employ to mobilize peasants; and when racist propaganda produced in the United States finds its way to the apartments of European skinheads. The modern state, which began its consolidation in opposition to its territorial enemies, is becoming increasingly permeable to nonterritorial movements. As a result, the social movement may be becoming an ex-prisoner of the state.

If this is true, what are the implications for the character of social movements and for social conflict in general? If nothing else, the characteristic pattern whereby political cycles result from the processing of challenges within national states may be extended over time and space by crossnational extension. Fundamentalist Islam is the most successful example: When the expansion of the Iranian revolution failed in the Iran–Iraq war, Afghanistan became the major field of action; when the Red Army left Kabul, fundamentalist militants moved on from Peshawar to Cairo, to Algiers and eventually to New York.[4] Where movements respond to political opportunities across state boundaries, they can escape the mediation and control of any single state.

As long as these expressions of integral religious nationalism were bounded within the Third World, Western governments and their citizens remained relatively indifferent. But with the attack by Islamic militants on the World Trade Center in New York in 1993, long-distance nationalism moved to the West. The diffusion of militant fundamentalism to the heart of world capitalism showed that, in the interdependent contemporary world, modernization does not equal secularization and that international trends deeply affect the internal order of states.

This leads to an even more worrying concern. Over the past two hundred years, there has been a slow, ragged but inexorable civilizing trend in the nature of collective action and in the state's means of controlling it. . . . [A]s modular repertoires linked social movements to the state, violent and direct forms of attack were increasingly replaced by the power of numbers, by solidarity and an informal dialogue between states and movements. The cycle of the 1960s, with its remarkably low level of violence and employment of nonviolent direct action, was the apotheosis of this trend. But the guerilla wars, the hostage takings and the ethnic conflicts of the past two decades must make us wonder whether the trend to a peaceful repertoire was no more than a historical parenthesis and is now being reversed.

The integralist beliefs—if not the violent methods—of militant Islam bear a striking resemblance to trends in Western culture: to politicized ministers who preach intolerance on Sunday morning television; to the "rescuers" of unborn fetuses who refuse to recognize women's rights to reproductive freedom; to orthodox attacks on secular values in education and personal life; and to xenophobic political parties that claim their nations' natural superiority. The methods are different, but how different are the French *Front National* or the Hungarian Way, from the zealots of Gush Emunim or the fanatics of the Party of God?

Citizens of modern states have lived through such "moments of madness" before. It is enough to remember that severed heads were paraded around the streets of Paris on pikes during the great democratic French Revolution, or that Jews were attacked in France and Germany during the Springtime of Freedom in 1848, to find parallels for the violence and intolerance that have emerged in the West since the 1980s. The concern raised by these more recent outbreaks is that—if, in fact a "movement society" *is* developing out of the social, economic and cultural changes of the late twentieth century—it will have a different cultural valence than the movements that broke out in Boston in 1765, in Paris in 1848 and in the nonviolent movements of the 1960s.

Is the New World Order that was supposed to result from the liberation of 1989 turning instead into a permanent state of violence and disorder? Have the resources for violent collective action become so widely accessible, integralist identities so widespread, and militants so freed of the national state that a permanent and violent movement society is resulting? Or will the current plethora of ethnic and religious movements be partially outgrown, partially domesticated and partially mediated by the political process, as in previous cycles of protest?

The violence and intolerance of the 1990s constitute a truly alarming trend. But this is not the first great wave of movement in history, nor will it be the last. If its dynamic comes to resemble the social movements that we have encountered in this [discussion], then its power will at first be ferocious, uncontrolled and widely diffused, but later ephemeral. If so, then like previous waves of movement, it will ultimately disperse "like a flood tide which loosens up much of the soil but leaves alluvial deposits in its wake" (Zolberg 1972: 206).

Notes

1. "No hint of subsequent radicalization, no echo of social conflict, no shadow of the Terror could mar this season of commemoration," observed historians Keith Baker and Steven Kaplan of the Bicentennial in their preface to Roger Chartier's *The Cultural Origins of the French Revolution*, p. xii. Even as they celebrated it, the French in 1989 were interring their Revolution. See Kaplan's *Adieu 1789*, which reads the Bicentennial as a celebratory rite for the funeral of the Revolution.
2. In a 1991 paper, Charles Tilly provocatively writes, "As Europeans unconsciously subvert the state in the very act of affirming its desirability, comparative-historical sociologists are unwittingly peripheralizing the state while declaring its centrality." See his "Prisoners of the State," p. 1.

3. The most articulate advocates of this global view of industrial conflict are Giovanni Arrighi, and Beverly Silver. See the former's "World Income Inequalities and the Future of Socialism," and the latter's "Class Struggle and Kondratieff Waves, 1870 to the Present," as well as her "Labor Unrest and Capital Accumulation on a World Scale."

4. See the account of the links between Afghan-trained Islamic militants and the attackers of the World Trade Center in the *New York Times*, August 11, 1993.

References

Anderson, Benedict (1990). "Language, Fantasy, Revolution: Java, 1900–1945," *Prisma* 50:25–39.

Baker, Keith Michael (1990). *Inventing the French Revolution. Essays on French Political Culture in the Eighteenth Century*. Cambridge and New York: Cambridge University Press.

Bunce, Valerie, and Dennis Chong (1990). "The Party's Over: Mass Protest and the End of Communist Rule in Eastern Europe," presented to the annual meeting of the American Political Science Association, San Francisco, Calif.

Drescher, Seymour (1987). *Capitalism and Antislavery: British Mobilization in Comparative Perspective*. Oxford and New York: Oxford University Press.

——. (1982). "Public Opinion and the Destruction of British Colonial Slavery," in James Walvin, ed., *Slavery and British Society, 1776–1846*. Baton Rouge: Louisiana State University Press, pp. 22–48.

——. (1991). "British Way, French Way: Opinion Building and Revolution in the Second French Slave Emancipation," *American Historical Review* 96:709–34.

——. (1994). "Whose Abolition? Popular Pressure and the Ending of the British Slave Trade," *Past and Present*.

Rosenau, James (1990). *Turbulence in World Politics: A Theory of Change and Continuity*. Princeton: Princeton University Press.

Tilly, Charles (1991). "Prisoners of the State." Working Paper No. 129, the Center for Studies of Social Change, the New School for Social Research, New York.

Zolberg, Aristide R. (1972). "Moments of Madness," *Politics and Society* 2:183–207.

 7.4

Bowling Alone: America's Declining Social Capital

Robert D. Putnam

This selection documents what Robert Putnam considers a fundamental change in the United States: that Americans are increasingly less likely to form voluntary associations (what he calls social capital). After "Bowling Alone" was published, Putnam became an instant celebrity: He was invited to meet with the president and became a frequent commentator on radio and television. He speculates in an

Robert D. Putnam, "Bowling Alone: America's Declining Social Capital," *Journal of Democracy* 6, No. 1 (Jan. 1995), 65–78. Reprinted by permission of the Sagalyn Agency.

account published elsewhere that the reason why his research became so widely reported was because it apparently confirmed a widespread concern that the American social fabric was weakening.

Not everyone agreed with Putnam's argument. Some critics argued that American society was weakening not because Americans were less likely to form associations but because of widening economic inequalities; other critics claimed that Putnam did not consider the role of government policies. Consider how Putnam's argument stands up to these criticisms.

M any students of the new democracies that have emerged over the past decade and a half have emphasized the importance of a strong and active civil society to the consolidation of democracy. Especially with regard to the postcommunist countries, scholars and democratic activists alike have lamented the absence or obliteration of traditions of independent civic engagement and a widespread tendency toward passive reliance on the state. To those concerned with the weakness of civil societies in the developing or post-communist world, the advanced Western democracies and above all the United States have typically been taken as models to be emulated. There is striking evidence, however, that the vibrancy of American civil society has notably declined over the past several decades.

Ever since the publication of Alexis de Tocqueville's *Democracy in America*, the United States has played a central role in systematic studies of the links between democracy and civil society. Although this is in part because trends in American life are often regarded as harbingers of social modernization, it is also because America has traditionally been considered unusually "civic" (a reputation that, as we shall later see, has not been entirely unjustified).

When Tocqueville visited the United States in the 1830s, it was the Americans' propensity for civic association that most impressed him as the key to their unprecedented ability to make democracy work. "Americans of all ages, all stations in life, and all types of disposition," he observed, "are forever forming associations. There are not only commercial and industrial associations in which all take part, but others of a thousand different types—religious, moral, serious, futile, very general and very limited, immensely large and very minute. . . . Nothing, in my view, deserves more attention than the intellectual and moral associations in America."[1]

. . . American social scientists of a neo-Tocquevillean bent have unearthed a wide range of empirical evidence that the quality of public life and the performance of social institutions (and not only in America) are indeed powerfully influenced by norms and networks of civic engagement. Researchers in such fields as education, urban poverty, unemployment, the control of crime and drug abuse, and even health have discovered that successful outcomes are more likely in civically engaged communities. Similarly, research on the varying economic attainments of different ethnic groups in the United States has demonstrated the importance of social bonds within each group. These results are consistent with research in a wide range of settings that demonstrates the vital importance of social networks for job placement and many other economic outcomes.

Meanwhile, a seemingly unrelated body of research on the sociology of economic development has also focused attention on the role of social networks. Some of this work is situated in the developing countries, and some of it elucidates the peculiarly successful "network capitalism" of East Asia.[2] Even in less exotic Western economies, however, researchers have discovered highly efficient, highly flexible "industrial districts" based on networks of collaboration among workers and small entrepreneurs. Far from being paleoindustrial anachronisms, these dense interpersonal and interorganizational networks undergird ultramodern industries, from the high tech of Silicon Valley to the high fashion of Benetton.

The norms and networks of civic engagement also powerfully affect the performance of representative government. That, at least, was the central conclusion of my own 20-year, quasi-experimental study of subnational governments in different regions of Italy.[3] Although all these regional governments seemed identical on paper, their levels of effectiveness varied dramatically. Systematic inquiry showed that the quality of governance was determined by longstanding traditions of civic engagement (or its absence). Voter turnout, newspaper readership, membership in choral societies and football clubs—these were the hallmarks of a successful region. In fact, historical analysis suggested that these networks of organized reciprocity and civic solidarity, far from being an epiphenomenon of socioeconomic modernization, were a precondition for it.

No doubt the mechanisms through which civic engagement and social connectedness produce such results—better schools, faster economic development, lower crime, and more effective government—are multiple and complex. While these briefly recounted findings require further confirmation and perhaps qualification, the parallels across hundreds of empirical studies in a dozen disparate disciplines and subfields are striking. Social scientists in several fields have recently suggested a common framework for understanding these phenomena, a framework that rests on the concept of *social capital*.[4] By analogy with notions of physical capital and human capital—tools and training that enhance individual productivity—"social capital" refers to features of social organization such as networks, norms, and social trust that facilitate coordination and cooperation for mutual benefit.

For a variety of reasons, life is easier in a community blessed with a substantial stock of social capital. In the first place, networks of civic engagement foster sturdy norms of generalized reciprocity and encourage the emergence of social trust. Such networks facilitate coordination and communication, amplify reputations, and thus allow dilemmas of collective action to be resolved. When economic and political negotiation is embedded in dense networks of social interaction, incentives for opportunism are reduced. At the same time, networks of civic engagement embody past success at collaboration, which can serve as a cultural template for future collaboration. Finally, dense networks of interaction probably broaden the participants' sense of self, developing the "I" into the "we," or (in the language of rational-choice theorists) enhancing the participants' "taste" for collective benefits.

I do not intend here to survey (much less contribute to) the development of the theory of social capital. Instead, I use the central premise of that rapidly growing body of work—that social connections and civic engagement pervasively influence our public life, as well as our private prospects—as the starting point for an empirical survey of trends in social capital in contemporary America. I concentrate here entirely on the American case, although the developments I portray may in some measure characterize many contemporary societies.

Whatever Happened to Civic Engagement?

We begin with familiar evidence on changing patterns of political participation, not least because it is immediately relevant to issues of democracy in the narrow sense. Consider the well-known decline in turnout in national elections over the last three decades. From a relative high point in the early 1960s, voter turnout had by 1990 declined by nearly a quarter; tens of millions of Americans had forsaken their parents' habitual readiness to engage in the simplest act of citizenship. Broadly similar trends also characterize participation in state and local elections.

It is not just the voting booth that has been increasingly deserted by Americans. A series of identical questions posed by the Roper Organization to national samples ten times each year over the last two decades reveals that since 1973 the number of Americans who report that "in the past year" they have "attended a public meeting on town or school affairs" has fallen by more than a third (from 22 percent in 1973 to 13 percent in 1993). Similar (or even greater) relative declines are evident in responses to questions about attending a political rally or speech, serving on a committee of some local organization, and working for a political party. By almost every measure, Americans' direct engagement in politics and government has fallen steadily and sharply over the last generation, despite the fact that average levels of education—the best individual-level predictor of political participation—have risen sharply throughout this period. Every year over the last decade or two, millions more have withdrawn from the affairs of their communities.

Not coincidentally, Americans have also disengaged psychologically from politics and government over this era. The proportion of Americans who reply that they "trust the government in Washington" only "some of the time" or "almost never" has risen steadily from 30 percent in 1966 to 75 percent in 1992.

These trends are well known, of course, and taken by themselves would seem amenable to a strictly political explanation. Perhaps the long litany of political tragedies and scandals since the 1960s (assassinations, Vietnam, Watergate, Irangate, and so on) has triggered an understandable disgust for politics and government among Americans, and that in turn has motivated their withdrawal. I do not doubt that this common interpretation has some merit, but its limitations become plain when we examine trends in civic engagement of a wider sort.

Our survey of organizational membership among Americans can usefully begin with a glance at the aggregate results of the General Social Survey, a scientifically conducted, national-sample survey that has been repeated 14 times over the last two decades. Church-related groups constitute the most common type of organization joined by Americans; they are especially popular with women. Other types of organizations frequently joined by women include school-service groups (mostly parent-teacher associations), sports groups, professional societies, and literary societies. Among men, sports clubs, labor unions, professional societies, fraternal groups, veterans' groups, and service clubs are all relatively popular.

Religious affiliation is by far the most common associational membership among Americans. Indeed, by many measures America continues to be (even more than in Tocqueville's time) an astonishingly "churched" society. For example, the United States has more houses of worship per capita than any other nation on Earth. Yet religious sentiment in America seems to be becoming somewhat less tied to institutions and more self-defined.

How have these complex crosscurrents played out over the last three or four decades in terms of Americans' engagement with organized religion? The general pattern is clear: The 1960s witnessed a significant drop in reported weekly churchgoing—from roughly 48 percent in the late 1950s to roughly 41 percent in the early 1970s. Since then, it has stagnated or (according to some surveys) declined still further. Meanwhile, data from the General Social Survey show a modest decline in membership in all "church-related groups" over the last 20 years. It would seem, then, that net participation by Americans, both in religious services and in church-related groups, has declined modestly (by perhaps a sixth) since the 1960s.

For many years, labor unions provided one of the most common organizational affiliations among American workers. Yet union membership has been falling for nearly four decades, with the steepest decline occurring between 1975 and 1985. Since the mid-1950s, when union membership peaked, the unionized portion of the nonagricultural work force in America has dropped by more than half, falling from 32.5 percent in 1953 to 15.8 percent in 1992. By now, virtually all of the explosive growth in union membership that was associated with the New Deal has been erased. The solidarity of union halls is now mostly a fading memory of aging men.[5]

The parent-teacher association (PTA) has been an especially important form of civic engagement in twentieth-century America because parental involvement in the educational process represents a particularly productive form of social capital. It is, therefore, dismaying to discover that participation in parent-teacher organizations has dropped drastically over the last generation, from more than 12 million in 1964 to barely 5 million in 1982 before recovering to approximately 7 million now.

Next, we turn to evidence on membership in (and volunteering for) civic and fraternal organizations. These data show some striking patterns. First, membership in traditional women's groups has declined more or less steadily since the mid-1960s. For example, membership in the national Federation of Women's Clubs is down by more than half (59 percent) since 1964, while membership in the League of Women Voters (LWV) is off 42 percent since 1969.[6]

Similar reductions are apparent in the numbers of volunteers for mainline civic organizations, such as the Boy Scouts (off by 26 percent since 1970) and the Red Cross (off by 61 percent since 1970). But what about the possibility that volunteers have simply switched their loyalties to other organizations? Evidence on "regular" (as opposed to occasional or "drop-by") volunteering is available from the Labor Department's Current Population Surveys of 1974 and 1989. These estimates suggest that serious volunteering declined by roughly one-sixth over these 15 years, from 24 percent of adults in 1974 to 20 percent in 1989. The multitudes of Red Cross aides and Boy Scout troop leaders now missing in action have apparently not been offset by equal numbers of new recruits elsewhere.

Fraternal organizations have also witnessed a substantial drop in membership during the 1980s and 1990s. Membership is down significantly in such groups as the Lions (off 12 percent since 1983), the Elks (off 18 percent since 1979), the Shriners (off 27 percent since 1979), the Jaycees (off 44 percent since 1979), and the Masons (down 39 percent since 1959). In sum, after expanding steadily throughout most of this century, many major civic organizations have experienced a sudden, substantial, and nearly simultaneous decline in membership over the last decade or two.

The most whimsical yet discomfiting bit of evidence of social disengagement in contemporary America that I have discovered is this: more Americans are bowling today than ever before, but bowling in organized leagues has plummeted in the last decade or so. Between 1980 and 1993 the total number of bowlers in America increased by 10 percent, while league bowling decreased by 40 percent. (Lest this be thought a wholly trivial example, I should note that nearly 80 million Americans went bowling at least once during 1993, *nearly a third more than voted in the 1994 congressional elections* and roughly the same number as claim to attend church regularly. Even after the 1980s' plunge in league bowling, nearly 3 percent of American adults regularly bowl in leagues.) The rise of solo bowling threatens the livelihood of bowling-lane proprietors because those who bowl as members of leagues consume three times as much beer and pizza as solo bowlers, and the money in bowling is in the beer and pizza, not the balls and shoes. The broader social significance, however, lies in the social interaction and even occasionally civic conversations over beer and pizza that solo bowlers forgo. Whether or not bowling beats balloting in the eyes of most Americans, bowling teams illustrate yet another vanishing form of social capital. . . .

Good Neighborliness and Social Trust

I noted earlier that most readily available quantitative evidence on trends in social connectedness involves formal settings, such as the voting booth, the union hall, or the PTA. One glaring exception is so widely discussed as to require little comment here: the most fundamental form of social capital is the family, and the massive evidence of the loosening of bonds within the family (both extended and nuclear) is well known. This trend, of course, is quite consistent with—and may help to explain—our theme of social decapitalization.

A second aspect of informal social capital on which we happen to have reasonably reliable time-series data involves neighborliness. In each General Social Survey since 1974 respondents have been asked, "How often do you spend a social evening with a neighbor?" The proportion of Americans who socialize with their neighbors more than once a year has slowly but steadily declined over the last two decades, from 72 percent in 1974 to 61 percent in 1993. (On the other hand, socializing with "friends who do not live in your neighborhood" appears to be on the increase, a trend that may reflect the growth of workplace-based social connections.)

Americans are also less trusting. The proportion of Americans saying that most people can be trusted fell by more than a third between 1960, when 58 percent chose that alternative, and 1993, when only 37 percent did. The same trend is apparent in all educational groups; indeed, because social trust is also correlated with education and because educational levels have risen sharply, the overall decrease in social trust is even more apparent if we control for education.

Our discussion of trends in social connectedness and civic engagement has tacitly assumed that all the forms of social capital that we have discussed are themselves coherently correlated across individuals. This is in fact true. Members of associations are much more likely than nonmembers to participate in politics, to spend time with neighbors, to express social trust, and so on.

The close correlation between social trust and associational membership is true not only across time and across individuals, but also across countries. Evidence from the 1991 World Values Survey demonstrates the following:[7]

1. Across the 35 countries in this survey, social trust and civic engagement are strongly correlated; the greater the density of associational membership in a society, the more trusting its citizens. Trust and engagement are two facets of the same underlying factor—social capital.
2. America still ranks relatively high by cross-national standards on both these dimensions of social capital. Even in the 1990s, after several decades' erosion, Americans are more trusting and more engaged than people in most other countries of the world.

3. The trends of the past quarter-century, however, have apparently moved the United States significantly lower in the international rankings of social capital. The recent deterioration in American social capital has been sufficiently great that (if no other country changed its position in the meantime) another quarter-century of change at the same rate would bring the United States, roughly speaking, to the midpoint among all these countries, roughly equivalent to South Korea, Belgium, or Estonia today. Two generations' decline at the same rate would leave the United States at the level of today's Chile, Portugal, and Slovenia.

Why Is U.S. Social Capital Eroding?

As we have seen, something has happened in America in the last two or three decades to diminish civic engagement and social connectedness. What could that "something" be? Here are several possible explanations, along with some initial evidence on each.

The movement of women into the labor force. Over these same two or three decades, many millions of American women have moved out of the home into paid employment. This is the primary, though not the sole, reason why the weekly working hours of the average American have increased significantly during these years. It seems highly plausible that this social revolution should have reduced the time and energy available for building social capital. For certain organizations, such as the PTA, the League of Women Voters, the Federation of Women's Clubs, and the Red Cross, this is almost certainly an important part of the story. The sharpest decline in women's civic participation seems to have come in the 1970s; membership in such "women's" organizations as these has been virtually halved since the late 1960s. By contrast, most of the decline in participation in men's organizations occurred about ten years later; the total decline to date has been approximately 25 percent for the typical organization. On the other hand, the survey data imply that the aggregate declines for men are virtually as great as those for women. It is logically possible, of course, that the male declines might represent the knock-on effect of women's liberation, as dishwashing crowded out the lodge, but time-budget studies suggest that most husbands of working wives have assumed only a minor part of the housework. In short, something besides the women's revolution seems to lie behind the erosion of social capital.

Mobility: The "re-potting" hypothesis. Numerous studies of organizational involvement have shown that residential stability and such related phenomena as homeownership are clearly associated with greater civic engagement. Mobility, like frequent re-potting of plants, tends to disrupt root systems, and it takes time for an uprooted individual to put down new roots. It seems plausible that the automobile, suburbanization, and the movement to the Sun Belt have reduced the social rootedness of the average American, but one fundamental difficulty with this hypothesis is apparent: the best evidence shows that residential stability and homeownership in America have risen modestly since 1965, and are surely higher now than during the 1950s, when civic engagement and social connectedness by our measures was definitely higher.

Other demographic transformations. A range of additional changes have transformed the American family since the 1960s—fewer marriages, more divorces, fewer children, lower real wages, and so on. Each of these changes might account for some of the slackening of civic engagement, since married, middle-class parents are generally more socially involved than other people. Moreover, the changes in scale that have swept over the American economy in these years—illustrated by the replacement of the corner grocery by the supermarket and now perhaps of the supermarket by electronic shopping at home, or the replacement of community-based enterprises by outposts of distant multinational firms—may perhaps have undermined the material and even physical basis for civic engagement.

The technological transformation of leisure. There is reason to believe that deep-seated technological trends are radically "privatizing" or "individualizing" our use of leisure time and thus disrupting many opportunities for social-capital formation. The most obvious and probably the most powerful instrument of this revolution is television. Time-budget studies in the 1960s showed that the growth in time spent watching television dwarfed all other changes in the way Americans passed their days and nights. Television has made our communities (or, rather, what we experience as our communities) wider and shallower. In the language of economics, electronic technology enables individual tastes to be satisfied more fully, but at the cost of the positive social externalities associated with more primitive forms of entertainment. The same logic applies to the replacement of vaudeville by the movies and now of movies by the VCR. The new "virtual reality" helmets that we will soon don to be entertained in total isolation are merely the latest extension of this trend. Is technology thus driving a wedge between our individual interests and our collective interests? It is a question that seems worth exploring more systematically.

What Is to Be Done?

The last refuge of a social-scientific scoundrel is to call for more research. Nevertheless, I cannot forbear from suggesting some further lines of inquiry.

♦ We must sort out the dimensions of social capital, which clearly is not a unidimensional concept, despite language (even in this essay) that implies the contrary. What types of organizations and networks most effectively embody—or generate—social capital, in the sense of mutual reciprocity, the resolution of dilemmas of collective action, and the broadening of social identities? In this essay I have emphasized the density of associational life. In earlier work I stressed the structure of networks, arguing that "horizontal" ties represented more productive social capital than vertical ties.[8]

◆ Another set of important issues involves macrosociological crosscurrents that might intersect with the trends described here. What will be the impact, for example, of electronic networks on social capital? My hunch is that meeting in an electronic forum is not the equivalent of meeting in a bowling alley—or even in a saloon—but hard empirical research is needed. What about the development of social capital in the workplace? Is it growing in counterpoint to the decline of civic engagement, reflecting some social analogue of the first law of thermodynamics—social capital is neither created nor destroyed, merely redistributed? Or do the trends described in this essay represent a deadweight loss?

◆ A rounded assessment of changes in American social capital over the last quarter-century needs to count the costs as well as the benefits of community engagement. We must not romanticize small-town, middle-class civic life in the America of the 1950s. In addition to the deleterious trends emphasized in this essay, recent decades have witnessed a substantial decline in intolerance and probably also in overt discrimination, and those beneficent trends may be related in complex ways to the erosion of traditional social capital. Moreover, a balanced accounting of the social-capital books would need to reconcile the insights of this approach with the undoubted insights offered by Mancur Olson and others who stress that closely knit social, economic, and political organizations are prone to inefficient cartelization and to what political economists term "rent seeking" and ordinary men and women call corruption.[9]

◆ Finally, and perhaps most urgently, we need to explore creatively how public policy impinges on (or might impinge on) social-capital formation. In some well-known instances, public policy has destroyed highly effective social networks and norms. American slum-clearance policy of the 1950s and 1960s, for example, renovated physical capital, but at a very high cost to existing social capital. The consolidation of country post offices and small school districts has promised administrative and financial efficiencies, but full-cost accounting for the effects of these policies on social capital might produce a more negative verdict. On the other hand, such past initiatives as the county agricultural-agent system, community colleges, and tax deductions for charitable contributions illustrate that government can encourage social-capital formation. Even a recent proposal in San Luis Obispo, California, to require that all new houses have front porches illustrates the power of government to influence where and how networks are formed.

The concept of "civil society" has played a central role in the recent global debate about the preconditions for democracy and democratization. In the newer democracies this phrase has properly focused attention on the need to foster a vibrant civic life in soils traditionally inhospitable to self-government. In the established democracies, ironically, growing numbers of citizens are questioning the effectiveness of their public institutions at the very moment when liberal democracy has swept the battlefield, both ideologically and geopolitically. In America, at least, there is reason to suspect that this democratic disarray may be linked to a broad and continuing erosion of civic engagement that began a quarter-century ago. High on our scholarly agenda should be the question of whether a comparable erosion of social capital may be under way in other advanced democracies, perhaps in different institutional and behavioral guises. High on America's agenda should be the question of how to reverse these adverse trends in social connectedness, thus restoring civic engagement and civic trust.

Notes

1. Alexis de Tocqueville, *Democracy in America*, ed. J.P. Maier, trans. George Lawrence (Garden City, N.Y.: Anchor Books, 1969), 513–17.

2. On social networks and economic growth in the developing world, see Milton J. Esman and Norman Uphoff, *Local Organizations: Intermediaries in Rural Development* (Ithaca: Cornell University Press, 1984), esp. 15–42 and 99–180; and Albert O. Hirschman, *Getting Ahead Collectively: Grassroots Experiences in Latin America* (Elmsford, N.Y.: Pergamon Press, 1984), esp. 42–77. On East Asia, see Gustav Papanek, "The New Asian Capitalism: An Economic Portrait," in Peter L. Berger and Hsin-Huang Michael Hsiao, eds., *In Search of an East Asian Development Model* (New Brunswick, N.J.: Transaction, 1987), 27–80; Peter B. Evans, "The State as Problem and Solution: Predation, Embedded Autonomy and Structural Change," in Stephan Haggard and Robert R. Kaufman, eds., *The Politics of Economic Adjustment* (Princeton: Princeton University Press, 1992), 139–81; and Gary G. Hamilton, William Zeile, and Wan-Jin Kim, "Network Structure of East Asian Economies," in Stewart R. Clegg and S. Gordon Redding, eds., *Capitalism in Contrasting Cultures* (Hawthorne, N.Y.: De Gruyter, 1990), 105–29. See also Gary G. Hamilton and Nicole Woolsey Biggart, "Market, Culture, and Authority: A Comparative Analysis of Management and Organization in the Far East," *American Journal of Sociology* (Supplement) 94 (1988): S52–S94; and Susan Greenhalgh, "Families and Networks in Taiwan's Economic Development," in Edwin Winckler and Susan Greenhalgh, eds., *Contending Approaches to the Political Economy of Taiwan* (Armonk, N.Y.: M.E. Sharpe, 1987), 224–45.

3. Robert D. Putnam, *Making Democracy Work: Civic Traditions in Modern Italy* (Princeton: Princeton University Press, 1993).

4. James S. Coleman deserves primary credit for developing the "social capital" theoretical framework. See his "Social Capital in the Creation of Human Capital," *American Journal of Sociology* (Supplement) 94 (1988): S95–S120, as well as his *The Foundations of Social Theory* (Cambridge: Harvard University Press, 1990), 300–21. See also Mark Granovetter, "Economic Action and Social Structure: The Problem of Embeddedness," *American Journal of Sociology* 91 (1985): 481–510; Glenn C. Loury, "Why Should We Care About Group Inequality?" *Social Philosophy and Policy* 5 (1987): 249–71; and Robert D. Putnam, "The Prosperous Community: Social Capital and Public Life," *American Prospect* 13 (1993): 35–42. To my knowledge, the first scholar to use the term "social capital" in its current sense was Jane Jacobs, in *The Death and Life of Great American Cities* (New York: Random House, 1961), 138.

5. Any simplistically political interpretation of the collapse of American unionism would need to confront the fact that the steepest decline began more than six years before the Reagan administration's attack on PATCO. Data from the General Social Survey show a roughly 40-percent decline in reported union membership between 1975 and 1991.

6. Data for the LWV are available over a longer time span and show an interesting pattern: a sharp slump during the Depression, a strong and sustained rise after World War II that more than tripled membership between 1945 and 1969, and then the post-1969 decline, which has already erased

virtually all the postwar gains and continues still. This same historical pattern applies to those men's fraternal organizations for which comparable data are available—steady increases for the first seven decades of the century, interrupted only by the Great Depression, followed by a collapse in the 1970s and 1980s that has already wiped out most of the postwar expansion and continues apace.

7. I am grateful to Ronald Inglehart, who directs this unique cross-national project, for sharing these highly useful data with me. See his "The Impact of Culture on Economic Development: Theory, Hypotheses, and Some Empirical Tests" (unpublished manuscript, University of Michigan, 1994).

8. See my *Making Democracy Work*, esp. ch. 6.

9. See Mancur Olson, *The Rise and Decline of Nations: Economic Growth, Stagflation, and Social Rigidities* (New Haven: Yale University Press, 1982), 2.

 7.5

The Future of Freedom: Illiberal Democracy at Home and Abroad

Fareed Zakaria

Zakaria claims that democratic political institutions can produce outcomes that diminish freedom because majorities may trample on the rights of minorities. The answer, he suggests, is to limit democracy by insulating political institutions, that is, reducing the influence of elections and other democratic procedures. Zakaria does not consider an opposite danger: that because institutions are insulated and unaccountable, they may abuse their power and limit freedom. A challenge for scholars and citizens, then, is to devise a way for institutions *both* to safeguard freedom *and* to be responsive and accountable. Any suggestions?

The twentieth century was marked by two broad trends: the regulation of capitalism and the deregulation of democracy. Both experiments overreached. They were sensible solutions to the problems of the time, unregulated capitalism and oligarchy. But as Evelyn Waugh pointed out in his comic novel *Scoop*, every good idea is valid "up to a point."

In the early years of the twentieth century, free markets and free trade seemed to be the inevitable way of the future. Countries around the world were trading

---

with one another, opening up their markets, indeed, their entire societies. Markets were on the march. But it turned out that those years before World War I, hyperinflation, and the Great Depression were a watershed for laissez faire. From then on, whenever a problem developed—economic, social, political—government intervention was the solution. Every crisis brought forth new regulations, and every regulation brought forth a new bureaucracy. As a result, for most of the twentieth century, capitalism was taxed, licensed, controlled, and even nationalized, so much so that by 1945 Britain's preeminent historian, A. J. P. Taylor, could assert, "Nobody believes in the American way of life—that is, private enterprise." In 1961, when Britain's Queen Elizabeth II visited Ghana, she was hailed as "the greatest socialist monarch in the world," which even her Tory government accepted as a compliment. When the conservative Republican Richard Nixon imposed wage and price controls on the U.S. economy in 1971 and announced, "We are all Keynesians now," he was reflecting the widespread view—even in America—that capitalism had to be intrusively managed by the state.

Democracy moved in the opposite direction. "The cure for the ailments of democracy," wrote the influential American philosopher John Dewey in 1927, "is more democracy." He was prescient. Most problems faced by most democracies during the twentieth century were addressed by broadening the franchise, eliminating indirect elections, reducing the strength of elite groups, and empowering more and more people in more and more ways. The results were thrilling. In America that meant blacks and women got the right to vote, senators were directly elected, parties chose their candidates on the basis of popular votes, and clubs changed their character and rules. The political history of the twentieth century is the story of ever-greater and more direct political participation. And success kept expanding democracy's scope. Whatever the ailment, more democracy became the cure.

The regulation of capitalism had gone overboard by the 1970s, resulting in heavy tax rates and Byzantine government controls. Over the last two decades, governments all over the world, from the United States to France to India to Brazil, have been deregulating industries, privatizing companies, and lowering tariffs. As the economic boom of the late 1990s unravels, there will be need for new regulation and a renewed appreciation of the role of government in capitalism. But few countries are likely to return to the bloated practices of a generation ago. The state has retreated from the commanding heights of the economy.

The deregulation of democracy has also gone too far. It has produced an unwieldy system, unable to govern or command the respect of people. Although none would dare speak ill of present-day democracy, most people instinctively sense a problem. Public respect for politics and political systems in every advanced democracy is at an all-time low. More intriguingly, in poll after poll, when Americans are asked what public institutions they most respect, three bodies are always at the top of their list: the Supreme Court, the armed forces, and the Federal Reserve System. All three have one thing in common: they are insulated from public pressures and operate undemocratically. It would seem that Americans admire these institutions precisely because they lead rather than follow. By contrast, Congress, the most representative and reflective of political institutions, scores at the bottom of most surveys. People view the pandering and the resulting paralysis with dismay, even disgust. Of course that does not stop them from celebrating the processes that have made such pandering inevitable.

Delegating Democracy

When the stakes are high we do not entrust day-to-day politics to ourselves. No democracy has ever conducted a war by weekly vote. The struggle against terrorism is, inevitably, being waged by governments that have been given much leeway by their societies. We now face new threats but also new and deep pressures on government. Democracies will have to demonstrate that they can cope with terrorism effectively, or else in many developing countries we will see the rise of a new authoritarianism. Developing countries, particularly in the Islamic world, will need to manage a difficult balancing act. They must remain strong enough to handle the new dangers of terrorism but yet be open and democratic enough that they don't create political opposition that morphs into extremism. In other words, they must be able to kill terrorists without breeding terrorism. When it works right, the state's power, legitimacy, and effectiveness can work together, each reinforcing the other, in a virtuous cycle. When things go awry, however, the virtuous cycle becomes vicious—and violent. Repression produces extremism, which produces more repression. Russia's approach to Chechnya is a sorry illustration of this downward spiral.

Globalization has produced a special set of challenges. The increasingly open world economy has forced governments to adopt disciplined policies that maintain fiscal stability over the long term. When they do not, markets punish countries faster and more severely than ever before, plunging currencies and stock markets into ruin. And yet long-term policies cause short-term pain—to voters. Demographic changes are pressing Western governments to reform their welfare states, in particular their benefits for the elderly. This will prove nearly impossible because senior citizens are politically powerful; they are well organized, contribute money, lobby hard, and vote regularly. Real reform, however, will inevitably mean trimming back their benefits. Governments will have to make hard choices, resist the temptation to pander, and enact policies for the long run. The only possible way that this can be achieved in a modern democracy is by insulating some decision-makers from the intense pressures of interest groups, lobbies, and political campaigns—that is to say, from the intense pressures of democracy.

It is already happening. The rise of independent central banks, like the U.S. Federal Reserve, over the last few decades is the clearest example of this trend.

In most advanced democracies, the government's most powerful economic lever is now exercised by an unelected body. And it works. Though they have their flaws, by and large independence of central banks has resulted in more responsible monetary policy. In part because of this discipline, the business cycle, which was once sharp and severe, has increasingly been smoothed out. The bust of 2000–2002, which followed the longest boom in half a century, is still (as of this writing) less extreme than many had feared. . . .

Less Is More

What we need in politics today is not more democracy but less. By this I do not mean we should embrace strongmen and dictators but rather that we should ask why certain institutions within our society—such as the Federal Reserve and the Supreme Court—function so well and why others—such as legislatures—function poorly. As it happens, Alan Blinder, a Princeton professor, pondered just this question in a fascinating essay in *Foreign Affairs* magazine in 1997.[1] Blinder had completed two stints in government, first at the White House on the Council of Economic Advisers and then at the Federal Reserve, where he served as vice chairman. He noted in his essay that policymaking at the White House was dominated by short-term political and electoral considerations, whereas policymaking at the Federal Reserve was concerned largely with a policy's social, economic, and legal merits. This difference in large part accounted for the consistently high quality of decision-making at the Fed.

Blinder argued that Federal Reserve decision-making was insulated from politics for three good reasons. First, interest rates are a technical subject that specialists are better equipped to handle than amateurs. Second, monetary policy takes a long time to work and so requires patience and a steady hand. Finally, the pain of fighting inflation (higher unemployment) comes well before the benefits (permanently lower costs of goods, lower interest rates, etc.). As a result, good interest-rate policy cannot be made in an atmosphere dominated by short-term considerations. But then Blinder admitted that "a nasty little thought kept creeping through my head: the argument for the Fed's independence applies just as forcefully to many other areas of government. Many policy decisions require complex technical judgments and have consequences that stretch into the distant future." He cited health care, environmental policy, and tax policy as just such cases.

Consider the U.S. federal income tax. In its first incarnation in 1914, the entire tax code was 14 pages long, and individuals' tax returns fit on a single page. Today the tax code runs over 2,000 pages, with 6,000 pages of regulations and tens of thousands of pages of rulings and interpretations. The Internal Revenue Service publishes 480 tax forms and 280 forms to explain them. It is unclear exactly how much it costs Americans to comply with these Byzantine rules; estimates go as high as $600 billion per year, but most scholars place the number at about $100 billion, or about 15 percent of income-tax revenue (about $375 to $450 per person per year). Dale Jorgenson, chairman of the Economics Department at Harvard, calculates that moving to a flat-rate tax on consumption would raise as much revenue as the current income-tax system while increasing economic growth by more than $200 billion a year.

The tax code has become time-consuming, complex, and expensive for a simple reason: democratic politics. It presents a golden opportunity for politicians to fund their favorite programs, groups, and companies without attracting much attention. An outright grant would be noticed; a small change in tax law will not. Corporations with very similar balance sheets can pay widely differing taxes, depending on whether they have effective lobbyists who can bully Congress into rewriting the code to their benefit. Often a new law is so narrowly written as to be in effect a subsidy to one particular company. Although each tax break might seem small, the overall cost is staggering, totaling more than $550 billion in forgone revenue for the federal government in 2001. Some of these "tax expenditures" are designed to support programs with broad public approval, but others—such as narrowly targeted tax breaks for industry—can only be described as corporate welfare.

Americans of all political stripes agree that the tax code is unwieldy, inefficient, and unfair. Yet no one believes it will ever be reformed, because it is embedded in democratic politics. Blinder points out that the three reasons that the Federal Reserve is independent all apply particularly strongly to tax policy. He proposes the creation of an independent federal tax authority, much like the Federal Reserve. Congress would give it broad directions and guidelines, and on this basis it would prepare tax legislation. Congress would then vote on the bill but no amendments would be allowed. Although hardly flawless, such a system would undoubtedly produce a better tax code than the one we have now.

The United States government already experiments with this kind of delegation in some areas. The president is usually given the authority to negotiate trade agreements, which are then presented to Congress as a complete package. Congress votes on the bill as a whole with no amendments allowed. Congress used a similar procedure in the early 1990s, when it needed to close dozens of military bases as the country demobilized after the Cold War. Faced with a crisis, legislators realized that the only way to arrive at a fair outcome was to take politics out of the process. Otherwise members of Congress would all be strongly in favor of closing bases, just not the ones in their districts. They delegated the task of determining which bases should be closed to a nonpartisan commission. The final list was presented to Congress for a single vote, up or down, with no changes permitted. These processes have all worked well, combining effective government with democratic control.

Delegation is the modern-day equivalent of the strategy that Homer's wandering hero, Ulysses, used as he sailed past the Sirens, whose singing made men cast themselves into the sea. Ulysses had his sailors fill their ears with wax so that they could not hear the Sirens' calls. For his part, he wanted to hear the music, so he had himself bound tightly to the mast of his ship and told his men that no matter what he said, they were not to untie him. As they passed the treacherous waters, Ulysses was seduced by the music and begged to be released. But the system worked. His men held to his initial orders and kept him bound. As a result, the boat and its sailors emerged safely from their trial. Politicians today should bind themselves more often to the ship of state as they pass through turbulent political waters.

The Highest Stakes

In developing countries the need for delegation is even greater because the stakes are often higher. Governments must demonstrate deep commitment and discipline in their policies or else markets quickly lose faith in them. They must focus on the long-term with regard to urban development, education, and health care, or their societies will slowly descend into stagnation or even anarchy. Far-sighted policies pay huge dividends; short-term patronage politics have immense costs.

In general dictators have not done better at these policies than democrats— far from it. Most dictators have ravaged their countries for personal gain. Scholars have asked whether democracy helps or hurts the economic growth of poor countries and, despite many surveys, have come to no conclusive answer.[2] But over the past fifty years almost every success story in the developing world has taken place under a liberal authoritarian regime. Whether in Taiwan, South Korea, Singapore, Chile, Indonesia, or even China, governments that were able to make shrewd choices for the long term were rewarded with strong economic growth and rising levels of literacy, life expectancy, and education. It is difficult to think of a Third World democracy that has achieved sustained growth rates like those of the countries listed above. Those that have gone down the path of reform are quickly stymied by the need to maintain subsidies for politically powerful groups. India has been unable to engage in sustained reform largely because its politicians will not inflict any pain—however temporary—on their constituents. As a result, for all its democratic glories, the country has slipped further and further behind on almost every measure of human development: life expectancy, infant mortality, health, literacy, education. It now ranks a shocking 124 (out of 173) on the United Nations 2002 human development index, behind China, of course, but even behind Guatemala, Bolivia, and Syria, and well behind Cuba. Surely it is time to ask whether democracies such as India, so lauded by Western intellectuals, are working for their people.

The solution is not to scuttle democracy in the Third World. Democracy has immense benefits regardless of its effects on development and growth. It also has real economic virtues. Although it does not achieve the best results, it usually protects against the worst. You may not get a Lee Kuan Yew through elections, but you will not get a Mobutu Sese Seko either. Yet cheerleading about democracy will not solve its problems. There must be a way to make democratic systems work so that they do not perennially produce short-term policies with dismal results. The stakes in poor countries are just too high.

Some form of delegation might be one solution. Central banks should become more powerful, a process that is already under way. Judges should have similar independent standing. In order to strengthen the judiciary and fight corruption, justice ministries and law-enforcement authorities should also be given more in-dependence. Many American institutions, such as the Federal Reserve System, the Securities and Exchange Commission, and the Federal Bureau of Investigation, have their leaders appointed to long terms (7–10 years) that do not coincide with the electoral cycle. This is done deliberately, to give them some distance from politics.

A crucial area in which a creative new arrangement might be possible is in the economic realm. Decision-making in this arena should be distanced from day-to-day politics. The finance minister in a Third World country should have the ability to present his annual budget as a package that cannot be amended, only approved or denied as a whole. (The United Kingdom, because of its parliamentary system and tight party discipline, does this informally, and as a result has a reputation for being able to enact effective fiscal policy.) One might even go further and allow the economics minister to be appointed to a longer term than the norm—as with the head of the Federal Reserve—so that when a political crisis triggers the fall of a government it does not automatically result in the collapse of economic reform. None of these measures will take politics out of the process entirely. Nor should they. Politics is healthy; it is how people assert their power in a democracy. You need political support for any policy, reformist or otherwise. Instead, the goal is simply to weaken the intense pressure of politics on public policy in the stressed circumstances of the Third World, to shift the balance somewhat to make the system work better. It will not always work better. Some ministers and bureaucrats will abuse the greater authority they are given. Others will pursue well-intentioned but foolish policies. But it will probably work better than the system now prevalent in most developing democracies, which has delivered so little to its people.

It is important to emphasize that these changes are utterly compatible with democracy. They delegate authority to institutions, but ultimate power rests with the people through their elected representatives. This check should be strengthened. Two-thirds majorities in legislatures should be able to override most of the special protections outlined above. Parliamentary committees should regularly oversee the work of all unelected bodies. In a sense these new arrangements are simply an extension of the way an administrative department, say the Department of Health and Human Services, works in the United States. It formulates and implements policies based on broad guidelines handed down by Congress. The legislature exercises ultimate control but leaves much of the policy to unelected bureaucrats. If it works for welfare policy, why not for taxes? Most of all politicians should defend these systems to the public, explaining that delegation can produce a reasonable balance between good government and democratic control. Given their appreciation (in the West, at least) of courts and central banks, clearly people understand this argument.

Delegation is not simply a phenomenon that exists in the political realm. In many other areas we face the same choice. Do we want to go down the path of loosening controls, bypassing mediators, and breaking down old standards—in economics and culture, for example—or do we want instead to retain and reshape some of the guides and buffers that have traditionally been part of our society? Technology has combined with ideology to offer the alluring prospect of a world without mediation. You can become your own stockbroker, newspaper editor, lawyer, and doctor. But do you want to? Attitudes on this matter are less giddy than they were during the boom years of the 1990s. People have begun to recognize that perhaps there is a reason that mediators have existed in so many different areas in so many ages. It turns out that most investors would gladly pay slightly higher fees for the proper execution of stock trades, for financial and investment advice, and even for old-fashioned hand-holding. Those with legal complaints and medical problems realized that self-diagnosis—by reading internet sites and participating in chat groups—is only so useful. In the world of journalism, the personal Web site ("blog") was hailed as the killer of the traditional media. In fact it has become something quite different. Far from replacing newspapers and magazines, the best blogs—and the best are very clever—have become guides to them, pointing to unusual sources and commenting on familiar ones. They have become new mediators for the informed public. Although the creators of blogs think of themselves as radical democrats, they are in fact a new Tocquevillean elite. Much of the Web has moved in this direction because the wilder, bigger, and more chaotic it becomes, the more people will need help navigating it.

Onward and Downward

But for all these encouraging signs, the broad trends still move us toward the unceasing democratization of society. Politics becomes more and more permeable, European societies become "Americanized," old institutions open up, professions and guilds die out, and technology continues to threaten most intermediaries. All of which will result in much good, as it has in the past. But it will also destroy parts of the fabric of our culture. The institutions and attitudes that have preserved liberal democratic capitalism in the West were built over centuries. They are being destroyed in decades. Once torn down they will not be so easy to repair. We watch this destruction without really being able to stop it—that would be undemocratic. But it will leave its mark on our politics, economics, and culture, all of which will increasingly be dominated by short-term interests and enthusiasms. Edmund Burke once described society as a partnership between the dead, the living, and the yet unborn. It is difficult to see in the evolving system who will speak for the yet unborn, for the future.

Meanwhile, public dissatisfaction with the effects of all these changes will continue to grow. If these problems build, eventually people will define democracy by what it has become: a system, open and accessible in theory, but ruled in reality by organized or rich or fanatical minorities, protecting themselves for the present and sacrificing the future. This is a very different vision from that of the enthusiasts of direct democracy, who say that the liberating new world we will live in will harken back to the city-states of ancient Greece. I leave it to the reader to judge whether Californian politics today resembles Athenian democracy in its prime. In any event, it is worth remembering that direct democracy was tried only in a few small cities in ancient Greece where a few thousand men were allowed to vote. It is also worth remembering that within a hundred years all those democracies collapsed into tyranny or chaos—frequently both.

Such gloom may seem far-fetched, but if current trends continue, democracy will undoubtedly face a crisis of legitimacy, which could prove crippling. Legitimacy is the elixir of political power. "The strongest is never strong enough to be the master," Jean-Jacques Rousseau observed, "unless he translates strength into right and obedience into duty." Only democracy has that authority in the world today. But it can lose its hold on our loyalties. The greatest danger of unfettered and dysfunctional democracy is that it will discredit democracy itself, casting all popular governance into a shadowy light. This would not be unprecedented. Every wave of democracy has been followed by setbacks in which the system is seen as inadequate and new alternatives have been proposed by ambitious leaders and welcomed by frustrated people. The last such period of disenchantment, in Europe during the interwar years, was seized upon by demagogues, many of whom capitalized on the public's disenchantment with democracy. It is worth remembering that the embrace of communism and fascism in the 1930s did not seem as crazy at the time as it does now. While the democracies were mired in depression and gloom, authoritarian states had mobilized their societies and were on the march.

Modern democracies will face difficult new challenges—fighting terrorism, adjusting to globalization, adapting to an aging society—and they will have to make their system work much better than it currently does. That means making democratic decision-making effective, reintegrating constitutional liberalism into the practice of democracy, rebuilding broken political institutions and civic associations. Perhaps most difficult of all, it requires that those with immense power in our societies embrace their responsibilities, lead, and set standards that are not only legal, but moral. Without this inner stuffing, democracy will become an empty shell, not simply inadequate but potentially dangerous, bringing with it the erosion of liberty, the manipulation of freedom, and the decay of a common life.

This would be a tragedy because democracy, with all its flaws, represents the "last best hope" for people around the world. But it needs to be secured and strengthened for our times. Eighty years ago, Woodrow Wilson took America into the twentieth century with a challenge to make the world safe for democracy. As we enter the twenty-first century, our task is to make democracy safe for the world.

Notes

1. Alan Blinder, "Is Government Too Political," *Foreign Affairs*, November/December, 1997.
2. There is a large and interesting literature on this topic. A good starting point would be the overview in United Nations Development Program, *Human Development Report 2002: Deepening Democracy in a Fragmented World* (New York: Oxford University Press, 2002), 56. All the works it cites are worth reading, but in particular see Adam Przeworski, Michael E. Alvarez, Jose Antonio Cheibub, and Fernando Limongi, *Democracy and Development: Political Institutions and Well-Being in the World, 1950–1990* (New York: Cambridge University Press, 2000).

 7.6

An Alternative to Progress

Bill McKibben

What does Gorasin, a remote village in Bangladesh, suggest about how to promote economic improvement in underdeveloped regions of the world? Bill McKibben claims that Gorasin has lessons aplenty to offer. Villagers in Gorasin have achieved progress by rejecting the advice offered by most economists and technical experts. Rather than shifting to high-value crops for export, involving the use of pesticides and genetically modified seed, they use traditional methods to produce food for local consumption.

Critics might reply that McKibben tends to idealize traditional village life. Farming by age-old methods can involve back-breaking labor and produce meager output. Nor does McKibben explain how villagers who raise subsistence crops (food grown for local consumption) can earn money to purchase necessities (like medicines) that are not produced in the village. Do you have any suggestions about how to resolve this dilemma?

The eastern end of the village of Gorasin, on the edge of the Louhajang River in the district of Taugail, in the nation of Bangladesh, has no store that we would recognize, no car, no electric lines, no television. No telephone. There are just small fields, a cow, some chickens, barefoot children,

---

banana palms swaying in the breeze. The call to prayer from a nearby muezzin drifts over the croplands. It is about as far from the center of the world as you can possibly get. And that may be the point.

Hovering over all the issues about the World Bank and the World Trade Organization and the spread of genetically modified crops, hovering over everything that's happened since the 1999 Battle of Seattle is a big question: Is there really any alternative to the General Course of things? Is there some imaginable future that does not lead through the eternal Westernization, the endless economic expansion, that is the gospel of our time? Is there some alternative to progress?

Gorasin is one of those places that suggests there might be. "Suggests" is about as strong as I'd like to get. Alternatives get quickly overwhelmed in the modern world, co-opted or submerged beneath the staggering flow of business as usual. But, at least right now, life in Gorasin is worth a look.

If we think about Bangladesh at all, it is as a basket case. A hundred and thirty million people crowded into an area the size of Wisconsin. Constant flooding, with the regular scattering of killer cyclones. A 10-letter word for woe.

If you ask the World Bank what needs to happen in Bangladesh, their answer—detailed in a report called "Bangladesh 2020"—is to turn it into another Thailand or, better yet, another Singapore: to ramp up its growth rate, produce crops like cut flowers for export, "manage" a "transition" to urbanization, and exploit its huge supply of cheap labor to allow a leap up the development ladder. "There is no alternative to accelerated growth." If you ask Monsanto, the key is high-yielding varieties of rice, including new genetically engineered strains: "golden rice," say, designed to eliminate vitamin A deficiency. If you ask international donor agencies, the secret is more microcredit, like the pioneering Grameen Bank projects that have captured worldwide attention in recent years. "If you want to work on misery, Bangladesh is the ultimate misery you can have," says Atiq Rahman, of the Bangladesh Center for Advanced Studies, a local NGO.

Those are the standard views: that Bangladesh lives in a state of backwardness that can be "fixed" through an application of technology, capital, exposure to the discipline of the markets. To quote from the World Bank report, "Backwardness in the form of cheap labor gives Bangladesh a strong competitive potential edge." In other words, an inexhaustible supply of poor people willing to work at low wages is its greatest asset. In the words of Rahman, who co-authored the Bank report, Bangladeshis are now at a "survival" stage and need to make a "quantum leap" to some higher level of development, a leap that inevitably leads to urbanization, an export-oriented economy, more fertilizer, big electric power plants. And when you look at the country's sad statistics for nutrition, for life expectancy, for literacy, then it's easy to defend the conventional wisdom: The average person dies at 60, and the infant mortality rate is 10 times that of the United States.

But there is another way of looking at things, a Gorasin way, one developed closer to home, less despairing and less grandiose at the same time. "People say that it's a miracle Bangladesh can survive its food and energy crises, that it somehow perseveres," Sajed Kamal, a solar energy educator, told me as we walked the town's fields. "The real miracle, though, is that you could contrive a way to have a food crisis. If you stick something in the ground here, it grows." So Bangladesh, it's worth noting, is able to feed itself.

Our guides that day were the people who lived in Gorasin, who lived in small huts, smaller than trailer homes. They were showing us sesame seed plants, loofah sponge gourds, eggplants, sugarcane, bamboo. Onions, pulses, all manner of local leafy greens. All grown without pesticides, without fertilizer, and without seed imported from the laboratories of the West. Gorasin sits in a large self-declared pesticide-free zone, one of several organic oases established around the country by adherents of the Nayakrisbi, or "New Agriculture" movement. The movement arose in response to numerous environmental hazards that the villagers believe were traceable to pesticides.

"When we women went to collect water, we would be affected," one villager was saying. She was twenty something, beautiful, gregarious. "Our skin would absorb the poisons. We would get itchiness, get gastric trouble. Now we've adopted our own solution. The water is pure again."

"The cows used to eat the grass and drop dead," one man added. "And then the villagers would fight each other."

"We grew up with a saying: 'We Bengalis are made of rice and fish,'" said another man. "Then the fish started catching diseases. We are not scientists, but we made the connection between pesticide and fish death. Since we've started organic farming, the fish are now healthier and more plentiful."

"A fertilized plant jumps up fast and falls right over," said a third. "Our plants are strong and healthy. Theirs, you eat it and you get sick. The minute you say 'Nayakrishi' in the market, though, people will pay more, because they know they're saving on health care."

A few miles away, at the Nayakrishi training school for the Tangail district, 25 varieties of papaya are growing. A hundred and twelve varieties of jackfruit, all cataloged by the farmers by taste, size, color, season, habitat. Wicker baskets and clay pots in a darkened shed contain 300 varieties of local rice, 20 kinds of bitter gourd, 84 varieties of local beans.

"Do you know how much it costs to build a gene bank like the ones where botanists store plant varieties?" asks Farhad Mazhar, a founder of the Center for Development Alternatives, known by its Bengali acronym, UBINIG, the Dhaka-based NGO that helped launch the Nayakrishi movement. "No scientist can afford to catalog hundreds of varieties of rice. But farmers are doing it as part of household activity. Our little seed station has more vegetables than the national gene bank, which spends millions. But we can do it for free."

For free, and in the process, they insist, they can rejuvenate village life. Farida Akhter, Mazhar's partner running UBINIG, is one of Bangladesh's leading feminists. She set up the nation's only women's bookstore and led a long fight against contraceptive abuses by international agencies. But if you ask her what single step would do the most to improve the lot of Bengali women, she does not hesitate: "I'd want rural women to have control over seeds again. That's women's power, or was before the multinationals started selling their new varieties in the last few decades. Traditionally, the woman is the one who knows what a good seed is, what will germinate, how to store it. Maybe they like the sound of the seed when they flick it, the weight of it on the winnowers, how it looks. They'll cut a seed with their teeth and listen to the sound it makes. They know how to dry it, how many times to put it under the sun, and whether to use the morning sun or the afternoon sun. Men used to discuss with their wives what kind of crop to raise for next year. But now they listen to the seed seller. The woman has become redundant, a burden."

Farhad Mazhar was in Seattle for the WTO protests. "I strongly believe in globalization," he says. "I'm not a national chauvinist. We need more interaction at the international level. We need cultural exchanges, all that sort of thing. But that's not happening here in Bangladesh, and it's not happening in all the other countries like us. We're just a source of raw materials." Certainly not a source of ideas. Ideas flow the other way.

Bangladesh became a country in 1971, following a brief civil war. "Civil war" is actually a misnomer: Pakistan, backed rhetorically by the United States, carried out what may have been the most efficient genocide of the 20th century, killing as many as 3 million Bengalis in nine months before a resistance army aided by Indian troops drove them out. That carnage was followed in short order by famine and cyclones. Then a military coup shut off the new nation's political life. Since then, Bangladesh has made the world news only sporadically, usually when the waters of the Ganges and the Brahmaputra overflow their banks. (Two or three thousand need to drown before it makes the back pages of American newspapers.) As a relatively calm Muslim country, without geopolitical significance and with a minuscule economy, it would be hard to imagine a less newsworthy place. But 1 human in 50 now lives there, and its grand history stretches back into the mists far enough to qualify it as a cradle of civilization. Still, for the rest of the planet, its only outstanding feature today is poverty.

"Poverty is the most salable commodity we have here," says Khushi Kabir, a longtime grassroots organizer. Experts jet in, stay at the Sheraton in Dhaka, issue reports, and leave. Local academics vie for "consultancies," making bids that sometimes require kickbacks to government officials. And the expert advice has often gone spectacularly wrong. A huge Flood Action Plan, for instance, called for ever-higher embankments to keep the rivers at bay. But Bangladesh is not Holland: The huge silt deposits kept raising riverbeds, and the floodwater that eventually topped the dikes had nowhere to drain. "One area in the southwest was underwater for 10 years," says Kabir.

Later, in an effort to curb diarrheal disease, UNICEF helped drill thousands of deep tube wells around the country and ran advertisements urging people to stop drinking surface water. But they neglected to sample the subsurface geology, and so tens of millions began drinking water contaminated with naturally occurring arsenic. The water has killed some already; others, disfigured by the melanoma lesions that arsenic causes, can no longer be given in marriage. UNICEF's new ads tell people not to drink from the tube wells.

Other international aid has worked better: The country's fertility rate has fallen quickly and the International Center for Diarrheal Disease Research has cut the incidence of cholera, which is endemic in the region. But local activists say the benefits aren't worth the costs: "Absolutely we would be better off if everyone trying to 'help' us just went home," says Mazhar. "If they did, then the people in the country would be able to come up with their own ideas." Those ideas would, necessarily, center on village life. Though Dhaka, a chaotic mega-city with a population uncountably north of 10 million, dominates the political life of the nation, 80 percent of Bengalis still live in rural areas. Which is not to say that they live in Iowa, or the Punjab, or any of the other places that the word rural conjures in our minds. In the first place, Bangladesh is almost as much liquid as solid. There is water everywhere you look, and much of the year many villages are accessible mostly by canoe. Land holdings tend to be tiny, many under an acre. And the place feels, to a Westerner, almost unbelievably crowded. The population density dwarfs that of India or China; it approaches the density of Hong Kong. Even in rural farming districts, there is simply no such thing as a lonely road. Rickshaws, bicycles, buses, draft animals, and pedestrians jam every vista. One Bengali said the reason his country did not excel at most international sports was simple: "Where is the room for a soccer pitch?"

That picture of a standingroom-only floodplain sounds pretty desperate to our ears, as if the population of our Eastern seaboard were ordered to somehow make a living in Chesapeake Bay. But at least for the moment this huge population of Bengalis manages to feed itself. Partly that's a result of the "Green Revolution," the rice strains that, whatever their toll in pesticides and fertilizers, have boosted grain yields. But mostly that's a function of the simple biology of a hot delta. Floods regularly renew the soil, the sun shines most of the year, and so fruit trees grow in two years to a girth that would require five decades on a New England hillside. Plants jump from the ground. There's an almost obscene lushness everywhere. And the large population means that there are plenty of people to manage that lushness, to help make the most of it.

Here's what I mean. We were sitting one day on the front porch of a one-acre organic farm about an hour from Dhaka. It was a hobby farm, whose owner was mostly concerned with his rosebushes. Still, without getting up, we could see guava, lemon, pomegranate, coconut, betel nut, mango, jackfruit, apple, lichee, chestnut, date, fig, and bamboo trees, as well as squash, okra, eggplant, zucchini, blackberry, bay leaf, cardamom, cinnamon, and sugarcane plants, not to mention dozens of herbs, far more flowers, and a flock of ducklings. A chicken coop produced not just eggs and meat, but waste that fed a fishpond, which in turn produced thousands of pounds of protein annually, and a healthy crop of water hyacinths that were harvested to feed a small herd of cows, whose dung in turn fired a biogas cooking system. "Food is everywhere, and in 12 hours it will double," Kamal said.

So what do you do with that kind of fertility? The World Bank report recommends that you figure out ways to grow "higher value" crops for export; they cite the Colombian cut-flower industry as an example. It could supply vegetables to other parts of Asia, "graduating from a minor supplier at present to a major player in the long term." That would probably generate the most money, cash that would be plowed into expanding the industries that could take advantage of the country's cheap labor pool.

Or you could follow UBINIG's advice and focus on farms like those of Gorasin. "Any 'development' policy here must give agriculture priority," says Farhad Mazhar. "Don't destroy it any further, because you've got no way to take care of those people." The choice you make will depend on your sense of the future. The sheer growth in human numbers—Bangladesh's population may double again by 2020—could mean that you have no choice but to make a mad dash for modernization, figuring out every possible way to convert your country's resources to cash. But it will also depend on how you see the people living in Bengali villages. Are they desperately poor? Or is, in Mazhar's words, "the whole Western construction of poverty" suspect? "The real question," he insists, "is, What are the livelihood strategies of the bulk of people, and what kind of development enhances or destroys those strategies?"

That is, do you want a few lightbulbs run off rooftop solar generators, or do you want to run electric lines to the three-quarters of the country that currently lacks them? Do you want more people moving to the cities, or do you want to develop an organic agriculture that can absorb more labor? Those are questions, not answers. Rahman, the development expert, says that rooftop solar is only a beginning: "Once people have the 'little power,' they want 'big power' from electric lines," he says. Even though big power in a poor country can imply expense, pollution, dependence.

Here's another way of asking the same thing: How do you address the problem of vitamin A deficiency? Large numbers of poor people around South Asia suffer from a variety of micronutrient deficiencies—their diets lack sufficient iron or zinc or vitamin A, also known as beta-carotene. If you don't get enough, you can go blind. In 1999, European researchers announced they had managed to genetically modify rice so that it would express vitamin A to anyone who ate a bowlful, as surely as if they had popped a vitamin pill. Within a year the major biotech companies had announced agreements to license the technology free of charge to poor nations. As Time magazine put it last year, "The biotech industry sees golden rice as a powerful ally in its struggle to win public acceptance." An industry group ran a massive ad campaign touting the new technology with a rapid-fire montage of children and farms against a backdrop of swelling music.

But the advertisements look a little different from the organic farms of the Bengali floodplain, where farmers insist they have a different solution to the problem. The Nayakrishi movement held a small seminar for peasant farmers on the new technology at an open-air meeting hall in the Tangail district one day while I was there. A Filipino agriculture expert discussed the plans—that by 2003 the International Rice Research Institute would be producing genetically modified seeds for them to plant. The farmers—illiterate, most of them—kept interrupting with questions and sermonettes. They weren't concerned about franken-foods. Instead, they instantly realized that the new rice would require fertilizer and pesticide. More to the point, they kept saying, they had no need of golden rice because the leafy vegetables they could grow in their organic fields provided all the nutrition they needed. "When we cook the green vegetables, we are aware not to throw out the water," said one woman. "Yes," said another. "And we don't like to eat rice only. It tastes better with green vegetables."

This is neither simplistic nor sentimental. In fact, there's plenty of evidence to show that as the Green Revolution spread in the last four decades, nutrient deficiency followed close behind. A plant like bathua, a leafy vegetable that provided beta-carotene to Indians for an eternity, becomes such a competitor of wheat once you start using chemical fertilizers that it requires herbicides to destroy it. A steady decline in the consumption per capita of vegetables, fruits, beans, and spices took place in Bangladesh even as the consumption of rice increased. Plants growing wild around the margins of Gorasin's fields provide massive quantities of vitamins A and C, or folic acid, iron, and calcium. But the spread of any high-yielding variety like golden rice tends to reduce that crop diversity. "There may or may not be issues of biosafety," said the Filipino expert. "The real question is, Do we really need this?"

Again, the answer depends on how you see the world. Maybe it's too late for Bangladesh to go back to a balanced diet, particularly in urban areas where bathua and amaranth are hard to come by. There's a kind of inevitability to the argument for a technological, capital-intensive future that comes from a scarcity of successful counterexamples. There aren't many places that have chosen an alternative path. Kerala, perhaps, the state of 30 million people in the south of India that has achieved Western levels of life expectancy, literacy, infant mortality, and fertility on an average income per capita of $300 per year. But the World Bank and Monsanto don't talk about Kerala; they talk about Thailand and Singapore.

"The Nayakrishi fields can be twice as productive as 'modern' agriculture," says Mazhar. "But I can't get anyone from the World Bank to come out and test my claims. We don't fit with the model." The Nayakrishi movement is small, with only tens of thousands of farmers in a nation with tens of millions. And although it is growing, it remains insubstantial against the sheer scale of Bangladesh. But Nayakrishi hints at other ways of addressing other issues, like energy: The Bangladesh Rural Advancement Committee has begun using microcredit programs to help peasants finance solar systems for their rooftops, and biogas generators for their cookstoves. The dung from three cows lets you cook all your meals for a day and frees you from crouching by the fireside to feed rice straw to the flame. That's a kind of progress that doesn't show up easily in anyone's statistics, but you can feel it in the strain on your back at the end of the day. It's a kind of progress that could conceivably mix with newer technologies. In his recent primer, *Food's Frontier: The Next Green Revolution*, Richard Manning notes that Western researchers are just beginning to focus more intensely on how people have grown food for generations.

There are few certainties when talking about the future of places like Bangladesh. Here's one, though: The most important Western export to Bangladesh in the next few decades will almost certainly be the higher sea level caused by global warming. When the Bay of Bengal rises a foot or two, the waters of the Ganges and the Brahmaputra will back up when they flood, unable to flow smoothly into the ocean. The Bay of Bengal rose a few inches higher than normal in 1998, and that year the floodwaters covered vast swaths of the country for as long as three months. Forget the fertility-promoting "normal" floods of the Bengali summer; this was 90 days of wading through thigh-deep water—more or less because Americans can't manage to stop driving Explorers. That near-geological force may be enough to end all these debates, to shut off the experimentation and innovation that offer curious and unexpected twists on what we've taken to calling development. Which would be the biggest shame of all.

The night we left Gorasin, we sat in the courtyard by everyone's small huts. The whole village of 35 or 40 people was on hand. Two babies were using a grapefruit as a ball, which every person in the village would roll back to them with great smiles. It takes a village to raise a child, indeed, and to raise a crop. And to raise a song, as well: One of the men, Akkas Ali, mentioned that he had written a hundred songs praising organic agriculture, tunes he and the other men had sung at local markets in an effort to convert other farmers. We ate fat bananas, and rosy grapefruit, and listened as the sun set.

"Nayakrishi has corrected my mistakes," he sang in a reedy Bengali, as the rest of the village clapped rhythmically.

"Food from Nayakrishi is so much better. No longer do I eat the poisons.

Why should I eat that life-destroying stuff? Bangladesh will come to an end, Unless you turn to Nayakrishi.

If you use organic fertilizer, the Almighty will be behind you, And you'll be having no more gastric problems."

As I say, the sun was setting over Gorasin. I have no idea if this represents a vision of the future, or a fragment of a fleeting past.

It depends on how you look at it.